MW01096921

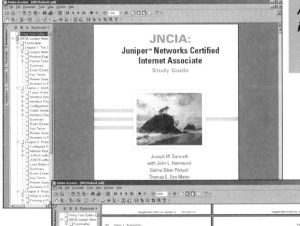

Access the entire book in PDF!

- Full search capabilities let you quickly find the information you need

- Complete with tables and illustrations

- Adobe Acrobat Reader 5.1 with Search included

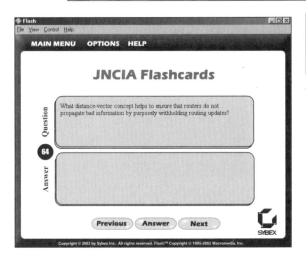

Reinforce understanding of key topics with flashcards for your PC, Pocket PC, or Palm handheld!

- Contains over 150 flashcard questions

- Runs on multiple platforms for usability and portability

- Quiz yourself anytime, anywhere!

SYBEX

OBJECTIVE	CHAPTER

SYBEX

JNCIA: Juniper Networks Certified Internet Associate Study Guide

Juniper Networks Certified Internet Associate, M-series, T-series Routers (JNCIA-M) exam (code JN0-201)

SYBEX

OBJECTIVE	CHAPTER

NOTE

Exam objectives are subject to change at any time without prior notice and at Juniper Networks' sole discretion. Please visit the Juniper Networks Technical Certification Program website (http://www.juniper.net/certification) for the most current exam objectives listing.

SYBEX

OBJECTIVE	CHAPTER

JNCIA:
Juniper Networks Certified Internet Associate
Study Guide

JNCIA:
Juniper™ Networks Certified
Internet Associate
Study Guide

Joseph M. Soricelli
with John L. Hammond
Galina Diker Pildush
Thomas E. Van Meter
and Todd M. Warble

San Francisco • London

SYBEX

Associate Publisher: Neil Edde
Acquisitions Editor: Maureen Adams
Developmental Editor: Colleen Strand
Production Editor: Mae Lum
Technical Editors: Steven T. Y. Wong, Bruno De Troch
Copyeditor: Liz Welch
Compositor: Judy Fung
Graphic Illustrator: Tony Jonick
CD Coordinator: Dan Mummert
CD Technician: Kevin Ly
Proofreaders: Emily Hsuan, David Nash, Laurie O'Connell, Yariv Rabinovitch, Nancy Riddiough, Monique Vandenberg
Indexer: Lynnzee Elze
Book Designers: Bill Gibson, Judy Fung
Cover Designer: Archer Design
Cover Illustrator/Photographer: Bruce Heinemann, PhotoDisc

Library of Congress Card Number: 2002111961

ISBN: 0-7821-4071-8

SYBEX

To Our Valued Readers:

As internetworking technologies continue to pervade nearly every aspect of public and private industry worldwide, the demand grows for individuals who can demonstrate they possess the skills needed to manage these technologies. Recognizing this need, Juniper Networks—the leading provider of Internet infrastructure solutions that enable ISPs and other telecommunications companies to meet the demands of Internet growth—recently restructured its certification program to provide a clear path for the acquisition of these skills. Sybex is proud to have partnered with Juniper Networks and worked closely with members of the Juniper Networks Technical Certification Program to develop this Official Study Guide for the Juniper Networks Certified Internet Associate certification.

Just as Juniper Networks is committed to establishing measurable standards for certifying those professionals who work in the cutting-edge field of internetworking, Sybex is committed to providing those professionals with the means of acquiring the skills and knowledge they need to meet those standards. It has long been Sybex's desire to help individuals acquire the technical knowledge and skills necessary to excel in the IT industry.

The authors and editors have worked hard to ensure that this Official Juniper Networks Study Guide is comprehensive, in-depth, and pedagogically sound. We're confident that this book will exceed the demanding standards of the certification marketplace and help you, the Juniper Networks certification candidate, succeed in your endeavors.

Good luck in pursuit of your Juniper Networks certification!

Neil Edde
Associate Publisher—Certification
Sybex, Inc.

This book is dedicated to my wife, Christine, whose patience and love has allowed me to pursue those things in my life that excite me. In addition, my family and friends have provided encouragement beyond words that have helped me reach this point in my life.
—Joseph M. Soricelli

To my beautiful wife of 33 years, Patricia. She deserves the best.
—John L. Hammond

I dedicate my work to my very special parents, my loving and devoted husband, and my children, David and Joseph, the angels of my life.
—Galina Diker Pildush

This is written for my lovely wife, Pam, and our daughter, Catherine Margaret— the cutest future engineer in the world!
—Thomas E. Van Meter

Acknowledgments

There are numerous people who deserve a round of thanks for assisting with this book. I would first like to thank Jason Rogan and Patrick Ames, who got this project started in the first place. Your guidance throughout this process has been invaluable. I would like to thank Colleen Strand, Mae Lum, Liz Welch, and Maureen Adams at Sybex. Colleen was instrumental in molding the tone of this book into the "Sybex way," Mae kept me on schedule (and sane), Liz made sure I was always talking in an active voice (and fixed grammatical errors), and Maureen helped get the whole thing rolling. Without their assistance and guidance, this book would still be a figment of my imagination. A very large thank-you goes out to the technical editors—Steven Wong and Bruno De Troch. Both Steven and Bruno worked very hard to make this book as accurate and complete as possible. Finally, I need to thank my fellow authors. Galina, John, Todd, and Tom all worked very hard on this book and had to put up with my nagging as well as my editing. All of you have made this book something I'm very proud of.

I would be remiss without acknowledging my colleagues and fellow JEDI at Juniper Networks. Both the old crew (Chris, Derek, John, Scott, Tim, and Tom) and the new crew (Harry, Jason, Matt, and Todd) have made Juniper an organization that I feel truly blessed to belong to.

Finally, a special thank-you belongs to Terry Slattery. Many years ago he took a chance on a young kid who didn't know all that much about networking. The organization I joined at that time had a number of role models who taught me a lot about this industry and about being a better person. I feel that I've now found my niche in life and I'm truly indebted to you.

—Joe

I would like to thank Hannes Gredler, Lenny Giuliano, and Amir Tabdili for answering my questions on IS-IS (Hannes) and multicasting (Lenny and Amir). Hannes particularly clarified L1/L2 multicast addresses and IS-IS Ethernet frame sizes, while Lenny and Amir both helped clarify exactly how designated routers work for multicasting and PIM questions in general. In case of any errors, it is solely my responsibility for mischaracterizing their answers.

—Tom

I would like to thank my parents, Lloyd and Jane, and my two brothers, Lloyd Jr. and Sandy, for all their support. I would like to thank Joe for his help and support during my contribution to this book. I would also like to thank my good friends for all their support and guidance. Finally, I want to thank all my excellent co-workers at Juniper.

—Todd

Sybex would like to thank electronic publishing specialist Judy Fung and indexer Lynnzee Elze for their valuable contributions to this book.

Contents at a Glance

Contents

Introduction

Greetings and welcome to the world of Juniper Networks. This introductory section serves as a location to pass on to you some pertinent information concerning the Juniper Networks Technical Certification Program. In addition, you'll find information about how the book itself is laid out and what it contains. Finally, we'll review some technical information that you should already know before reading this book.

Juniper Networks Technical Certification Program

The Juniper Networks Technical Certification Program (JNTCP) consists of two platform-specific, multitiered tracks. Each exam track allows participants to demonstrate their competence with Juniper Networks technology through a combination of written proficiency and hands-on configuration exams. Successful candidates demonstrate a thorough understanding of Internet technology and Juniper Networks platform configuration and troubleshooting skills.

The two JNTCP tracks focus on the M-series Routers & T-series Routing Platforms and the ERX Edge Routers, respectively. While some Juniper Networks customers and partners work with both platform families, it is most common to find individuals working with only one or the other platform. The two different certification tracks allow candidates to pursue specialized certifications, which focus on the platform type most pertinent to their job functions and experience. Candidates wishing to attain a certification on both platform families are welcome to do so, but are required to pass the exams from each track for their desired certification level.

 This book covers the M-series & T-series track. For information on the ERX Edge Routers certification track, please visit the JNTCP website at http://www.juniper.net/certification.

M-series Routers & T-series Routing Platforms

The M-series Routers certification track consists of four tiers. They include the following:

Juniper Networks Certified Internet Associate (JNCIA)   The Juniper Networks Certified Internet Associate, M-series, T-series Routers (JNCIA-M) certification does not have any prerequisites. It is administered at Prometric testing centers worldwide.

Juniper Networks Certified Internet Specialist (JNCIS)   The Juniper Networks Certified Internet Specialist, M-series, T-series Routers (JNCIS-M) certification also does not have any prerequisites. Like the JNCIA-M, it is administered at Prometric testing centers worldwide.

Juniper Networks Certified Internet Professional (JNCIP)   The Juniper Networks Certified Internet Professional, M-series, T-series Routers (JNCIP-M) certification requires that candidates first obtain the JNCIS-M certification. The hands-on exam is administered at Juniper Networks offices in select locations throughout the world.

Juniper Networks Certified Internet Expert (JNCIE)   The Juniper Networks Certified Internet Expert, M-series, T-series Routers (JNCIE-M) certification requires that candidates first obtain the JNCIP-M certification. The hands-on exam is administered at Juniper Networks offices in select locations throughout the world.

FIGURE I.1   JNTCP M-series Routers & T-series Routing Platforms certification track

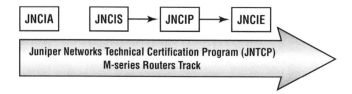

 The JNTCP M-series Routers & T-series Routing Platforms certification track covers the M-series and T-series routing platforms as well as the JUNOS software configuration skills required for both platforms. The lab exams are conducted using M-series routers only.

Juniper Networks Certified Internet Associate

The JNCIA-M certification is the first of the four-tiered M-series Routers & T-series Routing Platforms track. It is the entry-level certification designed for experienced networking professionals with beginner-to-intermediate knowledge of the Juniper Networks M-series and T-series routers and the JUNOS software. The JNCIA-M (exam code JN0-201) is a computer-based, multiple-choice exam delivered at Prometric testing centers globally for U.S.$125. It is a fast-paced exam that consists of 60 questions to be completed within 60 minutes. The current passing score is set at 70 percent.

70 Percent Seems Really Low!

The required score to pass an exam can be one indicator of the exam's difficulty, but not in the way that many candidates might assume. A lower pass score on an exam does *not* usually indicate an easier exam. Ironically, it often indicates the opposite—it's harder.

The JNTCP exams are extensively beta tested and reviewed. The results are then statistically analyzed based on multiple psychometric criteria. Only after this analysis is complete does the exam receive its appropriate passing score. In the case of the JNCIA-M exam, for example, requiring the passing score to be higher than 70 percent would mean that the exam's target audience would have been excluded from passing. In effect, the exam would have been more difficult to pass. Over time, as more exam statistics are collected, or the exam questions themselves are updated, the passing score may be modified to reflect the exam's new difficulty level. The end result is to ensure that the exams are passable by the members of the target audience for which they are written.

JNCIA-M exam topics are based on the content of the Introduction to Juniper Networks Routers, M-series (IJNR-M) instructor-led training course. Just as IJNR-M is the first class most students attend when beginning their study of Juniper Networks hardware and software, the JNCIA-M exam should be the first certification exam most candidates attempt. The study topics for the JNCIA-M exam include:

- System operation, configuration, and troubleshooting

- Routing protocols—BGP, OSPF, IS-IS, and RIP

- Protocol-independent routing properties

- Routing policy

- MPLS

- Multicast

 Please be aware that the JNCIA-M certification is *not* a prerequisite for further certification in the M-series Routers & T-series Routing Platforms track. The purpose of the JNCIA-M is to validate a candidate's skill set at the Associate level and it is meant to be a stand-alone certification fully recognized and worthy of pride of accomplishment. Additionally, it can be used as a stepping stone before attempting the JNCIS-M exam.

Juniper Networks Certified Internet Specialist

The JNCIS-M was originally developed as the exam used to prequalify candidates for admittance to the practical hands-on certification exam. While it still continues to serve this purpose, this certification has quickly become a sought-after designation in its own right. Depending on the candidates' job functions, many have chosen JNCIS-M as the highest level of JNTCP certification needed to validate their skill set. Candidates also requiring validation of their hands-on configuration and troubleshooting ability on the M-series and T-series routers and the JUNOS software use the JNCIS-M as the required prerequisite to the JNCIP-M practical exam.

The JNCIS-M exam tests for a wider and deeper level of knowledge than does the JNCIA-M exam. Question content is drawn from the documentation set for the M-series routers, the T-series routers, and the JUNOS software. Additionally, on-the-job product experience and an understanding of Internet technologies and design principles are considered to be common knowledge at the Specialist level.

The JNCIS-M (exam code JN0-302) is a computer-based, multiple-choice exam delivered at Prometric testing centers globally for U.S.$125. It consists of 75 questions to be completed in 90 minutes. The current passing score is set at 70 percent.

The study topics for the JNCIS-M exam include:

- Advanced system operation, configuration, and troubleshooting

- Routing protocols—BGP, OSPF, and IS-IS

- Routing policy

- MPLS
- Multicast
- Router and network security
- Router and network management
- VPNs
- IPv6

 There are no prerequisite certifications for the JNCIS-M exam. While JNCIA-M certification is a recommended stepping stone to JNCIS-M certification, candidates are permitted to go straight to the Specialist (JNCIS-M) level.

Juniper Networks Certified Internet Professional

The JNCIP-M is the first of the two one-day practical exams in the M-series Routers & T-series Routing Platforms track of the JNTCP. The goal of this challenging exam is to validate a candidate's ability to successfully build an ISP network consisting of seven M-series routers and multiple EBGP neighbors. Over a period of eight hours, the successful candidate will perform system configuration on all seven routers, install an IGP, implement a well-designed IBGP, establish connections with all EBGP neighbors as specified, and configure the required routing policies correctly.

This certification establishes candidates' practical and theoretical knowledge of core Internet technologies and their ability to proficiently apply that knowledge in a hands-on environment. This exam is expected to meet the hands-on certification needs of the majority of Juniper Networks customers and partners. The more advanced JNCIE-M exam focuses on a set of specialized skills and addresses a much smaller group of candidates. You should carefully consider your certification goals and requirements, for you may find that the JNCIP-M exam is the highest-level certification you need.

 The JNCIP-M certification is a prerequisite for attempting the JNCIE-M practical exam.

Juniper Networks Certified Internet Expert

At the pinnacle of the M-series Routers & T-series Routing Platforms track is the one-day JNCIE-M practical exam. The *E* stands for Expert and they mean it—the exam is the most challenging and respected of its type in the industry. Maintaining the standard of excellence established over two years ago, the JNCIE-M certification continues to give candidates the opportunity to distinguish themselves as the truly elite of the networking world. Only a few have dared attempt this exam, and fewer still have passed.

The new eight-hour format of the exam requires that candidates troubleshoot an existing and preconfigured ISP network consisting of 10 M-series routers. Candidates are then presented with additional configuration tasks appropriate for an expert-level engineer.

The JNCIE-M (exam code CERT-JNCIE-M) is delivered at one of several Juniper Networks offices worldwide for U.S.$1,250. The current passing score is set at 80 percent.

The study topics for the JNCIE-M exam *may* include:

- Expert-level system operation, configuration, and troubleshooting
- Routing protocols—BGP, OSPF, IS-IS, and RIP
- Routing protocol redistribution
- Advanced routing policy implementation
- Firewall filters
- Class of service
- MPLS
- VPNs
- IPv6
- IPSec
- Multicast

 Since the JNCIP-M certification is a prerequisite for attempting this practical exam, all candidates who pass the JNCIE-M will have successfully completed two days of intensive practical examination.

Registration Procedures

JNTCP written exams are delivered worldwide at Prometric testing centers. To register, visit Prometric's website at `http://www.2test.com` (or call 1-888-249-2567 in North America) to open an account and register for an exam.

The JNTCP Prometric exam numbers are:

- JNCIA-M—JN0-201
- JNCIS-M—JN0-302

JNTCP lab exams are delivered by Juniper Networks at select locations. Currently the testing locations are:

- Sunnyvale, CA
- Herndon, VA
- Amsterdam, Holland

Other global locations are periodically set up as testing centers based on demand. To register, send an e-mail message to Juniper Networks at `certification-testreg@juniper.net` and place one of the following exam codes in the subject field. Within the body of the message, indicate the testing center you prefer and which month you would like to attempt the exam. You will be contacted with the available dates at your requested testing center. The JNTCP lab exam numbers are:

- JNCIP-M—CERT-JNCIP-M
- JNCIE-M—CERT-JNCIE-M

Recertification Requirements

To maintain the high standards of the JNTCP certifications, and to ensure that the skills of those certified are kept current and relevant, Juniper Networks has implemented the following recertification requirements, which apply to both certification tracks of the JNTCP:

- All JNTCP certifications are valid for a period of two years.

- Certification holders who do not renew their certification within this two-year period will have their certification placed in *suspended mode*. Certifications in suspended mode are not eligible as prerequisites for further certification and cannot be applied to partner certification requirements.

- After being in suspended mode for one year, the certification is placed in *inactive mode*. At that stage, the individual is no longer certified at the JNTCP certification level that has become inactive and the individual will lose the associated certification number. For example, a JNCIP holder placed in inactive mode will be required to pass both the JNCIS and JNCIP exams in order to regain JNCIP status; such an individual will be given a new JNCIP certification number.

- Renewed certifications are valid for a period of two years from the date of passing the renewed certification exam.

- Passing an exam at a higher level renews all lower-level certifications for two years from the date of passing the higher-level exam. For example, passing the JNCIP exam will renew the JNCIS certification (and JNCIA certification if currently held) for two years from the date of passing the JNCIP exam.

- JNCIA holders must pass the current JNCIA exam in order to renew the certification for an additional two years from the most recent JNCIA pass date.

- JNCIS holders must pass the current JNCIS exam in order to renew the certification for an additional two years from the most recent JNCIS pass date.

- JNCIP and JNCIE holders must pass the current JNCIS exam in order to renew these certifications for an additional two years from the most recent JNCIS pass date.

The most recent version of the JNTCP Online Agreement must be accepted for the recertification to become effective.

JNTCP Nondisclosure Agreement

Juniper Networks considers all written and practical JNTCP exam material to be confidential intellectual property. As such, an individual is not permitted to take home, copy, or re-create the entire exam or any portions thereof. It is expected that candidates who participate in the JNTCP will not reveal the detailed content of the exams.

For written exams delivered at Prometric testing centers, candidates must accept the online agreement before proceeding with the exam. When taking practical exams, candidates are provided with a hard-copy agreement to read and sign before attempting the exam. In either case, the agreement can be downloaded from the JNTCP website for your review prior to the testing date. Juniper Networks retains all signed hard-copy nondisclosure agreements on file.

Candidates must accept the online JNTCP Online Agreement in order for their certifications to become effective and to have a certification number assigned. You can do this by going to the CertManager site at `http://www.certmanager .net/juniper`.

Resources for JNTCP Participants

Reading this book is a fantastic place to begin preparing for your next JNTCP exam. You should supplement the study of this volume's content with related information from various sources. The following resources are available for free and are recommended to anyone seeking to attain or maintain Juniper Networks certified status.

JNTCP Website

The JNTCP website (`http://www.juniper.net/certification`) is the place to go for the most up-to-date information about the program. As the program evolves, this website is periodically updated with the latest news and major announcements. Possible changes include new exams and certifications, modifications to the existing certification and recertification requirements, and information about new resources and exam objectives.

The site consists of separate sections for each of the certification tracks. The information you'll find there includes the exam number, passing scores, exam time limits, and exam topics. A special section dedicated to resources is also provided to supply you with detailed exam topic outlines, sample written exams, and study guides. The additional resources listed next are also linked from the JNTCP website.

CertManager

The CertManager system (`http://www.certmanager.net/juniper`) provides you with a place to track your certification progress. The site requires a username and password for access, and you typically use the information contained on your hard-copy score report from Prometric the first time you log in. Alternatively, a valid login can be obtained by sending an e-mail message to `certification@juniper.net` with the word **certmanager** in the subject field.

Once you log in, you can view a report of all your attempted exams. This report includes the exam dates, your scores, and a progress report indicating the additional steps required to attain a given certification or recertification. This website is where you accept the online JNTCP agreement, which is a required step to become certified at any level in the program. You can also use the website to request the JNTCP official certification logos to use on your business cards, resumes, and websites.

Perhaps most important, the CertManager website is where all your contact information is kept up-to-date. Juniper Networks uses this information to send you certification benefits, such as your certificate of completion, and to inform you of important developments regarding your certification status. A valid company name is used to verify a partner's compliance with certification requirements. To avoid missing out on important benefits and information, you should ensure your contact information is kept current.

Juniper Networks Training Courses

Juniper Networks training courses (`http://www.juniper.net/training`) are the best source of knowledge for seeking a certification and to increase your hands-on proficiency with Juniper Networks equipment and technologies. While attendance of official Juniper Networks training courses doesn't guarantee a passing score on the certification exam, it does increase the likelihood of your successfully passing it. This is especially true when you seek to attain JNCIP or JNCIE status, where hands-on experience is a vital aspect of your study plan.

Juniper Networks Technical Documentation

You should be intimately familiar with the Juniper Networks technical documentation set (`http://www.juniper.net/techpubs`). During the JNTCP lab exams (JNCIP and JNCIE), these documents are provided in PDF on your PC. Knowing the content, organizational structure, and search capabilities of these manuals is a key component for a successful exam attempt. At the time of this writing, hard-copy versions of the manuals are provided only for the hands-on lab exams. All written exams delivered at Prometric testing centers are closed-book exams.

Juniper Networks Solutions and Technology

To broaden and deepen your knowledge of Juniper Networks products and their applications, you can visit `http:///www.juniper.net/techcenter`. This website contains white papers, application notes, frequently asked questions (FAQ), and other informative documents, such as customer profiles and independent test results.

Group Study

The Groupstudy mailing list and website (`http://www.groupstudy.com/list/juniper.html`) is dedicated to the discussion of Juniper Networks products and technologies for the purpose of preparing for certification testing. You can post and receive answers to your own technical questions or simply read the questions and answers of other list members.

Tips for Taking Your Exam

Many questions on the exam have answer choices that at first glance look identical. Remember to read through all the choices carefully because "close" doesn't cut it. Although there is never any intent on the part of Juniper Networks to trick you, some questions require you to think carefully before answering. Also, never forget that the right answer is the *best* answer. In some cases, you may feel that more than one appropriate answer is presented, but the best answer is the *correct* answer.

Here are some general tips for exam success:

- Arrive early at the exam center, so you can relax and review your study materials.

- Read the questions *carefully*. Don't just jump to conclusions. Make sure that you're clear about *exactly* what each question asks.

- Don't leave any questions unanswered. They count against you.

- When answering multiple-choice questions that you're not sure about, use a process of elimination to eliminate the obviously incorrect answers first. Doing this greatly improves your odds if you need to make an educated guess.

- Mark questions that you're not sure about. If you have time at the end, you can review those marked questions to see if the correct answer "jumps out" at you.

After you complete the exam, you'll get immediate, online notification of your pass or fail status, a printed Examination Score Report that indicates your pass or fail status, and your exam results by section. (The test administrator will give you the printed score report.) Test scores are automatically forwarded to Juniper Networks within five working days after you take the test, so you don't need to send your score to them.

JNCIA Study Guide

Now that you know a lot about the JNTCP, we need to provide some more information about this text. We begin with a look at some topics and information you should already be familiar with and then examine what topics are in the book. Finally, we discuss how to utilize this resource and the accompanying CD.

What You Should Know Before Starting

If you are familiar with networking books, you might be a little surprised by the starting topic in Chapter 1. It is not the Open Systems Interconnection (OSI) model common to books in our industry, but instead the software that operates the router. In the following chapters, we dive headfirst into the details of running a network using the JUNOS software. This philosophy of *knowing the basics* is quite ingrained in the Juniper Networks Education courseware and certification exams, so we follow that assumption.

This means that you should be knowledgeable and conversant in the following topics:

OSI Model   The OSI model defines seven different OSI layers—Physical, Data Link, Network, Transport, Session, Presentation, and Application. This model allows vendors and engineers to develop products designed for a specific OSI level. The segmentation this provides splits the overall "problem" of networking into smaller, more manageable pieces. Each layer of the model has certain responsibilities assigned to it and interacts with its neighboring levels in a predefined manner.

Switches   Ethernet, Asynchronous Transfer Mode (ATM), and Frame Relay switches all operate at the Data Link layer (Layer 2) of the OSI model. You should understand the concept of a logical address and know how the local significance of those addresses plays a part in the scalability of the network.

Routers   Routers operate at the Network layer (Layer 3) of the OSI model. They connect separate IP subnets together and route packets across a network in a hop-by-hop manner.

Ethernet Networks   Ethernet networks are commonly referred to as a broadcast domain. This means that all connected hosts receive all transmissions on the physical media. Each host uses the destination Media Access Control (MAC) address of the Ethernet frame to determine which frame it should process. The MAC addresses on a segment are learned through the Address Resolution Protocol (ARP).

Point-to-Point Links   Point-to-point links in a network are often referred to as wide area network (WAN) links. This generalized term is used to describe the nature of a point-to-point link— it contains no end IP hosts. In a core network, point-to-point links connect two network devices. These devices can be ATM switches, Frame Relay switches, or network routers. These network links have the ability to use one of many Layer 2 encapsulations, including ATM, Frame Relay, the Point-to-Point Protocol (PPP), and High-Level Data Link Control (HDLC).

IP Addressing and Subnetting   IP hosts and routers use a common packet format for all data transmissions. This includes the destination and source IP address fields, which use a 32-bit address space. Humans often use a dotted decimal format to represent an IP address. The address contains a host portion and a network portion. For example, 192.168.1.1 /24 defines a network address of 192.168.1.0 and a host address of 1 on that subnet.

TCP   The Transmission Control Protocol (TCP) operates at the Transport layer (Layer 4) of the OSI model. It defines a common header format, which includes destination and source port numbers. TCP provides a connection-oriented session between two end hosts that is established using a three-way handshake. TCP also uses a sliding window for flow control between the hosts.

UDP   The User Datagram Protocol (UDP) also operates at the Transport layer (Layer 4) of the OSI model. Like TCP, it defines a common header format and uses destination and source port numbers. Unlike TCP, however, UDP provides a connectionless session between two end hosts that resembles a flowing packet stream. No reliability or flow control is provided to the hosts.

ICMP   The Internet Control Message Protocol (ICMP) uses the IP packet format to perform its functions. Therefore, we often describe it as operating at the Network layer of the OSI model.

The main function of ICMP is to generate error messages that should be acted upon by network devices.

Network Troubleshooting   Network engineers use ping, a function of ICMP, to verify connectivity in the network. Should a problem be found, a second useful tool is traceroute. Traceroute sends UDP messages in a hop-by-hop fashion and provides you with the exact route, and possible trouble spot, through your network.

If you feel that you need a refresher on these topics, please visit the Core Routing website listed in the "About the Authors and Technical Editors" section later in this introduction. You will find resources there that you may use to complete your knowledge base.

Scope of the Book

While it's easy to say that the book covers the objectives for the JNCIA-M exam, we anticipate that this book, like the exam itself, is only the beginning of your reading and learning about Juniper Networks products and the JUNOS software. To that end, we tried to begin each chapter with some basic theory concepts. In addition, the foundation for future learning is laid out in the protocol packet formats and detailed explanations of what they include. From there, we begin to explore the implementation details of the JUNOS software in relation to the chapter subject.

 All router output in the book was taken from JUNOS software versions 5.4 and 5.5.

To truly cover all there is to know about the JUNOS software and the Juniper Networks routers would take quite a few books. We currently have plans for writing only a few that relate, like this book, to the certification program. Therefore, you will notice a difference in the depth (or lack thereof) of detail from chapter to chapter. The material in some chapters is enough to satisfy your requirements for almost all of your certification needs, but is only the tip of the iceberg within that subject matter. In those cases, we discuss all we need and leave the rest to your own reading from other sources. Other topics, like routing protocols, require a deep understanding at all levels of the certification program. Those topics, in this book, are truly the basic concepts. We leave the rest of the knowledge needed to the forthcoming books in the series.

In the end, we hope that you get enough data to perform well on the JNCIA-M exam, but that you are left longing for more detailed and advanced information. That's a good sign; it is the mark of a great network engineer. Please know that additional resources are available to you and that more Sybex Study Guides are on the way to quench your thirst for knowledge.

What Does This Book Cover?

This book covers everything you need to know to pass the JNCIA-M exam. It teaches you how to configure and operate many protocols and features of the JUNOS software. While this material is helpful, we also recommend gaining some hands-on practice. We understand that accessing a live Juniper Networks router in a lab environment is difficult, but if you can manage it you'll retain this knowledge far longer in your career.

Each chapter begins with a list of the exam objectives covered, so make sure you read them over before getting too far into the chapter. The chapters end with some review questions that are specifically designed to help you retain the knowledge we discussed. Take some time to carefully read through the questions and review the sections of the chapter relating to any question you miss. The book consists of the following material:

- Chapter 1 introduces you to the basic components of the Juniper Networks Routers. We discuss the hardware composition of the chassis platforms and the details of the JUNOS software. This is where we discuss using the command-line interface (CLI) and how an IP packet flows through the router.

- Chapter 2 focuses on the types of interfaces supported by the JUNOS software. We discuss permanent and transient interfaces as well as provide configuration examples for both.

- Chapter 3 introduces you to a portion of the JUNOS software that affects the router as a whole—protocol-independent properties. Static, aggregate, generated, and Martian routes are some of the topics covered.

- Chapter 4 explores the basics of the JUNOS software policy framework. Routing policies on a Juniper Networks router are very powerful and perform numerous functions. We show you how to build and apply a policy on the router.

- Chapter 5 begins our journey into the IP routing protocols with the Routing Information Protocol (RIP). We attempt to discuss all aspects of RIP within the JUNOS software in this single chapter.

- Chapter 6 covers the Open Shortest Path First (OSPF) protocol. The format of the protocol packets, the basic operation, and some configuration details are discussed.

- Chapter 7 discusses the second link-state protocol used by the JUNOS software. Intermediate System to Intermediate System (IS-IS) is very similar to OSPF. We also discuss the packet formats, basic operations, and the configuration within the router. At the conclusion of the chapter, we compare and contrast IS-IS to OSPF.

- Chapter 8 explores the Border Gateway Protocol (BGP). BGP is an important portion of the JUNOS software, and we begin our coverage of it by detailing the protocol attributes. After a look at how BGP selects its routes, we discuss how to configure BGP in a multi-AS environment.

- Chapter 9 takes us in a bit of a different direction when we talk about multicast routing and forwarding on a Juniper Networks router. Multicast addresses for IP and Ethernet are explained as well as the forwarding differences between a dense-mode and a sparse-mode network. After that, we explore the operation and configuration of the Internet Group Management Protocol (IGMP) and Protocol Independent Multicast (PIM).

- Chapter 10 covers how the JUNOS software filters packets in an IP network. Firewall filters are similar to routing policies but are used for different purposes. In addition to packet filtering, you can sample, log, and rate-limit IP traffic.

- Chapter 11 ends the book with a discussion of Multiprotocol Label Switching (MPLS). This relatively new technology is growing ever more popular. We look at the reasons why it was created and the basics of its operation. Its implementation and configuration in the JUNOS software concludes the chapter.

How to Use This Book

This book can provide a solid foundation for the serious effort of preparing for the Juniper Networks Certified Internet Associate M-series routers (JNCIA-M) exam. To best benefit from this book, we recommend the following study method:

1. Take the Assessment Test immediately following this Introduction. (The answers are at the end of the test.) Carefully read over the explanations for any question you get wrong, and note which chapters the material comes from. This information should help you to plan your study strategy.

2. Study each chapter carefully, making sure that you fully understand the information and the test topics listed at the beginning of each chapter. Pay extra-close attention to any chapter where you missed questions in the Assessment Test.

3. Answer the review questions found at the conclusion of each chapter. (The answers appear at the end of the chapter, after the review questions.)

4. Note the questions that you answered correctly but that confused you. Also make note of any questions you answered incorrectly. Go back and review the chapter material related to those questions.

5. Before taking the exam, try your hand at the two bonus exams that are included on the CD accompanying this book. The questions in these exams appear only on the CD. This gives you a complete overview of what you can expect to see on the real thing. After all, the authors of this book are the people who wrote the actual exam questions!

6. Remember to use the products on the CD that is included with this book. The electronic flashcards and the Sybex exam-preparation software have all been specifically selected to help you study for and pass your exam.

7. Take your studying on the road with the *JNCIA Study Guide* eBook in PDF. You can also test yourself remotely with the electronic flashcards.

The electronic flashcards can be used on your Windows computer or on your Palm device.

8. Make sure you read the Key Terms list at the end of each chapter. The glossary includes all of the terms used in the book (as well as others), along with an explanation for each term.

To learn all the material covered in this book, you'll have to apply yourself regularly and with discipline. Try to set aside the same amount of time every day to study, and select a comfortable and quiet place to do so. If you work hard, you will be surprised at how quickly you learn this material. Before you know it, you'll be on your way to becoming a JNCIE. Good luck and may the force be with you!

What's on the CD?

We worked very hard to provide some really great tools to help you with your certification process. All of the following tools should be loaded on your workstation when you're studying for the test.

The Sybex Test Engine for JNCIA-M Exam Preparation

This test-preparation software prepares you to successfully pass the JNCIA-M exam. In this test engine, you'll find all of the questions from the book, plus two additional bonus exams that appear exclusively on the CD. You can take the assessment test, test yourself by chapter or exam objective, or take the two bonus exams that appear on the CD.

To find more test-simulation software for the Juniper Networks exams, explore the information at `http://www.boson.com`.

Electronic Flashcards for PC and Palm Devices

After you read the *JNCIA Study Guide*, read the review questions at the end of each chapter and study the practice exams included in the book and on the CD. But wait, there's more! Test yourself with the flashcards included on the CD. If you can get through these difficult questions and understand the answers, you'll know you're ready for the actual exam.

The flashcards include over 150 questions specifically written to hit you hard and make sure you are ready for the exam. Between the review questions, practice exams, and flashcards, you'll be more than prepared for the exam.

JNCIA Study Guide in PDF

Sybex is also offering the Juniper Networks Certification books on their accompanying CDs so you can read the books on your PC or laptop. The *JNCIA Study Guide* is on this CD in Adobe Acrobat format. Acrobat Reader 5.1 with Search is also included on the CD.

This will be extremely helpful to readers who travel and don't want to carry a book, as well as to readers who find it more comfortable to read from their computer.

JUNOS software Documentation in PDF

Finally, the Juniper Networks documentation set for version 5.3 is included on the CD so that you can read these manuals on your PC or laptop. The documentation set is in Adobe Acrobat format. Acrobat Reader 5.1 with Search is also included on the CD.

About the Authors and Technical Editors

You can reach all of the authors and technical editors through the Core Routing website at `http://www.corerouting.net`. This website includes links to e-mail the authors, a list of known errata, and other study material to aid in your pursuit of all the Juniper Networks certifications.

Joseph M. Soricelli is an Education Services Engineer at Juniper Networks Inc. He is JNCIE #14, a Juniper Networks Authorized Trainer, and CCIE #4803. He is a contributing author to *Juniper Networks Routers: The Complete Reference* and has written numerous training courses. He has worked with and trained carriers, telcos, and ISPs throughout his career in the networking industry.

John L. Hammond is an Education Services Engineer with Juniper Networks Inc., and has provided on-site training and course development for Juniper Networks since October 2000. John's first exposure to "routers" was in the 1970s with the United States Army Security Agency while stationed in Europe. In those days, the "routers" were lower-rank enlisted men who could read the seven-level code punched on paper tape. After leaving the Army, John worked for several major corporations as a field engineer and later spent eight years in the Technical Support department of a Silicon Valley startup. He began his teaching career after joining a Cisco Authorized Training Partner headquartered in Annapolis, Maryland in 1998.

Galina Diker Pildush, CCIE #3176, JNCIE #18, provides training and course development for Juniper Networks Inc. After earning her M.S. in Computer Science, she worked for 20 years for major international corporations in the areas of internetwork design, architecture, network optimization, implementation, project management, and training. She has been an academic teacher at York University and received her Routing and Switching CCIE certification in 1997. Upon achieving her CCIE certification, Galina dedicated a majority of her professional career to training and mentoring CCIE candidates by being a technical director for the Netgun Academy CCIE preparation program at Global Knowledge Network Inc. After joining Juniper Networks, Galina achieved one of the industry's toughest certifications, Juniper Networks Certified Internet Expert (JNCIE). Galina continues to teach at Juniper and enjoys the state-of-the-art technology. Her areas of interest and specialization are ATM, internetwork design and optimization, Voice over IP, VPNs, MPLS and wireless. She is the author of *Cisco ATM Solutions: Master ATM Implementation of Cisco Networks*.

Thomas E. Van Meter is a trainer in the Education Services department for Juniper Networks Inc. He has a B.S. from the U.S. Military Academy and an M.S. in Telecommunications and Computers from George Washington University. He was formerly a trainer and consultant at Chesapeake Computer Consultants Inc., and Automation Research Systems Ltd. He served in the U.S. Army for 10 years, mostly in infantry units, but his brief stint working as an automation officer and with satellite data communications started him down the Internet routing path. He currently teaches as an adjunct faculty member in the George Mason University M.S. program in Telecommunications. He is JNCIE #34 and CCIE #1769.

Todd M. Warble is a senior instructor for Juniper Networks Education Services. He has been delivering courses on the M-series routers since July of 2000. Todd is JNCIE #7 and also performs grading of the practical exam, as well as development of the written test.

Steven T. Y. Wong is currently a Customer Support Engineer in Juniper Networks Technical Assistance Center (JTAC), where he provides technical support to major ISPs. Before joining Juniper Networks, he worked for a regional system integrator and was responsible for providing consulting and technical support services to multinational enterprise customers and ISPs. Steven is

JNCIE #10 and CCIE #4353. He also holds a Master's degree and a Bachelor's degree in Electrical and Electronic Engineering from the Hong Kong University of Science and Technology.

Bruno De Troch is a Juniper Networks Technical Assistance Center (JTAC) engineer, supporting some of the major European ISPs and carriers. He started his career in networking as a Captain in the Belgian Armed Forces, managing the operations for their national data network. Bruno is a Juniper Networks Authorized Trainer and is JNCIE #15. He is married and has two children, both of whom he considers as his most valuable achievements.

Assessment Test

1. Which BGP attribute is used, by default, only when multiple routes arrive from the same neighboring AS?

   A. Local Preference

   B. MED

   C. AS Path

   D. Origin

2. How many route entries are advertised in a single RIPv2 Response message when MD5 authentication is used in the network?

   A. 23

   B. 24

   C. 25

   D. 26

3. Which interface name correctly represents an Ethernet interface that is located in port 2 on a PIC that is in slot 3 of the FPC, which is in slot 4 in the chassis?

   A. `fe-2/3/4`

   B. `fe-4/3/2`

   C. `fe-2/4/3`

   D. `fe-3/4/2`

4. How are RIPv2 Response messages advertised, by default?

   A. Unicast

   B. Multicast

   C. Broadcast

   D. Anycast

5. You are using an MPLS network to support Layer 3 VPNs. By default, which routing table is used to store information in this environment?

   A. `inet.3`

   B. `mpls.0`

   C. `bgp.l3vpn.0`

   D. `bgp.l2vpn.0`

6. By default, how many next-hop entries are placed into the forwarding table for each valid route?

   A. 1

   B. 2

   C. 3

   D. 4

7. How many prefixes will match `route-filter 192.168.0.0/16 upto /17`?

   A. 1

   B. 2

   C. 3

   D. 4

8. Which software process is responsible for operating all routing protocols?

   A. mgd

   B. chassisd

   C. rpd

   D. pfed

9. What is the largest usable metric allowed in a RIP Response message?

   A. 10

   B. 15

   C. 20

   D. 25

10. Which PIM interface mode must be used in an Auto-RP environment?

    A. Sparse mode

    B. Dense mode

    C. Sparse-dense mode

    D. Dense-sparse mode

11. What OSPF adjacency state is a router in after it receives a hello packet with its own router ID listed as a neighbor?

    A. `Init`

    B. `Start`

    C. `Down`

    D. `2-Way`

12. Which command allows you to view the networks advertised by each router in the OSPF area?

   A. `show ospf neighbor`

   B. `show ospf database detail`

   C. `show ospf interface`

   D. `show ospf statistics`

13. What ASIC is responsible for creating J-cells?

   A. PIC I/O Manager ASIC

   B. I/O Manager ASIC

   C. Distributed Buffer Manager ASIC

   D. Internet Processor ASIC

14. What are the criteria for the election of the Designated Intermediate System (DIS) on a broad-cast link?

   A. Highest priority followed by highest MAC address

   B. Lowest priority followed by highest MAC address

   C. Highest priority followed by lowest MAC address

   D. Lowest priority followed by lowest MAC address

15. What protocol family correctly configures an interface to support IS-IS within the JUNOS software?

   A. `iso`

   B. `isis`

   C. `clns`

   D. `clnp`

16. What CLI command allows the router to use all configuration changes you enter?

   A. `commit`

   B. `rollback`

   C. `save filename`

   D. `load filename`

17. Which configuration statement best summarizes the following routes and allows the router to forward IP traffic to the configured route?

- 172.16.13.0 /24
- 172.16.64.0 /19
- 172.16.32.0 /21
- 172.16.52.9 /32

A. set aggregate route 172.16.0.0/17

B. set aggregate route 172.16.0.0/18

C. set generate route 172.16.0.0/17

D. set generate route 172.16.0.0/18

18. By default, an IS-IS router will export which of the following routes from the routing table?

A. All Direct routes matching the IS-IS configuration

B. All IGP routes, including OSPF

C. All active routes in inet.0

D. No routes will be exported.

19. What protocol is used in a multicast network for communications between the hosts and the routers?

A. ICMP

B. IGMP

C. IRDP

D. IGRP

20. An IS-IS router uses which circuit ID to represent the loopback interface of the router?

A. 0x00

B. 0x01

C. 0x02

D. 0x03

21. What PIM state describes a source of 172.16.1.1 for the 228.202.100.1 /32 multicast group address?

A. (228.202.100.1, 172.16.1.1)

B. (228.202.100.1, 172.16.1.1, *)

C. (172.16.1.1, 228.202.100.1)

D. (*, 172.16.1.1, 228.202.100.1)

22. How would you get a Juniper Networks router to advertise IS-IS routes to an OSPF neighbor?

    A. Configure an import policy under [`edit protocols ospf`] that matches IS-IS routes and accepts them.

    B. Configure an export policy under [`edit protocols ospf`] that matches IS-IS routes and accepts them.

    C. Configure an import policy under [`edit protocols isis`] that matches IS-IS routes and accepts them.

    D. Configure an export policy under [`edit protocols isis`] that matches IS-IS routes and accepts them.

23. Where does a BGP router store information it should advertise to an EBGP peer?

    A. Adjacency-RIB-In

    B. Local-RIB

    C. Forwarding-RIB

    D. Adjacency-RIB-Out

24. You would like to implement a firewall filter to affect transit user traffic. On which interface should you apply the filter?

    A. `lo0.0`

    B. `fxp0.0`

    C. `fxp1.0`

    D. `fe-0/0/0.0`

25. Which firewall filter action drops packets that match a term and returns an ICMP message to the source of the packet?

    A. `accept`

    B. `discard`

    C. `dismiss`

    D. `reject`

26. Which of the following routers advertises a Type 7 LSA?

    A. ABR

    B. ASBR

    C. DR

    D. BDR

27. Which BGP attribute is set by the router that first announces a route and denotes the source of that route?

   A. Local Preference

   B. Origin

   C. MED

   D. AS Path

28. Which Juniper Networks router component is responsible for implementing a firewall filter?

   A. PIC I/O Manager ASIC

   B. I/O Manager ASIC

   C. Distributed Buffer Manager ASIC

   D. Internet Processor ASIC

29. An interface has multiple IP addresses configured within the same subnet. Which of the following statements is true concerning the interface's `preferred` address?

   A. It is the highest numbered address on the interface.

   B. It is the lowest numbered address on the interface.

   C. Each configured address is considered to be the `preferred` address.

   D. There is no `preferred` address.

30. What does an MPLS label value of 3 mean?

   A. IPv4 Explicit NULL

   B. Router Alert

   C. IPv6 Explicit NULL

   D. Implicit NULL

31. Which protocol can be used to set up a dynamic LSP using an explicit network path?

   A. IGP

   B. LDP

   C. BGP

   D. RSVP

32. Which of the following is a valid NET address?

   A. 49.0001.1921.6800.1001.01

   B. 49.1000.1111.0001.1921.6800.1001.00

   C. 49.abcd.efgh.1921.6800.1001.00

   D. 49.abcd.1921.6800.1001.01

33. What are the methods used by RSVP to maintain an established LSP? (Choose two.)

  A. It refreshes RSVP `Resv` messages upstream.

  B. It refreshes RSVP `Resv` messages downstream.

  C. It refreshes RSVP `Path` messages upstream.

  D. It refreshes RSVP `Path` messages downstream.

34. Which operating system is the JUNOS software kernel based on?

  A. Linux

  B. FreeBSD

  C. AIX

  D. Solaris

35. What logical binary representation is useful for understanding the operation of a JUNOS software route filter?

  A. Route tree

  B. Forwarding tree

  C. Binary tree

  D. Radix tree

Answers to Assessment Test

1. B. A BGP router only uses the MED attribute, by default, when multiple routes in the Adjacency-RIB-In table have arrived from the same neighboring AS. For more information, see Chapter 8.

2. A. By default, a Response message carries 25 route entries. When plain-text authentication is configured, one route entry is used to store the authentication data. Therefore, only 24 route entries can be advertised in this scenario. Using MD5 authentication, however, requires the use of two route entries, leaving a capacity of 23 RIP routes in the message. For more information, see Chapter 5.

3. B. The correct order is media type, FPC slot number, PIC slot number, and PIC port number. In this instance, this is displayed as `fe-4/3/2`. For more information, see Chapter 2.

4. B. RIPv2 defaults to advertising Response messages using the 224.0.0.9 /32 multicast group address. For more information, see Chapter 5.

5. C. By default, the JUNOS software stores VPN routing information advertised between Provider Edge routers in the `bgp.l3vpn.0` routing table. For more information, see Chapter 3.

6. A. The JUNOS software places a single next-hop entry into the forwarding table for each valid route in the routing table, by default. You can modify this behavior by configuring a routing policy within the `[edit routing-options forwarding-table]` configuration hierarchy. For more information, see Chapter 3.

7. C. The `upto` match type stops the evaluation of the route filter and matches the routes found at the specified level. This route filter matches the 192.168.0.0 /16, 192.168.0.0 /17, and 192.168.128.0 /17 routes. For more information, see Chapter 4.

8. C. The Routing Protocol Daemon (rpd) is in charge of operating all routing protocols in the JUNOS software. For more information, see Chapter 1.

9. B. The largest usable metric supported by RIP is 15. For more information, see Chapter 5.

10. C. The use of Auto-RP in a PIM network means that the 224.0.1.39 /32 and 224.0.1.40 /32 group addresses must be densely flooded throughout the network. All other multicast traffic must be forwarded using the RP and sparse-mode forwarding rules. This prompts the use of sparse-dense mode on all PIM interfaces. For more information, see Chapter 9.

11. D. When a router receives a hello packet with its router ID listed as a neighbor, it can guarantee that the sending router has received at least one OSPF packet from the local router. Therefore, bidirectional communication has been achieved and the local router will transition to the `2-Way` state. For more information, see Chapter 6.

12. B. Option B displays detailed information about the LSAs known to the local router. This information includes the networks advertised by all the routers within the OSPF area. For more information, see Chapter 6.

13. B. The I/O Manager ASIC is responsible for creating J-cells. For more information, see Chapter 1.

14. A. The two possible criteria for DIS election are priority and MAC address. The first tiebreaker is the highest priority, followed by the highest MAC address. For more information, see Chapter 7.

15. A. The iso protocol family is the only valid JUNOS software family and is used to configure an interface to support IS-IS. For more information, see Chapter 2.

16. A. The router uses information in the candidate configuration when you issue the commit command. For more information, see Chapter 1.

17. C. Both options A and C adequately summarize all of the routes given. However, a generated route contains an IP address as a next-hop value. This allows the router to forward IP traffic using the 192.168.0.0 /17 route. For more information, see Chapter 3.

18. A. By default, IS-IS advertises only Direct routes that match the subnets and interfaces you define in the IS-IS configuration of the router. For more information, see Chapter 4.

19. B. Host-to-router communications in a multicast network are handled by the Internet Group Management Protocol (IGMP). For more information, see Chapter 9.

20. B. The loopback and all point-to-point links share a value of 0x01. Broadcast links begin their unique numbering at 0x02, while the router itself always uses a circuit ID of 0x00. For more information, see Chapter 7.

21. C. PIM state is always displayed in a (Source, Group) fashion. Only option C uses this format. For more information, see Chapter 9.

22. B. In order to properly redistribute routes from IS-IS into OSPF, you must create a policy that matches on IS-IS routes and then apply that policy to OSPF. For more information, see Chapter 4.

23. D. The Adjacency-RIB-Out table stores all route advertisements to other BGP peers. For more information, see Chapter 8.

24. D. Firewall filters affect user transit traffic when they are applied to transient interfaces. Only option D (fe-0/0/0.0) represents a transient interface. For more information, see Chapter 10.

25. D. Both discard and reject drop packets in a filter term, but only reject returns an ICMP message back to the source of the IP packet. For more information, see Chapter 10.

26. B. An ASBR router injects external routing information into OSPF. When used in a not-so-stubby area, the ASBR generates Type 7 LSAs. For more information, see Chapter 6.

27. B. The Origin attribute is designed to inform all BGP routers as to the source of the route from the perspective of the originating router. For more information, see Chapter 8.

28. D. All firewall filters are implemented on the Internet Processor ASIC. For more information, see Chapter 10.

29. B. An interface contains a single preferred address per configured subnet and, by default, it is the lowest numerical prefix on the interface. For more information, see Chapter 2.

30. D. An MPLS label value of 3 represents an Implicit NULL, which informs the immediate upstream router to perform penultimate hop popping (PHP). For more information, see Chapter 11.

31. D. While both LDP and RSVP are MPLS signaling protocols, only RSVP supports the use of traffic engineering and explicit network paths. For more information, see Chapter 11.

32. B. Option B is the only correct NET address shown. Options A and D have a 0x01 for the selector byte, which must be 0x00. Option C contains characters that are not valid for a hexadecimal address. For more information, see Chapter 7.

33. A, D. RSVP refreshes Path and Resv messages every 30 seconds to maintain the soft state of the LSP in the network. Path messages are sent downstream, and Resv messages are sent upstream. For more information, see Chapter 11.

34. B. The JUNOS software kernel is based on the FreeBSD Unix operating system. For more information, see Chapter 1.

35. D. A radix tree is used to represent the operation of a JUNOS software route filter. For more information, see Chapter 4.

Chapter 1

The Components of a Juniper Networks Router

As we discussed in the Introduction, you should already have a grasp of basic networking concepts. This includes the layers of the Open Systems Interconnection (OSI) model, the format and layout of an IP packet, and the function of a router as a network device. Additionally, you should understand the operation of both the Transmission Control Protocol (TCP) and the User Datagram Protocol (UDP).

This chapter will introduce you to the basic components of the Juniper Networks family of routers. We start with a high-level examination of the two basic components of the system: the Routing Engine and the Packet Forwarding Engine. Next, we cover the specific details of the Routing Engine, including the JUNOS software modules, boot devices, and boot sequence pattern. In addition, we discuss the various modes of the software as well as some fail-over capabilities. We conclude with a discussion of the Packet Forwarding Engine ASICs and an example of a packet's flow through the router.

Let's first ensure that we have a common understanding of the terminology and an idea of how all the pieces fit together.

Juniper Networks Router Design

The central design principle of the Juniper Networks platform centers on a separation of the control and forwarding planes within the router. The Routing Engine and the Packet Forwarding Engine, respectively, represent these planes. You can see this design concept in Figure 1.1.

FIGURE 1.1   Juniper Networks router design

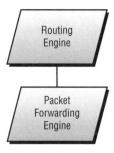

Let's examine each of these components in more detail.

Routing Engine Overview

The *Routing Engine* in a Juniper Networks router is the central location for control of the system. This is where the intelligence of the router operates. You perform software upgrades and maintenance on the Routing Engine. In addition, you interface with the Routing Engine for monitoring and configuring the router.

General Functions

Your experience with a Juniper Networks router begins with the Routing Engine. After connecting to the router, you supply authentication information (name and password) to the Routing Engine. After you're authenticated, you perform management and configuration operations within the Routing Engine. Troubleshooting tools like Telnet, ping, or traceroute operate from within the Routing Engine as well.

Since control of the router occurs in the Routing Engine, this is the logical location to store the JUNOS software. As such, the Routing Engine operates all routing protocols and makes all *routing table* decisions, building a master routing table with the best path to each destination selected. The router then places these best paths into the *forwarding table* on the Routing Engine and copies that same data into the forwarding table on the Packet Forwarding Engine. The forwarding table on the Packet Forwarding Engine allows the router to actually forward user data packets.

Physical Composition

The intelligence of the Routing Engine software is not matched by equally intelligent hardware. In fact, the physical components are widely available. Each Routing Engine is based on an Intel PCI motherboard. The actual components of each Routing Engine depend on the model you are using and include the following:

Routing Engine 2   The Routing Engine 2 is found in the Juniper Networks M-series routers (M5, M10, M20, M40, M40e, M160). It contains a 333MHz processor and 768MB of random access memory (RAM). File storage is handled by an 80MB internal flash drive and a 6.4GB traditional hard drive. When you use the Routing Engine 2 on an M40 router, it contains an LS 120 disk for external file storage; all other models use a removable PCMCIA flash card for this purpose.

Routing Engine 3   The Routing Engine 3 is found in the Juniper Networks T-series routers (T320 and T640). Additionally, recent versions of the JUNOS software support the use of this Routing Engine in the M5, M10, M20, M40e, and M160 routers. The Routing Engine 3 contains a 600MHz processor and 2GB of RAM. File storage is handled by a 128MB internal flash drive and a 30GB traditional hard drive. The Routing Engine 3 uses a removable PCMCIA flash card for external file storage.

The RAM memory in the Routing Engine stores routing tables, forwarding tables, link-state databases, and operational memory space for the JUNOS software. The internal flash drive stores the JUNOS software and configuration files for the router. The hard drive is used to store a backup copy of the JUNOS software, log files, traceoptions output (debug), and user files.

While the differences between the Routing Engine models certainly control how much storage capacity you have in the router, they do not affect the operation of the JUNOS software. The internal flash drive is used for the same purposes and the software builds routing tables in the amount of RAM available to it. In fact, each version of the JUNOS software operates across all Routing Engine models. You never need to worry about replacing the Routing Engine hardware and then having to find the right software version to support it.

The hardware in a Juniper Networks Routing Engine is generally composed of the most common components available at its time of construction. As the cost of hardware decreases over time, you can expect that newer versions of the Routing Engine will contain more powerful hardware. Regardless, the requirements of the router design allow the Routing Engine to function quite well using the hardware described here.

Packet Forwarding Engine Overview

The *Packet Forwarding Engine* is the central location for data packet forwarding through the router. The router's throughput speed and capacity are controlled by the specially designed hardware, which sets a Juniper Networks router apart from its competitors.

General Functions

Simply put, the Packet Forwarding Engine provides industry-leading performance in the forwarding of data packets across any interface in the router. Achieving this type of throughput requires dividing the forwarding plane of the router into multiple segments controlled by *application-specific integrated circuits (ASICs)*. The interaction of these ASICs provides the forwarding path within a Juniper Networks router.

The function of the Juniper Networks ASICs and their role in packet forwarding is covered in the section "Packet Forwarding Engine Components" later in this chapter.

Physical Composition

In contrast to the Routing Engine with its single motherboard and processor, the Packet Forwarding Engine contains a passive midplane as well as multiple boards and processors. Each circuit board is controlled by software that is fairly non-intelligent when compared to the JUNOS software on the Routing Engine.

The main portions of the Packet Forwarding Engine are the Physical Interface Card, the Flexible PIC Concentrator, and a switching control board. Each component contains an ASIC custom-designed by Juniper Networks engineers and manufactured by IBM. Each ASIC performs a specific function in the forwarding path of packets. (We discuss the specific functions of each ASIC in the section "Packet Flow" later in this chapter.)

Switching Control Board

The switching control board contains a PowerPC CPU and 64MB of RAM that operates the components of the circuit board itself, but doesn't participate in packet forwarding. An additional 8MB (or 16MB in recent versions of the circuit board) of synchronized static random access memory (SSRAM) contains the forwarding table for the router. The Internet Processor ASIC is located on the control board and accesses the forwarding table for route lookups. Additionally, the control board contains an ASIC designed for packet storage memory management.

> As a comparison, the 8MB of SSRAM on the switching control board holds approximately 450,000 forwarding table entries. As of this writing, the Internet has about 120,000 unique routing entries. This means that the Internet can double in size twice before you run out of storage capacity for your forwarding table.

Each router model uses a different name for the control board functionality. The possible names include:

Forwarding Engine Board (FEB) The *Forwarding Engine Board* is found in both the M5 and M10 platforms and integrates the circuit board with the FPC. Each router contains no more than one FEB, which is specific to either the M5 or the M10 chassis.

System Switching Board (SSB) The *System Switching Board* is found in the M20 platform. Each platform is configured to hold dual SSBs, but only one board is operational at any one time.

System Control Board (SCB) The *System Control Board* is found in the M40 platform. Each chassis contains no more than one SCB.

Switching and Forwarding Module (SFM) The *Switching and Forwarding Module* is found in the M40e and M160 platforms. Each M40e router can contain 2 SFMs, with only one operational at a time. The M160 router contains four SFMs working in parallel.

Memory Mezzanine Board (MMB) The *Memory Mezzanine Board* is found in the T320 and T640 platforms and is located on the FPC itself.

> The T320 and T640 platforms are designed with a different internal architecture for the Packet Forwarding Engine. The M-series platforms are the focus of this book, and we point out differences with the T-series platforms where appropriate.

Flexible PIC Concentrator

The *Flexible PIC Concentrator (FPC)* connects to both the switching control board and the router's interfaces within the Packet Forwarding Engine. A PowerPC CPU controls the FPC board, and it uses 64MB of RAM to operate the Embedded OS software. The PowerPC CPU doesn't participate in data packet forwarding, however. This is the function of a Juniper Networks ASIC, which is located on the FPC and interacts with the data packets as they enter and exit the router interfaces.

Physical Interface Card

The physical media in your network connects to the *Physical Interface Card (PIC)* in your router. Up to four individual PICs are contained on an FPC. A media-specific ASIC is located on each PIC.

Routing Engine Components

Let's now discuss the specific details and operation of the Routing Engine components. We start with the JUNOS software, examine the operation of the command-line interface (CLI), and finish with the fail-over capabilities of the Routing Engine.

Software Architecture

The JUNOS software is based on the FreeBSD Unix operating system. The open source software is modified and hardened by Juniper Networks engineers to operate in the router's specialized environment. For example, some executables have been deleted while other utilities were de-emphasized. Additionally, certain daemons were added to enhance the routing functionality. The result of this transformation is the *kernel*, the heart of the JUNOS software.

The kernel is responsible for operating multiple daemons that perform the actual functions of the router. Each daemon operates in its own protected memory space, which is also controlled by the kernel. This separation provides isolation between the processes and resiliency in the event of a process failure. This is important in a core routing platform since a single process failure does not cause the entire router to cease functioning. Some common daemons include:

Routing Protocol Daemon (rpd)   The router's protocols are controlled by the *Routing Protocol Daemon*. Its functionality includes all protocol messages, routing table updates, and implementation of routing policies.

Device Control Daemon (dcd)   The router's interfaces are configured and maintained by the *Device Control Daemon*. This process controls both the physical and logical properties of the interfaces.

Management Daemon (mgd)   The *Management Daemon* process controls all user access to the router. For example, the user's CLI is a client of mgd.

Chassis Daemon (chassisd)   The *Chassis Daemon* process controls the properties of the router itself, including the interaction of the passive midplane, the FPCs, and the control boards.

Packet Forwarding Engine Daemon (pfed)   The *Packet Forwarding Engine Daemon* process controls the communication between the Packet Forwarding Engine and the Routing Engine. For example, one of its functions is retrieving the interface input/output statistics from the Packet Forwarding Engine.

The kernel also generates specialized daemons as needed for additional functionality. Some examples include Simple Network Management Protocol (SNMP), Virtual Router Redundancy Protocol (VRRP), and Class of Service (CoS).

Software Components

The JUNOS software is actually made up of multiple pieces working together to control the router's functions. Each section of the software is referred to as a *package* and contains files specific to its particular function. The current packages found in each copy of the JUNOS software are:

jkernel   The *jkernel* package contains the basic components of the JUNOS software operating system.

jbase   The *jbase* package contains additions to the JUNOS software since the last revision of the jkernel package.

jroute   The *jroute* package contains the software that operates on the Routing Engine. This controls the Unicast routing protocols, the multicast routing protocols, and the Multiprotocol Label Switching (MPLS) signaling protocols. The package also contains the software for some daemons, such as mgd.

jpfe   The *jpfe* package contains the Embedded OS software that controls the components of the Packet Forwarding Engine.

jdocs   The *jdocs* package contains the complete JUNOS software documentation set.

jcrypto   The *jcrypto* package contains software that controls various security functions, such as IP Security (IPSec) and Secure Shell (SSH). This package is available only in U.S. and Canadian versions of the software.

jbundle   The *jbundle* package is a single file that contains all of the other packages we discussed previously.

Getting Help from Your Router

The jdocs package is an interesting topic to discuss. It contains the entire JUNOS software documentation set on your router and is accessed through the user CLI. It is a handy tool to keep at your disposal.

You can find conceptual information on network topics by using the help topic command. For example, let's say you'd like to know more about setting up Open Shortest Path First (OSPF) backbone areas. Here's how you'd access this information and what the router would tell you:

```
user@Merlot> help topic ospf area-backbone
```

Configure the Backbone Area

You must create a backbone area if your network consists of multiple areas. An ABR must have at least one interface in the backbone area, or it must have a virtual link to a router in the backbone area. The backbone comprises all area border routers and all routers that are not included in any other area. You configure all these routers by including the following area statement at the [edit protocols ospf] hierarchy level (for routing instances, include the statement at the [edit routing-instances routing-instance-name protocols ospf] hierarchy level):

```
[edit protocols ospf]
    area 0.0.0.0;
```

When you are ready to configure your router to support an OSPF area, you can view specific configuration information using the help reference command:

```
user@Merlot> help reference ospf area
```

area

      Syntax

    area area-id;

      Hierarchy Level

    [edit protocols ospf],
    [edit routing-instances routing-instance-name protocols ospf]

      Description

Specify the area identifier for this router to use when participating in OSPF routing. All routers in an area must use the same area identifier to establish adjacencies.

Specify multiple area statements to configure the router as an area border router. An area border router automatically summarizes routes between areas; use the area-range statement to configure route summarization. By definition, an area border router must be connected to the backbone area either through a physical link or through a virtual link. To create a virtual link, use the virtual-link statement.

> To specify that the router is directly connected to the OSPF backbone, include
> the area 0.0.0.0 statement.
>
>   Options
>
> area-id--Area identifier. The identifier can be up to 32 bits. It is common to
> specify the area number as a simple integer or an IP address. Area number 0.0.0.0
> is reserved for the OSPF backbone area.

The JUNOS software Naming Convention

The JUNOS software follows a specific naming convention of *package-major_version*
<stage>released_version-type. An example from the Merlot router shows this format:

```
user@Merlot> file list jbundle*
/var/home/user/jbundle-5.2R1.4-domestic-signed.tgz
/var/home/user/jbundle-5.2R2.3-domestic-signed.tgz
/var/home/user/jbundle-5.3R2.4-domestic-signed.tgz
```

 The command output shown here contains information explained in the
"Command-Line Interface" section later in this chapter.

This naming structure allows you to quickly determine if your version of the software supports a desired feature. The details of the naming convention are as follows:

package   This represents the specific portion of the JUNOS software contained in the file. Examples include jbundle, jroute, and jpfe.

major_version   This represents the major version of the JUNOS software located in the file. This is always shown in a two-integer format, as in 5.2 or 5.3.

stage   This single capital letter represents the type of software in the file. Possible values include:

- R—Publicly released software (most common)
- A—Alpha version of the software
- B—Beta version of the software
- I—Internal or test version of the software

released_version   Each major_version of the software may contain multiple releases. This field represents the specific release number contained in this file. The Merlot router shows several examples: 1.4, 2.3, and 2.4.

type   Each jbundle package contains an additional field that represents whether the jcrypto package is contained. jcrypto is included in files marked with *domestic* and is omitted in files marked as *export*.

In addition, all packages may include the *signed* notation. This means that the package file is protected using the MD5 algorithm. When you apply the package to the router, the router runs the algorithm and compares the MD5 hash result to the stored value in the file. The package is used only when the values match, thereby protecting you from corrupted software files.

Upgrading the Software

You upgrade the JUNOS software by using the request system software add *filename* command. This command loads a software file from some location, often the user's home directory, onto the internal flash on the Routing Engine. (Files and directories are discussed in the section "Manipulating Files on the Router" later in this chapter.) In the following example, we want to upgrade the Merlot router, which is currently running version 5.2R2.3, to version 5.3R2.4:

```
user@Merlot> show version brief
Hostname: Merlot
Model: m5
JUNOS Base OS boot [5.2R2.3]
JUNOS Base OS Software Suite [5.2R2.3]
JUNOS Kernel Software Suite [5.2R2.3]
JUNOS Packet Forwarding Engine Support [5.2R2.3]
JUNOS Routing Software Suite [5.2R2.3]
JUNOS Online Documentation [5.2R2.3]
JUNOS Crypto Software Suite [5.2R2.3]


user@Merlot> request system software add jbundle-5.3R2.4-domestic-signed.tgz
```

The command separates the jbundle package into its individual package components (jroute, jpfe, etc.), and the Routing Engine upgrades each package individually. If the new version relies on changes to the base operating system, the jbase package is also upgraded. Upon a successful completion, you must reboot the router to use the new software using the request system reboot command. You also have the option of an automatic reboot by using the *reboot* option in conjunction with the request system software add *filename* command. The process looks like this:

```
user@Merlot> request system software add jbundle-5.3R2.4-domestic-signed.tgz
reboot
Installing package '/var/home/lab/jbundle-5.3R2.4-domestic-signed.tgz' ...
Verified MD5 checksum of jbundle-5.3R2.4-domestic.tgz
```

```
Adding jbundle...
Verified MD5 checksum of jbase-5.3R2.4.tgz
Verified MD5 checksum of jboot-5.3R2.4
Verified MD5 checksum of jcrypto-5.3R2.4.tgz
Verified MD5 checksum of jdocs-5.3R2.4.tgz
Verified MD5 checksum of jkernel-5.3R2.4.tgz
Verified MD5 checksum of jpfe-5.3R2.4.tgz
Verified MD5 checksum of jroute-5.3R2.4.tgz
Auto-deleting old jroute...
Auto-deleting old jdocs...
Auto-deleting old jpfe...
Auto-deleting old jcrypto...
Restarting kmd ...
Auto-deleting old jkernel...
Adding jkernel...
Restarting watchdog ...
Adding jcrypto...
Adding jpfe...
Adding jdocs...
Adding jroute...
Saving package file in /var/sw/pkg/jbundle-5.3R2.4-domestic-signed.tgz ...
Saving state for rollback ...
Rebooting ...
shutdown: [pid 5584]

*** FINAL System shutdown message from root@HongKong-3 ***
System going down IMMEDIATELY
```

It is possible to upgrade a single JUNOS software package individually, but this practice is not recommended. Software packages operating at different version levels might have an interaction that causes unforeseen consequences. This type of upgrade should be completed only with the guidance of the Juniper Networks Technical Assistance Center (JTAC).

Boot Sequence

Whether installed at the factory or upgraded in your network, the router stores bootable copies of the JUNOS software in three possible locations: the internal flash disk, the hard drive, or the removable media. Each location has the ability to load the software into memory and boot the router, but the primary boot media is the internal flash disk. The hard drive is considered the secondary boot location, while the removable media is used for disaster-recovery purposes.

A "factory fresh" router has the most recent JUNOS software version installed on the internal flash disk as well as the removable media.

As the router boots, it first runs a power-on self-test (POST) to verify that the basic system components are operating normally. The router then locates a copy of the JUNOS software and loads it into memory. The boot sequence of the router is shown in Figure 1.2.

FIGURE 1.2   The JUNOS software boot sequence

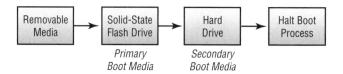

The removable media is the first boot location examined. If the router finds a copy of the JUNOS software there, it loads the software on the router. This presents a possible hazard in your network since all existing files and file systems on the router are erased during this process. This type of boot process returns the router to a factory default-type environment and should be used only for disaster recovery. If no removable media is present, the router loads the software from the internal flash disk. This is considered the normal boot operation and should occur at each router start.

It is possible for the internal flash disk to become corrupted or otherwise unusable. In this situation, the router uses the hard drive as its boot location and displays a message to alert you of this issue. You can see this as you log into the router:

To successfully boot the router from the hard drive, you first need to copy the JUNOS software and other critical files to it with the request system snapshot command.

```
Merlot (ttyp0)

login: user
Password:

--- JUNOS 5.3R1.2 built 2002-04-30 01:40:52 UTC
---
--- NOTICE: System is running on alternate media device (/dev/ad1s1a).
---

user@Merlot>
```

Should your router encounter a problem and boot from the hard drive, please contact the JTAC for assistance.

Command-Line Interface

At this point, we have the router booted and the appropriate software loaded on it. It is now time to monitor and configure the router using the *command-line interface (CLI)*.

The JUNOS software CLI contains two main modes: operational and configuration. The names adequately describe the functions permitted within each environment. Operational mode displays the current router status, and you use it for verifying and troubleshooting the router. Configuration mode, on the other hand, provides you with a method for altering the current environment.

Operational Mode

You enter *operational mode* on the router after a successful login attempt. The router prompt displays your status graphically:

```
user@Merlot>
```

The default prompt for the JUNOS software is a combination of your username and the router hostname. In our case, the username is `user` and the hostname of the router is `Merlot`. In addition, the > character tells you that you are in operational mode.

As with most router operating systems, the JUNOS software uses a command hierarchy paradigm within operational mode. This allows you to find only the information you request in a timely manner. Here we are accessing the top level of the operational-mode hierarchy on the Merlot router:

```
user@Merlot> ?
Possible completions:
  clear               Clear information in the system
  configure           Manipulate software configuration information
  file                Perform file operations
  help                Provide help information
  monitor             Real-time debugging
  mtrace              Trace multicast path from a source to a receiver
  ping                Ping a remote target
  quit                Exit the management session
  request             Make system-level requests
  restart             Restart a software process
  set                 Set CLI properties, date, time, craft display text
  show                Show information about the system
```

```
ssh                  Open a secure shell to another host
start                Start a software process
telnet               Telnet to another host
test                 Diagnostic debugging commands
traceroute           Trace the route to a remote host
```

You use this hierarchy level for several different purposes. For example, the `ping`, `telnet`, `traceroute`, and `ssh` commands allow the router to behave as an IP end host. The router generates these IP packets on the Routing Engine and sends them into the network through a particular interface. Commands such as `request`, `restart`, and `start` control the router's operations. In the "Upgrading the Software" section earlier in this chapter, we used the `request` command to load a new version of the JUNOS software.

You can view the router's current status by using the `show` command. The hierarchy located in this directory lets you access interface statistics, routing protocol information, and the current routing table. The `show` hierarchy directory on the Merlot router is:

```
user@Merlot> show ?
Possible completions:
  accounting         Show accounting profiles and records
  aps                Show APS information
  arp                Show system ARP table entries
  as-path            Show table of known AS paths
  bgp                Show information about BGP
  chassis            Show chassis information
  class-of-service   Show information about class of service
  cli                Show command-line interface settings
  configuration      Show configuration file contents
  connections        Show CCC connections
  dvmrp              Show information about DVMRP
  firewall           Show firewall counters and information
  helper             Show port-forwarding helper information
  host               Host name lookup service using domain name server
  igmp               Show information about IGMP
  ike                Show IKE information
  ilmi               Show ILMI information
  interfaces         Show interface information
  ipsec              Show IPSec information
  ipv6               Show information about IPv6
  isis               Show information about IS-IS
  l2circuit          Show information about Layer 2 circuits
  l2vpn              Show information about Layer 2 VPNs
  ldp                Show information about LDP
  log                Show contents of a log file
```

mpls	Show information about MPLS
msdp	Show information about MSDP
multicast	Show multicast information
ntp	Show Network Time Protocol information
ospf	Show information about OSPF
pfe	Show Packet Forwarding Engine information
pim	Show information about PIM
policer	Show interface policer counters and information
policy	Show policy information
rip	Show information about RIP
ripng	Show information about RIPng
route	Show routing table information
rsvp	Show information about RSVP
sap	Show session advertisement addresses
snmp	Show SNMP information
system	Show system information
task	Show routing protocol per-task information
ted	Show information about TED
version	Show software process revision levels
vrrp	Show VRRP information

Context-Sensitive Help

It is no accident that we've been utilizing the question mark (?) throughout this chapter to locate information. This character gives you *context-sensitive help* to navigate the command hierarchy. We often use the help function at a specific hierarchy level, but it also provides assistance in locating specific options within a particular level. For example, let's locate the possible commands starting with the letter i within the show hierarchy:

```
user@Merlot> show i?
Possible completions:
  igmp             Show information about IGMP
  ike              Show IKE information
  ilmi             Show ILMI information
  interfaces       Show interface information
  ipsec            Show IPSec information
  ipv6             Show information about IPv6
  isis             Show information about IS-IS
```

To see information about the Intermediate System to Intermediate System (IS-IS) routing protocol, let's use the question mark within the next level of the command hierarchy like so:

```
user@Merlot> show isis ?
```

```
Possible completions:
  adjacency          Show the IS-IS adjacency database
  database           Show the IS-IS link-state database
  hostname           Show IS-IS hostname database
  interface          Show IS-IS interface information
  route              Show the IS-IS routing table
  spf                Show information about IS-IS SPF calculations
  statistics         Show IS-IS performance statistics
```

   The context-sensitive help system is a powerful tool when you're learning the command hierarchy and locating specific commands. The router also provides another tool to assist you in learning the CLI—the command completion function, which we discuss next.

Command Completion

The JUNOS software CLI provides you with a *command completion* function. Each unique combination of characters at a particular hierarchy level expands into the full command when you use either the spacebar or the Tab key. For example, the characters sh are the most unique combination at the top of the operational hierarchy. You press the spacebar to complete the show command as follows:

user@Merlot> **sh<space>**ow

   We further complete our command with the letter c followed by the Tab key:

user@Merlot> **sh<space>**ow **c<tab>**
                             ^

```
'c' is ambiguous.
Possible completions:
  chassis            Show chassis information
  class-of-service   Show information about class of service
  cli                Show command-line interface settings
  configuration      Show configuration file contents
  connections        Show CCC connections
user@Merlot> show c
```

   The router returns an error message telling us that there are multiple commands in the show hierarchy that start with the letter c. The output informs you that 'c' is ambiguous and displays the possible commands that begin with the requested letter. The router maintains the command prompt at the position of the error and waits for you to enter more characters. We now complete our command:

user@Merlot> **sh<space>**ow **c<tab>**
                             ^

```
'c' is ambiguous.
```

```
Possible completions:
  chassis                 Show chassis information
  class-of-service        Show information about class of service
  cli                     Show command-line interface settings
  configuration           Show configuration file contents
  connections             Show CCC connections
user@Merlot> show cli
CLI complete-on-space set to on
CLI idle-timeout disabled
CLI restart-on-upgrade set to on
CLI screen-length set to 24
CLI screen-width set to 80
CLI terminal is 'vt100'
CLI is operating in enhanced mode
```

The router's parsing of the CLI during your command typing provides you with an immediate syntax check. With the CLI, you'll never type out a long command and then after you press Enter be told that you made an error at the beginning of the command.

 Real World Scenario

Easing into the JUNOS software CLI

The command completion functionality of the JUNOS software allows you to easily migrate from another vendor's software. Your mind and your fingers can still use the same keystrokes and produce the same results. For example, the command string sh rou completes into show route and displays the routing table:

```
user@Merlot> sh<space>ow rou<space>te

inet.0: 6 destinations, 6 routes (6 active, 0 holddown, 0 hidden)
+ = Active Route, - = Last Active, * = Both

10.0.24.2/32        *[Local/0] 10w2d 05:45:23
                       Local via so-0/3/0.0
10.0.31.0/24        *[Direct/0] 2w2d 06:42:26
                       > via fe-0/0/1.0
10.0.31.1/32        *[Local/0] 2w2d 06:42:26
                       Local via fe-0/0/1.0
172.64.0.0/16       *[Direct/0] 2w2d 06:50:26
                       > via fxp0.0
```

```
172.64.0.24/32      *[Local/0] 2w2d 06:50:26
                       Local via fxp0.0
192.168.24.1/32     *[Direct/0] 2w2d 06:42:26
                       > via lo0.0
```

The string sh int completes into show interfaces and displays the interfaces on the router:

```
user@Merlot> sh<space>ow int<space>erfaces

Physical interface: fe-0/0/0, Enabled, Physical link is Up
  Interface index: 11, SNMP ifIndex: 13
  Description: Where does this go
  Link-level type: VLAN-CCC, MTU: 1518, Speed: 100mbps, Loopback: Disabled,
  Source filtering: Disabled, Flow control: Enabled
  Device flags   : Present Running
  Interface flags: SNMP-Traps
  Current address: 00:90:69:6a:f0:00, Hardware address: 00:90:69:6a:f0:00
  Last flapped   : 2002-07-09 10:40:16 UTC (10w2d 06:24 ago)
  Input rate     : 0 bps (0 pps)
  Output rate    : 0 bps (0 pps)
  Active alarms  : None
  Active defects : None

(Note: Information deleted for brevity)
```

Since the JUNOS software was built to support IPv4 as its primary protocol, the only thing you have to erase from your mind is the use of ip in your commands:

```
user@Merlot> sh<space>ow ip
                       ^
'ip' is ambiguous.
Possible completions:
  ipsec             Show IPSec information
  ipv6              Show information about IPv6
user@Merlot> show ip
```

Editing Command Lines

The router stores operational mode commands in a history buffer as you type them. This allows you to repeat a command by accessing the previous version and pressing the Enter key. When the CLI and your terminal emulator agree to use vt100 as the character output, you can use the left, right, up, and down arrows. These keystrokes provide you with access to the CLI history and allow you to easily edit your previous commands. The Backspace key is also enabled in vt100 mode, and you use it to delete characters to the left of the cursor. To set your current terminal session to vt100 mode, use the following:

user@Merlot> **set cli terminal vt100**

Regardless of your current terminal type, the JUNOS software CLI responds to common *editor macros (Emacs)* keystrokes to edit the command line. Some of the more useful commands are shown in Table 1.1.

TABLE 1.1   Common Emacs Keystrokes

Command	Effect
Ctrl+P	Displays the previous line in the CLI history buffer and is equivalent to the Up arrow key.
Ctrl+N	Displays the next line in the CLI history buffer and is equivalent to the Down arrow key.
Ctrl+B	Moves the cursor back one character and is equivalent to the Left arrow key.
Ctrl+F	Moves the cursor forward one character and is equivalent to the Right arrow key.
Esc+B	Moves the cursor back one word at a time. The Esc key must be released and re-pressed for each keystroke.
Esc+F	Moves the cursor forward one word at a time. The Esc key must be released and re-pressed for each keystroke.
Ctrl+A	Moves the cursor to the beginning of the current command line.
Crtl+E	Moves the cursor to the end of the current command line.
Ctrl+W	Deletes the word to the left of the cursor.
Ctrl+X	Deletes the entire current command line.
Ctrl+L	Redraws the current command line.

Operational Command Variables

Now that you are exposed to the command hierarchy and you know how to get help from the CLI, you can operate your Juniper Networks router efficiently. The router, however, provides you with additional capabilities that you may find useful. One such option is the ability to attach variables to your commands through the use of the pipe key (|).

Each valid command in operational mode has this ability. You can see it as a final option when you use the context-sensitive help function:

```
user@Merlot> show cli ?
Possible completions:
  <[Enter]>             Execute this command
  authorization         Show authorization and authentication information
  history               Show list of previous commands
  |                     Pipe through a command
user@Merlot> show cli
```

The router's help system also works with the pipe functionality:

```
user@Merlot> show cli | ?
Possible completions:
  count                 Count occurrences
  display               Display additional information
  except                Show only text that does not match a pattern
  find                  Search for the first occurrence of a pattern
  hold                  Hold text without exiting the --More-- prompt
  match                 Show only text that matches a pattern
  no-more               Don't paginate output
  resolve               Resolve IP addresses
  save                  Save output text to a file
  trim                  Trim specified number of columns from start of line
user@Merlot> show cli
```

The options available to you include the following:

count   This option prompts the router to count the lines in the output. You see only a single line returned with the total count listed; for example, Count: 7 lines.

display   This option allows the router to show you additional data associated with the command. In operational mode, only the xml switch is accessible to view the Extensible Markup Language (XML) tags for each command.

except   This option allows you to omit any line in the output containing the text string you provide.

find   This option prompts the router to begin the output at the first occurrence of the text string you provide.

hold   The router automatically paginates its output based on the current terminal screen length. When the end of the output is reached, the router returns to the command prompt. This option prevents the router from automatically ending the pagination process when the end of the output is reached.

match   This option prompts the router to display only lines in the output containing the text string you provide.

no-more   This option causes the router to not paginate the output.

resolve   This option causes the router to resolve IP addresses in the output to hostnames, if possible. You must configure the router with the IP address of a domain name server to use this option effectively.

save   This option automatically saves the output to the filename you provide. You see a single line returned with the number of lines saved to the file; for example, `Wrote 27 lines of output to 'saved-file'`.

trim   This option prompts the router to omit the number of columns you supply from the output, beginning with the left-hand side of the output. You might use this command when your terminal width is small and you need to see data without a line wrap.

The router also gives you the ability to combine multiple pipe options together for maximum flexibility. Suppose you want to know how many logical interfaces on your router have an IP address configured. The `show interfaces terse` command supplies this information:

```
user@Merlot> show interfaces terse
Interface       Admin Link Proto Local                 Remote
fe-0/0/0        up    up
fe-0/0/0.100    up    up   ccc
fe-0/0/0.200    up    up   ccc
fe-0/0/1        up    up
fe-0/0/1.0      up    up   inet  10.0.31.1/24
fe-0/0/2        up    down
fe-0/0/3        up    down
so-0/3/0        up    up
so-0/3/0.0      up    up   inet  10.0.24.2             --> 0/0
                               mpls
so-0/3/1        up    down
so-0/3/2        up    down
so-0/3/3        up    down
fxp0            up    up
fxp0.0          up    up   inet  172.64.0.24/16
fxp1            up    up
fxp1.0          up    up   tnp   4
gre             up    up
ipip            up    up
lo0             up    up
lo0.0           up    up   inet  192.168.24.1          --> 0/0
lsi             up    up
mtun            up    up
```

```
pimd          up    up
pime          up    up
tap           up    up
```

You can find the IP addresses by displaying only lines with the inet string:

```
user@Merlot> show interfaces terse | match inet
fe-0/0/1.0      up    up    inet   10.0.31.1/24
so-0/3/0.0      up    up    inet   10.0.24.2          --> 0/0
fxp0.0          up    up    inet   172.64.0.24/16
lo0.0           up    up    inet   192.168.24.1       --> 0/0
```

Finally, you can allow the router to count the output lines for you:

```
user@Merlot> show interfaces terse | match inet | count
Count: 4 lines
```

We discuss the assignment of IP addresses to interfaces and the meaning of inet in Chapter 2, "Interfaces."

Modifying the Command Output

Each time you enter a command, the router generates the entire output before displaying any characters on your screen and stores that information in a buffer. When the display output is longer than your terminal length, the router paginates the output by displaying a prompt of ---(more 18%)---. Not only does this tell you that more information is to follow, but it also reveals how much of the output buffer you have seen. In our case, we've viewed 18 percent of the total output.

Each time the router stops at a page break, you have the option of modifying and manipulating the output. You access these features by pressing the **h** key at the (more) prompt. The list of options looks like this:

```
---(Help for CLI automore)---
    Clear all match and except strings:                          c or C
    Display all line matching a regexp:              m or M <string>
    Display all lines except those matching a regexp:  e or E <string>
    Display this help text:                                          h
    Don't hold in automore at bottom of output:                     N
    Hold in automore at bottom of output:                           H
    Move down half display:                          TAB, d, or ^D
    Move down one line:        Enter, j, ^N, ^X, ^Z, or Down-Arrow
    Move down one page:             Space, f, ^F, or Right-Arrow
```

```
Move to bottom of output:                                    G, ^E, or End
Move to top of output:                                       g, ^A, or Home
Move up half display:                                             u or ^U
Move up one line:          k, Delete, Backspace, ^P, or Up-Arrow
Move up one page:                                  b, ^B, or Left-Arrow
Quit automore:                                     q, Q, ^K, or Clear
Redraw display:                                                  ^L or ^R
Repeat a keystroke command 1 to 9 times:                     Meta-1..9
Repeat last search:                                                    n
Save output to a file:                             s or S <filename/url>
Search backwards thru the output:                           ?<string>
Search forwards thru the output:                            /<string>
---(End of Help)---
```

While the number of possible options and keystrokes is too numerous to detail here, we can point out some commonly used ones. You access the bottom (or end) of the output buffer with the Ctrl+E keystroke. This is useful when examining log files where new information is placed at the end of the file. You can move backward through any router output with the Ctrl+B sequence. This is handy for viewing information earlier in the output without retyping the command over again. You can exit from the output and return to the command line at any time by using the q key. Finally, you can search for a particular string in the output with the forward slash (/) key. This moves your prompt to the first occurrence of the supplied string and paginates the output at that point. This is similar to the find pipe variable.

Configuration Mode

At some point, you're going to want to configure your router. After all, a router without configured interfaces and routing protocols is a large hunk of steel and circuitry that doesn't accomplish much. You access the router's *configuration mode* hierarchy with either the configure or edit command:

```
user@Merlot> configure
Entering configuration mode

[edit]
user@Merlot#
```

As with operational mode, the router uses the prompt to visually show you that you are in configuration mode. The > is changed into the pound character (#), and your current level in the hierarchy is displayed above the router's hostname. The [edit] portion of the output on Merlot tells us that we are at the top of the configuration hierarchy. We can view the command options at this level with the context-sensitive help system:

```
[edit]
user@Merlot# ?
```

```
Possible completions:
  <[Enter]>           Execute this command
  activate            Remove the inactive tag from a statement
  annotate            Annotate the statement with a comment
  commit              Commit current set of changes
  copy                Copy a statement
  deactivate          Add the inactive tag to a statement
  delete              Delete a data element
  edit                Edit a sub-element
  exit                Exit from this level
  help                Provide help information
  insert              Insert a new ordered data element
  load                Load configuration from an ASCII file
  quit                Quit from this level
  rename              Rename a statement
  rollback            Roll back database to last committed version
  run                 Run an operational-mode command
  save                Save configuration to an ASCII file
  set                 Set a parameter
  show                Show a parameter
  status              Display users currently editing the configuration
  top                 Exit to top level of configuration
  up                  Exit one level of configuration
  update              Update private database
```

 Real World Scenario

Using the *run* Command

One very useful command that exists in configuration mode is run. When you use this command, the router allows you access to operational mode commands from within the configuration. This flexibility enables you to easily verify information on the router. Let's look at an example.

Suppose that you connect to a router using Telnet and enter configuration mode to enable the OSPF routing protocol. After navigating to the [edit protocols ospf] hierarchy directory, you can't recall the interface names on this particular router. You could look at a network map for this information, but this option is not always available. You are now left to ask the router for the information. A router from another vendor may require you to exit the configuration to use the show interfaces command. The JUNOS software, however, provides this ability from within the configuration:

[edit protocols ospf]

```
user@Merlot# run show interfaces
Physical interface: so-0/0/0, Enabled, Physical link is Up
  Interface index: 11, SNMP ifIndex: 13
  Description: Sydney to Sao Paulo
  Link-level type: PPP, MTU: 4474, Clocking: Internal, SONET mode,
  Speed: OC3, Loopback: None, FCS: 16, Payload scrambler: Enabled
  Device flags   : Present Running
  Interface flags: Point-To-Point SNMP-Traps
  Link flags     : Keepalives
  Keepalive settings: Interval 10 seconds, Up-count 1, Down-count 3
  Keepalive: Input: 27244 (00:00:06 ago), Output: 27293 (00:00:06 ago)
  LCP state: Opened
  NCP state: inet: Opened, inet6: Not-configured, iso: Opened, mpls: Opened
  CHAP state: Not-configured
  Last flapped   : 2002-09-30 12:12:42 UTC (3d 03:21 ago)
  Input rate     : 0 bps (0 pps)
  Output rate    : 0 bps (0 pps)
  SONET alarms   : None
  SONET defects  : None
(Note: Information deleted for brevity)
```

Another requirement that network engineers often encounter is the desire to examine the current routing table. Again, the router provides this ability from within configuration mode:

```
[edit protocols ospf]
user@Merlot# run show route

inet.0: 23 destinations, 24 routes (23 active, 0 holddown, 0 hidden)
+ = Active Route, - = Last Active, * = Both

1.1.1.0/24        *[OSPF/10] 00:40:41, metric 4
                   > via so-0/0/0.0
10.200.200.0/24   *[Direct/0] 1d 17:31:30
                   > via fe-0/3/0.0
10.200.200.1/32   *[Local/0] 3d 03:24:34
                     Local via fe-0/3/0.0
10.222.3.0/24     *[OSPF/10] 00:40:41, metric 3
                   > via so-0/0/0.0
10.222.5.2/32     *[Local/0] 3d 03:24:35
                     Reject
```

```
10.222.6.0/24       *[OSPF/10] 00:40:41, metric 2
                     > via so-0/0/0.0
10.222.44.0/24      *[OSPF/10] 00:40:41, metric 3
                     > via so-0/0/0.0
10.222.45.0/24      *[OSPF/10] 00:40:41, metric 3
                     > via so-0/0/0.0
(Note: Information deleted for brevity)
```

These are only two examples of using the run command to your advantage. Just keep in mind that this capability is usable for any operational-mode command within the JUNOS software.

Just because you've entered configuration mode, the router doesn't stop assisting you as it did in operational mode. The pipe variables are available with each command, the output paginates with the (more) prompt, and the Emacs editor strings are a usable feature in configuration mode. The CLI stills uses the command-completion function:

```
[edit]
user@Merlot# st<space>atus
Users currently editing the configuration:
  user terminal d0 (pid 23892) on since 2002-09-25 14:30:27 UTC
      [edit]
```

If you examine the command options for configuration mode, you'll notice that the st characters are the most significant way to access the status command. The output from the Merlot router shows the users who are currently in configuration mode, how long they have been in that mode, and what their current configuration hierarchy level is.

Navigating within the Hierarchy

One method for conceptually viewing the configuration mode hierarchy is in a vertical fashion, with the top of the directory structure at the top of a tree. Each branch of the tree below the root forms a subdirectory below it. As is common with a directory system, each top-level subdirectory can branch out into its own set of subdirectories, as shown in Figure 1.3.

You navigate downward through this structure to the next lower directory by using the edit command:

```
[edit]
user@Merlot# edit protocols

[edit protocols]
user@Merlot#
```

We continue into one of the next lower directories:

```
[edit protocols]
user@Merlot# edit ospf

[edit protocols ospf]
user@Merlot#
```

FIGURE 1.3   Configuration mode hierarchy directories

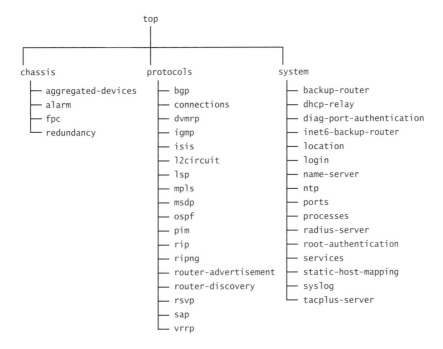

After reaching your desired directory, you can change the current configuration by using either the set or delete command as discussed in the next section, "Altering the Configuration."

The vertical nature of the configuration hierarchy requires you to always move in an up/down direction. We looked at how to move down to a directory, so let's see how to move up a directory. Quite simply, you use the up command to move up a directory level:

```
[edit protocols ospf]
user@Merlot# up

[edit protocols]
user@Merlot# up
```

```
[edit]
user@Merlot#
```

The JUNOS software allows you to reach any lower directory in the hierarchy by entering multiple directories with the edit command:

```
[edit]
user@Merlot# edit protocols ospf

[edit protocols ospf]
user@Merlot#
```

Conversely, the top command takes you to the top of the configuration hierarchy in a single step:

```
[edit protocols ospf]
user@Merlot# top

[edit]
user@Merlot#
```

Finally, if you are currently in a lower configuration directory, such as [edit protocols ospf], and you wish to move to a different directory, such as [edit routing-options static], you can do so by combining the top and edit commands:

```
[edit protocols ospf]
user@Merlot# top edit routing-options static

[edit routing-options static]
user@Merlot#
```

Altering the Configuration

While moving around the configuration hierarchy is a valuable skill, at some point you are going to want to actually configure the router. Each directory in the hierarchy may contain variables that you can add or remove from the configuration. Continuing our tree analogy results in these variables becoming the leaves on each branch of the tree. You enter new information into the configuration with the set command:

```
[edit]
user@router# edit system

[edit system]
user@router# set host-name Merlot
```

The router now has a hostname of Merlot instead of router. Notice that the *host-name* variable is actually in the [edit system] hierarchy directory. We used the edit command to move into that directory and then configured the hostname. In the previous section, "Navigating within the Hierarchy," we described the ability to add multiple directories to the edit command. The set command works in a similar manner. You can enter multiple directory names between the variable and the set command as long as the directories are in a direct downward line. Let's move back to the top of the hierarchy and change the hostname to Shiraz:

```
[edit system]
user@router# top

[edit]
user@router# set system host-name Shiraz
```

You can view the changes you've made to the configuration by issuing the show command. This command displays any configuration in your current directory and all subdirectories below your current location. Using this command at the top of the hierarchy displays the entire configuration:

```
[edit]
user@router# show
version 5.3R1.2;
system {
    host-name Shiraz;
    root-authentication {
        encrypted-password "$1$ZwtQb$cDpgAVcfDl/MLhTC1ZqQ4/"; # SECRET-DATA
    }
    login {
        user user {
            class super-user;
            authentication {
                encrypted-password "$1$/7NAOjwP$iwCrhoAqH38Kqh91AQFuY."; #
SECRET-DATA
            }
        }
    }
    radius-server {
        172.30.10.1;
    }
    services {
        telnet;
    }
    syslog {
        user * {
```

```
            any emergency;
        }
        file messages {
            any notice;
            authorization info;
        }
    }
}
```

To view the configuration just within the [edit system] directory, you may either move to that level with the edit command or add the hierarchy name to the show command from the top of the configuration:

```
[edit]
user@router# show system
host-name Shiraz;
root-authentication {
    encrypted-password "$1$ZwtQb$cDpgAVcfDl/MLhTC1ZqQ4/"; # SECRET-DATA
}
login {
    user user {
        class super-user;
        authentication {
            encrypted-password "$1$/7NAOjwP$iwCrhoAqH38Kqh91AQFuY."; # SECRET-DATA
        }
    }
}
radius-server {
    172.30.10.1;
}
services {
    telnet;
}
syslog {
    user * {
        any emergency;
    }
    file messages {
        any notice;
        authorization info;
    }
}
```

 **Real World Scenario**

Using the *set* Command

We discussed how you have the ability to use the set command from the top of the configuration to change variables in the configuration. As you become more proficient with using the JUNOS software CLI, you might start taking advantage of this capability. To assist you in this making this transition, let's examine some details of the router's output.

Suppose we begin configuring the router in the [edit system] directory. The possible options at that hierarchy level are:

```
[edit system]
user@router# set ?
Possible completions:
+ apply-groups          Groups from which to inherit configuration data
+ authentication-order  Order in which authentication methods are invoked
> backup-router         IPv4 router to use while booting
  compress-configuration-files  Compress the router configuration files
  default-address-selection  Use system address for locally originated traffic
> dhcp-relay            BOOTP/DHCP relay configuration
> diag-port-authentication  Authentication for the diagnostic port
  domain-name           Domain name for this router
+ domain-search         List of domain names to search
  host-name             Host name for this router
> inet6-backup-router   IPv6 router to use while booting
> location              Location of the system, in various forms
> login                 Users, their classes and passwords
  mirror-flash-on-disk  Mirror contents of the flash drive onto hard drive
> name-server           DNS name servers
  no-redirects          Disable ICMP redirects
  no-saved-core-context  Don't save context information for core files
> ntp                   Network Time Protocol services
> ports                 Craft interface RS-232 ports
> processes             Process control
> radius-server         RADIUS server configuration
> root-authentication   Authentication information for the root login
  saved-core-context    Save context information for core files
> services              System services
> static-host-mapping   Static host name database mapping
```

```
 > syslog                System logging facility
 > tacplus-server        TACACS+ server configuration
   time-zone             Time zone definition name (<continent>/<major-city>)
 [edit system]
 user@router# set
```

When you examine the output closely, you might notice that some command options are preceded with a character—either an angle bracket (>) or a plus sign (+). These characters, as well as their absence, carry a special meaning when you use the set command.

The angle bracket is used to designate lower-level directories. In our case, the name-server option is really a subdirectory of [edit system]. The plus sign shows command variables you can configure that may have multiple values assigned. For example, the authentication-order option tells the router how to authenticate users who log in. You can assign a single authentication method or multiple methods. Finally, some options do not have any characters preceding them. These are configurable variables, such as host-name, that may contain only a single possible value.

You remove variables from the configuration with the delete command. Examining the earlier output shows that the router is currently configured to communicate with a remote authentication (RADIUS) server at address 172.30.10.1. This requirement is no longer valid, so we remove it from the router's configuration and verify that it is deleted:

```
[edit]
user@router# delete system radius-server 172.30.10.1

[edit]
user@router# show system
host-name Shiraz;
root-authentication {
    encrypted-password "$1$ZwtQb$cDpgAVcfDl/MLhTC1ZqQ4/"; # SECRET-DATA
}
login {
    user user {
        class super-user;
        authentication {
            encrypted-password "$1$/7NAOjwP$iwCrhoAqH38Kqh91AQFuY."; # SECRET-DATA
        }
    }
}
```

```
services {
    telnet;
}
syslog {
    user * {
        any emergency;
    }
    file messages {
        any notice;
        authorization info;
    }
}
}
```

The Candidate Configuration

You may have noticed that we've been changing the hostname of the router but that the router's prompt hasn't changed. This brings us to a very important point concerning how a Juniper Networks router behaves. When you enter configuration mode, you are actually viewing (and changing) a file called the *candidate configuration*. The candidate configuration allows you to make configuration changes without causing operational changes to the current operating configuration, called the *active configuration*. The router implements the changes in the candidate configuration when you use the `commit` command. (We discuss this function in the "Using the `commit` Command" section later in this chapter.) This abstraction allows you the flexibility to alter your configuration without causing damage to your current network operations.

You may enter or exit configuration mode as many times as you wish without implementing your changes. If you do this several times, you may find that you've forgotten the exact changes you've made. In this situation, you can utilize a pipe command called `compare` in conjunction with the `show` command. This prompts the router to compare the current candidate configuration to the active configuration running on the router. Differences between the two files are displayed with either a plus (+) or a minus (–) sign. The plus sign represents variables in the candidate configuration that are not present in the active configuration; you've added them to the file. The minus sign shows the opposite; you've deleted variables from the file. In other words, the candidate configuration doesn't have items found in the active configuration.

Let's use this command on our router to see the difference between the candidate and active configurations:

```
[edit]
user@router# show | compare
[edit system]
-   host-name router;
+   host-name Shiraz;
```

We see that host-name Shiraz was added to the candidate configuration and that host-name router has been removed. This follows the configuration changes we implemented in the previous section, "Altering the Configuration."

The show | compare command displays only the differences between the two files. All other portions of the configuration files are not shown.

Saving and Loading Configuration Files

The fact that the candidate configuration is a file that you edit also provides other advantages to you. You can save the current candidate configuration to a file on the router. Alternatively, you can load existing files into the router. Let's examine one example of how to use these options.

Suppose you are burning in (initially configuring) a number of routers in your network. You might want to have the common configuration components from the first router saved to more easily configure the remaining routers. Let's configure the first router with the common elements and use the save command from the top of the configuration hierarchy:

```
[edit]
user@router# show
version 5.3R1.2;
system {
    host-name Shiraz;
    root-authentication {
        encrypted-password "$1$ZwtQb$cDpgAVcfDl/MLhTC1ZqQ4/"; # SECRET-DATA
    }
    login {
        user user {
            class super-user;
            authentication {
                encrypted-password "$1$/7NAOjwP$iwCrhoAqH38Kqh91AQFuY."; #
SECRET-DATA
            }
        }
    }
    services {
        telnet;
    }
    syslog {
        file messages {
            any notice;
            authorization info;
```

```
        }
    }
}
```

```
[edit]
user@router# save common
Wrote 24 lines of configuration to 'common'
```

The router creates (or overwrites) the file called ***common*** and places the candidate configuration in it. We place these configuration elements on other routers with the load command. You have two main options for loading the files—override and merge. As you might guess from their names, the override option completely erases the current candidate configuration and replaces it with the contents of the file you specify. The merge function combines the file with the candidate configuration. Elements in the file that are not in the candidate are added. Variables in the candidate configuration that are not in the merging file are left unchanged. When an item is in both the merging file and the candidate configuration, the router uses the value specified in the file.

On the next router to be configured, we use the load override command to enter the common configuration elements:

```
[edit]
root# show
system {
    syslog {
        user * {
            any emergency;
        }
        file messages {
            any notice;
            authorization info;
        }
    }
}
```

```
[edit]
root# load override common
load complete
```

```
[edit]
root# show
version 5.3R1.2;
system {
```

```
    host-name Shiraz;
    root-authentication {
        encrypted-password "$1$ZwtQb$cDpgAVcfDl/MLhTC1ZqQ4/"; # SECRET-DATA
    }
    login {
        user user {
            class super-user;
            authentication {
                encrypted-password "$1$/7NAOjwP$iwCrhoAqH38Kqh91AQFuY."; #
SECRET-DATA
            }
        }
    }
    services {
        telnet;
    }
    syslog {
        file messages {
            any notice;
            authorization info;
        }
    }
}
```

The previous output displays no hostname for the router. This is expected with a new router because no configuration has yet taken place.

Comparing the results of the load override command with the *common* file we saved earlier shows that only the elements detailed in the file are now in the candidate configuration. Specifically, the user * portion of the syslog directory is not in the *common* file and is removed. The load merge command provides you with different results:

```
[edit]
root# show
system {
    syslog {
        user * {
            any emergency;
        }
        file messages {
```

```
            any notice;
            authorization info;
        }
    }
}

[edit]
root# load merge common
load complete

[edit]
root# show
version 5.3R1.2;
system {
    host-name Shiraz;
    root-authentication {
        encrypted-password "$1$ZwtQb$cDpgAVcfDl/MLhTC1ZqQ4/"; # SECRET-DATA
    }
    login {
        user user {
            class super-user;
            authentication {
                encrypted-password "$1$/7NAOjwP$iwCrhoAqH38Kqh91AQFuY."; #
SECRET-DATA
            }
        }
    }
    services {
        telnet;
    }
    syslog {
        user * {
            any emergency;
        }
        file messages {
            any notice;
            authorization info;
        }
    }
}
```

The existing user * configuration remains as a result of the load merge command.

Real World Scenario

Cutting and Pasting Configuration Files

The ability to cut and paste portions of configuration files between routers is valuable when operating a network. Within the JUNOS software, you accomplish this with the `load merge terminal` command. In place of a file, the router expects you to enter keystrokes from the terminal directly. You may actually type portions of the configuration yourself, or more often paste text into the terminal window.

Suppose you have the following configuration within [edit protocols] on one of your routers:

```
[edit]
user@Shiraz# show | find protocols
protocols {
    bgp {
        group internal {
            type internal;
            local-address 192.168.16.1;
            neighbor 192.168.24.1;
            neighbor 192.168.12.1;
        }
    }
    ospf {
        area 0.0.0.0 {
            interface all;
            interface fxp0.0 {
                disable;
            }
        }
    }
}
```

You would like to copy the OSPF portion of the configuration to other routers in your network. To accomplish this, copy the output shown previously and place it into a text editor. Edit the text to look like the following:

```
protocols {
    ospf {
        area 0.0.0.0 {
            interface all;
```

```
            interface fxp0.0 {
                disable;
            }
        }
    }
}
```

You should ensure that all of the configuration hierarchy is accounted for—the router returns an error message if it does not receive the proper information. Type the **load merge terminal** command on your router and paste the text from your text editor into the router. After all of the text is entered, press Ctrl+D to close the paste window. You should see a load complete message if you are successful:

```
[edit]
user@Shiraz# load merge terminal
[Type ^D to end input]
protocols {
    ospf {
        area 0.0.0.0 {
            interface all;
            interface fxp0.0 {
                disable;
            }
        }
    }
}
load complete

[edit]
user@Shiraz#
```

After some practice to fully understand the procedure, you'll find this to be a valuable tool for operating and configuring your network.

Using the *commit* Command

We mentioned the commit command in the "The Candidate Configuration" section earlier in this chapter. Because no changes you make to the router become effective until you use this command, let's spend some time exploring its functionality.

Each time you commit your configuration, the router performs several tasks. The candidate configuration is examined for syntax and semantic problems and if any single problem exists, the candidate is not implemented. One example of a possible problem is referencing a routing policy without creating that policy. (We discuss routing policies in Chapter 4, "Routing Policy.") If the candidate configuration possesses no errors, the router then implements the new configuration and makes changes to the operating environment as needed. Finally, the existing active configuration is saved on the router for future use.

You now decide to implement the changes to the router's configuration:

```
[edit]
user@router# commit
commit complete

[edit]
user@Shiraz#
```

The commit complete message tells us that the process was successful. Notice a change of the router's hostname from router to Shiraz. We used the commit command from the top of the configuration hierarchy, but you can issue it from any level you wish. Unlike many other configuration mode commands that affect only the current configuration level and lower branches, the commit process always implements the entire configuration at once. Any errors encountered during a commit procedure result in no portion of the configuration changing.

Suppose that there was an error in the configuration we just committed. In that case, the router does not implement the changes we made and supplies an error message informing us of the problem:

```
[edit]
user@router# commit
Policy error: Policy Advertise-Routes referenced but not defined
error: configuration check-out failed

[edit]
user@router#
```

In addition to the configuration check-out failed message, we see that the router's hostname did not change. It appears that a policy called Advertise-Routes was referenced in the configuration without ever being created in the first place. We remove the offending policy and successfully commit the configuration.

```
[edit]
user@router# delete protocols ospf export Advertise-Routes

[edit]
user@router# commit
commit complete

[edit]
user@Shiraz#
```

Command Options

The commit command has several options you may use to alter its operation. Let's view them on the Shiraz router:

```
[edit]
user@Shiraz# commit ?
Possible completions:
  <[Enter]>              Execute this command
  and-quit               Quit configuration mode if commit succeeds
  at                     Time at which to activate the configuration changes
  check                  Check only, do not apply changes
  confirmed              Automatically rollback if not confirmed
  synchronize            Synchronize commit on both routing engines
  |                      Pipe through a command
[edit]
user@Shiraz# commit
```

The router always remains in configuration mode, by default, after committing the configuration. You may exit back to operational mode with the addition of the and-quit option:

```
[edit]
user@Shiraz# commit and-quit
commit complete
Exiting configuration mode

user@Shiraz>
```

> The router exits configuration mode only after a successful commit process. If any errors are encountered, they are reported and the router remains in configuration mode.

You can have the router verify the validity of the configuration without implementing the changes by using the check option. You might use this option after making a number of changes to the router and you want to be sure you have all of the required portions of the configuration in place. After running the syntax and semantic checks, the router does not implement the changes. You're either notified of a successful check or your errors are reported to you:

```
[edit]
user@Shiraz# commit check
configuration check succeeds

[edit]
user@Shiraz#
```

The syntax and semantic checks the router performs verify only that information is present in the configuration that allows the router to implement the candidate file. No verification is ever completed to see if the configuration actually does what you wanted it to do in the network; that is your job. If you are concerned that changes you made will either lock you out of your router or cause harm to the operation of the network, you should use the confirmed option. This option provides a safety net to the user in case of operational problems with your new configuration and is designed to allow the router to return to a working configuration automatically. After you issue the commit confirmed command, the router implements the changes you requested and starts a 10-minute timer. If you are happy with the new configuration, you must issue a normal commit command to stop the timer and end the operation of the confirmed option. If you don't stop the timer, the router automatically returns to the last operational configuration and implements those changes.

```
[edit]
user@router# commit confirmed
commit confirmed will be automatically rolled back in 10 minutes unless
confirmed
commit complete

[edit]
user@Shiraz#
```

The output of the commit confirmed command is no different from that of a normal commit operation. The router either reports an error or displays the commit complete message. Additionally, you have the option of altering the timer value used with the confirmed option. The possible values range from 1 minute to 65,535 minutes (45 days, 12 hours, and 15 minutes).

The last option you may use with the commit command is synchronize. When you have a router with two Routing Engines installed, you can have the router apply the candidate configuration to both Routing Engines.

```
[edit]
user@router# commit synchronize
re0: configuration check succeeds
re1: configuration check succeeds
re0: commit complete
re1: commit complete

[edit]
user@Shiraz#
```

This option is helpful in the event of a Routing Engine failure; the backup Routing Engine now has the latest operational parameters in the network.

We discuss the fail-over operation of the Routing Engine in the section "Routing Engine Redundancy" later in this chapter.

Restoring an Old Configuration

When the router commits a configuration, it also saves the existing configuration to a file. It is this saved file that the router uses during the commit confirmed process. This single file is not the only old configuration file saved, however. The JUNOS software saves up to nine previous configuration files for your use. The current active configuration is named junper.conf and is file number 0. The most recent active configuration is called juniper.conf.1.gz and is file number 1. This naming convention continues with each older file incrementing by 1 until the juniper.conf.9.gz file is reached.

You place one of these files into the candidate configuration with the rollback command. This command functions exactly like the load override command in that the existing candidate configuration is removed and the new file is put into its place. To actually implement the old configuration file, you must still issue the commit command to make the candidate configuration the new active configuration.

Suppose that we've altered the properties of the configuration on the Shiraz router. After committing the configuration, we realize that the new configuration is not performing as we wanted it to. So we load the most recent configuration and commit that change:

```
[edit]
user@Shiraz# rollback 1
load complete

[edit]
user@Shiraz# commit
commit complete

[edit]
user@Shiraz#
```

The router never automatically commits a rollback file for you. The only exception is a commit confirmed operation where the router issues both a rollback 1 and a commit command.

Manipulating Files on the Router

The JUNOS software stores multitudes of information in files on the router. Thus far, we've discussed configuration and rollback files, files we stored using the save command, and new versions of the JUNOS software itself. The router stores these files in various directories, including:

/config   This directory is located on the router's internal flash drive. It contains the active configuration (juniper.conf) and rollback files 1, 2, and 3.

/var/db/config   This directory is located on the router's hard drive and contains rollback files 4 through 9.

/var/tmp   This directory is located on the router's hard drive. It holds core files from the various daemons on the Routing Engines. Core files are generated when a particular daemon crashes and are used by Juniper Networks engineers to diagnose the reason for failure.

/var/log   This directory is located on the router's hard drive. It contains files generated by both the router's logging function as well as the traceoptions command.

/var/home   This directory is located on the router's hard drive. It contains a subdirectory for each configured user on the router. These individual user directories are the default file location for many JUNOS software commands.

/altroot   This directory is located on the router's hard drive and contains a copy of the root file structure from the internal flash drive. This directory is used in certain disaster-recovery modes where the internal flash drive is not operational.

/altconfig   This directory is located on the router's hard drive and contains a copy of the /config file structure from the internal flash drive. This directory is also used in certain disaster-recovery modes where the internal flash drive is not operational.

You can view the router's directory structure as well as individual files by issuing the file command in operational mode:

```
user@Shiraz> file ?
Possible completions:
  compare              Compare files (local)
  copy                 Copy files (local or remote)
  delete               Delete files from the system (local)
  list                 List file information (local)
  rename               Rename files (local)
  show                 Display file contents (local)
```

As you can see, the file command gives you several options for manipulating files, but we'll focus on the list option here to see the directory structure of the router. The default directory for the file list command is the home directory of the user logged into the router. In fact, the user's home directory is the default directory for the majority of the JUNOS software commands requiring a filename. We currently have the following files in our home directory on the Shiraz router.

```
user@Shiraz> file list
.ssh/
common
```

You have the ability to view the contents of other file directories by specifying the directory structure:

```
user@Shiraz> file list /config
juniper.conf
juniper.conf.1.gz
juniper.conf.2.gz
juniper.conf.3.gz
```

The router's context-sensitive help system is also available to assist you in locating the desired directory:

```
user@Shiraz> file list /?
Possible completions:
  <[Enter]>           Execute this command
  <path>              Path to list
  /COPYRIGHT          Size: 4735, Last changed: Mar 31 2001
  /altconfig/         Last changed: Dec 11 2001
  /altroot/           Last changed: Dec 11 2001
  /bin/               Last changed: Aug 26 08:49:25
  /boot/              Last changed: Oct 03 16:27:55
  /config/            Last changed: Oct 03 16:27:56
  /dev/               Last changed: Sep 30 12:10:56
  /etc/               Last changed: Oct 03 16:27:56
  /kernel             Size: 9302545, Last changed: Apr 30 02:00:21
  /mnt/               Last changed: Dec 11 2001
  /modules/           Last changed: Aug 26 08:43:17
  /packages/          Last changed: Aug 26 08:49:45
  /proc/              Last changed: Oct 04 10:20:32
  /root/              Last changed: Aug 26 08:47:33
  /sbin/              Last changed: Aug 26 08:49:45
  /tmp/               Last changed: Oct 03 16:27:55
  /usr/               Last changed: Dec 11 2001
  /var/               Last changed: Dec 27 2001
user@Shiraz> file list /var/?
Possible completions:
  <[Enter]>           Execute this command
  <path>              Path to list
```

```
/var/crash/        Last changed: Sep 16 09:03:30
/var/cron/         Last changed: Dec 27 2001
/var/db/           Last changed: Oct 03 16:27:56
/var/etc/          Last changed: Oct 03 16:27:56
/var/home/         Last changed: Oct 03 15:07:40
/var/log/          Last changed: Oct 03 16:27:56
/var/run/          Last changed: Oct 04 10:07:53
/var/sw/           Last changed: Dec 27 2001
/var/tmp/          Last changed: Sep 30 12:11:28
user@Shiraz> file list /var/log
messages
```

(Note: Information deleted for brevity)

Routing Engine Redundancy

Certain Juniper Networks routers have the ability to contain two Routing Engines in the physical chassis. For the M-series platforms, the M20, M40e, and M160 support this configuration. Only one of the Routing Engines is considered the *master* at any point in time, and it controls the router's operations. The other Routing Engine, the *backup*, is available in the chassis to provide fail-over capability should the master cease to function.

By default, the router does not automatically enable the backup Routing Engine to assume the master role. You have to enable this functionality:

```
[edit chassis]
user@Shiraz# set redundancy failover on-loss-of-keepalives


[edit chassis]
lab@SanJose# show
redundancy {
    failover on-loss-of-keepalives;
}
```

The master and backup Routing Engines begin generating keepalive signals to each other. If the backup Routing Engine fails to receive keepalives for 20 seconds (a non-configurable timer), it enters a message in the messages log file. After 300 seconds, the default fail-over timer, the backup Routing Engine attempts to assume the master role for the router. When it succeeds, an alarm is generated to notify you that the master Routing Engine failed.

You can adjust the fail-over timer to between 2 and 10,000 seconds by using the keepalive-time command. Here, we've decided that the Shiraz router should use a 30-second timer value:

```
[edit chassis]
user@Shiraz# set redundancy keepalive-time 30
```

```
[edit chassis]
lab@SanJose# show
redundancy {
    failover on-loss-of-keepalives;
    keepalive-time 30;
}
```

 Both the master and backup Routing Engines must be operating the same version of the JUNOS software for the redundancy process to function correctly.

Packet Forwarding Engine Components

We now investigate the details of the Packet Forwarding Engine. This is a shorter discussion than the components of the Routing Engine, since your interaction with the Packet Forwarding Engine is through the CLI and the JUNOS software. The components of the Packet Forwarding Engine fall into two main subsets: the Embedded OS software operating the circuit boards themselves and the ASICs actually participating in packet forwarding. After covering the details of these two components, we discuss examples of the data packet flow through the forwarding plane.

Embedded OS Software

As the router boots, the *Embedded OS software* (microcode) is downloaded from the Routing Engine to the CPUs on the circuit boards. Built by Juniper Networks engineers, the Embedded OS software contains a microkernel and individual threads that operate like the daemons on the Routing Engine. In stark contrast to the JUNOS software on the Routing Engine, the Embedded OS software on the Packet Forwarding Engine is fairly non-intelligent. It contains only enough capabilities to operate the control board, the FPCs, and the PICs. Perhaps most important, the Embedded OS software also begins the operation of the ASICs in the Packet Forwarding Engine.

Application-Specific Integrated Circuits

Each circuit board in the Packet Forwarding Engine contains at least one ASIC, with some boards containing multiple chips. It is the interaction of these ASICs that provide the forwarding path through the router and supply the industry-leading forwarding performance of Juniper Networks routers.

 For the remainder of this book, we focus only on the ASICs found within the M-series family of routers.

PIC I/O Manager ASIC

Each PIC in the router contains an individual *PIC I/O Manager ASIC* that is unique to the specific media type on the PIC. For example, a PIC with Asynchronous Transfer Mode (ATM) interfaces has a different ASIC than a PIC with Synchronous Optical Network (SONET)/Synchronous Digital Hierarchy (SDH) interfaces. The requirement for this individuality arises from the tasks of the ASIC.

The PIC I/O Manager ASIC handles media-specific tasks such as verifying data-link framing, detecting link-level errors, and generating link-level alarms. Specialized functions such as ATM segmentation and reassembly (SAR) takes place on the PIC ASIC as well.

Generally speaking, the PIC I/O Manager ASIC is responsible for removing data packets from the physical media and placing data packets back on the physical media. It connects directly to the I/O Manager ASIC on the FPC containing the PIC.

I/O Manager ASIC

Each FPC contains a single *I/O Manager ASIC* that connects to both the PIC I/O Manager ASIC and the Distributed Buffer Manager ASIC (which we discuss next) on the control board. The I/O Manager ASIC performs multiple functions on each data packet.

As a data packet enters the router, the I/O Manager ASIC verifies the integrity of both the Layer 2 and Layer 3 headers. Provided the data packet is valid, the ASIC removes the Layer 2 header and segments the packet into 64-byte units called a *J-cell*. The I/O Manager ASIC sends these J-cells to the Distributed Buffer Manager ASIC for storage in the shared memory pool.

Each I/O Manager ASIC in the router contributes memory to the shared memory packet storage on the router, controlled by the ASICs on the router's control board. The Distributed Buffer Manager ASIC instructs the I/O Manager ASIC to place and retrieve individual J-cells in the memory on its FPC.

On the outgoing side of the router, the I/O manager queues a special J-cell called the *result cell*. The result cell contains the next-hop information for the packet as well as other information about which queue to store the packet in. When the router is ready to send the data packet out an interface, the I/O manager ASIC receives all of the packet's J-cells from the packet buffer storage via the Distributed Buffer Manager ASIC. The I/O Manager ASIC re-forms the data packet and adjusts any protocol time-to-live (TTL) values before encapsulating the packet into the appropriate Layer 2 format. Finally, the packet is sent to the PIC I/O Manager ASIC for placement on the physical media.

Distributed Buffer Manager ASIC

Each control board in the router contains two *Distributed Buffer Manager ASICs*. The ASICs connect to the I/O Manager ASIC on the FPC and to the Internet Processor ASIC, which is also on the control board. The ASIC is logically split into two components, each with an important function. One of the ASICs, which we refer to as the Inbound Distributed Buffer Manager ASIC, is responsible for handling inbound J-cells. Its partner, the Outbound Distributed Buffer Manager ASIC, handles outbound J-cells.

The two ASICs work in conjunction with each other to store and retrieve J-cells in the shared packet buffer pool. In addition, the Inbound Distributed Buffer Manager ASIC also generates a special J-cell called the *notification cell*. The notification cell contains information from the data packet, such as source and destination IP addresses, source and destination port numbers, the incoming interface on the router, Quality of Service (QoS) settings, and the existing protocol TTL value of the packet. The ASIC then sends the notification cell to the Internet Processor ASIC.

Internet Processor ASIC

Every Juniper Networks router contains a single *Internet Processor ASIC* on the control board in the Packet Forwarding Engine. In many respects, the Internet Processor ASIC is the heart of the Packet Forwarding Engine. It is the only ASIC in the forwarding path that accesses the forwarding table, performs route lookups, and makes forwarding decisions. It receives notification cells from the Inbound Distributed Buffer Manager ASIC and transforms them into result cells after performing a route lookup. Additionally, the Internet Processor ASIC performs firewall packet filtering, enforces policy controls on data packets, and collects exception packets for transmission to the routing engine.

We discuss exception packets in the section "Exception Packets" later in this chapter.

Packet Flow

By understanding the functionality of the different ASICs in the Packet Forwarding Engine, you may already have a good idea of how a data packet flows through the forwarding path of the router. To provide a complete picture to use as a concise guide, we follow a unicast packet as it enters and then leaves the Packet Forwarding Engine. We then examine the differences in the forwarding path for multicast packets and discuss what exception packets are and how they are handled.

Unicast Packets

Each unicast packet received on a router's interface is treated in a similar fashion. At a high level, the packet is stored in the shared memory pool, a route lookup is performed, and the packet is transmitted out one of the router's interfaces. Figure 1.4 displays a simplified view of the Packet Forwarding Engine ASICs and their representation to each other.

FIGURE 1.4   Unicast packet flow

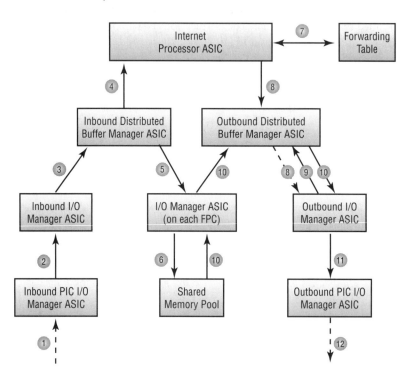

Let's use Figure 1.4 as a reference for the detailed steps of the unicast packet flow:

1. A data packet arrives on one of the router's interfaces. The PIC I/O Manager ASIC formulates the packet and performs link-layer error checking, if appropriate.

2. The PIC I/O Manager ASIC transmits the data packet, complete with Layer 2 and Layer 3 headers, to the I/O Manager ASIC on its FPC.

3. The I/O Manager ASIC verifies the integrity of the Layer 2 and Layer 3 headers. Provided a valid protocol packet remains, the I/O Manager ASIC removes the Layer 2 header and segments the data packet into 64-byte J-cells. It then sends those J-cells to the Inbound Distributed Buffer Manager ASIC.

4. The Inbound Distributed Buffer Manager ASIC begins to receive J-cells from the I/O Manager ASIC. The notification cell is built and is transmitted to the Internet Processor ASIC.

5. The J-cells that make up the data packet are stored in the shared memory pool. Each FPC supplies the physical components of the shared memory, and the Inbound Distributed Buffer Manager ASIC sends the packet's J-cells to all FPCs in the router on a round-robin basis.

6. The I/O Manager ASIC on each FPC receives the J-cells and stores them in its physical memory as instructed by the Inbound Distributed Buffer Manager ASIC.

7. While the J-cells are being stored in memory, the Internet Processor ASIC receives the notification cell and performs a route lookup in the forwarding table. The next-hop router along the path of the route and the outgoing interface on the router is determined. This next-hop information is stored in the notification cell, which now becomes the result cell.

8. The Internet Processor ASIC sends the result cell to the Outbound Distributed Buffer Manager ASIC, which examines the cell to locate the outgoing interface. The result cell is then sent to the appropriate FPC for queuing and transmission.

9. The I/O Manager ASIC queues the result cell and applies appropriate queuing mechanisms. When the result cell reaches the head of the queue, the I/O Manager ASIC requests the packet's J-cells from the Outbound Distributed Buffer Manager ASIC.

10. The Outbound Distributed Buffer Manager ASIC copies the J-cells from the packet storage buffer and sends them to the I/O Manager ASIC on the outgoing FPC.

11. The I/O Manager ASIC re-forms the data packet into a single unit and alters any protocol TTL values. The ASIC then appends the appropriate Layer 2 header information and sends the packet to the PIC I/O Manager ASIC.

12. The PIC I/O Manager ASIC performs any link-layer duties, if required, and transmits the data packet out the router's interface.

Multicast Packets

A Juniper Networks router handles multicast data packets in a very similar fashion to unicast packets. There is only one major difference between the two, so we won't repeat the packet flow steps in detail here.

Refer back to Figure 1.4 and the steps outlined in the previous section, and focus on steps 7 and 8. When the Internet Processor ASIC performs its route lookup on a multicast packet, it often finds multiple next-hop interfaces in the forwarding table. Information about all the outgoing interfaces is placed in the result cell and sent to the Distributed Buffer Manager ASIC. This ASIC examines the result cell and finds several outgoing interfaces. It generates a copy of the result cell for each interface and sends those cells to the appropriate I/O Manager ASICs on the FPCs. The queuing and transmission of the multicast packets at this point then follows the unicast packet steps outlined previously.

Exception Packets

The Packet Forwarding Engine can't process some data packets in your network in its normal fashion. A prime example of these packets is routing protocol updates addressed to the router itself. There is no outgoing interface for these packets; they should be sent to the Routing Engine instead. The CPU on the router's control board handles this type of traffic, called an *exception packet*.

Other forms of exception packets include:

- Packets addressed to the router, such as ICMP pings, Telnet, and SSH traffic

- Packets requiring the generation of an ICMP error message, including traceroute responses and destination unreachable messages

- Packets containing an IP Options field

The control board CPU handles different types of exception traffic differently. For example, routing protocol updates are sent to the Routing Engine over the fxp1 interface. Local delivery packets (Telnet, for example) and IP Options packets are sent to the Routing Engine as well. The control board CPU itself generates any ICMP error messages and sends them to the appropriate IP source address.

Summary

This chapter discussed the basic router design of a Juniper Networks router. We examined the basic functionality and components of both the Routing Engine and the Packet Forwarding Engine.

We further explored the Routing Engine with a look at the JUNOS software architecture, its naming convention, and operational parameters. Next, we discussed the router's CLI by examining the operational and configuration modes of the router. We saw how to navigate through the CLI, use the context-sensitive help system, understand the command completion process, and modify the output of commands. We then discussed the differences between the candidate and active configurations, including a look at the router's rollback functionality. We also examined the various ways to use the commit command and where the router stores configuration and user files.

We concluded the chapter by looking at the Packet Forwarding Engine. This discussion centered on how the ASICs and control boards forward user data packets through the router. We examined the handling of both unicast and multicast packets. Finally, we defined an exception packet and explained how the router handles them.

Exam Essentials

Understand the basic functions of the Routing Engine and the Packet Forwarding Engine. The Routing Engine is the intelligence of the router. It operates the routing protocols and builds a routing and forwarding table. The forwarding table is copied to the Packet Forwarding Engine, where the actual transmission of user data packets is handled.

Be able to identify the JUNOS software boot locations and the default boot sequence. The JUNOS software is stored on the internal flash drive, the internal hard drive, and the removable flash media. When the router begins to boot, the removable media is checked first, followed by the internal flash drive, and finally the internal hard drive.

Understand the JUNOS software commands associated with configuration files. You may save the router's configuration to the hard drive with the save command. The load command restores files to the candidate configuration. The candidate configuration becomes the active configuration with the commit command. You can easily return to a previous configuration with the rollback command.

Be able to identify the ASICs used in the Packet Forwarding Engine.   There are four main ASICs used in the Packet Forwarding Engine: the Internet Processor ASIC, the Distributed Buffer Manager ASIC, the I/O Manager ASIC, and the PIC I/O Manager ASIC.

Be able to describe the flow of a packet through the Packet Forwarding Engine.   A packet is received on an interface and is segmented into J-cells by the I/O Manager ASIC. The Distributed Buffer Manager ASIC stores the packet in the shared memory pool. The Internet Processor ASIC performs a route lookup and sends the result to the Distributed Buffer Manager ASIC, which forwards it to the outgoing I/O Manager ASIC. After queuing the packet, the I/O Manager ASIC receives the J-cells from the memory pool and re-forms the packet. It is sent to the outgoing PIC I/O Manager ASIC for transmission into the network.

Understand what an exception packet is and how the router handles those packets.   An exception packet could be a routing protocol update, a locally addressed packet, or a packet requiring the generation of an ICMP error message. The CPU on the router's control board handles these exception packets and performs the appropriate action.

Key Terms

Before you take the exam, be certain you are familiar with the following terms:

active configuration	`jdocs`
application-specific integrated circuits (ASICs)	`jkernel`
backup	`jpfe`
candidate configuration	`jroute`
Chassis Daemon (chassid)	kernel
command completion	Management Daemon (mgd)
command-line interface (CLI)	master
configuration mode	Memory Mezzanine Board (MMB)
context-sensitive help	notification cell
Device Control Daemon (dcd)	operational mode
Distributed Buffer Manager ASIC	package
editor macros (Emacs)	Packet Forwarding Engine
Embedded OS software	Packet Forwarding Engine Daemon (pfed)
exception packet	Physical Interface Card (PIC)
Flexible PIC Concentrator (FPC)	PIC I/O Manager ASIC
Forwarding Engine Board (FEB)	result cell
forwarding table	Routing Engine
I/O Manager ASIC	Routing Protocol Daemon (rpd)
Internet Processor ASIC	routing table
`jbase`	Switching and Forwarding Module (SFM)
`jbundle`	System Control Board (SCB)
J-cell	System Switching Board (SSB)
`jcrypto`	

Review Questions

1. What are the functions of the Routing Engine? (Choose three.)

    A. Operates routing protocols

    C. Segments data packets into J-cells

    C. Loads the JUNOS software

    D. Controls the CLI

2. Which router component is responsible for creating the forwarding table?

    A. Packet Forwarding Engine

    B. Routing Engine

    C. Flexible PIC Controller

    D. Physical Interface Card

3. The PIC I/O Manager ASIC is responsible for what function?

    A. Creating J-cells

    B. Performing route lookups

    C. Transmitting packets

    D. Storing packets in memory

4. The Internet Processor ASIC is responsible for what function?

    A. Creating J-cells

    B. Performing route lookups

    C. Transmitting packets

    D. Storing packets in memory

5. The I/O Manager ASIC is responsible for what function?

    A. Creating J-cells

    B. Performing route lookups

    C. Transmitting packets

    D. Creating notification cells

6. The Distributed Buffer Manager ASIC is responsible for what function?

    A. Creating J-cells

    B. Performing route lookups

    C. Transmitting packets

    D. Storing packets in memory

7.   A unicast packet is flowing through the Packet Forwarding Engine. Which ASIC receives the packet after the incoming PIC I/O Manager ASIC performs its functions?

  A. Incoming I/O Manager ASIC

  B. Outgoing I/O Manager ASIC

  C. Incoming Distributed Buffer Manager ASIC

  D. Outgoing Distributed Buffer Manager ASIC

8.   What component of the router is responsible for handling exception packets?

  A. Internet Processor ASIC

  B. Switching control board CPU

  C. Routing Engine

  D. Flexible PIC Controller CPU

9.   Which types of packets are considered exception packets? (Choose two.)

  A. IP packets with TTL=1

  B. HTTP packets

  C. SMTP packets

  D. Routing protocol updates

10.   Which JUNOS software daemon is responsible for operating the CLI?

  A. chassisd

  B. rpd

  C. mgd

  D. dcd

11.   Which JUNOS software daemon is responsible for controlling the routing protocols?

  A. chassisd

  B. rpd

  C. mgd

  D. dcd

12.   When issued from the top of the configuration hierarchy, which command creates a file called *saved-file* that contains the entire candidate configuration?

  A. `file save saved-file`

  B. `save saved-file`

  C. `run file save saved-file`

  D. `run save saved-file`

13. Which command places the `juniper.conf.5.gz` file in the candidate configuration?

➤**A.** `rollback 5`

B. `run rollback 5`

C. `load override juniper.conf.5.gz`

D. `load merge juniper.conf.5.gz`

14. Where does the router store each user's home directory?

A. `/var/db/config`

B. `/var/log`

C. `/var/home`

D. `/var/usr`

15. What is the primary boot media for the JUNOS software?

A. Removable media

B. Internal flash drive

C. External flash drive

D. Internal hard drive

16. What is the secondary boot media for the JUNOS software?

A. Removable media

B. Internal flash drive

C. External flash drive

D. Internal hard drive

17. Which command loads a new version of the JUNOS software into the internal flash drive?

A. `load upgrade` *filename*

B. `request system software add` *filename*

C. `load software` *filename*

D. `request system load` *filename*

18. Which Emacs keystroke takes the cursor to the beginning of the command line?

A. Ctrl+A

B. Ctrl+D

C. Ctrl+E

D. Ctrl+W

19. Which command allows you to paste text directly into the candidate configuration?

   A. `load override`

   B. `load override filename`

   C. `load merge`

   D. `load merge terminal`

20. When you're committing your configuration, what command allows the router to automatically return to a previous configuration?

   A. `commit`

   B. `commit and-quit`

   C. `commit check`

   D. `commit confirmed`

Answers to Review Questions

1. A, C, D.   The Routing Engine performs multiple functions, including operating the routing pro-tocols on the router, loading the JUNOS software, and controlling the CLI. The Packet Forward-ing Engine controls packet forwarding.

2. B.   The Routing Engine builds the master routing table, selects the best path to each route, and places those next hops into the forwarding table.

3. C.   The PIC I/O Manager ASIC is responsible for receiving and transmitting data packets from the physical media connected to the PIC.

4. B.   The Internet Processor ASIC consults the forwarding table on the control board to determine the next-hop router along the path to the destination.

5. A.   The I/O manager ASIC is responsible for multiple functions in the router. One of those is the creation of J-cells from the original data packet.

6. D.   The primary role of the Distributed Buffer Manager ASIC is storing and retrieving J-cells from the packet storage buffer.

7. A.   After receiving the packet from the physical media and performing any link-layer func-tions, the incoming PIC I/O Manager ASIC sends the packet to the incoming I/O Manager ASIC on its FPC.

8. B.   The CPU on the router's control board is responsible for handing exception packets. Some of those exception packets might reach the Routing Engine.

9. A, D.   Routing protocol updates and packets requiring an ICMP error message (TTL = 1) are con-sidered exception packets. A Juniper Networks router does not communicate using the HTTP or SMTP protocols. Therefore, these packets must be transiting the router and are handled by the Packet Forwarding Engine.

10. C.   The Management Daemon (mgd) is responsible for controlling the CLI process.

11. B.   The Routing Protocol Daemon (rpd) is responsible for all routing protocol activity on the router.

12. B.   The `save` command takes portions of the candidate configuration and places them in a file you specify. When used from the top of the hierarchy, this process saves the entire candidate configuration.

13. A.   Only the `rollback 5` command places the fifth rollback file in the candidate configuration. Options C and D will look for the `juniper.conf.5.gz` file in the user's home directory, where it is not stored by default.

14. C.   Each user configured on the router receives his or her own home directory in the `/var/home` section of the hard drive.

15. B.   The router's internal flash drive is the primary boot location for the JUNOS software.

16. D.   The router's internal hard drive is the secondary boot location for the JUNOS software.

17. B.   The `request system software add` *filename* command loads a copy of the JUNOS software onto the router's flash drive.

18. A.   To reach the beginning of the command line, use the Ctrl+A keystroke. Ctrl+E takes you to the end and Ctrl+W deletes the previous word. Ctrl+D closes your terminal during a `load merge terminal` operation.

19. D.   The `load merge terminal` command allows you to cut and paste configuration directly into the router.

20. D.   The `commit confirmed` command allows the router to return to the previous configuration automatically if you don't issue a regular `commit` within the default 10-minute timer.

Chapter

2

Interfaces

JNCIA EXAM OBJECTIVES COVERED IN THIS CHAPTER:

✓ Identify valid options for interface names and protocol families within the JUNOS software

✓ Describe the function of CLI commands used to monitor interfaces

In this chapter, we present the basic skills required to configure and monitor interfaces on a Juniper Networks router. We compare permanent and transient interfaces, and take a look at the JUNOS software interface nomenclature. Next, we discuss the physical and logical properties of different interface types, focusing on the configuration of protocol families and virtual circuits.

Once the foundation has been laid, we explore several configuration examples of interfaces. The chapter concludes with a presentation of the JUNOS software command-line interface (CLI) commands used to monitor the status of interfaces, verify their operation, and perform troubleshooting.

Types of Interfaces

A Juniper Networks platform contains two types of interfaces. Permanent interfaces are always present in each router, while transient interfaces are inserted in or removed from the router by a user.

Permanent Interfaces

The *permanent interfaces* on a Juniper Networks platform perform two vital roles—management and operation. The management functionality is performed primarily by the *fxp0* interface. This *Management Ethernet* interface provides you with an out-of-band method for connecting to the router. This connection uses utilities such as Secure Shell (SSH) and Telnet to allow a remote user to manage and configure the router.

The fxp0 interface on a Juniper Networks router does not provide forwarding capabilities for transit data packets. It is used only for user management connectivity to the router.

The operation of a Juniper Networks platform itself relies on the *Internal Ethernet* interface, *fxp1*. The fxp1 interface connects the Routing Engine to the Packet Forwarding Engine. This communications link is how routing protocol packets reach the Routing Engine to update the routing table. The forwarding table updates reach the Packet Forwarding Engine across this interface as well.

> The Internal Ethernet interface is configured, addressed, and enabled automatically when the JUNOS software boots. There is never a reason to configure or disable the fxp1 interface. Altering the default behavior can seriously impair the router's ability to perform its functions.

Transient Interfaces

When you talk about a router's interfaces, you often mean the interfaces that receive a user's data packet and then transmit that packet toward the final destination. For a Juniper Networks platform, these are *transient interfaces*. These interfaces are physically located on a *Physical Interface Card (PIC)* and can be inserted and removed from the router at any time. This property gives them their transient nature.

You must configure each transient interface before using it for operational purposes. In addition, the JUNOS software allows you to configure transient interfaces that are not currently in the physical chassis. As the software activates the router's configuration, it detects which interfaces are actually present and activates only those transient interfaces. Should you install new physical interfaces in the router (for which some configuration exists), the JUNOS software activates the parameters for that transient interface.

You will learn how to configure transient interfaces in the "Interface Properties" section later in this chapter. Next, we discuss the naming structure for transient interfaces.

> For the remainder of this book, any reference to the term *interface* should be interpreted as a transient interface. References to fxp0 and fxp1 as permanent interfaces will be explicitly stated.

Interface Naming

In Chapter 1, "The Components of a Juniper Networks Router," we saw that a router's interfaces are located on a PIC. The PIC is located on a particular *Flexible PIC Concentrator (FPC)*, which is inserted in a router's chassis. This physical placement of interfaces becomes quite important when we start referencing them within the configuration. Each interface receives a unique name based on this location in the router. Let's see how this works.

Interface Naming Structure

The JUNOS software follows a consistent naming structure of *media_type-fpc/pic/port*
.unit. The portions of the interface names include the following:

media_type   A two-character designator that uniquely identifies the type of physical interface

fpc   The physical slot in the chassis where the interface is located

pic   The slot on the FPC that contains the interface

port   The location on the PIC where the interface port is located

unit   The logical portion of the interface that contains properties, such as an IP address

   Let's examine each of these interface portions in more detail.

Media Types

The media type portion of the interface name allows the JUNOS software to identify each physical interface. The two-letter representation relates closely to the actual type of interface used. Several interface types are available; some of the more prevalent types are listed here:

ae   Aggregated Ethernet interface

as   Aggregated SONET/SDH interface

at   Asynchronous Transfer Mode (ATM) interface

ds   DS0 interface (including Multichannelized DS-3 interfaces)

e1   E1 interface (including Channelized STM-1 to E1 interfaces)

e3   E3 interface

es   Encryption interface

fe   Fast Ethernet interface

fxp   Management and Internal Ethernet interfaces

ge   Gigabit Ethernet interface

gr   Generic Route Encapsulation tunnel interface

ip   IP-over-IP encapsulation tunnel interface

lo   Loopback interface

so   SONET/SDH interface

t1   T1 interface (including Channelized DS-3)

t3   T3 interface (including Channelized OC-12 interfaces)

The fxp interfaces are the only current interface types that do not follow the two-letter designator format. These interfaces are special in their function, and this uniqueness is represented in their media type descriptor. The "Permanent Interfaces" section earlier in this chapter describes the fxp interfaces in more detail.

FPC Slot Numbers

The FPC slots in a Juniper Networks router begin at 0. Each router model contains a specific number of slots that range from 1 to 8. The slot number is printed directly on the router chassis. Figure 2.1 shows the FPC slots on the M40, M40e, M160, T320, and T640 platforms. These are numbered 0 through 7 in a left-to-right fashion.

FIGURE 2.1   Eight-slot chassis

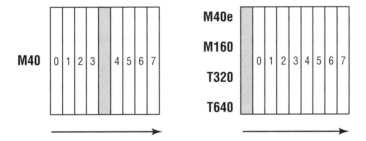

The M20 platform has four horizontal slots numbered 0 through 3, top to bottom. Figure 2.2 displays this pattern.

FIGURE 2.2   Four-slot chassis

The remaining router platforms, M5 and M10, share the same chassis platform, with each model supporting a different number of slots. The M5 has a single slot, numbered 0, while the M10 has two slots, numbered 0 and 1. Figure 2.3 shows these platforms and their slot numbers.

FIGURE 2.3   M5 and M10 chassis platforms

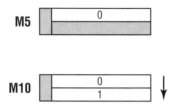

PIC Slot Numbers

PIC slot numbers also begin at 0 and have a maximum value of 3. They are physically printed on the FPC and represent the location of the PIC on the FPC module. The numbering scheme follows the physical layout of the Juniper Networks platforms. The vertical FPC slots use the same numbering, while the horizontal slots use a different one. Figure 2.4 details the differences between these patterns.

FIGURE 2.4   PIC slot numbering

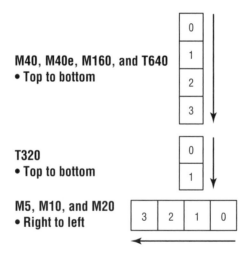

The vast majority of FPCs for a Juniper Networks platform contain four PIC slots (numbered 0 through 3). Some physical PICs are *quad-wide* and combine the PIC with an FPC in a single FPC slot. In this situation, the PIC slot number is always set to 0.

PIC Port Numbers

The physical media cable in your network (for example, Ethernet or SONET) actually connects to a port on the PIC. These ports are also numbered and represent a portion of the interface naming structure. The number of ports on a PIC varies, as does the numbering pattern on the PIC itself. The actual port numbers are physically printed on the PIC for accuracy. While it is not an exhaustive list, Figure 2.5 shows some of the different numbering schemes.

FIGURE 2.5 PIC port numbering

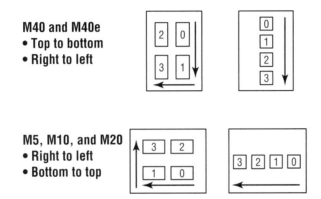

Logical Unit and Channel Numbers

The logical unit portion of the interface name corresponds to the unit number assigned within the interface configuration hierarchy. This value is a number in the range of 0 to 16384. Interfaces within the JUNOS software always contain a logical configuration, so some value is always present in the naming scheme. (We cover logical interface configuration in the "Logical Properties" section later in this chapter.)

Some physical interfaces use a channel number instead of a unit number to represent their logical configuration. For example, a nonconcatenated (that is, channelized) SONET/SDH OC-48 interface has four OC-12 channels, numbered 0 through 3. A channelized OC-12 interface has 12 DS-3 channels, numbered 0 through 11.

Interface Naming Examples

Now that we've gotten the details out of the way, let's see if we can bring the concepts together with some concrete examples. Suppose a router has two OC-3 PICs in slots 0 and 1 on an FPC in slot 1. Each of the PICs contains two ports. The names of these interfaces are:

- so-1/0/0.0
- so-1/0/1.0
- so-1/1/0.0
- so-1/1/1.0

When an FPC in slot 3 contains four OC-12 ATM PICs, the FPC becomes fully populated. Each PIC supports a single physical port. The interface names when each port has a single logical unit assigned are:

- at-3/0/0.0
- at-3/1/0.0
- at-3/2/0.0
- at-3/3/0.0

The OC-48 SONET FPC in an M40 router is an example of a quad-wide PIC. Should this PIC be installed in slot 6, it appears as PIC slot 0 with a single port 0. The JUNOS software representation becomes:

so-6/0/0.0

A channelized OC-12 PIC contains 12 logical DS-3 channels. When installed in PIC slot 2 on FPC slot 2, the channels are represented as:

- t3-2/2/0:0
- t3-2/2/0:1
- t3-2/2/0:2
- t3-2/2/0:3
- t3-2/2/0:4
- t3-2/2/0:5
- t3-2/2/0:6
- t3-2/2/0:7
- t3-2/2/0:8
- t3-2/2/0:9
- t3-2/2/0:10
- t3-2/2/0:11

Interface Properties

Interfaces in the JUNOS software contain both physical and logical properties. The actual media type (such as Ethernet or SONET) often determines the physical properties of the interface. An interface's logical properties represent the Layer 3 routing and Layer 2 transmission parameters needed to operate the interface in a network. Let's examine the physical properties first.

Physical Properties

Each interface in the router inherits certain default values for its physical properties. When the JUNOS software activates an interface, it assigns these values. The list of possible physical options and changes is exhausting, but a few values are more commonly used than others. These properties include the following:

Description   A user-defined text description is available for all interfaces. This is often used to describe the interface's purpose.

Diagnostic characteristics   Circuit-testing capabilities, such as loopback settings or Bit Error Rate Test (BERT) tests, are user-configured on a per-physical interface basis. (We discuss these tools in the "Useful Interface Commands" section later in this chapter.)

Encapsulation   Options for encapsulation types vary for different media types.

Frame check sequence (FCS)   This field is used for error-checking received packets. You can change the default value from a 16-bit field to a 32-bit mode.

Interface clock source   Point-to-point interfaces require a clocking source for synchronization purposes. Options here include `internal` (the default) or `external`.

Interface MTU size   The *maximum transmission unit (MTU)* of the physical interface can be changed. Each interface has a different default value; the possible range is 256 to 9192 bytes.

Keepalives   A *keepalive* is a physical-layer mechanism that is used to determine whether the interface is operating correctly. With the exception of ATM interfaces, each interface uses keepalives by default. You can disable this function.

Payload scrambling   Scrambling is a mechanism used for long-haul communications to assist in an error-free transmission. Most interfaces in the JUNOS software use a default value of `payload-scrambler`, but you can disable this function as well.

Real World Scenario

Connecting to Another Vendor's Router

When two Juniper Networks routers are connected, the default physical properties allow the network link to operate normally. However, the physical interface defaults do not always match the operational parameters of another vendor. In situations like this, you must change the operation of one side of the link to allow the connection to fully function.

One good example of this is connecting a SONET point-to-point link to a router from Cisco Systems. The default encapsulation type for a SONET link within the JUNOS software is the *Point-to-Point Protocol (PPP)*. A Cisco Systems router, on the other hand, uses a Cisco proprietary format of the *High-Level Data Link Control (HDLC)* protocol. The JUNOS software supports this HDLC format on point-to-point interfaces using the keyword `cisco-hdlc`. Once configured, your Juniper Networks router and Cisco Systems router can interoperate and pass user data traffic.

Logical Properties

Each and every interface within the JUNOS software requires at least one logical interface, called a *unit*. This is where all addressing and protocol information is configured. Some physical encapsulations allow only a single logical unit. PPP and Cisco-HDLC fall into this category. Logical interfaces, such as the loopback, and non-VLAN Ethernet also provide for only one logical unit. In both situations, the logical interface is assigned a unit value of 0.

Multiple logical interface units are often used in ATM, Frame Relay, and VLAN tagged Ethernet networks. In these cases, each logical unit is assigned a Virtual Circuit Identifier (VCI), Data-Link Connection Identifier (DLCI), or Virtual Local Area Network (VLAN) number, respectively. This system allows you to map multiple logical interfaces onto a single physical interface. The JUNOS software views each logical interface as a separate entity.

Common logical interface properties include a protocol family, logical Layer 3 addressing, MTU, and virtual circuit (Layer 2) addressing information.

Protocol Families

Each logical interface in the JUNOS software has the ability to support one or more *protocol families*. These families enable the logical interface to accept and process data packets for the router. Without their configuration, the interface drops any unknown transmissions. Currently four possible protocol families are available for your use:

inet   The *inet protocol family* supports IP version 4 (IPv4) packets.

inet6   To allow support for IP version 6 (IPv6) data packets, each interface can be configured with the *inet6 protocol family*.

iso   The Intermediate System to Intermediate System (IS-IS) routing protocol uses a data link encapsulation defined by the International Standards Organization (ISO). The *iso protocol family* allows the processing of these packet types. (IS-IS is discussed in greater detail in Chapter 7.)

mpls   The *mpls protocol family* provides support for processing packets encoded with a Multiprotocol Label Switching (MPLS) label. This label information allows the router to forward the data packet. (We discuss MPLS in greater detail in Chapter 11.)

Protocol Addresses

A *protocol address* is a logical Layer 3 value used to route user packets in a network. For example, an IPv4 address of 192.168.1.1 /24 is a protocol address. The JUNOS software allows addressing for the inet, inet6, and iso protocol families. The inet family provides the capability to assign multiple addresses to each logical unit, with each address equally represented on the interface. In this situation, you encounter the concepts of the *primary address* and the *preferred address*.

A single *primary address* is assigned to each interface. By default, it is the lowest numerical IP address configured. For example, 10.10.10.1 /24 is a lower value than 172.16.1.1 /24. The primary address is used as the source address of a packet when the destination address is not local to a configured subnet. Let's look at an example.

Cabernet has both 10.10.10.1 /24 and 172.16.1.1 /24 configured on its fe-0/0/0.0 interface. You use the ping command to form an IPv4 packet with a destination address of 192.168.100.10.

This packet is ready for transmission on the fe-0/0/0.0 interface. Since the destination address is not part of the interface's subnets, the primary interface address of 10.10.10.1 is used as the source IP address within the packet.

Unlike the primary address, a logical unit may have multiple preferred addresses at the same time. The *preferred address* is used when an interface has two addresses configured within the same subnet. The default selection of the preferred address is similar to the primary address in that the lowest numerical prefix is selected. The use of the preferred address is also similar in that it assists the interface in selecting the source IP address of a packet.

We've added the 172.16.1.100 /24 address to Cabernet's fe-0/0/0.0 interface. This time, we issue the ping command to the destination of 172.16.1.200. The outgoing subnet is known to the interface, so the primary address is not automatically used. The local address within the subnet is used instead, but in our case we have two addresses configured in the subnet. The preferred address of 172.16.1.1 is used in this case as the source IP address.

You will find examples of defining different protocol families, protocol addresses, and altering the primary and preferred addresses in the "Configuration Examples" section later in this chapter.

 Real World Scenario

Multiple Addresses on an Interface

The discussion on primary and preferred addresses for an interface brings up an interesting point. The JUNOS software allows multiple IP addresses on a logical unit. A Cisco Systems interface allows multiple IP addresses by using a concept called a *secondary address*. In this case, only the primary address is used for all interface functions. A Juniper Networks router, on the other hand, sees no functional difference between the addresses on its interfaces. All addresses are equal to the operating system. Each address forms routing protocol neighbor relationships, and each is advertised into the Interior Gateway Protocol (IGP).

This default behavior means that you must take care when changing IP addresses on an interface. Simply configuring the new address results in multiple addresses assigned to the interface. You have two main methods for avoiding this issue. First, you can remove the old address by using the delete command prior to configuring the new address. Second, you can change the old address to the new address by using the rename command.

The use of rename is covered in Chapter 4, "Routing Policy." In addition, Chapter 4 contains a sidebar titled "Other Uses for rename."

Protocol MTU

An MTU value can be configured for each logical unit in the router. The default values vary for each physical media type as well as for the protocol family configured.

Point-to-point interfaces   When you're using an encapsulation type of PPP, Cisco-HDLC, ATM, or Frame Relay, the default MTU for the inet and iso protocols is 4470 bytes. The mpls protocol family uses a value of 4458 bytes.

Broadcast interfaces   Both a Gigabit Ethernet and a Fast Ethernet interface share the same properties for protocol MTU sizes. The inet family uses 1500 bytes, the iso family uses 1497 bytes, and the mpls family uses 1488 bytes.

> The difference between the protocol MTU and the interface MTU discussed in the "Physical Properties" section earlier in this chapter is quite important. The interface MTU is the largest size packet able to be sent on the physical media. This value includes all Layer 2 overhead information, such as the destination MAC address on Ethernet, or the labels in an MPLS environment. The Cyclic Redundancy Check (CRC) information is not included in this value, however. Each encapsulation type has a payload field where higher-layer information is stored. This payload field is the size of the protocol MTU. This is the largest amount of logical protocol data, including the protocol header, able to be sent on a particular interface.

Virtual Circuit Addressing

An interface configured for use on an ATM, Frame Relay, or Ethernet VLAN network requires the addition of a Layer 2 virtual circuit address. We examine these options next.

ATM VPI and VCI

An *Asynchronous Transfer Mode (ATM)* network uses the concept of a virtual path and a virtual circuit to connect two devices. The path is represented by a *virtual path identifier (VPI)*, which can be thought of as a logical conduit between the devices. Each VPI in a network may contain multiple logical circuits represented by a *virtual circuit identifier (VCI)*, which is the actual connection between the devices.

Each logical unit in the router is assigned a VPI/VCI Layer 2 address. The path values range from 0 to 255, while the circuits on that path can be between 0 and 4089. These values are locally significant so that the two connected devices agree on their usage. The specific pair can then be used elsewhere in the ATM network, allowing for greater overall scalability.

As an example, assume that the Merlot router is connected to Riesling through an ATM interface. Ten logical units are created on the interface, each with a unique IPv4 address and VCI value. When data packets are passed between the two routers, the VCI address at Layer 2 helps determine which logical unit should receive and process the packet.

Frame Relay DLCI

In a manner similar to ATM, a *Frame Relay* network uses *data link connection identifiers (DLCIs)* to address packets at Layer 2. The DLCI value is the logical circuit between the two devices, which is also locally significant. Each logical interface unit assigned a DLCI becomes a Frame Relay *per-*

manent virtual circuit (PVC). Possible DLCI values range between 1 and 1022 with reserved ranges between 1 and 15 and between1008 and 1022.

Suppose that the routers Cabernet and Shiraz are communicating over a Frame Relay network. The logical circuit that connects them is assigned a DLCI value of 200 on each router. The DLCI provides enough addressing for a data packet to reach the other router and for the receiving router to process it with the appropriate logical unit.

Ethernet VLAN Tags

For broadcast-capable media, such as Fast Ethernet and Gigabit Ethernet, the JUNOS software supports a subset of the IEEE 802.1Q standard for channelizing an interface into multiple logical interfaces. These channels are referred to as *virtual local area networks (VLANs)*. A VLAN allows many hosts to connect to an Ethernet switch while maintaining separate logical subnets and broadcast domains. Each Ethernet interface on a Juniper Networks router can support up to 1024 VLANs. Gigabit and some Fast Ethernet interfaces use values in the range of 0 to 4094, while the rest of the Ethernet interfaces use values between 0 and 1023.

The operation of a VLAN is similar to the Layer 2 operation of ATM and Frame Relay. Two routers share a VLAN value, allowing data packets to be processed by the correct logical interface.

Disabling or Deactivating an Interface

Interfaces within the JUNOS software are automatically enabled for operation when configured in the router. To stop the operation of a particular interface, you may use one of two CLI commands—*disable* or *deactivate*. Both halt an interface without removing the current configuration in the router. This allows you to easily restart the interface when needed.

The difference between the commands is how the JUNOS software uses the configuration when the `commit` command is issued. Using the `disable` command at the [`edit interfaces` `interface-name`] hierarchy level allows the router to use the interface configuration. Operationally, the interface is viewed as down, or administratively disabled.

The `deactivate` command places an `inactive` tag next to the configuration in the router. As the `commit` command is issued, the JUNOS software completely ignores the configuration. Operationally, the interface has no configuration—as if you had never entered any commands at all.

Examples of using these commands are provided in the next section. In addition, we'll explore the configuration of protocol families and addresses.

The JUNOS software provides several methods to move the configuration of an interface to a new location. The rename and `insert` commands discussed in Chapter 1 are available. In addition, you can use the `deactivate` command to remove all knowledge of an interface's configuration. This is critical in a situation where duplicate IP addresses are used.

Configuration Examples

In this section, we'll discuss the commands required to perform some basic interface configuration. As a framework for our discussion, we'll examine how to configure each of the protocol families (inet, inet6, iso, mpls) to the router's interfaces. These basic examples allow you to get a feel for how the JUNOS software interacts with its transient interfaces.

To get started, Figure 2.6 shows the router Cabernet connected to Riesling and Merlot over some point-to-point interfaces. Only the hostname of Cabernet is currently configured.

FIGURE 2.6   Interface configuration sample network

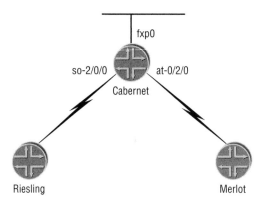

The output of the show interfaces terse command tells us which interfaces are currently installed in the router:

```
user@Cabernet> show interfaces terse
Interface       Admin Link Proto Local              Remote
fe-0/0/0        up    down
fe-0/0/1        up    down
fe-0/0/2        up    down
fe-0/0/3        up    down
at-0/2/0        up    down
at-0/2/1        up    down
so-2/0/0        up    down
so-2/0/1        up    down
so-2/0/2        up    down
so-2/0/3        up    down
ge-2/2/0        up    down
fxp0            up    down
fxp0.0          up    down
```

```
fxp1            up    up
fxp1.0          up    up    tnp    4
gre             up    up
ipip            up    up
lo0             up    up
lsi             up    up
mtun            up    up
pimd            up    up
pime            up    up
tap             up    up
```

Interfaces are always displayed in numerical order, from the lowest to the highest FPC slot number. Within that slot, the lowest PIC slot is shown first, and on an individual PIC the lowest port number is always first.

All interface configurations are completed at the [edit interfaces] hierarchy level. A generic interface configuration looks like this:

```
interfaces {
    interface-name {
        physical-properties;
        unit unit-number {
            logical-properties;
        }
    }
}
```

IP Version 4

We'll start building our network by configuring some interfaces with the inet protocol family and IPv4 addresses. We'll have an Ethernet broadcast interface, an ATM, and a SONET interface.

Broadcast Interfaces

The out-of-band management interface of fxp0 is first:

```
[edit interfaces fxp0]
user@Cabernet# set unit 0 family inet address 172.16.0.1/24
user@Cabernet# set description "This is the Ethernet management interface"
```

Notice that the logical IP address is configured within the family inet hierarchy directory and that the prefix length of the address is used, not the address mask. The prefix length is the number of bits in the network portion of the IP address. For example, a prefix length of /24 translates into 255.255.255.0. Forgetting to specify the prefix length results in the router assuming a length of 32 bits, or /32. The text description on the interface is enclosed in quotation marks to allow for the spaces in the text. This convention is consistent throughout the JUNOS software syntax.

It turns out that we made a mistake in assigning the fxp0 IP address. It should have an address of 172.16.1.1 /24. Because the inet family supports multiple addresses, simply entering the new address results in the interface having two IP addresses. We don't want this to happen, so let's first delete the old information and then correct our mistake:

```
[edit interfaces fxp0]
user@Cabernet# delete unit 0 family inet address 172.16.0.1/24
user@Cabernet# set unit 0 family inet address 172.16.1.1/24
```

While only a virtual entity, the loopback interface of the router closely simulates the operation of a broadcast interface. The configuration syntax is similar in nature, so we'll investigate it at this point. Both an IP address and a description are assigned:

```
[edit interfaces lo0]
user@Cabernet# set unit 0 family inet address 192.168.1.1/32
user@Cabernet# set description "This is the router's loopback interface"
```

One major difference of the loopback interface is the prefix length of the addresses—only a 32-bit prefix length is supported in the JUNOS software.

ATM Interfaces

Let's continue on and configure the interface to Merlot. All ATM interfaces in the JUNOS software require some configuration of physical properties: the maximum number of virtual circuits allowed on a virtual path and the encapsulation of the interface. We also assign a description to the interface:

```
[edit interfaces at-0/2/0]
user@Cabernet# set atm-options vpi 0 maximum-vcs 200
user@Cabernet# set encapsulation atm-pvc
user@Cabernet# set description "Connection to Merlot"
```

Then, we can configure the logical properties of the interface:

```
[edit interfaces at-0/2/0]
user@Cabernet# set unit 100 point-to-point
user@Cabernet# set unit 100 family inet address 10.0.1.1/24
user@Cabernet# set unit 100 vci 0.100
```

SONET Interfaces

SONET interfaces don't require any physical-level configuration, as did the ATM interface. We'll be adding some to our interface, however. A description is in order to provide for easier management and troubleshooting in the future. Also, a 32-bit FCS checksum is used to provide for a more reliable packet transmission.

```
[edit interfaces so-2/0/0]
user@Cabernet# set description "Connection to Riesling"
user@Cabernet# set sonet-options fcs 32
```

Recall from the "Logical Properties" section earlier in this chapter that a SONET interface uses a default encapsulation of PPP. Further, a PPP interface may have only a single logical unit assigned to it—unit 0. We now assign an IP address to our SONET interface:

```
[edit interfaces so-2/0/0]
user@Cabernet# set unit 0 family inet address 10.0.2.1/30
```

Configuration Verification

Let's check our progress so far by examining the candidate configuration file:

```
[edit interfaces]
user@Cabernet# show
at-0/2/0 {
    description "Connection to Merlot";
    encapsulation atm-pvc;
    atm-options {
        vpi 0 maximum-vcs 200;
    }
    unit 100 {
        point-to-point;
        vci 0.100;
        family inet {
            address 10.0.1.1/24;
        }
    }
}
so-2/0/0 {
    description "Connection to Riesling";
    sonet-options {
        fcs 32;
    }
    unit 0 {
        family inet {
            address 10.0.2.1/30;
        }
```

```
        }
    }
    fxp0 {
        description "This is the Ethernet management interface";
        unit 0 {
            family inet {
                address 172.16.1.1/24;
            }
        }
    }
    lo0 {
        description "This is the router's loopback interface";
        unit 0 {
            family inet {
                address 192.168.1.1/32;
            }
        }
    }
}
```

Operational Changes

Now that we have some configured interfaces, we can examine the operation of disabling or deactivating an interface. We first verify the current status of the so-2/0/0.0 interface:

```
user@Cabernet> show interfaces so-2/0/0 terse
Interface          Admin Link Proto Local                 Remote
so-2/0/0           up    up
so-2/0/0.0         up    up    inet  10.0.2.1/30
```

The up keyword in the Admin and Link columns shows that the interface is fully functional. Let's use the deactivate command to remove the operational configuration from the router:

```
[edit interfaces]
user@Cabernet# deactivate so-2/0/0

[edit interfaces]
user@Cabernet# show
inactive: so-2/0/0 {
    description "Connection to Riesling";
    sonet-options {
        fcs 32;
    }
    unit 0 {
```

```
        family inet {
            address 10.0.2.1/30;
        }
    }
}
```

The inactive tag proceeding the interface name shows that the configuration hierarchy is ignored when the commit command is issued. After this process, the output of show interfaces terse displays the logical configuration removed by the router:

```
user@Cabernet> show interfaces so-2/0/0 terse
Interface        Admin Link Proto Local            Remote
so-2/0/0         up    up
```

To return the interface to its normal operation, we'll need to remove the inactive tag. This is accomplished with the activate command:

```
[edit interfaces]
user@Cabernet# activate so-2/0/0

[edit interfaces]
user@Cabernet# show
so-2/0/0 {
    description "Connection to Riesling";
    sonet-options {
        fcs 32;
    }
    unit 0 {
        family inet {
            address 10.0.2.1/30;
        }
    }
}
```

The disable command has a different effect on an operational interface. It marks the interface as **down**, or administratively disabled. We'll explore this functionality through the use of the disable command on the fxp0 interface:

```
[edit interfaces]
user@Cabernet# set fxp0 disable

[edit interfaces]
user@Cabernet# show fxp0
description "This is the Ethernet management interface";
```

```
disable;
unit 0 {
    family inet {
        address 172.16.1.1/24;
    }
}
```

The output of the show interfaces terse command indicates that the physical interface fxp0 is now marked as down in the Admin and Link columns. This occurs due to the application of the disable keyword at the physical interface hierarchy level of the configuration:

```
user@Cabernet> show interfaces fxp0 terse
Interface       Admin Link Proto Local            Remote
fxp0            down  up
fxp0.0          down  down inet  172.16.1.1/24
```

Since the disable keyword is now a part of the configuration, we must remove that configuration option with the delete command:

```
[edit interfaces]
user@Cabernet# delete fxp0 disable
```

```
[edit interfaces]
user@Cabernet# show fxp0
description "This is the Ethernet management interface";
unit 0 {
    family inet {
        address 172.16.1.1/24;
    }
}
```

IPv6 Support

Internet Protocol version 6 (IPv6) is an evolutionary step from the current IPv4. It uses the best aspects of IPv4 and accounts for the lessons learned over the last number of years. To enable IPv6 on a logical interface, we add the protocol family inet6 as well as a 128-bit IPv6 address:

```
[edit interfaces at-0/2/0]
user@Cabernet# set unit 100 family inet6 address fec0:0:0:3002::2/64
```

```
[edit interfaces so-2/0/0]
user@Cabernet# set unit 0 family inet6 address fec0:0:0:1002::1/64
```

```
[edit interfaces lo0]
user@Cabernet# set unit 0 family inet6 address fec0:0:0:1006::1/128
```

The candidate configuration now shows that the new `family inet6` hierarchies have been added:

```
[edit interfaces]
user@Cabernet# show
at-0/2/0 {
    description "Connection to Merlot";
    encapsulation atm-pvc;
    atm-options {
        vpi 0 maximum-vcs 200;
    }
    unit 100 {
        point-to-point;
        vci 0.100;
        family inet {
            address 10.0.1.1/24;
        }
        family inet6 {
            address fec0:0:0:3002::2/64;
        }
    }
}
so-2/0/0 {
    description "Connection to Riesling";
    sonet-options {
        fcs 32;
    }
    unit 0 {
        family inet {
            address 10.0.2.1/30;
        }
        family inet6 {
            address fec0:0:0:1002::1/64;
        }
    }
}
fxp0 {
    description "This is the Ethernet management interface";
```

```
    unit 0 {
        family inet {
            address 172.16.1.1/24;
        }
    }
}
lo0 {
    description "This is the router's loopback interface";
    unit 0 {
        family inet {
            address 192.168.1.1/32;
        }
        family inet6 {
            address fec0:0:0:1006::1/128;
        }
    }
}
```

IS-IS Support

The IS-IS routing protocol uses Connectionless Network Protocol (CLNP) packets to send updates to neighboring routers. Each interface using the IS-IS protocol must be configured to accept and process these packets using the family iso command. In addition, the lo0 interface receives a protocol address to represent the routing node:

```
[edit interfaces at-0/2/0]
user@Cabernet# set unit 100 family iso

[edit interfaces so-2/0/0]
user@Cabernet# set unit 0 family iso

[edit interfaces lo0]
user@Cabernet# set unit 0 family iso address 49.0001.1921.6800.1001.00
```

You have now added the new protocol family to the appropriate logical unit:

```
[edit interfaces]
user@Cabernet# show
at-0/2/0 {
    description "Connection to Merlot";
    encapsulation atm-pvc;
```

```
    atm-options {
        vpi 0 maximum-vcs 200;
    }
    unit 100 {
        point-to-point;
        vci 0.100;
        family inet {
            address 10.0.1.1/24;
        }
        family iso;
    }
}
so-2/0/0 {
    description "Connection to Riesling";
    sonet-options {
        fcs 32;
    }
    unit 0 {
        family inet {
            address 10.0.2.1/30;
        }
        family iso;
    }
}
fxp0 {
    description "This is the Ethernet management interface";
    unit 0 {
        family inet {
            address 172.16.1.1/24;
        }
    }
}
lo0 {
    description "This is the router's loopback interface";
    unit 0 {
        family inet {
            address 192.168.1.1/32;
        }
        family iso {
            address 49.0001.1921.6800.1001.00
```

```
        }
    }
}
```

MPLS Support

MPLS provides a mechanism for forwarding data packets using a label value instead of an IP address. As was the case with IS-IS, you must configure each transit interface with a protocol family to allow processing of MPLS packets. You accomplish this by using the `family mpls` command; no protocol addressing is required for MPLS.

```
[edit interfaces at-0/2/0]
user@Cabernet# set unit 100 family mpls

[edit interfaces so-2/0/0]
user@Cabernet# set unit 0 family mpls
```

The candidate configuration now appears as such:

```
[edit interfaces]
user@Cabernet# show
at-0/2/0 {
    description "Connection to Merlot";
    encapsulation atm-pvc;
    atm-options {
        vpi 0 maximum-vcs 200;
    }
    unit 100 {
        point-to-point;
        vci 0.100;
        family inet {
            address 10.0.1.1/24;
        }
        family iso;
        family mpls;
    }
}
so-2/0/0 {
    description "Connection to Riesling";
    sonet-options {
        fcs 32;
    }
```

```
    unit 0 {
        family inet {
            address 10.0.2.1/30;
        }
        family iso;
        family mpls;
    }
}
fxp0 {
    description "This is the Ethernet management interface";
    unit 0 {
        family inet {
            address 172.16.1.1/24;
        }
    }
}
lo0 {
    description "This is the router's loopback interface";
    unit 0 {
        family inet {
            address 192.168.1.1/32;
        }
        family iso {
            address 49.0001.1921.6800.1001.00
        }
    }
}
```

Useful Interface Commands

The JUNOS software provides a number of operational mode CLI commands you can use to check the status and operation of the router interfaces. Some of the commands are specific to the JUNOS software, while a few are well-known IP tools, such as ping.

In the sections that follow, we examine the output of some show commands as well as the operation of some troubleshooting tools.

show interfaces extensive

The show interfaces extensive command displays all possible information about every interface currently installed in the router. You have the option of specifying a particular interface or a group of interfaces through a wildcard notation. For example, let's get some information about all SONET interfaces in the Cabernet router:

```
user@Cabernet> show interfaces so* extensive
Physical interface: so-2/0/0, Enabled, Physical link is Up
  Interface index: 17, SNMP ifIndex: 53, Generation: 16
  Link-level type: PPP, MTU: 4474, Clocking: Internal, SONET mode, Speed: OC3,
    Loopback: None,
  FCS: 32, Payload scrambler: Enabled
  Device flags   : Present Running
  Interface flags: Point-To-Point SNMP-Traps
  Link flags     : Keepalives
  Hold-times     : Up 0 ms, Down 0 ms
  Keepalive settings: Interval 10 seconds, Up-count 1, Down-count 3
  Keepalive statistics:
    Input : 52 (last seen 00:00:04 ago)
    Output: 54 (last sent 00:00:07 ago)
  LCP state: Opened
  NCP state: inet: Opened, inet6: Not-configured, iso: Not-configured, mpls:
    Not-configured
  CHAP state: Not-configured
  Last flapped   : 2002-06-11 17:14:27 UTC (3d 18:28 ago)
  Statistics last cleared: Never
  Traffic statistics:
   Input  bytes  :            254324             0 bps
   Output bytes  :            290551             0 bps
   Input  packets:              3122             0 pps
   Output packets:              4529             0 pps
  Input errors:
      Errors: 0, Drops: 0, Framing errors: 0, Runts: 0, Giants: 0,
      Bucket drops: 0, Policed discards: 235, L3 incompletes: 0,
      L2 channel errors: 0, L2 mismatch timeouts: 3, HS link CRC errors: 0,
      HS link FIFO overflows: 00
  Output errors:
      Carrier transitions: 0, Errors: 0, Drops: 0, Aged packets: 0,
      HS link FIFO underflows: 0

(Note: Information deleted for brevity)

  Logical interface so-2/0/0.0 (Index 4) (SNMP ifIndex 21) (Generation 11)
    Flags: Point-To-Point SNMP-Traps Encapsulation: PPP
```

```
Protocol inet, MTU: 4470, Flags: None, Generation: 19 Route table: 0
  Addresses, Flags: Is-Preferred Is-Primary
    Destination: 10.0.1/24, Local: 10.0.1.2, Broadcast: Unspecified,
      Generation: 26
```

Important information to gather from the output includes the current interface status: `Enabled, Physical link is Up`. This tells us that the interface is administratively started and that a physical wire is plugged into the PIC port. Some of the default SONET parameters are seen here, including the encapsulation type (PPP), the interface MTU (4474), the default clocking (`Internal`), and the operation (`Payload scrambler`). Our earlier configuration is being used since the FCS is currently set to a value of 32. Finally, an interface loopback has not been set, as noted by the keyword `None`.

 We cover interface and circuit testing using the Loopback command in the "Loopback Testing" section later in this chapter.

The other advantage to using the `show interfaces extensive` command is that you can view the actual data packets entering and leaving the interface. Traffic statistics are measured as `Input bytes`, `Output bytes`, `Input packets`, and `Output packets`. The statistics are displayed in both a total value column and a current bits-per-second column.

Following the statistics section are error counters for the interface. The `Input Errors` fields are:

Errors   Displays the sum of incoming frame aborts and FCS errors.

Policed discards   Displays the frames discarded due to an unrecognized format. This field normally reports received protocol packets that the JUNOS software does not understand. For example, if the `family iso` command were not used, then received IS-IS packets would increment this counter. In addition, protocols such as the Cisco Discovery Protocol (CDP) are not recognized and thus increment this counter.

L3 incompletes   Displays the number of times a received packet fails a Layer 3 header check. For example, a frame with fewer than 20 bytes of available IP header is discarded and the counter is incremented.

L2 channel errors   Displays the number of received packets with an unknown Layer 2 address. For example, a packet with DLCI100 as an address is discarded when that DLCI value is not configured on the interface.

L2 mismatch timeouts   Displays the number of malformed packets that cause the incoming interface to discard the frame as unreadable.

SRAM errors   Displays hardware errors in the static random access memory (SRAM) on the PIC itself. This should always be a value of 0. If not, the PIC is malfunctioning.

HS link CRC errors   Displays the errors on the internal router links between application-specific integrated circuits (ASICs).

The possible Output Errors in the display include the following:

Carrier transitions   Displays the number of times the interface has gone from a Down state to an Up state. A rapidly incrementing number in this field represents a network problem. Possibilities include the transmission line, the far-end system, or a malfunctioning PIC.

Errors   Displays the sum of outgoing frame aborts and FCS errors.

Drops   Displays the packets dropped by the output queue of the I/O Manager ASIC.

Aged packets   Displays the packets that remained in shared-packet synchronous dynamic random access memory (SDRAM) for so long that the system automatically purged them. The value in this field should never increment.

monitor interface

The monitor interface *interface-name* command displays per-second real-time statistics for a physical interface. The output of this command shows how often each field has changed since the command was executed. You can also view common interface failures, such as alarms, errors, or loopback settings.

```
user@Cabernet> monitor interface so-2/0/0

Cabernet               Seconds: 11              Time: 12:41:55
                                                Delay: 2/0/2
Interface: so-2/0/0, Enabled, Link is Up
Encapsulation: PPP, Keepalives, Speed: OC3
Traffic statistics:                                          Current delta
  Input bytes:            1103360 (40 bps)        [36]
  Output bytes:           1190328 (48 bps)        [26]
  Input packets:            13839 (0 pps)          [3]
  Output packets:           15246 (0 pps)          [2]
Encapsulation statistics:
  Input keepalives:           410                  [1]
  Output keepalives:          407                  [1]
  LCP state: Opened
Error statistics:
  Input errors:                 0                  [0]
  Input drops:                  0                  [0]
  Input framing errors:         0                  [0]
  Input runts:                  0                  [0]
  Input giants:                 0                  [0]
  Policed discards:           235                  [0]
  L3 incompletes:               0                  [0]
  L2 channel errors:            0                  [0]
```

```
L2 mismatch timeouts:            3                     [0]
Carrier transitions:             0                     [0]
Output errors:                   0  Output drops:  Z   [0]
```

```
Next='n', Quit='q' or ESC, Freeze='f', Thaw='t', Clear='c', Interface='i'
```

At the end of the output, you'll see a legend of keystrokes that allow you to control the display parameters. For example, pressing N switches the command to the next interface in the router. Pressing I allows you to enter the name of a specific interface. The counter information is updated every second. To examine the values more closely, press F to freeze the display. The counter values will still increment in the background, but your visual display will stop changing. Pressing T thaws the output and the current counter values are displayed and updated again. Pressing C clears the counter values within the output of this command, but does not change the values in the show interfaces output. You can end the display by pressing either Q or the Esc key.

Some of the fields in the output warrant further discussion:

Cabernet   Displays the current hostname of the router.

Seconds   Displays the time (in seconds) since the counters were set to zero. If the counters are not reset, this field displays the time the command has been running.

Time   Displays the current time on the router.

Interface   Describes the interface, including its name, status, and encapsulation.

Link   Provides the current status of the interface. Possible values are Up, Down, or Test.

Current delta   Displays the number of times the respective field has changed since the counters were set to zero.

Statistics   Displays interface statistics, such as alarms and errors.

monitor traffic

The monitor traffic command prints packet headers to your terminal screen for information sent or received by the Routing Engine. It is very similar in operation to the Unix *tcpdump* utility. The PPP keepalives on our so-2/0/0 interface are seen below:

```
user@Cabernet> monitor traffic interface so-2/0/0
Listening on so-2/0/0
15:09:05.467601 Out LCP echo request        (type 0x09  id 0x76  len 0x0008)
15:09:05.468244  In LCP echo reply          (type 0x0a  id 0x76  len 0x0008)
15:09:08.017283  In LCP echo request        (type 0x09  id 0x1a  len 0x0008)
15:09:08.017301 Out LCP echo reply          (type 0x0a  id 0x1a  len 0x0008)
15:09:15.667708 Out LCP echo request        (type 0x09  id 0x77  len 0x0008)
15:09:15.668403  In LCP echo reply          (type 0x0a  id 0x77  len 0x0008)
^C
```

```
6 packets received by filter
0 packets dropped by kernel
```

You use the Ctrl+C keystroke sequence to stop the output and return to the JUNOS software command prompt.

Using the monitor traffic command might affect your router performance. We recommend that you use this option only when other JUNOS software show commands don't resolve your problem and you need to prove that a packet is actually entering or leaving the router interface.

show arp

The show arp command displays the entries in the Address Resolution Protocol (ARP) table. This command is a useful troubleshooting tool for Ethernet networks, but shows only entries for hosts that the router has attempted to send traffic to. You use the clear arp command to remove entries from the table.

```
user@Cabernet> show arp
MAC Address         Address         Name            Interface
00:a0:a5:28:15:f5 172.16.0.1      172.16.0.1      fxp0.0
00:a0:a5:12:29:bd 172.16.5.1      172.16.5.1      fxp0.0
00:a0:a5:12:2a:4b 172.16.8.1      172.16.8.1      fxp0.0
Total entries: 3
```

ping

The ping *destination* command is a common troubleshooting tool used to check host reachability and network connectivity. It sends ICMP ECHO_REQUEST messages to elicit ICMP ECHO_RESPONSE messages from the specified host. A received response tells you that all intervening network components are operational between the local router and the destination host. In addition, the network layer of the destination host is operational.

```
user@Cabernet> ping 10.0.1.1
PING 10.0.1.1 (10.0.1.1): 56 data bytes
64 bytes from 10.0.1.1: icmp_seq=0 ttl=255 time=1.086 ms
64 bytes from 10.0.1.1: icmp_seq=1 ttl=255 time=0.934 ms
64 bytes from 10.0.1.1: icmp_seq=2 ttl=255 time=0.912 ms
64 bytes from 10.0.1.1: icmp_seq=3 ttl=255 time=0.920 ms
64 bytes from 10.0.1.1: icmp_seq=4 ttl=255 time=0.918 ms
64 bytes from 10.0.1.1: icmp_seq=5 ttl=255 time=0.980 ms
^C
```

```
--- 10.0.1.1 ping statistics ---
6 packets transmitted, 6 packets received, 0% packet loss
round-trip min/avg/max/stddev = 0.912/0.958/1.086/0.061 ms
```

Using the Ctrl+C keystroke sequence stops the operation of the ping command.

ping atm

When using ATM as a Layer 2 technology, you have the option of testing the connectivity of specific PVCs with the ping atm command. Individual 53-byte ATM cells are sent along the PVC and are returned by the terminating device at the far end. The command requires an outgoing interface and a VCI value at a minimum.

```
user@Cabernet> ping atm interface at-0/2/0 vci 100
53 byte oam cell received on (vpi=0 vci=100): seq=1
53 byte oam cell received on (vpi=0 vci=100): seq=2
53 byte oam cell received on (vpi=0 vci=100): seq=3
53 byte oam cell received on (vpi=0 vci=100): seq=4
53 byte oam cell received on (vpi=0 vci=100): seq=5
53 byte oam cell received on (vpi=0 vci=100): seq=6
53 byte oam cell received on (vpi=0 vci=100): seq=7
53 byte oam cell received on (vpi=0 vci=100): seq=8
^C
--- atmping statistics ---
8 cells transmitted, 8 cells received, 0% cell loss
```

As with most JUNOS software commands, the Ctrl+C keystroke terminates the operation. The OAM cells are transmitted end-to-end through the PVC. To test just a portion of the PVC, use the segment option.

traceroute

Another standard network troubleshooting tool is the traceroute command. We often use this when the result of the ping command shows that end-to-end network connectivity is not established. We can determine the actual network path taken by the IP packets and zero in on where the problem might exist.

```
user@Cabernet> traceroute 192.168.5.1
traceroute to 192.168.5.1 (192.168.5.1), 30 hops max, 40 byte packets
 1  10.0.2.2 (10.0.2.2)  0.432 ms  0.347 ms  0.320 ms
 2  192.168.5.1 (192.168.5.1)  1.210 ms  1.005 ms  0.919 ms
```

traceroute and the User Datagram Protocol

Since the JUNOS software is based on FreeBSD, it makes sense that the `traceroute` command uses User Datagram Protocol (UDP) packets in its operation. Most (if not all) Unix-based systems follow this format. It is worth investigating, or reviewing, how `traceroute` actually operates.

When the command is executed, three UDP packets are generated. Each packet uses the supplied end-host information as the destination IP address. The outgoing interface of the router is used as the source IP address. The time-to-live (TTL) value is set to 1 and the destination UDP port is set to 33434. These packets are then sent out into the network.

When the first network device receives the packets, it decrements the TTL field by 1. This results in a new TTL value of 0, which is unusable by an IP device. The network device drops the packet and returns an `ICMP TIME_EXCEEDED` message to the source IP address of the UDP packet (the local router's interface). The local router receives these ICMP messages and examines the Source IP Address field. We've now found the first network hop along our path!

The local router now sends out three new UDP packets with the same source and destination IP addresses. The UDP port number is incremented by 1 to 33435. The TTL is also incremented by 1 to a new value of 2. The second device along the path repeats the process above by dropping the packet and returning an ICMP message to the source. This process repeats itself (UDP port and TTL incrementing each time) for each network device along the path.

When the UDP packets finally reach the end system, they are received and not dropped. After all, the TTL may be set to 1 at that point, but no forwarding of the packet is involved. The IP network layer accepts the packet, since the destination IP address is its own interface. The UDP packet is then passed up to the transport layer. The UDP process examines the destination port number to determine whether a session is expecting inbound packets on that port. When no process is found, an ICMP message is again returned to the source IP address. This time, however, it is a `PORT_UNREACHABLE` message. When the local router receives this ICMP message, it knows that it has reached the far-end system and that the system is active at the network and transport layers.

Interface Diagnostic Commands

The JUNOS software uses two main types of diagnostic configuration to test the physical layer circuitry of an interface: the loopback and BERT tests. You can also use these tools to test the circuit connecting two routers. In this section, we show you how to configure these options and interpret the results using the output of various show commands.

Loopback Testing

The physical path of a network data circuit usually consists of a number of segments interconnected by devices that repeat and regenerate the transmission signal. These devices connect together in a symmetric pattern. That is, the transmit path on one device connects to the receive path on the next device, and vice versa. Should a circuit fault occur in the form of a line break or a signal corruption due to noise, it is possible to localize the problem by taking advantage of this symmetric segmented system. One of the physical transmission systems sets up a *line loopback*. Instead of transmitting the signal toward the far-end system, it immediately sends the signal back toward the originating router. Either the originating router sees the loop in the line or it does not. The detection of a loop is achieved when the originating router sees its own data link layer packets return.

If a line loop is set back toward a local router and it is detected, then the problem lies beyond the looping transmission device. Your next step is to set a loop *farther* away from the local router to locate the problem segment.

When a line loop is set back toward the local router and it is not detected, you can assume the problem lies somewhere between the router and the looped transmission device. In this case, your next troubleshooting step is to set a loop *closer* to the local router to localize the problem.

Loopback Types

The physical interface on a Juniper Networks router can be set to loop a circuit in either `local` or `remote` mode. Both options are configured as a physical interface property and affect the operation of a PIC and its ports.

local Loopback

When the interface is operating with a `local` loopback, the PIC transmits packets to the Channel Service Unit (CSU) built into the interface. These packets are passed onto the circuit toward the far-end system. On the inbound side, the PIC receives its own transmission back and ignores any data sent from the physical circuit and the CSU. A `local` loopback is useful for troubleshooting physical PIC errors. The operation is shown in Figure 2.7.

FIGURE 2.7   `local` loopback

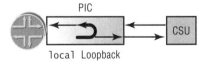

To view the operation of a loopback, we've added a new interface on Cabernet—t3-1/2/0. We first configure the interface for `local` loopback operation:

```
[edit interfaces t3-1/2/0]
user@Cabernet# set t3-options loopback local
```

```
[edit interfaces t3-1/2/0]
user@Cabernet# show
t3-options {
    loopback local;
}
```

After issuing a commit, we verify the current interface status with the show interfaces command:

```
user@Cabernet> show interfaces t3-1/2/0
Physical interface: t3-1/2/0, Enabled, Physical link is Up
  Interface index: 14, SNMP ifIndex: 18
  Link-level type: PPP, MTU: 4474, Clocking: Internal
  Speed: T3, Loopback: Local, CRC: 16, Mode: C/Bit parity
  Device flags   : Present Running Loop-Detected
  Interface flags: Point-To-Point SNMP-Traps
  Link flags     : Keepalives
  Keepalive settings: Interval 10 seconds, Up-count 1, Down-count 3
  Keepalive Input: 7230 (00:00:14 ago), Output: 7266 (00:00:09 ago)
  NCP state: Down, LCP state: Conf-req-sent
  Input rate    : 0 bps (0 pps), Output rate: 0 bps (0 pps)
  Active alarms  : None
  Active defects : None
  Logical interface t3-1/2/0.0 (Index 105) (SNMP ifIndex 29)
    Flags: Hardware-Down Point-To-Point SNMP-Traps, Encapsulation: PPP
    Protocol inet, MTU: 4470, Flags: Protocol-Down
      Addresses, Flags: Dest-route-down Is-Preferred Is-Primary
        Destination: 175.1.1.0/30, Local: 175.1.1.1
```

The Loopback: Local output shows us that our configuration was successful. In addition, the PPP keepalives transmitted on the interface are being received by the PIC, which results in a Loop-Detected message in the Device Flags field.

To return the interface to its normal operation, we remove the loopback keyword from the configuration:

```
[edit interfaces t3-1/2/0]
user@Cabernet# delete t3-options loopback
```

remote Loopback

The routers on each end of a transmission circuit are also participating in the circuit status. As such, one of the routers can initiate a line loopback toward its far-end partner. This type of environment tests all the intermediate transmission facilities.

When an interface is operating in a remote loopback mode, packets received from the physical circuit and CSU are received by the interface. In addition, those same packets are immediately retransmitted by the PIC back out toward the CSU and the circuit. This environment is displayed in Figure 2.8.

FIGURE 2.8 remote loopback

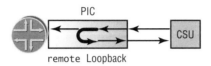

remote Loopback

In our example, Cabernet suspects a physical circuit problem between itself and the far-end router, so we decide to initiate a loop on Cabernet to test the line. The configuration looks like this:

```
[edit interfaces t3-1/2/0]
user@Cabernet# set t3-options loopback remote

[edit interfaces t3-1/2/0]
user@Cabernet# show
t3-options {
   loopback remote;
}
```

We now check the interface status:

```
user@Cabernet> show interfaces t3-1/2/0
Physical interface: t3-1/2/0, Enabled, Physical link is Up
  Interface index: 14, SNMP ifIndex: 18
  Link-level type: PPP, MTU: 4474, Clocking: Internal
  Speed: T3, Loopback: Remote, CRC: 16, Mode: C/Bit parity
  Device flags   : Present Running
  Interface flags: Point-To-Point SNMP-Traps
  Link flags     : Keepalives
  Keepalive settings: Interval 10 seconds, Up-count 1, Down-count 3
  Keepalive Input: 7245 (00:00:09 ago), Output: 7281 (00:00:04 ago)
  NCP state: Down, LCP state: Conf-req-sent
  Input rate     : 0 bps (0 pps), Output rate: 0 bps (0 pps)
  Active alarms  : None
  Active defects : None
  Logical interface t3-1/2/0.0 (Index 105) (SNMP ifIndex 29)
    Flags: Hardware-Down Point-To-Point SNMP-Traps, Encapsulation: PPP
    Protocol inet, MTU: 4470, Flags: Protocol-Down
```

```
         Addresses, Flags: Dest-route-down Is-Preferred Is-Primary
              Destination: 175.1.1.0/30, Local: 175.1.1.1
```

The Loopback: Remote output shows the expected configuration. Since Cabernet is not receiving its own keepalives, no Loop-Detected message is seen in the Device Flags field.

Once again, we return to normal operation by removing the loopback keyword from the configuration:

```
[edit interfaces t3-1/2/0]
user@Cabernet# delete t3-options loopback
```

BERT Testing

While a loopback test can verify the connectivity of a circuit, it can't track down poor signal quality due to noise on a line. This is the job of a *Bit Error Rate Test (BERT)*. Many of the interfaces in a Juniper Networks router support BERT testing. These include the T1/E1, T3/E3, CH DS3, CH OC-12, and CH STM-1 interfaces.

A BERT test requires a line loop to be in place on either the transmission devices or the far-end router. The local router generates a known bit pattern and sends it out the transmit path. The received pattern is then verified against the sent pattern. The higher the bit error rate of the received pattern, the worse the noise is on the physical circuit. When the position of the line loop is moved downstream toward the far-end router, you can easily find the troubled portion of the link.

A successful BERT test requires the interface to be configured with the duration of the test, the bit pattern to send on the transmit path, and the error rate to monitor when receiving the inbound pattern.

Configuring the BERT Parameters

The physical interface receives the configuration of the BERT parameters. You configure the duration of the test, the pattern to send in the bit stream, and the error rate to include in the bit stream with the bert-period, bert-algorithm, and bert-error-rate commands, respectively. We've configured Cabernet's BERT settings as follows:

```
[edit interfaces t3-1/2/0]
user@Cabernet# set t3-options bert-period 120
```

```
[edit interfaces t3-1/2/0]
user@Cabernet# set t3-options bert-algorithm all-ones-repeating
```

```
[edit interfaces t3-1/2/0]
user@Cabernet# set t3-options bert-error-rate 0
```

```
[edit interfaces t3-1/2/0]
user@Cabernet# show
```

```
t3-options {
    bert-algorithm all-ones-repeating;
    bert-error-rate 0;
    bert-period 120;
}
```

The run duration lasts from 1 to 240 seconds, with Cabernet running for 120 seconds. The error rate value is an integer between 0 and 7. The supplied value becomes an exponential and results in a final error rate between 10^{-0} (no errors) and 10^{-7}(1 error in 10 million received bits). The bit patterns to test are too numerous to mention here in detail. Cabernet has opted to send a pattern where every bit is set to a value of 1. Some of the more common testing patterns include:

all-ones-repeating   The transmitted pattern is 1111111111111111…

all-zeros-repeating   The transmitted pattern is 0000000000000000…

alternating-ones-zeros   The transmitted pattern is 1010101010101010…

alternating-double-ones-zeros   The transmitted pattern is 1100110011001100…

Starting and Stopping the Test

Once the BERT parameters are committed, you begin the test with the following command:

user@host> **test interface t3-1/2/0 t3-bert-start**

The test runs for the specified second duration as configured. Should you wish to terminate the test sooner, use the following command:

user@host> **test interface t3-1/2/0 t3-bert-stop**

BERT Test Results

You can view the results of the BERT test with the show interfaces extensive command. To immediately locate the BERT values in the output, use the JUNOS software pipe functionality. The find *string* option starts the output at the specified string:

```
user@Cabernet> show interfaces t3-1/2/0 extensive | find BERT
    BERT time period: 120 seconds, Elapsed: 120 seconds (completed)
    Algorithm: All ones, Repetitive (22), Error rate: 10e-0
    Bit count      :            0, Overflows: 0
    Error bit count:            0, Overflows: 0
    LOS status: OK, LOS count: 1, LOS seconds: 239
    . . .
```

In our example, it appears that the transmission lines are noise free between Cabernet and the looping device. The BERT test ran for all 120 seconds using the all-ones pattern. It found zero errors using the 10e-0 error rate.

Summary

In this chapter, we've seen that a Juniper Networks router has both permanent and transient interfaces. These interfaces use a distinct and common naming structure that relates directly to their physical location in the platform. We also discussed differences between the physical and logical properties of an interface. These properties translate into the operation of the specific physical media and the logical Layer 2 and 3 addressing of the interface.

We then looked at some examples of configuring the various protocol families within the JUNOS software. Next, we examined some commands used to verify the operation and status of an interface. Finally, we described two methods for testing the physical circuits connecting two routers—loopback and BERT testing.

Exam Essentials

Understand the JUNOS software interface naming convention.   The format consists of a two-character media type designator followed by the FPC slot number, the PIC slot number within an FPC, the port number on the PIC, and the logical unit. The format is `media_type-fpc/pic/port.unit`.

Know the differences between a permanent and a transient interface.   Each Juniper Networks router contains the `fxp0` and `fxp1` permanent interfaces. All interfaces contained on a PIC are considered transient because they can be removed at any time.

Be able to list the protocol families available for configuration on an interface.   The `inet`, `inet6`, `iso`, and `mpls` protocol families are configurable on a Juniper Networks interface.

Know the logical properties available on an interface.   Each interface in the JUNOS software requires some logical properties. These often include the Layer 3 and Layer 2 addressing information for enabling proper network operation.

Be able to identify the major fields in the `show interfaces extensive` command.   Information such as the current status, input/output byte and packet statistics, and input/output error counters are available in the command output.

Understand the interface diagnostic options available in the JUNOS software.   Both loopback and BERT testing help you locate trouble spots on a physical network circuit.

Key Terms

Before you take the exam, be certain you are familiar with the following terms:

Asynchronous Transfer Mode (ATM)

Bit Error Rate Test (BERT)

data link connection identifiers (DLCIs)

`deactivate`

`disable`

Flexible PIC Concentrator (FPC)

Frame Relay

`fxp0`

`fxp1`

High-Level Data Link Control (HDLC)

`inet` protocol family

`inet6` protocol family

Internal Ethernet

`iso` protocol family

keepalive

line loopback

Management Ethernet

maximum transmission unit (MTU)

`mpls` protocol family

permanent interfaces

permanent virtual circuit (PVC)

Physical Interface Card (PIC)

Point-to-Point Protocol (PPP)

preferred address

primary address

protocol address

protocol families

quad-wide

`tcpdump`

transient interfaces

unit

virtual circuit identifier (VCI)

virtual local area networks (VLANs)

virtual path identifier (VPI)

Review Questions

1. What is the correct order of elements in the JUNOS software interface naming convention?

   A. FPC, PIC, port, type

   B. Type, port, PIC, FPC

   C. Type, FPC, PIC, port

   D. Port, PIC, FPC, type

2. How are the FPC slot numbers for an M40e numbered?

   A. 0 through 3, top to bottom

   B. 0 through 7, left to right

   C. 0 through 7, top to bottom

   D. 1 through 8, left to right

3. How are the PIC slots numbered on an M20 FPC?

   A. 0 through 3, top to bottom

   B. 0 through 3, left to right

   C. 0 through 3, bottom to top

   D. 0 through 3, right to left

4. There are two different types of interfaces on a Juniper Networks router. What are they?

   A. Permanent and transient

   B. Transient and logical

   C. Physical and logical

   D. Permanent and logical

5. Which properties are examples of a physical interface configuration? (Choose three.)

   A. Keepalives

   B. IP Address

   C. Description

   D. FCS

6. Which properties are examples of a logical interface configuration? (Choose two.)

   A. DLCI number

   B. Scrambling

   C. FCS Value

   D. Protocol MTU

7. What prefix length is assigned to an IPv4 address if you do not specify one in the configuration?

    A. The command fails the syntax check.

    B. The command fails the commit check.

    C. The router assigns a /32 prefix length.

    D. The router assigns a classful network prefix length.

8. Which command displays the status of all SONET interfaces on the router?

    A. `show ip interfaces brief`

    B. `show sonet interfaces terse`

    C. `show interfaces so-* terse`

    D. `show so-* interfaces`

9. An interface has multiple IP addresses configured. Which of the following statements is true about the interface's primary address?

    A. It is the highest numbered address on the interface.

    B. It is the lowest numbered address on the interface.

    C. Each configured address is considered to be a primary address.

    D. There is no default primary address.

10. What is the result of using the `deactivate` command?

    A. The configuration is ignored and not applied.

    B. The interface configuration is marked `deactivated`.

    C. The physical interface status changes to Admin Down.

    D. The logical interface status changes to Admin Down.

11. In the `show interfaces extensive` output, which field displays framing errors?

    A. `Input Errors`

    B. `Input policed discards`

    C. `Input L2 channel errors`

    D. `Input HS link CRC errors`

12. Which field in the `show interfaces extensive` output displays received packets with a damaged IP header?

    A. `active alarms`

    B. `output carrier transitions`

    C. `input policed discards`

    D. `input L3 incompletes`

13. A Frame Relay interface is configured to support DLCI values 40, 50, and 60. Incoming frames show a DLCI 45. Which field in the `show interfaces extensive` output displays this information?

   A. `active alarms`

   B. `output carrier transitions`

   C. `input policed discards`

   D. `input L2 channel errors`

14. The `monitor traffic` command closely resembles what Unix-based utility?

   A. pwd

   B. ps –aux

   C. tcpdump

   D. ls –a–l

15. The `monitor traffic` command can evaluate traffic _____. (Choose two.)

   A. Inbound on interface `at-0/2/0.100` destined for the Routing Engine

   B. Outbound on interface `at-0/2/0.100` from the Routing Engine

   C. Inbound on interface `at-0/2/0.100` destined for interface `so-2/0/0.0`

   D. Outbound on interface `at-0/2/0.100` from interface `so-2/0/0.0`

16. Which command allows a network administrator to view locally sourced BGP keepalive packet headers on interface `so-2/0/0.0`?

   A. `monitor interface so-2/0/0.0`

   B. `monitor traffic interface so-2/0/0.0`

   C. `monitor bgp interface so-2/0/0.0`

   D. `tcpdump interface so-2/0/0.0`

17. When a `local` loopback is configured on an interface, which of the following statements is true?

   A. Traffic received on the interface is looped back to the other end of the link.

   B. Traffic sent on the interface is looped back to the router on another interface.

   C. Traffic sent by the router is looped back to the router on the same interface.

   D. Traffic received by the router is looped back to the router on the same interface.

18. What command is used to check the status of a configured loopback?

   A. `show interface terse`

   B. `show interface extensive`

   C. `monitor interface terse`

   D. `monitor interface extensive`

19. Which parameters are used for BERT testing? (Choose two.)

    A. `bert-algorithm`

    B. `bert-error-rate`

    C. `bert-pattern`

    D. `bert-seconds`

20. Which JUNOS software command starts a BERT test?

    A. `test interface t3-1/0/1 t3-bert-start`

    B. `interface test t3-1/0/1 t3-bert-start`

    C. `interface t3-1/0/1 t3-bert-start`

    D. `test interface t3-1/0/1 t3-bert-begin`

Answers to Review Questions

1. C. The correct order is media type, FPC slot number, PIC slot number, and PIC port number.

2. B. An M40e has eight vertical FPC slots. They are numbered 0 through 7, left to right.

3. D. An M20 has four PIC slots in each FPC. Since the FPC has a horizontal orientation, the PIC slots are numbered 0 through 3, right to left.

4. A. Juniper Networks routers have two types of interfaces: permanent and transient.

5. A, C, D. Only the protocol address is a logical property of an interface.

6. A, D. DLCIs and protocol MTU are both logical interface properties. Scrambling and description are physical properties.

7. C. In the absence of a prefix length, the router assumes a 32-bit prefix length for an IPv4 address.

8. C. An asterisk (*) may be used as a wildcard character. The command `show interface so-*` `terse` will display the status of all SONET interfaces on the router.

9. B. An interface contains only a single primary address and, by default, it is the lowest numerical prefix on the interface.

10. A. When an interface has been deactivated, the interface is marked `inactive` and the configuration statements are ignored when the candidate configuration is committed.

11. A. `Input Errors` are the sum of the incoming frame aborts and FCS errors.

12. D. The `input L3 incompletes` field is a counter that is incremented when the incoming packet fails Layer 3 (usually IPv4) checks of the header.

13. D. The `input L2 channel errors` field is a counter that increments when the software cannot find a valid logical interface for an incoming frame.

14. C. The Unix-based tcpdump utility closely resembles the `monitor traffic` command.

15. A, B. The `monitor traffic` command can be used to track any packets destined to, or coming from, the Routing Engine over a particular interface.

16. B. The command `monitor traffic interface so-2/0/0.0` allows you to view packet headers. `monitor interface so-2/0/0.0` displays packet, byte, and error counters in real time. Answers C and D are not valid JUNOS software commands.

17. C. Traffic sent by the router is looped back to the router on the same interface. A `remote` loopback will loop traffic received on the interface back to the other end of the link.

18. B. The command `show interface extensive` is used to check if an interface has a loopback set. Answer A displays only the interface up/down status and all logical configuration. Answers C and D are not valid JUNOS software commands.

19. A, B. The `bert-algorithm` parameter is used to specify the test pattern. The `bert-error-rate` parameter is used to examine the received pattern.

20. A. The correct command is `test interface t3-1/0/1 t3-bert-start`.

Chapter

3

Protocol-Independent Routing

JNCIA EXAM OBJECTIVES COVERED IN THIS CHAPTER:

- ✓ Describe configuration options for static and aggregate routes
- ✓ Identify the default routing tables and preference values
- ✓ Describe the options available for load balancing

In this chapter, we discuss the options available for IP routes that are not specific to a particular routing protocol. We first explore routes that are configured locally on the router. Then we investigate the various routing tables in the JUNOS software and learn how those tables select routes to use for forwarding. Finally, we explore how a Juniper Networks router handles the load balancing of user data packets.

Generally speaking, functions that are protocol independent affect the router as a whole. They are not specific to a particular routing protocol, such as Open Shortest Path First (OSPF) or Border Gateway Protocol (BGP). Routes that are manually configured on the router are a good example, so let's start there.

Configured Routes

Every network has a requirement for locally configured routes. These routes are not learned through a dynamic routing protocol but are manually entered by you, the administrator. Within the JUNOS software, locally configured routes include the following:

- Static routes
- Aggregated routes
- Generated routes

In a typical operating environment, you use a dynamic routing protocol to propagate and learn route information. Dynamic protocols offer many benefits, including prevention of routing loops and minimal user intervention. However, there is still a special role for nondynamic routing information. Let's examine these special situations as we take a look at static routes.

Static Routes

A *static route* within the JUNOS software is a route to a destination with an assigned next hop. If we want to place the route into the routing table, the next hop must be valid. This means that the router is able to forward packets using the next hop. We discuss options for valid next hops in the section "Next-Hop Options" later in this chapter.

Static routes are not affected by topology changes or new routing information. They are present in the routing table until you remove them through a configuration change. As a quick example, let's look at Figure 3.1. In this figure, Chardonnay is required to reach the subnets of 192.168.16.0 /24, 192.168.32.0 /24, and 192.168.48.0 /24. These routes are physically located behind the routers of Merlot, Riesling, and Cabernet, respectively. You may decide that a static route on Chardonnay for each destination can provide the connectivity you desire. The interface on Riesling that connects to Chardonnay would be the next hop for the static routes. Since the link between these two routers is the only physical path available to Chardonnay, the use of static routes in this example is perfectly acceptable. Should the link fail, no alternate paths would exist and Chardonnay would lose connectivity to those remote destinations. The problem with this simple example, of course, is scalability. As the network grows, Chardonnay will need to continually update its list of static routes to provide adequate connectivity.

FIGURE   3 . 1   Example of static route use

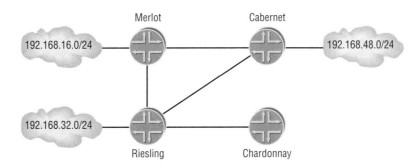

The Ideal Routing Protocol?

If you took a poll of network engineers and asked them for their reaction on building an entire network out of static routes, most would say something along the lines of "Are you out of your mind?" After all, static routes are an administrative hassle to build and maintain. They don't respond to dynamic changes in the network. Worst of all, they might require you to awake at 3 AM to a page about a connectivity problem due to a misconfigured static route!

If we forget about reality for a little while, a static routing solution might be the ideal routing protocol. It requires no convergence time and utilizes a minimum of router resources, such as memory and processing time. It supplies you with the ultimate control over packet forwarding. You've told each router what to do and they will each perform that function until powered down. If we could only reconfigure the static routes automatically, we would be completely happy.

> Okay, stop dreaming and come back to the real world. As with most things in network engineering, there is a trade-off. The advantages of static routes do not outweigh the disadvantages when it comes to widespread use. You can think of large networks as living, breathing entities. This dynamic nature of a living beast means that a dynamic solution is really the only choice.
>
> This is not to say that static routes do not have their place—they do! Many Internet service providers (ISPs) use static routes to supply connectivity to single-homed customers. Those customers, in turn, use static routes to provide connectivity to the Internet.

Using a static route when you have a single physical connection is a valid consideration. Let's examine Figure 3.2. Shiraz is a border router within Autonomous System 65001 with physical connections to five customer routers. Each of these customers has requested Internet connectivity from AS 65001. With just a single physical connection between each set of routers, a static route solution might be appropriate. Shiraz sets up five static routes, one for each customer. These routes are then advertised by a dynamic routing protocol to the other routers within AS 65001.

FIGURE 3.2   Static routes in a service provider

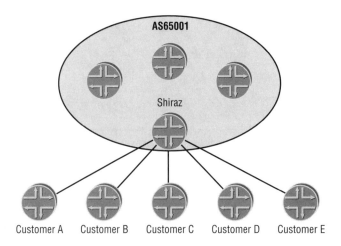

Each customer router configures a static route for each destination that it wishes to communicate with. This approach has the same limitation we discussed for Chardonnay in Figure 3.1; as the number of reachable destinations grows, the number of static routes also grows. An optimal solution to this problem is for the customer to configure a *default route* of 0.0.0.0 /0 as its only static route. The default route will provide connectivity to all possible destinations that the customers would ever wish to communicate with.

Now that we have a better understanding of why we'd want to use static routes, let's learn how to configure them within the JUNOS software.

Next-Hop Options

You must configure a valid and usable next hop for a static route before placing the route in the routing table. The JUNOS software provides six different options for a static route next hop:

Directly connected IP address   An IP address belonging to a physically connected subnet is often used as the next hop for a static route. The interface connected to the remote router is used to forward user packets.

Remote IP address   You can also use any known IP address in the network as a next hop. The local router performs a *recursive lookup* in the inet.0 routing table to find a physical next hop to the configured address. You enable this functionality by adding the *resolve* keyword when defining the IP address.

reject   The value *reject* is a configured null value. Route lookups that match a static route with a reject next hop are dropped.

discard   The value *discard* is also a configured null value. Route lookups matching this next-hop value are also dropped.

Qualified next hop   Routes utilizing a *qualified next hop* allow you to assign multiple IP address next hops and/or JUNOS software preference values to a single static route. This enables multiple versions of the same prefix to appear in the routing table at the same time. In effect, you end up with a *floating static route*. We discuss preference values in the section "JUNOS software Preference Values" later in this chapter.

Label switched path (LSP)   In a network configured to use Multiprotocol Label Switching (MPLS), a static route can be assigned an LSP as a next-hop value. All route lookups matching this next hop are forwarded using a label value instead of an IP address. See Chapter 11 for more about MPLS.

While we define both reject and discard as configured null values, their functionality is quite different. A route lookup matching a route with one of these next-hop values configured will drop the data packet from the network. The difference between the values lies in the local router's response to the drop action. A reject next hop will prompt the local router to send an ICMP message of "Destination Host Unreachable" to the source of the IP packet. This message notifies the remote router that the data packet was dropped from the network. A discard next hop does *not* send an ICMP message back to the source; it silently drops the packet from the network.

Real World Scenario

Floating Static Routes

The concept of a floating static route is not a new one to network engineers. In its simplest form, it is a backup route. A floating static route is often configured and ready to use at a moment's notice. It can provide redundancy for either a dynamically learned route or another static route.

So, what's *floating* about a floating static route? Well, to understand that we need to visualize the routing table in a vertical fashion. At the bottom of the table are versions of a route that are very *believable*. These versions should be used to forward packets if they are available. Other versions of the same route might also appear in the routing table but are considered less believable. These versions of the route appear in the middle of the routing table. At the top of the table are versions of the route that are very unbelievable but can be used if they are really needed. *Regular* static routes are normally very believable versions of a route. After all, you specifically configured this route so you must want to use it! So, a regular static route will appear at the bottom of the routing table. A floating static route, on the other hand, is a version of a route that is very *unbelievable*. When it is placed into the routing table, it floats from the bottom of the table to the top. Did you see it float up?

Now, what does all this have to do with routing? Simple; we want to make a version of a route available as a backup in case of a failure. Let's look at an example. Imagine that Router A has two physical paths available toward a destination of 10.0.0.0 /8. One of the paths uses Gigabit Ethernet while the other uses slower T1 links. Clearly, you would want your traffic to use the faster physical path if it is available. The problem is, when you assign both of the next hops to the static route, the local router thinks it can use both of them. This is not good!

A valid solution to this dilemma is to configure two different versions of the 10.0.0.0 /8 route. One of the static route versions will be very believable and will use the Gigabit Ethernet links. The other version will be less believable and will use the T1 links. User packets will now always use the faster links until they are no longer available, at which time they will use the slower links. A floating static route "solved" our administrative requirements.

Static Route Attributes

The next-hop value is only one possible attribute that you can assign to a static route. In addition, the JUNOS software allows you to assign various parameters to your static routes. Some of these are beneficial to the static routes themselves, such as a preference value for a floating static route. Other attributes benefit the dynamic routing protocols. For instance, BGP can use a community value assigned to a static route.

You configure static routes within the [edit routing-options] portion of the configuration hierarchy. Let's look at the basic syntax we use to configure a static route:

```
routing-options {
    static {
        defaults {
```

```
            static-options;
        }
        route destination-prefix {
            next-hop next-hop;
            qualified-next-hop address {
                metric metric;
                preference preference;
            }
            lsp-next-hop lsp-name {
                metric metric;
                preference preference;
            }
            static-options;
        }
    }
}
```

Notice that the attributes for a static route (`static-options`) appear within two separate hierarchies of the configuration. The `route` portion of the configuration is where the actual destination prefix is configured. The next hop and all additional attributes are configured within each route's directory. The `defaults` section of the configuration is used when each of the static routes should have the exact same attribute defined. You would use the `defaults` section, for example, when you want to have only floating static routes. Instead of configuring a `preference` value for each individual route, you define the attribute one time within the `defaults` section and each configured route inherits the attribute value. In accordance with the JUNOS software defaults of the configuration hierarchy defined in Chapter 1, "The Components of a Juniper Networks Router," attributes defined specifically within a `route` hierarchy are used instead of the same attribute defined within the `defaults` hierarchy.

Some of the options available for configuration on a static route are outlined here. Not every route requires the configuration of each attribute.

active This option tells the router to remove the route from the routing table if the next hop becomes unavailable; it is the default value for static routes.

as-path This option manually assigns the AS Path attribute to a static route and is useful when the route is redistributed into BGP. We cover route redistribution in Chapter 4, "Routing Policy."

community This option assigns a BGP community value to the route. It is also helpful when you're performing route redistribution.

install This option places usable static routes into the forwarding table on the Packet Forwarding Engine; it is the default value for static routes.

metric With this option, metric values assigned to static routes are used by the Routing Engine to select which version of a route to use. We discuss the selection of active routes in the routing table in the section "JUNOS software Preference Values" later in this chapter.

no-install   This option is the opposite of the `install` option. A static route with this attribute will not be placed into the forwarding table on the router.

no-readvertise   This option prevents a static route from being exported from the routing table and redistributed into another routing protocol using a routing policy.

no-retain   With this option, static routes are removed from the forwarding table if the routing process shuts down. This value is the default for static routes.

passive   The opposite of `active`, the `passive` option allows a static route to stay in the routing table if the next hop is unavailable.

preference   This option allows a static route to have a preference value other than the default of 5. Preference values are covered in the "JUNOS software Preference Values" section later in this chapter.

readvertise   The opposite of `no-readvertise`, this option allows a static route to be exported from the routing table and redistributed into another routing protocol. This value is the default for static routes.

retain   Routes configured with this option (the opposite of `no-retain`) will remain in the forwarding table if the routing process shuts down. This option helps to speed the start time of a router when a large number of static routes are configured.

Configuration Examples

We've now discussed what a static route is and options for its configuration. Let's now look at configuration examples within the JUNOS software. In Figure 3.3, we have the same network from Figure 3.1, but there are now IP addresses configured on the interfaces between Riesling and Chardonnay. To provide connectivity to the 192.168.16.0 /24 network, you configure Chardonnay like so:

```
[edit routing-options]
user@Chardonnay# set static route 192.168.16/24 next-hop 1.1.1.1
```

This results in the following configuration:

```
[edit routing-options]
user@Chardonnay# show
static {
    route 192.168.16.0/24 next-hop 1.1.1.1;
}
```

Since the assigned next hop of 1.1.1.1 is reachable through a directly connected interface, the static route should be active and visible in the `inet.0` routing table. We can verify this through the following command:

```
user@Chardonnay> show route protocol static
```

```
inet.0: 10 destinations, 15 routes (10 active, 0 holddown, 0 hidden)
+ = Active Route, - = Last Active, * = Both

192.168.16.0/24    *[Static/5] 00:02:28
                    > to 1.1.1.1 via fe-0/0/0.0
```

We configure the routes for 192.168.32.0 /24 and 192.168.48.0 /24 in a similar manner. Once completed, the routing table looks like this:

```
user@Chardonnay> show route protocol static

inet.0: 13 destinations, 15 routes (13 active, 0 holddown, 0 hidden)
+ = Active Route, - = Last Active, * = Both

192.168.16.0/24    *[Static/5] 00:03:58
                    > to 1.1.1.1 via fe-0/0/0.0
192.168.32.0/24    *[Static/5] 00:01:14
                    > to 1.1.1.1 via fe-0/0/0.0
192.168.48.0/24    *[Static/5] 00:01:14
                    > to 1.1.1.1 via fe-0/0/0.0
```

FIGURE 3.3   Static route sample network

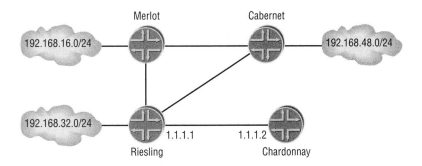

Chardonnay now has IP reachability to customers connected to its partner routers. Actually sending data packets to those customers will rely on a host of other factors, however. Does Riesling have valid routes to all the customers? Are the customer routes still valid? None of the answers to these questions are known to Chardonnay. Such is the case with static routes; you are given no visibility into the network. This is one main reason that administrators prefer to use dynamic protocols.

So, let's say that our sample network is configured to operate a routing protocol. You would still like the network to attempt to reach the customers if the dynamic protocol encounters a problem. Sounds like a job for a floating static route! In our case, we want all of our routes to float with a higher preference value. We configure Chardonnay with the following:

```
[edit routing-options]
user@Chardonnay# set static defaults preference 200
```

We check our routing table and see that our change took effect:

```
user@Chardonnay> show route protocol static

inet.0: 13 destinations, 15 routes (13 active, 0 holddown, 0 hidden)
+ = Active Route, - = Last Active, * = Both

192.168.16.0/24    *[Static/200] 00:03:58
                    > to 1.1.1.1 via fe-0/0/0.0
192.168.32.0/24    *[Static/200] 00:01:14
                    > to 1.1.1.1 via fe-0/0/0.0
192.168.48.0/24    *[Static/200] 00:01:14
                    > to 1.1.1.1 via fe-0/0/0.0
```

Remember that we discuss preference values later, in the "JUNOS software Preference Values" section.

Aggregated Routes

An *aggregate route* is the second form of a locally configured route within the JUNOS software. Once active in the `inet.0` routing table, aggregate routes will remain until you manually remove them from the configuration. We use aggregate routes to represent multiple IP routes with a single route announcement. In short, they promote route summarization. Let's look at Figure 3.4 as an example.

FIGURE 3.4   Example of aggregated route use

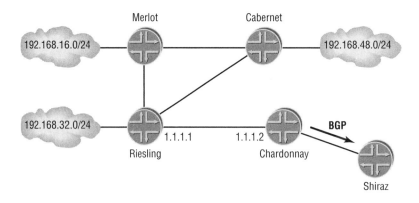

Chardonnay is now connected to Shiraz and has a requirement to advertise routing knowledge using BGP. While multiple methods are available to accomplish this task, we want to send Shiraz a single summarized route. This route represents all the customers connected to Merlot, Riesling, and Cabernet. The most precise summary available to fit this criterion is 192.168.0.0 /17. Once configured and active, this route is redistributed into BGP and advertised to Shiraz. (We discuss route redistribution in Chapter 4.)

Contributing Routes

The key to making an aggregate route active in the routing table is the presence of one or more *contributing routes*. A contributing route is an active route in the routing table that is more specific than the summary and shares the same most significant bits. In Figure 3.4, the 192.168.16.0 /24, 192.168.32.0 /24, and 192.168.48.0 /24 are all contributing routes to the aggregate route 192.168.0.0 /17. We can verify this in the routing table:

```
user@Chardonnay> show route protocol aggregate detail

inet.0: 23 destinations, 25 routes (23 active, 0 holddown, 0 hidden)
192.168.0.0/17 (1 entry, 1 announced)
        *Aggregate Preference: 130
                Next hop type: Reject
                State: <Active Int Ext>
                Age: 23
                Task: Aggregate
                Announcement bits (2): 0-KRT 5-Resolve inet.0
                AS path: I (LocalAgg)
                Flags:                  Depth: 0        Active
                AS path list:
                AS path: I  Refcount: 3
                Contributing Routes (3):
                        192.168.16.0/24     proto Static
                        192.168.32.0/24     proto Static
                        192.168.48.0/24     proto Static
```

When we use either the `detail` or `extensive` option of the `show route` command, all aggregate routes display the active routes that are currently contributing to the summary.

It seems we've skipped a step. We went from a discussion of aggregate route theory into a configured and active aggregate route. Let's now explore how we made that transition.

Next-Hop Options

All routes in the routing table must have a next-hop value assigned, and aggregate routes are no exception. Unlike with a static route, only two options are available within the JUNOS software for next-hop values:

reject The value *reject* is a configured null value. Route lookups that match an aggregate route with a reject next hop are dropped and an ICMP "Destination Host Unreachable" message is returned to the source of the packet. This is the default for aggregate routes.

discard The value *discard* is also a configured null value. Route lookups matching this next-hop value are also dropped.

Don't be alarmed that the only available next hops for an aggregate route will drop your data packets from the network. Keep in mind the purpose of this route—it is only representing other routes that are already in your routing table. These more specific routes will be the next hops actually used to forward the traffic. The only time that a drop will occur is when the aggregate route itself is the result of a routing table longest-match lookup.

Aggregate Route Attributes

All locally configured routes have attribute values that can be assigned to the route, and again, aggregate routes are no exception. You'll notice that many of the attributes of static routes also appear in the list for aggregate routes. This occurs since the JUNOS software routing table allows all types of routes to contain similar information. Before we list the attribute options, let's talk about the configuration syntax for an aggregate route. As with static routes, you configure aggregates within the [edit routing-options] configuration hierarchy. The basic syntax is as follows:

```
routing-options {
    aggregate {
        defaults {
            aggregate-options;
        }
        route destination-prefix {
            policy policy-name;
            aggregate-options;
        }
    }
}
```

The purpose of the `defaults` and `route` portions of the configuration is identical to our earlier discussion (see the "Static Route Attributes" section). You can configure all attributes of an aggregate route within either hierarchy, with the more specific reference being applied to the route.

Some of the available attributes for an aggregate route are outlined here. As before, each attribute need not be configured for each aggregate route. In fact, the most common configuration for an aggregate route requires that no additional attributes be assigned. We discuss the configuration later in the section "Configuration Examples."

`active`   This option tells the router to remove the route from the routing table if all contributing routes become unavailable. This value is the default for aggregate routes.

`as-path`   This option manually assigns the AS Path attribute and is useful when the route is redistributed into BGP. (We cover route redistribution in Chapter 4.)

`brief`   With this option, only the longest common sequences in the AS Path of all BGP contributing routes are transferred to the aggregate.

`community`   This option assigns a BGP community value to the route and is also helpful when you're performing route redistribution.

`full`   With this option, all AS values in the AS Path of BGP contributing routes are included in the aggregate. This value is the default for aggregate routes.

`metric`   With this option, metric values are assigned to allow the Routing Engine to select which version of a route to use when the route preference values are equal. To learn more about the selection of active routes in the routing table, see the section "JUNOS software Preference Values" later in this chapter.

`passive`   The opposite of `active`, the `passive` option will allow the route to stay in the routing table if no contributing routes are available.

`policy`   By default, all possible contributing routes to an aggregate will in fact contribute. A routing policy is defined to allow only certain contributing routes to contribute to an aggregate. Routing policies are covered in Chapter 4.

`preference`   This option allows an aggregate route to have a preference value other than the default of 130. We cover preference values in the "JUNOS software Preference Values" section later in this chapter.

Configuration Examples

We now look at the simple configuration we mentioned in the preceding section. Referring back to Figure 3.4, Chardonnay would enter the following command to configure the 192.168.0.0/17 route:

```
[edit routing-options]
user@Chardonnay# set aggregate route 192.168/17
```

This appears in the candidate configuration as:

```
[edit routing-options]
user@Chardonnay# show
aggregate {
    route 192.168.0.0/17;
}
```

Notice that no attributes were defined within the configuration. By default, the aggregate route will appear in the inet.0 routing table when at least one contributing route is in the routing table. We've made no other configuration changes, so the static routes should still be in the routing table and contributing to the aggregate. We can check this ourselves by using this command:

```
user@Chardonnay> show route protocol aggregate

inet.0: 11 destinations, 16 routes (11 active, 0 holddown, 0 hidden)
+ = Active Route, - = Last Active, * = Both

192.168.0.0/17      *[Aggregate/130] 00:01:52
                      Reject
```

Of course, the contributing routes can be verified as before:

```
user@Chardonnay> show route protocol aggregate detail

inet.0: 11 destinations, 26 routes (11 active, 0 holddown, 0 hidden)
192.168.0.0/17 (1 entry, 1 announced)
        *Aggregate Preference: 130
                Next hop type: Reject
                State: <Active Int Ext>
                Age: 3
                Task: Aggregate
                Announcement bits (2): 0-KRT 5-Resolve inet.0
                AS path: I (LocalAgg)
                Flags:                Depth: 0        Active
                AS path list:
                AS path: I  Refcount: 3
                Contributing Routes (3):
                        192.168.16.0/24      proto Static
                        192.168.32.0/24      proto Static
                        192.168.48.0/24      proto Static
```

Notice the default next hop of `reject` for this route. Recall that this is a configured null value that will drop user packets from the network. You have the ability within the JUNOS software to combine the summarization of aggregate routes with the IP forwarding capability of static routes. These are called generated routes; we discuss those next.

Generated Routes

A *generated route* is identical to an aggregate route in all but one way. Both forms of routes summarize routes, rely on contributing routes, and share most attribute values. In fact, the routing table views them as one protocol, `protocol aggregate`. The one difference between them is in the default next-hop attribute. Recall that an aggregate has a default next hop of `reject` with an option for `discard`. A generated route, on the other hand, has an IP address as its default next hop with an option for `discard`. With these two routes being mainly equal, we'll skip the listing of next-hop and attribute options. If you're curious, please refer to the "Aggregate Route Attributes" section. What is truly important is to focus on the one difference—the next-hop value.

Contributing Routes

A generated route needs at least one contributing route in the routing table to become active. These contributing routes, however, must either include an IP address for a next hop or be a connected point-to-point interface. Next-hop values of `discard` or `reject` on a route makes the route ineligible to contribute. Let's look at a more concrete example in Figure 3.5.

FIGURE 3.5 Example of generated route use

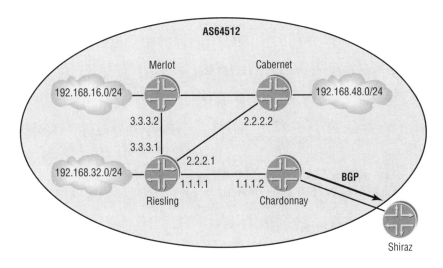

Riesling is communicating to the other routers in Autonomous System 64512 using the Intermediate System to Intermediate System (IS-IS) routing protocol. There are also static routes configured on Riesling that represent customers connected to that router. The current routing table looks like this:

```
user@Riesling> show route 192.168/16

inet.0: 10 destinations, 10 routes (10 active, 0 holddown, 0 hidden)
+ = Active Route, - = Last Active, * = Both

192.168.16.0/24     *[IS-IS/18] 00:16:27, metric 20, tag 2
                     > to 3.3.3.2 via fe-0/0/2.0
192.168.32.12/30    *[Static/5] 00:32:46
                      Reject
192.168.32.24/30    *[Static/5] 00:32:46
                     > to 10.10.10.1 via so-0/1/1.0
192.168.32.36/30    *[Static/5] 00:32:46
                      Discard
192.168.32.48/30    *[Static/5] 00:32:46
                     > to 10.10.10.1 via so-0/1/1.0
192.168.48.0/24     *[IS-IS/18] 00:11:04, metric 20, tag 2
                     > to 2.2.2.2 via fe-0/0/1.0
```

Riesling currently has six routes that are part of the 192.168.0.0 /16 subnet. Two of the routes are IS-IS learned routes while the other four are static routes. Of the static routes, only two of them contain IP next hops. A generated route of 192.168.0.0 /16 is configured like this:

```
[edit routing-options]
user@Riesling# set generate route 192.168/16
```

The new route appears in the `inet.0` routing table since contributing routes with IP next hops exist:

```
user@Riesling> show route 192.168/16

inet.0: 11 destinations, 11 routes (11 active, 0 holddown, 0 hidden)
+ = Active Route, - = Last Active, * = Both

192.168.0.0/16      *[Aggregate/130] 00:01:15
                     > to 3.3.3.2 via fe-0/0/2.0
192.168.16.0/24     *[IS-IS/18] 00:17:42, metric 20, tag 2
                     > to 3.3.3.2 via fe-0/0/2.0
192.168.32.12/30    *[Static/5] 00:34:01
                      Reject
```

```
192.168.32.24/30    *[Static/5] 00:34:01
                       > to 10.10.10.1 via so-0/1/1.0
192.168.32.36/30    *[Static/5] 00:34:01
                        Discard
192.168.32.48/30    *[Static/5] 00:34:01
                       > to 10.10.10.1 via so-0/1/1.0
192.168.48.0/24     *[IS-IS/18] 00:12:19, metric 20, tag 2
                       > to 2.2.2.2 via fe-0/0/1.0
```

A quick count of routes in this output reveals that there are four routes with IP next hops. We can verify that only these four actually contributed to the generated route by using the detail option with the show route command:

```
user@Riesling> show route protocol aggregate detail

inet.0: 11 destinations, 11 routes (11 active, 0 holddown, 0 hidden)
192.168.0.0/16 (1 entry, 1 announced)
        *Aggregate Preference: 130
                Nexthop: 3.3.3.2 via fe-0/0/2.0, selected
                State: <Active Int Ext>
                Age: 2
                Task: Aggregate
                Announcement bits (2): 0-KRT 5-Resolve inet.0
                AS path: I (LocalAgg)
                Flags:              Depth: 0        Active
                AS path list:
                AS path: I  Refcount: 4
                Contributing Routes (4):
                        192.168.16.0/24     proto IS-IS
                        192.168.32.24/30    proto Static
                        192.168.32.48/30    proto Static
                        192.168.48.0/24     proto IS-IS
```

Just as we suspected! The static routes of 192.168.32.12 /30 and 192.168.32.36 /30 did not contribute to the generated route. Their current next hops are reject and discard, respectively. At this point you might be wondering how the IP next hop of the generated route is selected. That's our next topic of discussion.

Primary Contributing Route

Each generated route selects one of the contributing routes to be the *primary contributing route*. This route is the contributor with the numerically smallest prefix. In the case of the

192.168.0.0 /16 route from Figure 3.5, the primary contributing route is 192.168.16.0 /24. The IP next hops of those two routes are identical:

```
user@Riesling> show route 192.168.16/24 exact

inet.0: 11 destinations, 11 routes (11 active, 0 holddown, 0 hidden)
+ = Active Route, - = Last Active, * = Both

192.168.16.0/24    *[IS-IS/18] 00:19:52, metric 20, tag 2
                    > to 3.3.3.2 via fe-0/0/2.0
```

```
user@Riesling> show route 192.168/16 exact

inet.0: 11 destinations, 11 routes (11 active, 0 holddown, 0 hidden)
+ = Active Route, - = Last Active, * = Both

192.168.0.0/16     *[Aggregate/130] 00:03:25
                    > to 3.3.3.2 via fe-0/0/2.0
```

The easy way to determine the primary contributing route is to use the show route detail command. The primary contributor will be listed first in the output. Notice that the 192.168.16.0 /24 route is at the top of the list:

```
user@Riesling> show route protocol aggregate detail

inet.0: 11 destinations, 11 routes (11 active, 0 holddown, 0 hidden)
192.168.0.0/16 (1 entry, 1 announced)
        *Aggregate Preference: 130
                Nexthop: 3.3.3.2 via fe-0/0/2.0, selected
                State: <Active Int Ext>
                Age: 6
                Task: Aggregate
                Announcement bits (2): 0-KRT 5-Resolve inet.0
                AS path: I (LocalAgg)
                Flags:              Depth: 0        Active
                AS path list:
                AS path: I  Refcount: 4
                Contributing Routes (4):
                        192.168.16.0/24     proto IS-IS
                        192.168.32.24/30    proto Static
                        192.168.32.48/30    proto Static
                        192.168.48.0/24     proto IS-IS
```

The automatic selection of the primary contributor is changed with the addition of a routing policy to the configuration. This policy should accept only the route you wish to be the primary. All other contributing routes should be rejected. Chapter 4 covers the details of constructing routing policies.

 Real World Scenario

Why Use a Generated Route?

It is a question that gets asked over and over again, so don't feel bad for asking. The examples in the chapter are constructed to show off the features of the JUNOS software, but do not necessarily represent real-world uses. Let's examine a potential use of a generated route.

Suppose you, an ISP, have a customer who would like to purchase service from you for Internet connectivity. This customer also has similar arrangements with other ISPs. You have been requested to use BGP to send this customer a default route (0.0.0.0 /0) *only* if your upstream connection to the Internet is working. The question then becomes, "How best to do this?" Let's examine the options:

- A default route already exists in your network. Depending on your network environment, this route may not represent your connectivity to the Internet. While functional and dynamic, this may not be the best choice.

- You can configure a static route, which will be active and advertised as long as the router has working interfaces. It will not be removed if your upstream connectivity is lost. This approach probably is not a good idea.

- You can configure an aggregate route, one that will represent your upstream connectivity but also represent your internal connectivity. (All possible routes will contribute to a default route!) The downside of an aggregate route is that route lookups matching the default will be dropped from the network. The only next-hop options are reject and discard. Unless the router connected to the customer has every possible route in its routing table, this is not likely an option.

- You can configure a generated route. The pros and cons are mostly the same as with an aggregate route. Of course, with an IP next hop, the generated route can forward packets matching the default route to some other destination. This sounds like the best option so far.

The only real issue with the generated route is that you need a way to ensure that the route disappears if your upstream connection is lost. This is solved with a routing policy. This policy should accept only a single route in your routing table that represents your connectivity. A route to the root DNS servers in the Internet might be a good one to choose. The policy should further reject all other routes from contributing to your generated route. In this fashion, the generated route will have only one possible contributing route—your upstream connectivity route. Should the route be lost from your routing table, the generated route is removed and you stop advertising a default route to your customer.

Martian Routes

Martian routes are network addresses that should not be globally routed in the Internet. Typically these are addresses reserved by a governing body such as the Internet Assigned Numbers Authority (IANA). The default list of martian routes in the JUNOS software is:

- Prefix bits of 0.0.0.0 /8 and more specific routes
- Prefix bits of 127.0.0.0 /8 and more specific routes
- Prefix bits of 128.0.0.0 /16 and more specific routes
- Prefix bits of 191.255.0.0 /16 and more specific routes
- Prefix bits of 192.0.0.0 /24 and more specific routes
- Prefix bits of 223.255.255.0 /24 and more specific routes
- Prefix bits of 240.0.0.0 /4 and more specific routes

Where Do Martians Come From?

Many of the routes on the Juniper Networks default martian list are derived from the IANA address space assignment list at http://www.iana.org/assignments/ipv4-address-space. The following list details the various reasons why the addresses were declared martian networks:

- Prefix bits of 0.0.0.0 /8 were reserved by IANA in September 1981.

- Prefix bits of 127.0.0.0 /8 were reserved by IANA in September 1981.

- Prefix bits of 128.0.0.0 /16 are used by various address registries and were reserved in May 1993.

- Prefix bits of 191.255.0.0 /16 are used by various address registries and were reserved in May 1993.

- Prefix bits of 192.0.0.0 /24 are used by various regional address registries and were reserved in May 1993.

- Prefix bits of 223.255.255.0 /24 were reserved by IANA in September 1981.

- Prefix bits of 240.0.0.0 /4 denote the traditional Class E address space and are used only for experimental purposes.

You might notice that the Request for Comments (RFC) 1918 private IP address space of 10.0.0.0 /8, 172.16.0.0 /12, and 192.168.0.0 /16 is not included in this list. This is due to the special treatment martian routes get within the JUNOS software. Let's discuss that in some more depth right now.

JUNOS software Implementation

A defined martian route within the JUNOS software is not allowed to be placed into a routing table. The local router can never forward packets to those destinations. Many networks rely on the use of the private IP address space and require those routes to appear in the routing table. Their inclusion in the default martian list would make their use impossible. To allow for maximum user flexibility, you have the ability to define additional martian routes. This is accomplished by using the following syntax:

```
routing-options {
    martians {
        prefix/prefix-length match-type allow;
    }
}
```

The **prefix** and **prefix-length** represent the actual route designated as a martian route. The **match-type** variable is required to define either a single route or a grouping of routes. We've listed the possible values for **match-type** here and discuss them in greater detail in Chapter 4:

- exact
- longer
- orlonger
- prefix-length-range
- through
- upto

The *allow* keyword removes a route from the default martian list and allow that route to be in the routing table.

Configuration Examples

Let's now take a quick look at the application of martian routes within the routing table. The current routing table from Riesling in Figure 3.5 is shown here:

```
user@Riesling> show route

inet.0: 15 destinations, 15 routes (15 active, 0 holddown, 0 hidden)
+ = Active Route, - = Last Active, * = Both

1.1.1.0/24         *[Direct/0] 02:03:31
                    > via fe-0/0/0.0
1.1.1.1/32         *[Local/0]  02:03:31
                     Local
```

```
2.2.2.0/24          *[Direct/0] 02:03:31
                       > via fe-0/0/1.0
2.2.2.1/32          *[Local/0]  02:03:31
                          Local
3.3.3.0/24          *[Direct/0] 02:03:31
                       > via fe-0/0/2.0
3.3.3.1/32          *[Local/0]  02:03:31
                          Local
10.10.10.0/24       *[Direct/0] 02:03:31
                       > via so-0/1/1.0
10.10.10.1/32       *[Local/0]  02:03:31
                          Local
192.168.0.0/16      *[Aggregate/130] 00:31:15
                       > to 3.3.3.2 via fe-0/0/2.0
192.168.16.0/24     *[IS-IS/18] 00:47:42, metric 20, tag 2
                       > to 3.3.3.2 via fe-0/0/2.0
192.168.32.12/30    *[Static/5] 01:04:01
                          Reject
192.168.32.24/30    *[Static/5] 01:04:01
                       > to 10.10.10.1 via so-0/1/1.0
192.168.32.36/30    *[Static/5] 01:04:01
                          Discard
192.168.32.48/30    *[Static/5] 01:04:01
                       > to 10.10.10.1 via so-0/1/1.0
192.168.48.0/24     *[IS-IS/18] 00:42:19, metric 20, tag 2
                       > to 2.2.2.2 via fe-0/0/1.0
```

We now define a martian route using the following command:

```
[edit routing-options]
user@Riesling# set martians 192.168/16 orlonger
```

This defines the 192.168.0.0/16 route and all more specific routes as martians. We can verify this with a show route command:

```
user@Riesling> show route

inet.0: 15 destinations, 15 routes (8 active, 0 holddown, 7 hidden)
+ = Active Route, - = Last Active, * = Both

1.1.1.0/24          *[Direct/0] 02:05:31
                       > via fe-0/0/0.0
```

```
1.1.1.1/32          *[Local/0]  02:05:31
                      Local
2.2.2.0/24          *[Direct/0] 02:05:31
                      > via fe-0/0/1.0
2.2.2.1/32          *[Local/0]  02:05:31
                      Local
3.3.3.0/24          *[Direct/0] 02:05:31
                      > via fe-0/0/2.0
3.3.3.1/32          *[Local/0]  02:05:31
                      Local
10.10.10.0/24       *[Direct/0] 02:05:31
                      > via so-0/1/1.0
10.10.10.1/32       *[Local/0]  02:05:31
                      Local


user@Riesling> show route hidden

inet.0: 15 destinations, 15 routes (8 active, 0 holddown, 7 hidden)
+ = Active Route, - = Last Active, * = Both


192.168.0.0/16      [Aggregate/130] 00:31:35
                      > to 3.3.3.2 via fe-0/0/2.0
192.168.16.0/24     [IS-IS/18] 00:48:02, metric 20, tag 2
                      > to 3.3.3.2 via fe-0/0/2.0
192.168.32.12/30    [Static/5] 01:04:21
                       Reject
192.168.32.24/30    [Static/5] 01:04:21
                      > to 10.10.10.1 via so-0/1/1.0
192.168.32.36/30    [Static/5] 01:04:21
                       Discard
192.168.32.48/30    [Static/5] 01:04:21
                      > to 10.10.10.1 via so-0/1/1.0
192.168.48.0/24     [IS-IS/18] 00:42:39, metric 20, tag 2
                      > to 2.2.2.2 via fe-0/0/1.0
```

We can also check the effect of our configuration by using this command:

```
user@Riesling> show route martians

inet.0:
            0.0.0.0/0  -- allowed
            0.0.0.0/8 orlonger -- disallowed
```

```
                127.0.0.0/8 orlonger -- disallowed
                128.0.0.0/16 orlonger -- disallowed
                191.255.0.0/16 orlonger -- disallowed
                192.0.0.0/24 orlonger -- disallowed
                223.255.255.0/24 orlonger -- disallowed
                240.0.0.0/4 orlonger -- disallowed
                192.168.0.0/16 orlonger -- disallowed
```

After we use the `rollback` command to return to our previous configuration, the routes of the 192.168.0.0 /16 subnet are once again in the `inet.0` routing table:

```
user@Riesling> show route

inet.0: 15 destinations, 15 routes (15 active, 0 holddown, 0 hidden)
+ = Active Route, - = Last Active, * = Both

1.1.1.0/24          *[Direct/0] 02:13:31
                     > via fe-0/0/0.0
1.1.1.1/32          *[Local/0]  02:13:31
                      Local
2.2.2.0/24          *[Direct/0] 02:13:31
                     > via fe-0/0/1.0
2.2.2.1/32          *[Local/0]  02:13:31
                      Local
3.3.3.0/24          *[Direct/0] 02:13:31
                     > via fe-0/0/2.0
3.3.3.1/32          *[Local/0]  02:13:31
                      Local
10.10.10.0/24       *[Direct/0] 02:13:31
                     > via so-0/1/1.0
10.10.10.1/32       *[Local/0]  02:13:31
                      Local
192.168.0.0/16      *[Aggregate/130] 00:41:15
                     > to 3.3.3.2 via fe-0/0/2.0
192.168.16.0/24     *[IS-IS/18] 00:57:42, metric 20, tag 2
                     > to 3.3.3.2 via fe-0/0/2.0
192.168.32.12/30    *[Static/5] 01:14:01
                      Reject
192.168.32.24/30    *[Static/5] 01:14:01
                     > to 10.10.10.1 via so-0/1/1.0
192.168.32.36/30    *[Static/5] 01:14:01
                      Discard
```

```
192.168.32.48/30    *[Static/5] 01:14:01
                      > to 10.10.10.1 via so-0/1/1.0
192.168.48.0/24     *[IS-IS/18] 00:52:19, metric 20, tag 2
                      > to 2.2.2.2 via fe-0/0/1.0
```

We've been using the output of the show route command to highlight the use of configured routes and martians. Let's now spend some time interpreting the keywords and symbols of the output.

JUNOS software Routing Tables

The JUNOS software provides multiple routing tables that are used to store routes for your network. Each table is represented within the output of the show route command. The software provides default tables that the operating system builds on an as-needed basis. These tables include the following:

- inet.0
- inet.1
- inet.2
- inet.3
- inet.4
- inet6.0
- mpls.0
- bgp.l3vpn.0
- bgp.l2vpn.0

Each of the default tables contains separate route information. Let's examine each of them in turn.

Table *inet.0*

The *inet.0* routing table is the table used to store IPv4 unicast routes. This is the table we've been using throughout this chapter. The router interfaces and all routing protocols place information into this table by default. This output is an example of routes that populate the inet.0 routing table:

```
user@Riesling> show route table inet.0

inet.0: 49 destinations, 49 routes (49 active, 0 holddown, 0 hidden)
+ = Active Route, - = Last Active, * = Both
```

```
10.0.8.0/24          *[Direct/0] 00:11:43
                     > via so-0/0/2.900
10.0.8.3/32          *[Local/0] 00:11:43
                     Local
172.16.16.0/21       *[Aggregate/130] 00:36:17
                     Reject
172.16.16.0/24       *[Static/5] 00:06:12
                     Reject
192.168.5.1/32       *[OSPF/10] 00:00:15, metric 1
                     > via so-0/0/2.900
192.168.6.0/24       *[IS-IS/18] 00:24:49, metric 10, tag 2
                     > to 10.0.0.1 via fe-0/0/0.0
192.168.10.0/24      *[BGP/170] 00:06:08, localpref 100
                        AS path: 1 I
                     > to 121.10.0.2 via at-0/1/0.100
```

Each route listing contains pertinent information you use to interpret the routing table. Some things to look for are:

Route status   Routes are marked with a status icon. Options include the active route (+), the last active route (–), both the current and last active routes (*), or inactive routes (no icon is used). In a steady state, routes are marked active with an asterisk or they are not active. Only the active routes are copied to the Packet Forwarding Engine.

Protocol name   Routes placed into the routing table are assigned a protocol name. This name tells you how the routing table learned the route. This name is also used by routing policies to advertise and filter routes. (Routing policy is covered in Chapter 4.)

Protocol preference   Each protocol is assigned a numerical value called a protocol preference. This preference value assists the routing table in selecting the active route when more than one version of a route exists.

Next hop information   Routes may be assigned more than one next-hop value. Each next hop instructs the router where to forward packets for each route. When multiple next hops exist, the routing table selects a single next hop to be placed in the forwarding table. This selected next hop is marked with a caret (>) in the output. Multiple next-hop values can be placed in the forwarding table. You'll learn more in the "Load Balancing" section later in this chapter.

Table *inet.1*

The *inet.1* routing table is the table used to store IPv4 multicast routes. This is often referred to as the *multicast forwarding cache*. Each (Source, Group) pair in the network is placed into this table. In this example of the inet.1 routing table, the multicast group 224.2.2.2 /32 is being advertised by a source located at 10.10.200.200 /32.

```
user@Riesling> show route table inet.1

inet.1: 1 destinations, 1 routes (1 active, 0 holddown, 0 hidden)
+ = Active Route, - = Last Active, * = Both

224.2.2.2,10.10.200.200/32*[PIM/105] 00:01:58
                        Multicast
```

Table *inet.2*

The *inet.2* routing table is also used to store IPv4 unicast routes. The use of those routes, however, is quite different from the inet.0 table. Routes in the inet.2 table are used by multicast routing protocols to prevent routing loops. This process is called the Reverse Path Forwarding (RPF) check and is covered in Chapter 9, "Multicast." Sample routes from the inet.2 routing table include:

```
user@Riesling> show route table inet.2

inet.2: 49 destinations, 49 routes (49 active, 0 holddown, 0 hidden)
+ = Active Route, - = Last Active, * = Both

10.0.8.0/24        *[Direct/0] 00:15:43
                    > via so-0/0/2.900
10.0.8.3/32        *[Local/0] 00:15:43
                     Local
10.0.9.0/24        *[Direct/0] 00:15:43
                    > via so-0/0/1.0
10.0.9.2/32        *[Local/0] 00:15:43
                     Local
10.0.10.0/24       *[Direct/0] 00:15:43
                    > via so-0/0/0.212
10.0.10.1/32       *[Local/0] 00:15:43
                     Local
```

Table *inet.3*

The *inet.3* routing table contains the egress IP address of a MPLS label switched path (LSP). (We show you how to create LSPs within the JUNOS software in Chapter 11.) The inet.3 routing table looks like this:

```
user@Riesling> show route table inet.3
```

```
inet.3: 1 destinations, 1 routes (1 active, 0 holddown, 0 hidden)
+ = Active Route, - = Last Active, * = Both

192.168.96.1/32    *[RSVP/7] 00:05:12, metric 20, metric2 0
                    > via so-0/0/3.0, label-switched-path to-the-egress
```

Table *inet.4*

The *inet.4* routing table stores information learned using the Multicast Source Discovery Protocol (MSDP). (Refer to Chapter 9 for more details on multicast networks.) The inet.4 routing table looks like this:

```
user@Riesling> show route table inet.4

inet.4: 1 destinations, 1 routes (1 active, 0 holddown, 0 hidden)
+ = Active Route, - = Last Active, * = Both

224.2.2.2,10.10.201.200/32*[MSDP/175/1] 00:00:45, from 192.168.20.1
                    > to 192.168.28.1 via fe-0/1/3.0
```

Table *inet6.0*

The *inet6.0* routing table contains IPv6 unicast routes. Here's a sample of the routing table:

```
user@Riesling> show route table inet6.0

inet6.0: 2 destinations, 2 routes (2 active, 0 holddown, 0 hidden)
+ = Active Route, - = Last Active, * = Both

fec0:0:0:2003::/64    *[Direct/0] 00:06:14
                      > via fe-0/0/1.0
fec0:0:0:2003::1/128  *[Local/0] 00:06:14
                        Local via fe-0/0/1.0
```

Table *mpls.0*

The *mpls.0* table is not actually a routing table but is instead a switching table. MPLS label values are stored in this table. You view the switching table using the show route command, so we've included it here. (In Chapter 11, we discuss how to use this table for MPLS forwarding.) The mpls.0 routing table looks like this:

```
user@Riesling> show route table mpls.0
```

```
mpls.0: 3 destinations, 3 routes (3 active, 0 holddown, 0 hidden)
+ = Active Route, - = Last Active, * = Both

0                       *[MPLS/0] 00:06:40, metric 1
                           Receive
1                       *[MPLS/0] 00:06:40, metric 1
                           Receive
100000                  *[RSVP/7] 00:06:18, metric 1
                         > via so-0/0/1.0, label-switched-path to-the-egress
```

Table *bgp.l3vpn.0*

The *bgp.l3vpn.0* routing table stores routing information in a Layer 3 virtual private network (VPN) environment. (The details of a VPN network are outside the scope of this book. Please consult the JUNOS software documentation for more information.) Here are sample routes from the bgp.l3vpn.0 routing table:

user@Riesling> **show route table bgp.l3vpn.0**

```
bgp.l3vpn.0: 13 destinations, 13 routes (13 active, 0 holddown, 0 hidden)
+ = Active Route, - = Last Active, * = Both

192.168.16.1:1:172.20.0.0/24
                        *[BGP/170] 14:28:30, localpref 100, from 192.168.5.1
                           AS path: 65000 I
                         > to 10.0.0.2 via fe-0/0/0.0, label-switched-path LSP
192.168.16.1:1:172.20.1.0/24
                        *[BGP/170] 14:28:30, localpref 100, from 192.168.5.1
                           AS path: 65000 I
                         > to 10.0.0.2 via fe-0/0/0.0, label-switched-path LSP
192.168.16.1:1:172.20.2.0/24
                        *[BGP/170] 14:28:30, localpref 100, from 192.168.5.1
                           AS path: 65000 I
                         > to 10.0.0.2 via fe-0/0/0.0, label-switched-path LSP
```

Table *bgp.l2vpn.0*

The *bgp.l2vpn.0* routing table stores routing information in a Layer 2 VPN environment. (Again, the details of a VPN network are outside the scope of this book. Please consult the JUNOS software documentation for more information.) Here are sample routes from the bgp.l2vpn.0 routing table:

user@Riesling> **show route table bgp.l2vpn.0**

```
bgp.l2vpn.0: 1 destinations, 1 routes (1 active, 0 holddown, 0 hidden)
+ = Active Route, - = Last Active, * = Both

192.168.24.1:1:4:1/96
                    *[BGP/170] 01:08:58, localpref 100, from 192.168.24.1
                     AS path: I
                  > to 10.0.16.2 via fe-0/0/1.0, label-switched-path LSP
```

JUNOS software Preference Values

As we mentioned in the previous section "JUNOS software Routing Tables," each route in the routing table is assigned a *protocol preference* value. These values assist the table in selecting the active route when an individual prefix is installed from multiple sources. The preference value informs the routing table which protocols are more believable, with a lower value preferred. The valid value range is between 0 and 4,294,967,295 (2^{32} -1). Table 3.1 lists the default preference values.

TABLE 3.1   JUNOS software Preference Values

Source or Protocol Name	Meaning	Preference Value
Direct	Subnet address of an interface	0
Local	Host address of a directly connected interface	0
Static	Static routes	5
RSVP	Resource Reservation Protocol	7
LDP	Label Distribution Protocol	9
OSPF Internal	Open Shortest Path First internal routes	10
IS-IS Level 1 Internal	Intermediate System to Intermediate System Level 1 internal routes	15
IS-IS Level 2 Internal	Intermediate System to Intermediate System Level 2 internal routes	18
RIP	Routing Information Protocol	100
PIM	Protocol Independent Multicast	105

TABLE 3.1   JUNOS software Preference Values *(continued)*

Source or Protocol Name	Meaning	Preference Value
Aggregate	Aggregate and generated routes	130
OSPF External	Open Shortest Path First external routes	150
IS-IS Level 1 External	Intermediate System to Intermediate System Level 1 external routes	160
IS-IS Level 2 External	Intermediate System to Intermediate System Level 2 external routes	165
BGP	Border Gateway Protocol	170
MSDP	Multicast Source Discovery Protocol	175

The reason for using a preference system within the routing table is quite simple. Each protocol has a separate method for determining the best path to every destination. For instance, the Routing Information Protocol (RIP) uses hop count while OSPF uses cost. These two methods are not directly comparable by the routing table. Should both protocols install a route in the table, an arbitrary criterion (the preference value) must be used to select the active route.

Load Balancing

The default installation of data in the forwarding table is one next hop per destination. A routing policy (which we discuss in more detail in Chapter 4) is the method by which we accomplish a change to this default. Let's examine the JUNOS software load-balancing defaults in more detail by examining Figure 3.6.

Merlot has two equal-cost paths through the network to the loopback address of Cabernet, 192.168.80.1 /32. We can verify this by using the following command:

```
user@Merlot> show route 192.168.80/24 terse

inet.0: 4 destinations, 4 routes (4 active, 0 holddown, 0 hidden)
+ = Active Route, - = Last Active, * = Both

A Destination       P Prf Metric 1   Metric 2    Next hop        AS path
* 192.168.80.1/32   I  18         20             10.222.10.2
                                                 >10.20.20.1
```

As we suspected, only one next hop is installed into the forwarding table:

```
user@Merlot> show route forwarding-table matching 192.168.80/24

Routing table:: inet
Internet:
Destination       Type RtRef Nexthop        Type Index NhRef Netif
192.168.80.1/32   user    0 10.20.20.0      ucst    26    30 so-0/0/3.0
```

FIGURE 3.6 Load-balancing sample network

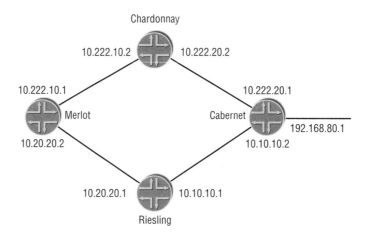

The currently assigned next hop for 192.168.80.1 /32 is Riesling's interface of 10.20.20.1. Recall from the "JUNOS software Routing Table" section earlier in this chapter that a caret marker (>) designates the next hop installed in the forwarding table. The captures from Merlot clearly show this correlation. To install both 10.20.20.1 and 10.222.10.2 as next hops, we configure the following policy:

```
[edit]
user@Riesling# show
policy-options {
    policy-statement please-load-balance-traffic {
        then {
            load-balance per-packet;
        }
    }
}
```

The policy called ***please-load-balance-traffic*** informs the forwarding table to accept all possible next hops from the routing table. This policy is then applied (and takes effect) to the router:

```
[edit routing-options]
user@Riesling# set forwarding-table export please-load-balance-traffic
```

Here's the effect of this configuration on the forwarding table:

```
user@Merlot> show route forwarding-table matching 192.168.80/24


Routing table:: inet
Internet:
Destination        Type RtRef Nexthop       Type Index NhRef Netif
192.168.80.1/32    user    0                ulst   30   14
                              10.222.10.0    ucst   20   19 so-0/0/0.0
                              10.20.20.0     ucst   26   22 so-0/0/3.0
```

Packets forwarded through Merlot toward Cabernet are sent across both next hops. The actual choice of a next hop is based on a microflow selection using the following Layer 3 criteria:

- Incoming interface
- Source IP address
- Destination IP address

We can enable additional criteria for the microflow selection of the forwarding table. These additional criteria are:

- Protocol (TCP or UDP)
- Source port number
- Destination port number

Internet Processor ASICs and Load Balancing

In Chapter 1, we discuss the differences between the original Internet Processor ASIC and the Internet Processor II ASIC. Within the scope of load balancing, there are additional differences we need to point out.

The first of these is the number of next-hop values per route in the forwarding table. The Internet Processor ASIC forwards packets across 8 equal-cost next hops. The Internet Processor II ASIC, however, is able to forward across 16 equal-cost next hops. The second difference between the two ASICs deals with the actual forwarding of user packets.

> The forwarding description described in this section is representative of the Internet Processor II ASIC and is based on a microflow. This means that all user packets that match a certain set of criteria will always follow the same path through the network. This assists end-user applications because it minimizes out-of-order packet delivery. The original Internet Processor ASIC forwards packets on a per-packet basis only. Each individual data packet is sent in a round-robin fashion via a different interface.

Summary

In this chapter, we've seen how to create static, aggregate, and generated routes within [edit routing-options]. We examined some scenarios where these routes might be used and how to activate them within the routing table.

We then analyzed the various routing tables within the JUNOS software and the types of routes each table contains. Next, we went over the selection of an active route using preference values. Finally, we discussed how the JUNOS software handles load balancing across multiple equal-cost paths through the network.

Exam Essentials

Be able to describe the next-hop options for static routes. Static routes require that a valid next hop be installed in the routing table. Possible values include an IP address, a configured null value, a label switched path, and a qualified next hop.

Identify methods for creating a summary route within the JUNOS software. Both an aggregate and a generated route will summarize more specific routes in the routing table. These more specific routes are also known as contributing routes.

Describe the treatment of martian routes. A defined martian route within the JUNOS software prevents that route from appearing in the routing table.

List the default routing tables used in the JUNOS software. There are multiple individual tables included in the output of the show route command. Some of these are inet.0, inet.3, inet6.0, and mpls.0.

Be able to identify the protocol preference values in the routing table. The preference values in the routing table describe the believability of individual protocols. These values assist the routing table in deciding among multiple versions of a route to a destination.

Understand the default JUNOS software load-balancing behavior. The default JUNOS software behavior for load balancing is to install a single next hop into the forwarding table. This default is altered through a routing policy.

Key Terms

Before you take the exam, be certain you are familiar with the following terms:

aggregate route	`inet.4`
`bgp.l2vpn.0`	`inet6.0`
`bgp.l3vpn.0`	martian routes
contributing routes	`mpls.0`
default route	primary contributing route
`discard`	protocol preference
floating static route	qualified next hop
generated route	`receive`
`inet.0`	recursive lookup
`inet.1`	`reject`
`inet.2`	`resolve`
`inet.3`	static route

Review Questions

1. Within the JUNOS software, what is the definition of a generated route?

    A. A route that is generated by a routing protocol

    B. A route that is generated by a remote router and advertised to the local router

    C. A route that is manually entered on the local router

    D. A route that is manually entered on a remote router

2. Given the following section of code:

    ```
    routing-options {
        generate {
            defaults {
                metric 5;
            }
            route 161.10.64.0/18;
            route 161.10.128.0/18;
            route 161.10.192.0/18;
            route 161.10.0.0/18;
            route 161.10.0.0/16 {
                metric 10;
            }
        }
    }
    ```

    what metric will the 161.10.0.0 /18 route have in `inet.0`?

    A. 5

    B. 10

    C. No metric will be assigned

    D. The metric from the primary contributing route

3. What is the difference between an aggregate route and a generated route?

    A. There is no difference.

    B. Aggregate routes have a default next hop of `reject`, while generated routes have an IP address next hop.

    C. The preference value of an aggregate route is better than the preference value of a generated route.

    D. An aggregate route is generated by BGP, while a generated route is manually created.

4. What is the default next hop assigned to a generated route?

   A. `reject`

   B. `discard`

   C. `receive`

   D. IP address of the primary contributing route

5. Which static route next-hop value represents a configured null?

   A. `receive`

   B. `discard`

   C. `label-switch-path`

   D. `qualified-next-hop`

6. What JUNOS software configuration statement allows a static route to use an IP address next hop from a remote router?

   A. `set static route 1.1.1.0/24 next-hop 10.10.10.1`

   B. `set static route 1.1.1.0/24 next-hop 10.10.10.1 resolve`

   C. `set static route 1.1.1.0/24 reject`

   D. `set static route 1.1.1.0/24 receive`

7. What type of route is not considered to be a locally configured route?

   A. Static

   B. Aggregate

   C. Generated

   D. Martian

8. Which configuration statement best summarizes the following routes?

   - 172.16.8.0 /24
   - 172.16.10.32 /30
   - 172.16.48.0 /20
   - 172.16.62.64 /26

   A. `set aggregate route 172.16.0.0/17`

   B. `set aggregate route 172.16.0.0/18`

   C. `set aggregate route 172.16.0.0/19`

   D. `set aggregate route 172.16.0.0/20`

9.   Manually created routes are placed into which routing table by default?

    A. `inet.0`

    B. `inet.2`

    C. `inet.3`

    D. `inet.4`

10.   Your router has learned about the 151.10.0.0 /16 route from protocols Static, RIP, OSPF, and IS-IS. Which version of the route will the router use?

    A. Static

    B. RIP

    C. OSPF

    D. IS-IS

11.   You have multicast traffic flowing through your router. Which routing table contains the multicast forwarding cache?

    A. `inet.0`

    B. `inet.1`

    C. `inet.2`

    D. `inet.3`

12.   What is the default route preference for OSPF internal routes?

    A. 9

    B. 10

    C. 15

    D. 18

13.   Which routes are most preferred by the JUNOS software routing table?

    A. Direct

    B. Aggregate

    C. BGP

    D. Static

14.   Which routing tables are used by MPLS? (Choose two.)

    A. `inet.1`

    B. `inet.2`

    C. `inet.3`

    D. `mpls.0`

15. Which routing table contains unicast routes for IPv6?

    A. `inet.0`

    B. `inet.6`

    C. `inet6.0`

    D. `inet6.6`

16. With load balancing enabled, how does the packet forwarding behavior differ between the Internet Processor ASIC and the Internet Processor II ASIC?

    A. There is no difference.

    B. Internet Processor ASIC load-balances by destination, while the Internet Processor II ASIC load-balances by packet.

    C. Internet Processor ASIC load-balances by packet, while the Internet Processor II ASIC load-balances by MAC address and destination IP address.

    D. Internet Processor ASIC load-balances by packet, while the Internet Processor II ASIC load-balances by a microflow.

17. What is the maximum number of next hops that the Internet Processor ASIC installs in the forwarding table?

    A. 6

    B. 8

    C. 10

    D. 16

18. What is the maximum number of next hops that the Internet Processor II ASIC installs in the forwarding table?

    A. 6

    B. 8

    C. 10

    D. 16

19. What criteria are used by default to form a microflow?

    A. A combination of source MAC address and destination MAC address

    B. A combination of source IP address, destination IP address, and destination MAC address

    C. A combination of source IP address, destination IP address, and incoming router interface

    D. A combination of source IP address, destination IP address, and source port number

20. Which of the following is a required element to configure load balancing in the JUNOS software?

   A. Routing policies

   B. Loopback interfaces

   C. Generated routes

   D. Static routes

Answers to Review Questions

1. C. Generated routes are configured routes that are local to an individual router. Only routing protocols transmit routes between routers.

2. A. Since no metric value is defined for the route itself, it will inherit the metric assigned in the `defaults` section. Recall that the `defaults` section assigns attributes for all routes.

3. B. The single biggest difference between an aggregate and a generated route is the default next-hop value. An aggregate route receives a `reject` next hop. A generated route inherits the IP address next hop of the primary contributing route.

4. D. A generated route inherits the IP address next hop of the primary contributing route. The primary contributor has the smallest numerical prefix.

5. B. A `discard` next hop will drop the packet from the network and *not* return an ICMP message to the source of the packet.

6. B. The `resolve` keyword allows a static route to perform a recursive lookup in the `inet.0` routing table. By default, the IP address of the next hop must be on a directly connected subnet.

7. D. While all of the options are configured within `[edit routing-options]`, only a martian route is not considered a locally configured route.

8. B. Both 172.16.0.0 /17 and 172.16.0.0 /18 adequately summarize the given routes. Answer B, 172.16.0.0 /18, is the best aggregate in that it does not include more routes than necessary.

9. A. All IPv4 unicast routing information is placed into the `inet.0` routing table by default. Locally configured routes are included in this group.

10. A. The preferred route will be the route with the lowest preference value. The default value for static routes is 5. This is better than OSPF (10 or 150), IS-IS (15, 18, 160, or 165), and RIP (100).

11. B. The (Source, Group) information of a multicast forwarding cache is stored in the `inet.1` routing table by default.

12. B. OSPF internal routes receive a preference value of 10 by default. LDP has a default of 9 while IS-IS uses both 15 and 18.

13. A. The preferred route will be the route with the lowest preference value. The default value for direct routes is 0. This is better than static (5), aggregate (130), and BGP (170).

14. C, D. MPLS stores information in both the `inet.3` and `mpls.0` routing tables. LSP egress addresses are placed into `inet.3` and MPLS label information is placed into `mpls.0`.

15. C. All IPv6 unicast routing information is placed into the `inet6.0` routing table by default.

16. D. When using multiple next hops, the main thing to recall about the behavior of the Internet Processor II ASIC is that packet forwarding is accomplished using a microflow computation.

17. B. The Internet Processor ASIC can install up to 8 next hops in the forwarding table for each route destination.

18. D. The Internet Processor II ASIC can install up to 16 next hops in the forwarding table for each route destination.

19. C. The Layer 3 information of source/destination IP address and incoming router interface are used to determine a microflow. We can also enable additional Layer 4 information of source/destination port number and protocol.

20. A. The configuration of load balancing within the JUNOS software requires the use of routing policies. A policy is created and then applied that tells the forwarding table to install multiple next hops for each route destination.

Chapter

4

Routing Policy

JNCIA EXAM OBJECTIVES COVERED IN THIS CHAPTER:

- ✓ Describe JUNOS software routing policy design considerations—import; export; terms; match criteria; actions; default actions; policy evaluation

- ✓ List the main reasons to create and apply policies

- ✓ Define the locations within a BGP configuration where a policy may be applied

- ✓ Identify the components of a route filter and the various match types

- ✓ Evaluate the outcome of a policy

In this chapter, we explore how you implement a basic routing policy in a Juniper Networks router. We first examine why you need a routing policy and when it would be appropriate to implement it. Then we see how to create policies and, finally, how to apply policies within the JUNOS software.

A routing policy is an integral part of any effective network. Without it, a network is subject to the rules of its Interior Gateway Protocol (IGP) and Border Gateway Protocol (BGP) configuration. Using routing policies allows you to modify or ignore the default behavior of the routing protocols. This gives you a significant amount of control over the routing behavior of the network. A complete understanding of how and when to use a routing policy is essential to running an optimal network, so let's start there.

What Is a Routing Policy?

Although it is tempting to jump right into configuring routing policies, we first need to understand why policies are needed and how they are implemented. In this section, we review the purpose of routing tables, the selection process for active routes, and reasons for modifying the selection process. After that, we consider how routing policies affect the router's view of the network.

The Routing Table

If you think back to *Routing 101*, you will recall that a router is a Layer 3 device that utilizes IP addresses to determine the best path to an end destination. The router works with the routing protocols to learn about the network's destinations. For the most part, the end goal of the routing protocols is the same—to learn about all possible routes and to send those routes to all possible neighbors. How this is actually accomplished varies, but the general goal remains the same.

A router stores all the routes (and paths) that it learns about in a routing table. The router then references this table to make forwarding decisions. As you saw in Chapter 3, "Protocol-Independent Routing," a Juniper Networks router uses *preference* as a selection process to determine the active route for each destination. Once the network installs this route in the forwarding table, it can simply forward all user packets out of the proper interface.

The active route plays another important role. The routing protocols will send the active routes in the routing table to all their neighbors. Through this learn-and-send process, each router is able to build its own map of the entire network. In a fully operational and converged network, all routers should see a valid path to any destination. This simple process is highly effective. In some cases, it works extremely well. So why change it?

Why Modify the Routing Table?

Using the default behavior of routing protocols is certainly enough to maintain connectivity in a simple network, but what happens when the network grows in complexity? A single protocol often cannot maintain enough information to ensure that all routers are utilizing the best paths available. The key word in the previous sentence is *best*. In short, different protocols define the best path differently. Making sure that the best path is taken, even in a small network, can be a very tricky proposition.

The JUNOS software routing policy framework is your tool to guarantee that the best path in your network is the one you want to use. It can override and alter the selections made by the routing protocols and inject new information into the network. Let's see how this might work.

Modifying the Default Protocol Route Selection

Distance-vector routing protocols rely on hop counts to determine the optimal path. This means that the protocol has no knowledge of the physical network topology. Figure 4.1 shows a simple distance-vector network. In the diagram, the router Shiraz sees Merlot via two distinct paths. The path via Cabernet costs two hops, while the path via Riesling costs three hops. Since the protocol selects the route with the fewest hops, Shiraz will install a route to Merlot via Cabernet. Of course, 99.9 percent of you would rather use the path via Riesling because of its larger bandwidth connections. Clearly, the distance-vector protocol did not choose our best path through the network.

FIGURE 4.1 A simple distance-vector network

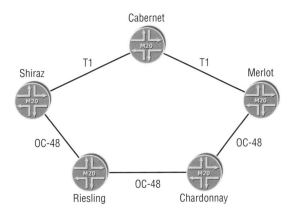

While this is a simple and contrived example, it does prove an important point. The routing protocols in your network will do only what they are configured to do, not what you want them to do! You would like the ability to change, or even ignore, any information in your routing table. This is a perfect situation for using a routing policy.

Redistributing Routes

You can also use routing policies to redistribute routes from one protocol into another. Remember, routing protocols advertise only routes that have been learned by that specific protocol. To move routes from one protocol into another, a policy is again required.

Figure 4.2 shows a simple multiprotocol network. Here, Shiraz is connected to a server farm that uses the Routing Information Protocol (RIP) for its network connectivity. Shiraz is also running Open Shortest Path First (OSPF) to communicate with the backbone network of Cabernet, Chardonnay, and Riesling. Without a policy, the RIP network will have no knowledge of the OSPF backbone. Similarly, the OSPF backbone will have no knowledge of the RIP server farm network. In essence, the networks are completely segmented from each other. One solution might be to use some default and static routes, but this is not scalable beyond our small network here. The preferred solution is to have all routers in the two networks utilize the routing protocols themselves for connectivity. After all, that's what they're there for!

FIGURE 4.2   A simple multiprotocol network

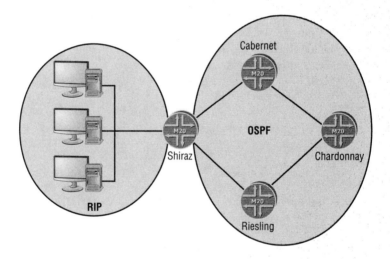

Route redistribution is a much more dynamic and scalable solution because it will allow the networks to expand without significant reconfiguration. To reach this goal, we place a routing policy on Shiraz to modify the protocol's default behavior. The policy allows the RIP process to advertise the OSPF learned routes and vice versa.

You may have noticed a trend by now. It looks like we can use a routing policy when we want to alter the default behavior of a protocol. In fact, you are right. With a policy, you can modify or ignore routes that are advertised to you as well as routes that you advertise to other neighbors. Don't forget that we can also use a routing policy to redistribute routes from one protocol into another.

Changing the Map

When you modify or ignore (suppress) the routes that are sent and received by the local router, you change the network map. It is extremely important that you understand which router's map you are changing.

By changing a route's properties prior to installing it into your routing table, you have modified how the local router perceives the network. If you change a route's properties prior to sending it to your neighbors, you will be modifying the remote router's perception of the network. So the question becomes, whose behavior do you want to modify? How might you apply a routing policy to accomplish that?

The application of a routing policy is always performed from the perspective of the routing table. Routes being placed into the routing table are said to be "inbound." Routes being extracted from the routing table are said to be "outbound." When your goal is to modify your view of the network, you need to apply a policy to all inbound routes. If your goal is to modify your neighbor's view of the network, you apply a policy to all outbound routes. In the section "Applying Routing Policies" later in this chapter, you'll see how to accomplish this within the JUNOS software. For now, it is important to keep the directionality of inbound and outbound very distinct.

Forming a Policy

There are two main steps to forming a routing policy—writing the policy and applying the policy. The focus for this section will be on writing your policies, including some best practices. We examine the various components of a routing policy and then discuss identifying routes of interest to you. Once you've identified the "interesting" routes, you need to do something with them. This is the job of an action. Finally, we look at the default policy already in place for each routing protocol.

Composing a Routing Policy

It probably goes without saying that before you compose your routing policy, you had better know what you are going to do with it. That concept is doubly important within the JUNOS software. A specific set of rules governs the processing of policies and how they are evaluated on the router. This evaluation process might lead you to decide to segment your policies, so let's take a look at that approach as well. Let's also discuss some industry best practices.

Policy Processing

All active routes in the routing table are evaluated individually against all applied routing policies. The policies are evaluated in order of application in a daisy-chain fashion called a *policy chain*. A route will proceed through each policy until a *match* is found for that route. In addition, the matching policy must also contain a *terminating action*.

Consider the block diagram in Figure 4.3. Notice that each policy contains three possible results:

- accept
- reject
- next policy

FIGURE 4.3 Block diagram of policy processing

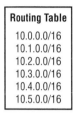

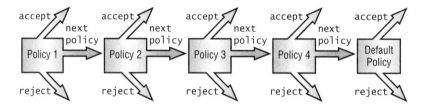

Both accept and reject are considered terminating actions and they have a special meaning—they stop the policy evaluation. The result of next policy simply means that the route should be evaluated by the next position in the policy chain. If you look closely at Figure 4.3, you will see that each policy chain has a default policy at the end. Further, that default policy does not have a next policy result. It will always end the policy evaluation.

We discuss default policies in the section "Default Policy" later in this chapter.

A Programming Language?

Those of you familiar with programming languages will likely compare the evaluation of a routing policy to an if-then-else loop. If a route matches a set of conditions, it then performs a set of defined actions. Otherwise, it continues on to the next set of conditions. This process continues until some final action is determined.

In some ways, you are right. The policy-chain evaluation does generally follow that model. There are some differences as well. So you should only use the model to frame your approach to creating a policy.

Using Figure 4.3 as a guide, the 10.0.0.0 /16 route is first evaluated against Policy 1. If the route doesn't match Policy 1, it moves to Policy 2 and is evaluated there. A nonmatch within Policy 2 causes the route to proceed to Policy 3. This process continues until the route encounters a terminating action.

The terminating results of `accept` and `reject` are represented by the JUNOS software keywords of `accept` and `reject`. When a route matches a policy with an action of `accept`, the route is used. Should a route match a policy with an action of `reject`, the route is ignored. By using this simple guide, you can easily determine which routes will be included in a routing table and which ones will be omitted.

Routing policies are constructed in a very systematic method to allow for maximum scalability and flexibility. A basic routing policy looks like this:

```
policy-options {
    policy-statement policy-name {
        from {
            match-conditions;
        }
        then {
            actions;
        }
    }
}
```

Notice that the policy is broken into the two sections we have been discussing. There are match conditions and there are actions. What you will not see is the implied result of `next policy`. By default, any route that does not fit the match conditions will proceed to the next applied policy. We discuss the specific match conditions and actions in the "Match Conditions" and "Actions" sections later in this chapter.

The JUNOS software policy configuration allows you to customize the names of your policies. This makes it easier to identify their purpose at a later time. This naming structure provides for some creativity on your part. While you can call your policy anything you want, it is recommended that you define the policy name so its intended use is self-evident. For example, a policy designed to tag routes from Customer A might be named *tag-customerA*.

The naming of policies and terms within the JUNOS software are case sensitive in nature. For example, `policy-a` is different from `Policy-A`, which is different from `PoLiCy-A`.

Policy Segmentation

As the complexity of your network grows, so will the number of your routing policies. A policy chain can be applied in numerous ways, but the order of its evaluation is always the same. If you want to use multiple policies to accomplish your goal, it is critical that you place them in the correct order. You can fix an out-of-order policy chain by using the `insert` command, which we talk about later in the "Useful JUNOS software Commands" section.

WARNING   The flexibility of creating multiple specific policies and then applying those policies in a policy chain brings with it an inherent complexity. You must be very conscious of the order in which your policies are applied. You could easily apply a routing policy that rejects an important route prior to a policy that is supposed to accept it. Once a route is rejected via a terminating action, it is not evaluated by any further policies.

You can simplify a complex policy chain somewhat by using a single routing policy to accomplish all of your goals. This means that your complex policy chain is now turned into a complex single policy with multiple, distinct sections. These policy sections are called *terms*. Within their policy, they are evaluated in a similar daisy-chain fashion like a policy chain. One benefit of this approach is that the same logic used to build the policy chain is used to build a multiterm policy. Figure 4.4 shows such a configuration. Here, a single policy, Policy 1, has been separated into multiple terms. These terms are now evaluated in a daisy-chain fashion in the order they are written.

FIGURE 4.4   A block diagram of policy evaluation using terms

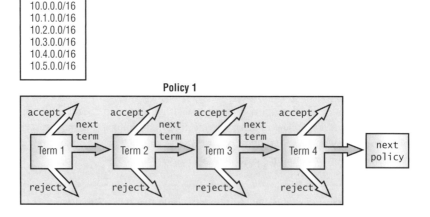

Using routing policies with terms allows you to avoid two possible pitfalls in your network. First, a single policy with multiple match conditions and actions can be applied to a protocol. This reduces the policy chain to the one configured policy and the implicit default policy, thereby eliminating an out-of-order policy evaluation. Second, you might often find it impossible to write an entire policy correctly on the first attempt. You will leave out some match criteria or actions. If you were using a large policy chain, fixing this would mean a new policy and possible issues with a sequence evaluation problem. The use of terms allows you to add this new information to your existing policy.

A multiterm policy looks similar to the following:

```
policy-options {
    policy-statement policy-name {
        term term-name {
            from {
                match-conditions;
            }
            then {
                actions;
            }
        }
        term term-name {
            from {
                match-conditions;
            }
            then {
                actions;
            }
        }
    }
}
```

Like the policies themselves, terms let you define a name to identify its purpose. Again, we highly recommend that the name you give the term be as descriptive as possible. This makes troubleshooting your configuration much easier.

A routing policy does not require the use of terms, but omitting them can cause you some heartburn later. The absence of a term in a policy means that the policy can contain only one set of match conditions and actions. If you ever want to add other match/action pairs in the future, you would need to delete and re-create the policy from scratch. If you create the policy using terms to begin with, however, adding a new set of conditions and actions is quite easy. The one thing to keep in mind is that new terms are always added to the end of the existing policy. If this is not the best location, you have the ability to move them within the policy by using the `insert` command. Again, you can find more information about the `insert` command in the "Useful JUNOS software Commands" section later in this chapter.

Now that you have seen the evaluation order of policy terms and policy chains, let's examine the details of an individual term. The logical place to start is with the match conditions that qualify a route for a policy action.

Match Conditions

To allow you to properly identify active routes in the routing table, the JUNOS software provides a number of match conditions for routing policies. You can identify these conditions within the policy by using the keyword *from* or *to*. We first examine the differences between from and to when using a match condition. Then we look at how to match on specific routes using route filters.

 It is worth emphasizing that a routing policy in the JUNOS software will evaluate only active routes in the routing table. All inactive routes located in the table will *not* be evaluated by a policy. We explain active versus nonactive routes in Chapter 3.

from and *to*

The match conditions available within the JUNOS software provide numerous ways to identify routes of interest. All of the criteria will be defined using either the from or the to syntax.

Table 4.1 details some of the possible match criteria that you can use in a routing policy. Specifically, they are items that are used with the from keyword. One useful match criterion is the neighbor address. Matching on the address of a neighbor is fairly intuitive. When used with the from keyword, routes that are sent by that address will match the policy. Look at this policy:

```
policy-options {
    policy-statement bgp-import {
        term coming-from-ISPA {
            from neighbor 2.2.2.2;
            then reject;
        }
    }
}
```

The term *coming-from-ISPA* specifies that the routes being received from the BGP neighbor of 2.2.2.2 should match this policy.

The protocol match condition is another widely used match criterion. This criterion essentially means, "How did the route get placed into the routing table?" Some of the options for the protocol match condition are listed in Table 4.1. While it is fairly obvious that matching on protocol ospf will locate all OSPF routes, using the protocol aggregate match criterion may not initially make sense. After all, aggregate routes are not found using a routing protocol—they are locally configured on the router. Just keep in mind that all routes in the routing table are assigned a protocol, as we discussed in Chapter 3. The protocol match condition looks for those assigned values only.

Table 4.1 lists a number of the match conditions used in routing policies, but by no means is it a complete list. Please consult the JUNOS software documentation for the complete list of all policy match conditions.

TABLE 4.1   *from* Match Conditions

Match Condition	Description
area *area-id*	Used in an export policy to identify routes learned from a particular area. (OSPF only)
as-path *name*	Identifies routes with the named AS Path. (BGP only)
community *[names]*	Identifies routes with the named community assigned. (BGP only)
level *level*	Used in an export policy to identify routes that are coming from a particular level. (IS-IS only)
local-preference *value*	Identifies the Local Preference value of BGP routes. (BGP only)
metric *metric*	Identifies routes with the specified metric. For BGP, the metric action identifies the MED route attribute.
neighbor *address*	Identifies the neighbor from which a route was learned.
next-hop *address*	Identifies routes with the specified physical next-hop address. For BGP routes, it identifies the BGP protocol next hop.
origin *value*	Identifies the BGP Origin attribute. (BGP only)
preference *preference*	Identifies routes with the specified preference.
protocol *protocol*	Identifies how the router learned the route. Possible options include: aggregate, bgp, direct, isis, ospf, rip, or static.
rib *routing-table*	Identifies the routing table where routes are located.

You can also use the level match criterion with the to keyword. This means that only the routes being sent to that level will match. Consider the following section of code:

```
policy-options {
    policy-statement isis-export {
        term sending-to-neighborA {
```

```
        to level 2;
        then accept;
    }
  }
}
```

The term **sending-to-neighborA** matches only on routes being sent to the ISIS level 2.

The to keyword has far fewer match conditions (as seen in Table 4.2) associated with it than does the from keyword. As such, it is not used very often in routing policies.

TABLE 4.2 *to* Match Conditions

Match Condition	Description
level *level*	Used in an export policy to identify routes that are going to a particular level. (IS-IS only)
rib *routing-table*	Identifies the routing table where candidate routes will be placed.

As you examine the various match criteria in the JUNOS software, it might appear that a number of them are associated with BGP routes. In fact, you would be correct to think so. This is due to the large amount of information contained within a BGP route. For example, a few of the BGP route properties include Local Preference, AS Path, Origin, and MED. In addition, you can tag BGP routes with a user-defined value called a *community*. By comparison, OSPF attributes only include metric and a user-defined tag field. We don't want to imply here, however, that a routing policy is not effective on an IGP—it is. We are simply saying that more match criteria is available for BGP.

Defining Multiple Criteria

As you build your policies, you may find it necessary to identify your "interesting" routes by using more than a single property. You accomplish this by specifying multiple match conditions within a policy term. This imposes a logical AND on your candidate route. It will match the policy term only if it also matches all of the specified conditions.

As an example, let's say that you wanted to accept all BGP routes from neighbor 1.1.1.1 only if the routes have a MED value of 10. You could configure a policy that looks like the following:

```
policy-options {
    policy-statement bgp-import {
        term coming-from-neighborA {
            from {
                neighbor 1.1.1.1;
                metric 10;
            }
            then accept;
        }
        term deny-other-neighborA {
            from neighbor 1.1.1.1;
            then reject;
        }
    }
}
```

The term *coming-from-neighborA* will match only routes that have been advertised from neighbor 1.1.1.1 and that also have a MED value of 10. These routes will be accepted into the routing table. To ensure that no other routes from that neighbor are accepted, you create a second term called *deny-other-neighborA*. This term looks for all other routes from neighbor 1.1.1.1 and rejects them. We use this "extra" term to avoid the processing of the default BGP policy that is implied at the end of the policy chain. To learn the implication of the default routing policies, see the section "Default Policy" later in this chapter.

Route Filters

The match criterion that we've looked at so far has selected groups of routes based on some general attributes. What happens if you know the exact route that you want? The way to match against a particular route in a policy is to use a *route filter*. To truly understand the operation of a route filter, you need to be familiar with a device used for binary number matching known as a *radix tree* (sometimes called a *radix trie*). In the sections that follow, we examine the IP route relationship, perform route lookups, and use a radix tree and route filters to match IP routes.

Radix Tree

Binary math is a necessary evil for computers since they can only understand voltage (a value of 1) or no voltage (a value of 0). This on/off concept leads us into a binary notation. A radix tree uses binary lookups to identify IP addresses (routes). Remember that an IP address is really a 32-bit number represented in a dotted decimal format for easy comprehension by humans. These 8-bit groupings can each have a value between 0 and 255. A radix tree can be a graphical representation of these binary numbers.

For example, look at Figure 4.5. This radix tree starts with no configured value (starts at 0) and is at the leftmost position of the binary IP address. This is shown as 0 /0, which is often referred to as the default route. Our first step is to look at the first position of the IP address. Since we are talking about binary here, it can have only one of two possible values—a 0 or a 1. Moving down the left branch represents a value of 0, while moving to the right represents a value of 1. Our first step is shown in Figure 4.6.

FIGURE 4.5   Beginning of a radix tree

FIGURE 4.6   Starting to build a radix tree

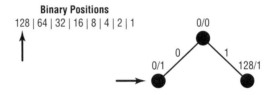

At the first position, the first octet of the IP address has a value of 00000000 or 10000000—a 0 or 128, respectively. This is represented in Figure 4.6 by the values 0 /1 and 128 /1. The second step of the tree is shown in Figure 4.7.

FIGURE 4.7   Radix tree build—step 2

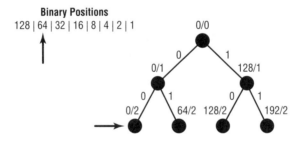

This second level of the tree has four possible binary values for the first octet: 00000000, 01000000, 10000000, and 11000000. These decimal values of 0, 64, 128, and 192 are represented by the IP addresses of 0 /2, 64 /2, 128 /2, and 192 /2 on the radix tree. This step-by-step process continues on for 33 total levels. In the end, we effectively represent every possible IP address.

The radix tree structure is also very helpful when locating a group of routes that all share the same most significant bits. Figure 4.8 shows the point in the radix tree that represents the 192.168.0.0 /16 network. All of the routes that are more specific than 192.168.0.0 /16 are shown in the highlighted section.

FIGURE 4.8   Locating a group of routes

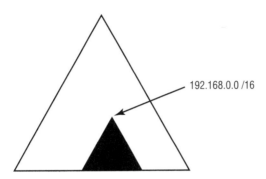

192.168.0.0 /16

If we now focus in on the specific structure of the radix tree that starts at 192.168.0.0 /16, then we'll see something similar to Figure 4.9.

While the figure stops at the 19th level of the tree, please be aware that it actually continues down to the 32nd level. This shortened version, however, will suffice for our discussion of route filters.

JUNOS software Syntax

To find a specific route, or a group of routes, within a routing policy you utilize the route filter match condition. The route filter syntax within the JUNOS software looks similar to the following:

```
route-filter prefix/prefix-length match-type actions;
```

The **prefix** and **prefix-length** variables are simply the reference point on the radix tree where you would like to start finding a route. One of six possible *match type* keywords describes the additional routes on the radix tree that will match the route filter. If any optional actions are defined, they will be processed immediately, allowing the policy to skip actions configured using the **then** statement. (See the section "Actions" later in this chapter for more on policy actions.)

FIGURE 4.9 Portion of the radix tree

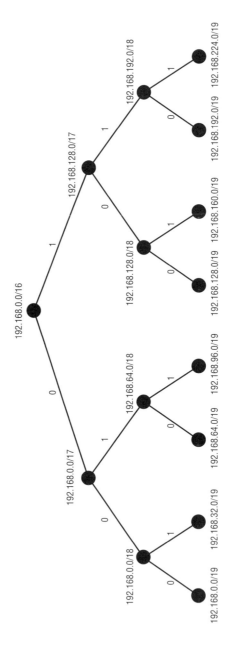

Each of the route filter match types locates a different set of routes on the radix tree. Let's take a look at each of the match types, along with a sample syntax output:

exact   The *exact* match type will locate only the route at the specified point in the tree.

The following route filter matches only the 192.168.0.0 /16 route—no other routes will be selected:

```
route-filter 192.168.0.0/16 exact;
```

orlonger   The *orlonger* match type will also match the route specified in the route filter. In addition, it will match all routes more specific than the specified route. This more specific match will continue until the bottom of the radix tree (the 32nd level) is reached. This match type is similar to a greater-than-or-equals-to operation in mathematics.

The following route filter matches the 192.168.0.0 /16 route and all routes below it in the radix tree:

```
route-filter 192.168.0.0/16 orlonger;
```

longer   The *longer* match type is similar to the `orlonger` match type. The difference between them is that `longer` will only match routes that are more specific than the specified route. This match type is analogous to the mathematical greater-than operation.

The following route filter matches only the routes below the 192.168.0.0 /16 route in the radix tree starting with 192.168.0.0 /17 and 192.168.128.0 /17:

```
route-filter 192.168.0.0/16 longer;
```

upto   The *upto* match type provides the router with a starting prefix and an ending prefix length. The match type locates the route specified in the route filter and starts to match all routes more specific than the specified route. The route matching stops when it reaches the level in the radix tree configured in the route filter. This behavior mimics the `orlonger` function except now we're specifying a bottom boundary in the tree lookup instead of letting it continue to the 32nd level of the tree.

The following route filter matches the 192.168.0.0 /16 route. It then starts matching all of the more specific routes until it reaches the 18th level of the tree and matches those routes. In this way, `upto` is an inclusive match type. If we look back at Figure 4.9, we'll see that this route filter locates seven total routes.

```
route-filter 192.168.0.0/16 upto /18;
```

prefix-length-range   Much like the relationship between `orlonger` and `longer`, the *prefix-length-range* and the `upto` match types are very similar. Recall that `upto` allows you to configure a bottom boundary in the radix tree lookup. `prefix-length-range` also provides this capability but adds to it the ability to specify a starting boundary in the radix tree as well. It is important to remember that all routes located by this match type will still share the same more significant bits as configured in the ***prefix/prefix-length*** portion of the route filter.

The following route filter starts looking for routes at the 192.168.0.0 /16 level of the radix tree. It starts to match routes at the 17th level of the tree and stops matching routes at the 18th level. Like upto, this is also an inclusive match type. Using Figure 4.9 as a reference again, we'll see that this route filter locates six total routes.

```
route-filter 192.168.0.0/16 prefix-length-range /17-/18;
```

through   The *through* match type is very different from the others we've talked about. The configuration for this match type requires you to specify both a starting route and an ending route. The route filter matches both of these routes exactly and then further locates only the routes on the radix tree that connect the two.

The following route filter matches the 192.168.0.0 /16 and 192.168.128.0 /19 routes. It also matches the 192.168.128.0 /17 and 192.168.128.0 /18 routes because they are the routes between the start and end points. A quick look back at Figure 4.9 can verify this.

```
route-filter 192.168.0.0/16 through 192.168.128.0/19;
```

While it's nice to talk about these match types in English, the descriptions can be very confusing. Figure 4.10 shows us the match types in a graphical format. This often helps to solidify the concept in our minds.

Real World Scenario

Route Aggregation in BGP

The longer route filter match type is useful when aggregating route information in BGP. Let's say that the local router is receiving the routes 192.168.1.0 /24, 192.168.2.0 /24, and 192.168.3.0 /24. You have created a local aggregate route of 192.168.0.0 /22 to summarize these routes. The aggregate route is being exported to your upstream BGP peer by an export policy using the from protocol aggregate match criteria. Unfortunately for you, the three more specific routes are also still being sent to that peer.

The default BGP policy (discussed in the "Default Policy" section later in this chapter) will match all BGP routes in the routing table and export them to all peers. This is not what you wanted to do administratively, but the defaults get in your way. Sounds like a job for a routing policy! Specifically, you need to match on all routes that are more specific than your aggregate route *without* also matching on your aggregate. One effective way to accomplish this is to add a term to the current policy that rejects routes that match route-filter 192.168.0.0/22 longer. The new term should be placed prior to the term that exports the aggregate route to effectively filter the more specific routes.

Using Multiple Route Filters

In the "from and to" section earlier in this chapter, we saw that the application of multiple match conditions in a term results in a logical AND operation. When multiple route filters are used in a single term, this process is changed somewhat. In this situation, the multiple route filters are evaluated much like a logical OR in that only one of the route filters will actually be the match criteria used. This one route filter is found by performing a longest-match lookup on the configured *prefix/prefix-length* within each route filter. Only after this longest-match lookup is completed will the match type be considered to see if a candidate route actually matches the policy term.

FIGURE 4.10   Route filter match types

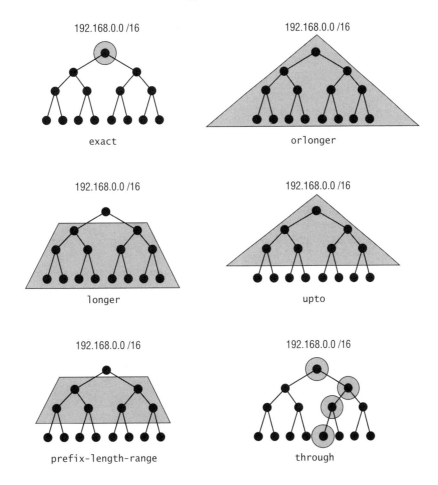

It is often mistakenly believed that the match type is included in the longest-match lookup of a route filter. In actuality, the routing policy evaluation evaluates only the *prefix/prefix-length* statement.

Let's investigate this concept a little more by looking at the following policy:

```
policy-options {
    policy-statement bgp-export {
        term coming-from-neighborA {
            from {
                route-filter 192.168.0.0/16 orlonger;
                route-filter 192.168.0.0/24 exact;
            }
            then accept;
        }
    }
}
```

When evaluating the 192.168.0.128 /25 route against this policy, we first perform our longest-match lookup on the configured route filters. The 192.168.0.0 /16 route filter and our candidate route share only the first 16 bits in common while the 192.168.0.0 /24 route filter shares 24 bits in common with our candidate route. Because 24 bits is clearly greater than 16, the second configured route filter will be the one we use as a match criterion for this term. Now it's time to worry about the match type. The 192.168.0.0 /24 route filter specifies the exact match type and our candidate route of 192.168.0.128 /25 is not an exact match. There-fore, 192.168.0.128 /25 does not match the criterion in the policy term, and it will be evaluated by the next policy in the policy chain. It is *not* evaluated against the first route filter in the policy.

Route Filters and Other Match Criteria

Within a policy term, multiple route filters can be paired with other types of match conditions. When this situation arises, the first operation must always be the longest-match lookup of the route filters—the logical OR. After the one route filter to be used is located, it can be combined with the other match conditions in the term using the logical AND operation. Only after the candidate route "passes" all of the configured match conditions will it proceed to the actions specified in the policy term. A policy that uses this type of configuration may look something like this:

```
policy-options {
    policy-statement bgp-export {
        term coming-from-neighborA {
            from {
                protocol bgp;          ┐
                metric 10;             ┘ AND
                route-filter 192.0.0.0/8 exact;       ┐
                route-filter 192.168.0.0/16 longer;   │ "OR"
                route-filter 10.222.12.0/24 longer;   ┘
            }
            then accept;
        }
    }
}
```

Absence of Match Criteria

Up to this point, we've talked about a lot of different match criteria that we can use in a policy term. All of these configuration options are, however, completely optional in their usage. You can configure a policy without either a `from` or a `to` match condition. Take this section of code:

```
policy-options {
    policy-statement ibgp-export {
        term accept-all-routes {
            then accept;
        }
    }
}
```

When no match criteria are used, every active route in the routing table will match the policy. In other words, the absence of match criteria means that all routes match. All routes then take the configured actions of the policy term. In the case of this particular policy, all routes would be accepted by the policy.

Finding routes in the routing table is only the first step in using a routing policy. After they are located, we must then decide what to actually do with them. This is the job of a policy action.

Actions

You've seen how to easily identify routes from the routing table using the JUNOS software match criteria. We now need to explore further the options that are available in the `then` portion of a policy for performing some sort of *action* on a candidate route. We first review the terminating actions before looking at using flow control within the policy evaluation. We then discuss how to modify the properties of our candidate route.

Terminating Actions

For the sake of completeness, let's take another look at the terminating actions of `accept` and `reject`. We first talked about these actions in the "Policy Processing" section earlier in this chapter. As we mentioned, the presence of a terminating action within a policy term will halt the evaluation of the policy chain. In addition, the terminating actions affect whether the routing information is used.

When a candidate route matches the criterion of an inbound policy term and the action of `accept` has been configured, that route is placed into the routing table. The `accept` action used in an outbound policy term means that the candidate route is advertised out of the routing table.

The function of the `reject` action is quite the opposite. An inbound policy term match with an action of `reject` does not place the route into the routing table. Likewise, the outbound action of `reject` does not advertise the route out of the routing table.

Flow Control

Instead of stopping the evaluation of a policy chain via a terminating action, you have the ability to alter the evaluation process. This is accomplished with a *flow control action* of `next term` or `next policy`. These actions allow a candidate route to break out of the normal daisy-chain policy evaluation. Look at this policy:

```
policy-options {
    policy-statement bgp-import {
        term coming-from-neighborA {
            from {
                neighbor 1.1.1.1;
                metric 10;
            }
            then next policy;
        }
        term deny-other-neighborA {
            from neighbor 1.1.1.1;
            then reject;
        }
    }
}
```

Routes arriving from the BGP neighbor of 1.1.1.1 that also have a MED of 10 will match the first policy term of ***coming-from-neighborA***. The configured action of `next policy` directs the candidate routes to the next policy in the policy chain without any other immediate actions taken. All other routes from neighbor 1.1.1.1 match the second policy term of ***deny-other-neighborA*** and are immediately rejected. This policy allows us to selectively avoid the daisy-chain processing for a portion of the received routes.

Action Modifiers

Before a candidate route is accepted or rejected by a terminating action, you can modify the attributes of the route. A partial list of possible modifying actions is shown in Table 4.3. Again, for a more complete listing, please refer to the JUNOS software documentation.

TABLE 4.3   Modifying Actions

Action	Description
`local-preference` *value*	Sets the BGP local preference attribute to the specified value. (BGP only)
`metric` *value*	Sets the metric to the specified value. Sets the BGP MED attribute to the specified value. (BGP only)

TABLE 4.3   Modifying Actions *(continued)*

Action	Description
next-hop *address*	Sets the next-hop value to the specified address. A keyword of self will cause the next-hop address to be replaced by one of the local router's addresses. Which address is used is determined by the routing protocol.
origin *value*	Sets the BGP Origin attribute to the specified value. (BGP only)
preference *value*	Sets the route's protocol preference to the specified value.

The modifying actions give you a great deal of control over the contents of the routing table. When you selectively manipulate the properties of certain routes, you can gain full control over your network's behavior. Look at the following policy:

```
policy-options {
    policy-statement bgp-import {
        term coming-from-neighborA {
            from {
                protocol bgp;
                neighbor 1.1.1.1;
            }
            then {
                metric 20;
                accept;
            }
        }
    }
}
```

All BGP routes received from the neighbor address of 1.1.1.1 have the MED attribute set to 20 and are installed into the routing table via the accept action.

Default Policy

Thus far in the chapter we've discussed how to build a routing policy to modify the default behavior of the routing protocols. Recall that these configured policies are evaluated before the default policy in a policy chain. It is now time to examine the default policies of the routing protocols. At first glance, the default policy concept sounds quite ominous. In reality, each of the default routing policies is in fact exactly how the routing protocol is designed to work. Let's take a closer look and maybe this will make more sense. We start with BGP and then look at the IGPs.

Border Gateway Protocol (BGP)

BGP is the routing protocol of the Internet and connects different Autonomous Systems (ASs) together. The protocol supports the mesh-like interconnection structure of the ISPs that comprise the Internet backbone. BGP is a very policy-driven protocol that gives you control over exactly what routes are received and sent to a peer. This translates into a possibly complex configuration of BGP. We examine the details of applying policies to BGP in the next section, but now let's look at how the protocol is designed to work by default.

When a BGP router receives routes from a peer, it is designed to accept all of the routes advertised to it. The router performs this function for each peer it is currently communicating with. Once the routes are stored in memory, the router selects the best path to each distinct network and installs those in the forwarding table. These best paths (active BGP routes in inet.0) are then advertised to its BGP peers. The specific routes advertised to each peer will depend on the local router's relationship with its peer. If the relationship is an internal one (both of the routers are in the same AS), then only routes originally received from an external peer will be advertised. The routes sent to an external peer are quite different, however. In this case, all active BGP routes will be sent to the external peer.

The default BGP import and export policies mirror this normal operation of BGP. The following summarizes these policies:

Import Policy (All Peers)   A BGP router will accept all non-looped BGP routes received from another BGP router.

Export Policy (External Peers)   A BGP router will advertise all active BGP routes in inet.0 to all configured external BGP peers.

Export Policy (Internal Peers)   A BGP router will advertise all active BGP routes in inet.0 to all internal peers if the routes were originally received from an external peer.

Internal Gateway Protocols

While at first you might think that all of the IGPs would have similar default policies, this is not the case. In fact, each of the three protocols (RIP, OSPF, and IS-IS) has very different import and export policies by default. Let's look at each of the protocols separately.

Routing Information Protocol (RIP)

The default import and export policies for the JUNOS software implementation of RIP do not follow a "normal" operation of a distance-vector protocol. The default import policy is to accept all routes advertised to the local router via RIP. The default export policy for RIP is to not advertise any routes to any neighbors. One main reason for this seemingly odd behavior is that a Juniper Networks router is designed to run in the core of the Internet and RIP is not well suited for that use. However, many customer implementations need to receive RIP routes in their networks from server farms or remote access servers. These routes would then be advertised to the rest of the network using a different routing protocol. The JUNOS software defaults for RIP support this functionality. For more on using RIP, see Chapter 5.

Open Shortest Path First (OSPF)

OSPF is a link-state routing protocol that mandates that each router in an OSPF area maintain an identical link-state database. Filtering out and rejecting incoming routing information could break this mandate, so import policies are not permitted. This means that there is no default import policy for OSPF.

The default export policy for OSPF is to reject all routes. While this sounds very similar to the default RIP export operation, things are actually quite different. OSPF advertises routing information in a format called a link-state advertisement (LSA). These LSAs contain the local router's networks and are generated by the protocol based on the current router configuration for OSPF and *not* on the routing table. In addition, these LSAs are flooded by the protocol on all operational OSPF interfaces. In this manner, all routers in the network receive a copy of each router's information without ever consulting the routing table. OSPF is covered in more detail in Chapter 6.

Intermediate System to Intermediate System (IS-IS)

Like OSPF, IS-IS is a link-state routing protocol. It also must maintain an identical link-state database on all routers in an IS-IS level. This once again means that import policies are not permitted and that there is no default import policy for IS-IS.

Route advertisements are also very similar to OSPF in that information is flooded throughout the network using an update packet called a link-state PDU (LSP). These LSPs are flooded throughout the network to all IS-IS routers using operational IS-IS interfaces. The difference with IS-IS, however, is how the local router populates its own LSP. In OSPF, this was accomplished via the router's configuration. For IS-IS, this information is actually retrieved from the routing table. To accommodate this difference, the default export policy for IS-IS is to export all direct routes configured for IS-IS. For more information on IS-IS, see Chapter 7.

Applying Routing Policies

Up to this point, we've talked about how to build your own routing policies, and we've examined the default policies for the protocols. We've also discussed how a network evaluates policies configured as a policy chain. We now need to examine how to actually apply these policies within the configuration so they do what we want. We start with the IGPs and finish this section with an examination of the multiple policy applications within BGP.

RIP Policy Application

Since RIP has both a default import and export policy, you may configure and apply your own policies to alter those defaults. You can apply RIP import policies at either the global or the neighbor level. This will affect routes from either all peers or a specific neighbor. Export policies, by contrast, may only be applied at the group level, allowing you to alter routing knowledge for a specific set of peers only.

Chapter 5 discusses the details about configuring RIP. For now, take a look at the syntax for applying policies:

```
protocols {
    rip {
        import [ policy1 policy2 ...];
        group test {
            export [ policy1 policy2 ...];
            neighbor fe-0/0/2.0 {
                import [ policy1 policy2 ...];
            }
        }
    }
}
```

Link-State IGP Policy Application

Policies are applied to both OSPF and IS-IS in an export fashion only. This follows the discussion in the "Default Policy" section earlier in the chapter where we said that the link-state protocols do not allow import policies to be configured. Both of the protocols apply their export policies at the global level so that all neighbors will receive the same routing information. This is also very consistent with the link-state database nature of the protocols. The basic syntax for the policy application is as follows:

```
protocols {
    isis {
        export [ policy1 policy2 ... ];
    }
    ospf {
        export [ policy1 policy2 ... ];
    }
}
```

As with RIP, you can find the details of the protocol configuration in later chapters. Chapter 6 examines OSPF, and Chapter 7 describes IS-IS.

BGP Policy Application

BGP provides you with a sort of "best of all worlds." You can utilize both import and export policies and you may apply those policies at the global, group, or neighbor level. A sample BGP configuration might look something like the following:

```
protocols {
```

```
bgp {
    import [ policy1 policy2 …];
    export [ policy1 policy2 …];
    group external-peers {
        type external;
        import [ policy1 policy2 …];
        export [ policy1 policy2 …];
        peer-as 65521;
        neighbor 1.1.1.1 {
            import [ policy1 policy2 …];
            export [ policy1 policy2 …];
        }
    }
}
```

Even this small sample seems very complex—just like everything else about BGP! We configured only one peer, but we were allowed three different places to apply import and export policies. To ensure the proper operation of the protocol, we need to make sure we understand which policies are applied to a given neighbor.

To correctly interpret which policy is applied to your BGP neighbor, simply remember that a more specific policy application always overrides a less specific application. The BGP global level is always the least-specific application. This is followed by the group-level application, then by the most-specific neighbor level. So, always start with the most-specific possibility when decoding your configuration. When you have a policy configured at the neighbor level, that policy will be applied and policies at other levels are ignored. Otherwise, look for a policy at the group level and apply any that are there, again ignoring any global policies. Finally, examine the global level of the configuration and use any policies found there. Let's look at a specific example to help sort this out:

```
[edit protocols bgp]
user@Shiraz# show
export [ set-comm prepend-as ];
group peer-as65221 {
    type external;
    import [ deny-martians find-custb ];
    export [ send-agg send-cust add-metric ];
    peer-as 65221;
    neighbor 1.1.1.1 {
        import [ deny-specifics set-lpref ];
    }
    neighbor 1.1.1.2;
```

```
    neighbor 1.1.1.3 {
        export [ set-med prepend-as ];
    }
}
group internal {
    type internal;
    local-address 2.2.2.10;
    import add-metric2;
    neighbor 2.2.2.2 {
        export send-transit;
    }
    neighbor 2.2.2.3;
    neighbor 2.2.2.4;
}
```

Here we configured two BGP groups; each group has three neighbors. We applied numerous import and export policies throughout the configuration. Let's start by examining some specific neighbors.

Neighbor 2.2.2.4 does not have any policies applied at its neighbor level, so we need to look at the group level. The group `internal` has a single import policy configured called ***add-metric2***. The router uses this configured policy followed by the default import BGP policy in its policy chain for this neighbor. This group, however, does not have any applied export policies. To locate any export policies, we need to examine the BGP global level. There we find both ***set-comm*** and ***prepend-as*** applied as export policies. These will be added to the default BGP export policy in the policy chain for this neighbor.

Neighbor 1.1.1.1 is in a different group in the configuration, so its policies may be different. This neighbor has both ***deny-specifics*** and ***set-lpref*** applied as import policies. As before, these will be combined with the default BGP import policy to complete the policy chain for this peer. While we haven't configured any export policies for this peer, three policies are configured at the group level for export: ***send-agg***, ***send-cust***, and ***add-metric***. With these policies added to the default BGP export policy, the local router has a complete policy chain to use for advertising routes to this peer.

Useful JUNOS software Commands

We've discussed the application of routing policies to the protocols and the concept of a policy chain. Let's now look at some JUNOS software commands. Both the *insert* and *rename* commands allow you to modify your configuration. Let's also examine some optional switches for the show route command that let you verify the operation of your policies.

Configuring Multiple Policies

There are two methods for configuring multiple policies within the JUNOS software. The first is to configure the individual policies one at a time, as follows:

```
[edit protocols ospf]
user@Shiraz# set export set-metric
[edit protocols ospf]
user@Shiraz# set export reject-area1
```

The second method is to configure all policies at once by enclosing the policy chain in square brackets ([ ]):

```
[edit protocols ospf]
user@Shiraz# set export [set-metric reject-area1]
```

Both options result in a configuration that looks like this:

```
protocols {
    ospf {
        export [ set-metric reject-area1 ];
    }
}
```

Many users prefer the second method of entering multiple policies at the same time since it allows you to see the policy chain order as you are creating the configuration. When you enter the policies one at a time, the last policy configured is placed at the end of the policy chain. Of course, both methods work equally well but one may save you troubleshooting time in the future.

insert

One possible drawback to the policy chain configured in the previous section is the order of the policies. For the sake of argument, let's say that the **set-metric** policy contains a terminating action that prevents routes from reaching the **reject-area1** policy. What you really wanted to do was to place the **reject-area1** policy first. The question then becomes how to change the policy chain order.

One possible solution is to delete the entire policy chain and reenter it in the proper order. This solution is quite valid but requires a lot of typing and reconfiguration. A second solution is to use the JUNOS software insert command to easily reorder the policies without a significant amount of additional work. The syntax of the insert command is:

```
[edit protocols protocol-name]
user@Shiraz# insert export policy-name1 before|after policy-name2
```

This allows you to first specify a policy to be moved, ***policy-name1***. You then decide if this policy should be placed before or after a second policy, ***policy-name2***. Let's see this command in action. Assume our configuration currently looks like this:

```
[edit protocols ospf]
user@Shiraz# show
export [ set-metric reject-area1 ];
area 0.0.0.0 {
    interface so-0/0/0.0;
    interface so-0/0/1.0;
    interface so-0/0/2.0;
}
```

Remember that we want to place ***reject-area1*** as the first in the policy chain. We enter the following command:

```
[edit protocols ospf]
userb@Shiraz# insert export reject-area1 before set-metric
```

This reorders the policy processing so that our configuration now looks like this:

```
[edit protocols ospf]
user@Shiraz# show
export [ reject-area1 set-metric ];
area 0.0.0.0 {
    interface so-0/0/0.0;
    interface so-0/0/1.0;
    interface so-0/0/2.0;
}
```

rename

Another JUNOS software command that is helpful for policy maintenance is rename. Recall that you have the ability to name your policies and terms to match their functions. If the policy is modified so that its function changes, you may want to change the name of the policy to match. This is a perfect use of the rename command. After all, without it you would be deleting your policy and retyping it all over again. Not a pretty thought!

The use of the rename command is very straightforward. Its syntax is:

```
[edit policy-options]
user@Shiraz# rename policy-statement name1 to policy-statement name2
```

The same command can be used to rename terms in a policy such as:

```
[edit policy-options policy-statement policy-name]
user@Shiraz# rename term term-name1 to term term-name2
```

Let's change the **reject-area1** policy we used earlier to the following:

```
[edit policy-options]
user@Shiraz# show
policy-statement reject-area1 {
    term area-1-routes {
        from area 1;
        then accept;
    }
}
```

We can see that the policy name no longer matches the purpose of the policy. After all, the policy is accepting routes and not rejecting them. To change the name of the policy, we enter the following command:

```
[edit policy-options]
user@Shiraz# rename policy-statement reject-area1 to policy-statement accept-area1
```

This renames the policy so that our configuration now looks like this:

```
[edit policy-options]
user@Shiraz# show
policy-statement accept-area1 {
    term area-1-routes {
        from area 1;
        then accept;
    }
}
```

 Real World Scenario

Other Uses for *rename*

While the rename command is helpful for managing policy and term names, it has other valuable uses. In the larger scope of things, this JUNOS software command can change the name of any current user-defined string in the candidate configuration. This includes interface names, unit numbers, and IP addresses.

Let's say that we've assigned the interface fe-0/0/0.0 an IP address of 10.10.10.1 /24. Because of a network topology change, we need to change this address to 172.16.10.1 /24. You enter configuration mode on the router and type:

```
[edit interfaces]
user@Shiraz# set fe-0/0/0 unit 0 family inet address 172.16.10.1/24
```

You have now added a second IP address to the interface and haven't removed the first one. In short, the JUNOS software default for family addresses is to *not* overwrite them in the configuration. The solution to this problem is to simply delete the first IP address by using:

```
[edit interfaces]
user@Shiraz# delete fe-0/0/0 unit 0 family inet address 10.10.10.1/24
```

Here's where the power of the rename command can come in handy. Just as with a routing policy, you do not have to first delete the old address and then enter the new one. You can simply rename the current address:

```
[edit interfaces fe-0/0/0 unit 0 family inet]
user@Shiraz# rename address 10.10.10.1/24 to address 172.16.10.1/24
```

This simple step is highly effective and can save you troubleshooting time in the future.

---

show route Options

Up to this point in the chapter, everything we've talked about has been focused on the local router and its policies. What we could really use now is a way to verify that our policies are working as we expect them to. Of course, we can visit the neighboring routers and examine their routing tables. Or we can use some JUNOS software options within the show route command. That sounds like more fun, so let's investigate that.

Recall that all policy processing is done from the perspective of the local routing table. This is graphically depicted in Figure 4.11. As routes are advertised to the local router, they pass through any import policies prior to being installed in the local routing table. You can view the received routes *before* the policies have been applied by using the *show route receive-protocol* command. Effectively, this is the view of your neighbor's routing table. Similarly, you can view outbound routes *after* any export policies have been applied by executing the *show route advertising-protocol* command. This shows you what your neighbor will receive from you.

These commands work very well with protocols that place and extract their routing information directly from the routing table—in other words, protocols like RIP and BGP. Recall from the discussion in the "Default Policy" section earlier that the link-state protocols flood their information in LSAs and LSPs. Since these updates do not use the routing table to propagate routing information, the advertising-protocol and receive-protocol options are ineffective. Let's use BGP to illustrate the use of these options.

FIGURE 4.11   Viewing policy results

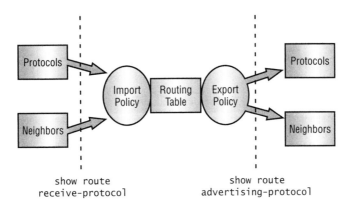

A sample network is shown in Figure 4.12. Shiraz is peering with Riesling via an internal BGP connection. Shiraz has three static routes that it is redistributing into IBGP via a routing policy called ***advertise-statics***. This policy appears in the configuration as:

```
[edit policy-options]
user@Shiraz# show
policy-statement advertise-statics {
    term find-static-routes {
        from protocol static;
        then accept;
    }
}
```

FIGURE 4.12   Sample BGP network

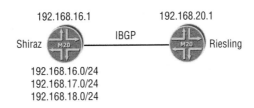

Shiraz's static routes appear in the local routing table as:

```
user@Shiraz> show route protocol static

inet.0: 13 destinations, 15 routes (13 active, 0 holddown, 0 hidden)
+ = Active Route, - = Last Active, * = Both
```

```
192.168.16.0/24    *[Static/5] 00:16:51, metric 0
                    Discard
192.168.17.0/24    *[Static/5] 00:16:51, metric 0
                    Discard
192.168.18.0/24    *[Static/5] 00:16:51, metric 0
                    Discard
```

To verify these static routes are correctly being advertised to Riesling, we use the show route advertising-protocol command:

```
user@Shiraz> show route advertising-protocol bgp 192.168.20.1 brief

inet.0: 13 destinations, 15 routes (13 active, 0 holddown, 0 hidden)
+ = Active Route, - = Last Active, * = Both

192.168.16.0/24
Self                    0           100 I
192.168.17.0/24
Self                    0           100 I
192.168.18.0/24
Self                    0           100 I
```

Remember that the default BGP export policy is to advertise only BGP routes. The appearance of these local static routes being advertised to Riesling means that the *advertise-statics* policy properly appears before the default policy in the export policy chain.

On the other side of the network, Riesling is using an import policy called *set-metric* that sets the BGP MED attribute to a value of 20. We should first verify that we are actually receiving routes from Shiraz. The output of the show route receive-protocol command displays:

```
user@Riesling> show route receive-protocol bgp 192.168.16.1 brief

inet.0: 13 destinations, 15 routes (13 active, 0 holddown, 0 hidden)
+ = Active Route, - = Last Active, * = Both

192.168.16.0/24
192.168.16.1            0           100 I
192.168.17.0/24
192.168.16.1            0           100 I
192.168.18.0/24
192.168.16.1            0           100 I
```

It appears that we are receiving the correct routes. The *set-metric* policy on Riesling appears in the configuration as:

```
[edit policy-options]
```

```
user@Riesling# show
policy-statement set-metric {
    term change-the-med-value {
        from {
            protocol bgp;
            neighbor 192.168.16.1;
        }
        then {
            metric 20;
            accept;
        }
    }
}
```

To verify that the import policy chain is working, we examine the local routing table on Riesling:

```
user@Riesling> show route protocol bgp brief

inet.0: 13 destinations, 15 routes (13 active, 0 holddown, 0 hidden)
+ = Active Route, - = Last Active, * = Both

192.168.16.0/24    *[BGP/170] 00:26:28, MED 20, localpref 100, from 192.168.16.1
                     AS path: I
                   > via so-0/0/0.0
192.168.17.0/24    *[BGP/170] 00:26:28, MED 20, localpref 100, from 192.168.16.1
                     AS path: I
                   > via so-0/0/0.0
192.168.18.0/24    *[BGP/170] 00:26:28, MED 20, localpref 100, from 192.168.16.1
                     AS path: I
                   > via so-0/0/0.0
```

Looks like the MED value has successfully been altered in our local routing table.

Summary

In this chapter, we saw how a router creates a routing table and why we might want to modify this default behavior using a routing policy. We explored how to create a policy using descriptive names and terms to ease future troubleshooting headaches. We looked at the default daisy-chain evaluation of a policy chain and how we would break out of that sequence.

We then analyzed the match conditions and actions used in a routing policy to identify routes and take some action (flow control or modification) on them. After that, we examined the default policy for each of the routing protocols. Then it came time to apply our configured policies. We analyzed the application of a policy to both the IGPs as well as BGP. Finally, we covered some of the commands available to you in the JUNOS software for managing policies.

Overall, we've seen that routing policy is an intricate part of life within a Juniper Networks environment. Throughout the course of this book, we will use routing policies again and again to enable features within the JUNOS software.

Exam Essentials

Be able to describe how routing policy manipulates the default routing behavior.   Policies consist of match/action pairs that allow you to specify routes of interest and manipulate the route properties. The policies are applied in a daisy-chain fashion to all routes in the routing table.

Understand that routing policy allows control of the network map.   Using both import and export policies controls how the local router and your neighbors view your network. Routes can be ignored, suppressed, or have attributes modified.

Know the various matching criteria available to locate a candidate route.   Various match criteria are used to locate a candidate route. Options include generic information (incoming interface), protocol-specific information (which protocol is using the route), or an individual route using a route filter.

Be able to identify the possible actions taken on a route.   Actions can suppress or advertise a route via `accept` and `reject`. They can also modify route properties and alter the default processing of a policy chain.

Understand that policy application varies for each protocol.   Each routing protocol allows its information to be modified differently. Some allow only an application at the global level while others permit per-group or per-neighbor applications.

Identify JUNOS software commands that provide for user flexibility.   Various commands allow you to rename and reorder policies as you see fit. They also provide the ability to view routes prior to and immediately after policy application.

Key Terms

Before you take the exam, be certain you are familiar with the following terms:

action	`prefix-length-range`
`exact`	`rename`
flow control action	route redistribution
`from`	route filter
`insert`	`show route advertising-protocol`
`longer`	`show route receive-protocol`
match	terminating action
match type	terms
`orlonger`	`through`
policy chain	`to`
preference	`upto`

Review Questions

1. By default, which routes are sent to an IBGP neighbor?

    A. All active routes in `inet.0`

    B. All active BGP routes

    C. All active BGP routes learned via IBGP neighbors

    D. All active BGP routes learned via EBGP neighbors

2. By default, an OSPF router will export which of the following routes from the routing table?

    A. All OSPF routes

    B. All IGP routes, including IS-IS

    C. All routes within `inet.0`

    D. No routes will be exported.

3. How would you block a route (10.0.0.0 /16) from a BGP neighbor?

    A. Apply an import policy that matches on 10.0.0.0 /16 and rejects it.

    B. Create a static route to 10.0.0.0 /16 with a next hop of `discard`.

    C. Create a firewall filter that blocks packets from that address.

    D. Apply an export policy that matches on 10.0.0.0 /16 and rejects it.

4. When is the default routing policy applied?

    A. During the evaluation of each applied policy

    B. Only when explicitly referenced

    C. At the beginning of every policy chain

    D. At the end of every policy chain

5. Why would you create an export policy? (Choose all that apply.)

    A. To send RIP routes to a RIP neighbor

    B. To suppress route advertisements

    C. To limit bandwidth to a neighbor

    D. To prevent denial-of-service attacks

6. How would you get a Juniper Networks router to advertise OSPF routes to an IS-IS neighbor?

   A. Configure an import policy under [`edit protocols ospf`] that matches OSPF routes and accepts them

   B. Configure an export policy under [`edit protocols ospf`] that matches OSPF routes and accepts them

   C. Configure an import policy under [`edit protocols isis`] that matches OSPF routes and accepts them

   D. Configure an export policy under [`edit protocols isis`] that matches OSPF routes and accepts them

7. You should use a routing policy to do which of the following? (Choose all that apply.)

   A. Suppress routes from route advertisements

   B. Discard BGP data packets

   C. Modify routes entering the routing table

   D. Ignore inbound OSPF routes

8. You can use an import policy to do which of the following? (Choose all that apply.)

   A. Ignore routes from an OSPF neighbor

   B. Ignore routes from an IS-IS neighbor

   C. Modify BGP attributes

   D. Ignore routes from a RIP neighbor

9. Which of the following would be the most specific policy application within BGP?

   A. Global level

   B. Group level

   C. Neighbor level

   D. Defaults level

10. Given the following section of code:

```
[edit protocols bgp]
lab@Shiraz# show
export [ set-comm prepend-as ];
group peer-as65221 {
    type external;
    import find-custb;
    export send-agg;
    peer-as 65221;
    neighbor 1.1.1.1 {
        import deny-specifics;
    }
```

```
    neighbor 1.1.1.2;
    neighbor 1.1.1.3 {
        export set-med;
    }
}
```

which import policy will be applied to neighbor 1.1.1.3?

A. set-med

B. deny-specifics

C. find-custb

D. send-agg

11. Given the following section of code:

```
[edit protocols bgp]
lab@Shiraz# show
export set-comm;
group peer-as65221 {
    type external;
    import find-custb;
    export send-agg;
    peer-as 65221;
    neighbor 1.1.1.1 {
        import deny-specifics;
    }
    neighbor 1.1.1.2;
    neighbor 1.1.1.3 {
        export set-med;
    }
}
```

which export policy or policies will be applied to neighbor 1.1.1.3?

A. set-med

B. deny-specifics

C. set-med and send-agg

D. set-med, send-agg, and set-comm

12. Which of the following would correctly identify all routes more specific than 10.0.0.0 /16?

A. route-filter 10.0.0.0/16 longer

B. route-filter 10.0.0.0/16 orlonger

C. route-filter 10.0.0.0/16 upto /32

D. route-filter 10.0.0.0/17 orlonger

13. Given the following section of code:

```
policy-options {
    policy-statement find-custA {
        term coming-from-neighborA {
            from {
                route-filter 10.0.0.0/16 exact;
                route-filter 10.2.0.0/24 exact reject;
                route-filter 10.1.0.0/16 longer;
                route-filter 10.0.128.0/17 orlonger {
                    metric 10;
                    accept;
                }
            }
            then {
                metric 20;
                accept;
            }
        }
    }
}
```

what will happen to the route 10.0.0.0 /17?

A. The route will be rejected.

B. The route will be accepted.

C. The route will be accepted with a metric of 10.

D. The route will proceed to the next policy for evaluation.

14. Which of the following will match on all prefixes that begin with 192.168 in the first two octets, and have a prefix length of /20–/24?

A. route-filter 192.168.0.0/20 through /24

B. route-filter 192.168.0.0/16 upto /24

C. route-filter 192.168.0.0/16 prefix-length-range /20-/24

D. route-filter 192.168.0.0/20 through 192.168.0.0/24

15. How many prefixes will match `route-filter 192.168.0.0/16 through 192.168.64/19`?

   A. 3

   B. 4

   C. 64

   D. 65

16. Which route filter would reject all routes more specific than a /24, but less specific than a /27 for the 10.0.0.0 /16 address space?

   A. `route-filter 10.0.0.0/25 upto /26 reject`

   B. `route-filter 10.0.0.0/25 through /26 reject`

   C. `route-filter 10.0.0.0/16 prefix-length-range /25-/26 reject`

   D. `route-filter 10.0.0.0/24 upto /27 reject`

17. Which command will allow you to see the effect of an export policy applied to a BGP neighbor?

   A. `show route protocol bgp`

   B. `show route protocol bgp next-hop` *address*

   C. `show route protocol bgp export-policy`

   D. `show route advertising-protocol bgp` *neighbor-address*

18. Which command will allow you to see the effect of an import policy applied to a BGP neighbor?

   A. `show route protocol bgp`

   B. `show route protocol bgp next-hop` *address*

   C. `show route protocol bgp import-policy`

   D. `show route receive-protocol bgp` *neighbor-address*

19. Given the following policy:

```
policy-statement bgp-import {
    from {
        route-filter 192.0.0.0/8 orlonger reject;
        route-filter 192.168.55.0/24 orlonger;
        route-filter 192.168.0.0/16 orlonger accept;
        route-filter 0.0.0.0/0 through 0.0.0.0/32 {
            metric 5;
            accept;
        }
    }
    then {
```

```
        metric 10;
        accept;
    }
}
```

what will happen to the route 192.168.192.0 /18?

A. It will be rejected.

B. It will be accepted.

C. It will be accepted with a metric of 10.

D. It will not match this policy.

20. Given the same policy as found in question 19, what will happen to the route 192.168.56.0 /24?

A. It will be rejected.

B. It will be accepted.

C. It will be accepted with a metric of 10.

D. It will not match this policy.

Answers to Review Questions

1. D. Only active BGP routes are advertised in BGP. In an IBGP session, only EBGP routes are sent.

2. D. By default, OSPF does not extract information from the routing table.

3. A. Import policies affect information received from network peers.

4. D. The routing protocols default policy is always applied at the end of the policy chain.

5. A, B. RIP will not send any routes by default. A policy is needed in order to send RIP routes to a RIP neighbor. Also, a policy is needed to suppress any route advertisements that would occur normally.

6. D. In order to properly redistribute routes from OSPF into IS-IS, you must create a policy that matches on OSPF routes and then export it into IS-IS.

7. A, C. You can use a routing policy to suppress routes as they are being sent to neighbors in route advertisements. You can also use a policy to modify routes as they enter the local routing table.

8. C, D. First, remember that the link-state protocols do not allow import policies. Second, inbound routing policy is used to modify routes or to ignore routes prior to being installed in the local routing table.

9. C. Within BGP, there are three main places where you can apply a policy: the global level, the group level, and the neighbor level. Of these, the neighbor level is the most specific option.

10. C. Since there is no import policy applied at the neighbor level, the router will next look at the group level. The policy *find-custb* is applied as an import policy at the group level and will therefore apply to neighbor 1.1.1.3.

11. A. Since neighbor 1.1.1.3 has a neighbor-level export policy applied, only that policy will be applied. This is due to the fact that the protocol default policy will be applied after *set-med*, which will terminate all route processing.

12. A. The longer keyword identifies all prefixes more specific than 10.0.0.0/16. If we used either the upto or orlonger keyword, the route 10.0.0.0/16 would also be included. The 10.0.0.0/17 orlonger option ignores the 10.0.128.0/17 point on the radix tree and all points more specific than it.

13. D. The route matches the first route filter since it is the longest match. The exact keyword forces the route filter to not match the criterion for the policy term so the route will drop to the next policy in the chain.

14. C. Only the prefix-length-range option allows you to specify a starting point and a range of prefixes to match. The upto option requires that the starting point be one of the matches, and the through option matches only the points that connect the ending point to the starting point.

15. B.   Remember that the `through` action matches only points that connect the starting point to the end point. This route filter would match routes 192.168.0.0/16, 192.168.0.0/17, 192.168.64.0/18, and 192.168.64.0/19.

16. C.   Only the `prefix-length-range` keyword allows you to specify a starting point and a range of prefixes that will match.

17. D.   To see routes after you have applied an export routing policy, you can use option D locally or telnet to the neighboring router and examine its routing table.

18. A.   To see the effect of an import routing policy, you need to look at your local routing table using `show route`. Using option D shows you the routes prior to your applied import policy.

19. B.   This route will first look for the longest match and find `route-filter 192.168.0.0/16 orlonger`. The route matches this route filter and executes the immediate action of `accept`.

20. B.   This route will first look for the longest match and find `route-filter 192.168.0.0/16 orlonger`. The route matches this route filter and executes the immediate action of `accept`.

Chapter 5

The Routing Information Protocol (RIP)

JNCIA EXAM OBJECTIVES COVERED IN THIS CHAPTER:

- ✓ Describe the basic characteristics of the RIP protocol
- ✓ Describe the enhancements included in the RIPv2 specification
- ✓ Define the message types used in RIP
- ✓ List the steps required to advertise routes into a RIP network

In this chapter, you'll learn about the most basic of IP routing protocols: the Routing Information Protocol (RIP). We begin with an overview of the protocol—its features and its limitations. Next, we cover the protocol's theory of operation, examine how neighbors are acquired, describe the two RIP packet types, and show you how RIPv2 solves some of the limitations of RIPv1. Finally, we look at how you can configure the JUNOS software to use RIP in the network.

In today's environment, fewer and fewer sites are running RIP for reasons that we discuss in this chapter. First, however, you need to have a basic understanding of how the protocol works.

Overview of RIP

RIP is a dynamic routing protocol that uses the shortest path computation algorithm known as the *Bellman-Ford algorithm*. RIP routers exchange routing information with their neighbors in the form of routing updates. These updates contain the length of the path to the destination (distance), as well as the address of the next router along the path (vector). RIP is also considered to be an Interior Gateway Protocol (IGP) because it is meant for intra-autonomous system routing. It is best used for homogenous networks (having similar interface speeds) of small to moderate size.

RIP has its roots in the protocols developed by Xerox at its Palo Alto Research Center (PARC). In the mid-1970s, Xerox developed the PARC Universal Protocol (PUP) for use on its experimental 3Mbps network that eventually became Ethernet. PUP was routed by another protocol called the Gateway Information Protocol (GWINFO). PUP evolved into the Xerox Network System (XNS) protocol suite, and GWINFO became the XNS Routing Information Protocol (XNS RIP). XNS RIP provided the foundation for other vendors' protocols, such as Novell's IPX RIP, AppleTalk's Routing Table Maintenance Protocol (RTMP), and, of course, IP RIP.

The evolving protocol gained large popularity when it was refined and shipped as the protocol accompanying the Berkeley Software Distribution (BSD) release 4.2 of Unix in 1982. More recent versions of the Unix operating system implement the protocol as either *routed* or *gated*. RIP's popularity led to its eventual standardization in 1988 by the Internet Engineering Task Force (IETF).

Since RIP was one of the first *distance-vector* protocols in the Internet, it will be helpful to examine its features in greater detail. Let's do that now.

RIP Standards

The use of RIP in IP networks is specified and standardized by three Requests for Comment (RFCs):

- RFC 1058, "Routing Information Protocol"

- RFC 2082, "RIP-2 MD5 Authentication"

- RFC 2453, "RIP Version 2"

RFC 1058 is the basic RFC of IP RIP (RIPv1). It specifies the limitations of the protocol, the operation of distance-vector algorithms, and features designed to stabilize the protocol. In addition, it describes the specifics of message formats, timers, and message processing. Compatibility issues, too, are discussed. Of course, this original RIP specification is over 10 years old. Two newer RFCs provide updates to the protocol's specifications.

The first is RFC 2082, which describes the use of an MD5 hash algorithm as an authentication mechanism. MD5 does provide a good security feature to protect your network, but it's only available with RIPv2.

If you want to bother with only one RFC about RIP, RFC 2453 is the one to read. This second update is the latest document to describe the extensions to the protocol. In addition to the RIPv2 enhancements, RFC 2453 contains virtually all the information from the original RIP specification, RFC 1058.

To access a particular RFC, go to `http://www.rfc-editor.org` and select the RFC Search link. You are presented with a number of criteria upon which to search. Simply enter your search criteria to find the RFC you're looking for.

RIP Features

RIP was designed to be a very "lightweight" protocol. That means that it can be operated on very basic machines (Unix hosts, for example) as well as sophisticated Internet routers. This portability between systems is due in large part to the features of the protocol:

- RIP routers use *UDP (User Datagram Protocol)* port 520 to send messages to their neighbors. UDP is sometimes referred to as "send and pray" because there is no reliable delivery mechanism inherent in UDP. In addition, the RIP specification does not provide its own mechanism for reliable delivery.

- RIP routers exchange packets with their neighbors; the packets contain network addresses and an associated metric, or hop count, to reach those addresses.

- The metric (hop count) is a measure of the distance from the source of the update to the destination network. Each hop in the path is assigned a value, which is typically 1. Most implementations (including the JUNOS software) let you alter this value.

- RIPv1 sends messages to the broadcast address (255.255.255.255) on broadcast-capable networks such as Ethernet. This means the RIP messages are sent to all devices on the subnet—including the RIP routers and all other hosts on the subnet, many of which do not need the information.

- RIP sends routing update messages at regular intervals (30 seconds) and when warranted by network topology changes.

- RIP uses an infinity metric to prevent routing loops, as described in the following section.

Infinity Metric

To prevent routing loops, the RIP protocol depends on a function known as "counting to infinity." A maximum metric (the *infinity metric*) is defined within the protocol, and all routes with a larger metric are deemed unusable. For RIP, the maximum hop count is defined as 15. If a router receives a RIP update with a metric value over 15 (that is, 16 or greater) after it is incremented, the router must throw the update away and the destination is considered unreachable.

For a closer look at the infinity metric, see Figure 5.1. Here, the routers are not implementing additional route-loop prevention measures such as *split horizon* and *triggered updates*. They are relying only on the infinity metric to stop a loop.

FIGURE 5.1   Counting to infinity: initial route advertisements

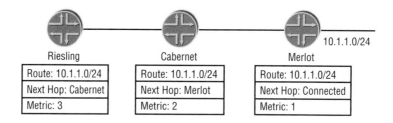

Merlot advertises the 10.1.1.0 /24 subnet to Cabernet with a metric of 1, which is in turn advertised to Riesling with a metric of 2. At this point, all three of the routers have converged on a common view of the network.

The route to the 10.1.1.0 /24 network disappears from Merlot's routing table, but before it can update its neighbors, it receives an update from Cabernet, which advertises the 10.1.1.0 /24 subnet with a metric of 2. Merlot now believes that it can reach the "lost" 10.1.1.0 /24 subnet through Cabernet and installs this route in its local routing table with a metric of 3.

Merlot now advertises its entire routing table to its neighbors again and informs Cabernet that it can reach the 10.1.1.0 /24 subnet with a metric of 3. From the perspective of Cabernet, Merlot is the current next hop for that subnet and Merlot is now advertising a larger metric of 3. Cabernet then updates its routing table to reflect this new metric. It will then advertise this new metric of 4 to all neighbors in its next update. This current situation can be seen in Figure 5.2.

FIGURE 5.2   Counting to infinity: a routing loop is formed.

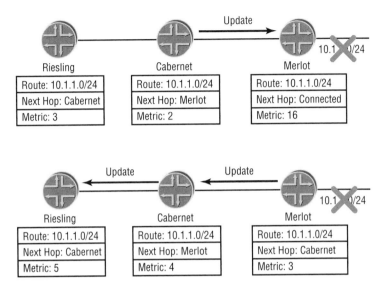

This cycle will continue until the defined infinity metric (16) is reached. At that point, all routers will agree that the 10.1.1.0 /24 subnet is unreachable and will remove it from their routing tables. Until that time, however, user data packets will still be forwarded based on this false information.

RIP Operations

Now that we have some basic terminology under our belts, we can begin looking at how RIP operates in a networking environment. We examine how a router sends and receives routing updates and look at some stability features built into RIP. A short discussion of various distance-vector timers follows. Finally, we explore some limitations of RIP and explain why many users choose not to run RIP in a large-scale network.

Input Processing

RIP routers can receive two types of messages from their neighbors: *Request messages* and *Response messages*. Each of these message types performs a specific function.

Request Messages

RIP routers receive Request messages from their neighbors. The purpose of a Request message is to ask for all or some part of the local router's current routing table. An optimum time to observe a Request message is when a router first boots up or its routing process is restarted. In this situation, the router will send a Request message to all its neighbors in order to populate its routing table as quickly as possible.

RIP routers process incoming Request messages entry by entry. Often, a Request message has a single entry in it with a metric of 16 and an address family identifier field that contains all zeros. This message translates into "Send me your entire routing table." A Request message, however, may contain one or more specific route entries. In this case, the local router consults its routing table for each of the destinations listed. If the destination is found, information about the route is sent by unicast back to the requesting router in a Response message. If the destination is not found, the metric field for the route is set to infinity (16) and is sent by unicast back to the requesting router.

Response Messages

A RIP router receives Response messages for one of three different reasons:

- In response to a Request message generated by the local router
- A regular (unsolicited) Response message sent by a neighbor
- A triggered update Response message sent by a neighbor

Regardless of the reason, all Response messages are processed in the same way. The first step performed by the local router after receiving a Response message is to validate the message by checking certain fields. For example, is the message from a valid RIP neighbor? Is the source address of the update on a directly connected network? If the answer to each of these questions is yes, then the message is accepted. Some validity checks cause the router to reject the updates. For instance, is the packet from one of the local router's own interfaces? It would not be good to process one of our own Response messages!

Next, the listed route entries are processed one by one. Each entry is checked for validity. Is the destination address of the update valid? Is the metric between 1 and 16?

Once an individual route entry is validated, the metric for that route is updated by adding to it the cost of the interface on which the message was received. The *interface cost* is usually 1. If the final metric is now larger than infinity, then the infinity metric of 16 becomes the metric.

The local router then consults its routing table to determine if there is already an explicit route to that destination. If no entry exists, then the received route is added to the table, except when the metric is currently set to infinity.

If the route does currently exist, the next-hop address of the route is checked. If the next hop of the received route is equal to the address in the routing table, the local router reinitializes the Timeout timer and compares the metrics of the two routes.

If the metric values are the same or the metric of the received route is higher, the existing route remains in the table and the router stops processing this route entry. Should the metric of the received route be lower than the current metric, then the router installs the new copy of the route with the lower metric and sends a triggered update. When the metric of the received route is the infinity metric, the local router starts the process to delete the route from the table.

Output Processing

RIP routers can both generate and send Request and Response messages. The use of Request messages for output is identical to that described in the preceding section on input processing.

A router may send a Response message to a neighbor in response to the following triggers:

- Processing of a Request message
- Expiration of the Update timer every 30 seconds (we explain Update timers in the section "Timers" later in this chapter)
- Resulting from a network topology change

Prior to sending the Response message, each route in the current routing table is examined. If the route should be included in the update due to local administrative controls, then the destination address and metric of the route are added to the message. Because of limitations in the size of a RIP packet, the Response message can contain no more than 25 entries, or routes. When there are more than 25 routes to be sent, the router must send multiple packets.

Stability Features

Modern RIP implementations include several features that add stability to the protocol. The features are all directed at minimizing the network convergence time (the time when all routers in the network have the same view). These are important features of the protocol.

Split Horizon

If Router A sends a route update to Router B that describes all of the entries in Router A's routing table, is it necessary for Router B to send that same information back to Router A? The answer is of course not; it is a waste of bandwidth. The concept of split horizon fixes this "problem." When the Update timer expires and a Response message is generated, split horizon prevents the local router from including any routes learned from a neighbor on the interface from which the message is being sent out. This technique also minimizes the time it can take to "count to infinity" because it prevents a router from advertising reachability to a down link through a neighbor that is actually further away and does not yet know the link is down.

The concept of split horizon is one simple method to solve the routing loop that we formed earlier in the chapter. In Figure 5.3, we have the same three routers—Merlot, Cabernet, and Riesling—but this time the routers are using split horizon to help prevent routing loops. The result is that Cabernet will never advertise the 10.1.1.0 /24 subnet back to Merlot. When the 10.1.1.0 /24 subnet disappears from Merlot's routing table, Merlot will not receive any updates for this route and will then be able to remove it from its routing table without forming a loop.

Split Horizon with Poisoned Reverse

The split horizon function can have additional functionality when the concept of *poisoned reverse* is added. In this case, instead of never advertising a route back to the neighbor it was learned from, the router advertises it with an infinity metric. This "poisoning" of the route provides robustness to the protocol because each router now has more information to use to make a routing decision. In the case of our routers in Figure 5.3, when 10.1.1.0 /24 is lost from its routing table, Merlot will know that Cabernet is not a viable alternate route since Cabernet will be actively advertising the 10.1.1.0 /24 subnet to Merlot with a metric of 16.

> The drawback of this process adds unnecessary protocol traffic to the network links. As such, the JUNOS software does not utilize this RIP feature.

FIGURE 5.3   Split horizon in action

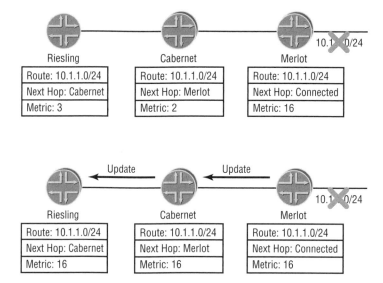

Triggered Updates

If a RIP router were to wait for a regular update interval to occur before notifying any neighbors of topology changes, the wait could be as long as 30 seconds. Clearly, this is not an optimum solution to topology-based notifications. The concept of triggered updates relaxes this timer "problem." In this case, a topology change for the local router will be announced immediately to all active neighbors. Each downstream RIP router will in turn send an almost immediate update to its neighbors using triggered updates. We say "almost immediate" because each router implements a short timer with triggered updates, which prevents the router from immediately sending multiple triggered updates individually. When a triggered update is received, the router waits for a short period of time, between 1 and 5 seconds, to see if other triggered updates arrive. If this occurs, the local router will bundle the updates and send them together to all neighbors. This reduces the computational burden of receiving and processing Response messages while helping speed the convergence of the RIP network.

Hold-Downs

The concept of a *hold-down* is not specifically mentioned in the RFCs for RIP. They are, however, widely used in routing implementations, including the JUNOS software. This real-world application is derived from one advantage of a hold-down—it prevents the propagation of bad routing information throughout the network. The *Hold-Down timer* is used when an update is received by the local router that contains a route from a peer with a higher metric (other than infinity) than the one in the current routing table. In addition, the current active route is using this peer as a next hop. In this case, a Hold-Down timer is started and the new information (with a higher metric) is not sent to the rest of the router's neighbors until the timer expires. In a sense, a hold-down has the opposite effect of a triggered update in that it slows down convergence in an attempt to ensure that only "good" routing knowledge is propagated.

Timers

RIP uses a number of timers in its operation, among them the Update timer, the Hold-Down timer, the Timeout timer, and the Garbage Collection timer.

A RIP router uses an *Update timer* to advertise its complete routing table (less split horizon) to all its neighbors. The JUNOS software uses 30 seconds as the default Update timer. Each timer cycle on the router is offset by a small random amount as it runs due to problems experienced in the past.

Randomizing Timers

Administrators of some networking environments have found that routers on a broadcast network tend to become synchronized in their updates. This has meant that all the RIP routers would process their Response messages simultaneously and attempt to transmit them all to the network. Of course, basic Ethernet theory tells us that only one packet at a time can be transmitted to the network. The multiple transmission attempts led to excessive collisions on the network, occurring every 30 seconds. Since collisions are something to avoid in a broadcast environment, vendors have randomized the timers within their software. This randomizing of timers occurs with virtually all JUNOS software timers, so we always mention the "intended" timer value without qualifying the statement by mentioning the timer randomization. What does this mean to you? If you are "sniffing" traffic on a network, don't be surprised when the actual time between packets varies on a regular basis.

We discussed the functionality of the Hold-Down timer in great detail in the previous section. Recall that it is the time a router should wait before advertising a route with a higher metric. The time value used for the Hold-Down timer within the JUNOS software is 180 seconds and is not configurable.

A RIP router uses both the Timeout and the Garbage Collection timers within the current routing table. The *Timeout timer* is used to ensure that the copy of the route is valid and usable. When the route is first installed in the table, this timer is initialized to 120 seconds, its maximum value. The timer value is updated when a Response message from a neighbor is processed and the route is maintained in the table. In this case, the timer is reset to 120. Since the Update timer runs every 30 seconds, the Timeout timer's maximum value of 120 seconds means that four RIP updates can be missed before the local router declares the route to be unusable. At this point, the metric is changed to infinity (16) and the route is advertised to all RIP neighbors.

Locally, the route is not removed from the routing table yet, and the Garbage Collection timer is initialized to a value of 0. The *Garbage Collection timer* runs to a maximum non-configurable value of 180 seconds, at which time the route will be removed from the routing table. These two timers allow the local router to have plenty of time to ensure that all downstream neighbors also know the route is down and unusable.

 **Real World Scenario**

RIP Timers in Action

While it is nice to define the various RIP timers and their values, it often doesn't make sense until you are talking about a real route. Let's explore how these timers interact with the 10.0.0.0 /8 route on a Juniper Networks router.

In our example, Router A sends the 10.0.0.0 /8 route with a metric of 5 to Router B in a RIP Response message. Router A sends this route every 30 seconds as defined by the Update timer. When Router B receives the route, it sets the Timeout timer to 120 seconds and begins to decrement it to 0. The next message from Router A (about 30 seconds later) prompts Router B to reset the Timeout timer to 120 seconds. Should Router A stop sending RIP messages, Router B waits until four update cycles have been missed, at which point the Timeout timer is at 0. Router B starts both the Hold-Down and Garbage Collection timers (both 180 seconds long), sets the metric for 10.0.0.0 /8 to 16, and places the route into holddown in the routing table. As the timers reach their maximum value of 180 seconds, the route is removed from the local routing table.

During the period of time in which a RIP route is in holddown, other RIP neighbors might advertise the same 10.0.0.0 /8 route to Router B. There are three variations on how Router B receives these routes and on its response to those messages. First, Router B receives the 10.0.0.0 /8 route with a lower metric than 5 from a neighbor on any operational interface. Router B immediately installs the new version of the route, sets the Timeout timer to 120 seconds, and advertises the new metric to all downstream neighbors.

Second, Router B receives the 10.0.0.0 /8 route with a higher metric than 5 on a different interface than the route currently in holddown. Router B waits for the Garbage Collection and Hold-Down timers to reach 180 seconds before using this new route advertisement. As the timers expire, the old version of the route is deleted and the next advertisement of the 10.0.0.0 /8 route from the new neighbor is installed in the routing table. The Timeout timer is set to 120 seconds and the route is advertised downstream.

Finally, the 10.0.0.0 /8 route is received by Router B with a higher metric than 5 on the same interface that the holddown route was received on. Router B immediately begins using this new version of the route. The Timeout timer is set to 120 seconds and the route is advertised to all downstream neighbors.

Limitations

So far, so good. We've looked at the RIP standards and some real-world enhancements in the form of timers and stability features. But why do many administrators still refuse to use RIP on a large scale? The answer lies in the various limitations of the protocol. Let's examine a few of them in some detail.

Scalability   RIP does not scale well for large networking environments. One issue is the maximum hop count used (discussed next). Another issue is the use of the 255.255.255.255 broadcast address for Response message updates in RIP version 1. On broadcast networks, this is quite disruptive to other IP (non-RIP) hosts.

Small hop count limit   Sixteen hops is the defined infinity metric that denotes an unreachable or unusable subnet. This value limits the size or "diameter" of the networks that can be built using RIP.

Slow convergence   Although triggered updates can help advertise new information into RIP, the timers can have the opposite effect. When a route needs to be removed from the protocol, the timer values for the Hold-Down, Timeout, and Garbage Collection timers can mean that a topology change at one end of the network may not be known at the other end of the network for several minutes.

Suboptimal routing   Since RIP routers utilize only the hop count as the metric, some suboptimal routing may occur. This occurs because hop count does not allow for dissimilar bandwidths, fewer delays, or less congestion on other alternate paths to a destination. When these alternate paths are available, RIP will always pick the one with the smallest hop count regardless of the interface speeds of the other path.

Nonhierarchical design   As the size of the RIP routing domain grows larger and approaches the maximum diameter of 15 routers, there is no mechanism to divide the domain into smaller, more manageable subdomains.

Classful routing protocol   RIPv1 is designed as a classful routing protocol and it does not transmit a subnet mask in the messages. The subnet masks must be assumed by one of two methods—either the subnet mask of the receiving interface address is used, or the classful network mask (that is, Class A, B, or C) is used.

Noncontiguous networks that are not visible   If a RIPv1 network has been segmented so that different subnets of the same classful network (Class B) are separated by a second classful network (Class A), the two separated sections of the Class B network will not have detailed visibility of each other. This occurs due to the automatic summarization described above.

The JUNOS software implementation does not summarize routes based on classful boundaries. Received routes are assigned a 32-bit host route mask prior to being placed in the routing table.

Variable-length subnet masks   RIPv1 routers do not support the ability to variably subnet the network using different mask lengths. This greatly limits the ability to conserve IP addressing space within a network.

Weak security   RIPv1 has no authentication mechanism available to verify that received Response messages have been sent by a "trusted" source.

Packet Types

Earlier we stated that RIP uses two packet types to send information to its neighbors:

Request   Sent to a neighbor to request that the neighbor send all or part of the neighbor's routing table. Requests are usually seen only at router startup or if the routing protocol is restarted.

Response   Sent as a reply to a neighbor's request packet or an unsolicited regular routing update. Most RIP packets are unsolicited Responses sent out at the 30-second Update timer interval.

Both the Request and the Response messages use the same packet format for all communications. So, when discussing packet types and field usage, the only real difference is whether a RIPv1 router or a RIPv2 router sends the packet.

The maximum size of an IP RIP packet is limited to 512 bytes. This means that an individual Request or Response message can contain no more than 25 entries. If a RIP router requires more space (in other words, it has more than 25 routes to send), then multiple packets must be used.

Version 1 Packet Format

RIPv1 packets are encapsulated in an UDP datagram; they contain a RIP specific header and up to 25 route entries. The format of the packet is shown in Figure 5.4.

FIGURE 5.4   RIPv1 packet format

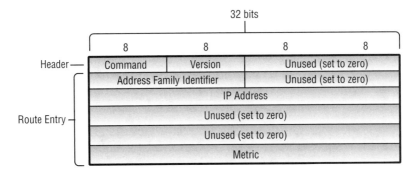

First, let's analyze the parts of the RIP header.

- The Command section comprises 1 octet. It indicates whether the packet is a Request or Response message, as follows:

  1   Request

  2   Response

  3   Traceon (obsolete)

  4   Traceoff (obsolete)

  5   Reserved

- The Version section (1 octet) is set to 1, for Version 1.
- The next section is unused and is set to 0 (2 octets).

  Now let's look at the components of the route entry portion of the packet. Each route entry consists of the following fields:

Address Family Identifier (2 octets)   This field is used to identify routing information for various protocols. It is set to 2 for IP.

Unused (2 octets)   This field is set to 0.

IP Address (4 octets)   This is the IP address of the destination network.

Unused (4 octets)   This field is set to 0.

Unused (4 octets)   This field is set to 0.

Metric (4 octets)   This field displays the number of hops traversed. The possible values are between 1 and 16, with a value of 16 representing an unreachable network.

Version 2 Packet Format

RIPv2 packets, like those in RIPv1, are encapsulated in a UDP datagram. They contain a RIP-specific header and up to 25 route entries. The format of the packet is shown in Figure 5.5.

FIGURE 5.5   RIPv2 packet format

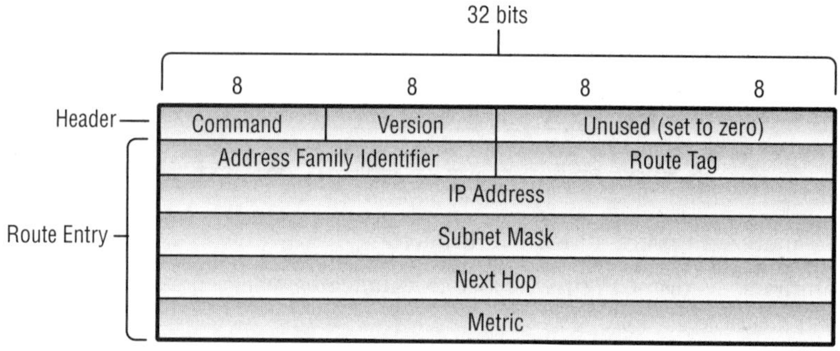

The RIPv2 header format is unchanged from RIPv1, except that the version number is now set to 2.

Each route entry in the RIPv2 packet consists of the following fields:

Address Family Identifier (2 octets)   Used to identify routing information for various protocols. Set to 2 for IP. If the Address Family Identifier (AFI) for the first entry of the packet is 0xFFFF, this field indicates that the entry contains authentication information.

Route Tag (2 octets)   Used to administratively "mark" a route. This can indicate whether the route is internal or external, or can be used in conjunction with routing policies.

IP Address (4 octets)   Contains the IP address of the destination network.

Subnet Mask (4 octets)   Contains the subnet mask of the destination network. Can also be set to 0 if no subnet mask was specified.

Next Hop (4 octets)   Contains the IP address of the next hop. Packets destined for the destination network should be sent to this address to be forwarded.

Metric (4 octets)   Provides the number of hops traversed. Its value must be between 1 and 16, with a value of 16 indicating an unreachable network.

RIPv2 Extensions

Version 2 of the RIP specification addresses some of the shortcomings of RIPv1. Since both versions use the same packet types and formats, RIPv2 is backward compatible with RIPv1. Notice that the previously unused fields in a RIPv1 packet are now used in a RIPv2 packet. If a RIPv1 router receives a RIPv2 packet, it just ignores those now populated fields. This allows version 1 and version 2 RIP routers to interoperate with each other.

Some of the enhancements that are included in the RIPv2 specification are:

VLSM support   By default, all RIPv2 Response updates include the subnet mask. This allows v2 routers to support variable-length subnet mask (VLSM) routing and provides for a classless network routing environment.

Multicast announcements   RIPv2 sends all Request and Response messages to a multicast address (224.0.0.9) instead of the 255.255.255.255 broadcast address. This provides for better scalability since only RIP-speaking routers (or hosts) need to process the packets.

Authentication   RIPv2 supports authentication by means of a password. This allows a RIP router to accept Response messages only from a "trusted" source. Although RFC 2453 specifies the use of a plain-text password only, the JUNOS software also supports the use of MD5 hashes, as defined in RFC 2082.

If you reexamine the message format of a RIPv2 packet, you will notice that authentication is communicated to neighboring routers through the use of a route entry. The AFI of the route entry is set to 0xFFFF, and the plain-text authentication password is encoded in the remainder of the fields. Therefore, the use of authentication means that any single update packet can contain a maximum of only 24 routes.

The use of MD5 authentication adds a 20-byte trailer to the length of the RIP message for encoding additional authentication data. Also, an additional route entry is used by the algorithm, reducing the total number of RIP routes to 23 in a single Response message.

Route tag   RIPv2 supports a 16-bit field called a route tag. This field was originally included to indicate whether the route was derived internally or externally to the RIP network. This field can also be used for other purposes, including administrative routing policy control.

Next hop address   RIPv2 allows the sending router to advertise the immediate next hop address for a route entry. Similar to an ICMP redirect message, this field is helpful in a broadcast environment to avoid an extra forwarding hop when the advertising RIP router is *not* the immediate next hop for the route.

JUNOS software Configuration

Now that we've covered the theory of how RIP should work, let's get to the "good stuff"—actually configuring the protocol within the JUNOS software.

By default, the RIP protocol is disabled on all Juniper Networks platforms. For a RIP router to exchange routes with other routers, you must first add RIP under the [edit protocols] section of the configuration hierarchy. Then, both RIP groups and RIP neighbors must be configured because RIP updates received from routers that have not been configured as RIP neighbors are ignored. Likewise, RIP routes are sent only to routers that have been configured as RIP neighbors. At this point, a RIP router will be able to receive all RIP routes advertised to it but will not advertise routes to any neighbors. This is caused by the default JUNOS software implementation of the RIP protocol. To have your RIP router advertise routes to any configured neighbor, you must write and apply a routing policy to your RIP configuration.

Many engineers are surprised by the defaults for RIP within the JUNOS software. Keep in mind that Juniper Networks routers were originally designed to operate in the core of the Internet. Most Internet providers are not using RIP as their IGP within their networks. These networks, however, might need to interface with a set of hosts (server farm) that is using RIP for connectivity. The JUNOS software was designed to receive those RIP routes and place them into the local routing table. From there, those routes could be redistributed into the core IGP within the provider's internal network.

Minimum RIP Configuration

A minimum RIP configuration must include at least the rip, group, and neighbor statements. All other RIP configuration statements are optional. (The term neighbor is a misnomer, by the way, in that you don't include the address of a neighbor but the name of the logical interface that connects to a neighbor or neighbors.) You include one neighbor statement for each logical interface on which you want to receive routes. The router imports all routes by default from this neighbor (that is, interface) but will not advertise any routes unless you write and apply a routing policy. Because of this, one might argue that the minimum configuration should include a policy and its relevant export statements. We explore this "enhanced" minimum configuration in the "Applying Export Policy" section later in this chapter.

Figure 5.6 shows the basic network map of the routers in the ACME Corporation network. The administrators at ACME have decided to use RIP to advertise routes in their network.

FIGURE 5.6   ACME Corporation network map

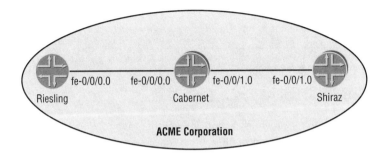

The following configuration for Cabernet allows it to receive RIP routes from both Riesling and Shiraz:

```
[edit protocols]
user@Cabernet# show
rip {
    group neighbor-routers {
        neighbor fe-0/0/0.0;
        neighbor fe-0/0/1.0;
    }
}
```

Once this configuration has been committed, we can view the operational status of RIP by using the show rip neighbor command. The results look like this:

```
user@Cabernet> show rip neighbor
                    Source         Destination   Send    Receive   In
Neighbor      State Address        Address       Mode    Mode      Met
--------      ----- -------        -----------   ----    -------   ---
fe-0/0/0.0    Up    172.16.1.2     224.0.0.9     mcast   both      1
fe-0/0/1.0    Up    172.16.2.1     224.0.0.9     mcast   both      1
```

At this point, however, none of the routers in the network have received any RIP routes. We can view all RIP routes in the routing table by using the show route protocol rip command, as follows:

```
user@Cabernet> show route protocol rip

inet.0: 10 destinations, 10 routes (10 active, 0 holddown, 0 hidden)
+ = Active Route, - = Last Active, * = Both
user@Cabernet>
```

This lack of routing information is due to the JUNOS software default for RIP route advertisements—which is to *not* advertise any routes. We need to configure some routing policies, so let's look at that next.

 **Real World Scenario**

Using RIP in the Real World

Based on the discussion in the previous section, you might be wondering what good it does you to have a router receive but not advertise RIP routes. The answer lies in what a Juniper Networks router uses RIP for—to inject routing information into the network core.

Keep in mind that the primary market for a Juniper Networks router is the core of a large network. For the reasons outlined in this chapter, RIP is not a suitable protocol for operating within the core of this environment. However, because RIP is a relatively straightforward protocol to implement, some network-capable devices communicate only with RIP—for example, a Remote Access Server (RAS) used for terminating modem dial calls.

A RAS device generates a 32-bit host route for each terminated call. Since each host route represents a user's address on the network, this reachability information needs to be advertised to the network core. Most large networks place all of their RAS devices on a single broadcast or switched infrastructure and allow each device to advertise, via RIP, which user addresses are currently connected. A router is also configured for RIP on the broadcast media to listen for these routing advertisements. The router can then redistribute the routes directly into the protocol operating in the network core. Another alternative is to configure some aggregate routes (the exact number depends on the number of RAS devices) on the router. The received RIP routes activate the aggregate route in the routing table, which is then redistributed into the network core.

Either of these options works very well with the JUNOS software RIP defaults. The RIP routes are received on the local router and are not required to be advertised to any other RIP-enabled devices in the network.

Applying Export Policy

By default, RIP does not export any routes from the local routing table to its neighbors. This includes the directly connected interfaces running the RIP protocol. To have RIP export routes, we must configure a routing policy within the [edit policy-options] portion of the configuration hierarchy. We then apply this policy to RIP at the group level.

You can define and apply more than one export policy to RIP. If no routes match any configured policies, the local router uses the RIP default policy, which does not export any routes to its neighbors. Export policies are applied after all RIP configuration options, such as metric-out, have been applied.

Let's say Cabernet would like to advertise the directly connected RIP interfaces to its neighbors. In addition, it would like to advertise transit RIP routes between Riesling and Shiraz. We have created two routing policies to accomplish these goals. We then apply these policies to RIP at the group level, as shown here:

```
[edit policy-options]
user@Cabernet# show
policy-statement connected-routes {
    term advertise-routes {
        from protocol direct;
        then accept;
    }
}
policy-statement transit-rip-routes {
    term advertise-routes {
        from protocol rip;
        then accept;
    }
}


[edit protocols]
user@Cabernet# show
rip {
    group neighbor-routers {
        export [connected-routes transit-rip-routes];
        neighbor fe-0/0/0.0;
        neighbor fe-0/0/1.0;
    }
}
```

Riesling now has knowledge of the RIP routes from Cabernet, including the routes from Shiraz:

```
user@Riesling> show route protocol rip

inet.0: 27 destinations, 27 routes (27 active, 0 holddown, 0 hidden)
+ = Active Route, - = Last Active, * = Both

172.16.2.0/24      *[RIP/100] 00:07:25, metric 2
                    > to 172.16.1.2 via fe-0/0/0.0
192.168.8.1/32     *[RIP/100] 00:07:25, metric 2
                    > to 172.16.1.2 via fe-0/0/0.0
```

```
192.168.24.1/32    *[RIP/100] 00:00:25, metric 3
                   > to 172.16.1.2 via fe-0/0/0.0
```

Applying Import Policy

The JUNOS software allows you to filter routes being imported by the local router from its neighbors. You can use import policies to reject unwanted routes or to alter the metric on routes received from certain neighbors. To accomplish these goals, you create a routing policy, which you then apply to the RIP configuration. If you specify more than one policy, they are evaluated in order (first to last) and the first matching policy is applied to the route. If no match is found, the local router imports all usable RIP routes from all neighbors.

In addition to its current configuration, Cabernet would like to reject all routes within the 192.168.0.0 /16 subnet from Riesling. In the following code snippet, we've created a policy within [edit policy-options] and applied it to only the neighbor statement for Riesling:

```
[edit policy-options]
user@Cabernet# show
policy-statement filter-Riesling {
    term filter-routes {
        from {
            protocol rip;
            route-filter 192.168.0.0/16 orlonger;
        }
        then reject;
    }
}

[edit protocols]
user@Cabernet# show
rip {
    group neighbor-routers {
        export [connected-routes transit-rip-routes];
        neighbor fe-0/0/0.0 {
            import filter-Riesling;
        }
        neighbor fe-0/0/1.0;
    }
}
```

Modifying the Incoming Metric

All routes received within a Response message from a configured neighbor will, by default, be added to the routing table if the metric is below infinity (16). Recall that the routing table metric is the sum of the advertised metric and the local metric cost. The JUNOS software default for the local metric cost is 1. You can modify this default cost on either a neighbor or global basis by using the `metric-in` command.

> **WARNING** Take care when using the `metric-in` command. Raising the metric over the default of 1 can place a limit on the distance the route can propagate. Remember that if the new metric ever becomes 16, the route will be considered unreachable.

Let's say Riesling would like all RIP routes received from Cabernet to have the metric increased by 5. So, we configure the `metric-in` command within the `neighbor` statement relating to Cabernet:

```
[edit protocols]
user@Riesling# show
rip {
    group neighbor-routers {
        export [connected-routes];
        neighbor fe-0/0/0.0 {
            metric-in 5;
        }
    }
}
```

In a previous output, the 172.16.2.0 /24 route was displayed with a metric of 2 in Riesling's routing table. After we apply the `metric-in` command, that metric increases to 6:

```
user@Riesling> show route protocol rip

inet.0: 27 destinations, 27 routes (27 active, 0 holddown, 0 hidden)
+ = Active Route, - = Last Active, * = Both

172.16.2.0/24      *[RIP/100] 00:08:25, metric 6
                    > to 172.16.1.2 via fe-0/0/0.0
192.168.8.1/32     *[RIP/100] 00:08:25, metric 6
                    > to 172.16.1.2 via fe-0/0/0.0
192.168.24.1/32    *[RIP/100] 00:01:02, metric 7
                    > to 172.16.1.2 via fe-0/0/0.0
```

Modifying the Outgoing Metric

After you've configured the appropriate policies, RIP advertises routes to neighbors configured with the `neighbor` statement. You can increase the metric of locally-generated routes on a per-group basis by using the `metric-out` command. These routes, your loopback address, and other directly connected subnets are advertised with a metric equal to the value configured using `metric-out`.

Suppose Shiraz would like all local routes advertised to Cabernet to have their current metric set to 3. Here, we've configured the `metric-out` command within the group level for Cabernet:

```
[edit protocols]
user@Shiraz# show
rip {
    group neighbor-routers {
        metric-out 3;
        export [connected-routes transit-rip-routes];
        neighbor fe-0/0/1.0;
    }
}
```

We can see this change by issuing the `show route` command on Riesling. Within the ACME network, only the loopback address of 192.168.24.1 /32 is being advertised by Shiraz into the network. This is the only route affected in the Riesling routing table.

```
user@Riesling> show route protocol rip

inet.0: 27 destinations, 27 routes (27 active, 0 holddown, 0 hidden)
+ = Active Route, - = Last Active, * = Both

172.16.2.0/24      *[RIP/100] 00:19:33, metric 6
                    > to 172.16.1.2 via fe-0/0/0.0
192.168.8.1/32     *[RIP/100] 00:19:33, metric 6
                    > to 172.16.1.2 via fe-0/0/0.0
192.168.24.1/32    *[RIP/100] 00:06:04, metric 9
                    > to 172.16.1.2 via fe-0/0/0.0
```

Configuring Authentication

By default, authentication between RIP neighbors is disabled within the JUNOS software. You can configure it globally for all peers or on a peer-by-peer basis within the `neighbor` configuration hierarchy. Authentication can be quite useful in a networking environment since RIP will accept all Response messages received on a configured interface, a practice that could be potentially dangerous.

To configure authentication, you need to use both the `authentication-type` and the `authentication-key` commands. `authentication-key` is the password to use for authentication, and `authentication-type` is the method you use to authenticate your neighbor. The JUNOS software supports two authentication methods:

Simple authentication   Uses a plain-text password that is included in the transmitted packet. The receiving router uses its configured password to verify the packet. This is not a secure method of authentication because any protocol analyzer could capture a packet and view the plain-text password. It will, however, prevent the receipt of RIP messages from "untrusted" sources.

MD5 authentication   Sends the result of a one-way hashing algorithm in the transmitted packet. The password (plain-text or encrypted) never appears "on the wire." The receiving router uses its authentication key (password) and the same algorithm to calculate its one-way hash value and compares it with the one in the packet. If they are identical, the packet is authenticated and the update will be processed. If the values differ, the router discards the packet.

In this example, all routers in our network would like to enable MD5 authentication globally for all neighbors with a configured password of **test**:

```
[edit protocols]
user@Cabernet# show
rip {
    authentication-type md5;
    authentication-key " $9$09-40hrW87Vs4xN"; # SECRET-DATA
    group neighbor-routers {
        export [connected-routes transit-rip-routes];
        neighbor fe-0/0/0.0;
        neighbor fe-0/0/1.0;
    }
}
```

Within the JUNOS software, all passwords are encrypted within the configuration files. This helps to enhance security since it prevents capture of a password through the casual viewing of a configuration file.

Controlling Route Preference

The JUNOS software default for the preference of RIP routes within the routing table is 100. The routing table uses the preference values to select the best route when multiple protocols are advertising the same destination prefix. The local router selects the route with the lowest preference value and installs it into the forwarding table. The preference value of an individual route is within the range of 0 to 4294967295 (2^{32}-1).

To modify the default RIP preference value, include the `preference` command at the group level of the RIP configuration. In the following example, Shiraz would like its local RIP routes to have a preference of 90. This configuration will alter the routes only on Shiraz because the preference value is local to each router and is not transmitted within a RIP Response message. It looks like this:

```
[edit protocols]
user@Shiraz# show
rip {
    group neighbor-routers {
        preference 90;
        export [connected-routes transit-rip-routes];
        neighbor fe-0/0/1.0;
    }
}

user@Shiraz> show route protocol rip

inet.0: 29 destinations, 30 routes (29 active, 0 holddown, 0 hidden)
+ = Active Route, - = Last Active, * = Both

172.16.1.0/24      *[RIP/90] 00:21:48, metric 2
                    > to 172.16.2.1 via fe-0/0/1.0
192.168.8.1/32     *[RIP/90] 00:21:48, metric 2
                    > to 172.16.2.1 via fe-0/0/1.0
192.168.16.1/32    *[RIP/90] 00:21:48, metric 3
                    > to 172.16.2.1 via fe-0/0/1.0
```

Configuring Update Messages

By default, all RIP routers will advertise RIPv2 messages via multicast to all configured neighbors. In addition, all routers are able to receive both RIPv1 and RIPv2 messages. You can alter the inbound defaults by using the `receive` *receive-options* command. The `send` *send-options* command alters the outbound defaults. Both of these commands are configured at either the global or the neighbor level.

The *receive-options* values are:

both   Accept RIPv1 and v2 packets.

none   Do not receive RIP packets.

version-1   Accept only RIPv1 packets.

version-2   Accept only RIPv2 packets.

The *send-options* values are:

broadcast   Broadcast RIPv2 packets (RIPv1 compatible).

multicast   Multicast RIPv2 packets.

version-1   Broadcast RIPv1 packets.

none   Do not send RIP updates.

Our ACME corporation network has been extended to communicate with a partner network that is represented by the Merlot router. This is shown in Figure 5.7.

FIGURE 5.7   ACME Corporation and partner

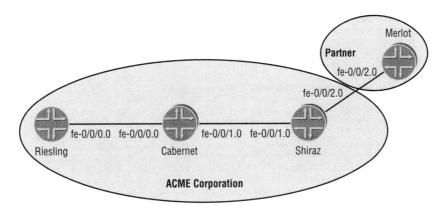

Merlot is able to communicate using the RIPv1 specification only, so Shiraz has added both the send and receive options within its neighbor statement for Merlot:

```
[edit protocols]
user@Shiraz# show
rip {
    group neighbor-routers {
        export [connected-routes transit-rip-routes];
        neighbor fe-0/0/1.0;
        neighbor fe-0/0/2.0 {
            send version-1;
            receive version-1;
        }
    }
}
```

Shiraz now communicates with Merlot using RIPv1 and with Cabernet using RIPv2. Additionally, Shiraz translates the routing updates from either neighbor into the appropriate RIP version.

Configuring the Number of Route Entries in an Update Message

You can increase the default size of the RIP Response messages to include more than 25 route entries in each Update message. The maximum number of route entries you can advertise is 255 in a single message. You can change the default by using the message-size command at either the global or the neighbor level.

For example, suppose Riesling would like to advertise a maximum of 100 route entries in a single Response message to all configured neighbors:

```
[edit protocols]
user@Riesling# show
rip {
    message-size 100;
    group neighbor-routers {
        export [connected-routes];
        neighbor fe-0/0/0.0 {
            metric-in 5;
        }
    }
}
```

Accepting Packets Whose Reserved Fields Are Nonzero

Recall that the Request and Response messages for both RIPv1 and RIPv2 were identical. The difference between them was in the use of the message fields. RIPv1 viewed many fields as reserved, while the RIPv2 specification used those same fields for subnet mask, next hop, and so forth.

An RIPv1 router expects the reserved fields to contain zeroes and will discard any received packets with nonzero values. In addition, a RIPv2 router will discard any received packet with a nonzero value in a field that must be set to zero. The JUNOS software allows you to alter this behavior so that the RIP process can receive packets that are being sent in violation of the RFC 1058 and RFC 2453 specifications. You can do this with the no-check-zero command.

Suppose Shiraz is connecting to a partner network on interface so-1/0/0.0 to a RIP router that may not adhere to the correct standards. To guarantee that all possible RIP packets will be received, Shiraz configures no-check-zero at the global RIP level:

```
[edit protocols]
```

```
user@Shiraz# show
rip {
    no-check-zero;
    group neighbor-routers {
        export [connected-routes transit-rip-routes];
        neighbor fe-0/0/1.0;
        neighbor so-1/0/0.0;
    }
}
```

Summary

This chapter discussed the operational aspects of the RIP routing protocol. We covered issues related to timers, routing loops, and protocol limitations. We also examined the protocol enhancements specified in RIPv2, including authentication, multicast updates, route tagging, specific next hops, and support for variable-length subnet masks.

After investigating how these features were designed to work, we showed you how to configure the protocol on a Juniper Networks router. We examined a basic configuration for exchanging routes in the network and included examples that showed how to activate and use configuration knobs within the JUNOS software.

Exam Essentials

Be able to describe the characteristics of a distance-vector protocol.   Each router has knowledge only of its immediate next-hop routers (the vector) and what routes are available through those routers. Each advertised route contains a metric (hop count) detailing the cost (distance) to reach the destination network.

Be able to identify the infinity metric.   The largest usable metric allowed in a RIP network is 15. A metric of 16 is considered unreachable and is defined as the infinity metric.

Know the stability features of RIP.   The operation of split horizon, triggered updates, and a Hold-Down timer is critical to avoiding routing loops in a distance-vector protocol.

Understand the timer values used in RIP.   A RIP router will advertise its entire routing table to all configured neighbors on a regular cycle. This regular update is controlled by the Update timer, which runs every 30 seconds.

Be familiar with the protocol enhancements of RIPv2. The version 2 specification for RIP contains several enhancements that allow RIP to operate in today's networking environment. Included in the update is support for VLSM, authentication, route tagging, next hop address, and multicast updates.

Know how to advertise RIP routes within the JUNOS software. The default operation of RIP within the JUNOS software is to receive routes but *not* to advertise routes. Route advertisement using RIP can be accomplished only with the use of a routing policy configured within [edit policy-options].

Key Terms

Before you take the exam, be certain you are familiar with the following terms:

Bellman-Ford algorithm	Request messages
distance-vector	Response messages
Garbage Collection timer	split horizon
Hold-Down timer	Timeout timer
infinity metric	triggered updates
interface cost	UDP (User Datagram Protocol)
poisoned reverse	Update timer

Review Questions

1. What is the defined infinity metric for RIP?

    A. 14

    B. 15

    C. 16

    D. 17

2. What distance-vector concept keeps a RIP router from advertising routes to the next-hop neighbor for those routes?

    A. Poisoned reverse

    B. Split horizon

    C. Count to infinity

    D. Hold-down

3. Which RIP function will speed convergence times in a network?

    A. Triggered updates

    B. Hold-down

    C. Split horizon

    D. Count to infinity

4. RIP updates are sent using _____.

    A. TCP port 250

    B. TCP port 520

    C. UDP port 250

    D. UDP port 520

5. Which two timers are started when the local router misses four update messages?

    A. Update

    B. Hold-Down

    C. Timeout

    D. Garbage Collection

6. RIPv2 updates are sent to a destination address of _____.

    A. 224.0.0.5

    B. 224.0.0.6

    C. 224.0.0.9

    D. 224.0.0.10

7. Which RIPv2 enhancement takes advantage of the subnet mask field in Update messages?

   A. Authentication

   B. Multicast updates

   C. Route tag

   D. Variable-length subnet masks

8. RIPv2 allows a network administrator to assign an arbitrary value to a RIP route. What function allows this?

   A. Authentication

   B. Route Tag field

   C. Next-hop address

   D. Multicast updates

9. RIPv2 is considered to be backward compatible with RIPv1. How is this accomplished?

   A. Authentication support

   B. Identical message formats

   C. Multicast updates

   D. RIPv2 is not compatible.

10. When you're using authentication, the password data is encoded within which message field?

   A. Option

   B. Version

   C. Route Tab Entry

   D. Route Entry

11. When would a RIP router send a Request message?

   A. When the routing process terminates

   B. When the routing process activates

   C. At the end of the Update timer

   D. At the end of the Hold-Down timer

12. When would a RIP router send a Response message?

   A. When the routing process terminates

   B. When the routing process activates

   C. At the end of the Update timer

   D. At the end of the Hold-Down timer

13. Which field allows RIPv2 to support VLSM?

    A. Next Hop

    B. Subnet Mask

    C. Metric

    D. Route Tag

14. What is the maximum number of route entries in a RIPv1 update?

    A. 23

    B. 24

    C. 25

    D. 26

15. What JUNOS software command allows a router to receive RIP messages?

    A. `metric-in`

    B. `metric-out`

    C. `neighbor`

    D. `export`

16. By default, the JUNOS software implementation of RIP will not advertise routes to neighbors. What will allow the router to advertise routes?

    A. Applying an import policy

    B. Applying an export policy

    C. Configuring neighbors

    D. Configuring `send` options

17. What configuration option will allow a RIP router to increase the metric of routes in a Response message from a neighbor?

    A. `no-check-zero`

    B. `message-size`

    C. `metric-in`

    D. `metric-out`

18. What two methods of authentication does the JUNOS software support?

    A. Plain-text password

    B. Authentication header

    C. MD5 hash algorithm

    D. Encapsulating payload

19. What two configuration options should be configured to allow a RIP router to communicate with a neighbor using only RIPv1?

A. message-size

B. send

C. neighbor

D. receive

20. What command should be used to advertise more than 25 routes in a Response message?

A. no-check-zero

B. neighbor

C. message-size

D. send broadcast

Answers to Review Questions

1. C.   Since the maximum hop count permitted in the RIP protocol is 15, the defined infinity metric is 1 larger than that—16.

2. B.   Split horizon is a loop-prevention mechanism that prevents a RIP from advertising routes to a neighbor if that neighbor is the active next hop for the route.

3. A.   Instead of waiting for the expiration of the Update timer before advertising any routes to neighbors, a triggered update will let a router send a Response message for a new or recently "lost" route.

4. D.   There is no reliable acknowledgment mechanism for RIP. As such, it uses the User Datagram Protocol (UDP) for all messages. Those messages are sent to port 520.

5. B, D.   When a RIP router misses four Response messages, both the Hold-Down and Garbage Collection timers are started. These timers allow all downstream routers in the network to know the route is no longer usable.

6. C.   RIPv2 messages are sent to the multicast address of 224.0.0.9. Other routing protocols, such as OSPF (224.0.0.5, 224.0.0.6) and EIGRP (224.0.0.10), use the other multicast addresses listed.

7. D.   Since the subnet mask is explicitly advertised in all RIPv2 messages, each router does not have to "assume" a mask locally. This provides support for VLSM in a RIP network.

8. B.   Like a BGP community, the Route Tag field in a RIP message allows a network administrator to assign an arbitrary value to a route. This provides a method for "tagging" a route for the purposes of routing policy.

9. B.   Both RIPv1 and RIPv2 use the same message formats. This allows the protocols to interoperate and provides for backward compatibility.

10. D.   RIPv2 authentication data is passed to all neighbors in a Route Entry field. The AFI of the entry is set to 0xFFFF, with the remaining fields containing the configured password.

11. B.   When the routing process activates, a RIP router will send a Request message to all neighbors asking for their entire routing table.

12. C.   Response messages can be sent for a variety of reasons, but often they are a result of the Update timer expiring.

13. B.   The Subnet Mask field in a RIPv2 update message provides support for VLSM.

14. C.   Since RIPv1 does not support authentication, at most 25 route entries can be advertised in a Response message.

15. C.   A RIP router will not receive or send messages until the `neighbor` command is configured. Recall that the interface must be used as the variable for this command.

16. B.   Until a routing policy is configured within `policy-options` and applied within the RIP hierarchy, a RIP router will only receive routes; no routes will be advertised prior to this occurring.

17. C. By default, a RIP router will increase by 1 the metric of all received routes. To increase this value, use the `metric-in` command, which you can configure at either the global or the neighbor level.

18. A, C. While the RIP RFCs specify support only for a plain-text password, the JUNOS software also allows a network administrator to use a MD5 hash algorithm. This provides better security in a network since only messages from "trusted" neighbors will be accepted.

19. B, D. By default, a Juniper Networks router will send RIPv2 messages. It will receive both version 1 and version 2 messages. To alter this default, use both the `send` and `receive` commands. The options for these commands will allow the router to send version 1 messages as well as receive version 1 messages.

20. C. To increase the number of route entries in an update message, use the `message-size` command. This will allow up to 255 entries to be sent in a single message.

Chapter

6

Open Shortest Path First (OSPF)

JNCIA EXAM OBJECTIVES COVERED IN THIS CHAPTER:

- ✓ Define the functions of OSPF packet types
- ✓ Define the functions of OSPF area types
- ✓ Define the functions of OSPF router types
- ✓ Identify the steps required to form an OSPF adjacency
- ✓ Identify the election criteria for an OSPF DR
- ✓ Describe the functions of the DR and BDR
- ✓ Identify CLI commands used to monitor and troubleshoot an OSPF network

In this chapter, we examine the Open Shortest Path First (OSPF) routing protocol. You'll get a high-level view of the protocol design, but we also discuss basic configuration and trouble-shooting commands used in a Juniper Networks environment.

We start by taking a look at how a link-state routing protocol provides interconnectivity within a network, exploring the underlying principles that govern how OSPF determines the best path to a destination. We follow this with a detailed discussion of the OSPF packet types and how two OSPF neighbors form an adjacency. We examine the evolution of an OSPF network and look at several methods that allow you to scale your OSPF deployment. This includes a review of OSPF link-state advertisements (LSAs), types of OSPF areas, and the various router designations within an OSPF network.

Throughout the chapter, we look at useful JUNOS software commands used to implement an OSPF network. Finally, we review some helpful troubleshooting and verification commands you can use.

Basic OSPF Operation

Before delving into the specific details of OSPF, let's look at the theory behind its operation as well as the overall goals of the protocol. First, we discuss how a router utilizes a link-state routing protocol, and then we examine the exchange of link-state databases. We also discuss how the router uses the database to find a path to each destination.

Link-State Protocol Review

Once a link-state router begins operating on a network link, information associated with that logical network is added to its local *link-state database*. The local router then sends Hello messages on its operational links to determine whether other link-state routers are operating on the interfaces as well. When a remote router is located, the local router attempts to form an adjacency. This adjacency enables the two routers to advertise summary link-state database information to each other. This exchange is not the actual detailed database information, but is truly a summary of the data. Each router evaluates the summary data against its local link-state database to verify that it has the most up-to-date information. Should one side of the adjacency realize that it requires an update, that router requests the new information from the adjacent router. The update includes the actual data contained in the link-state database. This exchange process continues until both routers have identical link-state databases.

This common view of the link-state database forms the basis of the network topology. Each router uses the *Dijkstra Algorithm* to process the database information into a path to each destination in the network. Every link-state router uses the same algorithm to process its database, requiring each router to maintain consistent information to get the same results. This concept of a consistent database is a core requirement for link-state protocols and allows the protocols to ensure a loop-free topology. Since no loops exist, each router then makes consistent forwarding decisions for user data packets. Ensuring the proper advertisement of link-state updates and propagating these updates correctly are the only barriers to preventing loops.

OSPF Defined

The IETF has written numerous documents to define the behavior of routing protocols. This ensures that vendor implementations are consistent and interoperable. OSPF is no exception to this rule. The OSPF working group was formed in 1987 and has released numerous Requests for Comment (RFC), including RFC 1247, "OSPF Version 2," which describes the routing behavior of OSPFv2, the basic foundation of the protocol. The most up-to-date RFC is published as RFC 2328, "OSPF Version 2," and contains all the latest updates and modifications to the protocol. It is backward-compatible with each of the previous documents that specify OSPFv2.

Some of the more interesting RFCs include:

- RFC 1131, "OSPF Specification," describes the first iteration of OSPF and was used in initial tests to determine whether the protocol worked. This RFC led to the creation of two working code bases that were used in test beds.

- RFC 1247, "OSPF Version 2," addresses a number of issues discovered during the initial rollout of OSPFv1 and modified the protocol to allow for future modifications without generating backward-compatibility issues. OSPFv2 is not compatible with OSPFv1.

- RFC 1584, "Multicast Extensions to OSPF," provides extensions to OSPF for the support of multicast IP traffic.

- RFC 1587, "The OSPF NSSA Option," describes the operations of a not-so-stubby area.

- RFC 1850, "OSPF Version 2 Management Information Base," allows network management of OSPF using the Simple Network Management Protocol (SNMP).

- RFC 2328, "OSPF Version 2," details the latest update to OSPFv2.

For a complete list of all RFCs pertaining to OSPF, please refer to the IETF website at www.ietf.org.

Packet Types

We now examine the basic components that allow OSPF to communicate and distribute the information needed to determine routes to all end destinations. After discussing the packet header, we offer a detailed look at the structure of the five packet types used in OSPF.

Common Packet Header

All OSPF packets share a common 24-octet header. This header allows the receiving router to determine whether the packet is valid and should be processed.

Figure 6.1 shows the OSPF header fields, which include the following:

Version (1 octet)   This field details the current version of OSPF used by the local router. It is set to a value of 2, the default value.

Type (1 octet)   This field specifies the type of OSPF packet. Possible values include:

- 1—Hello packet
- 2—Database descriptor
- 3—Link-state request
- 4—Link-state update
- 5—Link-state acknowledgment

Packet Length (2 octets)   This field displays the total length, in octets, of the OSPF packet.

Router ID (4 octets)   The router ID of the advertising router appears in this field.

Area ID (4 octets)   This field contains the 32-bit area ID assigned to the interface used to send the OSPF packet.

Checksum (2 octets)   This field displays a standard IP checksum for the entire OSPF packet, excluding the 64-bit authentication field.

Authentication Type (2 octets)   The specific type of authentication used by OSPF is encoded in this field. Possible values are:

- 0—Null authentication
- 1—Simple password
- 2—MD5 cryptographic authentication

Authentication (8 octets)   This field displays the authentication data to verify the packet's integrity.

Hello Packet

To establish and maintain a neighbor relationship, an OSPF-speaking router determines whether any directly connected routers also speak OSPF. The router sends an *OSPF hello packet* out all configured interfaces and awaits a response. The hello packet, type code 1, is addressed to the AllSPFRouters multicast address of 224.0.0.5 for broadcast and point-to-point connections. Other connection types unicast the hello packet to their neighbor. Figure 6.2 details the format of the hello packet.

FIGURE 6.1   The OSPF common header

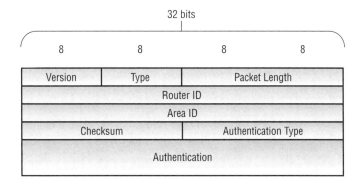

FIGURE 6.2   The OSPF hello packet

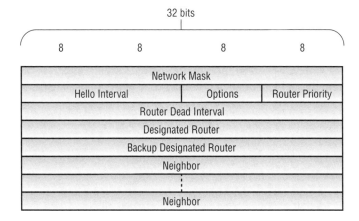

The packet includes the following fields:

Network Mask (4 octets)   This field contains the subnet mask of the advertising OSPF interface. Unnumbered point-to-point interfaces and virtual links set this value to 0.0.0.0.

Hello Interval (2 octets)   This field displays the value of the *hello interval* requested by the advertising router. Possible values range from 1 to 255, with a default value of 10 seconds.

Options (1 octet)   The local router advertises its capabilities in this field. Each bit in the Options field represents a different function. The various bit definitions are:

   Bit 7   The DN bit is used for loop prevention in a Virtual Private Network (VPN) environment. An OSPF router receiving an update with the bit set does not forward that update.

Bit 6 The O bit indicates that the local router supports opaque LSAs.

Bit 5 The DC bit indicates that the local router supports Demand Circuits. The JUNOS software does not use this feature.

Bit 4 The EA bit indicates that the local router supports the External Attributes LSA for carrying BGP information in an OSPF network. The JUNOS software does not use this feature.

Bit 3 The N/P bit describes the handling and support of not-so-stubby LSAs.

Bit 2 The MC bit indicates that the local router supports multicast OSPF LSAs. The JUNOS software does not use this feature.

Bit 1 The E bit describes the handling and support of external LSAs.

Bit 0 The T bit indicates that the local router supports TOS routing functionality. The JUNOS software does not use this feature.

Router Priority (1 octet) This field contains the priority of the local router. The value is used in the election of the designated router and backup designated router. Possible values range from 0 to 255, with a default value of 128.

Router Dead Interval (4 octets) This field shows the value of the *dead interval* requested by the advertising router. Possible values range from 1 to 65,535. The JUNOS software uses a default value of 40 seconds.

Designated Router (4 octets) The interface address of the current designated router is displayed in this field. A value of 0.0.0.0 is used when no designated router has been elected.

Backup Designated Router (4 octets) The interface address of the current backup designated router is displayed in this field. A value of 0.0.0.0 is used when no backup designated router has been elected.

Neighbor (Variable) This field displays the router ID of all OSPF routers for which a hello packet has been received on the network segment.

 The hello packet does not use all of the bit values defined in the Options field description above. We have included the definitions here as a reference guide.

Waiting on OSPFv3

One reason for moving to version 3 of OSPF is scalability of the protocol. Each time we need a new OSPF feature, we have to assign it a bit in the Options field. We already have bits assigned for multicast LSA, opaque LSA, TOS routing, and so forth. The problem is simple; we've used up all the bits in the Options field. As a result, the network community is having a difficult time scaling the protocol and adding new functionality.

Database Description Packet

After discovering its neighbors, the local router begins to form an adjacency with each neighbor (as discussed in the "Forming Adjacencies" section later in this chapter). This adjacency process requires that each router advertise its local database information. An OSPF router uses the *Database Description (DD) packet* for this purpose.

The DD packet, type code 2, summarizes the local database by sending LSA headers to the remote router. The remote router analyzes these headers to determine whether it lacks any information within its own copy of the link-state database. Figure 6.3 details the format of the DD packet.

FIGURE 6.3   The OSPF Database Description packet

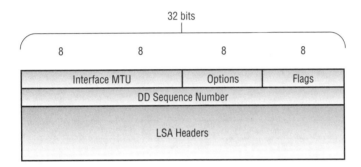

The fields include the following:

Interface MTU (2 octets)   This field contains the MTU value, in octets, of the outgoing interface. When the interface is used on a virtual link, the field is set to a value of 0x0000.

Options (1 octet)   The local router advertises its capabilities in this field. The bit values are discussed in the "Hello Packet" section earlier in this chapter.

Flags (1 octet)   This field provides an OSPF router with the capability to exchange multiple DD packets with a neighbor during an adjacency formation. The flag definitions include the following:

Bits 3 through 7   These bit values are currently undefined and must be set to a value of 0.

Bit 2   The I bit, or Initial bit, designates whether this DD packet is the first in a series of packets. The first packet has a value of 1, while subsequent packets have a value of 0.

Bit 1   The M bit, or More bit, informs the remote router whether the DD packet is the last in a series. The last packet has a value of 0, while previous packets have a value of 1.

Bit 0   The MS bit, or Master/Slave bit, is used to indicate which OSPF router is in control of the database synchronization process. The master router uses a value of 1, while the slave uses a value of 0.

DD Sequence Number (4 octets)   This field guarantees that all DD packets are received and processed during the synchronization process through use of a sequence number. The Master router initializes this field to a unique value in the first DD packet, with each subsequent packet being incremented by 1.

LSA Headers (Variable)   This field carries the LSA headers describing the local router's database information. Each header is 20 octets in length and uniquely identifies each LSA in the database. Each DD packet may contain multiple LSA headers.

Link-State Request Packet

During the database synchronization process, the local router may find that it is missing information or that its local copy is out of date. The local router acquires the needed database information by sending a *link-state request packet* to its neighboring router. This packet contains identifiers that uniquely describe the requested LSA. An individual link-state request packet may contain either a single set of identifiers or multiple sets to request multiple LSAs. The format of the link-state request packet, type code 3, is shown in Figure 6.4.

FIGURE 6.4   The OSPF link-state request packet

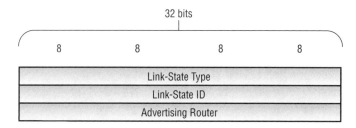

The unique LSA identifiers are:

Link-State Type (4 octets)   This field displays the type of LSA being requested. The possible type codes include:

- 1—Router LSA
- 2—Network LSA
- 3—Network summary LSA
- 4—ASBR summary LSA
- 5—AS external LSA
- 6—Group membership LSA
- 7—NSSA external LSA
- 8—External attributes LSA
- 9—Opaque LSA (link-local scope)
- 10—Opaque LSA (area scope)
- 11—Opaque LSA (AS scope)

Link-State ID (4 octets)   This field encodes information specific to the LSA. Each different type of advertisement places different information here.

Advertising Router (4 octets)   The router ID of the OSPF router that first originated the LSA is encoded in this field.

Link-State Update Packet

Information in the link-state database is populated through a *Link State Advertisement (LSA)*. Each LSA contains routing, metric, and topology information to describe a portion of the OSPF network. The local router advertises LSAs within a *link-state update* packet to its neighboring routers. This packet is reliably flooded throughout the network until each router has a copy. In addition, the local router advertises a link-state update packet in response to a link-state request for information. A link-state update, type code 4, is shown in Figure 6.5.

FIGURE 6.5   The OSPF link-state update packet

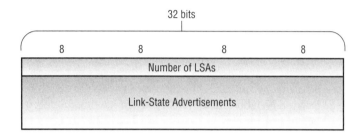

The two fields in the packet are:

Number of LSAs (4 octets)   This field displays the number of LSAs carried within the link-state update packet.

Link-State Advertisements (Variable)   The complete LSA is encoded within this variable-length field. Each type of LSA has a common header format along with specific data fields to describe its information. A link-state update may contain a single LSA or multiple LSAs.

Link-State Acknowledgment Packet

The *reliable* part of the OSPF reliable flooding paradigm arises from the fact that each router is required to explicitly acknowledge the receipt of each LSA. The local router accomplishes this with the *link-state acknowledgment* packet. The packet, type code 5, simply contains the common OSPF header followed by a list of LSA headers. This variable-length field allows the local router to acknowledge multiple LSAs using a single packet. Figure 6.6 displays the format of the link-state acknowledgment packet.

FIGURE 6.6   The OSPF link-state acknowledgment packet

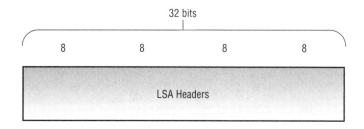

Forming Adjacencies

Now that we've discussed the specific OSPF packet types, let's explore their usage during the formation of an adjacency. This allows us to understand the interaction of the packet types as well as what the specific portions of the packets actually do.

Adjacency States

During the adjacency formation process, two OSPF routers transition through several states prior to becoming operational neighbors. The possible states include:

Down *Down* is the starting state for all OSPF routers. A start event, such as configuring the protocol, transitions the router to the Init state. The local router may list a neighbor in this state when no hello packets have been received within the specified router dead interval for that interface.

Init The *Init* state is reached when an OSPF router receives a hello packet but the local router ID is not listed in the received Neighbor field. This means that bidirectional communication has not been established between the peers.

Attempt The *Attempt* state is valid only for Non-Broadcast Multi-Access (NBMA) networks. It means that a hello packet has not been received from the neighbor and the local router is going to send a Unicast hello packet to that neighbor within the specified hello interval period.

2-Way The *2-Way* state indicates that the local router has received a hello packet with its own router ID in the Neighbor field. Thus, bidirectional communication has been established and the peers are now OSPF *neighbors*.

ExStart In the *ExStart* state, the local router and its neighbor establish which router is in charge of the database synchronization process. The higher router ID of the two neighbors controls which router becomes the master.

Exchange In the *Exchange* state, the local router and its neighbor exchange DD packets that describe their local databases.

Loading Should the local router require complete LSA information from its neighbor, it transitions to the *Loading* state and begins to send link-state request packets.

Full The *Full* state represents a fully functional OSPF adjacency, with the local router having received a complete link-state database from its peer. Both neighboring routers in this state add the adjacency to their local database and advertise the relationship in a link-state update packet.

These OSPF neighbor states can be seen in Figure 6.7.

FIGURE 6.7   Forming an OSPF adjacency

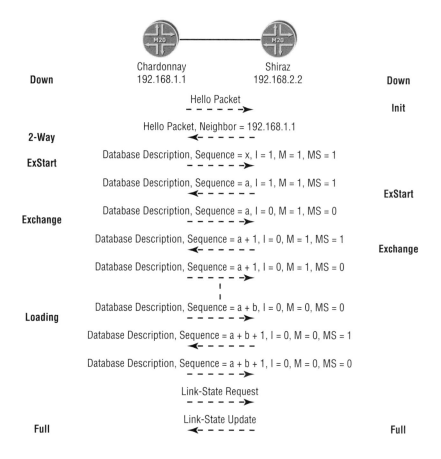

Down	Chardonnay 192.168.1.1	Shiraz 192.168.2.2	Down

Hello Packet
- - - - - ➤

Init

Hello Packet, Neighbor = 192.168.1.1
◄- - - - -

2-Way

Database Description, Sequence = x, I = 1, M = 1, MS = 1
- - - - - ➤

ExStart

Database Description, Sequence = a, I = 1, M = 1, MS = 1
◄- - - - -

ExStart

Database Description, Sequence = a, I = 0, M = 1, MS = 0
- - - - - ➤

Exchange

Database Description, Sequence = a + 1, I = 0, M = 1, MS = 1
◄- - - - -

Exchange

Database Description, Sequence = a + 1, I = 0, M = 1, MS = 0
- - - - - ➤
I
I

Database Description, Sequence = a + b, I = 0, M = 0, MS = 0
- - - - - ➤

Loading

Database Description, Sequence = a + b + 1, I = 0, M = 0, MS = 1
◄- - - - -

Database Description, Sequence = a + b + 1, I = 0, M = 0, MS = 0
- - - - - ➤

Link-State Request
- - - - - ➤

Link-State Update

Full   ◄- - - - -   **Full**

Figure 6.7 shows a generalized adjacency formation process and is not meant to represent every possible scenario in an OSPF network.

Example OSPF Adjacency

Figure 6.7 shows the Shiraz router with a complete link-state database. The Chardonnay router is configured and initialized into the network. The following steps then occur:

1. Chardonnay initiates the conversation by sending a hello packet to Shiraz using the 224.0.0.5 multicast address. The DR and BDR fields are set to 0.0.0.0 and the Neighbor field is empty because Chardonnay has yet to receive any OSPF packets from Shiraz.

2. Shiraz transitions to the Init state (bidirectional communication has not been established) and responds to Chardonnay with a hello packet. Shiraz lists the router ID of Chardonnay, 192.168.1.1, in the Neighbor field of the packet and sets the DR and BDR fields to 0.0.0.0.

3. Chardonnay briefly transitions to the 2-Way state (bidirectional communication has been established), but quickly moves to the ExStart state. Chardonnay and Shiraz are now OSPF neighbors. At this point, Chardonnay sends a DD packet to Shiraz. The flags of the DD packet are set to negotiate the Master/Slave relationship to determine which router controls the synchronization process. The I bit, the M bit, and the MS bit are all set to 1; Chardonnay is starting the conversation, has more information to send, and is going to control the conversation. In addition, a sequence number (x) is chosen to identify the DD packets in this conversation.

4. Shiraz has a higher router ID (192.168.2.2) than Chardonnay and should be the Master for the process. It therefore responds with its own DD packet using a different sequence number (a). Shiraz also sets the I, M, and MS bits to 1 to designate its role in the synchronization process.

5. Chardonnay recognizes Shiraz's higher router ID and role as the Master by generating a new DD packet containing the sequence number advertised by Shiraz (a) and having both the MS and I bits set to 0. At this time, Chardonnay transitions to the Exchange state.

6. Having completed the Master/Slave negotiation process, Shiraz also transitions to the Exchange state and begins sending DD packets with higher sequence numbers that contain the database information.

7. Chardonnay acknowledges the receipt of all DD packets by sending its own DD packets with the same sequence number. These new DD packets contain the information in Chardonnay's link-state database. As each router receives a DD packet, it notes which LSA headers in the received packet are not in its own local database. This header information is contained in a memory structure called the *link-state request list*.

8. Shiraz receives a DD packet with the M bit set to 0, which indicates that Chardonnay has sent all of the information in its database. Shiraz examines its link-state request list and finds no entries. It then transitions to the Full state and continues sending DD packets to Chardonnay.

9. Chardonnay continues to advertise DD packets with the M bit set to 0 to Shiraz as acknowledgments. This indicates that it is still receiving DD packets from Shiraz and potentially adding information to its link-state request list. When Shiraz finally sends a DD packet with the M bit set to 0, Chardonnay examines its request list and finds multiple headers for which it needs information.

10. Chardonnay transitions to the Loading state and begins requesting its missing data structures using link-state request packets. It receives the needed information from Shiraz in the form of a link-state update packet. This process continues until Chardonnay has emptied the link-state request list, at which point it transitions to the Full state.

After both peers reach an OSPF adjacency state of Full, they maintain that adjacency using hello packets at the specified hello interval. Changes to the link-state database on either router are advertised using a link-state update; reliability is assured with a link-state acknowledgment packet.

Real World Scenario

Troubleshooting an Adjacency Formation

We've taken a fairly quick look at the formation of an OSPF adjacency. When everything is operating properly, forming an adjacency is quite simple. Unfortunately, things can sometimes be different in the real world. Let's look at three possible scenarios where your adjacency does not get to the Full state.

When an OSPF router first receives a hello packet, it verifies that the data in some fields matches its own locally configured information. Should any of the checked data be different, the hello packet is discarded and not processed. The data fields verified are the Area ID, Authentication, Network Mask (on broadcast networks), Hello Interval, Router Dead Interval, and Options fields. In situations where this information differs, the neighbor remains in the Down state because it can't process your advertised hello. These types of neighbors are not visible with any JUNOS software show command.

Firewalls and packet filters often cause OSPF to have trouble forming a neighbor relationship. For example, say the remote router you're trying to form an adjacency with has an inbound filter applied to its loopback interface. This filter allows only diagnostic pings and Secure Shell (SSH) traffic into the router for security reasons. Unfortunately for you, your partner forgot about allowing the IP routing protocols through the filter. In this situation, the remote router sends you a hello packet. You do not see your router ID in the Neighbor field and transition to the Init state. You then generate your own hello packet and send it to your neighbor, who doesn't receive it because of the filter. At the expiration of the hello interval, the remote router sends another hello packet to you. Again, your router ID is not listed in the Neighbor field. You remain in the Init state and send your own hello packet to the remote router. This process continues until the filter is altered on the remote router to allow OSPF packets (protocol ID 89) through.

Finally, your OSPF adjacency might get stuck in the ExStart state. This occurs due to a final check the routers perform. In the DD packet, each router advertises the IP MTU of the interface it is using. Should the local and remote routers not agree on the MTU of the network link, the database synchronization process stops and both neighbors remain in the ExStart state. This increases the robustness of the protocol because fragmentation of the OSPF packets no longer occurs. In an environment where both peers have the same interface type and default MTU settings, this situation rarely occurs. One classic example of this scenario is when two peers are connected using a Frame Relay–to–ATM connection. One peer uses Frame Relay encapsulation while the other peer is using ATM encapsulation. The intervening carrier makes the transition from one encapsulation type to the other. The default MTUs for these links do not match, and the OSPF adjacency sticks in the ExStart state unless you manually change one side or the other.

Evolution of an OSPF Network

We've now examined how a link-state protocol operates at a high level. In addition, we explored how OSPF forms neighbor relationships and synchronizes its link-state databases. We now need to look at the actual data within the database itself. This information is encoded within an LSA.

To help you correlate the LSA types with their use, we'll base our discussion on a sample network. This allows us to see how the LSA advertises the status of a router and its connected subnets. Other discussion points include scaling your OSPF network and advertising external routing information. Let's start with the basics first.

The Router LSA

The first step in building an OSPF network is advertising the networks connected to the local router. This information is contained in the *router LSA*, type code 1, which displays data about the local router. This includes all links connected to the router, the metrics of those interfaces, and the OSPF capabilities of the router.

> Throughout the remainder of this chapter, we follow the common industry nomenclature by referring to LSAs by both their name (router LSA) as well as their type code (Type 1 LSA).

Figure 6.8 shows two routers, Shiraz and Chardonnay, in an OSPF network. Each generates a router LSA and places it into its local database. After becoming adjacent, both Shiraz and Chardonnay flood the Type 1 LSA to each other. This describes the directly connected networks of the router, including the loopback interfaces.

FIGURE 6.8   Exchanging router LSAs

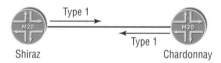

This is a fairly simple example, but consider a larger network consisting of multiple routers, as depicted in Figure 6.9.

As Shiraz now floods its Type 1 LSA into the network, Chardonnay re-floods the LSA to its connected neighbors. This is the expected behavior of a link-state protocol, because each router must maintain an identical link-state database. Figure 6.9 shows the router LSA only for Shiraz, but a similar procedure occurs for each router in the network. The end result is that each router has nine Type 1 LSAs in its local database, one for each router.

FIGURE 6.9   Flooding the router LSA

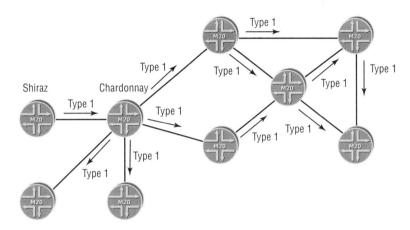

Broadcast Networks

In the "Forming Adjacencies" section earlier in this chapter, we discussed how two OSPF routers become neighbors. Each set of connected routers performs this peer-to-peer process. Broadcast segments in a network, such as an Ethernet link, pose a special problem to link-state protocols and their peer-to-peer nature. Multiple routers on the same physical segment share the resources of that link and produce a lot of redundant information.

Figure 6.10 shows an Ethernet segment with five routers physically attached: Sangria, Chardonnay, Cabernet, Shiraz, and Merlot. Each router on the segment sees an OSPF hello packet from all other routers because the packet is addressed to 224.0.0.5, AllSPFRouters. This prompts each router to form an adjacency with every other router on the segment, as seen in Figure 6.10. This default behavior results in 10 separate adjacencies formed for this single broadcast link.

FIGURE 6.10   OSPF peering on broadcast media

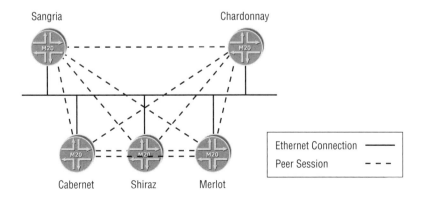

The ramifications of this process are twofold. First, each router reports the same set of information, the Ethernet link, to the rest of the OSPF network. Second, and perhaps more damaging, every router floods LSAs to each of its adjacent neighbors using the 224.0.0.5 multicast address. Using Figure 6.10 as a reference, assume that the Shiraz router receives a router LSA from some other router in the network. Shiraz floods that router LSA to each of its neighbors: Sangria, Chardonnay, Cabernet, and Merlot. Each of the four LSAs used the multicast destination address, so each router received the exact same LSA four times. To complicate matters, each of the four receiving routers re-floods the LSA to each of its adjacent neighbors, causing the duplication process to continue. This is clearly not an effective use of resources.

Designated Routers

OSPF avoids these problems through the use of a router known as the *designated router (DR)*. Each broadcast segment in an OSPF network elects a designated router to act as the main point of contact for the network segment. Each router on the link must become adjacent with the DR, which handles all LSAs for the network. Each router sends the DR information using a new multicast destination address of 224.0.0.6, AllDRRouters. The designated router generates a *network LSA*, type code 2, to represent the broadcast segment to the rest of the network. Like the router LSA, the Type 2 LSA has an area-flooding scope ensuring that each router in the area receives a copy for the link-state database.

The use of a designated router virtually eliminates the excess flooding of LSAs on the segment at the expense of introducing a single point of failure—the DR itself. Avoiding this potential pitfall requires the election of another router on the segment, the *backup designated router (BDR)*. The BDR also listens to the 224.0.0.6 multicast address and monitors the operations of the DR. Additionally, the BDR forms a Full adjacency relationship with all other routers on the segment. Should a problem arise with the designated router, the BDR immediately assumes the role of the DR for the segment. This mechanism provides for stability in the network.

Figure 6.11 displays the adjacencies formed on a broadcast segment when the DR (Sangria) and BDR (Chardonnay) routers are operational. While the total number of adjacencies didn't drop dramatically—from 10 to 7—the savings in LSA flooding is what proves useful in this environment. When the Shiraz router now receives a router LSA from some other router in the network, it floods it only to the 224.0.0.6 address for the DR and the BDR. The designated router re-floods the LSA to the segment using the 224.0.0.5 address. Because each of the routers has an adjacency only with the DR/BDR pair, no further flooding of the LSA across the segment is needed, preserving the resources of the network.

DR Elections

Although the designated router is a logical responsibility, it is in fact an actual router on the broadcast segment. Some process is required to determine which router should assume this responsibility. This is the function of the designated router election.

A DR election occurs when no operational designated router is present. This information is gleaned from the hello packet field where the current DR address is encoded. The election of a DR is based on two separate criteria: the *router ID* and the *router priority* of each router. An

OSPF hello packet, complete with header, provides the required data. The router priority of all participating routers is examined first, with the highest priority router becoming the DR. Any router reporting a priority value of 0 is ineligible to become either the DR or the BDR. In the event of a priority tie, the router ID of each router is then examined. Again, the highest value results in that router becoming the designated router.

Once a DR is elected for the segment, the remaining routers then elect the backup designated router for redundancy. The same criteria are used for this process—the router priority followed by the router ID. The failure of the current designated router causes the BDR to transition to the role of DR. A new election is performed to determine the new backup designated router.

FIGURE 6.11 Peering to the DR

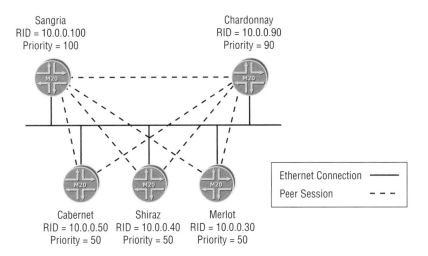

The network in Figure 6.11 shows the router priority and router ID for the routers attached to the Ethernet segment. Assuming that the routers start within 40 seconds of each other, Sangria becomes the DR with its router priority of 100. The second highest priority value of 90 belongs to Chardonnay, making it the backup designated router. If Sangria disappears from the network, Chardonnay assumes the role of DR and a new election takes place. The Cabernet, Shiraz, and Merlot routers all share a priority of 50, so the router ID of each router is compared. Cabernet's router ID of 10.0.0.50 is numerically higher than the other routers and it becomes the new BDR.

The wait time for electing the first designated router on the segment arises from an OSPF timer called the WaitTimer. It is set to the router dead interval (40 seconds by default) and helps to guarantee that all operational routers have the opportunity to receive and send hello packets before the election occurs.

When Sangria returns to the network, it does not automatically assume the DR role again. It receives a hello packet detailing Chardonnay as the current DR and Cabernet as the current BDR. Only when Cabernet becomes the DR (due to a failure of Chardonnay) does the priority of Sangria come into play and it is elected the new BDR. Cabernet will then have to fail in order for Sangria to once again become the designated router on this broadcast segment. This process is considered to be *non-deterministic* because the router with the best criteria is not guaranteed to be the designated router.

Scaling an OSPF Network

As the number of routers in the network grows, so does the amount of information in the link-state database. Additionally, each router requires more bandwidth and resources to flood the LSAs throughout the network. OSPF has mechanisms to limit the flooding scope of the LSAs and scale the network.

The building block for scaling an OSPF network is the concept of an *area*. OSPF areas limit the flooding of LSAs and control the size of the link-state database by retaining that data within the area boundary. Specific routers control this flooding process and allow certain information across the area boundary. Specifically, a network summary LSA is used to allow other portions of the OSPF network to retain database knowledge of the new area. We'll explore each of these concepts in some more detail.

OSPF Areas

The primary purpose of an OSPF area is scalability of the protocol. Boundaries are defined in the network to limit the flooding of specific LSA types. Each newly created area is assigned a unique 32-bit area ID value. This is represented in a quad-octet format of 0.0.0.0, much like an IP address. Although the router works with area numbers in this fashion, most humans prefer to use whole numbers, such as area 0.

 The JUNOS software automatically converts decimal values into quad-octet format. Area 0 becomes area 0.0.0.0, while area 300 becomes 0.0.1.44.

One of the newly defined areas, the *backbone area*, forms the core of the network. All other OSPF areas must connect to the backbone area. The backbone connects all areas and redistributes all non-backbone routing information between the areas.

The breakup of the OSPF network into areas also affects each router's local link-state database. It is no longer identical to the databases on every other router in the domain, which appears at odds with the core tenet of link-state protocols. This apparent contradiction is resolved through a more concise definition of this requirement. Within OSPF, the link-state database must be identical on all routers within an area.

Router Types

The roles and responsibilities of specific OSPF routers are defined by their location in the network. The router types include:

Internal router   A router that maintains all operational interfaces within a single area is known as an *internal router*. An internal router may belong to any OSPF area.

Backbone router   A router that has at least one interface in area 0 is known as a *backbone router*.

Area border router   The *area border router (ABR)* connects one or more OSPF areas to the backbone. This means that at least one interface is within area 0 while another interface is in another area. The ABR plays a very important role in an OSPF network. We'll see its responsibilities grow as we scale and expand our routing domain.

Autonomous System boundary router   An *Autonomous System boundary router (ASBR)* injects external routing knowledge into an OSPF network. ASBRs are discussed in more detail in the "Non-OSPF Routes" section later in this chapter.

Figure 6.12 displays our sample network with two areas, area 0 and area 10. Shiraz, Merlot, and Riesling are completely within area 10, making them internal area routers. Cabernet, on the other hand, is an internal backbone router because all its interfaces are within area 0. The Chardonnay router has interfaces in both area 10 and the backbone, making it an ABR.

FIGURE 6.12   Designating area boundaries

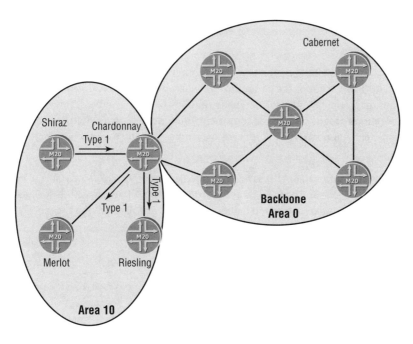

The area boundaries in Figure 6.12 result in router and network LSAs from area 10 remaining in that area. When Shiraz floods a Type 1 or Type 2 LSA into area 10, Chardonnay no longer floods those LSAs to all its OSPF neighbors. Instead, only other area 10 routers receive them—Merlot and Riesling, in our case. The reduced flooding scope introduces a problem for Cabernet, and other backbone routers, because they no longer receive network and metric information about Shiraz. OSPF mitigates this issue by allowing the ABR, Chardonnay, to advertise the required information in another LSA type.

 Real World Scenario

Design Considerations

The use of OSPF areas is an effective tool in minimizing the flooding scope of LSAs. Placing area boundaries and determining which routers become ABRs can be quite arbitrary, but the good network architect should consider some factors.

One easy decision point involves physical connectivity and topology of the network. If you have a central campus and several regional offices, it might make sense to partition the network along those same lines. Forcing a logical OSPF design that differs greatly from your topology might cause more problems in the long run.

Additionally, it is generally a good idea to have more than one ABR connecting an area to the backbone. The lack of dual ABRs presents a single point of failure in your design. Should one of the routers fail, its partner maintains connectivity as well as a valid forwarding path. With only a single ABR, its failure segments the area from the backbone, and the area destinations become unreachable.

The resources and bandwidth capabilities of the routers in your network are other factors to consider. The ABRs must support a larger link-state database than the area routers. Calculating the SPF algorithm against this larger database requires more resources. Of course, some of these considerations greatly depend on the size of your network. In a stable network, a Juniper Networks router can support over 200 routers in a single area and maintain multiple links to different areas.

Finally, the backbone routers might pass more user traffic along their links since all inter-area traffic flows through the backbone and not directly between the non-backbone areas. This generally means that more powerful backbone routers and higher-speed links are placed in the backbone area.

Network Summary LSA

Routing knowledge crosses an area boundary in an OSPF network by using a *network summary LSA*, type code 3. By default, each Type 3 LSA matches a single router LSA or network LSA on a one-for-one basis. This correlation is taken a step further in that the network summary LSA also has an area-flooding scope. This means that an OSPF router floods the LSA only to other routers in its same area. Figure 6.13 illustrates this concept.

FIGURE 6.13   Flooding network summary LSAs

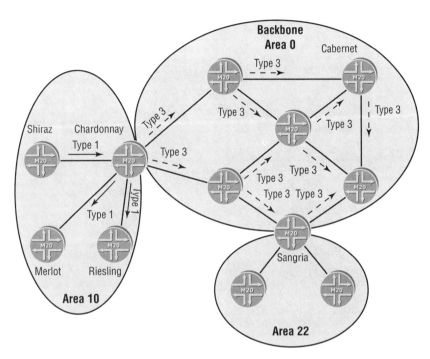

Shiraz is advertising its router LSA within area 10. Its flooding scope keeps the LSA contained to Chardonnay, Merlot, and Riesling, as we discussed in the "Router Types" section earlier in this chapter. Chardonnay's role as an ABR allows it to generate a network summary LSA that contains the subnet information in the Type 1 LSA of Shiraz. This new Type 3 LSA is flooded into the backbone. All area 0 routers, including Cabernet and Sangria, receive this information and place it in their local databases. After running the SPF algorithm, the backbone routers have reachability to Shiraz and its connected subnets.

The flooding scope of the Type 3 LSA does cause a problem, however. A closer examination of Figure 6.13 shows that Sangria, the ABR for area 22, is not flooding the Type 3 LSA from Chardonnay into that non-backbone area. To provide for this type of situation, OSPF allows Sangria to generate its own network summary LSA that matches the information in Chardonnay's version. Again, this generation of new LSAs is performed on a one-for-one basis. Sangria then floods the new Type 3 LSA into area 22.

Figure 6.14 shows the end result of this new LSA flooding: Every router in the OSPF network has reachability to every other router through a combination of router and network summary LSAs.

FIGURE 6.14 Generating new Type 3 LSAs

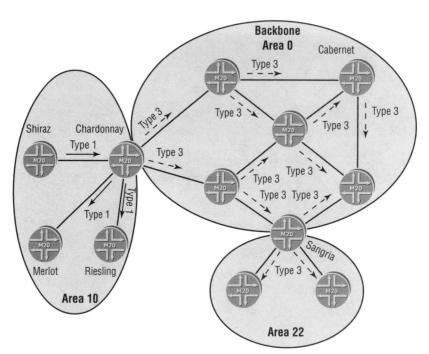

Non-OSPF Routes

Both the router and network summary LSAs are effective at propagating internal OSPF routing knowledge throughout the network. They are not capable, however, of carrying external routing information. The *AS external LSA*, type code 5, was defined for this explicit purpose.

External routes in an OSPF network can come in multiple forms. Perhaps we need to redistribute some static routes, or we recently purchased a network that is not currently running OSPF. Some portions of our own network—a server farm, for example—may be incapable of running OSPF internally. In any case, we have a requirement for reachability to these networks from our OSPF routers.

Figure 6.15 shows Cabernet now connected to a server farm network, making it an ASBR. Each external network is advertised into OSPF in a separate Type 5 LSA. Unlike the router, network, and network summary LSAs, the AS external LSA has a domain-flooding scope. This means that the ABR no longer stops the flooding process, but instead continues it into its respective areas. A look at Figure 6.15 shows this flooding process; Shiraz receives the same unique LSA as do the routers in area 22.

FIGURE 6.15   Injecting non-OSPF networks

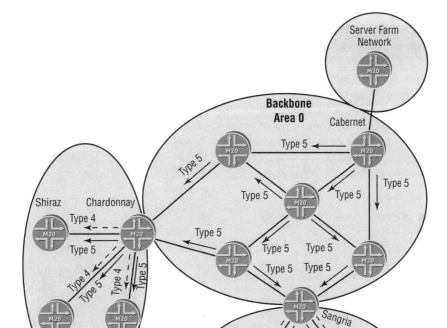

While the Type 5 LSA provides the network information necessary to reach the external networks, the OSPF routers may not automatically begin using that data. The address of the ASBR, Cabernet in our case, must be known in the link-state database via a router LSA. Chardonnay, Sangria, and the other backbone routers meet this criterion, because they share an area 0 database with Cabernet. It is the routers in area 10 and 22 that are currently not able to utilize the AS external LSA.

Once again, the ABR solves our problem by generating a new LSA type. For each ASBR reachable by a router LSA, the ABR creates an *ASBR summary LSA*, type code 4, and injects in into the appropriate area. This LSA provides reachability information to the ASBR itself. Like a Type 3 LSA, the ASBR summary LSA has area scope and is generated by an ABR. Using Figure 6.15 as a guide, Chardonnay generates a Type 4 LSA and floods it to Shiraz, Merlot, and Riesling. Sangria accomplishes the same task for area 22. All OSPF routers in the domain now have routing knowledge of the server farm network, and each router is able to use the information in the AS external LSA.

Additional Scaling Techniques

In our example, the creation of areas assisted in scaling the size of our OSPF network through a reduction in LSA flooding requirements and processing. It did not, however, affect the size of the link-state database itself. Each router in the network still has information in its database for each internal and external route. Some vendor implementations may have trouble with a large database, particularly older or smaller-scale routers. For networks in this situation, you may alter the behavior of an OSPF area to reduce the size of the link-state database. Three varieties of areas accomplish this: a stub area, a totally stubby area, and a not-so-stubby area.

We examine each of these area types in turn, using Figure 6.16 as a starting point. In this figure, both the ABRs of Chardonnay and Sangria are flooding summary LSAs, ASBR summary LSAs, and AS external LSAs into their respective areas. The Type 3 LSAs represent backbone networks as well as networks from the opposite area. The Type 5 LSAs are for the server farm networks, while the Type 4 LSAs represent the ASBR of Cabernet.

FIGURE 6.16   A full OSPF database

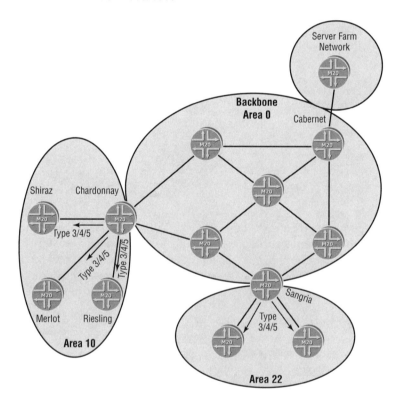

Stub Areas

An OSPF *stub area* provides for a smaller link-state database by restricting the presence of AS external LSAs within the area. Since a single Type 5 LSA is generated for each external route, the potential number of LSAs in an OSPF network can be quite sizeable. Some OSPF areas do not benefit from the explicit routing knowledge provided by the Type 5 LSAs.

The Shiraz router in area 10, for example, may have 5,000 external routes in its database. Each of those routes uses Chardonnay, the ABR, as the next hop in the routing table. From a reachability standpoint, Shiraz can send user data packets using these explicit routes or by using a default 0.0.0.0 /0 route that also points to Chardonnay. Either way, the data packets reach the ABR, which has explicit routing knowledge of the external routes and forwards the packets through the backbone to the ASBR. The disadvantage of forwarding potentially unroutable packets is outweighed by the large reduction in the size of the link-state database and the internal processing that database requires.

The responsibility for enforcing an OSPF stub area rests with the ABR. Under normal circumstances, the ABR re-floods the Type 5 LSAs into the area. When configured as a stub area, however, the ABR simply does not flood the AS external LSAs into the area. To provide the required IP reachability, the ABR should instead generate a summary LSA for the default route and inject that into the stub area.

Figure 6.17 shows area 10 as a stub area. Chardonnay is no longer forwarding the AS external LSAs into the area. Type 3 LSAs representing internal OSPF networks continue to be flooded, and Chardonnay generates its 0.0.0.0 /0 summary LSA for area 10 as well. The area routers Shiraz, Merlot, and Riesling still have reachability to the server farm networks, and the link-state database on those routers has been greatly reduced.

FIGURE 6.17 An OSPF stub area

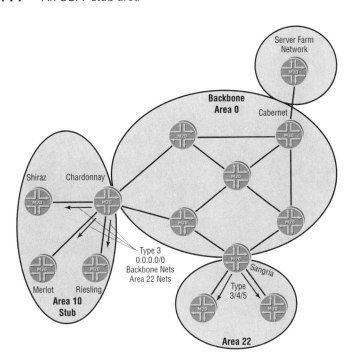

A closer examination of Figure 6.17 also reveals that Chardonnay is no longer generating ASBR summary LSAs as well. Recall from the "Non-OSPF Routes" section earlier in this chapter that the Type 4 LSAs allow OSPF routers simply to use the AS external LSAs in their databases. In a stub environment, the Type 5 LSAs are not present in the area routers, so the need for the ASBR summary LSAs is moot. The ABR, therefore, stops generating those LSAs as well.

Totally Stubby Areas

The stub area concept is expanded and carried one step further with a *totally stubby area*. A summary LSA default route replaces the Type 5 LSAs in the stub area. The area routers forward all external traffic to the ABR. This single ABR is also the exit point for all backbone and inter-area traffic. This allows us to further reduce the link-state database by preventing the generation of summary LSAs on the ABR.

In Figure 6.18, we've changed area 10 into a totally stubby area. The ABR, Chardonnay, has stopped creating and flooding Type 3 LSAs for the backbone and for area 22 routes. The default Type 3 LSA is generated to provide reachability to all routes outside area 10. The basic operation of the stub area did not change in this situation. Types 4 and 5 LSAs are still not present in the area 10 routers. Shiraz, Merlot, and Riesling have only LSAs originated in area 10 and the default summary LSA in their databases.

FIGURE 6.18   An OSPF totally stubby area

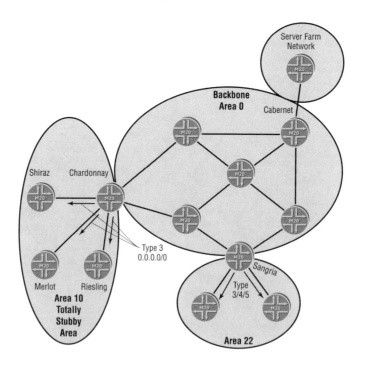

Not-So-Stubby Area

The exclusion of AS external LSAs in a stub area means that an ASBR is not permitted to operate within the confines of that area. This restriction may prove beneficial in the majority of circumstances, but the possibility exists for an exception. Suppose that your OSPF network requires connectivity to a partner that is using RIP within its network. Because of physical necessity, this partner can connect only to the Muscat router in area 22. The routers in this area have been suffering from similar database issues that caused area 10 to become stub. The plan was to make area 22 a stub area as well, but the new requirement for an ASBR may negate this change. This exact set of circumstances led to the development of the *not-so-stubby area (NSSA)*.

A not-so-stubby area is an OSPF stub area that allows some external routes to be present in the database. This is accomplished with a new *NSSA external LSA*, type code 7. The Type 7 LSA carries external routing information from the ASBR within the NSSA. It has an area flooding scope, so only routers in the NSSA receive the Type 7 LSA. The external routing information within the LSA is converted by the ABR into an AS external LSA at the area boundary. The ABR floods the Type 5 LSA into the OSPF domain, and no other routers in the network are aware of the NSSA configuration.

Area 22 in our sample network is configured as an NSSA, as seen in Figure 6.19. The Muscat router is connected to the partner network and is injecting Type 7 LSAs into area 22. These are flooded within the area to all other OSPF routers. Sangria, the ABR, converts the Type 7 LSA into an AS external LSA. It then floods the new Type 5 LSA into the backbone. In addition, Sangria generates a Type 4 LSA, because the ASBR is in another area, and floods that into area 0 as well. The operation of the rest of the OSPF network does not change based on the NSSA configuration in area 22, and IP reachability is achieved by all internal and external networks.

OSPF Configuration

The configuration of an OSPF network on a Juniper Networks router is an extremely straightforward task. The router simply needs to know which interfaces are assigned to which OSPF areas. All configuration is accomplished within the [edit protocols ospf] hierarchy.

Single OSPF Area

The most basic OSPF network is a single-area design, so let's start there. Figure 6.20 shows a single-area OSPF network.

FIGURE 6.19   An OSPF not-so-stubby area

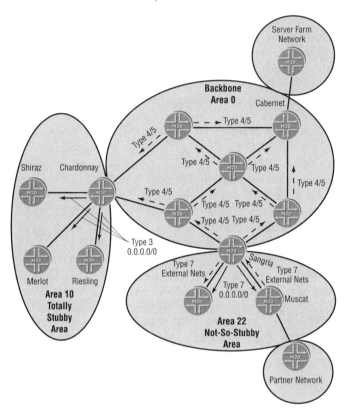

FIGURE 6.20   An OSPF single-area network

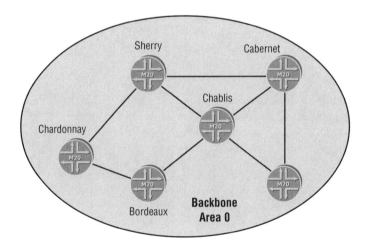

The Chablis router in area 0 is a backbone router with all interfaces within the area. This allows you to configure OSPF using two commands:

```
[edit protocols ospf]
user@Chablis# set area 0 interface all
user@Chablis# set area 0 interface fxp0 disable
```

This results in the configuration of Chablis appearing like so:

```
[edit protocols ospf]
user@Chablis# show
area 0.0.0.0 {
    interface all;
    interface fxp0.0 {
        disable;
    }
}
```

Instead of explicitly specifying each of the interfaces on Chablis that should run OSPF, we have informed the router to operate the protocol on all configured IPv4 interfaces. To prevent the router from forming OSPF adjacencies across the management interface of fxp0.0, we explicitly disabled that interface in the configuration.

Within the configuration of a protocol, any reference to a specific interface supersedes the parameters of the interface all statement.

The opposite approach of configuration is taken with the Chardonnay router; each interface is referenced explicitly:

```
[edit protocols ospf]
user@Chardonnay# set area 0 interface so-0/0/1
user@Chardonnay# set area 0 interface at-0/1/0.100
```

This results in the following configuration:

```
[edit protocols ospf]
user@Chardonnay# show
area 0.0.0.0 {
    interface so-0/0/1.0;
    interface at-0/1/0.100;
}
```

Each physical interface and logical unit number, if appropriate, is configured within the desired area. The so-0/0/1 interface connects Chardonnay to the Sherry router. The logical unit was omitted from the set command because the JUNOS software assumes a unit value of 0 if none is provided. The same process is not as effective for the connection to the Bordeaux router. This connection is using an ATM *virtual circuit identifier (VCI)* of 100 on logical unit 100. Had the logical unit not been specified, the router would have assumed unit 0 and Chardonnay wouldn't have been able to communicate with Bordeaux.

Multiple OSPF Areas

The configuration of a multiarea OSPF network is not much different than that of a single-area network. All area routers and backbone routers place all interfaces within their respective areas. It is the ABRs that have the extra work to do. Figure 6.21 shows a multiarea OSPF network.

FIGURE 6.21 An OSPF multiarea network

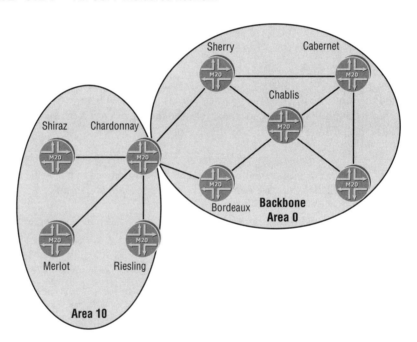

Our single-area network has grown and Chardonnay has become an ABR for area 10 with connections to the routers of Shiraz, Merlot, and Riesling. The configuration of Chardonnay for area 0 is already completed. We now add the interfaces within area 10:

```
[edit protocols ospf]
user@Chardonnay# set area 10 interface so-0/0/2
user@Chardonnay# set area 10 interface so-0/0/0
user@Chardonnay# set area 10 interface so-0/0/3
```

Chardonnay's configuration now appears as:

```
[edit protocols ospf]
user@Chardonnay# show
area 0.0.0.0 {
    interface so-0/0/1.0;
    interface at-0/1/0.100;
}
area 0.0.0.10 {
    interface so-0/0/2.0;
    interface so-0/0/0.0;
    interface so-0/0/3.0;
}
```

JUNOS software Commands

After deploying and configuring the OSPF network, you must verify the operation of the network. Additionally, you may need to do some network troubleshooting. The JUNOS software provides many show commands to use for this purpose. We'll examine a few of the basic commands, using Figure 6.21 as a sample network.

Troubleshooting Your Configuration

Once you've committed your configuration to the router and returned to the user operational mode, you may find that the network isn't quite right. Configuration issues often appear as problems with your OSPF interfaces and neighbors. We have the ability to verify these issues within the software.

show ospf interface

The first troubleshooting step is often to determine the state of the local router's interfaces. Each configured OSPF interface must be operational before any packets are sent. A non-operational interface means that no neighbors will be located, no adjacencies will form, and the link-state database won't be populated. The show ospf interface command provides insight into this information:

```
user@Chardonnay> show ospf interface
Interface          State    Area        DR ID        BDR ID       Nbrs
at-0/1/0.100       PtToPt   0.0.0.0     0.0.0.0      0.0.0.0      1
so-0/0/1.0         PtToPt   0.0.0.0     0.0.0.0      0.0.0.0      1
so-0/0/0.0         PtToPt   0.0.0.10    0.0.0.0      0.0.0.0      1
so-0/0/2.0         PtToPt   0.0.0.10    0.0.0.0      0.0.0.0      1
so-0/0/3.0         PtToPt   0.0.0.10    0.0.0.0      0.0.0.0      1
```

The various fields in the command output are:

Interface   Configured OSPF interfaces that are physically present in the router are displayed in this column. Failure to properly enter a logical unit value results in the interface not appearing in this output.

State   The current state of the interface is displayed in this column. Possible values include:

- BDR—The local router is the backup designated router.
- Down—The interface is not currently operational.
- DR—The local router is the designated router.
- DRother—The local router is neither the DR nor the BDR.
- PtToPt—This is a point-to-point interface.

Area   This field displays the current area ID assigned to the interface.

DR ID   The router ID of the current designated router is displayed in this column. Point-to-point interfaces use a value of 0.0.0.0.

BDR ID   The router ID of the current backup designated router is displayed in this column. Point-to-point interfaces use a value of 0.0.0.0.

Nbrs   The value in this column represents the total number of OSPF neighbors discovered across this interface.

show ospf neighbor

Once you are certain the interfaces are properly assigned and operational, you should check the status of the neighbor's adjacency by using the show ospf neighbor command:

```
user@Chardonnay> show ospf neighbor
  Address         Interface          State    ID            Pri  Dead
  10.0.1.46       at-0/1/0.100       Full     10.0.1.103    128  36
  10.0.1.34       so-0/0/1.0         Full     10.0.1.102    128  35
  10.0.1.9        so-0/0/0.0         Full     10.0.1.21     128  38
  10.0.1.5        so-0/0/2.0         Full     10.0.1.22     128  32
  10.0.1.1        so-0/0/3.0         Full     10.0.1.23     128  39
```

The fields in this output represent:

Address   The physical interface IP address of the neighbor is displayed in this column.

Interface   This column shows the OSPF interface that the neighbor is reachable across.

State   The current OSPF adjacency state is displayed here. The possible state values are discussed in the "Forming Adjacencies" section earlier in this chapter.

ID   This field shows the router ID of the neighbor. This is used with the Pri field to elect a DR or BDR on a broadcast segment.

Pri   The router priority is displayed in this field. This value is used with the ID field to elect a DR or BDR on a broadcast or NBMA segment.

Dead   The time remaining until the OSPF neighbor is declared unreachable appears in this column. Each received hello packet resets this timer to the router dead interval value.

clear ospf neighbor

It may be necessary to reset the peer session to a neighbor. This may occur if the remote router is malfunctioning or if you want to refresh the link-state database with new information. This is accomplished with the `clear ospf neighbor` *neighbor-address* command. The optional *neighbor-address* switch clears that specific neighbor. The `clear ospf neighbor` command, with no switches, clears all OSPF neighbors.

Troubleshooting the Routing Protocol

After the local router has found its neighbors and formed its adjacencies, flooding of LSAs ensues. This populates the link-state database and the Dijkstra calculation is performed. In addition, the periodic transmission of hello and link-state update packets is performed to maintain the adjacencies and the consistency of the database. Various commands provide some visibility to these processes.

show ospf database

The `show ospf database` command is an excellent tool in troubleshooting OSPF. If the information is not in the database, it will not appear in the routing table. The output shows summary information about each LSA on a per-area basis:

```
user@Shiraz> show ospf database

    OSPF link state database, area 0.0.0.10
 Type      ID                Adv Rtr          Seq        Age  Opt  Cksum  Len
Router   *10.0.1.21        10.0.1.21        0x80000004  2965  0x2  0x3407  60
Router   10.0.1.22         10.0.1.22        0x80000004  2971  0x2  0xb58a  60
Router   10.0.1.23         10.0.1.23        0x80000008  2800  0x2  0x2f12  60
Router   10.0.1.101        10.0.1.101       0x8000000c  1328  0x2  0x6d4   108
Summary  10.0.1.0          10.0.1.101       0x80000005   728  0x2  0x3525  28
ASBRSum  10.0.1.105        10.0.1.101       0x80000006   128  0x2  0xf976  28
    OSPF external link state database
 Type      ID                Adv Rtr          Seq        Age  Opt  Cksum  Len
Extern   192.168.1.0       10.0.1.105       0x80000034   306  0x2  0xe5da  36
Extern   192.168.2.0       10.0.1.105       0x80000034     5  0x2  0xdae4  36
Extern   192.168.3.0       10.0.1.105       0x80000033  1206  0x2  0xd1ed  36
Extern   192.168.4.0       10.0.1.105       0x80000033   907  0x2  0xc6f7  36
```

The fields in the command output represent the following information:

Type   The LSA type is displayed in this field. The possible names include:

- Router—Type 1 router LSA
- Network—Type 2 network LSA
- Summary—Type 3 network summary LSA
- ASBRSum—Type 4 ASBR summary LSA
- Extern—Type 5 AS external LSA
- NSSA—Type 7 NSSA external LSA

ID   This field shows the Link-State ID field from the LSA. This value is used to provide uniqueness for each LSA. Entries marked with an asterisk (*) are LSAs generated by the local router.

Adv Rtr   The router ID of the originating router for each LSA is displayed in this field.

Seq   The sequence number assists the router to determine the most recent version of the LSA.

Age   This field displays the current age of the LSA. All LSAs begin with a lifetime of 0 and increment to a defined MaxAge of 3600 seconds. Each LSA must be refreshed before the MaxAge value is reached.

Opt   The Options field from the OSPF header is displayed in this column. The possible bit values are discussed in the "Hello Packet" section earlier in this chapter.

Cksum   The calculated checksum value of the LSA is stored in this field. Each router calculates a new checksum when the LSA is received and verifies the value against the received value to ensure packet integrity.

Len   This field displays the total length of the LSA.

clear ospf database

By default, stale information in the link-state database is purged once the LSA Age reaches the MaxAge of 3600 seconds. You can start this process manually with the clear ospf database command. This command deletes all information in your local link-state database. Newly flooded LSAs repopulate the database, and the local router recalculates the SPF algorithm. The use of the *purge* option sets all LSAs in the current database to the MaxAge of 3600 and floods that information into the network. Again, newly flooded LSAs repopulate the database.

In our example, once the link-state database on Shiraz is purged, we issue show ospf database to display the new LSAs with ages of 2 and 3 seconds:

```
user@Shiraz> clear ospf database purge

user@Shiraz> show ospf database

    OSPF link state database, area 0.0.0.10
```

Type	ID	Adv Rtr	Seq	Age	Opt	Cksum	Len
Router	*10.0.1.21	10.0.1.21	0x80000003	2	0x0	0x54e9	60
Router	10.0.1.101	10.0.1.101	0x80000003	3	0x0	0x1b4a	84
Summary	0.0.0.0	10.0.1.101	0x80000002	3	0x0	0x2ab9	28
Summary	10.0.1.0	10.0.1.101	0x80000002	3	0x0	0x5906	28

WARNING The use of the `clear ospf database` command removes information from your local OSPF database in the hopes that your neighbors advertise routing information back to the local router. Additionally, each OSPF adjacency is reset. This is a disruptive procedure that causes the local router to lose routing information, if only temporarily. This command should be used with caution on production networks.

show ospf log

The `show ospf log` command displays how often the SPF algorithm is being initiated and how long each operation takes to finish. Certain OSPF events repeating themselves in rapid succession may be a sign of an inadvertently injected routing loop or an LSA that is taking too long to propagate across the network. Most commonly, a network link that is flapping consistently causes the router to recalculate SPF on a rapid basis.

The output of the `show ospf log` command displays the most recent occurrence of each OSPF event. The longest instance of each category is also displayed. Finally, you can view a history of events the local router has performed.

```
user@Shiraz> show ospf log
```

```
   Last instance of each event type
When        Type         Elapsed
00:17:29    SPF          0.000073
00:17:29    Stub         0.000067
00:17:29    Interarea    0.000025
00:17:29    External     0.000003
00:17:29    NSSA         0.000003
00:17:29    Cleanup      0.000083

   Maximum length of each event type
When        Type         Elapsed
01:17:57    SPF          0.000116
00:22:41    Stub         0.000365
20:00:18    Interarea    0.000132
01:19:43    External     0.000042
```

```
19:17:29        NSSA            0.000014
19:17:29        Cleanup         0.000715


   Last 100 events
When            Type            Elapsed


01:19:48            Total       0.000182
01:19:43        SPF             0.000090
01:19:43        Stub            0.000086
01:19:43        Interarea       0.000030
01:19:43        External        0.000042
01:19:43        NSSA            0.000004
…[output truncated]
```

show ospf statistics

The show ospf statistics command displays counters based on the OSPF packet type. Both the total number of packets and the number in the last 5 seconds is shown. Additionally, you can see the total number of LSA retransmissions with this command. If this value rapidly increases, it means your OSPF neighbor is not acknowledging its receipt of your LSAs. The remote router is either overworked or malfunctioning. Finally, the number and types of errors seen by the local router are displayed:

```
user@Shiraz> show ospf statistics
```

Packet type	Total		Last 5 seconds	
	Sent	Received	Sent	Received
Hello	24	45	0	0
DbD	24	16	0	0
LSReq	6	7	0	0
LSUpdate	375	2260	0	0
LSAck	2236	368	0	0

```
LSAs retransmitted: 2, last 5 seconds: 0

Flood queue depth: 0
Total rexmit entries: 0, db summaries: 0, lsreq entries: 0

Receive errors:
  25 stub area mismatches
  4 nssa mismatches
```

Viewing OSPF Routes

The purpose of utilizing OSPF as a routing protocol is to place routes in the routing table for forwarding traffic. The SPF algorithm generates the routes based on information found in the link-state database. The JUNOS software provides the ability to view those routes after the SPF calculation and after they are placed in the routing table.

show ospf route

The show ospf route command displays the results of the SPF algorithm. These are the routes that OSPF is handing off to the routing table. Each destination route includes a type (internal versus external), the LSA type used to find the route, a metric, and an outgoing interface name or IP address:

```
user@Chardonnay> show ospf route
Prefix            Path   Route   NH    Metric  NextHop      Nexthop
                  Type   Type    Type          Interface    addr/label
10.0.1.21/32      Intra  Router  IP    1       so-0/0/0.0
10.0.1.102/32     Intra  Router  IP    1       so-0/0/1.0
10.0.1.103/32     Intra  Router  IP    1       at-0/1/0.100
10.0.1.104/32     Intra  Router  IP    2       at-0/1/0.100
                                               so-0/0/1.0
10.0.1.105/32     Intra  AS BR   IP    2       so-0/0/1.0
10.0.1.106/32     Intra  Router  IP    3       at-0/1/0.100
                                               so-0/0/1.0
```

show route protocol ospf

The show route protocol ospf command displays routes after they have been placed in the routing table. As such, each route is displayed in a similar format to routes from other protocols. Additionally, each route may not be placed in the forwarding table due to the JUNOS software protocol preference values.

The Chardonnay router has OSPF routes in the routing table that are not marked as active. The 10.0.1.0/30 route is a good example. Most likely, Chardonnay also has a Direct route to this same subnet and prefers that version due to its preference value of 0.

```
user@Chardonnay> show route protocol ospf

inet.0: 34 destinations, 40 routes (34 active, 0 holddown, 0 hidden)
+ = Active Route, - = Last Active, * = Both

10.0.1.0/30        [OSPF/10] 03:02:40, metric 1
                   > via so-0/0/3.0
10.0.1.4/30        [OSPF/10] 03:02:40, metric 1
                   > via so-0/0/2.0
```

```
10.0.1.8/30        [OSPF/10] 03:02:40, metric 1
                   > via so-0/0/0.0
10.0.1.21/32       *[OSPF/10] 02:25:42, metric 1
                   > via so-0/0/0.0
10.0.1.32/30       [OSPF/10] 03:02:40, metric 1
                   > via so-0/0/1.0
192.168.1.0/24     *[OSPF/150] 03:02:40, metric 0, tag 0
                   > via so-0/0/1.0
192.168.2.0/24     *[OSPF/150] 03:02:40, metric 0, tag 0
                   > via so-0/0/1.0
192.168.3.0/24     *[OSPF/150] 03:02:40, metric 0, tag 0
                   > via so-0/0/1.0
192.168.4.0/24     *[OSPF/150] 03:02:40, metric 0, tag 0
                   > via so-0/0/1.0
224.0.0.5/32       *[OSPF/10] 5d 17:20:57, metric 1
```

 A detailed explanation of this output is discussed in Chapter 3, "Protocol-Independent Routing." This chapter also includes an explanation of the JUNOS software preference values.

Summary

In this chapter, we reviewed the mechanisms behind a link-state routing protocol. We then explored how OSPF applies these principles by first establishing adjacencies and then flooding network information. We saw how OSPF stores the information in the link-state database and uses the Dijkstra SPF Algorithm to determine the best path to an end destination.

We discussed the various OSPF packet types and how each packet plays a role in forming an adjacency. We then discussed the different types of LSAs used by OSPF. Our discussion focused on a sample network that grew from a single area into multiple areas. Our network grew to connect to external networks, leading to an examination of the various OSPF area types.

Finally, we saw how to configure OSPF on a Juniper Networks router and reviewed several commands that the JUNOS software makes available for the monitoring and troubleshooting of an OSPF network.

Exam Essentials

Be able to describe the OSPF packet types.   OSPF has five different packet types: hello, Database Description, link-state request, link-state update, and link-state acknowledgment.

Define the functions of the various OSPF area types.   An OSPF stub area prevents the flooding of Type 4 and Type 5 LSAs. A totally stubby area restricts the flooding of Type 3 LSAs by the ABR. An otherwise stub area may have external routes injected by an ASBR if configured to be a not-so-stubby area. These routes are carried in a Type 7 LSA.

Identify the different types of OSPF routers.   The four basic types of OSPF routers include an internal router, a backbone router, an area border router, and an Autonomous System boundary router.

Describe the steps for forming an OSPF adjacency and the possible adjacency states.   Two OSPF routers become adjacent when they exchange hello and Database Description packets, at a minimum. The adjacency process follows a specified set of steps that result in various adjacency states. Those states include `Down`, `Attempt`, `Init`, `2-Way`, `ExStart`, `Exchange`, `Loading`, and `Full`.

Identify the election criteria for an OSPF DR.   The two criteria used to elect a designated router are the router priority and the router ID.

Be able to describe the different link-state advertisements.   The JUNOS software utilizes six different LSA types: router, network, network summary, ASBR summary, AS external, and NSSA external LSAs.

Key Terms

Before you take the exam, be certain you are familiar with the following terms:

2-Way	internal router
area	link-state acknowledgment
area border router (ABR)	Link State Advertisement
AS external LSA	link-state database
ASBR summary LSA	link-state request list
Attempt	link-state request packet
Autonomous System boundary router (ASBR)	link-state update
backbone area	Loading
backbone router	neighbors
backup designated router (BDR)	network LSA
Database Description (DD) packet	network summary LSA
dead interval	not-so-stubby area (NSSA)
designated router (DR)	NSSA external LSA
Dijkstra Algorithm	OSPF hello packet
Down	router ID
Exchange	router LSA
ExStart	router priority
Full	stub area
hello interval	totally stubby area
Init	virtual circuit identifier (VCI)

Review Questions

1. How does an OSPF router confirm that its neighbor has received a link-state update?

    A. It relies on the underlying TCP protocol to acknowledge receipt.

    B. It receives a link-state update with an incremented sequence number.

    C. It receives a link-state update with the same sequence number it sent.

    D. It receives a link-state acknowledgment packet containing header information for the LSAs that it sent.

2. Which OSPF packet is used to summarize the link-state database during adjacency formation?

    A. Link-state advertisement

    B. Database Description

    C. Link-state request

    D. Link-state update

3. Should an OSPF link fail, which packet would advertise the network change?

    A. Link-state advertisement

    B. Database Description

    C. Link-state request

    D. Link-state update

4. Which of the following is not a reason to deploy areas in your OSPF network?

    A. To scale the size of the network

    B. To reduce the number of DRs

    C. To minimize processor utilization

    D. To minimize database size

5. A stub area eliminates which type of LSA?

    A. Type 1

    B. Type 2

    C. Type 3

    D. Type 4

6. A not-so-stubby area is used if you want to allow what kind of LSA?

    A. NSSA external

    B. Summary

    C. AS external

    D. Router

7. Which of the following routers serves as a gateway to external networks?

   A. ABR

   B. ASBR

   C. DR

   D. BDR

8. Which router will convert Type 7 LSAs into Type 5 LSAs?

   A. ABR

   B. ASBR

   C. DR

   D. BDR

9. If a router has one interface in the backbone area and four interfaces in non-backbone areas, what kind of router is it?

   A. ABR

   B. ASBR

   C. DR

   D. BDR

10. Two routers forming an adjacency have just finished exchanging DD packets. What happens next?

   A. They exchange hello packets to agree on authentication.

   B. They exchange LSAs when their network changes.

   C. They send link-state requests to get additional database information.

   D. They transition to an `ExStart` adjacency.

11. What state is a router in after it receives a hello packet with no known neighbors listed?

   A. `Init`

   B. `Start`

   C. `Down`

   D. `2-Way`

12. When sending its DD packet, the local router sets the MS bit to 1. What does this mean?

   A. The router is claiming to be the DR.

   B. The router is trying to control the database exchange.

   C. The router has additional information to send.

   D. The router has no more information to send.

13. Four OSPF routers come online at the same time. Based on the properties shown, which router would be elected DR?

   A. Priority = 50, router ID = 10.0.1.10

   B. Priority = 50, router ID = 10.0.100.100

   C. Priority = 25, router ID = 10.0.1.100

   D. Priority = 100, router ID = 1.0.1.10

14. Assume that the current DR has a router priority of 100. When will it lose control of the DR responsibility?

   A. When a router with a higher priority joins the network

   B. When a router with a higher router ID joins the network

   C. When a router with a higher interface address joins the network

   D. When it stops sending hello packets

15. What is the default router priority in the JUNOS software?

   A. 0

   B. 32

   C. 64

   D. 128

16. Which router originates a Type 2 LSA?

   A. DR

   B. BDR

   C. ABR

   D. ASBR

17. Which router plays backup to the node in control of a broadcast network?

   A. DR

   B. BDR

   C. ABR

   D. ASBR

18. You want to know which routers in your network are injecting external routes. Which command would be helpful?

   A. `show ospf neighbor`

   B. `show ospf gateway`

   C. `show ospf database`

   D. `show ospf statistics`

19. Which command allows you to verify that your interfaces are configured for the correct OSPF areas?

   A. `show ospf neighbor`

   B. `show ospf database`

   C. `show ospf interface`

   D. `show ospf statistics`

20. Which OSPF command provides information about connected routers?

   A. `show ospf neighbor`

   B. `show ospf adjacency`

   C. `show ospf interface`

   D. `show ospf statistics`

Answers to Review Questions

1. D.   OSPF handles its own acknowledgments via the link-state acknowledgment packet. The packet contains the LSA headers that describe the LSAs that are being acknowledged.

2. B.   The Database Description packet is used during adjacency formation to summarize the OSPF database. Based on the summarized database, the receiving router will request additional information via request packets. Detailed information will be provided via an update packet, which is acknowledged by an acknowledgment packet.

3. D.   When a network experiences a change, a link-state update packet is used to advertise the new status in the network.

4. B.   A DR is used on broadcast networks and serves as the primary point of contact to minimize point-to-point peering and bandwidth utilization. Establishing an OSPF area will not affect whether a DR is needed.

5. D.   A stub area is used to eliminate the existence of AS external Type 5 LSAs. When Type 5 LSAs are not allowed in a stub area, then the Type 4 LSAs that describe the location of the ASBR are not needed either.

6. A.   A not-so-stubby area is used when you want to allow external routes into a stub area. The definition of a stub area eliminates Type 5 LSAs. Since Type 3 and Type 1 LSAs already exist in a stub area, you are trying to allow NSSA external LSAs, or Type 7 LSAs.

7. B.   An ASBR injects AS external LSAs into the OSPF domain. These LSAs contain non-OSPF network information.

8. A.   The ABR to a not-so-stubby area will convert Type 7 LSAs to Type 5 LSAs by default. This is necessary since Type 7 LSAs can exist only in an NSSA.

9. A.   A router with at least one interface in the backbone and any number of interfaces in non-backbone areas is an area border router.

10. C.   When routers forming an adjacency finish exchanging DD packets, they start sending request packets, if needed, to acquire additional database information for unknown or out-of-date LSAs.

11. A.   When a router receives a hello packet with no known neighbors, it is a sign that a new neighbor is looking for OSPF-speaking devices. This is the first communication that the local router is receiving from the new neighbor, so the local router will transition to the Init state.

12. B.   When a router sets the MS bit to 1, it is attempting to control the exchange of DD packets.

13. D.   Even though this router has the lowest router ID, router priority is the first tiebreaker in DR election. This router's priority is the highest of all shown.

14. D.   In OSPF, DR ownership is nonpreemptive. This means that the only time a DR will lose control of its responsibilities is when it ceases to function properly.

15. D.   The JUNOS software default router priority setting is 128.

16. A. Only a designated router can originate the Type 2 LSA for a broadcast or NBMA network.

17. B. The backup designated router is responsible for monitoring the network segment and the DR. In the event of a DR failure, the BDR is to take over as DR.

18. C. By viewing the OSPF database, you can look for AS external summary LSAs. These will list the routers that are injecting non-OSPF routes into your network.

19. C. Answer C will show you directly which area each interface is configured for. While the other options may give you clues that the interface is not properly configured, they will not tell you which area each interface is configured for.

20. A. Only answer A will provide you with information regarding neighboring OSPF routers. Answer B is not a valid command, while answers C and D detail information about the local router.

Chapter

7

Intermediate System to Intermediate System (IS-IS)

JNCIA EXAM OBJECTIVES COVERED IN THIS CHAPTER:

✓ Describe ISO network addressing as it applies to IS-IS

✓ Define the functions of IS-IS PDUs

✓ Describe characteristics of IS-IS adjacencies

✓ Describe the election of the Designated Intermediate System

✓ Describe the steps required to configure IS-IS

✓ Identify CLI commands used to monitor and troubleshoot an IS-IS network

In this chapter, we explore the Intermediate System to Intermediate System (IS-IS) routing protocol. Many texts assume the reader has knowledge of other link-state protocols such as Open Shortest Path First (OSPF). We don't make that assumption, and discuss IS-IS from the ground up. To start, we take a big-picture view of what the protocol provides; this includes basic design of IS-IS networks and network addressing. Our generic coverage of link-state protocols helps set the stage for how IS-IS works. We then discuss specific details about IS-IS states, IS-IS adjacencies, and the Designated Intermediate System (DIS) election on broadcast links. After that, we take a look at various configuration, verification, and troubleshooting commands. Finally, we briefly compare IS-IS to OSPF.

Let's begin with an overview of the IS-IS protocol.

Overview of IS-IS

The International Standards Organization (ISO) calls a router an *intermediate system*. A host is referred to as an *end system* by the ISO. Since routers connect hosts in the IP world, intermediate systems connect end systems in an ISO network. IS-IS was originally designed to support the Connectionless Network Protocol (CLNP) and was later adapted to support IP reachability. Both the IP and CLNP information is carried within the payload of the IS-IS routing updates. The Juniper Networks implementation of IS-IS supports only IP routing, so we focus on this aspect of the protocol for the remainder of this chapter.

The Juniper Networks implementation of IS-IS is fully interoperable with other vendor implementations that utilize both the CLNP and IP protocol stacks.

Throughout our discussion, we use the single sample network shown in Figure 7.1.

Four routers make up this entire IS-IS network. An Ethernet segment interconnects Cabernet, Merlot, and Shiraz. These routers are configured within IS-IS area 47.0005.80.8300. Riesling is connected via point-to-point links to Cabernet and Merlot. Riesling is in a different IS-IS area, 49.0001. We discuss the significance of the area values and connectivity of the routers in the "Addressing" section later in this chapter.

FIGURE 7.1   IS-IS sample network

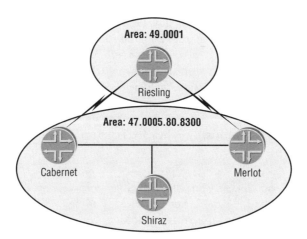

Link-State Review

Before we start our discussion of the IS-IS particulars, a brief review of link-state protocol concepts is in order. Once a link-state router starts operating on a network link, information associated with its logical networks is added to its *link-state database* by the local router. *Hello messages* are then sent by the router on all operational links to determine whether other routers are using the same protocol. If additional routers are located, both attempt to form an *adjacency* with each other. The routers use this adjacency to advertise summary database information to each other. This is not the actual database information but is truly a summary of the data. Each router checks this summary list to verify that it has the most up-to-date information. Should one of the routers require an information update, it sends a request to its neighbor for a link-state update. The update includes the actual data contained in the link-state database. This exchange process continues until both routers have identical link-state databases.

This common view of the link-state database forms the basis of the network topology. Each router uses the *Dijkstra Algorithm* to process the database information into a path from the local router to each remote destination. Every router uses the same algorithm to process its database; therefore, each router must have consistent information to get proper results. This consistent database concept is a central tenet of link-state protocols and allows the protocols to ensure a loop-free topology. Each router then makes consistent forwarding decisions for user data packets. In this state—a sort of network nirvana—no routing loops exist in the network. Ensuring the advertisement and consistency of link-state updates as well as propagating these updates quickly remains the only barrier to preventing loops.

IS-IS Levels

Let's start examining some further details of how IS-IS transmits its information to other routers in the network. We've previously stated that each link-state router must maintain a consistent link-state database. More specifically, each database within an *IS-IS level* must be identical. The ISO committee uses the term *level* to represent an arbitrary boundary or grouping of routers. Since the database in each level is the same, that level becomes the farthest distance that a link-state update can propagate. It follows that the Dijkstra Algorithm is then calculated by the local router using the information in the database within a specific level. IS-IS routers exchange link-state information with each other based on their level configuration—either Level 1 or Level 2.

Level 2

Two IS-IS routers form an adjacency and share database information when both ends of their common link are configured for Level 2. Let's take a look at Figure 7.2. All of the interfaces on Riesling are within the defined Level 2 area. In addition, both Cabernet and Merlot have an interface within that same Level 2 area. The dotted line represents the shared topology knowledge within the Level 2 link-state databases on the routers. The area values are different on the routers (49.0001 and 47.0005.80.8300), but the only requirement for a Level 2 adjacency is that each end of the link reside within Level 2.

Level 1

The requirements for a Level 1 adjacency are a bit different. Two IS-IS routers form an adjacency when each end of the common network link is configured for Level 1 and the IS-IS area value of each router is identical. Figure 7.3 displays a Level 1 area. All interfaces on Shiraz and a single interface on Cabernet and Merlot reside within Level 1. Cabernet, Merlot, and Shiraz all share an IS-IS area value of 47.0005.80.8300. This common area value allows adjacencies to form and updates to be exchanged. As before, all interfaces bounded by the dotted line exchange link-state updates.

When the common link between Cabernet and Riesling is configured for Level 1, no IS-IS adjacency forms since the area values of the two routers are different. Only a Level 2 adjacency can form between these two routers.

FIGURE 7.2   IS-IS Level 2 coverage

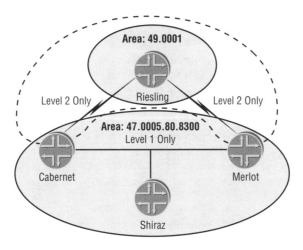

FIGURE 7.3   IS-IS Level 1 coverage

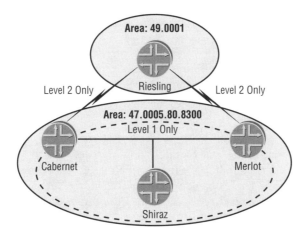

Both Cabernet and Merlot have two link-state databases. One database contains the Level 1 data while the other contains the Level 2 information. The Dijkstra Algorithm is calculated within each level database.

 **Real World Scenario**

Good Network Design?

In examining Figures 7.2 and 7.3, you might wonder if we had a reason for placing the IS-IS levels in specific places. The short answer is "sort of." We used some general rules, but level placement in a live network depends on a number of factors. Let's talk about what the figures represent.

Cabernet, Shiraz, and Merlot share an area address and reside in the same administrative domain. This is probably because a common Ethernet network interconnects them all. Cabernet and Merlot each connect to Riesling over wide area network (WAN) links. This leads to the possibility that the opposite ends of the links may be within different areas. In fact, Figure 7.2 shows this to be the case.

We've discussed here some general comments about how routing domains may be inter-connected. An Ethernet network between two or more routers doesn't mean that they will reside in the same administrative domain and IS-IS level. Likewise, a WAN link between two routers doesn't ensure that the routers are in different administrative domains.

Design Considerations

The design of a level topology depends on network scalability and personal preference. For a small network (fewer than 100 or 200 routers), you might decide to place all routers within the same level. For a larger network (hundreds of routers), you might decide to use multiple levels. The core/backbone routers comprise one level (Level 2) while smaller sets of routers are in several other levels (Level 1). These smaller sets sometimes exist in different physical locations.

Level 1 and Level 2 Operation

The ISO committee designed the level hierarchy for large network topologies requiring multiple levels. Level 1 routers contain IP routes for their specific level and maintain a default route (0.0.0.0 /0) toward a backbone network. Level 2 routers are devices that serve as the backbone routers. Level 2 routers have complete routing knowledge of the entire network. An individual IS-IS router can be one of the following:

- Level 1 router (L1)
- Level 2 router (L2)
- Level 1 and Level 2 router (L1/L2)—JUNOS software default

Level 2 routers share route knowledge with each other about all areas of the network. In a hierarchical network design, at least one router is both an L1 and an L2 router. Each router maintains a complete link-state database for each level configured. An L2 router connected to another L2 router in a different area sets the attached bit in its L1 updates. An L1 router that receives an update with the attached bit set assumes that the L2 router has reachability to the remainder of the network. The L1 router installs a 0.0.0.0 /0 default route locally that points to the L2 router as a next hop. Since all Level 1 routers have explicit knowledge of routes within their area, the default route is used only to reach routes outside the Level 1 area.

An Example of a Multilevel Network

Let's explore the operation of a multilevel IS-IS network in greater detail. Look at the network in Figure 7.4.

Suppose an ISP in Europe has routers in multiple countries with major concentrations in the metropolitan areas of London and Rome. The routers within London share an area address of 49.0002 and are configured for Level 1. Likewise, the routers within Rome share an area address of 49.0001 and are also configured for Level 1. The remaining routers have different area addresses (49.0003 and 49.0004), but they are all configured for Level 2. This configuration imposes a logical hierarchy to the network.

FIGURE 7.4   IS-IS level hierarchy

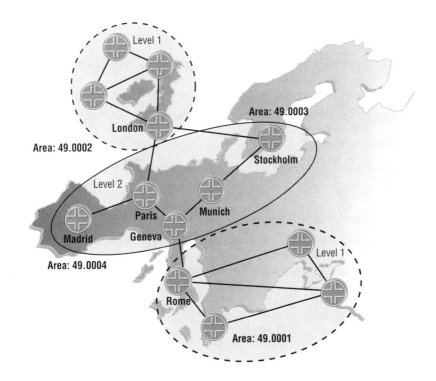

A router in London reaches a route in the Rome metropolitan area through the Level 2 backbone area. The London router forwards all inter-area traffic to the London L1/L2 router using its local default route. Recall that the L1/L2 router prompts this default route through the advertisement of the attached bit. The Level 2 backbone routers have complete link-state knowledge of all routes in the network. The London L1/L2 router forwards the user traffic from the London L1 router across the backbone to the Rome L1/L2 router. This router then forwards the traffic to the Rome L1 router.

Summary of IS-IS Levels

To summarize, the level boundaries determine the extent of propagation for link-state updates. All routers within a level maintain a complete link-state database of all other routers in the same level. Each router then uses the Dijkstra Algorithm to efficiently determine the shortest path from the local router to all routes in the link-state database.

Addressing

We've been referencing IS-IS area values up to this point. These area values are encoded in the IS-IS address of the router called the *Network Entity Title (NET)*. Let's now explore the details of IS-IS addressing. IS-IS uses the standard Network Service Access Point (NSAP) addressing as defined in ITU X.213. The size of the NSAP address varies from 8 to 20 bytes in length. There are three major parts to the address structure: area, system ID, and N-selector. The format of the NET is shown in Figure 7.5.

The first part of the address indicates the IS-IS area value. This field begins with the *Authority and Format Indicator (AFI)*, is followed by the Initial Domain Identifier, and finishes with the *Domain-Specific Part (DSP)*. The AFI byte indicates the governing body that administers the address space and assigns addresses. Networks often use 0x49 as their AFI, which represents the private NSAP address space. The NSAP private addresses are analogous to the private IP address space defined in RFC 1918. Your network requires a registered address only when Connectionless Network Protocol (CLNP) routing is desired with another network. The JUNOS software default does not route CLNP packets, so using private NSAP area addresses is perfectly fine.

NSAP Addressing

There are two major forms of registered NSAP addresses. The British Standards Institute administers the International Code Designator (ICD) address space. Each country has an address registration authority that administers the Data Country Code (DCC) address space. Each registered address space begins with a different value: 0x47 for ICD and 0x39 for DCC. Within the United States, you can order your own NSAP address (mine is 0x47.0005.80.8300). The Initial Domain Identifier (IDI) follows the AFI. The remaining area field indicates the DSP. In total, the combination of the AFI, IDI, and the DSP provides the complete area address.

Now that the alphabet soup is out of the way, let's talk about what this really means. First, think about your assigned IP address space. A registration authority decided that you should use certain bits to represent your network. The remainder of the address space is yours to subnet. In ISO-speak, your assigned address space is the combination of AFI and IDI numbers. You can subnet your network using the remainder of the area address, the DSP, as you see fit.

FIGURE 7.5   Network Entity Title format

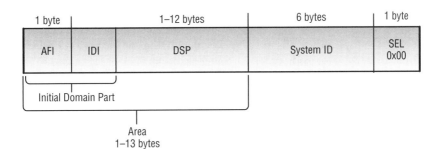

The field containing the *system ID* appears immediately after the Area field. The system ID uniquely identifies the router to the network. You can think of it as the host portion of the address. You are free to place any value in this field, but there are some common practices. The first is to use the Media Access Control (MAC) address of a broadcast interface as the system ID. This method guarantees uniqueness but carries with it the problem of user readability. A second method helps administrators more easily read the system ID. This approach uses an IP address assigned to the router (typically the router ID) to represent the ID value. You pad the address with leading zeros to provide 12 characters. As an example, assume our loopback address is 172.16.10.1 /32. We pad each dotted decimal value so that the address now reads 172.016.010.001 /32. The JUNOS software always uses a length of 6 bytes for the System ID field, which is also 12 characters long (in hexadecimal notation). Our padded IP address now fits neatly into the System ID field and provides us with an easy way to identify an IS-IS router in our network.

The last portion of the NET address is the *N-selector (SEL)* byte. The selector is used to distinguish different data services operating on the same router. A Juniper Networks router sends updates with a selector value of either 0x00 or some nonzero value. The 0x00 value is advertised in updates that represent the router itself, its links, and its neighbors. This type of update is always advertised into the network. A nonzero value is sent in updates for which the local router is acting as a pseudonode on a broadcast network. We discuss pseudonodes in the "Protocol Data Units" section later in this chapter. In following our analogy to IP addressing, the selector byte is similar to the function of the TCP/UDP port number in that it represents different logical processes.

Now that we understand what the pieces are, let's discuss how the JUNOS software comprehends the assigned NET address. You want to start reading the address from the right-hand side. The first byte is the selector, the next 6 bytes are the system ID, and the rest of the address is the area. It helps to interpret the address in this manner since the area value can range from 1 to 13 bytes in length.

Protocol Specifics

To this point, we've talked about link-state protocols, IS-IS levels, and addressing. Let's now begin discussing more specific details of the protocols. We look at the various IS-IS adjacency states first, followed by a discussion of how a router sends network data in a link-state update. We then explore the election process for the Designated Intermediate System (DIS) and finish with a look at the Protocol Data Units (PDUs) used by IS-IS in its operation.

IS-IS Adjacency States

If you recall our generic link-state discussion at the beginning of this chapter, two routers must first agree to exchange information before actually exchanging that data. This agreement to communicate is called an *adjacency*. The method for forming an adjacency is simple: two connected routers exchange IS-IS Hello messages. There are six possible states for an IS-IS adjacency:

New   This state is seen when the IS-IS adjacency process is just beginning. Start events could include router boot-up or initial configuration.

One-Way   Your IS-IS router transitions to this state after sending an IS-IS Hello PDU. In addition, any received hellos do not contain the local router's address as a neighbor.

Initializing   When a local router sees itself in a neighbor's hello, it transitions to this state. This state shows that bidirectional communications are established.

Up   This is a fully functioning state for IS-IS. An adjacency relationship is formed and the databases have been exchanged.

Down   This represents a nonfunctioning adjacency. An IS-IS router moves to this state for one of several reasons, including area mismatches, expiration of the hold time, and authentication failures.

Reject   Upon an authentication failure, an IS-IS router will transition between this state and the Down state.

General IS-IS Information Exchange

Now that our routers (Router A and Router B) have agreed to communicate, they then start exchanging information. Each router starts sending its partner a complete list of the information in its link-state database. The data exchanged at this time is the number of each link-state PDU in the database. This number is very similar to the table of contents for a book. If you are missing a chapter, you ask for that chapter number. Likewise, if Router A does not have a copy of a particular link-state PDU that Router B advertised, it asks for the missing information. Additionally, Router A might find that Router B has more updated information in its database, so Router A asks for the latest data. In both cases, Router B sends the complete data set related to the requested PDU. In this manner, both Router A and Router B generate complete copies of the link-state database. Recall that this is a critical concept for a link-state protocol like IS-IS. This process is represented in Figure 7.6.

FIGURE 7.6   IS-IS startup sequence

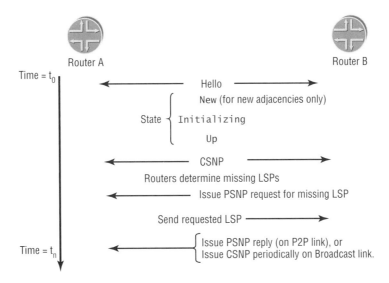

Router A and Router B are forming an adjacency and exchanging the information in their databases. The specific steps of this process are:

1. IS-IS Hello messages are exchanged to form an adjacency.

2. Each router sends a Complete Sequence Number PDU (CSNP) to its peer. These contain a complete summary listing of the link-state database, including sequence numbers and the age of each data segment.

3. Router B determines that it is missing information from its database and sends a Partial Sequence Number PDU (PSNP) to Router A.

4. Router A responds to this request with a link-state PDU (LSP) containing the requested information.

5. Router B issues either a PSNP (on a point-to-point link) or a CSNP (on a broadcast link) to inform Router A that the advertised link-state PDU was received. This acknowledgement is a critical step because it guarantees the reliable flooding of database information to all routers in the network.

Router B issues a CSNP on a broadcast link only when it's the Designated Intermediate System for that link. We discuss the election of the DIS in the "Designated Intermediate System" section later in this chapter.

Protocol Data Units

We'll now talk about the details of each IS-IS *Protocol Data Unit (PDU)*. We've been discussing some of the PDUs already, but this section contains an exhaustive look at each type.

FIGURE 7.7 IS-IS common PDU header

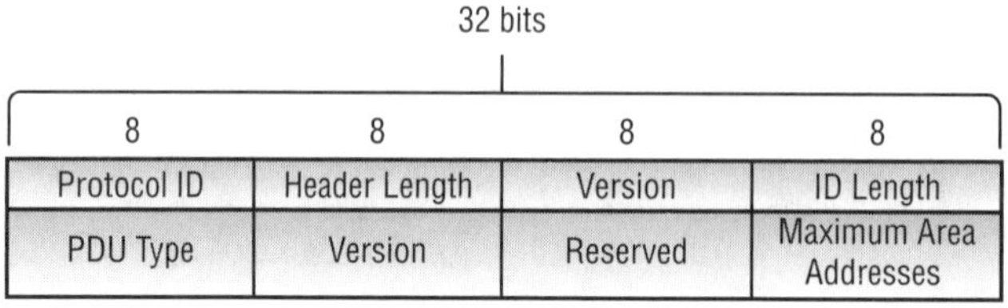

Each PDU shares a common header, illustrated in Figure 7.7. The header consists of the following fields:

Protocol ID (1 octet) This field is set to a constant value of 0x83 and designates that the higher-level data belongs to IS-IS.

Header Length (1 octet) This field indicates the total length, in octets, of the IS-IS headers. It includes both the common IS-IS header and any PDU-specific headers that follow.

Version/Protocol ID Extension (1 octet) This field is set to a constant value of 0x01. The IS-IS specification defines this field as an extension area for the Protocol ID data. The JUNOS software does not implement this function.

ID Length (1 octet) This field is used to inform other systems of the system ID length. For backward compatibility, the default length of 6 bytes is represented with the constant value of 0x00. The JUNOS software does not use a larger ID size, so this field is set to a constant value of 0x00.

PDU Type (1 octet) This field designates the PDU carried after the common header. The first 3 bits are set to 0. The remaining bit combinations include:

- Level 1 LAN Hello (15)
- Level 2 LAN Hello (16)
- Point-to-Point Hello (17)
- Level 1 link-state PDU (18)
- Level 2 link-state PDU (20)
- Level 1 Complete SNP (24)
- Level 2 Complete SNP (25)
- Level 1 Partial SNP (26)
- Level 2 Partial SNP (27)

Version (1 octet) This field is set to a constant value of 0x01, the current IS-IS version.

Reserved (1 octet) This field is set to a constant value of 0x00 and is ignored on receipt.

Maximum Area Addresses (1 octet) This field is set to a constant value of 0x00. It informs other systems how many area addresses are supported by the local router. A value of 0 means that no more than three area addresses are assigned to this router.

Details of each PDU type follow the common header. The information within the PDUs is encoded in a format called a *triple* (Type, Length, Value). IS-IS makes extensive uses of this format (often abbreviated as TLV) to convey information within its messages.

 Real World Scenario

Why Use a TLV Encoding Scheme?

The Type, Length, Value (TLV) format might at first glance appear to be unnecessary overhead. After all, each small piece of transmitted data is encoded in this format, resulting in larger transmissions between routers. It turns out, though, that this disadvantage is outweighed by the usefulness of the TLV format. TLVs allow the protocol to extend its capabilities and functionality very easily. For example, as new data formats were defined to support Traffic Engineering over Multiprotocol Label Switching, only a new TLV structure—not an entirely new PDU format—had to be defined. In addition, an IS-IS router ignores TLVs it does not support and uses the TLVs it does understand. Protocols based on message types alone do not have this luxury. The message type is either accepted or it is not. So although a TLV format adds more overhead to a specific data transmission, it makes the use of the protocol simpler in the long run.

IS-IS LAN Hello PDU

We've previously stated that IS-IS routers exchange *IS-IS Hello (IIH) PDUs* to establish an adjacency. While the purpose of the Hello PDU is the same, there are three different formats the router can use. One is for point-to-point links, and the two others are for broadcast links—one each for Level 1 and Level 2. Recall from the "IS-IS Levels" section earlier that L1 routers must share the same area address to form an adjacency, while L2 routers do not have this limitation. The separate LAN Hello PDUs simply tell the receiving router to check or ignore this information.

L1 LAN Hello PDUs are multicast to the "All L1 ISs" address of 01:80:c2:00:00:14. L2 routers share a separate multicast address "All L2 ISs" of 01:80:c2:00:00:15. Both LAN Hello PDUs share a common packet format, as shown in Figure 7.8.

The IS-IS LAN Hello PDU consists of the following fields:

Circuit Type (1 octet) The first 6 bits are set to 0. The remaining bits designate the level at which the interface is operating: L1 (0x01), L2 (0x02), or L1/L2 (0x03). PDUs with a value of 0x00 in this field are ignored.

Source ID (6 octets) This field designates the sender of the IIH. The field is set to the 6-byte system ID of the sending router.

Holding Time (2 octets)   The value in this field represents the amount of time each neighboring router should wait before terminating the adjacency after the last received IS-IS Hello PDU from this neighbor.

PDU Length (2 octets)   The value in this field represents the total length of the IS-IS Hello PDU. The field is set to a constant value of 1492 bytes (0x05D4).

Priority (1 octet)   The first bit is set to 0. The remainder of the byte designates the value used for the election of the DIS. The default value for the JUNOS software is 64.

LAN ID (7 octets)   This field designates the ID of the current DIS on the broadcast circuit. The field is set to the 6-byte system ID and 1-byte circuit ID of the DIS.

TLVs (Variable)   This field contains information about the sending router, including the area address, neighbor ID, authentication, and interface addressing.

 We discuss circuit ID values in the *"show isis interface"* section later in this chapter.

FIGURE 7.8   IS-IS Hello PDU (broadcast links)

```
                              32 bits
                                |
      ┌────────────────────────────────────────────────────┐
        8            8            8            8
      ┌──────────────┬────────────────────────────────────┐
      │ Circuit Type │              Source ID              │
      ├──────────────┴──────────────────────┬─────────────┤
      │      Source ID (continued)          │ Holding Time│
      ├──────────────┬──────────────────────┼─────────────┤
      │ Holding Time │        Length         │  Priority   │
      │ (continued)  │                       │             │
      ├──────────────┴───────────────────────┴─────────────┤
      │                    LAN ID                           │
      ├──────────────────────────────────────┬─────────────┤
      │         LAN ID (continued)            │    TLVs     │
      ├──────────────────────────────────────┴─────────────┤
      │                 TLVs (continued)                    │
      └─────────────────────────────────────────────────────┘
```

If you refer back to Figure 7.1, Shiraz is advertising an IS-IS LAN Hello on its `fe-0/0/0.0` interface:

```
May  2 22:50:54 Sending L1 LAN IIH on fe-0/0/0.0
May  2 22:50:54      max area 0, circuit type 11
May  2 22:50:54      neighbor 0:90:69:64:90:1f
May  2 22:50:54      neighbor 0:90:69:99:9c:0
May  2 22:50:54      No change in DR
May  2 22:50:54      hold time 9, priority 64, circuit id Shiraz.02
May  2 22:50:54      speaks IP
May  2 22:50:54      speaks IPv6
May  2 22:50:54      IP address 10.0.8.1
May  2 22:50:54      area address 47.0005.8083.00 (6)
```

Relevant portions of the output have been highlighted. You see the Circuit Type, Circuit ID, Hold Time, and Priority fields. Shiraz is advertising a hold time of 27 seconds. This is the default value for the JUNOS software on LAN interfaces unless the local router is the DIS. Hello PDUs are advertised every (hold time / 3) seconds, so the default Hello timer is 9 seconds.

Shiraz is also advertising a local DIS priority of 64, the JUNOS software default. This is the first tiebreaker for the election of the DIS, which we explain in the next section.

Designated Intermediate System

The concept of a *Designated Intermediate System (DIS)* is an important one when you're learning about IS-IS and link-state protocols. It helps to reduce the amount of data in the link-state database and aid in the processing of the shortest path first (SPF) calculation. We're examining its functionality here since a DIS is elected only on a broadcast-capable link.

Broadcast links in a network pose a special issue for link-state protocols. Using the example described earlier in this chapter in the "General IS-IS Information Exchange" section, each IS-IS router on the link forms an adjacency with every other router and advertises that information into the network. This requires information advertisements on the order of $N^*(N-1)$, where N is the number of routers on the link. Many texts refer to this amount of data as $O(N^2)$ updates. This adds unnecessary information and overhead to the protocol because each router is advertising the exact same information.

You can mitigate this situation by introducing a pseudonode that represents the broadcast link to the rest of the network. The pseudonode will advertise the neighbor relationships of all routers in its database update; the actual routers advertise a relationship with only the pseudonode.

Let's examine Figure 7.9. Without a pseudonode on this network, Shiraz advertises a relationship with Merlot, Riesling, and Cabernet. All other routers follow this same procedure. This $O(N^2)$ advertisement grows the database size exponentially as the number of routers on the broadcast link grows. When a pseudonode is introduced on the link, all routers only advertise a relationship to that node. The database size now grows on $O(N)$ as the number of routers grows.

FIGURE 7.9   Designated Intermediate System updates

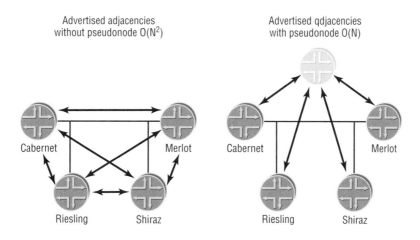

Advertised adjacencies without pseudonode $O(N^2)$

Advertised qdjacencies with pseudonode $O(N)$

Cabernet   Merlot   Riesling   Shiraz

Cabernet   Merlot   Riesling   Shiraz

Within IS-IS, the elected pseudonode is called the DIS. The election process is very determin-istic since the router with the best (highest) criteria is always the DIS. The first criterion checked is the advertised *DIS priority* of the router. The priority range is between 0 and 127, with a JUNOS software default of 64. When two or more nodes share priority values, the second cri-terion checked is the MAC address of the advertising router.

The Hello and hold-time timer values are changed for elected DIS routers. The 27-second hold time is reduced to 9 seconds. The Hello timer is still (hold time / 3), which results in a Hello PDU every 3 seconds. These quicker intervals allow the non-DIS routers to notice the loss of the DIS in a timely manner and elect a new DIS.

IS-IS Point-to-Point Hello PDU

IS-IS adjacencies on point-to-point links are also formed through the advertisement of Hello PDUs. On broadcast links, separate PDUs have been defined for Level 1 and Level 2. Only a single Hello PDU is defined for point-to-point links. The desire to be adjacent with a neighbor at L1, L2, or L1/L2 is encoded in the Circuit Type field within the PDU itself. The format of the PDU is shown in Figure 7.10.

FIGURE 7.10   IS-IS Hello PDU (point-to-point links)

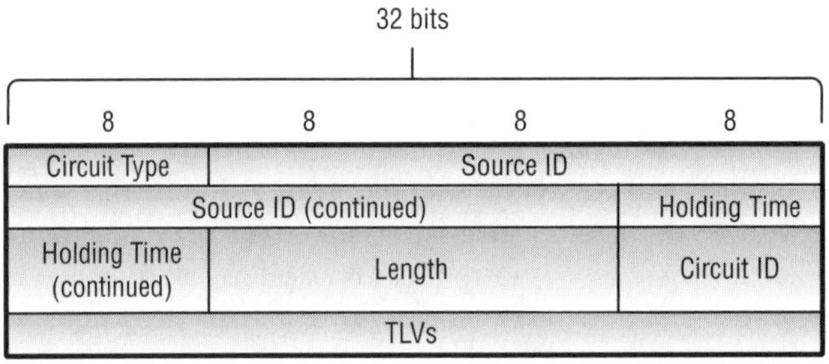

The IS-IS point-to-point Hello PDU consists of the following fields:

Circuit Type (1 octet)   The first 6 bits are set to 0. The remaining bits designate the level at which the interface is operating: L1 (0x01), L2 (0x02), or L1/L2 (0x03). PDUs with a value of 0x00 in this field are ignored.

Source ID (6 octets)   This field designates the sender of the IIH. It is set to the 6-byte system ID of the sending router.

Holding Time (2 octets)   The value in this field represents the amount of time each neighbor-ing router should wait before terminating the adjacency after the last received IS-IS Hello PDU.

PDU Length (2 octets)   The total length of the IS-IS Hello PDU is encoded in this field. The field is set to a constant value of 1492 bytes (0x05D4).

Circuit ID (1 octet)   This field designates the specific ID of the local router's interface. All point-to-point interfaces share a value of 0x01 within the JUNOS software.

TLVs (Variable)   This field contains information about the sending router, including the area address, authentication, and interface addressing.

We discuss circuit ID values in the "*show isis interface*" section later in this chapter.

In our example, Riesling is advertising an IS-IS point-to-point Hello on its e3-0/2/0.101 interface. It wants to form only a Level 2 adjacency with Cabernet, its neighboring router:

```
May   2 22:52:12 Sending PTP IIH on e3-0/2/0.101
May   2 22:52:12     max area 0, circuit type l2
May   2 22:52:12     ptp adjacency tlv length 15
May   2 22:52:12     neighbor state up
May   2 22:52:12     our extended local ciruit id 9
May   2 22:52:12     neighbor sysid Cabernet
May   2 22:52:12     neighbor extended local circuit id 5
May   2 22:52:12     speaks IP
May   2 22:52:12     speaks IPv6
May   2 22:52:12     IP address 192.168.1.1
May   2 22:52:12     area address 49.0001 (3)
```

 Real World Scenario

IS-IS Hello PDUs and Data-Link MTUs

You may notice that both the LAN and point-to-point Hello PDUs have preset lengths assigned to them. This arises from the fact that an IS-IS router does not resize any PDU to match the maximum transmission unit (MTU) on an interface. Therefore, each interface must support the transmission of the maximum IS-IS PDU of 1492 bytes. To enforce this requirement, the IS-IS Hello PDUs are padded to this maximum value. If the hello gets to the neighboring router, the connecting interface supports the maximum PDU size. Should the hello not be received by the neighboring router, no adjacency forms and this link is not used by IS-IS.

A point-to-point interface assumes a payload size of 1500 bytes but subtracts the transmission overhead of the High-Level Data Link Control (HDLC) broadcast frame (1 byte), an unnumbered information control field (1 byte), and the PPP Protocol ID field (2 bytes). This leaves 1496 bytes for IS-IS to operate within, 4 bytes more than the size of the Hello PDU for a point-to-point interface.

Broadcast links also begin with a 1500-byte payload field but have different overhead require-ments. Juniper Networks and other router vendors use the IEEE 802.2 Logical Link Control (LLC) encoding for IS-IS packets on broadcast interfaces. The 802.2 LLC format assumes 3 bytes of data, one each for the destination service access point (DSAP), the source service access point (SSAP), and the control field. This leaves 1497 bytes available while the Hello PDU is using only 1492 bytes. (The 5 bytes of difference are left to account for the option that a vendor might use an Ethernet SNAP header for IS-IS. This would use an additional 5 bytes of user payload, leaving IS-IS with only 1492 bytes available to it.) Therefore, the maximum PDU size of a Hello PDU for a broadcast link is set to 1492 to account for this possibility.

The following information is not specific to IS-IS but involves more detail in the Ethernet encap-sulation techniques used in networking. If you want to focus only on IS-IS, return to the chapter text at this point. For you true network nerds out there, please read on.

The IEEE 802.2 committee defined three methods for using the LLC in an Ethernet network. Type 1, unacknowledged connectionless service, uses the data-link layer as a stream of data. There is no inherent connection established to transmit the data reliably. Type 2 is a connection-oriented mode service that allows for a connection establishment, some data transfer, and a dis-connect sequence. This is very much like the functions of TCP for Ethernet. Finally, Type 3 is for acknowledged connectionless service where the receiving side sends messages to the sender to verify its receipt.

While Types 2 and 3 are valuable in a network using IBM's System Network Architecture (SNA), modern implementations of Ethernet use only Type 1 LLC encoding. Higher layers of the protocol stack assume responsibility for connections between systems. The Ethernet net-work should send the data in an unsequenced fashion. A Type 1 packet uses a control field value of 0x03 in the LLC header. When added to the default DSAP and SSAP values of 0xFE, the entire 802.2 LLC header for an IS-IS broadcast packet is 0xFE-FE-03.

For further reading, refer to *Handbook of Computer Communications Stan-dards*, William Stallings (Macmillan, 1990), pp. 76-87.

Complete Sequence Number PDU

The *Complete Sequence Number PDU (CSNP)* contains a complete listing of the link-state PDUs in the link-state database of the local router. The CSNP provides an identifier, a lifetime, a sequence number, and a checksum for each piece of information in the database. A CSNP is sent periodically on both broadcast and point-to-point links to maintain database correctness. In addition, CSNPs are advertised between two neighbors during the formation of an adjacency.

As with the IS-IS LAN Hello PDUs, there are separate CSNPs for Level 1 and Level 2 used on all media types. Level 1 PDUs are multicast to the "All L1 ISs" address of 01:80:c2:00:00:14. Level 2 PDUs are multicast to the "All L2 ISs" address of 01:80:c2:00:00:15. Figure 7.11 shows the format of the CSNP.

FIGURE 7.11   IS-IS Complete Sequence Number PDU

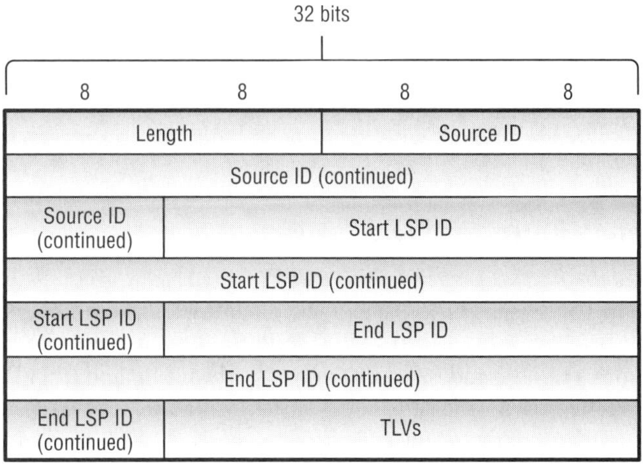

```
                            32 bits

         8            8            8            8
   ┌──────────────────────────────────────────────────┐
   │          Length          │        Source ID       │
   ├──────────────────────────────────────────────────┤
   │               Source ID (continued)               │
   ├──────────────┬────────────────────────────────────┤
   │  Source ID   │            Start LSP ID             │
   │ (continued)  │                                     │
   ├──────────────┴────────────────────────────────────┤
   │            Start LSP ID (continued)                │
   ├──────────────┬────────────────────────────────────┤
   │ Start LSP ID │             End LSP ID              │
   │ (continued)  │                                     │
   ├──────────────┴────────────────────────────────────┤
   │             End LSP ID (continued)                 │
   ├──────────────┬────────────────────────────────────┤
   │  End LSP ID  │                TLVs                 │
   │ (continued)  │                                     │
   └──────────────┴────────────────────────────────────┘
```

The fields of the CSNP include:

Length (2 octets)   The total length of the CSNP, in octets, is encoded in this field.

Source ID (7 octets)   This field designates the sender of the CSNP. It is set to the 6-byte system ID and 1-byte circuit ID (0x00) of the sending router.

Start LSP ID (8 octets)   This field is set to a constant value of 0x0000.0000.0000.00-00. It designates the smallest possible LSP ID value.

End LSP ID (8 octets)   This field is set to a constant value of 0xFFFF.FFFF.FFFF.FF-FF. It designates the largest possible LSP ID value.

TLVs (Variable)   This field contains the summary database information from the local router.

Here, Cabernet has received a CSNP from Riesling on its e3-0/2/0.101 interface:

```
May  2 22:49:51 Received L2 CSN, source Riesling, interface e3-0/2/0.101
May  2 22:49:51     LSP range 0000.0000.0000.00-00 to ffff.ffff.ffff.ff-ff
May  2 22:49:51     packet length 83
May  2 22:49:51     LSP Riesling.00-00 lifetime 916
May  2 22:49:51     sequence 0x42 checksum 0x60a7
May  2 22:49:51     Matched database, matching sequence numbers
May  2 22:49:51     LSP Merlot.00-00 lifetime 1160
May  2 22:49:51     sequence 0x3c checksum 0xb88d
May  2 22:49:51     Matched database, matching sequence numbers
May  2 22:49:51     LSP Cabernet.00-00 lifetime 801
May  2 22:49:51     sequence 0x3d checksum 0xc376
May  2 22:49:51     Matched database, matching sequence numbers
```

Each segment of Riesling's database contains the LSP ID, a sequence number, a lifetime value, and a checksum. The combination of these data segments uniquely identifies each LSP in the network. As Cabernet receives the CSNP, it checks the database entries against its own local link-state database. If some advertised information is missing, Cabernet requests the specific LSP details using a Partial Sequence Number PDU.

At this point, Cabernet's local database matches the advertised LSP information. The JUNOS software designates a match with the `Matched database, matching sequence numbers` message.

Partial Sequence Number PDU

An IS-IS router uses the *Partial Sequence Number PDU (PSNP)* to request LSP information from a neighbor. The PSNP is also used to explicitly acknowledge the receipt of a received LSP on a point-to-point link. On a broadcast link, CSNPs are used as implicit acknowledgments.

The PSNP has both a Level 1 and Level 2 variety, like the CSNP and IIH PDUs. On broadcast networks, Level 1 PSNPs are multicast to the "All L1 ISs" address of 01:80:c2:00:00:14 and Level 2 PSNPs are multicast to the "All L2 ISs" address of 01:80:c2:00:00:15. The format of the PSNP is shown in Figure 7.12.

FIGURE 7.12   IS-IS Partial Sequence Number PDU

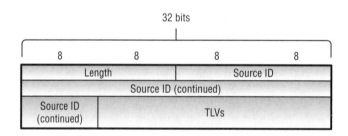

A Partial Sequence Number PDU includes the following fields:

Length (2 octets)   The total length of the PSNP, in octets, is encoded in this field.

Source ID (7 octets)   This field designates the sender of the PSNP. It is set to the 6-byte system ID and 1-byte circuit ID (0x00) of the sending router.

TLVs (Variable)   This field contains the requested database information or the LSP being acknowledged.

Here, Cabernet has received another CSNP from Riesling on its `e3-0/2/0.101` interface:

```
May  9 15:22:21 Received L2 CSN, source Riesling, interface e3-0/2/0.101
May  9 15:22:21    LSP range 0000.0000.0000.00-00 to ffff.ffff.ffff.ff-ff
May  9 15:22:21    packet length 83
```

```
May  9 15:22:21      LSP Riesling.00-00 lifetime 1194
May  9 15:22:21      sequence 0x336 checksum 0x9a76
May  9 15:22:21      Missing LSP, requesting
May  9 15:22:21 Sending L2 PSN on interface e3-0/2/0.101
May  9 15:22:21      LSP Riesling.00-00 lifetime 1192
May  9 15:22:21      sequence 0 checksum 0x9a76
May  9 15:22:26 Received L2 LSP Riesling.00-00, interface e3-0/2/0.101
May  9 15:22:26      from Riesling
May  9 15:22:26      sequence 0x336, checksum 0x9a76, lifetime 1188
<information removed>
May  9 15:22:26      New LSP, adding to database
May  9 15:22:26 Sending L2 PSN on interface e3-0/2/0.101
May  9 15:22:26      LSP Riesling.00-00 lifetime 1186
May  9 15:22:26      sequence 0x336 checksum 0x9a76
```

As Cabernet compares the CSNP to its local database, it determines that the Riesling.00-00 LSP is missing. Cabernet issues a PSNP for the missing LSP, which Riesling returns in a link-state PDU (which we describe in the next section). The received LSP of Riesling.00-00 is installed in Cabernet's database and an acknowledgement PSNP is returned to Riesling.

Link-State PDU

Thus far, we've been talking about the link-state database from numerous perspectives. IS-IS routers have formed adjacencies and compared their databases. Complete and Partial Sequence Number PDUs have been sent between routers to synchronize the databases. We've failed to discuss the actual database information to this point. Let's now tackle this subject.

A *link-state PDU (LSP)* contains information about each router in the network and its connected interfaces. Metric and IS-IS neighbor information is also included. Figure 7.13 shows the format of the link-state PDU.

FIGURE 7.13   IS-IS link-state PDU

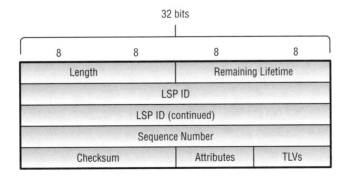

A link-state PDU includes the following fields:

Length (2 octets)   The total length of the LSP is encoded in this field.

Remaining Lifetime (2 octets)   This field lists the amount of time, in seconds, each router should consider the LSP active. The JUNOS software default lifetime value is 1200 seconds.

LSP ID (8 octets)   This field uniquely identifies the LSP throughout the network. The value is a combination of the system ID (6 bytes), circuit ID (1 byte), and LSP Number value.

Sequence Number (4 octets)   This field is set to the current version number of the LSP. The initial number is 0x01 and is incremented each time the originating router updates the LSP.

Checksum (2 octets)   This field contains the checksum value of the PDU fields after the Remaining Lifetime.

Attributes (1 octet)   This field contains multiple settings related to the state of the local router. The specific bit positions are:

Bit 7   Partition bit. Set to 0 and not supported by the JUNOS software.

Bit 6   Attached bit for error metric. Set to 0 and not supported by the JUNOS software.

Bit 5   Attached bit for expense metric. Set to 0 and not supported by the JUNOS software.

Bit 4   Attached bit for delay metric. Set to 0 and not supported by the JUNOS software.

Bit 3   Attached bit for default metric. Used by an L2 router to advertise connectivity to the IS-IS backbone into an L1 area.

Bit 2   Overload bit. Used to alert other IS-IS routers to not use the information advertised in this LSP.

Bits 0 and 1   Designates the capabilities of the router. An L1 router sets these to 0x01. An L1/L2 router or L2 router sets these to 0x03.

TLVs (Variable)   This field contains the summary database information from the local router.

In the "Partial Sequence Number PDU" section earlier in this chapter, we showed an IS-IS exchange between Riesling and Cabernet. Cabernet requested an LSP from Riesling using a PSNP and Riesling responded. The actual LSP information was removed from the earlier capture and is included here:

```
May  9 15:22:26 Received L2 LSP Riesling.00-00, interface e3-0/2/0.101
May  9 15:22:26     from Riesling
May  9 15:22:26     sequence 0x336, checksum 0x9a76, lifetime 1188
May  9 15:22:26     max area 0, length 263
May  9 15:22:26     no partition repair, no database overload
May  9 15:22:26     IS type 3, metric type 0
May  9 15:22:26     area address 49.0001 (3)
May  9 15:22:26     speaks IP
```

```
May  9 15:22:26     IP router id: 192.168.0.1
May  9 15:22:26     IP address 192.168.0.1
May  9 15:22:26     dyn hostname Riesling
May  9 15:22:26     IS neighbor Merlot.00, metric: 10
May  9 15:22:26       IP address: 192.168.2.1
May  9 15:22:26       Neighbor's IP address: 192.168.2.2
May  9 15:22:26     IS neighbor Cabernet.00, metric: 10
May  9 15:22:26       IP address: 192.168.1.1
May  9 15:22:26       Neighbor's IP address: 192.168.1.2
May  9 15:22:26     IP prefix: 192.168.0.1/32 metric 0 up
May  9 15:22:26     IP prefix: 192.168.1.0/30 metric 10 up
May  9 15:22:26     IP prefix: 192.168.2.0/30 metric 10 up
May  9 15:22:26     IP prefix: 192.168.0.0/24 metric 10 up
May  9 15:22:26     IP prefix: 192.168.1.0/24 metric 10 up
May  9 15:22:26     IP prefix: 200.0.3.0/24 metric 10 up
```

The highlighted portion of the output shows the sequence number, lifetime, checksum, and overload setting. The IS type, currently set to 3, shows that Riesling is capable of communicating at both Level 1 and Level 2. Also included are the IS-IS neighbors of Merlot and Cabernet with appropriate IP addressing information. You can also observe the IP subnets and metrics advertised by Riesling.

Common TLVs

Each of the IS-IS PDUs we have discussed contained some TLV triples. While the entire listing of TLV values is outside the scope of this book, the list below points out some common TLVs. You can observe many of these in the Riesling output in the "Link-State PDU" section earlier in this chapter.

- TLV 1—Area Addresses
- TLV 2—IS Reachability
- TLV 6—IS Neighbors
- TLV 8—Padding
- TLV 9—LSP Entry
- TLV 10—Authentication
- TLV 128—IP Internal Reachability
- TLV 129—Protocols Supported
- TLV 130—IP External Reachability
- TLV 132—IP Interface Address
- TLV 137—Dynamic Hostname Mapping

Command-Line Interface

Up to this point in the chapter, we've been talking about IS-IS from a theoretical point of view. Let's now discuss how to use the protocol on a Juniper Networks router. We first look at the configuration of the protocol; then we examine some JUNOS software commands you can use to troubleshoot the operation of IS-IS.

Configuration Commands

The configuration of IS-IS within the JUNOS software requires three main steps. You first assign a NET ID to the router. Then you configure each router interface using the `family iso` command. Finally, you configure the protocol itself within [edit protocols]. Let's examine each step in more detail.

Network Entity Title Assignment

Recall from the "Addressing" section earlier in this chapter that the ISO NSAP address encodes the system ID of the router and its area address. This information is critical to allow an IS-IS adjacency to form. You should configure the router's NET ID on a reliable and stable router interface; that way, an interface failure does not mean the loss of the NET address. It is currently a best practice to assign the NET ID to the router's loopback interface (lo0).

This command assigns a NET ID to Merlot's lo0 interface:

```
[edit interfaces lo0 unit 0]
user@Merlot# set family iso address 47.0005.8083.0000.1921.6800.5001.00
```

This results in the following configuration:

```
[edit interfaces lo0]
user@Merlot# show
unit 0 {
    family inet {
        address 192.168.5.1/32;
    }
    family iso {
        address 47.0005.8083.0000.1921.6800.5001.00;
    }
}
```

Remember to set the N-Selector byte to a value of 0x00 to allow your IS-IS adjacencies to form.

Configuring Physical Interfaces

An interface on a Juniper Networks router accepts only IP packets by default. To allow other protocol types to enter the router, you must configure the interface to recognize those packets. This means that each interface must be aware that IS-IS packets with a Network-Layer Protocol ID value of 0x83 are important. You use the `family iso` command to accomplish this, as shown in the following:

```
[edit]
user@Cabernet# set interfaces fe-0/1/0 unit 0 family iso
user@Cabernet# set interfaces e3-0/2/0 unit 101 family iso
```

Cabernet now has two transit interfaces capable of running the IS-IS protocol. This is verified when we issue the `show interfaces terse` command:

```
user@Cabernet> show interfaces terse
Interface       Admin Link Proto Local                 Remote
fe-0/1/0        up    up
fe-0/1/0.0      up    up    inet  10.0.8.3/24
                            iso
fe-0/1/1        up    down
fe-0/1/2        up    down
fe-0/1/3        up    down
e3-0/2/0        up    up
e3-0/2/0.101    up    up    inet  192.168.1.2/30
                            iso
e3-0/2/1        up    down
e3-0/2/2        up    down
e3-0/2/3        up    down
fxp0            up    up
fxp0.0          up    up    inet  172.25.41.111/25
fxp1            up    up
fxp1.0          up    up    tnp   4
gre             up    up
ipip            up    up
lo0             up    up
lo0.0           up    up    inet  192.168.16.1          --> 0/0
                            iso   47.0005.8083.0000.1921.6801.6001.00
lsi             up    up
```

The presence of the `iso` keyword within the logical interface portion of the fe-0/1/0 and e3-0/2/0 interfaces verifies the success of the configuration.

Configuring the Protocol

The final step in operating IS-IS within the JUNOS software is enabling the route protocol daemon, rpd, to process IS-IS messages. You enable rpd within the [edit protocols isis] portion of the configuration hierarchy. Each configured IS-IS interface operates at both Level 1 and Level 2 by default. To prevent IS-IS from forming an adjacency at a particular level, you must use the disable command. Let's examine some different methods for configuring the protocol. Figure 7.14 shows our sample network and the IS-IS level each interface should use.

FIGURE 7.14 IS-IS network-level configuration

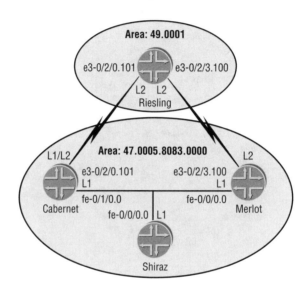

Riesling

We've configured Riesling to use only Level 2 IS-IS packets to communicate with its neighbors:

```
[edit protocols]
user@Riesling# show
isis {
    level 1 disable;
    interface e3-0/2/0.101;
    interface e3-0/2/3.100;
    interface lo0.0;
}
```

The configuration of level 1 disable at the global IS-IS level allows individual interfaces to be listed without requiring you to explicitly disable the level for each. This is a common practice for routers that use only one of the two possible levels. Interface `lo0.0` is configured to allow adjacencies to form with the neighboring routers. Recall from the "Network Entity Title Assignment" section earlier in this chapter that the area address in the NET ID was placed on the loopback interface. Neighbor adjacencies form only when the NET ID is on an operational IS-IS interface.

Cabernet

IS-IS adjacencies for Cabernet operate at both Level 1 and Level 2 with its neighbors. Its configuration is as follows:

```
[edit protocols]
user@Cabernet# show
isis {
    interface fe-0/1/0.0 {
        level 2 disable;
    }
    interface e3-0/2/0.101;
    interface lo0.0;
}
```

Interface `lo0.0` is included, as before, to advertise the NET ID to its neighbors. The inclusion of `level 2 disable` within the configuration of interface `fe-0/1/0.0` allows only IS-IS Level 1 packets to be sent and limits this neighbor relationship to an L1 adjacency. Cabernet sends both L1 and L2 IS-IS Hello PDUs to Riesling based on the default interface parameters for interface `e3-0/2/0.101`. Because Riesling is configured to only use Level 2, only an L2 adjacency will form between these routers.

Shiraz

The single interface on Shiraz is operating with its neighbors at Level 1 only. The configuration for Shiraz is:

```
[edit protocols]
user@Shiraz# show
isis {
    level 2 disable;
    interface all;
    interface fxp0.0 {
        disable;
    }
}
```

The configuration of `level 2 disable` at the global IS-IS level mirrors the configuration of Riesling. It again allows individual interfaces to be listed without requiring the explicit disabling of the IS-IS level for each. We've used the keyword `all` in Shiraz's configuration to allow IS-IS to operate on any interface configured with the `family iso` command. This is a common configuration when an IS-IS router is using every router interface.

Merlot

We've configured Merlot to use Level 2 with Riesling and Level 1 with all other routers:

```
[edit protocols]
user@Merlot# show
isis {
    interface e3-0/2/3.100 {
        level 1 disable;
    }
    interface all {
        level 2 disable;
    }
    interface fxp0.0 {
        disable;
    }
}
```

We've also configured Merlot with the `interface all` command, which allows all operational IS-IS capable interfaces to use the protocol. These interfaces use only Level 1 packets to form adjacencies with Shiraz and Cabernet. We've configured interface `e3-0/2/3.100` separately for Level 2 operations to Riesling. The listing of an individual interface within the IS-IS configuration overrides the more generic use of `interface all`. This is very similar to the JUNOS software default of a more specific parameter application taking precedence over a less specific application. The exception here is that both of the applications occur within the same configuration hierarchy.

There is one IS-IS configuration option that can't be overridden with a more specific application. When you set `level 2 disable` at the global IS-IS level, this will cause all interfaces on the router to never use Level 2 PDUs. A specific interface reference to `level 1 disable` (which normally activates Level 2) does not take effect. In essence, no adjacencies ever form on the interface you specified. Only use the global application when you really mean it!

Disabling the *fxp0* Interface

You may recall from Chapter 1, "The Components of a Juniper Networks Router," that the `fxp0` interface on a Juniper Networks router has a special purpose. It should be used only for out-of-band access to the Routing Engine. Packets can't be forwarded from a transit interface across the backbone of the router and out the management interface. However, `fxp0` is still an operational interface on the router and IS-IS adjacencies can be formed using this interface.

Using Figure 7.14 as a guide, imagine that the fxp0 interfaces of Shiraz and Riesling are con-figured for IS-IS and an L2 adjacency forms between those routers. Riesling now believes that it has a direct connection to Shiraz, when in fact it should not. Packets transiting Riesling and destined for Shiraz will attempt to be forwarded out the management interface, but will in fact be dropped from the network. Compounding this issue is the fact that both Shiraz and Riesling advertise their relationship into the IS-IS network and other routers view this "virtual" connec-tion as a viable network link.

In short, nothing good can come from enabling the fxp0 interface within a routing protocol. Therefore, it is a good practice to explicitly disable the management interface when using the interface all syntax.

Verification and Troubleshooting Commands

Once IS-IS is configured on your network, you probably want to know if it is working correctly. The JUNOS software provides command-line interface (CLI) commands that verify and assist in troubleshooting your configuration.

In Figure 7.15, we've added some IP addressing information to our sample network. We use this common diagram to explore the various commands.

FIGURE 7.15   IS-IS network addressing

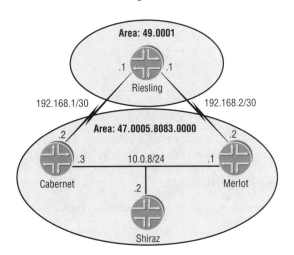

show isis adjacency

You can verify that your IS-IS adjacencies are working by using the show isis adjacency command. This is often the first command you'll use when troubleshooting IS-IS. When a neigh-bor appears in the output, you can safely assume that packets are traversing the physical inter-face, IS-IS PDUs have been exchanged, and the link-state databases are synchronized.

```
user@Cabernet> show isis adjacency
Interface           System          L State          Hold (secs) SNPA
e3-0/2/0.101        Riesling        2 Up                      23
fe-0/1/0.0          Shiraz          1 Up                       7  0:90:69:99:9c:0
fe-0/1/0.0          Merlot          1 Up                      24  0:90:69:97:c4:0
```

The column entries provide important information to you at a glance.

Interface   This identifies the logical interface on which IS-IS has formed an adjacency. If an expected entry is not listed here, first verify that the interface is configured within [edit protocols isis]. A second possible cause of this problem results from omitting the family iso command on that interface.

System   The automatic system ID-to-router hostname mapping is shown here. Until this resolution occurs, the system ID value itself is displayed.

L (Level)   This indicates the IS-IS adjacency level with that neighbor. Possible values are 1, 2, or 3. A value of 3 indicates both a Level 1 and a Level 2 adjacency on a point-to-point interface. A "!" symbol next to a level value denotes no IP information is present on the interfaces. Remember that a Juniper Networks router uses only CLNP packets to form an IS-IS adjacency.

State   Indicates the current state of the IS-IS adjacency. Possible values include:

- Up
- Down
- New
- One-Way
- Initializing
- Rejected

Hold   Displays the time remaining before the local router removes the IS-IS adjacency.

SNPA   The Sub-Network Point of Attachment (SNPA) is the data-link address used to reach the neighbor on a broadcast media. Ethernet links use the MAC address of the neighbor as the SNPA.

show isis adjacency detail

Adding the detail option to the show isis adjacency command provides additional information about each IS-IS adjacency:

```
user@Cabernet> show isis adjacency detail
Riesling
  Interface: e3-0/2/0.101, Level: 2, State: Up, Expires in 25 secs
  Priority: 0, Up/Down transitions: 1, Last transition: 08:18:11 ago
  Circuit type: 3, Speaks: IP, IPv6
  Restart capable: No
  IP addresses: 192.168.1.1
```

```
Shiraz
  Interface: fe-0/1/0.0, Level: 1, State: Up, Expires in 8 secs
  Priority: 64, Up/Down transitions: 1, Last transition: 00:06:21 ago
  Circuit type: 1, Speaks: IP, IPv6, MAC address: 0:90:69:99:9c:0
  Restart capable: No
  LAN id: Shiraz.02, IP addresses: 10.0.8.2
```

The first line of the output for each neighbor closely resembles the normal adjacency output. Additional information gathered from this command includes the configured (DIS) priority value. Riesling is advertising a value of 0 on the point-to-point link (because no DIS is elected on this interface), while Shiraz is advertising a value of 64 on the Ethernet link. The Circuit Type entry details the local level configuration of the router. Cabernet's interface is configured for a circuit type of 3 (both L1 and L2), but the actual adjacency is reporting only Level 2. Riesling is either configured for only L2, or an IS-IS area mismatch occurred at Level 1 between the two routers. The Ethernet link to Shiraz shows the MAC address (SNPA) of the neighbor as well as the address of the LAN pseudonode—Shiraz.02.

clear isis adjacency

The clear isis adjacency command enables you to remove an IS-IS adjacency from the local router. New IS-IS Hello PDUs and sequence number PDUs are exchanged and the adjacency is reestablished. This is helpful to guarantee that "fresh" information is entered in the link-state database correctly. Using the clear isis adjacency command itself clears all adjacencies; adding a neighbor's hostname clears just that single adjacency.

```
user@Shiraz> show isis adjacency
Interface          System        L State        Hold (secs) SNPA
fe-0/0/0.0         Cabernet      1 Up                    26 0:90:69:64:90:1f
fe-0/0/0.0         Merlot        1 Up                    23 0:90:69:97:c4:0

user@Shiraz> clear isis adjacency Cabernet

user@Shiraz> show isis adjacency
Interface          System        L State        Hold (secs) SNPA
fe-0/0/0.0         Cabernet      1 Initializing         26 0:90:69:64:90:1f
fe-0/0/0.0         Merlot        1 Up                    22 0:90:69:97:c4:0

user@Shiraz> show isis adjacency
Interface          System        L State        Hold (secs) SNPA
fe-0/0/0.0         Cabernet      1 Up                    26 0:90:69:64:90:1f
fe-0/0/0.0         Merlot        1 Up                    21 0:90:69:97:c4:0
```

After verifying the current adjacencies, Shiraz clears its connection with Cabernet. As the adjacency starts to reform, the Initializing state quickly appears since the neighboring router lists the local router in its IS-IS Hello PDU.

show isis interface

After you use the show isis adjacency command and see no neighbors, the show isis interface command is the next best troubleshooting command available. It displays the interfaces that are currently operational from the local router's perspective.

```
user@Cabernet> show isis interface
IS-IS interface database:
Interface            L CirID Level 1 DR      Level 2 DR       L1/L2 Metric
e3-0/2/0.101         3  0x1 Point to Point   Point to Point      10/10
fe-0/1/0.0           1  0x2 Shiraz.02        Disabled            10/10
lo0.0                0  0x1 Passive          Passive              0/0
```

Each of the columns in the output indicate the IS-IS configuration and operation of the interfaces.

Interface   This identifies the logical interface on which IS-IS is operating. Entries not listed here are often caused by a misconfiguration within [edit protocols isis] or a missing family iso command on that interface.

L (Level)   This indicates the IS-IS levels each interface is configured to support. Possible values are 0,1, 2, or 3. A value of 0 indicates that all operational IS-IS levels are currently in passive mode. A value of 3 indicates that both Level 1 and Level 2 are operating on the interface.

CirID   Each IS-IS interface is assigned a circuit ID value to identify the interface within the link-state database. The loopback interface and all point-to-point links share the locally significant value of 0x01. Each broadcast link receives a unique value starting at 0x02 and incrementing by 1 for each new interface.

Level 1 DR / Level 2 DR   Each interface lists the known DISs (if any) for that link. The loopback interface is always listed as passive since no IS-IS adjacency can ever form on this virtual interface. No DIS is ever elected on a point-to-point link, so the listing there is always Point to Point. Each broadcast interface displays the known DIS for that interface. All interfaces that are not configured for a particular IS-IS level show Disabled in this column.

L1/L2 Metric   The advertised metrics of each interface are displayed here. IS-IS uses a default interface metric of 10 for both Levels 1 and 2. The maximum metric value is a 6-bit value of 63. Each IS-IS router is capable of calculating a total path cost of 1023, or 10 bits.

show isis hostname

You can use the show isis hostname command to verify the dynamic hostname resolution of system ID values. This command is helpful when you suspect that multiple IS-IS routers have an identical system ID configuration.

```
user@Cabernet> show isis hostname
IS-IS hostname database:
System ID      Hostname                          Type
1921.6800.0001 Riesling                          Dynamic
```

```
1921.6800.5001 Merlot                           Dynamic
1921.6800.8001 Shiraz                           Dynamic
1921.6801.6001 Cabernet                         Static
```

show isis spf log

The show isis spf log command shows the history of SPF calculations (Dijkstra Algorithm), why it was performed, and the duration of the calculation. A constant and rapid SPF calculation is sometimes caused by a flapping interface in your network. The show isis spf log command can pinpoint the router that is connected to the interface because each flap causes a new link-state PDU to be generated.

```
user@Cabernet> show isis spf log
 IS-IS level 1 SPF log:
Start time          Elapsed (secs) Count Reason
Thu May  2 21:07:12      0.000205    1 Periodic SPF
Thu May  2 22:32:32      0.000225    1 Updated LSP Shiraz.00-00
Thu May  2 22:33:09      0.000171    1 Updated LSP Shiraz.02-00
Thu May  2 22:33:16      0.000177    3 Updated LSP Shiraz.02-00

 IS-IS level 2 SPF log:
Start time          Elapsed (secs) Count Reason
Thu May  2 22:24:46      0.000166    1 Periodic SPF
Thu May  2 22:33:10      0.000125    1 Updated LSP Cabernet.00-00
Thu May  2 22:33:11      0.000134    1 Updated LSP Merlot.00-00
Thu May  2 22:33:23      0.000127    1 Updated LSP Cabernet.00-00
```

 Remember that the SPF algorithm operates as the local router receives new LSPs. Topology changes result in an Updated LSP. The regular refreshing of LSPs in the network results in the Periodic LSP.

show isis statistics

The show isis statistics command is helpful to verify that IS-IS packets are being transmitted, received, and processed by the local router:

```
user@Cabernet> show isis statistics
IS-IS statistics for Cabernet:
```

PDU type	Received	Processed	Drops	Sent	Rexmit
LSP	301	301	0	101	0
IIH	1676	96	1580	25	0
CSNP	6695	6446	0	5989	0

```
PSNP                57          57           0          94          0
Unknown              0           0           0           0          0
Totals            8729        6900        1580        6209          0

Total packets received: 8729 Sent: 6184

SNP queue length: 0 Drops: 0
LSP queue length: 0 Drops: 0
SPF runs: 165
Fragments rebuilt: 103
LSP regenerations: 75
Purges initiated: 5
```

show isis route

The handy show isis route command displays the results of the SPF calculation before the routes are placed into the JUNOS software routing table. Although the same information can be gathered from the output of show route protocol isis, this command places an IS-IS slant on the data to aid in troubleshooting. For example, the next-hop router is displayed by IS-IS hostname and not IP address. The type of the metric (internal versus external) can also be seen. Finally, each route shows the exact SPF calculation used (the version) to select the route from the database.

```
user@Cabernet> show isis route
 IS-IS routing table                      Current version: L1: 84 L2: 85
 Prefix           L Version Metric Type Interface    Via
 192.168.0.0/24   2    85      20 int  e3-0/2/0.101 Riesling
 192.168.2.0/30   2    85      20 int  e3-0/2/0.101 Riesling
 192.168.5.0/24   1    84      20 int  fe-0/1/0.0   Merlot
 192.168.10.0/24  1    84      20 int  fe-0/1/0.0   Shiraz
 192.168.11.0/24  1    84      20 int  fe-0/1/0.0   Shiraz
 200.0.3.0/24     2    85      20 int  e3-0/2/0.101 Riesling
 200.0.6.0/24     1    84      20 int  fe-0/1/0.0   Merlot
 200.0.7.0/24     1    84      20 int  fe-0/1/0.0   Shiraz
```

show isis database

The show isis database command, along with its *detail* and *extensive* variations, is the final stop in troubleshooting IS-IS. Simply put, if information is not in the database, then it will never appear in the routing table. This version of the command displays summary information on a per-level basis. Each link-state PDU shows its name, remaining lifetime, and attributes:

```
user@Cabernet> show isis database
IS-IS level 1 link-state database:
LSP ID                          Sequence Checksum Lifetime Attributes
```

```
Merlot.00-00                        0x31    0x781a      1049 L1 L2 Attached

Shiraz.00-00                        0x39     0xf8b       835 L1
Shiraz.02-00                        0x37    0x7611       941 L1
Cabernet.00-00                      0x2d    0xc362      1015 L1 L2 Attached
   4 LSPs


IS-IS level 2 link-state database:
LSP ID                    Sequence Checksum Lifetime Attributes
Riesling.00-00              0x3c    0x6ca1      1120 L1 L2
Merlot.00-00               0x37    0xc288      1047 L1 L2
Cabernet.00-00             0x37    0x66d9      1015 L1 L2
   3 LSPs
```

show isis database detail

The *detail* option for the show isis database command provides more information about each LSP in the link-state database. The advertised prefixes from each router, the metric for each route, and the origin (internal versus external) of each route is visible when you issue this command.

```
user@Cabernet> show isis database detail
IS-IS level 1 link-state database:

Merlot.00-00  Sequence: 0x31, Checksum: 0x781a, Lifetime: 919 secs
   IS neighbor:             Shiraz.02 Metric:      10
   IP prefix:           200.0.6.0/24 Metric:      10 External
   IP prefix:         192.168.7.0/24 Metric:      10 External
   IP prefix:         192.168.6.0/24 Metric:      10 External
   IP prefix:         192.168.5.0/24 Metric:      10 External
   IP prefix:         192.168.5.1/32 Metric:       0 Internal
   IP prefix:            10.0.8.0/24 Metric:      10 Internal
```

show isis database extensive

You use the show isis database extensive command to view each piece of data advertised from each router into the IS-IS network. In addition to the information shown using show isis database detail, the *extensive* option provides the LSP header information as well as each TLV triple advertised. We'll examine only a single Level 1 LSP, Merlot.00-00. The entire link-state database from our small sample network takes over six pages to display.

```
user@Cabernet> show isis database extensive
IS-IS level 1 link-state database:
Merlot.00-00  Sequence: 0x31, Checksum: 0x781a, Lifetime: 969 secs
```

```
IS neighbor:                    Shiraz.02 Metric:      10
IP prefix:                   200.0.6.0/24 Metric:      10 External
IP prefix:                 192.168.7.0/24 Metric:      10 External
IP prefix:                 192.168.6.0/24 Metric:      10 External
IP prefix:                 192.168.5.0/24 Metric:      10 External
IP prefix:                192.168.5.1/32 Metric:       0 Internal
IP prefix:                    10.0.8.0/24 Metric:      10 Internal

Header: LSP ID: Merlot.00-00, Length: 222 bytes
  Allocated length: 222 bytes, Router ID: 192.168.5.1
  Remaining lifetime: 969 secs, Level: 1,Interface: 4
  Estimated free bytes: 0, Actual free bytes: 0
  Aging timer expires in: 969 secs
  Protocols: IP

Packet: LSP ID: Merlot.00-00, Length: 222 bytes, Lifetime : 1198 secs
  Checksum: 0x781a, Sequence: 0x31, Attributes: 0xb <L1 L2 Attached>
  NLPID: 0x83, Fixed length: 27 bytes, Version: 1, Sysid length: 0 bytes
  Packet type: 18, Packet version: 1, Max area: 0

TLVs:
  Area address: 47.0005.8083.00 (6)
  Speaks: IP
  Speaks: IPv6
  IP router id: 192.168.5.1
  IP address: 192.168.5.1
  Hostname: Merlot
  IS neighbor: Shiraz.02, Internal, Metric: default 10
  IS neighbor: Shiraz.02, Metric: default 10
    IP address: 10.0.8.1
  IP prefix: 10.0.8.0/24, Internal, Metric: default 10
  IP prefix: 192.168.5.1/32, Internal, Metric: default 0
  IP prefix: 10.0.8.0/24 metric 10 up
  IP prefix: 192.168.5.1/32 metric 0 up
  IP external prefix: 192.168.5.0/24, Internal, Metric: default 10
  IP external prefix: 192.168.6.0/24, Internal, Metric: default 10
  IP external prefix: 192.168.7.0/24, Internal, Metric: default 10
  IP external prefix: 200.0.6.0/24, Internal, Metric: default 10
  IP prefix: 192.168.5.0/24 metric 10 up
  IP prefix: 192.168.6.0/24 metric 10 up
```

```
    IP prefix: 192.168.7.0/24 metric 10 up
    IP prefix: 200.0.6.0/24 metric 10 up
  No queued transmissions
```

Comparison to OSPF

IS-IS and Open Shortest Path First (OSPF) are the main protocols ISPs use within their routing domains. These two protocols share many similarities but have distinct differences as well. Let's finish our discussion of IS-IS by examining these points.

The similarities between IS-IS and OSPF include:

Link-state protocols　Both protocols are based on the concept of a link-state database. Network information is flooded throughout the network, and each router maintains a complete copy of this data.

Hierarchical network designs　The flooding of information is bounded by the design of the network. Both protocols support a hierarchical design concept that bounds the update flooding. The IS-IS level is comparable to an OSPF area.

Hello protocol for adjacencies　Network link information is advertised after two routers form an adjacency relationship. The concept of a hello packet is common to both IS-IS and OSPF. This hello packet forms and maintains the adjacency.

Pseudonode election on broadcast media　To reduce the amount of information in the link-state database, both protocols utilize the concept of a pseudonode on broadcast links. A router is elected to represent the link to the remainder of the network.

IS-IS and OSPF approach these basic operational concepts in different ways. These differences include:

Election of a new pseudonode　Within IS-IS, the election of the pseudonode is deterministic—the router with the best criteria will always become the DIS. In addition, there is no provision or requirement for a backup DIS.

OSPF approaches this issue from a different perspective. The Designated Router (DR) may not be the router with the best criteria—which makes it a nondeterministic system. New elections are conducted only upon the failure of the current DR, resulting in a new backup DR. The previous BDR automatically assumes the DR responsibility.

Routing propagation　An entire link-state PDU is readvertised upon a network change in an IS-IS network. A similar change in an OSPF network, however, means that only a specific link-state advertisement (LSA) need be flooded.

Formatting Updates　IS-IS updates contain multiple (Type, Length, Value) triples to advertise information. The addition of a new TLV makes the protocol very easy to alter since an IS-IS router uses only the TLVs it understands. OSPF routers process only known Link-State Advertisements (LSA) and a protocol alteration requires a new standardized LSA definition that all vendors can agree on.

Reliance on IP   Two IS-IS routers can form an adjacency without the presence of IP addressing since NSAP addresses and CLNP processing are all that are required. OSPF, on the other hand, uses its own IP protocol number, so a valid IP addressing structure is required.

Summary

In this chapter, we reviewed the basic concepts behind the operation of link-state protocols. For IS-IS, this means that routers form adjacencies, flood network information into the network, and use the Dijkstra (shortest path first) Algorithm to calculate the total cost to each node in the network. You can configure an IS-IS network to support multiple levels that provide an information-flooding boundary.

We then discussed the data packets used by IS-IS routers. Once adjacent using IS-IS Hello PDUs, the routers synchronize their databases using Complete Sequence Number PDUs and Partial Sequence Number PDUs. This synchronization process advertises only the header information of the database contents. The actual network data is advertised within a Link-State PDU and is flooded throughout the network.

Finally, we covered the configuration and operation of IS-IS on a Juniper Networks router. We found that there are three major steps to configuring the protocol: NET ID assignment, interface configuration, and protocol setup. The JUNOS software provides several commands that you can use to verify adjacencies, protocol configuration, and database contents.

We wrapped up our discussion with a comparison of IS-IS and OSPF (covered in Chapter 6) by considering the similarities and differences between these two important protocols.

Exam Essentials

Be able to identify the portions of an IS-IS NSAP address.   The NET ID assignment to an IS-IS router is critical to the correct operation of the protocol. The NET ID contains the router's area address, system ID, and N-selector information. The N-selector must always be set to 0x00.

Know the various Protocol Data Units used by an IS-IS router.   Four main PDUs are advertised in an IS-IS network: the Hello, Link-State, Complete Sequence Number, and Partial Sequence Number PDUs.

Understand how an IS-IS adjacency is formed.   The two IS-IS levels have different criteria for forming an adjacency. Both require a unique system ID, while a Level 1 adjacency also dictates a common area address.

Be able to describe the election criteria for the Designated Intermediate System.   On a broadcast network, a single router is elected to represent the link information to the network. This router is chosen based on the highest configured priority, with the highest SNPA being the only tiebreaker.

Understand the steps required to configure IS-IS.   Configuring the protocol on a Juniper Networks router requires three main steps. First, you assign the NET ID; then, you configure each interface to support IS-IS. Finally, you tell the routing process which interfaces to operate across.

Identify the JUNOS software commands that validate the operation of IS-IS.   Various commands allow you to check the status of adjacencies, interfaces, and the link-state database.

Key Terms

Before you take the exam, be certain you are familiar with the following terms:

adjacency	IS-IS level
Authority and Format Indicator (AFI)	link-state database
Complete Sequence Number PDU (CSNP)	link-state PDU (LSP)
Designated Intermediate System (DIS)	N-selector (SEL)
Dijkstra Algorithm	Network Entity Title (NET)
DIS priority	Partial Sequence Number PDU (PSNP)
Domain-Specific Part (DSP)	Protocol Data Unit (PDU)
Hello messages	system ID
intermediate system	triple
IS-IS Hello (IIH) PDUs	

Review Questions

1. Which of the following would be considered a *private* NSAP address?

   A. 37.1010.1921.6806.4001.00

   B. 39.0001.1921.6806.4001.00

   C. 47.1010.1921.6806.4001.00

   D. 49.0001.1921.6806.4001.00

2. What is the size of the system ID on a Juniper Networks router?

   A. 3 bytes

   B. 6 bytes

   C. 13 bytes

   D. 20 bytes

3. An IS-IS router uses which circuit ID to represent the node itself within the network?

   A. 0x00

   B. 0x01

   C. 0x02

   D. 0x03

4. An IS-IS router uses which PDU to request information missing in its database?

   A. Hello

   B. Link-State

   C. Complete Sequence Number

   D. Partial Sequence Number

5. The IS-IS Hello PDU is used for what network function?

   A. To advertise information about connected networks

   B. To form an adjacency with a neighbor

   C. To inform the network about connected IS-IS routers

   D. To prevent database information from flooding beyond the defined IS-IS levels

6. Information about the local link-state database is exchanged with a neighbor during an adjacency formation. Which PDU accomplishes this?

   A. Hello

   B. Link-State

   C. Complete Sequence Number

   D. Partial Sequence Number

7. A link-state PDU advertises information using what format?

   A. Type, Length, Value (TLV) encoding

   B. Link-state advertisement (LSA) types

   C. Connectionless Network Protocol structures

   D. Link-layer encapsulation

8. An IS-IS router with a NET ID of `49.1234.4321.1921.6801.6001.00` can form a Level 1 adjacency with which other system?

   A. `49.4321.1921.6806.4001.00`

   B. `49.4321.1921.6801.6001.00`

   C. `49.1234.4321.1921.6806.4001.00`

   D. `49.1234.4321.1921.6801.6001.00`

9. Which IS-IS adjacency state shows that bidirectional communication has occurred but that the link-state databases are still converging?

   A. New

   B. One-Way

   C. Initializing

   D. Up

10. An authentication failure prompts which IS-IS adjacency state to appear?

   A. New

   B. Down

   C. Initializing

   D. Reject

11. What is the primary criterion for the election of the Designated Intermediate System (DIS) on a broadcast link?

   A. Highest system priority

   B. Lowest system priority

   C. Highest MAC address

   D. Lowest MAC address

12. The following four routers are adjacent on a broadcast link. Which router is elected the Designated Intermediate System?

   A. Priority of 25 and MAC address of 00:90:69:90:50:11

   B. Priority of 64 and MAC address of 00:90:69:96:87:46

   C. Priority of 64 and MAC address of 00:90:69:56:70:79

   D. Priority of 127 and MAC address of 00:90:69:31:55:91

13. What is the default priority value assigned to all IS-IS interfaces?

   A. 0

   B. 63

   C. 64

   D. 127

14. Which interface is primarily used for the assignment of the NET ID?

   A. lo0

   B. fxp0

   C. fe-0/0/0.0

   D. so-0/0/0.0

15. Given the following configuration:

```
protocols {
    isis {
        level 1 disable;
        interface all;
        interface fxp0.0 {
            disable;
        }
    }
}
```

which statement is correct?

   A. Only adjacencies on interface fxp0.0 will be established.

   B. All operational interfaces will form only Level 1 adjacencies (except fxp0.0).

   C. All operational interfaces will form only Level 2 adjacencies (except fxp0.0).

   D. All operational interfaces will form both Level 1 and Level 2 adjacencies.

16. Which command allows a logical interface to accept and process IS-IS packets?

   A. family inet

   B. family iso

   C. family isis

   D. family clnp

17. Which command allows you to see the result of the SPF calculation before routes are sent to the routing table?

    A. `show isis route`

    B. `show isis adjacency`

    C. `show isis database`

    D. `show route protocol isis`

18. You suspect that your neighbor may not be properly advertising its connected networks. Which command best troubleshoots this problem?

    A. `show isis route`

    B. `show isis database detail`

    C. `show isis interface`

    D. `show isis statistics`

19. Which command displays the circuit IDs assigned by the local router as well as information about elected DIS routers?

    A. `show isis route`

    B. `show isis interface`

    C. `show isis adjacency`

    D. `show isis statistics`

20. Which IS-IS command provides information about connected routers?

    A. `show isis adjacency`

    B. `show isis spf log`

    C. `show isis interface`

    D. `show isis statistics`

Answers to Review Questions

1. D. The presence of 49 in the Authority Format Indicator (AFI) position marks this NSAP address as a private address.

2. B. All IS-IS routers, by definition, support a variable-length field between 1 and 8 bytes. The JUNOS software implementation uses only a default value of 6.

3. A. The router node is always assigned a circuit ID of 0x00. This value is placed within the selector byte of a NET ID. Point-to-point links share a value of 0x01, while broadcast links begin their unique numbering at 0x02.

4. D. The Partial Sequence Number PDU (PSNP) is used during the adjacency formation process when one of the routers determines its database is not synchronized.

5. B. The Hello PDU forms adjacencies with network neighbors at either Level 1 or Level 2. The remaining functions are accomplished using a link-state PDU.

6. C. The Complete Sequence Number PDU (CSNP) is used to inform other IS-IS routers of the contents of the local router's database. This header information allows neighbors to determine if they have a complete and updated set of data.

7. A. The TLV structure is the basis for all IS-IS LSP information. This encoding allows for easy protocol scalability.

8. C. Only option C provides the same area address as that of the local router and a unique system ID. These are the two requirements of forming a Level 1 adjacency.

9. C. When the local router sees itself in a neighbor's link-state PDU, it understands that bidirectional communication is achieved. This is a critical step before a fully functional adjacency is established.

10. D. The rejected state is seen when two routers have an authentication failure or an area mismatch.

11. A. The two possible criteria for DIS election are priority and MAC address. The first tiebreaker is the highest system priority, followed by the highest MAC address.

12. D. The IS-IS router with the highest configured priority is always elected the DIS on the broadcast segment.

13. C. The possible priority range is from 0 to 127; the JUNOS software default value is 64.

14. A. To ensure that the NET ID is always reachable, you should assign it to the loopback interface. Options C and D are transit interfaces and susceptible to physical failure. The fxp0 interface is not used because only network management traffic should use this interface.

15. C. The presence of the level 1 disable command at the global IS-IS level allows only Level 2 adjacencies to form.

16. B. The family iso command is the protocol family assigned to interfaces within the JUNOS software.

17. A. To see routes after a SPF run, use the command show isis route. Option D shows the routes *after* they are placed into the routing table.

18. B. A detailed examination of the database will always display the networks advertised by all IS-IS routers.

19. B. Only show isis interface provides you with information about elected DIS routers and circuit IDs on a per-interface basis.

20. A. Only show isis adjacency details information about other routers in the network. The remaining commands display data about the local router only.

Chapter 8

Border Gateway Protocol (BGP)

JNCIA EXAM OBJECTIVES COVERED IN THIS CHAPTER:

- ✓ Define the basic operation and functionality of BGP
- ✓ Describe the different BGP neighbor states
- ✓ Define the functions of BGP packet types
- ✓ Define the functions of BGP attributes
- ✓ Identify the steps of the BGP Route Selection Algorithm
- ✓ Describe the default action for BGP route advertisements to EBGP and IBGP peers
- ✓ Describe the steps required to configure BGP
- ✓ Identify CLI commands used to monitor and troubleshoot a BGP network

This chapter explores the Border Gateway Protocol (BGP). This routing protocol is used extensively in the Internet to connect ISP networks. We start with an examination of how BGP forms peer relationships with neighboring routers. This is followed by a discussion of the packets used to exchange information and how a BGP router uses the route information. After exploring some BGP route attributes, we finish by looking at how BGP is configured within the JUNOS software.

Overview of BGP

BGP was created to achieve some specific goals. First, it needed to support the meshlike connectivity of ISP networks. It also required extensive policy controls to enforce the administrative policies of each ISP. It needed the ability to reliably transmit routing information between BGP peers. Finally, the protocol required the ability to scale route advertisements beyond a few thousand routes. Version 4 of the protocol accomplishes each of these goals.

Network Connectivity

In the early days of the Internet, connectivity between networks was regimented and hierarchical. For example, the ARPANET dictated a single backbone that provided transport services for each connected network. The Exterior Gateway Protocol (EGP) was used for inter–Autonomous System (AS) communications. It provided no loop prevention and sent its entire routing table in regular broadcasted updates. At the time, EGP satisfied the requirements of the Internet. As the ARPANET was disbanded and the Internet grew, this hierarchy grew into the concept of a tiered network design. Small networks (Tier 3 ISPs) connected upstream to larger regional networks (Tier 2 ISPs). The regional systems would, in turn, connect to the major ISPs (Tier 1 providers). Regional exchanges points were established to allow the Tier 1 ISPs to interconnect among themselves. This basic concept is shown in Figure 8.1.

The purpose of the Internet also changed during this timeframe from a research-type network to a commercial data-transport system. This transition forced many networks into providing better and faster service to their customers, necessitating a change in the design. Some ISPs began to connect to multiple upstream providers. Most Tier 1 ISPs connected to other peers outside the exchange points and in multiple locations.

The Internet growth also meant that more reachable prefixes were advertised to the network on a regular basis. This increased routing traffic as well as a more meshlike structure spelled the end of EGP. It simply was not designed for this type of environment. BGP, on the other hand, was created for just this situation. It provides loop prevention through an attribute called the AS Path, which is a collection of AS numbers through which a particular route has passed.

FIGURE 8.1   The tiered Internet design

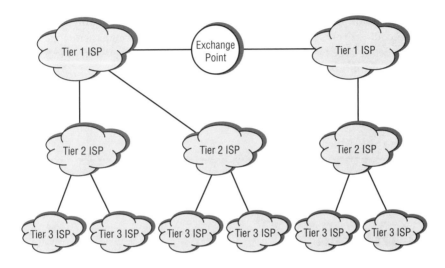

 An Autonomous System, in reality, is a set of routers under the control of a single administrative domain. An individual domain may have more than one AS number assigned to it. On the other hand, a single AS number can belong only to a single domain. For our purposes, we assume that an AS means a single number assigned to a single administrative domain.

The use of this attribute also leads to a common description of BGP as a *path-vector proto-col*. In a distance-vector network, such as the Routing Information Protocol (RIP), each router knows how far away a route is (the distance) and the direction to send a packet for that route (the vector). In a BGP network, on the other hand, each router knows the networks a route has traversed (the path) and the direction to send a packet for the route (the vector).

Policy Control

The use of the Internet for commercial traffic also requires that ISPs have extensive control over route advertisements and traffic patterns. The requirements for this control can come in many forms. For example, a government agency might dictate that all traffic originating and terminating within a specific country must use networks only within that country. If this set of networks is not naturally the best path toward the destination, the ISPs need a method for changing route attributes to make it the best path.

Another example might occur when two ISPs connect to each other on a private link outside an exchange point. In this situation, one of the networks might desire only certain routes from its peer. These routes could be the specific customers of the Tier 1 ISP, or a subset of the customer routes.

Another use of policy control occurs when some network links are not used for primary data traffic flows. Suppose a Tier 3 ISP purchases connectivity to a second upstream peer for use as a backup link. This link should be used only when its primary upstream link is not operational. The Tier 3 ISP could advertise its routes on this backup link but make them appear less attractive to the Internet at large by altering certain attributes. This dual advertisement provides for a faster fail-over of traffic should the primary link fail.

BGP accounts for each of these situations. It allows for explicit inbound and outbound policy controls on a per-peer basis. These controls permit an ISP to block or advertise particular routes. Each ISP may also alter a number of attributes to change the attractiveness of a particular route to its peers.

 The basic BGP attributes are discussed in the section "BGP Attributes," later in this chapter.

Reliable Transport

The size of the modern-day Internet routing table (over 100,000 routes) and the need for a high level of availability require the Internet routing protocol to guarantee its transmissions. This guarantee is not for actual user data traffic but for the protocol transmissions itself. BGP accomplishes this goal by utilizing the Transmission Control Protocol (TCP) as its underlying transport mechanism. This greatly differs from some Interior Gateway Protocols (IGPs), such as Open Shortest Path First (OSPF) and Intermediate System to Intermediate System (IS-IS), where the reliability is built into the protocol itself. When two BGP peers establish a session on *TCP port 179*, they get a connection-oriented and reliable stream of data between them. The peers can then rely on TCP for the following services:

Acknowledgments   After sending a segment, a retry timer starts decrementing until a receipt acknowledgment is received from the other end of the connection. When the timer reaches 0, the segment is retransmitted. The far-end acknowledgment is actually delayed up to 1 second to determine if any data should be sent along with the acknowledgment.

Segmentation   The BGP data is segmented, if necessary, into smaller sizes for transmission across the network.

Checksums   A checksum is maintained on both the TCP header and BGP data to ensure an error-free transmission. Should the received checksum differ from the advertised value, the segment is discarded. No acknowledgment is sent to the source, and the segment is retransmitted.

Data sequencing   TCP sequence numbers allow the receiving peer to reorder the BGP data in the event of an out-of-sequence receipt.

Flow control   Each BGP peer advertises its available buffer space to allow the far end of the session to send only a specific amount of data.

Real World Scenario

Is BGP Really a Routing Protocol?

This question can often start a very heated discussion between two network engineers—in large part because there is no clear answer to the question. Your particular answer is defined by your beliefs and experiences.

On one hand are the people who answer yes. After all, the end result of using BGP is the advertisement of IP routes. A router places these routes into the routing table after determining which version of the route is the best. The router then forwards user data packets based on the table's information.

People on the other side of the issue consider BGP to be an application of IP. Traditional routing protocols have their own protocol number. As such, they are part of the IP environment. Since BGP uses TCP for its transmissions, it actually performs its job as an application, like Telnet. The difference between the applications is the data transmitted between the end hosts. Telnet provides character-based terminal access to the far-end host. BGP, on the other hand, provides route knowledge to the far-end host. There is simply no difference.

We won't try to sway your vote to one side or the other. We'll simply attempt to discuss the facts of what BGP does and how it does it. The rest is up to you.

Routing Table Scalability

The rapid growth of the Internet routing table requires any inter-AS protocol to scale effectively. The original EGP specification required that each router advertise its entire routing table space on a regular cycle. This is similar to RIP in its operation and carries with it the scalability issues of a traditional distance-vector protocol. BGP uses a route advertisement mechanism that is more comparable to OSPF or IS-IS.

When two BGP peers establish a connection, they initially advertise their entire routing knowledge to each other. After this initial exchange, updates occur only on an as-needed basis. Updates are sent only when new information is learned or existing information is no longer valid. This change-based system provides the best possible scalability for the Internet's routing protocol.

When Will BGP Be Updated?

The current version of BGP is version 4, originally defined in 1995. No newer versions of the protocol have been introduced since then, due in large part to the adaptability of the protocol. As network needs have changed, the base specification has been modified to meet the new requirements. This means that no new version of BGP is needed for the foreseeable future.

A number of Requests for Comment (RFC) define the current BGP specification. These RFCs include:

- RFC 1771, "A Border Gateway Protocol (BGP-4)"

- RFC 1772, "Application of the Border Gateway Protocol in the Internet"

- RFC 1966, "BGP Route Reflection: An Alternative to Full-Mesh I-BGP"

- RFC 1997, "BGP Communities Attribute"

- RFC 2270, "Using a Dedicated AS for Sites Homed to a Single Provider"

- RFC 2385, "Protection of BGP Sessions through the TCP MD5 Signature Option"

- RFC 2439, "BGP Route Flap Damping"

- RFC 2842, "Capabilities Advertisement with BGP-4"

- RFC 2858, "Multiprotocol Extensions for BGP-4"

- RFC 2918, "Route Refresh Capability for BGP-4"

- RFC 3065, "AS Confederations for BGP"

Additionally, the JUNOS software supports various Internet Engineering Task Force (IETF) drafts for BGP. Two of these include:

- "BGP Extended Communities Attribute", IETF draft-ramachandra-bgp-ext-communities-04.txt

- "Graceful Restart Mechanism", IETF draft-ietf-idr-restart-01.txt

To locate IETF drafts, go to http://www.ietf.org/ID.html and search for a draft or examine a complete index of all current drafts.

Theory of Operation

BGP advertises routing knowledge between two routers. The type of relationship between those routers is determined by whether they are in the same AS. The establishment of this relationship and the actual advertisement of routes are controlled by various BGP packet types. The local router makes a routing decision based on the received routing knowledge. These decisions are then advertised to other BGP routers in the network. The routing decisions are based on a number of variables, including various route attributes and local policy controls.

We cover each of these major aspects in more detail throughout this section. Let's begin with a look at how BGP forms relationships with its neighboring routers.

Peers

BGP exchanges its routing information between two routers, called *peers* or *neighbors*. This connection is logical in nature and relies on the establishment of a TCP session between the peers. The session is established across a direct physical link or a number of intermediate links. Figure 8.2 shows each of these situations.

FIGURE 8.2 BGP peer relationships

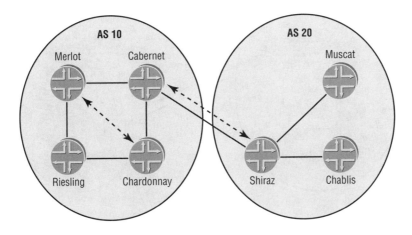

The Cabernet and Shiraz routers are joined by a direct physical connection. This connectivity implies that IP reachability is easily achieved between the two peers and that TCP can establish its session. On the other hand, the Merlot and Chardonnay routers are connected only via an intermediate router. In this situation, IP reachability between the peers must be supplied by some other means. Often this is handled by the IGP within the AS, but a static route is also a feasible solution.

Figure 8.2 also shows the different forms of logical connections used by BGP. One option connects two routers in different AS networks, like the Cabernet-Shiraz session. The second option is for two routers in the same AS to establish a session; this is represented by the Merlot-Chardonnay connection. While TCP sessions are established based on the IP reachability between two peers, BGP uses each type of session in a different manner.

External BGP Sessions

When two BGP routers are in different AS networks, the session between them is considered an *external BGP (EBGP)* connection. By default, an EBGP connection is formed between directly connected peers. This requirement is enforced by setting the time-to-live (TTL) of the IP packet to 1, thereby not permitting an intermediate router to forward the BGP packet.

Once the EBGP session is established, the two peers can begin to exchange routing knowledge with each other. All active BGP routes learned from other EBGP sessions are advertised. In addition, all active BGP routes learned from internal BGP peers are advertised.

Figure 8.3 shows the default EBGP route advertisements. The 10.100.0.0 /16 route is advertised from the Sherry router to Shiraz via an EBGP session. The 10.200.0.0 /16 route is advertised to Shiraz by the Muscat router, which is an internal peer. Both routes are currently active in Shiraz's routing table and are advertised to Cabernet using an EBGP advertisement.

FIGURE 8.3   EBGP route advertisements

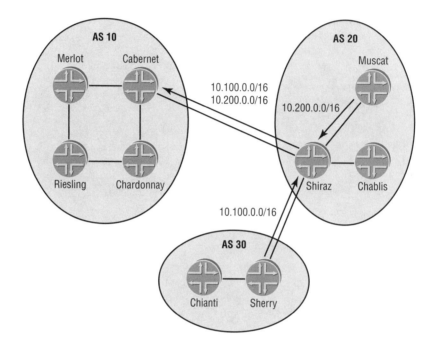

Internal BGP Sessions

The connection of two BGP routers within the same AS is called an *internal BGP (IBGP)* connection. Unlike the EBGP variety, there is no requirement for physical connectivity between IBGP peers. The TTL of the BGP packets is set to 64 to allow for connectivity across an AS. In fact, a great majority of IBGP sessions are between routers that are not directly connected.

 Real World Scenario

Internal BGP Design Considerations

Most ISP networks run BGP on all routers in their AS. Of course, any customer-facing router runs the protocol to announce routing information, but this design rule holds true for core routers as well. One reason for this setup is the avoidance of black-holing user data traffic. Let's look at a simple example.

Suppose that AS 65000 consists of three routers (A, B, and C) connected together in a chain; A connects to B, which connects to C. AS 65000 uses OSPF as its IGP for internal reachability. Router A has an external BGP session with AS 64777, and Router C has an EBGP session with AS 64888. Additionally, Routers A and C have an IBGP session between them. The administrators of AS 65000 choose to not have Router B participate in BGP because of a concern over router resources. It receives a default 0.0.0.0 /0 route from both Router A and Router C for reachability to the Internet at large.

So far, so good. Each router in the AS has usable routes in its routing table for Internet destinations. The problem occurs when a user connected to Router B wants to connect to www.juniper.net. The data packet arrives at Router B, and a routing table lookup is performed. Router B finds two copies of the default route and must choose one. Let's assume it selects Router C and forwards the packet. Router C then performs a route lookup and finds an explicit route to www.juniper.net through its IBGP peer—Router A. Router C forwards the packet to Router A, using Router B as the physical path to its peer.

You may already see the problem developing, but let's finish the process. Router B receives a data packet destined for www.juniper.net. It doesn't realize that it just forwarded this packet a second ago and performs a route lookup. It once again finds two default routes and forwards the packet back to Router C. Congratulations; we have just established a routing loop!

One obvious solution to this problem is establishing an IBGP session from Router B to both Router A and Router C. Once established, Router B has an explicit route for www.juniper.net. It no longer forwards the user data packets to Router C, but to Router A instead. The routing loop has been averted.

IBGP peers rely on the IGP knowledge within the AS network. In general, the TCP session between IBGP peers across the network uses the IP routing tables of intermediate nodes to establish itself. More specifically, this session is established using the loopback addresses of the peers for stability and resiliency. This common practice allows the IBGP session to remain operational in the event of a network outage.

Once the IBGP session is established, routes are exchanged between the peers. By default, only active BGP routes learned from EBGP peers are advertised across an IBGP session.

The default IBGP advertisement rules are shown in Figure 8.4. The Cabernet and Riesling routers are IBGP peers. Cabernet is learning both the 10.100.0.0 /16 and 10.200.0.0 /16 routes from Shiraz, an EBGP peer. Both of these routes are then readvertised to Riesling across the IBGP session. The Riesling router is also learning about the 172.30.1.0 /24 route from an IBGP peer—Chardonnay. This route is not advertised to the other AS 10 routers because it violates the advertisement rules for IBGP peers.

The restriction on advertising an IBGP-learned route to another IBGP peer causes an interesting problem within AS 20, as seen in Figure 8.5.

FIGURE 8.4   IBGP route advertisements

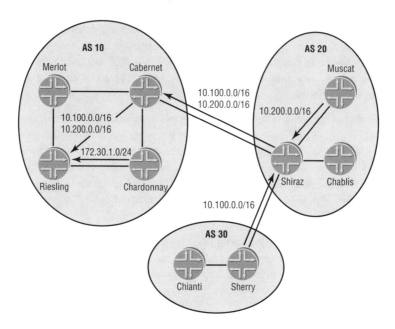

FIGURE 8.5   The IBGP full-mesh requirement

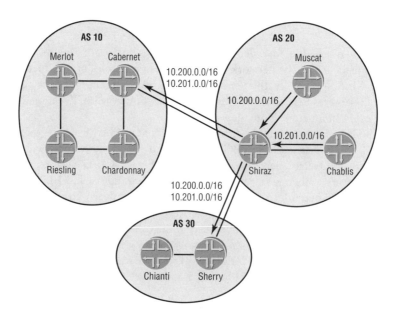

Both the Muscat and Chablis routers have an IBGP session with Shiraz, but not with each other. The 10.200.0.0 /16 route is advertised by Muscat, and the 10.201.0.0 /16 route is sent by Chablis. Shiraz receives both routes and advertises them to its EBGP peers of Cabernet and Sherry. By default, it does not advertise those routes back to its IBGP peers. This results in both Chablis and Muscat having no knowledge of other routes within the AS.

The resolution to this dilemma is the establishment of an IBGP session between Muscat and Chablis. Remember that IBGP peers do not need to be physically connected. Once established, both Muscat and Chablis advertise their routes to each other directly, in addition to advertising to Shiraz. The end result is an *IBGP full-mesh* within AS 20. This full-mesh concept is considered a best practice within an ISP network to maintain route reachability.

 Real World Scenario

Why Do We Need an IBGP Full-Mesh?

In Figure 8.5, we saw a graphic need for an IBGP full-mesh due to the default advertisement rules for IBGP peers. But the question about why the advertisement rules are in place is still a valid one.

The first, and easiest, answer is because the RFC says so. If you are happy with that response, please read no further. Personally, we never find those types of answers satisfying, so let's see if we can dig a little further.

The underlying reason for the full-mesh requirement stems from the use of the AS Path attribute. In the "Network Connectivity" section earlier in this chapter, we discussed the AS Path attribute as the method BGP uses for loop prevention. Each BGP router examines this attribute when it receives a route from a peer. If the local router's AS number is listed in the attribute, then the route has already been through this AS. The local router then drops the route advertisement to prevent the formation of a routing loop.

Having said all that, we still haven't answered the question! Okay, here it is. The AS Path attribute is modified only when a route is advertised between EBGP peers, not IBGP peers. So, if BGP were to allow an IBGP router to advertise an IBGP-learned route to another IBGP peer, we could easily form a routing loop.

As an example, suppose that Cabernet, Merlot, Riesling, and Chardonnay in Figure 8.5 are all IBGP peers across the physical connections only (Cabernet and Riesling are not peers, for example). In addition, suppose we allow the IBGP peers to advertise routes to other IBGP peers. When Cabernet receives the 10.200.0.0 /16 route from Shiraz, it advertises that route to Merlot and Chardonnay. Those two routers select Cabernet's version of the route as the best and forward it to Riesling. At this point, two versions of the same route have arrived on Riesling, which must choose between them. Riesling opts for the Merlot version and forwards the route to Chardonnay, which prefers the same version. Chardonnay then forwards the route to Cabernet, which announced the route in the first place!

Cabernet now has a decision to make between the versions from Shiraz and Chardonnay. Using the version from Chardonnay installs a routing loop in AS 10. User data packets from Merlot arrive at Cabernet, which forwards them to Chardonnay. Route lookups on Chardonnay forward the packets to Riesling, which forwards them back to Merlot. Unfortunately, Cabernet doesn't have the ability to foresee this danger through its loop avoidance mechanism, the AS Path. Neither the route from Shiraz nor the route from Chardonnay lists AS 10 in the AS Path attribute. Allowing the AS 10 routers to announce routes among themselves destroys the guarantee of a loop-free topology.

So, the BGP designers decided to not allow you to shoot yourself in the foot by preventing IBGP learned routes from being advertised to other IBGP peers.

Establishing Relationships

Now that we've established the basic concepts of BGP peering, let's take a closer look at how the sessions are actually formed. BGP uses a Finite State Machine model when forming a peer relationship. Here are the possible BGP states:

Idle   *Idle* is the initial neighbor state, in which it rejects all incoming session requests. After the BGP process starts, a TCP session is initiated to the remote peer. The local router transitions to the Connect state and begins to listen for a connection initiated by the remote router.

Connect   In the *Connect* state, the local router is waiting for the TCP session to be completed. If it is successful, the local router sends an Open message to the peer and transitions to the OpenSent state.

Should the TCP connection attempt fail, the local router resets the ConnectRetry timer and transitions to the Active state.

If the ConnectRetry timer reaches 0 while the local router is in the Connect state, the timer is reset and another connection attempt is made. The local router remains in the Connect state.

Active   In the *Active* state, the local router is trying to initiate a TCP session with its peer. If the session establishes successfully, an Open message is sent and the local router transitions to the OpenSent state.

If the TCP session fails to establish, the local router initiates another session, sets the ConnectRetry timer to 0, and transitions back to the Connect state.

Attempts by the remote router to connect from an unexpected IP address for the session causes the local router to refuse the connection. The local router remains in the Active state and resets the ConnectRetry timer.

OpenSent   The *OpenSent* state is reached upon a successful TCP establishment. The local router sends a BGP Open message and waits for an Open message from the remote peer.

When a valid Open message is received, the local router begins to send Keepalive messages to the remote router. The BGP peers negotiate the session parameters and the local router transitions to the `OpenConfirm` state.

Should a TCP disconnect be received while in this state, the local router terminates the BGP session, resets the ConnectRetry timer, and transitions back to the `Active` state.

OpenConfirm   When the local router receives a valid Open message from the remote peer, the *OpenConfirm* state is reached. The local router sends Keepalive messages to the peer and waits for a Keepalive message in return.

Established   The *Established* state is achieved when a Keepalive message is received while in the `OpenConfirm` state. This is the final state of a peer relationship and designates a fully operational connection.

Two BGP peers can exchange routing information only when the `Established` state is reached. All other BGP peering states designate a nonfunctional session.

Message Types

In the previous section, we discussed some BGP message types that were exchanged between two peers. In total, BGP defines four messages types: Open, Update, Notification, and Keepalive. Each message contains a 19-octet fixed-size header, as seen in Figure 8.6.

FIGURE 8.6   BGP message header

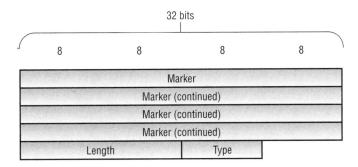

The header consists of the following fields:

Marker (16 octets)   This field is set to all 1s to detect a loss of synchronization. An Open message with authentication configured contains the authentication data for the session.

Length (2 octets) The total length of the BGP message is encoded in this field. Possible values range from 19 to 4096.

Type (1 octet) The type of BGP message is located in this field. Four type codes have been defined:

- 1 for an Open message
- 2 for an Update message
- 3 for a Notification message
- 4 for a Keepalive message

Let's now examine each of the BGP message types in more detail.

The Open Message

The *Open message* is the first packet BGP sends to a peer after the TCP connection has been established. It allows the two peers to negotiate the parameters of the peer session. These parameters include the BGP version, the hold time for the session, authentication data, refresh capabilities, and support for multiple *Network Layer Reachability Information (NLRI)*.

The message format is shown in Figure 8.7. After the common BGP header, the remaining fields include the following:

Version (1 octet) This field contains the current version of the peer. The default value is 4 and is set automatically.

Local Autonomous System (2 octets) The sender's AS value is encoded in this field.

Hold Time (2 octets) The sender places its proposed hold-time value here, and the two peers negotiate this value to the lower of the two proposals. The default value for the JUNOS software is 90 seconds, with a possible range between 6 and 65,535 seconds.

Each peer divides the negotiated hold time by 3 to calculate the Keepalive timer for the session.

BGP Identifier (4 octets) The local Router ID of the peer is encoded in this field. This uniquely identifies the router to the network.

Optional Parameters Length (1 octet) This field specifies the total length of the Optional Parameters field. A value of 0 indicates that no parameters are included in the message.

Optional Parameters (Variable) This variable-length field encodes any optional parameters used by the local peer. Possibilities include support for route refresh, authentication, and various NLRI. Each parameter is encoded in a (Type, Length, Value) triple. The parameter's type and length fields are 1 octet each and are followed by a variable-length value field.

FIGURE 8.7   The BGP Open message

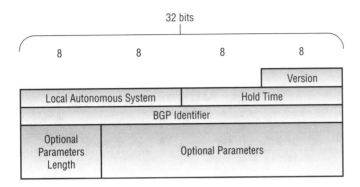

The Update Message

Routing information is sent and withdrawn in BGP using the *Update message.* If needed, each message contains information previously advertised by the local router that is no longer valid. The same message may also contain new information advertised to the remote peer.

Each Update contains a single set of BGP attributes and all routes using those attributes. This format reduces the total number of packets routers send between BGP peers when exchanging routing knowledge.

The various attributes used by BGP are discussed in the "BGP Attributes" section later in this chapter.

Figure 8.8 shows the format of the Update message. The following fields follow the common BGP header:

Unfeasible Routes Length (2 octets)   This field specifies the length of the Withdrawn Routes field that follows. A value of 0 designates that no routes are being withdrawn with this Update.

Withdrawn Routes (Variable)   This field lists the routes previously announced that are now being withdrawn. Each route is encoded as a (Length, Prefix) tuple where the length is the number of bits in the subnet mask and the prefix is the IPv4 NLRI.

Total Path Attributes Length (2 octets)   This field specifies the length of the Path Attributes field that follows. A value of 0 designates that no routes are being advertised with this message.

Path Attributes (Variable)   The attributes of the path advertisement are contained in this field. Each attribute is encoded as a (Type, Length, Value) triple.

Network Layer Reachability Information (Variable)   This field lists the routes advertised to the remote peer. Each route is encoded as a (Length, Prefix) tuple where the length is the number of bits in the subnet mask and the prefix is the IPv4 route.

FIGURE 8.8   The BGP Update message

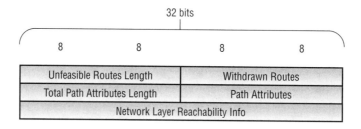

The Notification Message

When a BGP peer detects an error within the session, it sends a *Notification message* to the remote router and immediately closes both the BGP and TCP sessions. The format of the message is shown in Figure 8.9.

FIGURE 8.9   The BGP Notification message

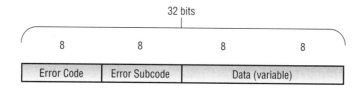

In addition to the common BGP header, the Notification message contains the following:

Error Code (1 octet)   This field specifies the type of BGP error seen by the local router. Six error codes have been defined:

- 1 for a Message Header Error
- 2 for an Open Message Error
- 3 for an Update Message Error
- 4 for Hold Time Expired
- 5 for a Finite State Machine Error
- 6 for a Cease

Error Subcode (1 octet)   This field contains more specific information about the error. For example, within the Open Message Error type code, Authentication Failure is a possible subcode.

Data (Variable)   This field is used to assist the administrator in troubleshooting the error. The contents of the field depend on the specific error code and subcode.

One common reason for a Notification message is intervention by a user. When you manually clear a BGP connection, you generate a Cease (Error Code 6) Notification message on the local router. The BGP and TCP sessions are torn down and reestablished. In addition, a configuration change that alters the parameters of an existing session will generate a Cease message by the local router.

The Keepalive Message

A BGP *Keepalive message* contains only the 19-octet message header and no other data. These messages are exchanged at one-third the negotiated hold-time value for the session, if necessary. The advertisement of an Update message within the keepalive period resets the timer to 0. In short, a Keepalive is sent only in the absence of other messages for a particular session.

Should the local router not receive a Keepalive or Update message within the hold-time period, a Notification message of *Hold Time Expired* is generated and the session is torn down.

Routing Information Bases

At this point, we've explored how a BGP router forms peer sessions with both external and internal peers and what routes are advertised to each peer. We've also looked at the message types used to actually form those peer relationships and advertise routes. We now need to explore the internal processes of how the local router receives, selects, and advertises specific routing information.

Each BGP router establishes memory locations in which to store routing knowledge. These are collectively known as a *Routing Information Base (RIB)*. A BGP peer maintains three categories of RIBs: the Adjacency-RIB-In, the Local-RIB, and the Adjacency-RIB-Out. Let's discuss each of these in further detail.

Adjacency-RIB-In

An *Adjacency-RIB-In* table is created on the local router for each established BGP peer. All routes received from the peer are placed in the appropriate memory table. There's one notable exception to this rule: Routes containing an AS Path loop are immediately discarded by the local router.

After receiving an Update message, the local router implements any applied import routing policies. These policies may alter the values of existing attributes, add new attributes, or discard specific routes. The router then examines all Adjacency-RIB-In tables for the best path advertisement to each unique destination. We discuss the specific method of selecting the best path in the "Route Selection Process" section later in this chapter.

Local-RIB

The best path to each destination is stored in the *Local-RIB* table. These are the routes that the local router uses to forward user data traffic. Only a single path advertisement per destination is placed in this table.

Adjacency-RIB-Out

Each established BGP peer also creates its own *Adjacency-RIB-Out* table for outbound route advertisements. Only routes currently located in the Local-RIB are eligible to be placed in this outbound database. In other words, a BGP router advertises only routes that it is currently using to forward data traffic.

By default, all Local-RIB routes are placed in each Adjacency-RIB-Out table. You can alter this behavior by applying export routing policies. A policy may add, alter, or remove attributes from each route. In addition, a policy may suppress a route from being advertised to a specific peer.

The Route Selection Process

As the local router scans the Adjacency-RIB-In tables for routing knowledge, it parses the feasible routes through a selection algorithm to determine the best path to each destination. The main criteria for this selection algorithm are the various BGP attributes, which we discuss in the next section, "BGP Attributes." Each vendor uses a slightly different algorithm, because the specifications dictate only the attributes to use with their possible values. We'll focus on how a Juniper Networks router makes its decisions.

If only a single version of a route exists in the inbound databases, that route is placed in the Local-RIB table and used for data forwarding. When multiple routes exist, they are grouped to evaluate their attributes. Each step in the selection algorithm attempts to eliminate all but one of the feasible routes to a destination. If multiple routes still exist after a particular step, the next step is executed. In this manner, the algorithm runs for only as long as it needs to.

The steps of the BGP selection algorithm are as follows:

1. The Next Hop attribute value for each route must be reachable in the local routing table; otherwise, the local router discards the route.

2. The router selects the route with the highest Local Preference attribute value.

3. The router selects the route with the shortest AS Path length.

4. The router selects the route with the smallest Origin attribute value.

5. The router selects the route with the smallest Multiple Exit Discriminator attribute value. This step is executed, by default, only for routes from the same neighboring AS.

6. The router selects routes learned from an EBGP peer over routes learned from an IBGP peer. If the remaining routes are all EBGP-learned routes, the router skips to step 9.

7. The router selects the route with the smallest IGP metric to the advertised BGP Next Hop.

8. If Route Reflection is used for IBGP peering, the router selects the route with the shortest Cluster-List length.

9. The router selects the route from the peer with the smallest numerical Router ID.

10. The router selects the route from the peer with the smallest numerical Peer Address.

BGP Attributes

The selection of a BGP route for data forwarding is highly dependent on the value of the path attributes. Each attribute is encoded in an Update message using a TLV triple. The Type portion of the TLV is a 2-octet field representing the following:

Optional Bit (Bit 0)   An attribute is either well known (a value of 0) or optional (a value of 1).

Transitive Bit (Bit 1)   Optional attributes can be either nontransitive (a value of 0) or transitive (a value of 1). Well-known attributes are always transitive.

Partial Bit (Bit 2)   Only optional transitive attributes use this bit. A 0 means each BGP router along the path recognized this attribute. A 1 means that at least one BGP router along the path did not recognize the attribute.

Extended Length Bit (Bit 3)   This bit sets the size of the TLV Length portion to one octet (a value of 0) or two octets (a value of 1).

Unused (Bits 4–7)   These bit positions are not used and must be set to 0.

Type Code (Bits 8–15)   The specific kind of attribute is encoded in this 1-octet field.

The attribute type bits result in four main categories of BGP attributes: well-known mandatory, well-known discretionary, optional transitive, and optional nontransitive.

BGP routers must recognize all of the well-known attributes, which must be included with all routes. Discretionary attributes may or may not be included on a particular route. BGP routers do not have to understand optional attributes but must readvertise them based on their transitive setting. Transitive attributes are advertised to all BGP peers, while nontransitive attributes may be discarded if the local router doesn't recognize them.

We now discuss some of the BGP attributes in further detail.

Next Hop

Next Hop, attribute type code 3, is a well-known mandatory attribute. It supplies each BGP router with the IP address of the next hop to the route destination. The local router performs a recursive lookup in the routing table to locate a route to the BGP next hop. The result of this recursive lookup is the physical next hop assigned to the BGP route in the routing and forwarding tables.

Reachability to the Next Hop attribute is critical to the operation of BGP. Recall from the previous section "The Route Selection Process" that a route whose Next Hop is not known is unusable to the local router. Care should be taken to maintain reachability because this attribute, by default, is modified only when a route is advertised across an EBGP peer session. Figure 8.10 shows an EBGP route advertisement.

FIGURE 8.10   An EBGP Next Hop change

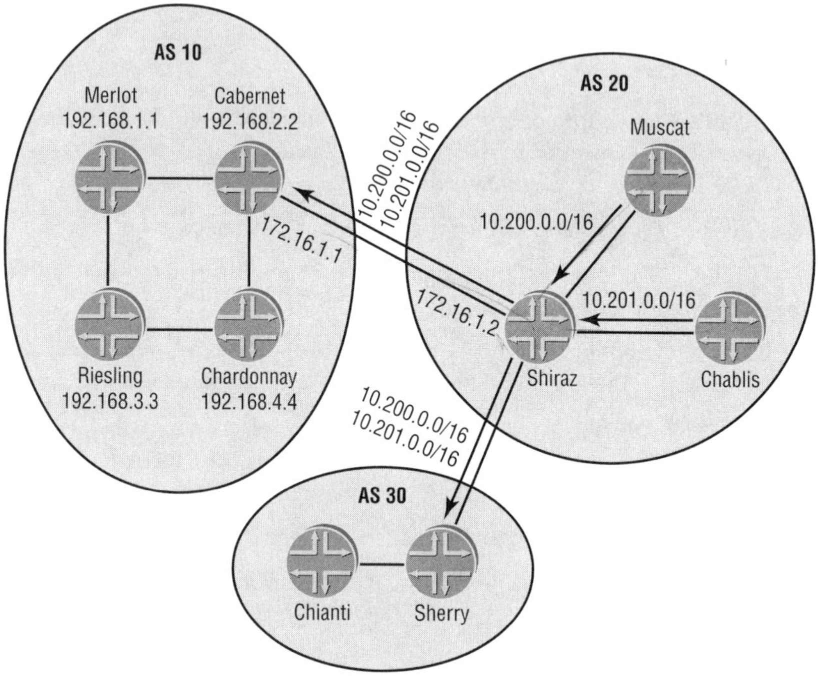

The Shiraz and Cabernet routers are EBGP peers in AS 10 and AS 20, respectively. As we discussed in the "Peers" section earlier in this chapter, they are directly connected and the BGP session is established between the 172.16.1.1 and 172.16.1.2 addresses. As Shiraz advertises the 10.200.0.0 /16 and 10.201.0.0 /16 routes to Cabernet, it changes the Next Hop attribute to the IP address on its side of the session—172.16.1.2 in our example. Cabernet is directly connected to the 172.16.1.0 /24 subnet, so reachability to the Next Hop is achieved.

Figure 8.11 shows an IBGP peer session between Cabernet and Riesling. When Cabernet advertises those same routes across that peer session, the Next Hop attribute is not changed—it is still 172.16.1.2. Chances are that Riesling does not have a route to the 172.16.1.0 /24 subnet because it is outside the AS boundary. This lack of reachability causes the 10.200.0.0 /16 and 10.201.0.0 /16 routes to become unusable to Riesling.

NOTE   A Juniper Networks router marks these types of routes as hidden. You can view them by using the show route hidden command.

FIGURE 8.11   An IBGP Next Hop advertisement

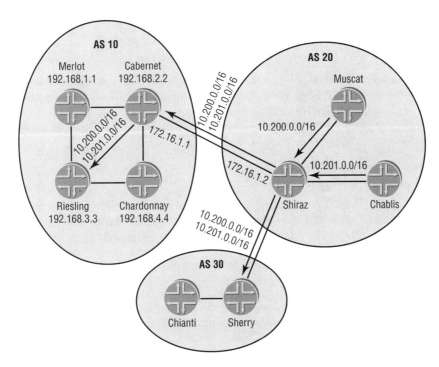

   To resolve this issue, the administrators of AS 10 must alter their current environment. There are five viable methods for providing reachability to the BGP Next Hop:

Setting the Next Hop attribute   Considered by many to be a best practice for an IBGP peer session, this method allows the advertising router to change the value of the Next Hop attribute.

In Figure 8.11, Cabernet and Riesling are peers using their loopback addresses of 192.168.2.2 and 192.168.3.3. Cabernet changes the Next Hop to its peer address of 192.168.2.2 prior to advertising routes to Riesling. The BGP peer session was established using reachability from Riesling to 192.168.2.2. The Next Hop attribute inherently becomes reachable and the advertised routes are now usable.

Using an IGP passive interface   In this scenario, the interface connecting the EBGP peers is configured to operate in passive mode within the IGP of the AS. This allows the IGP to advertise the external subnet as an internal route without establishing an adjacency between the EBGP peers. All routers in the AS now have reachability to the Next Hop advertised by the EBGP-speaking router.

Configuring an export policy   The end result of this approach is exactly the same as operating the external interface in passive mode. The difference lies in the method of advertising the interface's subnet. In this instance, an export policy is configured within the IGP to advertise the Direct routes from the routing table. The external interface of the EBGP-speaking router now appears as an external IGP route on all routers in the AS and reachability to the Next Hop is achieved.

Establishing an IGP adjacency   While a viable technical solution to solving Next Hop reachability, this is not a recommended practice for an ISP. This process involves establishing an IGP adjacency between the EBGP peers. The external subnet is automatically advertised to the IGP as part of this process and the Next Hop is reachable.

There is great risk involved in this process, however, because the IGPs are inherently trusting. All information advertised by the IGP from the neighboring AS is used without question and your internal routing tables may now contain routes you do not wish to use.

Using static routes   This approach carries with it the advantages and disadvantages of using static routes in place of your IGP. Static routes are simple and easy to configure but require manual input into all routers in the AS. You must configure a separate static route for each Next Hop for which reachability is required.

Local Preference

Local Preference, attribute type code 5, is a well-known discretionary attribute. All BGP routers must understand Local Preference, but it is not required on every route. In fact, Local Preference is only used within the confines of an AS—no value is advertised to an EBGP peer.

Administrators use the Local Preference attribute to designate the exit point out of the AS. Two factors make the Local Preference attribute well suited for this task. First, every router within the AS has a Local Preference value assigned to all routes. Second, this attribute is the first tiebreaker used in the BGP route selection algorithm. Therefore, each BGP router in the network makes the same selection decision and all user data traffic flows to the router advertising the highest Local Preference value. By default, each route within an AS receives a Local Preference value of 100. Possible values range from 1 to 4,294,967,295.

AS Path

AS Path, attribute type code 2, is a well-known mandatory attribute. The attribute contains a sequenced list of AS numbers that represent the networks the route has transited.

This attribute is modified only when a route is advertised to an EBGP peer. During this process, the local router adds its AS number to the attribute. The new value is prepended to (added to the front of) the existing path attribute. This means that the AS Path is actually read in a right-to-left manner. Examining a route with the path 65001 65100 65250 tells us it was originally advertised to BGP by AS 65250. It was then advertised to a router in AS 65100, transited AS 65001, and finally arrived in the local AS 64699. When you advertise this route to an EBGP peer, you modify the path to become 64999 65001 65100 65250.

In the "Network Connectivity" section earlier in this chapter, we discussed the AS Path attribute as a method for preventing routing loops. It is also used as a tiebreaker in the route selection algorithm. Each AS number represents a length of 1 with the shortest number of AS hops in a path being preferred. For example, the AS Path 65000 65001 has a length of 2. It is shorter than the path 65100 65200 65300 but longer than the path 64800.

In an attempt to influence traffic flows into your network, you can artificially lengthen the AS Path attribute. You do this when you advertise a route to an EBGP peer. Instead of adding your local AS number one time to the path, you add it several times. Assuming a local AS number of 64699, in our earlier example the default prepend action results in an AS Path length of 4 (64999 65001 65100 65250). Alternatively, you can prepend your AS number three times to result in an AS Path length of 6 (64999 64999 64999 65001 65100 65250).

Origin

Origin, attribute type code 1, is a well-known mandatory attribute. The Origin code designates the source of the route into BGP.

BGP routers receive and readvertise BGP routes by default, using the rules we outlined in the "Peers" section earlier in this chapter. However, the protocol does not naturally advertise non-BGP routes. Somewhere in the Internet, each route was explicitly configured for advertisement into BGP. For a Juniper Networks router, this is accomplished with an export policy, as we discussed in Chapter 4, "Routing Policy."

The first BGP router to advertise a route assigns a value to the Origin attribute to alert other routers as to the source of that route. The route selection algorithm may use this value as a tie-breaker, with a lower value being preferred. The current specification dictates three possible Origin values:

IGP   The route was originally learned by an IGP on the source router. IGP is displayed with the character "I" and is encoded as a value of 0.

EGP   The route was originally learned by the EGP protocol. EGP is displayed with the character "E" and is encoded as a value of 1.

Incomplete   The route's source was unknown to the initial BGP router. Incomplete is displayed with the character "?" and is encoded as a value of 2.

The Origin letter code (I/E/?) is displayed at the end of the AS Path attribute. Therefore, an Origin of IGP appears as 65499 65000 I in the router's output.

The JUNOS software always assigns an Origin code of IGP to all routes advertised using an export policy.

Multiple Exit Discriminator

Multiple Exit Discriminator (MED), attribute type code 4, is an optional nontransitive attribute. As such, BGP routes may not carry this attribute at all. Those that do, however, retain it only within the confines of a particular AS. This means that a MED attribute received from an EBGP peer is advertised to all IBGP peers and all routers may use the encoded value. MED values received from IBGP peers, however, are not readvertised to an EBGP peer. In other words, the router on the edge of the AS removes the attribute prior to sending the route.

By default, the MED attribute is only compared for routes received from the same neighboring AS. For example, suppose the route 192.168.100.0 /24 is received from AS 65000 and AS 65400. Any MED values associated with these routes are not comparable by the route selection algorithm since the first AS in the AS Path is not the same. On the other hand, should the 172.16.200.0 /24 route be received from two different routers in AS 64600, the MED values can be compared as a tiebreaker.

The JUNOS software interprets the absence of a MED as a value of 0.

Community

Community, attribute type code 8, is an optional transitive attribute. It is used to administratively group routes for a common policy action. For example, a BGP import policy might alter the Local Preference of all routes received with a certain community value assigned.

The attribute is encoded as a four-octet value where the first two octets represent an AS number and the remaining two octets represent a locally defined value. The Community attribute is displayed in the format 65001:1001.

🌐 Real World Scenario

The BGP Attributes in Action

While it is nice to have a definition of the attributes and talk about their purpose, nothing drives home their use like an example. Let's reexamine the BGP route selection algorithm using a sample router.

Suppose a BGP router in AS 65001 peers with six different neighbors. Each neighbor advertises the 10.0.0.0 /8 route to the local router with various attributes defined. The received routes are:

- Peer A: Local Preference—100; AS Path—64777 64888; Origin—I; MED—10

- Peer B: Local Preference—200; AS Path—64777 64888; Origin—I; MED—5

- Peer C: Local Preference—200; AS Path—64777 64888 64999; Origin—I; MED—15

- Peer D: Local Preference—200; AS Path—64777 64888; Origin—I; MED—25

- Peer E: Local Preference—200; AS Path—64777 64888; Origin—?; MED—20

- Peer F: Local Preference—200; AS Path—64777 64888 64999 65000; Origin—I; MED—30

The local router examines the Adjacency-RIB-In tables and locates these versions of the 10.0.0.0 /8 route. The router then uses the BGP route selection algorithm to decide which version should be used for forwarding traffic and placed into the Local-RIB table.

Assuming that the BGP Next Hop for each route is reachable in the routing table, the local router first examines the Local Preference attribute. It finds that the route from Peer A has a value of 100, while every other version of the route has a value of 200. A higher Local Preference value is preferred over a lower value, so the router removes Peer A from its list of candidates.

The router then examines the AS Path length of the remaining routes. Peers B, D, and E advertised a path length of 2. Peer C's version of the route has a path length of 3, and Peer F advertised a path length of 4. A shorter AS Path length is preferred, and the router removes Peers C and F from the list of candidates.

The Origin attribute of the remaining routes from Peers B, D, and E is now evaluated. The local router finds the routes from Peers B and D to have an Origin of IGP (I), while the route from Peer E has an Origin of Incomplete (?). The IGP Origin is preferred over the Incomplete Origin, and the router removes Peer E from the candidate list.

The next attribute considered by the router is the Multiple Exit Discriminator. Before examining the value of the attribute, the router first must decide if the candidate routes were advertised from the same neighboring AS. Peer B's route was last in AS 64777, as was the route from Peer D. These routes meet the required criteria, and the router finds that the MED of Peer B's route is 5. This is lower than the MED value 25 on Peer D's route. A lower MED value is preferred, and the router removes Peer D from the candidate list.

With only a single route remaining to be evaluated, the local router has found the best path to 10.0.0.0/8. The route is placed into the Local-RIB table, and user data packets are forwarded to the BGP next hop advertised by Peer B.

Juniper Networks Implementation

We've discussed the basic theoretical aspects of using BGP on a Juniper Networks router. Next we examine the steps required to configure the protocol and advertise routes to various peers. There are multiple theories, methods, and commands you can use in your configuration. This provides you with the most flexibility in operating your router. We focus here only on basic steps and procedures.

The JUNOS software provides for configuration options at the global BGP level, at the peer-group level, or at a specific neighbor level. It is often a best practice to group your peers into peer groups for ease of administering routing policies. We follow this practice throughout the remainder of this chapter.

Establishing Peer Relationships

Before any routes are advertised or attributes modified, you must first establish your BGP peer sessions. In the "Peers" section earlier in this chapter, we discussed the differences between an EBGP and an IBGP peer session. As you might suspect, the configurations of these peer sessions are different as well. One common aspect to both, however, is the local AS number.

Assigning an AS Number

The first step toward configuring BGP is to tell the router its local AS number. You configure this value in the [edit routing-options] hierarchy. Figure 8.12 shows the Shiraz router within AS 20.

FIGURE 8.12   A BGP sample network

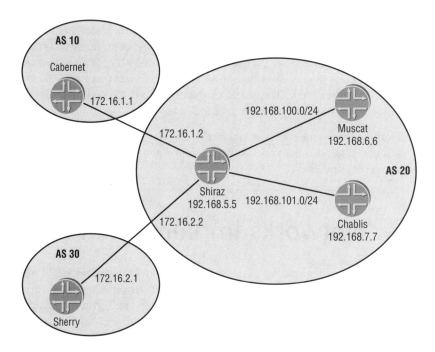

The autonomous-system command assigns the local AS number like so:

```
[edit]
user@Shiraz# set routing-options autonomous-system 20
```

The JUNOS software stores the AS number in the central routing-options hierarchy to allow for easier configuration. All BGP peers in the global routing instance inherit this value. In addition, other instances of BGP on the router (possibly within a VPN) use this common value.

Configuring an EBGP Peer Session

An external BGP peer session requires that the routers be directly connected to each other. Figure 8.12 shows the Cabernet router in AS 10 and the Sherry router in AS 30. Both routers are physically connected to Shiraz in AS 20.

A peer group called **ebgp-peers** has been created on Shiraz for the EBGP peer sessions to Cabernet and Sherry. The IP address and AS number of each peer is explicitly configured:

```
[edit protocols bgp group ebgp-peers]
user@Shiraz# set neighbor 172.16.1.1 peer-as 10
user@Shiraz# set neighbor 172.16.2.1 peer-as 30
```

We also inform the router whether the peer-group members are EBGP peers or IBGP peers by using the **type** command. This allows the group to perform the default attribute changes if required.

```
[edit protocols bgp group ebgp-peers]
user@Shiraz# set type external
```

The resulting configuration looks like this:

```
[edit protocols bgp]
user@Shiraz# show
group ebgp-peers {
    type external;
    neighbor 172.16.1.1 {
        peer-as 10;
    }
    neighbor 172.16.2.1 {
        peer-as 30;
    }
}
```

The configurations for Cabernet and Sherry mirror the peer-group setup and explicit configuration found on Shiraz:

```
[edit]
user@Cabernet# show
routing-options {
    autonomous-system 10;
}
protocols {
    bgp {
        group AS-20 {
            type external;
```

```
            peer-as 20;
            neighbor 172.16.1.2;
        }
    }
}


[edit]
user@Sherry# show
routing-options {
    autonomous-system 30;
}
protocols {
    bgp {
        group AS-20 {
            type external;
            peer-as 20;
            neighbor 172.16.2.2;
        }
    }
}
```

Configuring an IBGP Peer Session

In the "Peers" section earlier in this chapter, we explained that IBGP peers require only IP reachability to form a peer session. Often that reachability is achieved through an IGP within the AS. Using Figure 8.12 as a guide, we see that AS 20 consists of the Shiraz, Muscat, and Chablis routers. OSPF is configured within the domain, and Shiraz has IGP routes to the other routers:

```
user@Shiraz> show route protocol ospf

inet.0: 14 destinations, 15 routes (14 active, 0 holddown, 0 hidden)
+ = Active Route, - = Last Active, * = Both

192.168.6.6/32      *[OSPF/10] 00:00:06, metric 1
                    > to 192.168.100.2 via ge-0/2/0.0
192.168.7.7/32      *[OSPF/10] 00:00:06, metric 1
                    > via at-0/1/0.100
```

A new peer group called ibgp-peers has been created on Shiraz. The IP addresses of Muscat and Chablis are configured and the peer group is designated as an internal group by using the type command:

```
[edit protocols bgp group ibgp-peers]
```

```
user@Shiraz# set type internal
user@Shiraz# set neighbor 192.168.6.6
user@Shiraz# set neighbor 192.168.7.7
```

The loopback addresses of the IBGP peers are used to provide redundancy and resiliency to the internal BGP network. Should a physical interface address be configured, its failure would cause the peer session to drop. In our case, as long as the router is reachable through any means, the BGP session remains established. The use of loopback addresses for peer sessions also requires an additional configuration step on Shiraz. We inform the BGP process of our own loopback address by using the `local-address` command:

```
[edit protocols bgp group ibgp-peers]
user@Shiraz# set local-address 192.168.5.5
```

The configuration on Shiraz now looks like this:

```
[edit protocols bgp]
user@Shiraz# show
group ebgp-peers {
    type external;
    neighbor 172.16.1.1 {
        peer-as 10;
    }
    neighbor 172.16.2.1 {
        peer-as 30;
    }
}
group ibgp-peers {
    type internal;
    local-address 192.168.5.5;
    neighbor 192.168.6.6;
    neighbor 192.168.7.7;
}
```

Both the Muscat and Chablis routers have a similar `ibgp-peers` configuration to establish an IBGP full-mesh within AS 20.

We didn't configure an AS number for the IBGP peers because we used the `type internal` command. This command informs the router that the local AS number in `routing-options` should be used for these peer sessions.

🌐 Real World Scenario

Using *local-address*

It might seem strange to you that configuring an IBGP session requires more commands than an EBGP session does. After all, these peers are inside your own AS, and you trust their services, so it should be easy to set up. The truth is that it has nothing to do with trust, but rather with the method that BGP operates.

Each peer session requires that the peer's IP address and AS number be explicitly configured in order for the session to become established. This information is exchanged in Open messages during session establishment and must be agreed on for the session to come up. The setting of AS numbers is straightforward in the configuration. It is the IP address of the peer that causes a possible issue.

One basic principle of IP packets is that each contains a source and destination IP address. When a router generates an IP packet itself, the source IP address becomes the address of the outbound interface. For EBGP peers, this default behavior is fine because the peers are connected and are peering across that interface address. IBGP peers, on the other hand, are peering to the loopback address of the remote router. Let's look at a small example.

Router A and Router B want to become IBGP peers using their loopback addresses of 1.1.1.1 and 2.2.2.2, respectively. When Router A sends its Open message to 2.2.2.2, the source IP address of the packet is the outgoing interface, say 10.10.10.1. Router B receives this Open message and compares the source address of the packet to its list of configured peers. Router B does not find a configuration for 10.10.10.1 and rejects the Open message. Router B performs this same process in reverse, with Router A rejecting the Open message from Router B. Two routers in this situation remain in the BGP `Active` state forever, a clear indication of this problem.

The resolution to this issue is the `local-address` command. Its function is quite simple—it changes the source IP address of the BGP messages. In our example, Router A configures `local-address 1.1.1.1` within its peer session to Router B. The BGP Open message now lists 1.1.1.1 as the source IP address of the packet. Router B receives the message and compares the source address to its list of configured peers. It now finds a match for Router A and responds to the Open message with a BGP Keepalive message. The two peers can now become established and advertise routing knowledge to each other.

Verifying Your BGP Sessions

Now that the configuration of our peers is complete, we would like to verify that the peer sessions are actually established and operational. There are three main commands available in the JUNOS software to accomplish this. Each provides different levels of information to the user. Let's examine them in greater detail using Figure 8.12 as a guide.

show bgp summary

The show bgp summary command provides you with a good snapshot of the protocol on your router. This is often the command you use to determine if your peer sessions are established. The Shiraz router has configured two EBGP and two IBGP peers. The output below reveals the state of each peer:

```
user@Shiraz> show bgp summary
Groups: 2 Peers: 4 Down peers: 0
Table          Tot Paths  Act Paths Suppressed    History Damp State    Pending
inet.0              12         12          0           0         0            0
Peer             AS      InPkt     OutPkt    OutQ   Flaps Last Up/Dwn State
172.16.1.1       10       428        430       0       0    3:33:00 4/4/0
172.16.2.1       30       428        430       0       0    3:32:56 4/4/0
192.168.6.6      20       392        392       0       0    3:14:30 2/2/0
192.168.7.7      20       390        391       0       0    3:14:02 2/2/0
```

The command output is separated into a summary section and a detailed section for the specific peers. Within the summary area, you can see the number of peer groups and peers configured. You also can determine some routing information for received BGP routes. In the case of Shiraz, 12 path advertisements have been received from peers, and all 12 are currently active and being used to forward user traffic.

The specific peer portion of the show bgp summary output contains the following fields:

Peer   The configured peer address for each peer is listed in this field.

AS   The configured AS number for each peer is listed here.

InPkt   This field lists the total number of BGP messages received from the peer.

OutPkt   This field lists the total number of BGP messages sent to each peer.

OutQ   This field displays the number of BGP messages queued and waiting to be sent to a peer. This number is usually 0 because the queue is emptied quickly. A high and constant value in this column may indicate a problem with the peer session.

Flaps   This field specifies the number of times the peer session has been closed and reestablished.

Last Up/Dwn   This field displays the amount of time since the peer last changed state from Established to any other BGP state, or to Established from any other BGP state.

State   This field shows the current BGP state of the peer. When the session reaches the Established state, routing information is displayed instead of a keyword. The routes are shown in the format <# Active>/<# Received</<# Damped>. For example, Shiraz has received four routes from its peer at 172.16.2.1. All four routes are currently active in the routing table and none of them have been damped.

show bgp group

To view the configured peer groups on your router, use the show bgp group command. This displays each group's name, type, and configured peers. The output from Shiraz shows:

```
user@Shiraz> show bgp group
Group Type: External                    Local AS: 20
  Name: ebgp-peers
  Total peers: 2        Established: 2
  172.16.1.1+179
  172.16.2.1+179
  Route Queue Timer: unset Route Queue: empty

Group Type: Internal    AS: 20        Local AS: 20
  Name: ibgp-peers
  Total peers: 2        Established: 2
  192.168.6.6+1910
  192.168.7.7+1127
  Route Queue Timer: unset Route Queue: empty
```

The IP addresses displayed are the configured BGP peer addresses. The additional information details the TCP port number used for the session. For example, Shiraz is peering with 172.16.2.1 and the remote port number is 179. This tells you that Shiraz established the peer session because it is using the well-known port for BGP. The situation is a bit different for the 192.168.6.6 peer, whose remote TCP port is 1910. The far-end router initiated the session to Shiraz using the well-known BGP port number.

show bgp neighbor

To receive the most detailed information about your BGP peers, use the show bgp neighbor command. The output from Shiraz for just the 172.16.1.1 peer is as follows:

```
user@Shiraz> show bgp neighbor 172.16.1.1
Peer: 172.16.1.1+179  AS 10    Local: 172.16.1.2+1028 AS 20
  Type: External    State: Established    Flags: <>
  Last State: OpenConfirm   Last Event: RecvKeepAlive
  Last Error: None
  Options: <Preference HoldTime PeerAS Refresh>
  Holdtime: 90 Preference: 170
  Number of flaps: 0
  Peer ID: 192.168.2.2      Local ID: 192.168.5.5      Active Holdtime: 90
  Keepalive Interval: 30
  Local Interface: so-0/0/1.0
  NLRI advertised by peer: inet-unicast
```

```
NLRI for this session: inet-unicast
Peer supports Refresh capability (2)
Table inet.0 Bit: 10000
  Send state: in sync
  Active prefixes: 4
  Received prefixes: 4
  Suppressed due to damping: 0
Last traffic (seconds): Received 13    Sent 13    Checked 13
Input messages:  Total 438     Updates 4       Refreshes 0      Octets 8473
Output messages: Total 440     Updates 4       Refreshes 0      Octets 8526
Output Queue[0]: 0
```

The output of this command contains a wealth of information, including the following:

- The peer address and AS number of the peer
- Configured hold time (`Holdtime`) and negotiated hold time (`Active Holdtime`)
- Router ID values for each peer
- The number of active and received routes
- The number of packets and the amount of octets sent to and received from the peer

Viewing Routing Knowledge

BGP routers by default advertise only active BGP routes in the routing table. This creates a sort of chicken-and-egg problem. A route can appear in the routing table as a BGP route only if it is received from a BGP peer, but a BGP peer can only advertise a route if it's already in the routing table as a BGP route.

Injecting Routes into BGP

The solution to this problem is the explicit advertisement of other routes into BGP. For a Juniper Networks router, this is accomplished with an `export` routing policy.

Figure 8.13 shows some BGP routes advertised into AS 20 by Muscat and Chablis. Each router has local static routes representing customer networks that are injected with a routing policy called ***send-statics***. The policy configuration on Muscat is:

```
[edit]
user@Muscat# show policy-options
policy-statement send-statics {
    term find-static-routes {
        from protocol static;
        then accept;
    }
}
```

FIGURE 8.13 BGP routing knowledge

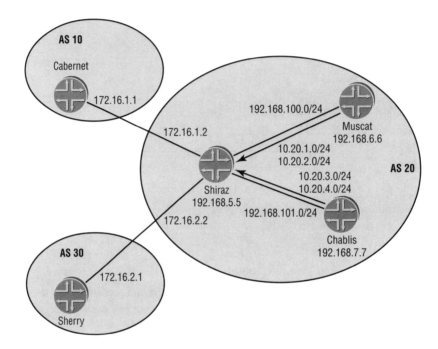

The policy is applied to BGP using the export command:

```
[edit protocols bgp group ibgp-peers]
user@Muscat# set export send-statics
```

The resulting configuration looks like this:

```
[edit protocols bgp]
user@Muscat# show
group ibgp-peers {
    type internal;
    local-address 192.168.6.6;
    export send-statics;
    neighbor 192.168.5.5;
    neighbor 192.168.7.7;
}
```

Viewing Received Routes

The routes that are received from each established BGP peer are stored in the Adjacency-RIB-IN tables. Within the JUNOS software, this is actually part of the routing table. Database pointers are used to keep the routing knowledge separate. You can view the routes advertised by a peer on the local router by using the show route receive-protocol bgp *neighbor-address* command.

The routes advertised from Chablis, whose peer address is 192.168.7.7, are as follows:

```
user@Shiraz> show route receive-protocol bgp 192.168.7.7

inet.0: 26 destinations, 27 routes (26 active, 0 holddown, 0 hidden)
+ = Active Route, - = Last Active, * = Both

10.20.3.0/24
192.168.7.7                      0         100 I
10.20.4.0/24
192.168.7.7                      0         100 I
```

Both the 10.20.3.0 /24 and 10.20.4.0 /24 routes are being received. The BGP Next Hop is 192.168.7.7 for both routes. Other BGP attributes visible in the output include a MED of 0, a Local Preference of 100, and an Origin of IGP.

Viewing Advertised Routes

The same routes are visible from the perspective of Chablis. They are also stored in the routing table with database pointers representing the Adjacency-RIB-Out. You can view this information by using the show route advertising-protocol bgp *neighbor-address* command:

```
user@Chablis> show route advertising-protocol bgp 192.168.5.5

inet.0: 21 destinations, 22 routes (13 active, 0 holddown, 8 hidden)
+ = Active Route, - = Last Active, * = Both

10.20.3.0/24
Self                             0         100 I
10.20.4.0/24
Self                             0         100 I
```

The main difference in this output is the listing of the BGP Next Hop attribute as Self. This represents the peer address of the router, 192.168.7.7 in our case. It is common to view this representation when using this command.

Viewing Local Routes

The representation of the BGP Local-RIB database is the routing table on your router. You can view this information by using a simple show route command. Of course, this shows you all the routes known to your router. To view just the BGP-learned routes, add the *protocol bgp* option.

The BGP routes on Shiraz are:

```
user@Shiraz> show route protocol bgp

inet.0: 26 destinations, 27 routes (26 active, 0 holddown, 0 hidden)
+ = Active Route, - = Last Active, * = Both

10.10.1.0/24       *[BGP/170] 00:23:21, MED 0, localpref 100
                      AS path: 10 I
                    > to 172.16.1.1 via so-0/0/1.0
10.10.2.0/24       *[BGP/170] 00:23:21, MED 0, localpref 100
                      AS path: 10 I
                    > to 172.16.1.1 via so-0/0/1.0
10.10.3.0/24       *[BGP/170] 00:23:21, MED 0, localpref 100
                      AS path: 10 I
                    > to 172.16.1.1 via so-0/0/1.0
10.10.4.0/24       *[BGP/170] 00:23:21, MED 0, localpref 100
                      AS path: 10 I
                    > to 172.16.1.1 via so-0/0/1.0
10.20.1.0/24       *[BGP/170] 02:37:11, MED 0, localpref 100, from 192.168.6.6
                      AS path: I
                    > to 192.168.100.2 via ge-0/2/0.0
10.20.2.0/24       *[BGP/170] 02:37:11, MED 0, localpref 100, from 192.168.6.6
                      AS path: I
                    > to 192.168.100.2 via ge-0/2/0.0
10.20.3.0/24       *[BGP/170] 02:36:34, MED 0, localpref 100, from 192.168.7.7
                      AS path: I
                    > via at-0/1/0.100
10.20.4.0/24       *[BGP/170] 02:36:34, MED 0, localpref 100, from 192.168.7.7
                      AS path: I
                    > via at-0/1/0.100
10.30.1.0/24       *[BGP/170] 00:24:18, MED 0, localpref 100
                      AS path: 30 I
                    > to 172.16.2.1 via so-0/0/0.0
10.30.2.0/24       *[BGP/170] 00:24:18, MED 0, localpref 100
                      AS path: 30 I
                    > to 172.16.2.1 via so-0/0/0.0
```

```
10.30.3.0/24        *[BGP/170] 00:24:18, MED 0, localpref 100
                       AS path: 30 I
                     > to 172.16.2.1 via so-0/0/0.0
10.30.4.0/24        *[BGP/170] 00:24:18, MED 0, localpref 100
                       AS path: 30 I
                     > to 172.16.2.1 via so-0/0/0.0
```

All of the BGP attributes are visible when you use the `show route detail` command. We'll examine just the 10.20.3.0 /24 route advertised from Chablis:

```
user@Shiraz> show route 10.20.3/24 detail

inet.0: 26 destinations, 27 routes (26 active, 0 holddown, 0 hidden)
10.20.3.0/24 (1 entry, 1 announced)
        *BGP    Preference: 170/-101
                Source: 192.168.7.7
                Nexthop: via at-0/1/0.100, selected
                Protocol Nexthop: 192.168.7.7 Indirect nexthop: 8458088 44
                State: <Active Int Ext>
                Local AS:    20 Peer AS:    20
                Age: 2:39:44    Metric: 0        Metric2: 1
                Task: BGP_20.192.168.7.7+1127
                Announcement bits (3): 0-KRT 3-BGP.0.0.0.0+179 4-Resolve inet.0
                AS path: I
                Localpref: 100
                Router ID: 192.168.7.7
```

The two attributes not explicitly listed by name are MED and Next Hop. The MED value is encoded within the `Metric` output and is currently set to 0. The `Metric2` field displays the current IGP cost to the BGP Next Hop and is set to 1. The Next Hop is listed as the `Protocol Nexthop` output and is 192.168.7.7, the peer address of the IBGP peer. This notation differentiates the attribute from the physical forwarding next hop (`at-0/1/0.100`) displayed in the `Nexthop` field.

Solving Next Hop Reachability

During our earlier discussion of the BGP attributes, we found that possible issues existed with establishing reachability to the BGP Next Hop attribute. This is especially noticeable for IBGP peer sessions since the attribute is changed, by default, only across EBGP sessions. Figure 8.14 shows that Cabernet in AS 10 and Sherry in AS 30 are advertising routes to Shiraz in AS 20.

FIGURE 8.14   Next Hop reachability

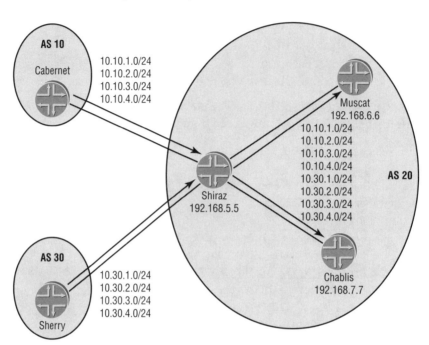

As shown here, the routes are visible in the local routing table of Shiraz:

```
user@Shiraz> show route protocol bgp terse
```

```
inet.0: 26 destinations, 27 routes (26 active, 0 holddown, 0 hidden)
+ = Active Route, - = Last Active, * = Both
```

A Destination	P Prf	Metric 1	Metric 2	Next hop	AS path
* 10.10.1.0/24	B 170	100	0	>172.16.1.1	10 I
* 10.10.2.0/24	B 170	100	0	>172.16.1.1	10 I
* 10.10.3.0/24	B 170	100	0	>172.16.1.1	10 I
* 10.10.4.0/24	B 170	100	0	>172.16.1.1	10 I
* 10.20.1.0/24	B 170	100	0	>192.168.100.2	I
* 10.20.2.0/24	B 170	100	0	>192.168.100.2	I
* 10.20.3.0/24	B 170	100	0	>at-0/1/0.100	I
* 10.20.4.0/24	B 170	100	0	>at-0/1/0.100	I
* 10.30.1.0/24	B 170	100	0	>172.16.2.1	30 I
* 10.30.2.0/24	B 170	100	0	>172.16.2.1	30 I
* 10.30.3.0/24	B 170	100	0	>172.16.2.1	30 I
* 10.30.4.0/24	B 170	100	0	>172.16.2.1	30 I

A detailed examination of a route from Cabernet and Sherry reveals that the BGP Next Hop is currently set to the addresses 172.16.1.1 and 172.16.2.1, respectively:

```
user@Shiraz> show route 10.10.1/24 detail

inet.0: 26 destinations, 27 routes (26 active, 0 holddown, 0 hidden)
10.10.1.0/24 (1 entry, 1 announced)
        *BGP    Preference: 170/-101
                Source: 172.16.1.1
                Nexthop: 172.16.1.1 via so-0/0/1.0, selected
                State: <Active Ext>
                Local AS:    20 Peer AS:    10
                Age: 57:35      Metric: 0
                Task: BGP_10.172.16.1.1+179
                Announcement bits (3): 0-KRT 3-BGP.0.0.0.0+179 4-Resolve inet.0
                AS path: 10 I
                Localpref: 100
                Router ID: 192.168.2.2
```

```
lab@Shiraz> show route 10.30.1/24 detail

inet.0: 26 destinations, 27 routes (26 active, 0 holddown, 0 hidden)
10.30.1.0/24 (1 entry, 1 announced)
        *BGP    Preference: 170/-101
                Source: 172.16.2.1
                Nexthop: 172.16.2.1 via so-0/0/0.0, selected
                State: <Active Ext>
                Local AS:    20 Peer AS:    30
                Age: 58:40      Metric: 0
                Task: BGP_30.172.16.2.1+179
                Announcement bits (3): 0-KRT 3-BGP.0.0.0.0+179 4-Resolve inet.0
                AS path: 30 I
                Localpref: 100
                Router ID: 192.168.8.8
```

Following the rules outlined in the "Peers" section earlier in this chapter, Shiraz advertises all active EBGP-learned routes to both its IBGP peers. The specific routes advertised to Chablis include:

```
user@Shiraz> show route advertising-protocol bgp 192.168.7.7

inet.0: 26 destinations, 27 routes (26 active, 0 holddown, 0 hidden)
+ = Active Route, - = Last Active, * = Both
```

```
10.10.1.0/24
172.16.1.1                      0            100 10 I
10.10.2.0/24
172.16.1.1                      0            100 10 I
10.10.3.0/24
172.16.1.1                      0            100 10 I
10.10.4.0/24
172.16.1.1                      0            100 10 I
10.30.1.0/24
172.16.2.1                      0            100 30 I
10.30.2.0/24
172.16.2.1                      0            100 30 I
10.30.3.0/24
172.16.2.1                      0            100 30 I
10.30.4.0/24
172.16.2.1                      0            100 30 I
```

As per the BGP defaults, the Next Hop attribute was not changed as the routes were advertised to the IBGP peer. Let's see what routes Chablis actually received from Shiraz:

```
user@Chablis> show route receive-protocol bgp 192.168.5.5

inet.0: 21 destinations, 22 routes (13 active, 0 holddown, 8 hidden)

user@Chablis>
```

At first glance, it appears that Chablis did not receive any routes. A closer examination, however, reveals that some routes are currently marked as hidden. We can view these routes with the show route hidden command:

```
user@Chablis> show route hidden

inet.0: 21 destinations, 22 routes (13 active, 0 holddown, 8 hidden)
+ = Active Route, - = Last Active, * = Both

10.10.1.0/24        [BGP/170] 01:04:41, MED 0, localpref 100, from 192.168.5.5
                      AS path: 10 I
                      Unusable
10.10.2.0/24        [BGP/170] 01:04:41, MED 0, localpref 100, from 192.168.5.5
                      AS path: 10 I
                      Unusable
10.10.3.0/24        [BGP/170] 01:04:41, MED 0, localpref 100, from 192.168.5.5
                      AS path: 10 I
                      Unusable
```

```
10.10.4.0/24        [BGP/170] 01:04:41, MED 0, localpref 100, from 192.168.5.5
                        AS path: 10 I
                        Unusable
10.30.1.0/24        [BGP/170] 01:05:38, MED 0, localpref 100, from 192.168.5.5
                        AS path: 30 I
                        Unusable
10.30.2.0/24        [BGP/170] 01:05:38, MED 0, localpref 100, from 192.168.5.5
                        AS path: 30 I
                        Unusable
10.30.3.0/24        [BGP/170] 01:05:38, MED 0, localpref 100, from 192.168.5.5
                        AS path: 30 I
                        Unusable
10.30.4.0/24        [BGP/170] 01:05:38, MED 0, localpref 100, from 192.168.5.5
                        AS path: 30 I
                        Unusable
```

It appears as though we've found our missing routes, but the routes are currently listed as Unusable. A closer look at the 10.10.1.0 /24 route reveals a vital clue:

```
user@Chablis> show route hidden 10.10.1/24 extensive

inet.0: 21 destinations, 22 routes (13 active, 0 holddown, 8 hidden)
10.10.1.0/24 (1 entry, 0 announced)
        BGP     Preference: 170/-101
                Next hop type: Unusable
                State: <Hidden Int Ext>
                Local AS:    20 Peer AS:     20
                Age: 1:07:23    Metric: 0
                Task: BGP_20.192.168.5.5+179
                AS path: 10 I
                Localpref: 100
                Router ID: 192.168.5.5
                Indirect nexthops: 1
                        Protocol Nexthop: 172.16.1.1 Indirect nexthop: 0 -
```

The BGP Next Hop of 172.16.1.1 is Unusable. It appears the recursive lookup did not find a route to the Next Hop. We can verify this with a show route command:

```
user@Chablis> show route 172.16.1.1


user@Chablis>
```

In the "BGP Attributes" section earlier in this chapter, we listed five viable methods for solving this problem. Let's follow the best practice recommendation and alter the Next Hop attribute on Shiraz as the routes are advertised to the IBGP peers. We accomplish this by applying an export routing policy to BGP. We first build the policy on Shiraz:

```
[edit]
user@Shiraz# show policy-options
policy-statement next-hop-self {
    term change-the-attribute {
        from protocol bgp;
        then {
            next-hop self;
        }
    }
}
```

The policy called *next-hop-self* matches all active BGP routes in the routing table. The action dictates that the Next Hop attribute be changed to the value self. In the "Viewing Advertised Routes" section earlier in this chapter, we explained that the keyword self translates into the local peer address for the BGP session. Shiraz is using its loopback address of 192.168.5.5 to peer with Chablis, so this address is used as the Next Hop value.

The attribute should be changed only as the routes are advertised to the peers and not for Shiraz itself. An export policy application within the IBGP peer group accomplishes this goal:

```
[edit protocols bgp]
user@Shiraz# set group ibgp-peers export next-hop-self

[edit protocols bgp]
user@Shiraz# show
group ebgp-peers {
    type external;
    neighbor 172.16.1.1 {
        peer-as 10;
    }
    neighbor 172.16.2.1 {
        peer-as 30;
    }
}
group ibgp-peers {
    type internal;
    local-address 192.168.5.5;
    export next-hop-self;
```

```
    neighbor 192.168.6.6;
    neighbor 192.168.7.7;
}
```

Do not apply a next-hop-self policy as an import policy for an EBGP peer. This results in all received routes being marked as hidden in the routing table, because a recursive lookup is not performed for EBGP peers.

A check of the routes advertised to Chablis reveals the Next Hop set to the value self:

user@Shiraz> **show route advertising-protocol bgp 192.168.7.7**

```
inet.0: 26 destinations, 27 routes (26 active, 0 holddown, 0 hidden)
+ = Active Route, - = Last Active, * = Both


10.10.1.0/24
Self                        0        100 10 I
10.10.2.0/24
Self                        0        100 10 I
10.10.3.0/24
Self                        0        100 10 I
10.10.4.0/24
Self                        0        100 10 I
10.30.1.0/24
Self                        0        100 30 I
10.30.2.0/24
Self                        0        100 30 I
10.30.3.0/24
Self                        0        100 30 I
10.30.4.0/24
Self                        0        100 30 I
```

Chablis is now receiving the routes as:

user@Chablis> **show route receive-protocol bgp 192.168.5.5**

```
inet.0: 21 destinations, 22 routes (21 active, 0 holddown, 0 hidden)
+ = Active Route, - = Last Active, * = Both


10.10.1.0/24
192.168.5.5                 0        100 10 I
```

```
10.10.2.0/24
192.168.5.5                     0            100 10 I
10.10.3.0/24
192.168.5.5                     0            100 10 I
10.10.4.0/24
192.168.5.5                     0            100 10 I
10.30.1.0/24
192.168.5.5                     0            100 30 I
10.30.2.0/24
192.168.5.5                     0            100 30 I
10.30.3.0/24
192.168.5.5                     0            100 30 I
10.30.4.0/24
192.168.5.5                     0            100 30 I
```

Chablis already had reachability to 192.168.5.5 to form the peer session. Therefore, the received routes are no longer hidden and now appear in the local routing table with the proper Protocol Nexthop listed:

```
user@Chablis> show route protocol bgp terse

inet.0: 21 destinations, 22 routes (21 active, 0 holddown, 0 hidden)
+ = Active Route, - = Last Active, * = Both

A Destination      P Prf   Metric 1   Metric 2  Next hop         AS path
* 10.10.1.0/24     B 170      100            0 >at-0/0/0.100     10 I
* 10.10.2.0/24     B 170      100            0 >at-0/0/0.100     10 I
* 10.10.3.0/24     B 170      100            0 >at-0/0/0.100     10 I
* 10.10.4.0/24     B 170      100            0 >at-0/0/0.100     10 I
* 10.20.1.0/24     B 170      100            0 >at-0/0/0.100     I
* 10.20.2.0/24     B 170      100            0 >at-0/0/0.100     I
* 10.30.1.0/24     B 170      100            0 >at-0/0/0.100     30 I
* 10.30.2.0/24     B 170      100            0 >at-0/0/0.100     30 I
* 10.30.3.0/24     B 170      100            0 >at-0/0/0.100     30 I
* 10.30.4.0/24     B 170      100            0 >at-0/0/0.100     30 I


user@Chablis> show route 10.10.1/24 detail

inet.0: 21 destinations, 22 routes (21 active, 0 holddown, 0 hidden)
10.10.1.0/24 (1 entry, 1 announced)
        *BGP    Preference: 170/-101
                Source: 192.168.5.5
```

```
Nexthop: via at-0/0/0.100, selected
Protocol Nexthop: 192.168.5.5 Indirect nexthop: 8463088 56
State: <Active Int Ext>
Local AS:    20 Peer AS:    20
Age: 1:30:07    Metric: 0        Metric2: 1
Task: BGP_20.192.168.5.5+179
Announcement bits (2): 0-KRT 4-Resolve inet.0
AS path: 10 I
Localpref: 100
Router ID: 192.168.5.5
```

Summary

In this chapter, we looked at some of the reasons BGP was created: connectivity of AS networks, policy control, reliable transport, and scalability of the Internet. We then discussed how BGP routers form peer relationships and how routes are advertised between EBGP and IBGP peers. Following that was a discussion of the BGP message types exchanged between two routers.

We then examined how a BGP router stores its routes in various RIBs. The routes in the Adjacency-RIB-In are then parsed through a route selection algorithm to find the best path to each destination. We then examined the attributes used in the algorithm.

Finally, we explored how to configure and operate BGP on a Juniper Networks router. We explained various show commands used to verify connectivity. We then discussed how to source routes into BGP using a routing policy and talked about CLI commands used to view routing knowledge. We ended with an examination of a Next Hop reachability problem and one potential solution.

Exam Essentials

Describe why BGP is used for interdomain routing.   BGP provides the Internet with the ability to connect AS networks in a mesh environment, allows for explicit policy control, and reliably transmits routing knowledge across the Internet.

Identify the different forms of BGP peering.   A BGP router can peer with a neighbor in a different AS using EBGP. It may also peer with other routers in its own AS using IBGP.

Describe the BGP message types.   There are four message types used in BGP. They include the Open, Update, Notification, and Keepalive messages.

Identify the various routing information bases used by BGP.   There are three main databases used to store BGP routes: the Adjacency-RIB-In, the Local-RIB, and the Adjacency-RIB-Out tables.

List the steps of the BGP route selection algorithm.   Each BGP router uses only one path advertisement to a destination. That singular path is located using a specific set of tiebreaking rules. Many steps include the comparison of BGP attributes.

Describe the major BGP attributes and their functions.   Some of the BGP attributes are Next Hop, Local Preference, AS Path, Origin, and Multiple Exit Discriminator.

Key Terms

Before you take the exam, be certain you are familiar with the following terms:

`Active` state	Multiple Exit Discriminator (MED)
Adjacency-RIB-In	neighbors
Adjacency-RIB-Out	Network Layer Reachability Information (NLRI)
AS Path	Next Hop
Community	Notification message
`Connect` state	Open message
`Established` state	`OpenConfirm` state
external BGP (EBGP)	`OpenSent` state
IBGP full-mesh	Origin
`Idle` state	path-vector protocol
internal BGP (IBGP)	peers
Keepalive message	Routing Information Base (RIB)
Local Preference	TCP port 179
Local-RIB	Update message

Review Questions

1. BGP uses Transmission Control Protocol (TCP) as its transport. What is the port number?

    A. 176

    B. 179

    C. 181

    D. 173

2. After the initial route exchange, does BGP send incremental or complete updates on a regular basis?

    A. BGP sends incremental updates only when needed.

    B. BGP sends complete updates to ensure that the routing information is accurate.

    C. BGP sends both complete and incremental updates to ensure the accuracy of routing.

    D. BGP does not send any updates after the initial data exchange.

3. What description best describes BGP?

    A. It is a path-vector protocol.

    B. It is a distance-vector protocol.

    C. It is a link-state protocol.

    D. It is a hybrid routing protocol.

4. What are two characteristics of a default EBGP peer session?

    A. Peers belong to different AS networks.

    B. Peers belong to the same AS network.

    C. Peers must be directly connected.

    D. Peers do not need to be directly connected.

5. What are two characteristics of an IBGP peering?

    A. Peers belong to different AS networks.

    B. Peers belong to the same AS network.

    C. Peers must be directly connected.

    D. Peers do not need to be directly connected.

6. Why must EBGP peers be directly connected, by default?

    A. An IGP does not operate between AS networks.

    B. The Next Hop attribute gets changed when routes are exchanged between the peers.

    C. The IP TTL of BGP messages is set to 1.

    D. They do not have to be directly connected.

7. What is one use of the AS Path attribute?

   A. To determine if a route is active in the routing table

   B. To prevent routing loops

   C. To establish a BGP peer session

   D. To prevent a denial-of-service attack

8. What BGP state denotes a fully operational session?

   A. OpenSent

   B. OpenConfirm

   C. Established

   D. Active

9. How do the advertisement rules differ for IBGP and EBGP peers?

   A. EBGP peers advertise only active routes, while IBGP peers advertise all routes.

   B. EBGP peers advertise routes learned from both EBGP and IBGP peers, while IBGP peers do not advertise IBGP-learned routes.

   C. IBGP and EBGP routers advertise all routes to all peers.

   D. IBGP peers advertise routes learned from both IBGP and EBGP peers, while EBGP peers do not advertise EBGP-learned routes.

10. What is the purpose of the Notification message?

   A. To notify a peer that it has completed sending all the routing updates

   B. To notify peers that a route's attributes are changing

   C. To open a BGP connection

   D. To notify a peer that an error has been detected

11. What two things about the Local Preference attribute set it apart from the other BGP attributes?

   A. A lower Local Preference is preferred over a higher one.

   B. A higher Local Preference is preferred over a lower one.

   C. Local Preference attempts to affect inbound traffic flows.

   D. Local Preference attempts to affect outbound traffic flows.

12. What command displays routes that are in the Adjacency-RIB-Out table?

   A. `show route advertising-protocol bgp` *neighbor-address*

   B. `show route bgp advertising-protocol` *neighbor-address*

   C. `show route receive-protocol bgp` *neighbor-address*

   D. `show route bgp receive-protocol` *neighbor-address*

13. What command displays routes that are in the Adjacency-RIB-In table?

    A. `show route advertising-protocol bgp` *neighbor-address*

    B. `show route bgp advertising-protocol` *neighbor-address*

    C. `show route receive-protocol bgp` *neighbor-address*

    D. `show route bgp receive-protocol` *neighbor-address*

14. What BGP attribute is checked first in the route selection algorithm?

    A. Local Preference

    B. Origin

    C. Next Hop

    D. AS Path

15. What method of resolving Next Hop reachability is considered a best practice?

    A. Using static routes

    B. Altering the attribute value

    C. Using the IGP passive option

    D. Using an export policy to advertise `Direct` routes

16. By default, what BGP attribute is evaluated only when two path advertisements are received from the same neighboring AS?

    A. Local Preference

    B. Multiple Exit Discriminator

    C. Next Hop

    D. AS Path

17. Which of the listed BGP attributes is evaluated last in the BGP Route Selection Algorithm when determining the best path advertisement for a route?

    A. AS Path

    B. Router ID

    C. IGP metric cost

    D. Preference of EBGP routes over IBGP routes

18. What is the purpose of the Keepalive message?

    A. To begin the peer relationship

    B. To request an Update message

    C. To acknowledge a Notificaton message

    D. To maintain the BGP peer session

19. What action does the local router take after sending a Notification message to a remote peer?

   A. Sends a Keepalive message to the peer.

   B. Sends an Update message to the peer.

   C. Terminates the peer session.

   D. No action is taken.

20. Why is a full-mesh peer session required for IBGP peers?

   A. Because an IGP is needed to establish the peering sessions.

   B. IBGP peers do not send each other IBGP-learned routing updates to prevent routing loops.

   C. EBGP peers won't advertise their routes until a full mesh is established.

   D. To preserve the Next Hop attribute.

Answers to Review Questions

1. B. BGP uses TCP port 179.

2. A. BGP sends incremental updates only as path advertisements change.

3. A. BGP is referred to as a path-vector routing protocol. It uses AS Path information to determine the direction to forward traffic.

4. A, C. By default, EBGP peers belong to different AS networks and must be directly connected.

5. B, D. IBGP peers belong to the same AS network and can be separated by other routers.

6. C. By default, EBGP peers must be directly connected because EBGP packets have a TTL value of 1.

7. B. BGP uses the AS Path attribute to prevent routing loops.

8. C. Only in the `Established` state can a BGP router exchange routing updates.

9. B. EBGP peers advertise routes learned from both EBGP and IBGP peers, while IBGP peers do not advertise IBGP-learned routes.

10. D. A BGP peer sends a notification message when an error is detected.

11. B, D. A higher Local Preference is a better system and is used by administrators to affect outbound traffic flows.

12. A. The Adjacency-RIB-Out table contains routes being advertised to a peer. The correct command syntax is `show route advertising-protocol bgp` *neighbor-address*.

13. C. The Adjacency-RIB-In table contains routes received from a peer. The correct command syntax is `show route receive-protocol bgp` *neighbor-address*.

14. C. The BGP route selection algorithm first determines if reachability to the Next Hop attribute exists before checking any other attributes.

15. B. While all options are viable methods for solving reachability issues, altering the Next Hop attribute to the value `self` is considered a best practice.

16. B. By default, the MED attribute is checked only for routes from the same neighboring AS.

17. B. Of the listed attributes, the Router ID is the lowest tiebreaker within the route selection algorithm.

18. D. BGP peers send Keepalive messages to maintain the BGP peer session.

19. C. After sending a Notification message, the local router closes the peering session and attempts to reestablish.

20. B. IBGP peers must be fully meshed, because IBGP peers do not send each other routing updates for routes learned from another IBGP peer. Since the AS Path attribute is not modified within an AS, this prevents routing loops.

Chapter

9

Multicast

JNCIA EXAM OBJECTIVES COVERED IN THIS CHAPTER:

✓ Identify the differences between the operation of a dense-mode and a sparse-mode protocol

✓ Define the reverse path forwarding (RPF) process and explain its importance

✓ Describe the operation of the IGMP protocol

✓ Describe the operation of the PIM protocol

✓ Describe PIM-SM RP options—static; Auto-RP; bootstrap router

In this chapter, we examine the concepts and operation of a multicast routing network. You'll get a high-level view of why we use multicast forwarding, and you'll learn the basic components of a multicast network.

We start by taking a look at the special addressing structure for multicast addresses. We follow this with a detailed discussion on how a multicast router prevents forwarding loops. The differences between a dense-mode network and a sparse-mode network are then covered. Next, we examine the details of the Internet Group Management Protocol (IGMP) and how it operates. This includes a look at the capabilities available with each version of the specification. We also discuss the details of the Protocol Independent Multicast (PIM) specification and explain the various methods for electing a rendezvous point.

Next, we show you a configuration example from a sample network operating in the different multicast modes. Finally, we review some helpful JUNOS software commands you can use to troubleshoot and verify your network.

Multicast Overview

In a networking environment, you have three main methods for transmitting data from one host to another: unicast, broadcast, and multicast. Up to this point in the book, we have been assuming that the data transmissions are unicast in nature. A single source sends a stream of traffic to a single destination. The intervening routers forward the traffic based on the destination IP address encoded in the IP packet.

Both broadcast and multicast follow a one-to-many forwarding paradigm where a single host transmits a single data stream and multiple hosts receive the traffic. The difference between a broadcast and a multicast transmission lies in which hosts process the traffic. A broadcast transmission assumes that all hosts wish to receive the data stream. Each host must process the broadcast packet before deciding if it wants the traffic. Unwanted transmissions are discarded, but the host's resources (CPU and memory) are wasted in making this decision.

A multicast transmission is also a single stream of traffic, but it assumes that only certain hosts on the network wish to receive the traffic. These hosts request a connection from the network, and the intervening routers forward the traffic to just those devices. This concept is very similar to the operation of both television and radio transmissions. The stations send their data (TV show or radio program) into the airwaves. Interested devices tune into the appropriate channel to receive just the programming they desire. Other devices in the same domain need not receive the traffic if they don't want to—they simply tune to a different channel or turn themselves off.

Let's explore the options for transmitting data to multiple end stations and see why multicast is the best option available.

Unicast Transmissions

In a unicast network, the source of the traffic needs to generate multiple sets of the same information when it wants to send that traffic to multiple hosts.

Figure 9.1 shows a source host connected to the Cabernet router that is transmitting a video stream to four different receiving hosts throughout the network. It begins transmitting its four data streams into the network. These transmissions cause the link between the Cabernet and Merlot routers to carry the same data within the four separate traffic flows. As the traffic reaches the Merlot router, one stream is forwarded to Receiver 1, one stream is forwarded to the Shiraz router, and two data streams are forwarded to the Riesling router. Shiraz, in turn, forwards its data stream to Receiver 2, while Riesling forwards its two data streams to Receiver 3 and Receiver 4.

FIGURE 9.1   Unicast forwarding to multiple hosts

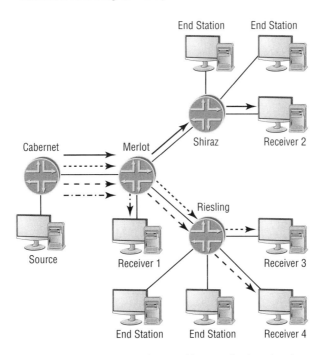

While the four receiving stations get their data traffic, we also burden the network needlessly. The Cabernet-Merlot and Merlot-Riesling physical links carry the same data multiple times, resulting in an overall loss of bandwidth in the network. Additionally, the routers themselves have to receive, process, and transmit additional packets. This could cause a resource drain within the router itself or congestion in the network as the outgoing interfaces fill up with the unneeded packets.

Broadcast Transmissions

We can easily mitigate the bandwidth and resource problems in the network encountered with a unicast transmission by using a broadcast transmission instead. In this instance, the source host sends a single stream of data traffic into the network, addressed to all possible hosts.

Figure 9.2 shows our same network using a broadcast transmission from the source connected to Cabernet. The source PC sends a single stream of traffic into the network, which Cabernet forwards to Merlot. As the traffic is received, Merlot replicates the data into multiple separate streams. A single stream is forwarded to Receiver 1, one stream is forwarded to the Shiraz router, and a third is forwarded to Riesling. Shiraz has multiple hosts connected to it and forwards the traffic to each of them, including Receiver 2. Riesling also forwards the traffic to all of its connected hosts, including Receiver 3 and Receiver 4.

FIGURE 9.2   Broadcast forwarding to multiple hosts

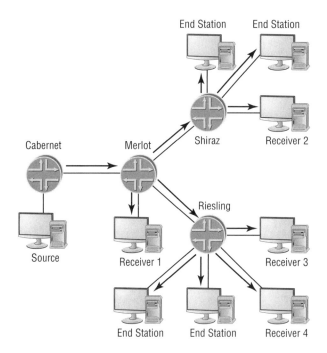

Overall, this system works well for the network. The routers, their links, and their interfaces process each unique data packet only once. We save bandwidth in the network and lessen the resource consumption on the routers. Unfortunately, we introduced another burden. Some end-station devices in the network received and processed the data stream when they didn't wish to receive it at all. While this may seem like a small consequence, remember that your PC has to expend CPU resource time to discard these unwanted packets. Additionally, we have scalability issues to worry about. As the number of traffic sources grows, the burden on the end stations grows proportionately.

Multicast Transmissions

Using a multicast transmission combines the best aspects of both unicasts and broadcasts. We get the network resource savings of the broadcast model while also gaining the end-station resource savings of the unicast model.

Figure 9.3 shows the benefits of using multicast to forward traffic to multiple hosts. Our same host connected to Cabernet is again transmitting the same data stream to the same receiving hosts. Like our broadcast network, the source sends only a single stream of traffic into the network. Cabernet forwards the data stream to Merlot, which replicates the packets into multiple streams. Merlot forwards one stream to Receiver 1, a second to Shiraz, and a third to Riesling. Shiraz forwards its traffic only to Receiver 2 and not to the other end stations. Riesling, like Merlot, replicates the data stream into two branches. One stream is forwarded to Receiver 3 and the other to Receiver 4.

FIGURE 9.3   Multicast forwarding to multiple hosts

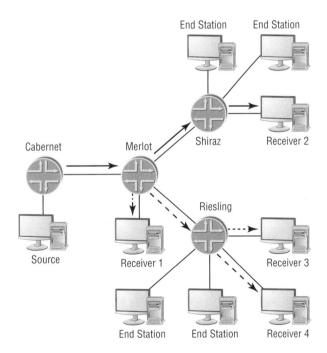

Multicast Addressing

To correctly forward multicast traffic to the appropriate hosts in the network, we need a special set of addressing rules. This allows the network routers to forward and replicate the traffic only where it is needed. In addition, it allows only specific end stations to receive and process the data stream. These two requirements are handled by special IP addresses and Ethernet MAC addresses, respectively.

IP Group Addresses

An end station wishing to receive a multicast transmission sends a request to the network that forwards packets matching a specific destination IP address to it. This address is similar to a TV or radio channel and can be requested by multiple hosts. The source station generates the data packets and places this special IP address, called a *group address*, in the destination field of the IP header. Each multicast data stream is uniquely identified by the combination of the traffic source and the group address, represented by the notation (S,G).

 When the multicast source is not known, a 0.0.0.0 notation or the wildcard character * replaces the source field. The multicast representation becomes (0.0.0.0,G), or more commonly (*,G).

The Internet Assigned Numbers Authority (IANA) has reserved a range of address space specifically designed for use with multicasting. Any IP address containing a 1110 in the first four address bits is a multicast group address. In a classful addressing context, this address space is represented by Class D addresses. When you convert the group addresses to a decimal number, the first octet of the address is between 224 and 239. Specifically, the IANA multicast range is 224.0.0.0 through 239.255.255.255. Figure 9.4 shows the multicast group address in a binary format.

FIGURE 9.4 Multicast group address

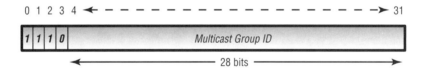

As is the case with the address space used for unicast transmissions, certain portions of the multicast group addresses are reserved for special purposes. One such group is all addresses within the 224.0.0.0 /24 subnet. These groups are restricted to a local physical media, which means that a router does not forward the datagram to other portions of the network. We enforce this restriction by setting the Time-to-Live (TTL) field to the value 1.

The group addresses in this range are often referred to as well-known addresses because many applications and routing protocols make use of its capability. Some of the more common addresses used from the 224.0.0.0 /24 subnet are:

224.0.0.1 /32   The 224.0.0.1 /32 address represents all IP hosts on the subnet. Each router and PC connected to the physical media receives the datagram and processes the packet.

224.0.0.2 /32   The 224.0.0.2 /32 address is used to reach all IP routers on the subnet. Only connected routers receive packets addressed to this destination. End-user PCs do not listen for these packets.

224.0.0.5 /32   The Open Shortest Path First (OSPF) routing protocol uses the 224.0.0.5 /32 address to communicate with all OSPF-speaking routers on the subnet.

224.0.0.6 /32   OSPF also uses the 224.0.0.6 /32 group address. The designated router and backup designated router receive packets addressed to this destination.

224.0.0.9 /32   Version 2 of the Routing Information Protocol (RIP) uses this address to communicate with other RIPv2 routers on the subnet.

224.0.0.13 /32   The 224.0.0.13 /32 group address is specifically used by multicast-speaking routers. All devices operating version 2 of the Protocol Independent Multicast (PIM) protocol receive packets addressed to this destination.

224.0.0.18 /32   The 224.0.0.18 /32 group address is used by routers operating the Virtual Router Redundancy Protocol (VRRP). This protocol allows multiple routers to share an IP address on an Ethernet subnet.

224.0.0.22 /32   Multicast-enabled routers also use the 224.0.0.22 /32 group address to communicate with all devices using version 3 of the Internet Group Management Protocol.

A second address block reserved by IANA is the 232.0.0.0 /8 address space. These addresses are used for *source-specific multicasting (SSM)*, which is supported in version 3 of IGMP. SSM allows an end station to request and receive data streams for a multicast group from a specific source of the traffic. Under normal circumstances, an end host only requests a connection to the group address and it is connected to the metrically closest source of the traffic.

The 233.0.0.0 /8 address space was set aside by IANA to support an addressing scheme known as GLOP. This system provides you with the ability to map an Autonomous System number to a specific set of multicast group addresses, much like an IP subnetting scheme. The AS number is converted to binary and is placed into the middle two octets of the group address. The administrators of the specific AS statically allocate the addresses in the final octet of the group address as needed. The purpose of the GLOP addressing scheme is to easily identify the source autonomous system of multicast traffic using an AS number for control and accounting purposes. While a Juniper Networks router does not actively monitor and control the use of GLOP multicast addresses, we recommend that you do not use the 233.0.0.0 /8 address range unless you intend to implement GLOP addressing in your network.

The term GLOP is not an acronym, nor is it short for some other term. It is simply the name given to this method of allocating group addresses.

The final reserved address space we discuss here is the 239.0.0.0 /8 range. These addresses are locally assigned by an administrator and are locally significant to that specific multicast domain. They do not cross the boundaries of the domain. You can think of these addresses as being roughly equivalent to the RFC 1918 addresses for unicast IP traffic; you can use any of the addresses in the range as long as you use them only within domains that you control.

Please visit www.iana.org/assignments/multicast-addresses for a complete list of reserved multicast addresses.

Ethernet Addresses

As multicast traffic reaches the edge of the network, the router transmits the data stream out each interface where hosts exist that have indicated their desire to receive the traffic. Generally speaking, this final transmission is over an Ethernet network where the multicast traffic is encapsulated in a Layer 2 frame. This situation carries with it the possibility of wasting resources on the local subnet. Let's take a closer look.

In a unicast transmission, the router determines the destination Media Access Control (MAC) address of the end station by using the Address Resolution Protocol (ARP). An ARP request is broadcast onto the Ethernet network, and the appropriate end station responds with its MAC address. The router then forwards the frame using this MAC address as the destination address. Using ARP for multicast is problematic because the potential list of stations wishing to receive the multicast data can change at any time as hosts enter or leave the multicast group. To account for this, the router could perform an ARP on a regular basis. However, the ARP request is a broadcast to the network, and all hosts on the segment must process the packet. Again, this causes a burden on the end stations—the very thing we were trying to avoid. Regardless of how it determines the destination MAC address, when the router sends the data stream to each end station individually, we defeat the purpose of multicast altogether. In the end, we are transmitting the data multiple times on the segment.

The basic operation of an Ethernet network means that each end station begins to receive all traffic transmitted on the wire. After interpreting the destination MAC address of the frame, most stations stop receiving the packet altogether. This means that when the router sends the same data multiple times, not only is the bandwidth of the segment wasted but the hosts actually receive portions of the data multiple times. To explore this problem in some more detail, suppose that we have four hosts on the Ethernet segment that would like to receive the 224.7.7.7/32 group address. The router encodes the data into the Ethernet frame, places the MAC address of Receiver 1 in the destination field, and transmits the frame onto the segment. All hosts on the network receive the frame, but only Receiver 1 processes the traffic. The router then repeats this process for the other receivers for the first packet of multicast data. This quadruple replication is repeated for each packet in the multicast data stream. Clearly, this is not a good use of our network resources.

To avoid these issues, we have a predefined process for encoding a specific multicast group address within an Ethernet destination MAC address. Once this occurs, the router needs to transmit each data packet onto the network only once and each interested end station receives the data only once. Finally, there is no need for the router or the hosts to perform an ARP request.

To determine the multicast MAC address for a specific group, we take the last 23 bits of the multicast group address and prepend a single 0 bit to them. These 24 bits now form the lower half of the 48-bit MAC address. The upper half of the address is derived from the assigned organizationally unique identifier (OUI) of 0x00:00:5E. When we use this OUI for multicast on an Ethernet segment, we need to set the Broadcast/Multicast bit to the value 1. This bit alerts receiving hosts that a broadcast or multicast frame is arriving. It is the first bit received from the network since all Ethernet transmissions are accomplished by sending the least significant bit (LSB) first. When we account for the LSB transmission, the actual OUI on the network becomes 0x01:00:5E. Figure 9.5 shows a multicast frame for an Ethernet network.

FIGURE 9.5 Multicast Ethernet frame

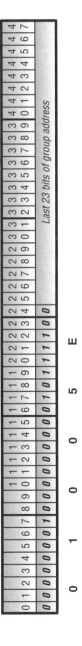

Suppose that we have multiple hosts on a network that all desire to listen to the same news conference over the network. The multicast group address for the conference is 224.7.7.7 /32, meaning that the last 23 bits of the group address are 0x07:07:07. When we combine this with the multicast MAC address of 0x01:00:5E, we find that the resulting destination address for the news conference is 0x01:00:5E:07:07:07. The router transmits frames with this address as the destination, and each host copies these same frames from the Ethernet network. Figure 9.6 shows this translation process.

FIGURE 9.6   Multicast group address to MAC address translation

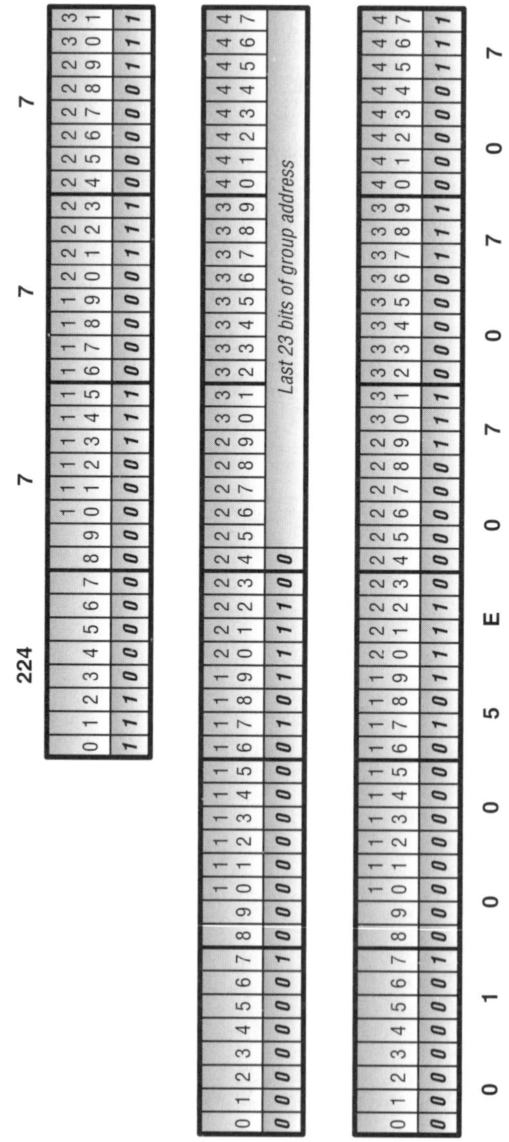

Can I Tune in the Wrong Channel?

A closer examination of how to build an Ethernet frame for multicast traffic might reveal a small problem. The uniqueness of each multicast group address is composed of the 28 bits following the common 1110 of the address range. We use only 23 of those 28 bits, however, in the multicast Ethernet frame. It is theoretically possible that a single host could receive two different multicast streams when it really wanted only one of them.

For example, the last 23 bits of the 230.129.16.1 /32 group address are 0x01:11:01. This is identical to the last 23 bits of the 224.1.16.1 /32 group address. When encoded within an Ethernet multicast frame, the destination MAC address for both groups is 0x01:00:5E:01:11:01. To the network interface card (NIC) on the PC, all frames with that destination MAC address are received and processed by the CPU. Most often, the end user does not notice this problem since the applications themselves won't use traffic from another stream. However, the back-end resources of the PC are taxed by the extra burden, which might result in a slower response to the user.

The 5-bit difference between the multicast group address and the Ethernet MAC address results in 32 possible address overlaps. In the scope of 268,435,456 possible multicast group addresses, the chance of an overlap occurring on a single Ethernet network is about .00001 percent.

Multicast Forwarding

So far, we've discussed the concept of using multicast in a network and explored the options for addressing the data packets. Let's now begin to focus on how the network itself actually forwards the data packets from the source to the receivers. We start by examining how to avoid a forwarding loop in the network. We then look at the two methods for transmitting multicast data in a network—dense mode and sparse mode.

Reverse Path Forwarding

The basic function of a router is the examination of an IP destination address and the forwarding of data to the next-hop router along the path. In a multicast network, this process is not effective because the destination IP address of the packets is the multicast group address. From the perspective of the router, the packets may have to be sent out multiple interfaces. In fact, the default behavior of a multicast router is to forward the data packet out all interfaces except the one where the packet was received. This behavior has the potential for forming a forwarding loop in the network.

Figure 9.7 shows a multicast source connected to the Shiraz router transmitting a data stream into the network. Shiraz uses the default multicast forwarding mechanism described earlier and sends the traffic to the Muscat router. Muscat has two neighboring routers, so it replicates the data stream and forwards the traffic to both of them. The traffic is not sent back to Shiraz because the interface connecting Muscat to it is the interface where the traffic was received. At this point, both the Riesling and Chardonnay routers receive the multicast traffic. Riesling checks for neighbors on its downstream interfaces, where it did not receive the traffic, and finds both Merlot and Cabernet. Riesling forwards the traffic to both of them. The Chardonnay router, on the other hand, has only a single downstream router in Merlot and forwards the multicast traffic to it.

FIGURE 9.7   Multicast forwarding loop

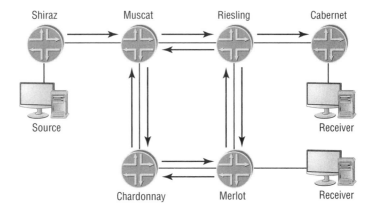

We now reach a critical juncture in the propagation of the data stream. The Merlot router receives two separate sets of multicast traffic—one from Chardonnay and the other from Riesling. Logically, we know that these data streams are in fact the same, but the router only sees the traffic as being multicast in nature. It receives one stream from Riesling and sends it downstream to Chardonnay. Merlot receives the other stream from Chardonnay and forwards it downstream to Riesling. At this point, we've formed a forwarding loop between Muscat, Riesling, Chardonnay, and Merlot. Each router continues to forward the same data stream endlessly around the network.

The method by which we break this forwarding loop is called a *reverse path forwarding (RPF)* check. While each multicast packet contains the same common destination group address, it also contains a unique source IP address. This address is the source of the data stream, and we use this information to determine whether the received multicast packet should be forwarded downstream. As the router receives the traffic, it examines the source IP address in the IP header. A lookup is then performed in a special RPF routing table for that address. The router is performing a simple check— "If I were to reverse the path of this packet and send it back to the source, would I send it out the interface I received the packet on?" When the result of this query affirms that the receiving interface is the best path back to the source, the router is assured that a forwarding loop is not forming and forwards the data stream out all of its downstream interfaces. Should the RPF check return a negative result, the router breaks any potential forwarding loops and drops all multicast packets it receives on that interface from that specific source. Let's examine this process with an example.

Figure 9.8 shows our same topology with the same multicast source, which begins to send out multicast traffic to Shiraz. As the traffic is received, Shiraz checks the source IP address of the packets against the RPF table. It finds that the receiving interface is in fact the best path back to the source because it is directly connected to the router. Shiraz then forwards the multicast traffic downstream to Muscat. Again, as Muscat receives the multicast packets, it performs an RPF check. The best path back to the source is through Shiraz, so the traffic is not forming a loop. Muscat forwards the traffic downstream to both Chardonnay and Riesling. The RPF check on both Chardonnay and Riesling finds that Muscat is the best path back to the multicast source, so they also forward the multicast data downstream.

FIGURE 9.8   Reverse path forwarding check

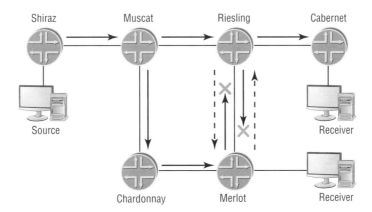

It was at this point in our earlier example that the forwarding loop was formed. Merlot receives two copies of the same multicast data—one from Chardonnay and the other from Riesling. This time, however, the RPF check prevents the loop from forming. Merlot compares the source IP address of the traffic against the RPF table and finds that Chardonnay is the best path back to the source. Merlot begins to drop all multicast traffic from the source it receives on the interface to Riesling and informs the Riesling router to stop sending that particular traffic stream. Since the Chardonnay interface passes the RPF check, Merlot forwards the traffic downstream to Riesling. The data stream received on Riesling's interface to Merlot is checked against the RPF table. We've already determined that the best path from Riesling to the source is through Muscat, so the packets sent by Merlot are dropped from the network. Riesling also instructs Merlot to stop forwarding the multicast data stream along that link. In the end, no multicast traffic is sent along the link connecting Riesling to Merlot.

The JUNOS software, by default, uses the inet.0 routing table to perform RPF checks.

Dense-Mode Forwarding

Dense mode multicast routing protocols assume that every user segment in the network wants to receive the data stream. The type of data forwarding used in a dense-mode environment is very efficient when you know that a large number of receivers exists.

Figure 9.9 shows a network consisting of 10 routers using a dense mode routing protocol. A multicast source is connected to the Shiraz router, and two receivers are currently connected to the group address—one each connected to Merlot and Cabernet. As the source begins transmitting data traffic destined for the multicast group address, the routers in the network flood the traffic to each segment in the network. This flooding process follows the rules of the RPF mechanism for forwarding multicast traffic.

FIGURE 9.9   Dense-mode flooding

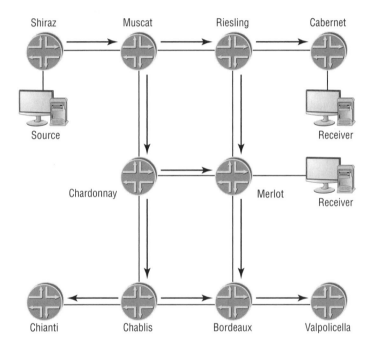

A quick look at Figure 9.9 shows that every router in the network doesn't need to receive the data stream. Only Merlot, Cabernet, and the routers along the path back to the source should be forwarding the traffic. Any router in a dense-mode network may prune itself from the forwarding path by sending a message to its upstream peer. This process occurs for all routers that do not need to receive the traffic.

Figure 9.10 shows the dense-mode prune process. The Chianti router has no connected receivers, so it sends a prune message to Chablis, its upstream neighbor. (Prune messages are discussed in the section "Sparse-Mode Operation" later in this chapter.) The Chablis router also receives a prune message from Bordeaux, its other downstream neighbor. Because both routers downstream of Chablis have pruned themselves from the forwarding path, Chablis sends its own prune message upstream to Chardonnay.

FIGURE 9.10   Dense-mode pruning

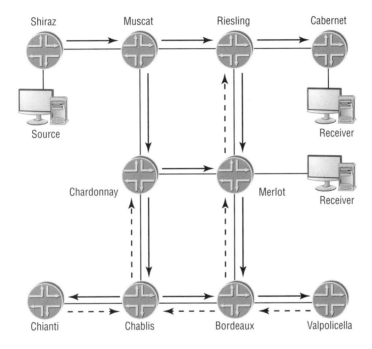

The *flood and prune* process occurs in a dense-mode network every three minutes (JUNOS software default timer). This ensures that any new hosts arriving on the network begin to receive the multicast traffic during the next flood process. The downside of the flood and prune process is that routers have to explicitly request to stop receiving the data stream when they have no receivers connected downstream. When you have a smaller number of receivers, you also have a larger number of routers pruning themselves from the forwarding path. Hence, a dense-mode network is better suited for an environment where almost all connected hosts would like to receive the data stream.

Figure 9.11 shows the end result of a dense-mode flood and prune. This *source-based tree* has the multicast source at the top of a forwarding tree. Each network segment forwarding the traffic forms a branch of the tree while the end-station hosts form the leaves of the source-based tree.

Distance Vector Multicast Routing Protocol (DVMRP), PIM dense mode, and Multicast Open Shortest Path First (MOSPF) all use dense-mode forwarding to send multicast packets to interested end stations.

FIGURE 9.11   Source-based tree

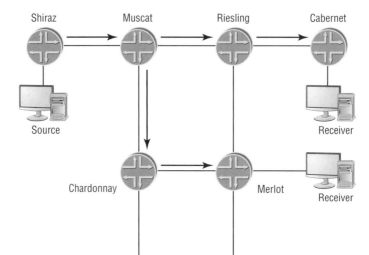

Sparse-Mode Forwarding

Sparse mode multicast routing protocols are exactly the opposite of dense-mode protocols in their assumptions. A sparse-mode multicast network assumes that very few receivers exist for each group address. As such, routers in a sparse-mode network must explicitly request that the data stream be forwarded to them. Additionally, one of the routers in the network performs a special function as a connection point between the source and the receiver. This *rendezvous point (RP)* combines knowledge of the group's source with the requests from the receiver.

Figure 9.12 shows our network after we converted to a sparse-mode protocol, with the Chablis router designated as the RP for the domain. The receivers connected to Merlot and Cabernet request a connection to the multicast group address. This prompts both Merlot and Cabernet to send a message to Chablis, the RP, requesting that they be added to the forwarding path of the group. Chablis also receives the data traffic from Shiraz, which is connected to the source, through a unicast tunnel. Once the multicast traffic from the source and the requests from the receivers connect at the rendezvous point, the traffic is forwarded through the network. This *shared tree* has the RP at the top of the forwarding tree with the network segments and receivers as the branches and leaves, respectively. This is often referred to as the *rendezvous point tree (RPT)* in a sparse-mode network.

FIGURE 9.12 Shared tree forwarding

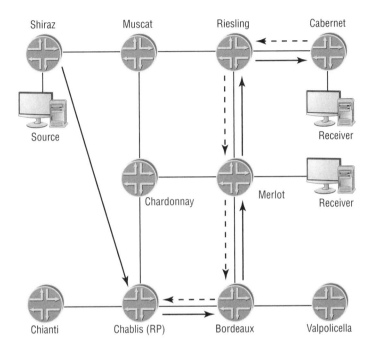

As Merlot and Cabernet begin to receive the multicast traffic, they examine the source of the multicast traffic and find that it is the host connected to Shiraz. Each router then determines whether the current forwarding path is its best path to the source, and neither router finds this to be the case. Both Merlot and Cabernet then send a request to the multicast source itself, asking for the group data stream to be sent to them directly.

Figure 9.13 shows the Merlot and Cabernet routers sending requests to the multicast source. Once the data stream is received directly from the source, the routers prune themselves from the shared tree. This is accomplished by sending a prune message to the rendezvous point, Chablis.

The actual operation of a sparse-mode multicast network is much more involved than our high-level example here. We discuss the details of this process in the "Sparse-Mode Operation" section later in this chapter.

FIGURE 9.13 Sparse mode shortest path tree

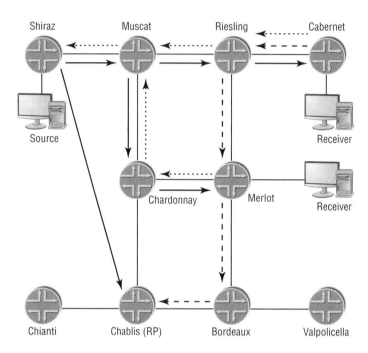

Multicast Protocols

We've discussed forwarding of traffic in a multicast network using both dense-mode and sparse-mode paradigms. The process involves requests for traffic, prune messages advertised upstream, and knowledge of the neighboring routers. All of this communication is made possible through the use of multicast routing protocols. We have a protocol that operates between the hosts and the routers and a protocol that operates within the network itself between the routers. We first examine the host-to-router communications and conclude with an intra-router protocol.

Internet Group Management Protocol

Multicast end stations communicate with the network routers using the *Internet Group Management Protocol (IGMP)*. This protocol allows receivers to request a multicast data stream from a particular group address. A local router on the host's subnet, the *designated router*, translates the request into a multicast routing protocol packet and forwards it to an appropriate source for the group. The basic function of IGMP is to allow an end station to join a multicast group, remain connected to the group address, and leave the multicast group. There are currently three versions of IGMP defined for your use. Each version handles these functions slightly differently, with the newer versions providing more features and functionality. Let's examine the operation of each in more detail.

> The designated router is the router with the lowest PIM priority value. The router with the highest interface IP address on the segment wins all priority ties.

IGMP Version 1

Version 1 of the IGMP specification, defined in RFC 1112, provides the most basic services to a multicast host. One message type allows the end stations to join and remain attached to a multicast group, while a second provides a multicast router the ability to retain knowledge of which groups are active on the network segment. The IGMPv1 message format is shown in Figure 9.14.

FIGURE 9.14 IGMPv1 messages

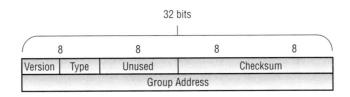

The various field definitions are:

Version The Version field is set to the value 1 for all IGMPv1 messages.

Type The Type field designates the actual IGMPv1 message being sent. The value 1 is a Host Membership Query, and the value 2 represents a Host Membership Report.

Unused This 1-octet field is undefined and should contain all zeros.

Checksum This field displays a standard IP checksum value for the IGMP packet.

Group Address The multicast group address is encoded in this field when used in a Host Membership Report. A Host Membership Query contains all zeros in this field.

When a multicast receiver decides to join a particular group address, it generates a *Host Membership Report* message. This packet is addressed to the multicast group being joined and is received by all hosts in the group, including the designated router. The network routers then attempt to locate a source for the group and transmit the multicast stream to the local segment. To ensure that network resources are not being wasted, the *querier router* for the segment generates a *Host Membership Query* and transmits it on the segment every 125 seconds (JUNOS software default timer). The Query message is addressed to the 224.0.0.1/32 group address representing all hosts on the segment. Each host that receives the Query message starts a random timer between 0 and 10 seconds. When the timer expires, the host generates a Report message for the group it is currently attached to. Should a host receive a Report for its group before the local timer expires, it knows that other hosts are active on the segment. The local host stops its timer and does not send its own Report message. This process helps keep the IGMP protocol traffic at a minimum on the segment.

The querier router is the router with the lowest interface IP address on the segment.

The IGMPv1 specification does not provide an explicit notification method when a host leaves a multicast group. When this happens, the host silently stops listening to the group address and no longer responds to Query messages from the router. After 260 seconds (4 minutes and 20 seconds), the querier router assumes that no hosts are left on the segment and the multicast data stream is stopped. This timeout value is calculated using the formula of (robustness variable × query interval) + (1 × query response interval). We already know the values of the query interval (125 seconds) and the query response interval (10 seconds). The JUNOS software default value of the robustness variable is 2, which means that the formula is (2 × 125) + (1 × 10) = 260 seconds.

IGMP Version 2

The potential for unneeded forwarding of multicast traffic with IGMPv1 led engineers to enhance the protocol with version 2, defined in RFC 2236. IGMPv2 is backward compatible with version 1 and includes the ability for a host to explicitly notify the router that it is leaving the group address. There is a similar message structure to IGMPv1, which we see in Figure 9.15.

FIGURE 9.15   IGMPv2 messages

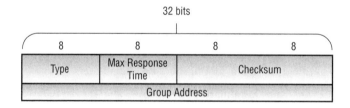

The message fields include:

Type   The Type field designates the actual IGMPv2 message being sent. The four possible values are:

- 0x11 represents a Membership Query. This includes both a General Query as well as a Group-Specific Query.
- 0x12 is used for backward compatibility and is a Version 1 Membership Report.
- 0x16 is used to send a Version 2 Membership Report.
- 0x17 represents a Leave Group message from a host.

Max Response Time   This 1-octet field informs the receiving hosts how long the router waits for a Membership Report for the multicast group. This field is set to a default value of 10 seconds.

Checksum   This field displays a standard IP checksum value for the IGMP packet.

Group Address   The multicast group address is encoded in this field when used in all IGMPv2 messages except a General Query.

The initial join process for IGMPv2 does not change. The host generates a Version 2 Membership Report message addressed to the multicast group. The local router locates an available source and begins transmitting the data stream onto the segment. The querier router also generates a General Query message every 125 seconds and transmits it to the 244.0.0.1 /32 group address representing all hosts. The Query message contains the maximum response time value of 10 seconds, which the hosts use as their maximum random timer value before sending a Report message. As before, a Report message received by a host before its timer expires causes that host to not send its own Report message.

The most significant change to the IGMP specification comes when the host decides to leave the multicast group. The end station now generates a Leave Group message addressed to the 224.0.0.2 /32 group address representing all routers on the segment. When the querier router receives the Leave message, it generates a Group-Specific Query message addressed to the group being left. The maximum response time in the Group Query is set to 1 second. Should the router not receive a Report message in that 1-second time frame, it assumes that no hosts remain on the segment and it stops transmitting the multicast data.

IGMP Version 3

Version 3, the most recent modification of the IGMP specification, is defined in RFC 3376. Previous versions of the protocol only allowed the end stations to request multicast traffic from any source using a (*,G) notation. IGMPv3 now allows the host to request traffic from a specific host in the network. In addition, the end system can also specify a list of sources that it should not receive the multicast traffic from. These changes provide support for the use of source-specific multicasting within the 232.0.0.0 /8 group address range.

Protocol Independent Multicast

While *Protocol Independent Multicast (PIM)* is not the only multicast routing protocol, it is the most popular and prevalent in the industry. Therefore, we focus solely on the operation of PIM in a multicast network. The independent portion of PIM arises from the fact that it relies on other sources of routing information (OSPF, BGP, etc.) to perform its RPF checks and other functions.

Calling PIM a routing protocol is technically a misnomer since it doesn't actually build a routing table itself. We refer to it in this way because it essentially replaced actual multicast routing protocols such as DVMRP and MOSPF.

PIM originally operated in two different modes for a single multicast group address: dense and sparse. We discussed the forwarding of multicast traffic using each of these modes in an earlier section in this chapter, "Multicast Forwarding." Recall that a dense-mode network utilizes a flood and prune philosophy to forward its traffic while a sparse-mode network takes advantage of a common meeting point called the rendezvous point. The PIM operational modes are now completely separate protocol specifications where each PIM router maintains state information that includes the upstream interface (RPF interface), the downstream interface(s), and the multicast group information as either a (*,G) or a (S,G). Both PIM protocols use a common packet header as well as some common address encoding formats. Let's explore these in more detail.

Specially formatted packets for PIM are a function of the version 2 specification. PIMv1 uses the frame format of IGMP to send information between neighbors. All future references to PIM protocol packets refer to PIMv2 only.

Common Protocol Components

Every PIM message contains a common header format, as shown in Figure 9.16.

FIGURE 9.16 PIM header format

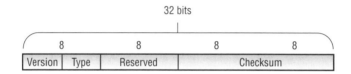

The field values are:

Version The Version field displays the current operating PIM version, which is set to the value 2.

Type This 4-bit field encodes the type of PIM message being sent. The possible values include:

0 The PIM Hello message is type code 0. It is addressed to the 224.0.0.13/32 group address (all PIM routers).

1 The PIM Register message is type code 1. It is unicast to the rendezvous point for the multicast domain.

2 The PIM Register-Stop message is type code 2, and it is unicast to the router connected to the multicast source.

3 The PIM Join/Prune message is type code 3. It is sent to the 224.0.0.13/32 group address (all PIM routers) to create or remove state in the network.

4 The PIM Bootstrap message is type code 4. It is sent to the 224.0.0.13/32 group address (all PIM routers) by the domain's bootstrap router to distribute RP information.

5 The PIM Assert message is type code 5. It is addressed to the 224.0.0.13/32 group address (all PIM routers) and is used to determine which PIM router should forward multicast traffic to a broadcast network when multiple routers are present.

6 The PIM Graft message is type code 6 and is used only in a dense-mode network. The Graft message reconnects a router to the forwarding tree. It is sent to the 224.0.0.13 /32 group address (all PIM routers).

7 The PIM Graft-Ack message is type code 7 and is also only used in a dense-mode network. The Graft-Ack message is unicast to the source of a Graft message and acknowledges its receipt.

8 The PIM Candidate-RP-Advertisement message is type code 8. It is unicast to the bootstrap router for the multicast domain and is used to help select the rendezvous point for the network.

Reserved This 1-octet field is not used and should be set to all zeros.

Checksum This field displays a standard IP checksum value for the entire PIM packet, except for the data field in a Register message.

Some portion of each PIM message pertains to specific multicast sources, group addresses, or destination routers (in the case of unicast transmissions). Each of these address types has a special encoding format that we'll examine in turn.

While at first glance, this may seem like too much information, we hope that its inclusion here saves the repetitive listing of the same fields in each PIM packet definition.

A unicast address is encoded within PIM using the format shown in Figure 9.17.

FIGURE 9.17 Encoded Unicast address

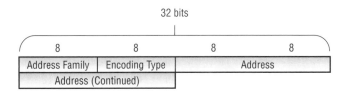

The various fields are:

Address Family This field displays the specific type of address encoded in the Address field. The value 1 represents IPv4.

Encoding Type This field represents a special encoding scheme for the address, if appropriate. The native IPv4 encoding (IP address) is represented by the value 0.

Address The actual unicast IP address is displayed in this field.

A multicast group address is encoded within PIM using the format shown in Figure 9.18.

FIGURE 9.18 Encoded group address

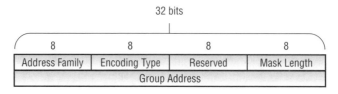

The various fields are:

Address Family This field displays the specific type of address encoded in the Address field. A value of 1 represents IPv4.

Encoding Type This field represents a special encoding scheme for the address, if appropriate. The native IPv4 encoding (IP address) is represented by the value 0.

Reserved This 1-octet field is not used and must be set to all zeros.

Mask Length This field displays the length of the subnet mask for the multicast group address.

Group Address The multicast group address is displayed in this field.

A multicast source address is encoded within PIM using the format shown in Figure 9.19.

FIGURE 9.19 Encoded source address

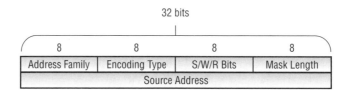

The various fields are:

Address Family This field displays the specific type of address encoded in the Address field. The value 1 represents IPv4.

Encoding Type This field represents a special encoding scheme for the address, if appropriate. The native IPv4 encoding (IP address) is represented by the value 0.

S/W/R Bits This 1-octet field is used to advertise information about how the PIM routers should handle the message. The first 5 bits in this field must be set to zero. They are followed by the Sparse bit, the Wildcard bit, and the RPT bit.

Sparse bit The S bit is set to the value 1 to represent the sparse-mode operation of PIM.

Wildcard bit The WC bit determines whether the source of the multicast group is known. The value 0 means that the state is (S,G), while an unknown source of (*,G) is represented by the value 1. All PIM messages sent to the RP must set this bit to 1.

RPT bit   The RPT bit determines where the message should be sent. The value 0 instructs the routers to forward the message to the source of the group. Messages sent to the RP for the network have the value 1.

Mask Length   This field displays the length of the subnet mask for the multicast source address.

Source Address   The multicast source address is displayed in this field.

Join and Prune Messages

The (S,G) state in a PIM sparse-mode network is maintained with a Join/Prune message. When a router wants to be added to a forwarding tree, it sends a *Join message* to its upstream router to the source of the traffic. Additionally, a Join message is sent to the rendezvous point when the exact source is not known, a (*,G) state. The *Prune message* has the opposite effect on the forwarding tree. It removes both the (*,G) and (S,G) PIM states from the upstream router.

A single message definition contains both join and prune information. The actual message may contain only join information (a Join message) or only prune information (a Prune message). The packet may also contain both join and prune information together. The format of the Join/Prune message is shown in Figure 9.20.

FIGURE 9.20   PIM Join/Prune message

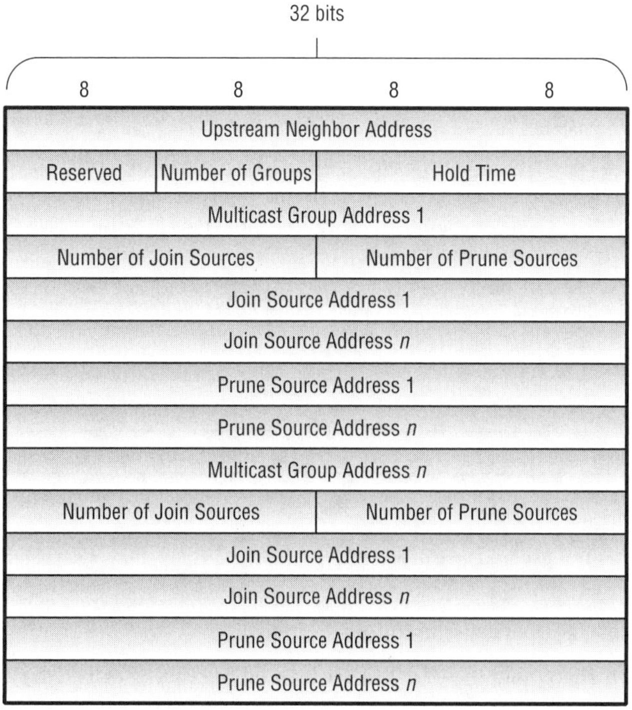

The fields of a Join/Prune message are:

Upstream Neighbor Address   The address of the upstream neighbor is placed here using the encoded unicast address format.

Reserved   This 1-octet field is not used and must be set to all zeros.

Number of Groups   This field displays the number of multicast group addresses present in the message.

Hold Time   This field displays the amount of time, in seconds, that the upstream neighbor should maintain the PIM state. The range of values is between 0 and 65,535 seconds, with a default value of 210. This value is unique to the JUNOS software and is not configurable.

Multicast Group Address   The group address of the multicast traffic is displayed in this field using the encoded group address format.

Number of Join Sources   This field displays the number of source addresses associated with the particular multicast group to add PIM state for.

Number of Prune Sources   This field displays the number of source addresses associated with the particular multicast group to remove PIM state for.

Join Source Address   The source address for each join request is placed in this field using the encoded source address format.

Prune Source Address   The source address for each prune request is placed in this field using the encoded source address format.

Register Message

The router connected to a traffic source encapsulates the multicast data into unicast packets and sends them to the rendezvous point for the domain. These *Register messages* allow the RP to forward native multicast traffic along the shared tree to the appropriate receivers. The format of the Register message is shown in Figure 9.21.

FIGURE 9.21   PIM Register message

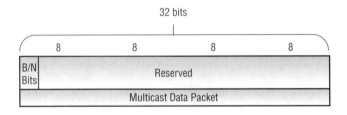

The Register message contains the following fields:

B/N Bits   This 2-bit field includes the Border bit and the Null Register bit.

Border bit   When the router sending the Register message is directly connected to the source, it sets the Border bit to the value 0. Otherwise, the bit is set to 1, which means that the source is not directly connected.

Null Register bit   The Null Register bit is normally set to the value 0. When the sending router wants to probe the RP, it sets the bit to 1. The probe process allows the router to check with the RP to see if it should actually send the multicast traffic in a Register message. This process continues until the multicast source stops generating its data stream and allows the RP to maintain knowledge of the active multicast source.

Multicast Data Packet   The multicast packets from the source are placed in this field for transmission to the RP. A null register message does not populate this field.

Register Stop Message

The RP for the domain uses the *Register Stop message* to inform the sending router to stop using Register messages to send multicast data to the RP. One reason this might occur is if the RP has not received any PIM Join messages for the group being sent in the Register message. A second reason might be that the RP was previously forwarding the data stream but received a PIM Prune message and no longer has any valid receivers in the network. Finally, the RP itself may be receiving the data stream from the source as native multicast packets. The format of the Register Stop message is shown in Figure 9.22.

FIGURE 9.22   PIM Register Stop message

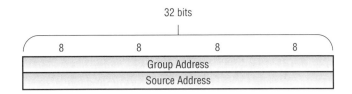

The Register Stop message contains the following fields:

Group Address   The address of the multicast group is displayed here in the encoded group address format.

Source Address   The multicast source address is placed here in the encoded unicast address format.

Sparse-Mode Operation

The operation of a PIM sparse-mode network can be segmented into three distinct areas. The first is the connection of the multicast receivers to the shared tree using Join messages and the receipt of data packets along that path. The second portion is the forwarding of the multicast packets from the source to the RP. Lastly, the receiver establishes a *shortest path tree (SPT)* to the source with Join messages and removes itself from the shared tree with Prune messages.

Generally speaking, the establishment of the shared tree and the forwarding of packets to the RP can occur in any order. The RP might receive Register messages and have no Join state from receivers. Conversely, the RP might receive Join messages from a downstream neighbor, but have no multicast packets to send. Regardless of this fact, let's cover the separate portions of the operation in the order we laid out earlier.

Establishing the Shared Tree

When an end station decides that it would like to receive multicast traffic, it generates an IGMP Report message for the group address it wishes to receive traffic for. The designated router for the segment (also the last-hop router on the forwarding path) generates a PIM Join message and forwards it to the RP. Each router along the path to the RP establishes a (*,G) state for the group address. This state includes the address itself, the downstream interface to the receiver, and the upstream interface to the RP. When the RP receives the PIM Join from downstream, it also installs a (*,G) state. If a valid multicast source is known, the RP begins forwarding native multicast packets to the receiver along the shared tree. At this point, each router along the path also installs an (S,G) state entry because an explicit source is now known. As the data stream reaches the last-hop router, it also installs an (S,G) state and forwards the packets to the receiver.

While multicast packets are flowing along the shared tree, all RPF checks are performed against the address of the RP, not the multicast source.

Forwarding Packets to the RP

When a multicast source has traffic to send, it begins to generate that traffic and forwards it to its local LAN. A PIM router on that network, the first-hop router in the forwarding path, encapsulates the traffic in a PIM Register message and sends it to the RP. If the RP has a current (*,G) state for the received group address, it de-encapsulates the traffic and forwards it along the shared tree. If no (*,G) state exists, the RP generates a Register Stop message and sends it to the first-hop router. This causes the first-hop router to stop sending the traffic to the RP and to start a 60-second timer. As the timer expires, the first-hop router generates a Register message that contains no multicast traffic, but has the Null Register bit set (often referred to as a *Null Register message*). The RP once again determines what state exists for the advertised group address and takes the appropriate action. If the first-hop router again receives a Register Stop, it starts its timer again.

This process of sending Null Register and Register Stop messages between the first-hop router and the RP continues until the source stops sending traffic.

Establishing the Shortest Path Tree

Once the last-hop router learns about a source for the data stream it is forwarding to the receiver, it connects itself to the shortest path tree for that (S,G). The last-hop router generates a PIM Join message with the (S,G) state defined and forwards it to an upstream router to the source. Each intermediate router forwards the Join message while also establishing an (S,G) state locally. When the first-hop router receives the Join message, it also establishes an (S,G) state and begins forwarding native multicast packets along the newly created SPT.

When the last-hop router begins to receive the traffic stream from the SPT, it then removes itself from the shared tree. A PIM Prune message is generated and sent upstream along the shared tree towards the RP. The intermediate routers along the shared tree remove the (S,G) from their database and forward the Prune message to the RP. When the RP receives the message, it also removes its (S,G) state and stops forwarding the multicast traffic along the shared tree. If this leaves the RP with no receivers for the multicast group, it generates a Register Stop message and sends it to the first-hop router.

Forwarding PIM Joins Upstream

We have assumed that no PIM state exists on any router during this discussion. This is not always the case, however. In the real world, it is entirely possible for some routers to have an existing (S,G) state for the requested multicast group address. When this happens, the intermediate router stops forwarding the Join upstream to the RP or first-hop router. Instead, it adds the neighbor to its list of downstream interfaces and begins to forward the multicast traffic to that neighbor.

Rendezvous Point Options

We've discussed the function of the rendezvous point in a sparse-mode network many times thus far. In fact, it is a critical component of a multicast network. What we haven't done is discuss how the routers in the network know what the RP address actually is. There are three ways for a sparse-mode network to learn the address of the RP: through a static configuration, through a dynamic process called Auto-RP, or through a PIM specification known as the bootstrap router. Let's explore each of these options.

Static

As the name implies, a *static RP* configuration means that you manually configure the address of the RP on each router in your network. This approach carries with it similar advantages and disadvantages to using static routes as your Interior Gateway Protocol. The biggest advantage is that you know exactly which router will always be the RP. Additionally, there is no protocol overhead to be concerned about. Of course, the biggest disadvantage is the lack of dynamic failover. If the RP in your network fails, you need to reconfigure each router with the address of the new rendezvous point.

Auto-RP

Auto-RP is a proprietary dynamic advertisement mechanism developed by Cisco Systems that is supported in the JUNOS software. It is capable of supporting redundant candidate RP routers in the multicast domain. One router in the network, the *mapping agent*, performs a special function. It selects the operational RP for the network and advertises this decision to the network. The PIM routers learn the RP address via this message.

The operation of Auto-RP is fairly straightforward. Each router that you configure to be a rendezvous point begins generating *Cisco-RP-Announce* messages addressed to the 224.0.1.39 /32 group address. These Announce messages are transmitted through the network in a dense-mode fashion, ensuring that each router receives a copy. The mapping agent for the network listens for the various Announce messages and makes a decision as to which router is the RP. By default, the candidate RP with the highest IP address is chosen as the RP for the network. The mapping agent then advertises this decision to the network in a *Cisco-RP-Discovery* message addressed to the 224.0.1.40 /32 group address. Like the Announce message, the Discovery message is propagated in a dense-mode fashion throughout the network.

The dynamic fail-over capability of Auto-RP arises from the mapping functionality. If the selected RP stops operating, its Announce messages no longer arrive at the mapping agent. The mapping router then selects a new RP for the network and advertises that selection to the network in a Discovery message.

Bootstrap Router

The original specification of PIM version 2 defined a dynamic RP announcement mechanism called the *bootstrap router (BSR)*. The end goal of the bootstrap router process is very similar to the outcome of the Auto-RP system. Multiple candidate RP routers advertise their capabilities to the network. A single router, the bootstrap router, collects the advertisements and advertises the RP information to the network.

 The bootstrap router process is now defined in a separate Internet Draft. Please see www.ietf.org/ID.html for the latest version of this specification.

A multicast network can support only a single BSR at any point in time, but multiple candidate routers may be operational simultaneously. Each candidate BSR advertises a priority value to the network using PIM Bootstrap messages addressed to the 224.0.0.13 /32 group address (all PIM routers). The candidate BSR with the highest priority value is elected as the BSR for the domain.

Once elected, the BSR collects *Candidate-RP-Advertisements* from any router configured as a rendezvous point. The Advertisement messages are Unicast directly to the BSR by the candidate RP routers. Unlike the Auto-RP mapping agent, which selects a single RP, the BSR advertises all valid RP routers in a message called the *RP-Set*. This message contains the address of the RP, the possible group addresses that RP supports, and a priority value. The BSR advertises the RP-Set to the network as a PIM message, where all of the multicast routers receive it. Each individual router then makes its own decision about which RP should be used for which multicast group address. This process allows multiple RP routers to operate simultaneously and load-balances the protocol traffic across those routers.

While the description of the RP-Set may sound a little chaotic, there is actually a defined process for selecting the RP for a group address. The tie-breaking steps are:

1. Choose the candidate RP advertising the most specific range of addresses. For example, say a router receives an IGMP Report message for the 224.100.1.1 /32 group address. The two candidate RP routers in the RP-Set have advertised group ranges of 224.0.0.0 /4 and 224.100.0.0 /16, respectively. The PIM router chooses the RP advertising the 224.100.0.0 /16 range because it is more specific.

2. Choose the candidate RP with the highest advertised priority in the RP-Set.

3. Choose the candidate RP that is returned by the bootstrap hash algorithm. Each PIM router using the bootstrap router process has the capability to operate a hash mechanism to choose the RP. Information such as the candidate RP address and the group address is combined with a defined mask value and run through the algorithm.

4. Choose the candidate RP with the highest IP address from the remaining list of candidates.

It is possible to have multiple RP election mechanisms operating simultaneously. In this instance, the JUNOS software prefers the RP found using bootstrap routing over Auto-RP, which is preferred to a static configuration.

JUNOS software Commands

We've seen how to forward multicast traffic in a network, and we've covered the operational theory of IGMP and PIM. Let's now examine the implementation of the multicast protocols within the JUNOS software, using Figure 9.23 as a reference for this section. We begin with the configuration of IGMP. Then we discuss the establishment of PIM on the router and examine the various options for configuring the rendezvous point. Finally, we explore some useful commands for verifying and troubleshooting your multicast network.

FIGURE 9.23   Multicast network

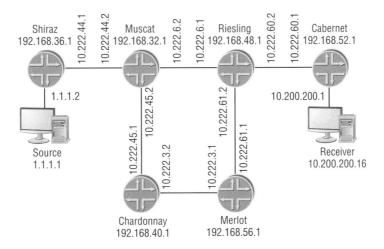

IGMP Configuration

The basic configuration of IGMP within the JUNOS software is quite simple: do nothing. Each operational broadcast interface on the router that is running PIM automatically enables IGMPv2 on that interface. The Cabernet router is currently configured for PIM, so we can verify that the interface to the receiver is operational with the show igmp interface command:

```
user@Cabernet> show igmp interface
Interface          State      Querier         Timeout Version Groups
fxp0.0             Up         10.250.0.113    None      2       0
so-0/0/0.0         Disabled                   0         2       0
so-0/0/1.0         Disabled                   0         2       0
fe-0/3/0.0         Up         10.200.200.1    None      2       0

Configured Parameters:
IGMP Query Interval (1/10 secs): 1250
IGMP Query Response Interval (1/10 secs): 100
IGMP Last Member Query Interval (1/10 secs): 10
IGMP Robustness Count: 2

Derived Parameters:
IGMP Membership Timeout (1/10 secs): 2600
IGMP Other Querier Present Timeout (1/10 secs): 2550
```

It appears that IGMP is operational and the appropriate broadcast interfaces are in an Up state. The fe-0/3/0.0 interface connects to the receiver, and Cabernet is currently the IGMP querier for that network segment. The point-to-point interfaces on the router generally do not connect to multicast receivers, so they become Disabled by default. Finally, the management interface of fxp0.0 is enabled. We've previously discussed the best practice of disabling protocols on the fxp0.0 interface, so let's do that for IGMP as well:

```
[edit protocols]
user@Cabernet# set igmp interface fxp0 disable

[edit protocols]
user@Cabernet# show igmp
interface fxp0.0 {
    disable;
}
```

We verify that the `fxp0.0` interface is no longer operating IGMP:

```
user@Cabernet> show igmp interface
Interface            State    Querier        Timeout Version Groups
fxp0.0               Disabled                      0    2       0
so-0/0/0.0           Disabled                      0    2       0
so-0/0/1.0           Disabled                      0    2       0
fe-0/3/0.0           Up       10.200.200.1    None      2       0

Configured Parameters:
IGMP Query Interval (1/10 secs): 1250
IGMP Query Response Interval (1/10 secs): 100
IGMP Last Member Query Interval (1/10 secs): 10
IGMP Robustness Count: 2

Derived Parameters:
IGMP Membership Timeout (1/10 secs): 2600
IGMP Other Querier Present Timeout (1/10 secs): 2550
```

If you are required to use a different version of IGMP, individual interfaces can be configured with the `version` command. Suppose the receiver connected to the Cabernet router is now capable of using IGMPv3 and would like to utilize some of its features. We alter the configuration of interface `fe-0/3/0.0` like so:

```
[edit protocols]
user@Cabernet# set igmp interface fe-0/3/0 version 3

[edit protocols]
user@Cabernet# show igmp
interface fxp0.0 {
    disable;
}
interface fe-0/3/0.0 {
    version 3;
}

[edit protocols]
user@Cabernet# run show igmp interface
Interface            State    Querier        Timeout Version Groups
fxp0.0               Disabled                      0    2       0
so-0/0/0.0           Disabled                      0    2       0
so-0/0/1.0           Disabled                      0    2       0
fe-0/3/0.0           Up       10.200.200.1    None      3       0
```

```
Configured Parameters:
IGMP Query Interval (1/10 secs): 1250
IGMP Query Response Interval (1/10 secs): 100
IGMP Last Member Query Interval (1/10 secs): 10
IGMP Robustness Count: 2

Derived Parameters:
IGMP Membership Timeout (1/10 secs): 2600
IGMP Other Querier Present Timeout (1/10 secs): 2550
```

PIM Configuration

The most common configuration for PIM on a Juniper Networks router is simply enabling the interfaces themselves within the [edit protocols pim] hierarchy. Each interface is configured to operate in dense, sparse-dense, or sparse mode. Let's briefly examine each of these configuration options and then explore the methods for configuring the PIM rendezvous point.

Dense Mode

Dense-mode PIM is the default operation mode in the JUNOS software for all interfaces. As such, the configuration is very straightforward. Referring back to Figure 9.23, let's use the keyword all to enable dense-mode PIM on the Chardonnay router:

```
[edit protocols]
user@Chardonnay# set pim interface all
user@Chardonnay# set pim interface fxp0 disable

[edit protocols]
user@Chardonnay# show pim
interface all;
interface fxp0.0 {
    disable;
}
```

We verify our configuration with the show pim interfaces command:

```
user@Chardonnay> show pim interfaces
Instance: PIM.master

Name         Stat Mode   V State  Priority DR address      Neighbors
at-0/1/1.0   Up   Dense  2 P2P                                     0
lo0.0        Up   Dense  2 DR            1 192.168.40.1            0
so-0/0/0.0   Up   Dense  2 P2P                                     0
```

Beginning with version 5.5 of the JUNOS software, the default mode for PIM has changed to sparse mode.

Sparse-Dense Mode

The JUNOS software provides the ability for a PIM interface to operate in both sparse and dense modes simultaneously. This flexibility is helpful during a network transition from dense-to sparse-mode PIM where some multicast groups are operating in dense mode while others are operating in sparse mode. In addition, it is a requirement when you're using Auto-RP as a rendezvous point election mechanism.

Each interface configured for *sparse-dense* operates in sparse mode for all nonconfigured groups. You use the `dense-groups` command to inform the router which groups should be treated in a dense-mode fashion. Let's configure the Merlot router in Figure 9.23 (shown earlier) for PIM in sparse-dense mode. To support the operation of Auto-RP, let's also configure 224.0.1.39 /32 and 224.0.1.40 /32 as our two PIM dense groups:

```
[edit protocols]
user@Merlot# set pim interface all mode sparse-dense
user@Merlot# set pim interface fxp0 disable
user@Merlot# set pim dense-groups 224.0.1.39
user@Merlot# set pim dense-groups 224.0.1.40

[edit protocols]
user@Merlot# show pim
dense-groups {
    224.0.1.39/32;
    224.0.1.40/32;
}
interface all {
    mode sparse-dense;
}
interface fxp0.0 {
    disable;
}
```

As before, we can verify our configuration with the `show pim interfaces` command:

```
user@Merlot> show pim interfaces
Instance: PIM.master
```

Name	Stat	Mode	V	State	Priority	DR address	Neighbors
lo0.0	Up	SparseDense	2	DR	1	192.168.56.1	0
so-0/0/0.0	Up	SparseDense	2	P2P			0
so-0/0/2.0	Up	SparseDense	2	P2P			0

Sparse Mode

Configuring your router for sparse-mode PIM is identical to the other PIM configurations we've discussed. Let's configure the Riesling router for PIM sparse mode:

```
[edit protocols]
user@Riesling# set pim interface all mode sparse
user@Riesling# set pim interface fxp0 disable

[edit protocols]
user@Riesling# show pim
interface all {
    mode sparse;
}
interface fxp0.0 {
    disable;
}

[edit protocols]
user@Riesling# run show pim interfaces
Instance: PIM.master


Name           Stat Mode      V State    Priority DR address      Neighbors
lo0.0          Up   Sparse    2 DR              1 192.168.48.1            0
so-0/0/0.0     Up   Sparse    2 P2P                                      0
so-0/0/1.0     Up   Sparse    2 P2P                                      0
so-0/0/2.0     Up   Sparse    2 P2P                                      0
```

The real effort and complexity of configuring PIM sparse mode is the establishment of the rendezvous point. There are two main steps in this process—the configuration of the local RP and the advertisement of that RP to the network.

Local RP Configuration

Recall from the section "Protocol Independent Multicast" earlier in this chapter that the rendezvous point must have the capability of de-encapsulating tunneled packets from the multicast source. A Juniper Networks router requires a Tunnel Services PIC to perform this function, and we use the show chassis command to verify its existence.

```
user@Riesling> show chassis fpc pic-status
Slot 0 Online
   PIC 0    4x OC-3 SONET, MM
   PIC 2    1x Tunnel
   PIC 3    4x F/E, 100 BASE-TX
```

The Riesling router has a Tunnel Services PIC, so we make it the rendezvous point for the domain. Within the [edit protocols pim rp] configuration hierarchy, we inform Riesling that it should be the rendezvous point by using the loopback address in conjunction with the local command:

```
[edit protocols]
user@Riesling# set pim rp local address 192.168.48.1
```

```
[edit protocols]
user@Riesling# show pim
rp {
    local {
        address 192.168.48.1;
    }
}
interface all {
    mode sparse;
}
interface fxp0.0 {
    disable;
}
```

Real World Scenario

Troubleshooting a Local RP Setup

Let's assume that you've configured your new RP router with the pim rp local address *address* command and committed your configuration. Using one of the RP election mechanisms (static, Auto-RP, or BSR), each PIM router in your domain has learned that the local router is the RP. A multicast source begins to send traffic and several interested receivers are online. Unfortunately, the traffic is not getting from the source to the clients. There are several problems that might be causing this to occur.

One problem might be that the first-hop router is not receiving the multicast traffic from the directly connected source. We check the interface statistics on that router and see that it is receiving large amounts of traffic on the appropriate interface. The first-hop router knows which router is the RP for the domain, so we can assume that it is forwarding the traffic in Register messages to the local RP router.

A second problem might be that the (*,G) PIM state is not established from the last-hop routers toward the local RP. After examining the state on each router, we find that the correct (*,G) state is installed. Also, the correct interfaces (according to the RPF tables) have been used to send the Join messages to the RP.

The remaining issues reside at the local RP itself. The Join messages might not be reaching the RP from the last-hop routers, or the Register messages from the first-hop router are not arriving. The obvious place to start checking is the PIM Join state and we find the appropriate (*,G) installed for the group address. This leaves us with the communication between the RP and the first-hop router.

Recall that native multicast data is encapsulated into a Register message by the first-hop router and is sent to the RP as a unicast packet. The RP must then de-encapsulate that Register message before forwarding any multicast traffic along the shared tree toward the receivers. We use the show chassis fpc pic-status command and find that our local RP router doesn't have a Tunnel PIC installed. Without it, the RP can't de-encapsulate the Register message.

The JUNOS software automatically creates encapsulation and de-encapsulation interfaces for this PIM function when a Tunnel PIC is installed. However, the lack of a Tunnel PIC doesn't generate an error message. While you may find this odd, remember that the router always allows you to enter configuration information for transient interfaces that are not physically present in the router. Once we insert our Tunnel PIC into the local RP router, the de-encapsulation interface (pd-1/0/1.32768, for example) is created, the Register messages are received, and the RP begins forwarding the multicast traffic down the shared tree toward the receivers.

Static RP

Once the rendezvous point for the domain is configured, each router in the network needs to *learn* which router is the RP. Perhaps the simplest way to accomplish this goal is to explicitly configure every router with the address of the RP. Unfortunately, the static RP configuration carries with it the disadvantages of static routes. You have no dynamic fail-over available to you if the RP were to stop operating, and the configuration is active until you manually change it.

We've already made Riesling the RP for the domain. We now configure each router with the static command in the [edit protocols pim rp] configuration hierarchy. We supply the address of the RP (Riesling's loopback address) to enable the routers to forward PIM Join and Prune messages as needed. Each of the routers in Figure 9.23 (shown earlier) contains an identical configuration, so we examine just the Chardonnay router here:

```
[edit protocols]
user@Chardonnay# set pim rp static address 192.168.48.1

[edit protocols]
user@Riesling# show pim
rp {
```

```
    static {
        address 192.168.48.1;
    }
}
interface all {
    mode sparse;
}
interface fxp0.0 {
    disable;
}
```

We verify our configuration with the show pim rps command. This informs you of all known RP routers in the network, how the local router learned about the RP, and what multicast group addresses that particular RP supports:

```
user@Chardonnay> show pim rps
Instance: PIM.master

RP address      Type      Holdtime Timeout Active groups Group prefixes
192.168.48.1    static           0  None               0 224.0.0.0/4
```

Chardonnay now knows that 192.168.48.1 (Riesling) is the RP via a static configuration. In addition, the 224.0.0.0/24 output in the Group prefixes column tells Chardonnay that Riesling supports all of the possible multicast group addresses.

After configuring a router as a local RP, there is no need to also configure a static address on that router. The local router automatically displays its own address as being learned via static in the show pim rps output.

Auto-RP

Auto-RP is one of two dynamic methods for propagating RP knowledge throughout your multicast network. It is perhaps the most difficult RP configuration to set up, because it requires multiple commands on each router in the network. The three main steps involved are:

- Each router must configure all PIM interfaces for sparse-dense mode and configure some Auto-RP options. Additionally, each router must allow the 224.0.1.39/32 and 224.0.1.40/32 group addresses to operate in dense mode.

- At least one router must be configured as the RP, and that router must advertise its information into the network.

- At least one router must be configured to select the RP from a list of candidates. That decision must then be advertised to the multicast domain.

Within the [edit protocols pim rp] configuration hierarchy, you use the auto-rp command to tell the router how to participate in the Auto-RP network. Three options are available for the command:

discovery The discovery option is the most basic Auto-RP configuration. It allows the router to listen for announcements from the mapping agent in the network and use any received RP information.

announce The announce option also allows the local router to listen for mapping announcements. In addition, the local router informs the network that it is configured to be a rendezvous point for the domain.

mapping The mapping option allows the router to perform all Auto-RP functions. It can listen for announcements from other mapping agents in the network, it can advertise a local RP configuration to the domain, and it can perform the Auto-RP mapping function.

In the network shown earlier in Figure 9.23, we configure Auto-RP for the domain. Riesling is the RP for the network, and Muscat is the Auto-RP mapping agent. All of the other routers should propagate the Auto-RP messages and listen for the mapping messages from Muscat. The Shiraz, Chardonnay, Merlot, and Cabernet routers all share a similar configuration, so we examine just the Merlot router as an example:

```
[edit protocols]
user@Merlot# set pim interface all mode sparse-dense
user@Merlot# set pim interface fxp0 disable
user@Merlot# set pim dense-groups 224.0.1.39
user@Merlot# set pim dense-groups 224.0.1.40
user@Merlot# set pim rp auto-rp discovery

[edit protocols]
user@Merlot# show pim
dense-groups {
    224.0.1.39/32;
    224.0.1.40/32;
}
rp {
    auto-rp discovery;
}
interface all {
    mode sparse-dense;
}
interface fxp0.0 {
    disable;
}
```

The Riesling router is already configured as a local RP, so we add only the Auto-RP configuration steps to it:

```
[edit protocols]
user@Riesling# set pim interface all mode sparse-dense
user@Riesling# set pim dense-groups 224.0.1.39
user@Riesling# set pim dense-groups 224.0.1.40
user@Riesling# set pim rp auto-rp announce

[edit protocols]
user@Riesling# show pim
dense-groups {
    224.0.1.39/32;
    224.0.1.40/32;
}
rp {
    local {
        192.168.48.1;
    }
    auto-rp announce;
}
interface all {
    mode sparse-dense;
}
interface fxp0.0 {
    disable;
}
```

Finally, we configure the Muscat router as the Auto-RP mapping agent for the domain:

```
[edit protocols]
user@Muscat# set pim interface all mode sparse-dense
user@Muscat# set pim interface fxp0 disable
user@Muscat# set pim dense-groups 224.0.1.39
user@Muscat# set pim dense-groups 224.0.1.40
user@Muscat# set pim rp auto-rp mapping

[edit protocols]
user@Muscat# show pim
dense-groups {
```

```
        224.0.1.39/32;
        224.0.1.40/32;
    }
    rp {
        auto-rp mapping;
    }
    interface all {
        mode sparse-dense;
    }
    interface fxp0.0 {
        disable;
    }
```

We verify the operation of the network with the show pim rps command and the optional *detail* variable. A check of the Cabernet router shows that an RP has been learned through auto-rp:

```
user@Cabernet> show pim rps
Instance: PIM.master


RP address      Type      Holdtime Timeout Active groups Group prefixes
192.168.48.1    auto-rp        150     131             2 224.0.0.0/4
```

Riesling is the RP for the multicast domain and it is supporting all possible multicast group addresses. A non-zero value appears in the Active groups column, so it appears that some multicast traffic is actually flowing in the network. We can determine which group addresses are using this RP, from Cabernet's perspective, by adding the detail option:

```
user@Cabernet> show pim rps detail
Instance: PIM.master


RP: 192.168.48.1
Learned from 192.168.32.1 via: auto-rp
Time Active: 00:04:05
Holdtime: 150 with 128 remaining
Group Ranges:
        224.0.0.0/4
Active groups using RP:
        224.7.7.7
        224.8.8.8

        total 2 groups active
```

We configured Muscat (192.168.32.1) as the Auto-RP mapping agent for the domain. The output from Cabernet tells us that the address of the RP was learned from Muscat using auto-rp. We see something interesting when we use the show pim rps command on Riesling:

```
user@Riesling> show pim rps
Instance: PIM.master

RP address      Type      Holdtime Timeout Active groups Group prefixes
192.168.48.1    auto-rp        150     136             2 224.0.0.0/4


192.168.48.1    static           0    None             2 224.0.0.0/4
```

Since Riesling was configured with the **announce** option, it also listened for the mapping messages from Muscat. It received those messages and installed 192.168.48.1 as an RP address. It also has that same address listed as being learned from a static configuration. We didn't make a mistake earlier; this is a normal output for an RP router. The local configuration appears as a static-learned RP in the output of this command.

Bootstrap Router

The bootstrap router is the second method for dynamically propagating RP knowledge in your network. The configuration of a bootstrap router relies on a sparse-mode PIM network as configured in the "Sparse Mode" section earlier in this chapter. This provides the basis for sending PIM bootstrap messages between the routers in the network. The bootstrap election is dependent on the highest configured router priority in the multicast domain. In the case of a priority tie, the router with the highest router ID is elected the BSR.

For our sample network, Riesling is again the RP. Both the Chardonnay and Riesling routers are configured with a non-zero priority value. All other routers in the network do not configure a priority and inherit the default value of 0, making them ineligible to become the bootstrap router. The Riesling router already has its local RP and basic PIM configuration in place. We now assign a priority value of 50:

```
[edit protocols]
user@Riesling# set pim rp bootstrap-priority 50

[edit protocols]
user@Riesling# show pim
rp {
    local {
        192.168.48.1;
    }
    bootstrap-priority 50;
}
interface all {
```

```
    mode sparse;
}
interface fxp0.0 {
    disable;
}
```

The Chardonnay router receives a priority value of 100:

```
[edit protocols]
user@Chardonnay# set pim rp bootstrap-priority 100
```

```
[edit protocols]
user@Chardonnay# show pim
rp {
    bootstrap-priority 100;
}
interface all {
    mode sparse;
}
interface fxp0.0 {
    disable;
}
```

We verify the operation of the network with the show pim rps command. We check the Muscat router and see that an RP has been learned through bootstrap:

```
user@Muscat> show pim rps
Instance: PIM.master


RP address       Type      Holdtime Timeout Active groups Group prefixes
192.168.48.1     bootstrap      150      131               2 224.0.0.0/4
```

After configuring the routers with their bootstrap priorities, we can check the election process with the show pim bootstrap command. The output contains information about both the network bootstrap router as well as the local router's configuration. We first examine the Muscat router:

```
user@Muscat> show pim bootstrap
Instance: PIM.master


BSR            Pri Local address  Pri State      Timeout
192.168.40.1   100 192.168.32.1     0 InEligible     132
```

Both the BSR and the first `Pri` columns display information about the elected bootstrap router—Chardonnay (192.168.40.1) has a priority value of 100. The remaining columns represent Muscat's local configuration. Its priority value of 0 makes it `InEligible` to become the bootstrap router. We next view the output of the Riesling router.

```
user@Riesling> show pim bootstrap
Instance: PIM.master


BSR             Pri Local address  Pri State     Timeout
192.168.40.1    100 192.168.48.1    50 Candidate      75
```

Again, we see that Chardonnay is the bootstrap router with its priority of 100. The local bootstrap configuration shows that Riesling has a bootstrap priority of 50 and is currently a `Candidate`. Finally, the output for Chardonnay shows that it is both the current bootstrap router and its local state is `Elected`:

```
user@Chardonnay> show pim bootstrap
Instance: PIM.master


BSR             Pri Local address  Pri State     Timeout
192.168.40.1    100 192.168.40.1   100 Elected        95
```

show pim neighbors

To view the neighboring routers in the network, we use the `show pim neighbors` command. Each active PIM neighbor is displayed with its physical IP address. In addition, the output displays the local router's interfaces with a timeout value of 65,535:

```
user@Cabernet> show pim neighbors
Instance: PIM.master


Interface      DR priority Neighbor addr  V Mode        Holdtime Timeout
lo0.0                    1 192.168.52.1   2 SparseDense     65535        0
so-0/0/0.0              1 10.222.60.1    2 SparseDense     65535        0
so-0/0/0.0              1 10.222.60.2    2 Unknown           105       81
fe-0/3/0.0              1 10.200.200.1   2 SparseDense     65535        0
```

The Mode of the 10.222.60.2 neighbor is currently Unknown because this information is not transmitted in a PIM message into the network.

show pim join extensive

The show pim join extensive command provides a wealth of information about the current state of your multicast network. In addition to the multicast group address and the multicast source, you gain visibility of the interfaces used to forward the data streams:

```
user@Cabernet> show pim join extensive
Instance: PIM.master

Group           Source          RP              Flags
224.7.7.7       0.0.0.0         192.168.48.1     sparse,rptree,wildcard
    Upstream interface: so-0/0/0.0
    Upstream State: Join to RP
    Downstream Neighbors:
        Interface: fe-0/3/0.0
            10.200.200.1    State: Join   Flags: SRW  Timeout: Infinity

224.8.8.8       0.0.0.0         192.168.48.1     sparse,rptree,wildcard
    Upstream interface: so-0/0/0.0
    Upstream State: Join to RP
    Downstream Neighbors:
        Interface: fe-0/3/0.0
            10.200.200.1    State: Join   Flags: SRW  Timeout: Infinity
```

Each multicast group address is displayed with its source, if known. The 0.0.0.0 notation in our output informs us that the source address is not known to Cabernet. This coincides with the fact that the Upstream State: is currently listed as Join to RP. This tells you that the local router has forwarded PIM Join messages to the RP and has joined the shared tree (rptree). When the data traffic from the RP begins to flow, Cabernet expects to receive it on so-0/0/0.0, its upstream interface. The traffic is then forwarded out the downstream interface, fe-0/3/0.0, to its neighbor at 10.200.200.1.

show pim source

One method for viewing the active multicast sources in the network is by using the show pim source command. The address of each source is listed in addition to the interface the local router expects to receive traffic on:

```
user@Shiraz> show pim source
Instance: PIM.master

RPF Address     Prefix/length      Upstream interface    Neighbor address
1.1.1.1         1.1.1.0/24         fe-0/3/0.0            Direct
192.168.48.1    192.168.48.1/32    so-0/0/0.0           10.222.44.2
```

The Shiraz router is connected to the multicast source of 1.1.1.1 /32, which is listed as Direct. Additionally, the address of the current RP, 192.168.48.1 /32, is listed because packets might be received when Shiraz connects to a shared tree for a particular group address.

show multicast rpf

To view the reverse path forwarding table used by the router during multicast forwarding, you use the show multicast rpf command. The output displays the IP subnet, the protocol installing the route, and the interface the multicast traffic should be received on. We can see the default usage of the inet.0 routing table.

```
user@Cabernet> show multicast rpf
Multicast RPF table: inet.0

Source prefix       Protocol    RPF interface    RPF neighbor
1.1.1.0/24          OSPF        so-0/0/0.0       (null)
10.200.200.0/24     Direct      fe-0/3/0.0
10.200.200.1/32     Local
10.222.3.0/24       OSPF        so-0/0/0.0       (null)
10.222.5.2/32       Local
10.222.6.0/24       OSPF        so-0/0/0.0       (null)
10.222.44.0/24      OSPF        so-0/0/0.0       (null)
10.222.45.0/24      OSPF        so-0/0/0.0       (null)
10.222.60.0/24      Direct      so-0/0/0.0
10.222.60.1/32      Local
10.222.61.0/24      OSPF        so-0/0/0.0       (null)
10.250.0.0/16       Direct      fxp0.0
10.250.0.119/32     Local
192.168.32.1/32     OSPF        so-0/0/0.0       (null)
192.168.36.1/32     OSPF        so-0/0/0.0       (null)
192.168.40.1/32     OSPF        so-0/0/0.0       (null)
192.168.48.1/32     OSPF        so-0/0/0.0       (null)
192.168.52.1/32     Direct      lo0.0
192.168.56.1/32     OSPF        so-0/0/0.0       (null)
200.200.200.1/32    OSPF        so-0/0/0.0       (null)
224.0.0.2/32        PIM
224.0.0.5/32        OSPF
224.0.0.13/32       PIM
```

show multicast route

The show multicast route command is one of two commands you use to verify known multicast group addresses and their sources. The output displays the group, its source, and information about incoming/outgoing interfaces on the router:

```
user@Cabernet> show multicast route
Group          Source prefix      Act Pru InIf  NHid  Session Name
224.7.7.7      1.1.1.1          /32 A   F   4     56
224.8.8.8      1.1.1.1          /32 A   F   4     56
```

show route table inet.1

The show route table inet.1 command is the other command you use to verify multicast group addresses and their sources known to your router. Like other routing table output, the installing protocol, a route preference, and the route itself are displayed:

```
user@Cabernet> show route table inet.1

inet.1: 2 destinations, 2 routes (2 active, 0 holddown, 0 hidden)
+ = Active Route, - = Last Active, * = Both

224.7.7.7,1.1.1.1/32*[PIM/105] 00:27:49
                    Multicast
224.8.8.8,1.1.1.1/32*[PIM/105] 00:27:49
                    Multicast
```

show multicast usage

Many multicast show commands provide insight into the operation of your domain. However, they often only prove that the PIM or IGMP protocols are operating correctly. To truly view the amount of multicast traffic flowing in your network, use the show multicast usage command. The output provides information on the number of packets and bytes seen for each multicast group address known to the router:

```
user@Cabernet> show multicast usage
Group          Sources Packets        Bytes
224.7.7.7      1       70             19880
224.8.8.8      1       68             19312
```

Summary

In this chapter, we explored the operation of a multicast routing network. This included a high-level view of why multicast forwarding is more efficient to reach multiple hosts from a single source of traffic. We also discussed the basic components of a multicast network, which include identifying multicast group addresses and translating those addresses into an Ethernet MAC address.

We examined the forwarding functions of a dense-mode network, with its flood and prune process, as well as a sparse-mode network and the rendezvous point. We saw how a multicast receiver connects to and leaves a multicast group using IGMP. We then discussed the PIM specification, the various message types, the interaction of multicast routers, and the basic operation of a sparse-mode network. Following that was a look at the three methods for choosing a rendezvous point in the network—static, Auto-RP, and bootstrap router.

We finished our multicast discussion by examining configuration examples from Juniper Networks routers operating in dense and sparse modes. In addition, we detailed some JUNOS software commands used to troubleshoot and verify the operation of a multicast network.

Exam Essentials

Be able to describe the characteristics of a dense-mode multicast network. A dense-mode multicast network floods and prunes data traffic every three minutes. Each router in the network must explicitly prune itself from the forwarding tree if it doesn't wish to receive traffic. In addition, a dense-mode network assumes that a large number of interested receivers exist for each multicast group address.

Be able to describe the characteristics of a sparse-mode multicast network. A sparse-mode multicast network utilizes the services of a rendezvous point. This connection router receives traffic from a source and requests from receivers, and places them together. A sparse-mode network assumes that a small number of interested receivers exist for each multicast group address. This requires each multicast router to explicitly add itself to the forwarding tree to receive traffic.

Be able to define the function of the Reverse Path Forwarding check. Each multicast router performs a Reverse Path Forwarding (RPF) check for each multicast packet it receives. The source of the data stream is examined and checked against a table to determine whether the receiving interface is the best path back to the source. If the check returns positively, a forwarding loop is not forming and the router can forward the packet downstream.

Be able to identify the basic function of IGMP. IGMPv1 defines the Query and Report message types. This allows a host to join a multicast group and provides the router with a method to verify the continued existence of interested receivers. Hosts leave the group address silently, leading to potentially long periods of time before traffic stops flowing onto the segment. IGMPv2 addresses this problem by defining Group-Specific Query and Leave messages. Hosts can then explicitly inform the router to stop forwarding traffic.

Be able to describe the operation of a PIM sparse-mode network.   A sparse-mode PIM network operates in three main phases. First, the last-hop router joins the shared tree and receives multicast packets from the RP. Next, the first-hop router forwards multicast packets over a tunnel to the RP using Register messages. Finally, the last-hop router joins the shortest path tree rooted at the first-hop router and prunes itself off the shared tree.

Be able to identify the three rendezvous point advertisement mechanisms.   The three methods used to propagate RP information to the network are static configuration, Auto-RP, and the bootstrap router mechanism.

Key Terms

Before you take the exam, be certain you are familiar with the following terms:

Auto-RP	Protocol Independent Multicast (PIM)
bootstrap router (BSR)	Prune message
Candidate-RP-Advertisements	querier router
Cisco-RP-Announce	Register message
Cisco-RP-Discovery	Register Stop message
dense mode	rendezvous point (RP)
designated router	rendezvous point tree (RPT)
flood and prune	reverse path forwarding (RPF)
group address	RP-Set
Host Membership Query	shared tree
Host Membership Report	shortest path tree (SPT)
Internet Group Management Protocol (IGMP)	source-based tree
Join message	source-specific multicasting (SSM)
mapping agent	sparse mode
Null Register message	static RP

Review Questions

1. Which term accurately describes the operation of a dense-mode network?

   A. Join and graft

   B. Graft and join

   C. Flood and prune

   D. Prune and flood

2. A dense-mode forwarding tree is built from the source to each of the receivers. What is the name of this tree?

   A. Shared tree

   B. Source-based tree

   C. Wildcard tree

   D. Flooding tree

3. How often does a dense-mode flood occur?

   A. Every 30 seconds

   B. Every 1 minute

   C. Every 3 minutes

   D. Every 5 minutes

4. When a multicast host is receiving packets from the rendezvous point, what type of tree is it joined to?

   A. Shared tree

   B. Source-based tree

   C. Wildcard tree

   D. Flooding tree

5. What does RPF stand for in a multicast network?

   A. Reverse protocol forwarding

   B. Reverse protocol flooding

   C. Reverse path forwarding

   D. Reverse path flooding

6. Which multicast group address range is reserved for source-specific multicast (SSM)?

   A. 224.0.0.0 /8

   B. 232.0.0.0 /8

   C. 233.0.0.0 /8

   D. 239.0.0.0 /8

7. When a multicast group address is placed in an Ethernet frame, how many bits of the address are used?

   A. 21 bits

   B. 23 bits

   C. 26 bits

   D. 28 bits

8. What is the OUI assigned to an Ethernet multicast frame?

   A. 0x00:00:5E

   B. 0x01:00:5E

   C. 0x00:11:5E

   D. 0x01:11:5E

9. Which version of IGMP provides support for source-specific multicast?

   A. IGMP

   B. IGMPv2

   C. IGMPv3

   D. IGMPv4

10. Which PIM message type does a router send to the RP to notify it about a multicast source?

    A. Join

    B. Prune

    C. Graft

    D. Register

11. Which PIM message type does a router send to the RP when it receives an IGMP message from a receiver requesting traffic?

    A. Join

    B. Prune

    C. Graft

    D. Register

12. Which PIM message type does a router send upstream to request that a neighbor stop sending multicast traffic?

   A. Join

   B. Prune

   C. Graft

   D. Register

13. What PIM state describes an unknown source for the 224.100.1.1 /32 multicast group address?

   A. (*,224.100.1.1)

   B. (*, *, 224.100.1.1)

   C. (224.100.1.1, *)

   D. (224.100.1.1, *, *)

14. Which version of IGMP first provided support for an end station to explicitly leave a multicast group?

   A. IGMP

   B. IGMPv2

   C. IGMPv3

   D. IGMPv4

15. Which rendezvous point mechanism is an integrated part of the PIMv2 specification?

   A. Local RP

   B. Static RP

   C. Auto-RP

   D. Bootstrap router

16. Which rendezvous point mechanism requires the flooding of information using dense-mode PIM?

   A. Local RP

   B. Static RP

   C. Auto-RP

   D. Bootstrap router

17. Which rendezvous point mechanism does not advertise information to neighboring PIM routers?

   A. Local RP

   B. Static RP

   C. Auto-RP

   D. Bootstrap router

18. Four routers in a network have a bootstrap priority configured. Which router will become the bootstrap router for the network?

    A. Router A = 5

    B. Router B = 10

    C. Router C = 15

    D. Router D = 20

19. Which multicast group address does Auto-RP use to advertise a local RP configuration to the network?

    A. 224.0.0.2

    B. 224.0.0.13

    C. 224.0.1.39

    D. 224.0.1.40

20. Which multicast group address does Auto-RP use to advertise the mapping of the RP to the network?

    A. 224.0.0.2

    B. 224.0.0.13

    C. 224.0.1.39

    D. 224.0.1.40

Answers to Review Questions

1. C. A dense-mode network floods multicast traffic into the network on a regular cycle. The routers that don't want to receive the traffic prune themselves from the forwarding tree.

2. B. When multicast traffic is flowing from a source to its receivers, it is using a source-based tree.

3. C. The dense mode flood and prune process occurs every 3 minutes.

4. A. A shared tree is built from the RP in the network to each multicast receiver.

5. C. The reverse path forwarding (RPF) check is performed before any multicast packets are transmitted to the network.

6. B. The 232.0.0.0 /8 address range is reserved by the IANA for use with source-specific multicast. The 224 /8 address space is not currently reserved. The 233 /8 range is for GLOP addressing, and the 239 /8 range is reserved for local administrative use.

7. B. The last 23 bits of the multicast group address are used to complete the MAC address in an Ethernet frame used for multicast traffic.

8. B. All Ethernet frames carrying multicast traffic use the 0x01:00:5E OUI as part of the destination MAC address.

9. C. IGMPv3 is the first version to provide support for source-specific multicasting.

10. D. A PIM router sends a Register message to the RP when it detects a new multicast source in the network.

11. A. The receipt of an IGMP message by a PIM router causes the generation of a PIM Join message. The Join message is sent to either a source of the traffic or the RP for the domain.

12. B. To stop the flow of multicast traffic, a PIM router sends a Prune message upstream along either the shared tree or the shortest path tree.

13. A. PIM state is always displayed in a (Source, Group) fashion. Only option A uses this format.

14. B. IGMPv2 was the first version to provide support for group-specific leave messages from the end station.

15. D. The PIMv2 specification details the operation of the bootstrap router as a dynamic method for propagating knowledge of the RP in a multicast domain.

16. C. Auto-RP uses the 224.0.1.39 and 224.0.1.40 multicast groups to flood RP knowledge in a dense-mode fashion.

17. B. The static RP process requires configuration on each router. It does not dynamically advertise or receive information from neighboring routers.

18. D. The router with the highest bootstrap priority is always the bootstrap router for the network.

19. C. Auto-RP advertises a local RP configuration using the 224.0.1.39 multicast group address.

20. D. Auto-RP advertises the RP mapping to the network using the 224.0.1.40 multicast group address.

Chapter 10

Firewall Filters

JNCIA EXAM OBJECTIVES COVERED IN THIS CHAPTER:

- ✓ Describe firewall filter concepts—input; output; match conditions; actions; action modifiers; syntax
- ✓ Identify the differences between a transit firewall filter and a Routing Engine firewall filter
- ✓ Identify CLI commands used to monitor and troubleshoot firewall filter operation

Firewall filters in a networking environment perform many functions, including restricting access to specific network resources. Additionally, filters are associated with protecting the network against denial-of-service (DoS) attacks and preventing spoofing of legal IP addresses. The JUNOS software also uses firewall filters to provide you with accounting information and to enable features such as filter-based forwarding.

This wide range of topics is a lot to cover in a single chapter, so we focus on the basic construction and application of a firewall filter on a Juniper Networks router. First, we examine why firewall filters are needed and when it is appropriate to implement them. We then see how to construct and apply a firewall filter, and discuss the differences between using a filter on user transit traffic versus protecting the Routing Engine. Finally, we demonstrate some JUNOS software CLI commands used to monitor and troubleshoot the firewall filter operation.

Firewall Filter Overview

Before we begin to examine the details of implementing and configuring a firewall filter in the JUNOS software, we should first discuss the larger picture of network security. The concept of network security means different things to different people. To some, guaranteeing that a packet's contents are secure and unreadable is security. This is the driving precept behind the IP Security (IPSec) protocols developed by the Internet Engineering Task Force (IETF). Other network administrators would like to ensure that only acceptable personnel access specific services. Generally speaking, a stateful firewall controls this type of access, examining the Layer 3 and Layer 4 headers as well as the packet's data. The firewall normally has the ability to check domain name service (DNS) queries, validate web browser requests, and monitor that TCP sessions do not remain active longer than required by the applications. Neither function is the focus of this chapter. Instead, we examine a final form of security—the packet filter.

You may already be familiar with the role a packet filter plays in a network; other router vendors often call this an *access list*. The JUNOS software uses the term *firewall filter* to describe the function of examining only the Layer 3 and Layer 4 headers on a packet-by-packet basis. The filter makes a decision, based on rules you configure, as to whether the packet should be forwarded or dropped by the router. The important distinction between a firewall filter and a stateful firewall is that the filter doesn't examine the packet's data nor does it monitor the activity of the TCP sessions transiting the router. The filter simply makes the binary decision about forwarding the packet, allowing you to control access to resources in your network.

Implementing a Firewall Filter

Although we understand the general function of a packet filter in examining a packet's headers, it is important to comprehend how the filter is implemented on a Juniper Networks router. The firewall filter utilizes the functionality of the custom-designed *Internet Processor ASIC*. Our discussion of a packet's flow through the Packet Forwarding Engine in Chapter 1, "The Components of a Juniper Networks Router," detailed that the Internet Processor ASIC receives only the notification cell to perform its route lookup. This cell contains the Layer 3 and Layer 4 header information required by the filter, but it does not hold any information about the packet's data. While this lack of data keeps the router from performing stateful firewall activities, realize that stateful monitoring is not the role your router should perform in the network.

The Internet Processor ASIC provides industry-leading forwarding rates for transit user traffic while simultaneously supporting complex filtering, packet sampling, and rate-limiting features. The Internet Processor ASIC supports a wealth of Layer 3 and Layer 4 packet-matching conditions, actions, and action modifiers using a JUNOS software syntax that is quite similar to the syntax of the policy framework discussed in Chapter 4, "Routing Policy."

Each Juniper Networks M-series and T-series router contains an Internet Processor ASIC. You can verify its existence by using the show chassis hardware command:

```
user@Shiraz> show chassis hardware
Hardware inventory:
Item            Version  Part number  Serial number    Description
Chassis                  50375            M5
Midplane        REV 03   710-002650   HF1437
Power Supply A   Rev 04   740-002497   LK22981         AC
Display         REV 04   710-001995   HF1278
Host                                  8a00000749a99a01  teknor
FEB             REV 08   710-002503   AL0781          Internet Processor II
FPC 0
  PIC 0         REV 04   750-002992   HC5418          4x F/E, 100 BASE-TX
  PIC 1         REV 03   750-002971   HE5256          4x OC-3 SONET, MM
```

Implementing a firewall filter within the JUNOS software is a two-step process: You first define the firewall filter and then apply it to an interface. The filter definition uses various match conditions, including the incoming interface on the router, IP address fields, protocol types, port numbers, and other header bit fields. As a packet matches the specified conditions, actions are performed to accept, discard, log, count, or sample the packet.

Writing the Firewall Filter

Although there are two steps to implementing a firewall filter, we focus on writing the filter in this section. Simply put, you may not apply a filter until it is built. We examine the various components of a firewall filter at a high level and see how the router evaluates the filter. We then explore the possible match conditions and the actions to be taken if there is a match within the filter.

Processing Filters

Much like a routing policy, a firewall filter has a specific set of rules that govern its processing within the JUNOS software. Unlike a policy, however, only a single firewall filter may be applied to any interface. Consequently, there is no concept of a firewall filter chain. The router evaluates all packets individually against the specific filter applied to each interface.

> We use the generic term *interface* throughout this chapter to represent both the physical and logical portions of an interface in the JUNOS software.

The JUNOS software provides a very systematic method for constructing a firewall filter. This allows you the maximum scalability and flexibility in using the router's capabilities. You configure a filter for IPv4 packets within the [edit firewall family inet] configuration hierarchy. The basic syntax of a firewall filter is:

```
firewall {
    family inet {
        filter filter-name {
            term term-name {
                from {
                    match-conditions;
                }
                then {
                    actions;
                    action-modifiers;
                }
            }
        }
    }
}
```

The JUNOS software requires the use of terms in a firewall filter and each term may contain both match criteria and actions. The router evaluates the configured match conditions to determine whether an IP packet meets all of the criteria of the filter. If it does, the router performs any defined actions for the filter. The specific match conditions and actions are discussed in the "Match Conditions" and "Actions" sections, respectively, later in this chapter.

The JUNOS software allows you to customize the names of your firewall filters so you can easily identify their purpose at a later time. For example, a filter designed to deny ICMP pings from Customer A might be named **no-ping-customerA**.

We recommend that you assign self-explanatory names to your filters so that their purpose is evident at a glance. A defined naming structure can help you accomplish this goal.

Segmenting Filters

The lack of a firewall filter chain within the JUNOS software means that you have to write complex filters with multiple terms to accomplish your goals. The basic firewall filter syntax is simply expanded with multiple terms:

```
firewall {
    family inet {
        filter filter-name {
            term term-name {
                from {
                    match-conditions;
                }
                then {
                    actions;
                    action-modifiers;
                }
            }
            term term-name {
                from {
                    match-conditions;
                }
                then {
                    actions;
                    action-modifiers;
                }
            }
        }
    }
}
```

The multiple terms are evaluated in the order they are configured. New terms are always added to the end of the existing filter. If this is not their desired location, you move them within the filter by using the insert command (discussed later in this chapter).

While the requirement of using terms may appear restrictive, realize that there is a side benefit to their use. You'll often find it difficult to write a firewall filter and have it perform flawlessly on your first attempt. Invariably, some match criteria and/or actions are left out. Using terms allows you to add new information and rearrange the terms of your existing filter.

The Default Action

Each firewall filter in the JUNOS software contains a hidden term that causes a single final action for all filters. This final action is to discard all packets and can be interpreted as:

```
term implicit-rule {
    then {
        discard;
    }
}
```

This term does not appear in your configuration, but is applied by the router on all filters. The lack of any from match conditions results in all packets performing the defined action: the silent discard of those packets.

Many users configure this term within their filter for readability and to remember that its actions always take place.

Match Conditions

Before writing a meaningful firewall filter, you must understand what information an IP packet contains. Additionally, the type of IP user traffic entering your router is also good information to have at hand. These two data sets provide the basis for the JUNOS software match conditions for firewall filters. You can identify these criteria by using the from syntax. Unlike with a routing policy, there is no to keyword.

The various match conditions are broken down into three categories: numeric ranges, address fields, and IP header bit fields. We examine all three next in some detail.

Numeric Range Match Conditions

One very common criteria used in a firewall filter is the protocol number and port number of the IP packet. These values readily translate into specific applications and programs used in the Internet. For example, you may want all web-based traffic to be accepted but all ICMP (ping) traffic to be rejected. The values contained in the IP header are configured within the filter like this:

```
[edit firewall family inet]
user@Shiraz# show
```

```
filter port-number {
    term deny-telnet {
        from {
            protocol 6;
            port 23;
        }
        then {
            reject;
        }
    }
}
```

The term ***deny-telnet*** specifies that all packets with a protocol number of 6 (TCP) and port number of 23 (Telnet) should be rejected. The use of both the protocol and port number ensures that the correct traffic is rejected. The router does not assume that specific applications are either TCP or UDP based; you must configure that knowledge explicitly to ensure that your filter does not accept or reject unwanted traffic.

The JUNOS software allows you to use syntax keywords instead of numerical values for many well-known protocol and port numbers. Here we've reconfigured our ***port-number*** filter using this system:

```
[edit firewall family inet]
user@Shiraz# show
filter example-filter-1 {
    term deny-telnet {
        from {
            protocol tcp;
            port telnet;
        }
        then {
            reject;
        }
    }
}
```

Both the ***example-filter-1*** and ***port-number*** filters perform the same function. You may use either the numeric values or the keywords, or both, in a single firewall filter. Many users find the keywords easier to interpret and troubleshoot, so we use that method throughout the remainder of the chapter.

A single filter term may contain multiple port numbers, if desired. For example, suppose you want both Telnet and SMTP traffic to be accepted. Using two terms for this filter works as expected:

```
[edit firewall family inet]
user@Shiraz# show
filter example-filter-2 {
    term allow-telnet {
        from {
            protocol tcp;
            port telnet;
        }
        then accept;
    }
    term allow-mail {
        from {
            protocol tcp;
            port smtp;
        }
        then accept;
    }
}
```

However, the JUNOS software allows you to combine multiple numeric values within a single match criterion by using the bracket notation:

```
[edit firewall family inet]
user@Shiraz# show
filter example-filter-2 {
    term allow-telnet-and-mail {
        from {
            protocol tcp;
            port [ telnet smtp ];
        }
        then accept;
    }
}
```

The router evaluates the **allow-telnet-and-mail** term as meaning that all TCP traffic with a port number of 23 or 25 (SMTP) is to be accepted. Table 10.1 details the possible *numeric range match conditions* that you use in a firewall filter.

TABLE 10.1   Numeric Range Match Conditions

Match Condition	Description
keyword-except	Negates a match—for example, destination-port-except **number**.
destination-port **number**	The TCP or UDP destination port field. You cannot specify both the port and destination-port match conditions in the same term. Normally, you use this condition in conjunction with the protocol match statement to determine which protocol is being used on the port. Some common text synonyms and their port numbers are listed here: bgp (179), bootpc (68), bootps (67), domain (53), finger (79), ftp (21), ftp-data (20), http (80), https (443), kerberos-sec (88), ldap (389), msdp (639), netbios-dgm (138), netbios-ns (137), netbios-ssn (139), nntp (119), ntp (123), pop3 (110), pptp (1723), radius (1812), rip (520), smtp (25), snmp (161), snmptrap (162), socks (1080), ssh (22), syslog (514), tacacs-ds (65), telnet (23), or tftp (69).
dscp **number**	The Differentiated Services codepoint. The Diffserv protocol uses the type of service (ToS) byte in the IP header. The most significant six bits of this byte form the Diffserv codepoint (DSCP). In place of the numeric value, you can specify one of the following text synonyms (the field values are also listed): The Expedited Forwarding RFC defines one codepoint: ef (46). The Assured Forwarding RFC defines 4 classes, with 3 drop precedences in each class, for a total of 12 codepoints: af11 (10), af12 (12), af13 (14), af21 (18), af22 (20), af23 (22), af31 (26), af32 (28), af33 (30), af41 (34), af42 (36), or af43 (38).
fragment-offset **number**	The fragment offset field.
icmp-code **number**	The ICMP code field. This value or keyword provides more specific information than the icmp-type condition. Because the value's meaning depends on the associated icmp-type, it must also be specified along with the icmp-code.

TABLE 10.1 Numeric Range Match Conditions *(continued)*

Match Condition	Description
icmp-type *number*	The ICMP packet type field. Normally, you specify this match in conjunction with the protocol match condition to determine which protocol is being used on the port. In place of the numeric value, you can specify one of the following text synonyms (the field values are also listed): echo-reply (0), echo-request (8), info-reply (16), info-request (15), mask-request (17), mask-reply (18), parameter-problem (12), redirect (5), router-advertisement (9), router-solicit (10), source-quench (4), time-exceeded (11), timestamp (13), timestamp-reply (14), or unreachable (3).
interface-group *group-number*	The interface group on which the packet was received. An interface-group is a set of one or more logical interfaces.
packet-length *bytes*	The length of the received packet, in bytes. The length refers only to the IP packet, including the packet header, and does not include any Layer 2 encapsulation overhead.
port *number*	The TCP or UDP source or destination port field. You cannot specify both the port match and either the destination-port or source-port match conditions in the same term. Normally, you specify this match in conjunction with the protocol match statement to determine which protocol is being used on the port. In place of the numeric value, you can specify one of the text synonyms listed under destination-port.
precedence *ip-precedence-field*	The IP precedence field. The precedence bits are the three most significant bits in the type of service (ToS) byte in the IP header. In place of the numeric field value, you can specify one of the following text synonyms (the field values are also listed): critical-ecp (0xa0), flash (0x60), flash-override (0x80), immediate (0x40), internet-control (0xc0), net-control (0xe0), priority (0x20), or routine (0x00).
protocol *number*	The IP protocol field. In place of the numeric value, you can specify one of the following text synonyms (the field values are also listed): egp (8), esp (50), gre (47), icmp (1), igmp (2), ipip (4), ipv6 (41), ospf (89), pim (103), rsvp (46), tcp (6), or udp (17).

TABLE 10.1   Numeric Range Match Conditions *(continued)*

Match Condition	Description
source-port *number*	The TCP or UDP source port field. You cannot specify the port and source-port match conditions in the same term. Normally, you specify this match in conjunction with the protocol match statement to determine which protocol is being used on the port. In place of the numeric field, you can specify one of the text synonyms listed under destination-port.

The JUNOS software allows you to enter an inclusive range of values. The criterion port 6-25 means all values between 6 and 25.

Some of the conditions in Table 10.1, such as port, icmp-code, and icmp-type, state that they are normally used in conjunction with a protocol match. This is an important recommendation and ensures the proper operation of your filter.

Address Match Conditions

No filtering system would be complete without the ability to watch for IP addresses, and the JUNOS software is no exception to that rule. You can use both the source and destination IP addresses of a packet as a match condition. Consider the following filter:

```
[edit firewall family inet]
user@Shiraz# show
filter example-filter-3 {
    term deny-subnets {
        from {
            source-address {
                10.1.1.0/24;
                172.16.0.0/16;
            }
            destination-address {
                192.168.1.0/24;
            }
        }
```

```
    then {
        reject;
    }
  }
}
```

The **deny-subnets** term rejects any packets that have a destination address in the 192.168.1.0/ 24 subnet where the source address is in either the 10.1.1.0/24 or the 172.16.0.0/16 subnet. The router interprets an address condition as a complete set of subnet addresses; all possible addresses in the subnet may match.

You may specify multiple address prefixes in a filter term. The router performs a longest match lookup on the specified addresses, much like a routing table lookup. As such, only a single prefix in a term produces a match.

 Don't let the from address syntax confuse you into thinking that the router is interpreting the directionality of the packet. The syntax checks both the source and destination address fields, as shown in **example-filter-3**. Think of the from/then filter syntax as really meaning if/then.

Table 10.2 lists the available *address match conditions* in the JUNOS software.

TABLE 10.2   Address Match Conditions

Match Condition	Description
address *prefix*	The IP source or destination address field. You cannot specify both the address and the destination-address or source-address match conditions in the same term.
destination-address *prefix*	The IP destination address field. You cannot specify the destination-address and address match conditions in the same term.
destination-prefix-list *prefix-list*	The IP destination prefix list field. You cannot specify the destination-prefix-list and prefix-list match conditions in the same term.
prefix-list *prefix-list*	The IP source or destination prefix list field. You cannot specify both the prefix-list and the destination-prefix-list or source-prefix-list match conditions in the same term.

TABLE 10.2 Address Match Conditions *(continued)*

Match Condition	Description
source-address *prefix*	The IP source address field. You cannot specify the source-address and address match conditions in the same rule.
source-prefix-list *prefix-list*	The IP source prefix list field. You cannot specify the source-prefix-list and prefix-list match conditions in the same term.

For information on how to configure a prefix list, refer to the *JNCIS Study Guide*, also from Sybex (forthcoming).

Bit Field Match Conditions

The JUNOS software uses *bit field match conditions* to determine whether particular bits in the Layer 3 and Layer 4 headers are set. These header fields include the IP options, TCP flags, and IP fragmentation fields. For bit field matches, you specify a syntax keyword representing the field to check and then supply the bit value in hexadecimal notation. Optionally, you can use a text synonym to represent the bit value being checked.

The three filters shown here accomplish the same task of allowing return TCP traffic back into your network. The difference between them is in the syntax options used to accomplish the goal.

```
[edit firewall family inet]
user@Shiraz# show
filter example-filter-4 {
    term allow-tcp-established-ack {
        from {
            protocol tcp;
            tcp-flags 0x10;
        }
        then accept;
    }
    term allow-tcp-established-rst {
        from {
            protocol tcp;
```

```
                tcp-flags 0x04;
            }
            then accept;
        }
    }
filter example-filter-5 {
    term allow-tcp-established {
        from {
            protocol tcp;
            tcp-flags "(ack|rst)";
        }
        then accept;
    }
}
filter example-filter-6 {
    term allow-tcp-established {
        from {
            protocol tcp;
            tcp-established;
        }
        then accept;
    }
}
```

Table 10.3 details the JUNOS software bit field match conditions.

TABLE 10.3   Bit Field Match Conditions

Match Condition	Description
fragment-flags *number*	IP fragmentation flags. In place of the numeric field value, you can specify one of the following keywords (the field values are also listed): dont-fragment (0x4000), more-fragments (0x2000), or reserved (0x8000).
ip-options *number*	IP options. In place of the numeric value, you can specify one of the following text synonyms (the field values are also listed): loose-source-route (131), record-route (7), router-alert (148), strict-source-route (137), or timestamp (68).

TABLE 10.3 Bit Field Match Conditions *(continued)*

Match Condition	Description
`tcp-flags` *number*	TCP flags. Normally, you specify this match in conjunction with the `protocol` match statement to determine which protocol is being used on the port. In place of the numeric value, you can specify one of the following text synonyms (the field values are also listed): ack (0x10), fin (0x01), push (0x08), rst (0x04), syn (0x02), or urgent (0x20).
`first-fragment`	The first fragment of a fragmented packet. This condition does not match unfragmented packets.
`is-fragment`	This condition matches if the packet is a trailing fragment; it does not match the first fragment of a fragmented packet. To match both first and trailing fragments, you can use two terms, or fragment-range 0-8191.
`tcp-established`	TCP packets other than the first packet of a connection. This is a synonym for (ack | rst). This condition does not implicitly check that the protocol is TCP. To check this, specify the protocol tcp match condition.
`tcp-initial`	First TCP packet of a connection. This is a synonym for (syn & !ack). This condition does not implicitly check that the protocol is TCP. To check this, specify the protocol tcp match condition.

In both Table 10.3 and **example-filter-5** earlier, we used the concept of a *logical operator*. These operators allow you to construct complex Boolean operations in a firewall filter. You configure these operators using a double-quote notation:

```
[edit firewall family inet]
user@Shiraz# show
filter example-filter-7 {
    term allow-tcp-initial {
        from {
            protocol tcp;
            tcp-flags "syn & !ack";
        }
        then accept;
    }
}
```

The list of logical operators is shown in Table 10.4.

TABLE 10.4 Bit Field Logical Operators

Logical Operator	Description
(...)	Grouping
!	Negation
& or +	Logical AND
| or ,	Logical OR

Real World Scenario

A Useful First Filter Term

One type of traffic is almost always accepted by an inbound firewall filter: the traffic that your network originates. After all, if your users can't access resources outside your network, they lose the ability to browse the Internet or send e-mail. These two applications use TCP as their underlying protocol, and this is our focus for interacting with a firewall filter.

Remember that the essence of a TCP connection is a three-way handshake between hosts. This means that a user sends out a TCP packet with the SYN flag set indicating its desire to form a connection. The receiving host responds to this request with its own TCP packet. This returning data has both the SYN and ACK flags set indicating that the remote host is acknowledging the initial transmission and would like to set up its own connection to the local host.

Should this return TCP packet not reach the local host, the connection is not established and the application does not function. Allowing this return packet through your inbound firewall filter is a must. You have multiple methods for solving this issue. You could build a term that accepts the return packet by application. The problem with this solution is administration of the firewall. Every time a new application is required, you have to modify your filter settings. Alternately, you could accept the return packet by either the source or destination IP address. Again, there is an administration headache with this solution. You also encounter a scalability issue in that the number of potential hosts sending the return traffic is quite large.

Many networks solve this problem by assuming that all traffic originated by your local network is *safe*. Of course, there are inherent risks with this assumption. Some of your users could be hackers using your network as a home base. Other users might unknowingly download viruses or other harmful applications. In general, though, this assumption of safe local traffic holds true. In this case, the filter configuration is quite simple: You allow the first term in your filter to accept the return TCP traffic. You can see an example of this in the *example-filter-6* filter earlier in this section. In that filter, the initial term watches for protocol tcp as well as tcp-established. The keyword tcp-established is a synonym for a TCP packet that has either the ACK or the RST flag set. Both of these flags indicate a return TCP packet to a local host that originated the session.

The Absence of Match Criteria

Up to this point, we talked about the different match criteria we can use in a firewall filter term. All of these options are, however, completely optional in their usage. You can configure a filter without a match condition:

```
[edit firewall family inet]
user@Shiraz# show
filter example-filter-8 {
    term accept-all-packets {
        then accept;
    }
}
```

When no match criteria are used, all packets will match the filter term. In other words, the *absence* of match criteria means that all packets match and the configured actions are implemented. In the case of *example-filter-8*, all IP user data packets are forwarded.

 Real World Scenario

A Common Last Term

When constructing a firewall filter, you must take one of two philosophical approaches. One option is to allow into your network only packets that you know are good and reject everything else. The opposite approach is to reject known bad packets and to accept everything else. Both of these options have advantages and disadvantages that we won't get into here. We also will not be taking sides in this war. Instead, we focus on a useful and common last filter term when you want to explicitly deny known bad packets.

In this situation, your filter contains multiple terms with varying match conditions. The actions in those terms are either reject or discard, depending on your desires. The issue that arises is the implicit final filter action of then discard. Unless you manually alter the evaluation, the filter drops all packets that have not matched a configured term. Clearly, this is not what you intended.

The easy solution to this dilemma is to add a term to the end of your filter with no match criteria listed. This term should have the terminating action of then accept configured. Additionally, it would be wise to add either the log or *syslog* action modifier to that final term. This logging function proves useful when you realize that you have discovered a new set of bad packets that you want your filter to drop. The log files contain all the information you need to build a new filter term and configure the appropriate match criteria.

Actions

Identifying packets using the JUNOS software match conditions is only the first step in building a firewall filter. Once you've located the packets, you must then decide what to do with them. This is the job of a filter *action*.

All filter actions are configured within the then portion of the filter term. The JUNOS software has three main types of actions you can use: terminating, flow-control, and action modifiers. We explore these possibilities in the following sections.

Terminating Actions

A *terminating action* halts all evaluation of a firewall filter for a particular IP packet. The router performs the specified action and no further terms are examined. Three actions exist within this category: accept, discard, and reject.

The router forwards IP packets through a filter when the *accept* action is used. The opposite function, packet drop, is performed when either the *discard* or *reject* action is configured. The difference between discard and reject is in the response of the router to the dropping of the packet.

When a packet is dropped as a result of the discard action, the router accomplishes this task silently. This is generally a good option when your filter is used to protect against potential intruders. The reject action prompts the router to return an administratively-prohibited ICMP error message back to the source address in the packet's header. If your goal is to keep unauthorized traffic out of your network, you might not want to inform a potential intruder that you use firewall filters to block traffic.

To assist you, the JUNOS software provides the ability to return other ICMP error messages back to the IP source when you use reject. These alternative messages may be useful if a suspected hacker is monitoring ICMP return messages for helpful information. In many cases, the default error message is a clear sign to a hacker that a firewall filter has been reached. Table 10.5 details the possible ICMP options configurable with the reject action.

TABLE 10.5   reject Message Options

ICMP Message Type	Notes
administratively-prohibited	Default
bad-host-tos	
bad-network-tos	
host-prohibited	
host-unknown	
host-unreachable	
network-prohibited	
network-unknown	
network-unreachable	
port-unreachable	
precedence-cutoff	
precedence-violation	
protocol-unreachable	
source-host-isolated	
source-route-failed	
tcp-reset	If you specify tcp-reset, a Transmission Control Protocol (TCP) reset is returned if the packet is a TCP packet. Otherwise, nothing is returned.

Flow-Control Actions

You have the ability to alter the default filter evaluation process in the JUNOS software. The *flow-control action* next term allows the router to perform some actions on the packet and then evaluate the following term in the filter. The action was designed to circumvent an implicit accept that was associated with the filter terms. When you omit the then statement or use an action modifier (discussed in the next section) within a filter term, the router accepts all packets that match the configured criteria.

To illustrate the need for the flow-control action, let's look at an example. Suppose that you have an inbound filter configured on your router. You would like to log information about all received traffic on that interface. The filter should then reject telnet traffic but accept all other traffic. You might logically configure a filter that looks like this:

```
[edit firewall family inet]
user@Shiraz# show
filter example-filter-9{
    term log-all-packets {
        then log;
    }
    term deny-telnet {
        from {
            protocol tcp;
            port telnet;
        }
        then {
            reject;
        }
    }
    term accept-everything-else {
        then accept;
    }
}
```

The only action configured in the *log-all-packets* term is log. When the router evaluates that term, it adds the implicit accept action and all IP packets are forwarded through the filter. Clearly, this is not what you wanted. One simple solution is to simply add the log action to the other existing terms:

```
[edit firewall family inet]
user@Shiraz# show
filter example-filter-9{
    term deny-telnet {
        from {
            protocol tcp;
            port telnet;
        }
        then {
            log;
            reject;
        }
    }
```

```
        term accept-everything-else {
            then {
                log;
                accept;
            }
        }
    }
}
```

While you solved the immediate issue, this is not a scalable solution. Imagine if your filter grew to 100 or even 1000 terms. Placing the log action in each term is no longer a simple fix. This situation is a perfect use for the next term action. Within *example-filter-9*, you configure this action in the *log-all-packets* term. The router now logs information on all packets and passes them to the following terms for further evaluation. The *deny-telnet* term now rejects the telnet traffic and all other traffic is forwarded by the *accept-everything-else* term:

```
[edit firewall family inet]
user@Shiraz# show
filter example-filter-9{
    term log-all-packets {
        then {
            log;
            next term;
        }
    }
    term deny-telnet {
        from {
            protocol tcp;
            port telnet;
        }
        then {
            reject;
        }
    }
    term accept-everything-else {
        then accept;
    }
}
```

Action Modifiers

The JUNOS software may perform other functions on an IP packet being evaluated by a firewall filter. Some of these actions include incrementing a counter, logging information about the IP header locally, sampling the packet data, or sending information to a remote host using the Unix syslog functionality.

You can include any combination of action modifiers in a single filter term. Each term carries with it an implicit accept action if no other terminating or flow-control actions are configured. Let's take a look at the available action modifiers.

count

A numerical packet counter is configured within a filter to track particular traffic types. All counters operate within the Internet Processor ASIC, so forwarding performance is not affected by their usage. You configure the count action and supply the name of the counter to increment:

```
[edit firewall family inet]
user@Shiraz# show
filter inbound-from-peer {
    term count-traffic {
        from {
            source-address {
                10.0.0/24;
            }
        }
        then {
            count traffic-counter;
            accept;
        }
    }
}
```

The ***inbound-from-peer*** filter counts all packets with a source address contained in the 10.0.0.0/24 subnet. The specific counter that should be incremented is named ***traffic-counter***.

log

Logging packet data is useful when you're monitoring ongoing network events in real time. The router can collect data contained in the IP header by using the log action. The information is stored in a memory-resident buffer that is 500 lines deep. The buffer works on a first-in, first-out basis, so the oldest data is overwritten by the newest data:

```
[edit firewall family inet]
user@Shiraz# show
filter log-tcp-flow-start {
    term count-syn {
        from {
            protocol tcp;
            tcp-initial;
        }
```

```
        then {
            log;
            accept;
        }
    }
}
```

The ***log-tcp-flow-start*** filter matches only on the first packet in a TCP connection. The header information of these packets is written to the buffer log and the packet is forwarded. The log buffer is not stored on the router's hard disk and can be accessed only with the `show firewall log` command. (We discuss this CLI command in the "JUNOS software Commands" section later in this chapter.)

sample

Statistical sampling examines a user-specified percentage of the traffic traversing the router. This data can assist you in planning for future capacity, evaluating your network design, and deploying new physical circuits. Sampling theory states that statistical sampling is quite accurate when you select the sampling parameters properly.

Within the JUNOS software, you configure a filter to sample incoming traffic on a transit interface by using the `sample` command:

```
[edit firewall family inet]
user@Shiraz# show
filter sample-peer-traffic {
    term peer-connections {
        from {
            source-address {
                10.10.0.0/16;
                172.30.45.0/24;
                192.168.164.0/20;
            }
        }
        then {
            sample;
            accept;
        }
    }
}
```

The ***sample-peer-traffic*** filter samples all IP packets originating from one of the configured peer subnets. The router then forwards the IP packets through the filter.

Packet data is written to a file based on the `sampling` setting specified under `[edit forwarding-options]`. The file is sent to a remote host using cflowd version 5 or 8. For more information regarding cflowd and its use, go to www.caida.org/tools.

syslog

To overcome the limitation of the memory buffer used with the `log` action, the JUNOS software provides a similar ability with the `syslog` command. The IP header information is now sent to the hard drive on the Routing Engine using the normal Unix syslog process:

```
[edit firewall family inet]
user@Shiraz# show
filter log-tcp-flow-start {
    term count-syn {
        from {
            protocol tcp;
            tcp-initial;
        }
        then {
            syslog;
            accept;
        }
    }
}
```

We modified the ***log-tcp-flow-start*** filter to store the header information of the packets to the hard drive instead of the memory log buffer. The logged data is contained within the `messages` file and provides us with the ability to maintain a historical record of the stored packets.

Applying Firewall Filters

Thus far, we've talked about how to build your own firewall filters and terms as well as the defaults for the JUNOS software. We also discussed how the router evaluates from the first term to the last term in order until it finds a match. To make your filter useful, you must apply it to an interface on the router.

Each logical unit on the router may contain a single input and a single output filter. There is no requirement to build a separate filter for each application. In fact, you should configure as many reusable filters as possible to ease administration and troubleshooting in your network. Once you apply your filter, the Internet Processor ASIC examines every packet received or forwarded on that interface against the match conditions of the filter terms. When the router finds a match, it takes the appropriate actions.

You apply each filter within the [edit interfaces] directory appropriate to your situation. The fe-0/0/0.0 interface here has both an input and an output filter configured:

```
[edit interfaces fe-0/0/0]
user@Shiraz# show
description "Connection to AS 65000";
unit 0 {
    family inet {
        filter {
            input AS65000-inbound-filter;
            output AS65000-outbound-filter;
        }
        address 10.10.10.1/24;
    }
}
```

When you access the router remotely using an in-band interface (not fxp0.0) and you are creating firewall filters, it might be a good idea to use the commit confirmed 1 command when you have finished. Should your new filter sever your in-band connection, the router performs a rollback for you one minute later to allow you to regain access.

Protecting the Routing Engine

Firewall filters configured on a router's transit interfaces only evaluate user packets that are flowing directly from one interface to another. These types of filters protect the network as a whole from unauthorized access and other threats. The core routers themselves, however, are left somewhat unprotected from unauthorized management access and other harmful effects. You can achieve this type of protection by applying a firewall filter to the lo0 interface, which protects the Routing Engine itself.

The CPU on the router's switching control board actually implements this filter. Therefore, this single filter processes all packets received on any transit interface before they are sent to the Routing Engine.

Traditionally, two types of tools are used in a layered fashion to protect core routers. The first line of defense is the router's remote access management policy, which is essentially a list of IP addresses. Management access to the router, like Telnet or SSH, requires a source IP address on the list of approved addresses. After the source IP address is verified, a second tool, such as remote authentication dial-in user service (RADIUS) provides a second layer of security. A firewall filter protecting the Routing Engine is a powerful replacement for the list of approved addresses.

Figure 10.1 shows the difference between a filter applied to the loopback interface as opposed to one configured on a transit interface. The application of the filter to an interface on a Physical Interface Card (PIC) affects only transit user traffic. Configuring a filter for the lo0 interface affects and protects the Routing Engine.

FIGURE 10.1 Transit versus Routing Engine filters

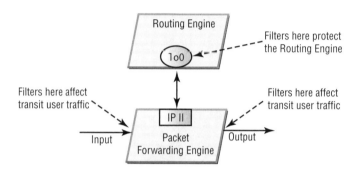

You configure a Routing Engine filter the same way you do all other filters:

```
[edit interfaces lo0]
user@Shiraz# show
unit 0 {
    family inet {
        filter {
            input protect-routing-engine;
        }
        address 192.168.1.1/32;
    }
}
```

Firewall filters applied to the lo0 interface to protect the Routing Engine must allow routing protocol traffic to be forwarded through the filter. The implicit discard in every filter can cause disastrous and unintentional effects in your network.

Rate Policing

The JUNOS software uses firewalls filters not only to drop or accept data packets but also to rate-limit those packets. *Rate policing* enables you to limit the amount of traffic that passes into or out of a particular interface. You can use a policer to thwart denial-of-service (DoS) attacks or to enforce a service contract with a customer.

A firewall filter using a policer still employs the normal match conditions of addresses, protocols, ports, and so forth to determine which specific traffic on an interface should be subject to rate limiting. To apply rate limiting for all packets on an interface, you either omit any from match criteria in a firewall filter or apply the policer itself directly to the interface. Before we begin using our policers, however, we must first understand the configuration steps in building one.

Rate Limits

Policing uses two different types of values to rate-limit user traffic. The first is the bandwidth-limit value, which is the average number of bits per second permitted in the range of 32Kbps to 32Gbps. The second is burst-size-limit, which is the amount of data allowed to exceed the given bandwidth constraints. This value is configured as the number of bytes allowed between 1500 and 100,000,000 (100MB).

Only the IP packet and the IP header are calculated by the bandwidth-limit and burst-size-limit options.

The JUNOS software policing function employs a *token-bucket algorithm*, which enforces a limit on the average usable bandwidth while allowing bursts of traffic up to a specified maximum value. This type of system allows an interface a certain amount of bursty traffic before packets are discarded by supplying token credits on a regular time sequence up to the maximum defined by the burst-size-limit value. At a high level, the algorithm works as follows:

1. As the policer evaluates each data packet, the current bandwidth of the interface is checked against the bandwidth-limit value.

2. If the traffic flow is above the limit, the size of the packet (in bytes) is compared against the current credits in the token bucket.

3. Should the packet size be smaller than the current credit, the policer accepts the packet and reduces the current credit by that packet's size. Otherwise, the policer rejects the packet.

The router deals with traffic that doesn't meet the constraints of a policer in two main ways. The packet is either silently discarded or its internal JUNOS software control information is altered. This internal information is either the *Packet Loss Priority (PLP)* bit or the *forwarding class* of the packet. By altering these values, you affect the probability that the packet is dropped by the outbound interface when it becomes congested.

The use of the PLP bit and the forwarding class for affecting traffic flows is beyond the scope of this book.

Setting the *burst-size-limit*

The Juniper Networks Technical Assistance Center (JTAC) suggests setting the `burst-size-limit` equal to the amount of traffic forwarded by the interface in 5 milliseconds. Let's look at an example.

Suppose you have a Gigabit Ethernet interface in your router. The interface can receive 1000 megabits per second. The `burst-size-limit` is entered in bytes per second, so we translate 1000Mbps into 125MBps. That further translates into 125,000KBps and finally 125,000,000Bps. In a single millisecond, the interface receives 125,000 bytes, so a total of 625,000 bytes are received in 5 milliseconds. The policer statement becomes `burst-size-limit 625000`.

Filter Policers

By using a policer in conjunction with a firewall filter, you can rate-limit specific types of traffic flowing across an interface. Should a packet not exceed the defined rate limit, the router processes it through the remainder of the filter term. If the packet exceeds the policer limits, it is either discarded or altered based on the current router configuration.

A simple firewall filter using a policer might look like this:

```
[edit firewall family inet]
user@Shiraz# show
filter limit-ftp {
    policer policer-1 {
        if-exceeding {
            bandwidth-limit 400k;
            burst-size-limit 100k;
        }
        then discard;
    }
    term ftp {
        from {
            source-address {
                10.2.3/24;
            }
```

```
            protocol tcp;
            destination-port [ftp ftp-data];
        }
        then {
            policer policer-1;
            accept;
        }
    }
    term accept-all {
        then accept;
    }
}
```

The *limit-ftp* filter rate-limits FTP traffic from hosts on the 10.2.3.0 /24 subnet only. All other user traffic is accepted by the *accept-all* term. The policer, named *policer-1*, is placed at the beginning of the filter by the router. It contains the rate limit values of 400Kbps of bandwidth and a burst size of 100KB. FTP traffic exceeding the policer parameters uses the configured action of discard.

If you apply the *limit-ftp* filter to multiple inbound interfaces, the policer definition is shared among those interfaces. This means that the aggregate of the interface bandwidths is combined before the router checks the policer parameters. You can create a separate instance of the policer for each separate interface by using the interface-specific command like this:

```
[edit firewall family inet]
user@Shiraz# show
filter limit-ftp {
    interface-specific;
    policer policer-1 {
        if-exceeding {
            bandwidth-limit 400k;
            burst-size-limit 100k;
        }
        then discard;
    }
    term ftp {
        from {
            source-address {
                10.2.3/24;
            }
            protocol tcp;
```

```
                destination-port [ftp ftp-data];
        }
        then {
            policer policer-1;
            accept;
        }
    }
    term accept-all {
        then accept;
    }
}
```

Interface Policers

A policer may also be configured directly on an interface to rate-limit all traffic flows. This allows you the flexibility of a single configured policer applied to multiple interfaces, each with its own instance of the policer. You configure this policer directly within the [edit firewall] configuration hierarchy:

```
[edit firewall]
user@Shiraz# show
policer police-all-traffic {
    if-exceeding {
        bandwidth-limit 10m;
        burst-size-limit 100k;
    }
    then {
        discard;
    }
}
```

The *police-all-traffic* policer discards all traffic above the limits of 10Mbps of bandwidth and 100KB of burst capacity. You can then apply the policer to a transit interface, such as fe-0/0/0.0:

```
[edit interfaces fe-0/0/0]
user@Shiraz# show
description "Connection to Customer-A";
unit 0 {
```

```
    family inet {
        policer {
            input police-all-traffic;
            output police-all-traffic;
        }
        address 10.100.1.1/24;
    }
}
```

The same policer is applied in both the inbound and outbound directions. Additionally, you can mix the interface policers and firewall filters together on a single interface. This allows you to police all traffic flows while still securing your network with a filter:

```
[edit interfaces fe-0/0/0]
user@Shiraz# show
description "Connection to Customer-A";
unit 0 {
    family inet {
        filter {
            input filter-customer-A;
        }
        policer {
            input police-all-traffic;
            output police-all-traffic;
        }
        address 10.100.1.1/24;
    }
}
```

JUNOS software Commands

Now that you have a handle on creating and applying your firewall filters, let's examine some useful JUNOS software commands. These commands allow you to monitor your filter operation as well as troubleshoot issues in your network. We first look at show and clear commands specific to firewall filters and then revisit the insert and rename commands to modify your configuration.

show firewall

The show firewall command displays counter and policer statistics for all firewall filters. You can include the name of a specific filter, as in show firewall filter *filter-name*, to view just the statistics for that filter:

```
user@Shiraz> show firewall
Filter/Counter          Packet count          Byte count
protect-re
  deny                              46              2791
  icmp                               0                NA
```

Here, we've applied a filter named ***protect-re*** on the Shiraz router. This particular filter is utilizing two different counters, ***deny*** and ***icmp***, that supply byte and packet counts.

In examining the output more closely, you might notice that the ***icmp*** counter lists NA in the Byte count column. In reality, the counter is not incrementing this field since it is a policer configured within the firewall filter. By default, the Internet Processor ASIC automatically creates a counter to record traffic in excess of a policer's profile. The name of the policer is used in this output as the name of the counter.

show firewall log

The show firewall log command displays entries in the memory-resident buffer or kernel cache. The router stores information in this buffer when the log filter action is used. The cache holds no more than 500 entries and wraps data when it is full. There is no CLI command to clear the firewall log. Here is some sample output:

```
user@Shiraz> show firewall log
Time      Filter A Interface       Pro Source address  Destination address
11:56:47 pfe     A so-0/1/0.0      OSP 200.0.0.2       224.0.0.5
11:56:43 pfe     A so-0/1/1.0      OSP 200.0.0.1       224.0.0.5
11:56:42 pfe     A fe-0/0/1.0      TCP 10.0.8.2        10.0.8.1:179
```

The Filter column displays the name of the filter that logged the particular entry, if the filter name is known. The Routing Engine is fully aware of filter names and enters data in this field for traffic generated by it and logged by a transit filter. The Internet Processor ASIC on the Packet Forwarding Engine is not aware of filter names and reports pfe as the filter name for all packets logged by a filter action and sent to the memory buffer.

The column titled A between the Filter and Interface columns represents the action performed by the filter for the particular packet. Possible entries in this column are A (accept), R (reject), and D (discard).

The log buffer also displays information about the packet's ingress interface, protocol, source IP address, destination IP address, and port numbers.

> The ingress interface displayed is not necessarily the interface to which the filter has been applied. For example, the filter logging the data may be an egress filter on the router.

You may also add the *detail* keyword to the show firewall log command to get more information:

```
user@Shiraz> show firewall log detail
2001-09-03 11:57:42 UTC, Filter: pfe, Action: accept
    Interface: so-0/1/1.0, Protocol: OSPF, Length: 64
    Source: 200.0.0.1, Destination: 224.0.0.5
2001-09-03 11:57:42 UTC, Filter: pfe, Action: accept
    Interface: fe-0/0/1.0, Protocol: TCP, Length: 52
    Source: 10.0.8.2:1024, Destination: 10.0.8.1:179
```

show log messages

The show log messages command displays syslog entries in the file called messages. The messages file is the default logging location for all router event information and can be quite large. Firewall filter entries are sent using the syslog info level and have the code FW associated with them, allowing you to more easily search for them. To see the firewall output only, pipe the router output to match on the FW code:

```
user@Shiraz> show log messages | match FW
Sep  2 16:38:39 router scb FW: fe-0/0/2.0   A  tcp 10.0.2.1 192.168.5.1  1026
23 (2 packets)
Sep  2 16:38:40 router scb FW: fe-0/0/2.0   A ospf 10.0.2.1 224.0.0.5      0
0 (1 packets)
Sep  2 16:38:40 router scb FW: fe-0/0/2.0   A  tcp 10.0.2.1 192.168.5.1  1026
23 (2 packets)
```

> The individual entries in the messages file are contained on a single line, allowing the match pipe option to function. The particular output in the text was gathered using a terminal width of 80 characters. Because each line is longer than the terminal width, we see the apparent multiple-line entries.

As with the show firewall log command, syslog entries indicate the ingress interface, protocol, ports, and addresses for the stored packets.

clear firewall

You use the clear firewall *counter-name* command to reset the counters associated with your firewall filters. You can clear an individual counter, an individual filter, or all filters on the router. The appropriate command arguments control the specific action:

```
user@Shiraz> clear firewall ?
Possible completions:
  all                   Clear all firewall counters
  counter               Counter name
  filter                Filter name
```

show interfaces filters

The show interfaces filters command displays all firewall filters configured on all interfaces on the router. You can optionally specify a particular interface by adding the interface name to the command, such as show interfaces filters *interface-name*:

```
user@Shiraz> show interfaces filters
Interface       Admin Link Proto Input Filter       Output Filter
fe-0/0/0        up    up
fe-0/0/0.0      up    up    inet  filter-1
   filter-2
fe-0/0/1        up    up
fe-0/0/1.0      up    up    inet  filter-3
   filter-4
fe-0/0/2        up    down
fe-0/0/3        up    down
```

show interfaces policers

The show interfaces policers command displays all policers applied on the router's interfaces. Again, a particular interface is viewed with the show interfaces policers *interface-name*:

```
user@Shiraz> show interfaces policers
Interface       Admin Link Proto Input Policer       Output Policer
fe-0/0/0        up    up
fe-0/0/0.0      up    up    inet  fe-0/0/0.0-in-policer
```

```
    fe-0/0/0.0-out-policer
fe-0/0/1        up    up
fe-0/0/1.0      up    up    inet  fe-0/0/1.0-in-policer
    fe-0/0/1.0-out-policer

fe-0/0/2        up    down
fe-0/0/3        up    down
```

show policer

The show policer command displays the names of all policers configured on the router. Additionally, the router displays the interfaces where the policer is being used as well as the total number of packets processed by the policer:

```
user@Shiraz> show policer
Policer: so-2/2/0.0-in-policer
    so-2/2/0.0-in-policer
                    0 packets
Policer: so-2/2/0.0-out-policer
    so-2/2/0.0-out-policer
                  238 packets
```

Both the show interfaces policers and the show policer commands display the name of the policer in the format of *interface.unit*-in-policer or *interface .unit*-out-policer. This naming syntax is used regardless of the policer name configured within the [edit firewall] hierarchy.

insert

Assume you wrote a multiterm firewall filter called **test-filter** and applied it to an interface. When you tested its operation, things just didn't seem to work the way you thought they would. After a closer examination of the configuration, you notice that **term 1** should have been **term 2** and vice versa. One possible solution is to delete the entire firewall filter and reenter it in the proper order. A better solution is to use the JUNOS software *insert* command to easily reorder the terms.

The syntax of the insert command is:

```
[edit]
user@host# insert value-1 before|after value-2
```

In the particular case of the **test-filter** firewall, either of the following commands solve the problem:

```
[edit firewall family inet filter test-filter]
user@Shiraz# insert term 1 after term 2
```

or

```
[edit firewall family inet filter test-filter]
user@Shiraz# insert term 2 before term 1
```

rename

The JUNOS software *rename* command is just as handy as the `insert` command. Just like renaming a routing policy name or an interface's IP address, you can rename your firewall filters and their terms. Using the `rename` command is very straightforward:

```
[edit firewall family inet]
user@Shiraz# rename filter filter-name1 to filter filter-name2
```

```
[edit firewall family inet filter filter-name]
user@Shiraz# rename term term-name1 to term term-name2
```

Summary

In this chapter, we saw how firewall filters allow you to filter packets based on their header components and to perform specific actions on those packets. The Internet Processor ASIC provides filtering capabilities on transit user traffic. Transit filters are useful for providing packet filtering, thwarting denial-of-service (DoS) attacks, preventing address spoofing, and implementing rate limiting. Filters may also be configured to protect the Routing Engine, its routing protocols, and its services, such as Telnet and SSH.

Firewall filters consist of one or multiple terms, each containing a set of match conditions using the `from` configuration syntax. After a packet matches the term's criteria, you can perform terminating actions, flow-control actions, or action modifiers.

After the filters are configured, they are then applied to the router's logical interfaces. A single interface unit may contain filters for inbound and outbound traffic.

The JUNOS software provides several useful `show` commands that allow you to check whether your filters are working properly. Additionally, you can use the `insert` and `rename` commands to alter your existing filter configurations.

Exam Essentials

Be able to describe firewall filter concepts.   Firewall filters consist of match/action pairs that allow you to target specific packets of interest and forward, reject, or silently discard them.

Understand that firewall filters allow control of traffic entering and leaving the router or Routing Engine.   Using both input and output filters controls how user transit traffic flows (or doesn't flow) through the router. A filter can also provide access control to the Routing Engine itself.

Know the various matching criteria available to identify specific packets.   Various match criteria are used to identify packets. Possible options include IP addresses, protocol and port numbers, and other bit fields in the IP and TCP headers.

Be able to identify the possible actions taken when packets match a filter term.   Actions can allow the packet to be forwarded, rejected, or silently discarded via the `accept`, `reject`, and `discard` actions. Additional actions include flow control through the `next term` action and modifiers such as `count`, `log`, `syslog`, and `sample`.

Understand the use of action modifiers.   You gather additional information about the contents of a packet by using the action modifiers of `count`, `log`, and `sample`.

Identify JUNOS software commands that verify firewall filter operation.   There are a number of operational `show` commands that allow you to ensure the firewall filters are working properly. Additionally, various configuration commands let you rename filters and reorder terms as needed.

Key Terms

Before you take the exam, be certain you are familiar with the following terms:

`accept`	logical operator
action	numeric range match conditions
address match conditions	Packet Loss Priority (PLP)
bit field match conditions	rate policing
`discard`	`reject`
firewall filter	`rename`
flow-control action	`syslog`
forwarding class	terminating action
`insert`	token-bucket algorithm
Internet Processor ASIC	

Review Questions

1. What are the components of a firewall filter? (Choose three.)

    A. Match conditions

    B. Actions

    C. Action modifiers

    D. Stateful monitoring

2. Which item is not a firewall filter action?

    A. accept

    B. discard

    C. next filter

    D. reject

3. Where would you apply a filter to protect the Routing Engine?

    A. fxp0.0

    B. fxp1

    C. lo0

    D. lo0.0

4. Which command might be best used when testing firewall filters through an in-band connection?

    A. commit

    B. commit and-quit

    C. commit confirmed

    D. commit confirmed 1

5. Firewall filters can be used to accept, discard, or reject packets based on _____. (Choose three.)

    A. IP address

    B. MAC address

    C. Protocol type

    D. Well-known port name

6. What is the rule regarding applying firewall filters on a single interface?

    A. Multiple filters per logical unit in each direction (input and output)

    B. One filter per logical unit in each direction (input and output)

    C. One filter per physical interface

    D. One filter per IP address, per logical interface in each direction (input and output)

7. Which action should be used to silently drop packets that match a term in a firewall filter?

    A. `accept`

    B. `discard`

    C. `dismiss`

    D. `reject`

8. A firewall filter is written and applied as an input filter on the `lo0.0` interface. What types of traffic will this action affect? (Choose two.)

    A. Inbound packets destined for a remote network

    B. Locally destined SSH sessions

    C. RIP update packets

    D. Transiting ICMP echo requests

9. When applying a firewall filter to the `lo0.0` interface, you should be careful to do which of the following?

    A. Allow routing protocol traffic.

    B. Allow transit traffic to enter on `fxp0.0`.

    C. Allow transit traffic to exit on `fxp0.0`.

    D. Restrict the number of telnet sessions to 5.

10. A firewall filter is applied as an input filter on a transit interface. Which types of traffic are affected? (Choose three.)

    A. Inbound traffic that is transiting the router

    B. Outbound traffic that has transited the router

    C. Traffic destined for the Routing Engine

    D. Traffic destined for the interface address on which the filter is applied

11. Which command can be used to display information about packets that have been logged with the `log` firewall filter action?

    A. `show firewall`

    B. `show firewall log`

    C. `show log`

    D. `show log messages`

12. Which command can be used to display information about packets that have been logged with the `syslog` firewall filter action?

    A. `show firewall`

    B. `show firewall log`

    C. `show log`

    D. `show log messages`

13. Which command clears all counters for the firewall filter named `service-restriction` only?

   A. `clear firewall`

   B. `clear firewall service-restriction`

   C. `clear firewall counter service-restriction`

   D. `clear firewall filter service-restriction`

14. What is the default action when using an action modifier?

   A. `accept`

   B. `discard`

   C. `reject`

   D. There is no default action.

15. If a packet does not match any terms in an applied firewall filter, the packet is _____.

   A. Forwarded to the destination IP address

   B. Silently discarded

   C. Thrown away and an ICMP message sent to the source IP address

   D. Sent to the Routing Engine for further processing

16. What items must be specified when configuring rate policing? (Choose two.)

   A. `bandwidth-limit`

   B. `burst-size-limit`

   C. `packet-size-limit`

   D. `time-period`

17. What is the default ICMP message sent to the IP source address of the packet when the action is `reject`?

   A. `administratively-prohibited`

   B. `host-prohibited`

   C. `network-prohibited`

   D. `port-prohibited`

18. Which statement is true when using a match condition of `port telnet`?

   A. It is not necessary to include `protocol tcp` as a match condition.

   B. It is necessary to include `protocol tcp` as a match condition.

   C. The router automatically checks for TCP as the protocol when `port telnet` is used as a match condition.

   D. The firewall stanza will not pass the `commit` checker.

19. Which action modifier logs packet matches to the hard drive on the Routing Engine?

　A. count

　B. log

　C. syslog

　D. next term

20. When using policers, which of the following is possible for packets exceeding the limits of the policer? (Choose three.)

　A. They are discarded.

　B. They have their PLP bit set.

　C. They have their forwarding class modified.

　D. They are dropped from the network and an ICMP message is sent to the source address.

Answers to Review Questions

1. A, B, C. Match conditions, actions, and action modifiers are all components of a firewall filter in the JUNOS software.

2. C. The flow-control action available with a firewall filter is `next term`, not `next filter`. Options A, B, and D are all terminating actions.

3. D. Although the loopback interface is the location where Routing Engine filters are used, the actual application of the filter occurs on the logical unit portion, `lo0.0`.

4. D. The default timer for the `commit confirmed` command is 10 minutes. Using `commit confirmed 1` allows you quicker access to the router in case of a configuration error.

5. A, C, D. A firewall filter in the JUNOS software operates on the Internet Processor ASIC, which evaluates only IP header information. Only options A, C, and D are contained in the IP header. The Internet Processor ASIC never sees the MAC address of packets.

6. B. Each logical unit on the router may have a single input and a single output filter applied at any one time.

7. B. Both `discard` and `reject` drop packets in a filter term, but only `discard` does so silently.

8. B, C. Firewall filters applied to the `lo0.0` interface evaluate only packets destined for or originating on the router itself. Only options B and C match this description.

9. A. All routing protocol traffic must be received by the Routing Engine to be effective. One common error when configuring filters is not accepting the routing protocol traffic.

10. A, C, D. Input firewall filters applied to transit interfaces affect only traffic entering the router, regardless of its destination.

11. B. The `log` filter action sends information to the memory buffer cache on the Routing Engine. You can view the buffer's contents with the `show firewall log` command.

12. D. The `syslog` filter action sends information to the hard drive storage file called `messages`. You can view the file with the `show log messages` command.

13. D. Only the `clear firewall filter service-restriction` command will clear all counters on the given firewall.

14. A. When using an action modifier in a filter term, the default terminating action is `accept`.

15. B. The implicit final term in a filter matches all packets with an action of `discard`. This action silently discards packets from the network.

16. A, B. The two values configured in a policer are `bandwidth-limit` and `burst-size-limit`.

17. A. The `reject` filter action sends an ICMP message of `administratively-prohibited` back to the source IP address of the packet.

18. B.   The router does not automatically check for the type of protocol for a given packet. It is best to include a protocol match condition, such as `protocol tcp`, to guarantee your filter is working properly.

19. C.   The `syslog` action modifier sends information to the hard drive storage on the Routing Engine.

20. A, B, C.   A policer action may discard packets, modify the PLP bit, or alter the forwarding class information in a packet.

Chapter 11

Multiprotocol Label Switching (MPLS)

JNCIA EXAM OBJECTIVES COVERED IN THIS CHAPTER:

- ✓ Define the functions of the following MPLS terms: LSP; LSR; ingress; transit; penultimate; egress

- ✓ Describe the differences between a static and a signaled LSP

- ✓ Define the functions of RSVP attributes

- ✓ Describe the relationship between BGP and MPLS

- ✓ Compare the differences between a strict and a loose ERO

In this chapter, we discuss Multiprotocol Label Switching (MPLS). This topic has gained a lot of importance and popularity in the last few years. A primary reason for this growth is that MPLS is seen by many Internet engineers as a method to support multiple services over a common IP infrastructure. We won't get into the marketing and hype of what MPLS might be used for. Instead, we look at how and why MPLS was first created. Then, we discuss the basic terms and concepts, as well as the various types and methods of MPLS connections. Finally, we explore how to configure, set up, and monitor MPLS connections in the JUNOS software.

The Creation of MPLS

The use of MPLS in the Internet today is a little different from the use for which it was created. Initially, engineers designed the MPLS technology to enhance the speed and time it took a router to perform a route lookup. This speed enhancement would in turn reduce the transit delays across the Internet.

Traditional routers performed their operations in software using a central CPU architecture. Both routing protocol maintenance and traffic forwarding using a route lookup followed this pattern. As network bandwidth and capacity grew, routers of this type had a harder time maintaining efficient operations. Routing vendors felt that adapting some ATM concepts for IP routing could alleviate these bottlenecks. ATM switches performed traffic forwarding in hardware, not software. Forwarding paths were preestablished through the ATM switched network, and traffic flows were switched using a fixed-sized cell header length of 5 bytes. These concepts formed the basis for MPLS, which used a fixed-size header length and forwarded traffic based on a switching table along a predetermined path.

Before MPLS could see widespread deployment in a production environment, the landscape of the Internet had changed. Some routers were no longer performing route lookups in software. Routing vendors had used advances in silicon technology to create hardware-based application-specific integrated circuit (ASIC) routing tables. As a result, routers could now route as fast as, if not faster than, ATM switches could switch. Thus, MPLS was left without a reason to exist. Luckily, another problem arose in which a technology like MPLS could prove useful—traffic engineering.

The History of Traffic Engineering and MPLS

In a network, *traffic engineering* is the ability to control how packets get from one edge of the network to the other. Voice, LAN, and WAN networks each carry with them some form of traffic engineering. The various methods have been oftentimes crude or sometimes quite elegant. We focus on engineering methods available to ISPs and WAN networks because this is where MPLS is most often used. As we'll see, early forms of traffic engineering were very rudimentary.

IP Routing

In the dark ages of the Internet, say 1990, backbones consisted mainly of dedicated leased lines at speeds between 1.544Mbps (T1) and 44.736Mbps (T3). Each network had only a few routers and links, enabling administrators to use Interior Gateway Protocol (IGP)–based metrics to control traffic flows.

Figure 11.1 shows a sample network using this system. In this network, the router Cabernet uses the Muscat-Merlot link and the Merlot-Riesling link to reach both the Riesling and Chardonnay routers. Let's say our traffic statistics show that the Merlot-Riesling link is heavily over-utilized and is causing a large transit bottleneck in the network. In an attempt to resolve this issue and engineer the traffic flow, we change the IGP metric of the Merlot-Riesling link to 6, as shown in Figure 11.2.

FIGURE 11.1   IGP-based network

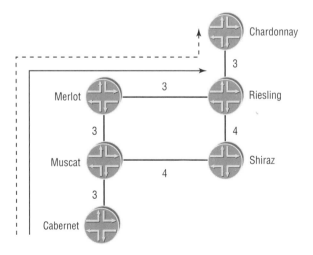

FIGURE 11.2   IGP-based traffic engineering

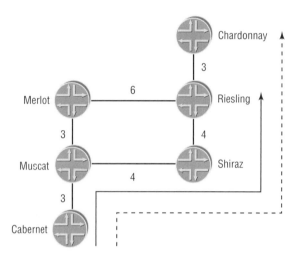

We've successfully solved the utilization problem on the Merlot-Riesling link. However, we've also created another problem. All traffic destined for both Riesling and Chardonnay now uses the Muscat-Shiraz and Shiraz-Riesling links. All we've really accomplished is moving the bottleneck to another set of links. Clearly, using IGP metrics for traffic engineering doesn't provide for fine-grained control. We need a better method. One option, ATM networks, is discussed next.

ATM and Overlay Networks

During the mid-1990s, ISPs saw traffic levels across their backbones rise dramatically. The Internet was growing in popularity, and more users and websites meant more traffic. The IGP-routed core didn't provide enough interface speed or deterministic control to face these new traffic patterns. Most ISPs turned to ATM as a core technology. Interface speeds for ATM networks started at OC-3 (155.52Mbps) and grew to OC-12 (622.08Mbps). In addition, the ATM core used virtual circuits (VCs) to logically connect the routers, as shown in Figure 11.3.

FIGURE 11.3   ATM overlay network–logical view

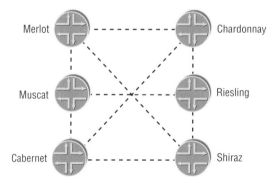

Each VC connection in the network appears as a point-to-point interface from the perspective of the router. In reality, however, the physical ATM connectivity may be quite different. Figure 11.4 shows this second set of connections.

FIGURE 11.4   ATM overlay network–physical view

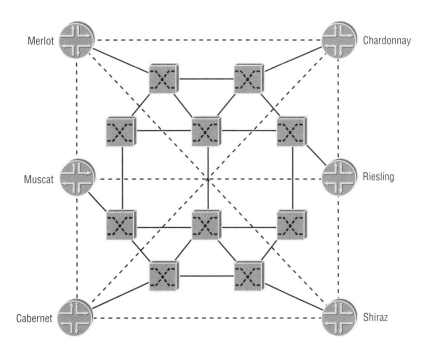

This environment was commonly called an *overlay network*, since multiple distinct networks were operating in parallel. (In our example, the ATM network routes packets and cells at Layer 2, while the IP network routes packets between distinct VCs at Layer 3.) From a traffic engineering perspective, an overlay network provided for better control because the physical path was determined by the VC setup and not by the IGP metrics between the routers. When the traffic statistics revealed that a physical link was overutilized in an overlay network, the ATM VC connection was moved to another path. The IP network and its routers, however, did not see this change and happily routed packets over the VC using the IGP metrics.

Overlay networks also provided other benefits to the ISPs. One such benefit was the ability to gather statistics on a per-VC basis. In an IGP-routed core, the statistics on a physical link showed only the total amount of traffic across that connection. You didn't know who the recipients of the packets were or what types of traffic were using the link. When ATM VCs were introduced into this picture, the statistics on that physical media had some segmentation to them. Each VC on the link connected two routers, and traffic flows between those routers were now visible.

Of course, the overlay network solution had its drawbacks as well. Each of the networks (ATM and IP) required engineers and support staff who specialized in their operation, placing a drain on company resources. The separation of knowledge in the overall network also meant that the switches and routers couldn't share responsibility for engineering traffic flows. Finally, there was the issue of the ATM *cell tax*. Each 53-byte ATM cell forwarded through the network carried with it a 5-byte header and 48 bytes of payload. The transmission of the ATM headers added up to a significant amount of bandwidth. For example, it took two cells to send a 64-byte IP packet across the network. The total bandwidth used by these cells was 106 bytes. The extra 42 bytes of used transmission capacity was not beneficial to the network as a whole and represented almost 40 percent of wasted bandwidth. While this is an extreme case, the ATM cell tax averaged between 10 and 20 percent.

ISPs were willing to live with the drawbacks of the overlay model as long as the disadvantages were outweighed by the benefits, namely the higher interface speeds. This benefit started to dwindle at the end of the 1990s as backbone traffic increased at a steady rate. ATM interface speeds remained at OC-12 capacity with no increase in sight. The main barrier to a faster interface was the hardware responsible for the ATM segmentation and reassembly (SAR) process. ATM vendors found it very difficult to produce OC-48 and OC-192 SAR hardware at an affordable price. Consequently, neither of these speeds was ever brought to market in large quantities. Faster speeds were needed to handle the increased traffic flows.

SONET and MPLS

As the end of the 1990s approached, router vendors were able to produce interfaces that operated with the Synchronous Optical Network (SONET) specification. This allowed interface and backbone speeds to increase to OC-48/STM-16 (2488.32Mbps/2.5Gbps) and OC-192/STM-48 (9953.28Mbps/10Gbps) capacity. While ISPs were happy with this development, they wanted to enjoy the benefits of the ATM overlay network model as well. This became the function of MPLS.

In an MPLS-based network, only IP knowledgeable devices exist to route traffic across the network. The routers are connected with point-to-point WAN interfaces running an IGP. This type of model is seen in Figure 11.5.

FIGURE 11.5   MPLS and IP–based network

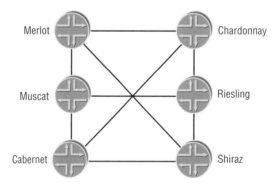

At first glance, this looks like a regular IGP-routed core with faster interfaces. However, the addition of MPLS as an operating protocol greatly alters the operation of the network. Each router now has the ability to create a label switched path (LSP) to any other router in the network. This path can traverse any number of physical links in the network.

Figure 11.6 shows an MPLS path from Cabernet to Chardonnay. This new network path physically uses the Cabernet-Muscat, Muscat-Merlot, and Merlot-Chardonnay links instead of the directly connected Cabernet-Chardonnay link. Like an ATM VC, this is a logical connection that provides connectivity between two routers. It is able to move to other physical links should traffic statistics reveal a bottleneck in the network. It also has the ability to provide statistics on a per-path basis. These are all benefits that ISPs received from the overlay network model.

FIGURE 11.6   MPLS network path

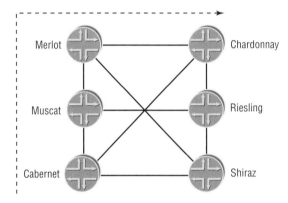

An MPLS-based network also mitigates many of the disadvantages of an overlay network. The ability to use any physical transmission media allows higher backbone and interface capacity. In addition, the ATM cell tax is eliminated. The removal of ATM also reduces the network support costs—all traffic now uses the IP-based network.

The use of MPLS as a forwarding mechanism provides ISPs with an even finer-grained method for traffic engineering than they received from ATM. The traffic using an MPLS network path is now a single IP subnet. Let's contrast this to an ATM VC in the overlay network. Multiple logical VCs were able to use a single physical link, and statistics from those connections showed traffic flows between two individual routers. In an MPLS network, multiple paths can exist between those two routers, with individual IP subnets using different paths. Traffic flows between the routers are now visible to the ISP on a per-destination basis.

Now that we've examined why MPLS is being used today, let's explore how it actually works.

MPLS Operations

MPLS is still an evolving protocol, but it is supported by the vast majority of routing vendors. As a new creation, it has its own set of terms and operational parameters to use for proper operation. In this section, we discuss the MPLS terminology and then look at methods for establishing MPLS network paths.

Multiprotocol Label Switching Standards

The JUNOS software currently supports the following RFCs and Internet drafts:

- RFC 2702, "Requirements for Traffic Engineering over MPLS"

- RFC 3031, "Multiprotocol Label Switching Architecture"

- RFC 3032, "MPLS Label Stack Encoding"

- Internet draft draft-ietf-isis-traffic-02.txt, "IS-IS Extensions for Traffic Engineering"

- Internet draft draft-katz-yeung-ospf-traffic-04.txt, "Traffic Engineering Extensions to OSPF"

- Internet draft draft-ietf-mpls-icmp-02.txt, "ICMP Extensions for Multiprotocol Label Switching"

Internet drafts are limited in scope and are updated on a frequent basis. Please check www.ietf.org for the current names and status of listed drafts.

Terminology

The path created in an MPLS network is called a label switched path. Each MPLS enabled router in the network is considered a label switching router. Finally, the actual forwarding of packets is accomplished using a header value that contains a numeric label value. Let's take a closer look at what these terms actually mean.

Label Switched Path (LSP)

Each network path created by the MPLS protocol is a *label switched path (LSP)*. This path is a unidirectional entity that typically exists within a single autonomous system or domain. This one-way traffic flow is different from that of many ATM VCs, which are usually established in a bidirectional manner. The use of a unidirectional system allows you ultimate control of your traffic but does require LSPs to be established in both the transmit and receive directions for total traffic engineering in the network.

> ## Real World Scenario
>
> ### Are We Running Out of Acronyms?
>
> So, an MPLS network path is called a label switched path (LSP). You may recall from Chapter 7, "IS-IS," that the acronym LSP also means a link-state PDU. Clearly, the networking world has run out of usable acronyms. We first started using acronyms from other industries. ATM is both Asynchronous Transfer Mode as well as an Automatic Teller Machine (where you get money from the bank). Now we need to reuse our own internal acronyms. The Internet is about to collapse!
>
> Well, that's not actually true, but it makes a great story for non-networking people. In reality, we haven't run out of acronyms. We've just reused one for a good cause!
>
> The point of all this bantering is to make sure that you are certain of your surroundings before using the term LSP. In a mixed crowd, some people may hear *link-state PDU* while others might hear *label switched path*. Within the course of this chapter, LSP means a label switched path.

Label Switching Routers (LSR)

Each IP router that supports the MPLS protocol is called a *label switching router (LSR)*. An LSR understands the MPLS header and the values encoded within it. The LSR is also responsible for the actual forwarding of user data traffic through the established LSP.

There are four different types of LSRs: ingress, transit, penultimate, and egress. Figure 11.7 shows an established LSP with each type of LSR displayed.

FIGURE 11.7   MPLS router types

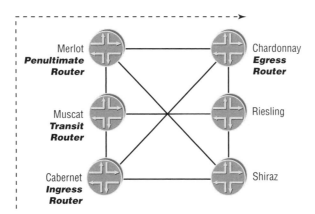

The unidirectional LSP is set up from Cabernet to Chardonnay. As such, Cabernet is the ingress router and Chardonnay is the egress router. All other routers within the LSP are considered transit routers. In Figure 11.7, both Muscat and Merlot are transit routers. However, Merlot is also the last router prior to the egress router, making it the penultimate router. Each LSR type performs specific functions within the LSP operation. Let's examine these a little closer.

Ingress Router

The *ingress router* in an LSP is the only entry point for user data traffic into MPLS. Native IPv4 packets are encapsulated into the MPLS protocol at this location by way of a *label push operation*. Once encapsulated, packets flow to the egress of the LSP in a downstream fashion. Hence, the ingress router is upstream from the perspective of the data flow.

Each LSP in a network must have an ingress router. In addition, only a single ingress router may exist per LSP.

Transit Router

All routers located in the middle of an LSP are considered *transit routers*. An individual path can contain between 0 and 253 such routers. In the sample LSP in Figure 11.7, two transit routers exist, Muscat and Merlot. Should an LSP be configured between Cabernet and Shiraz, no transit routers would exist.

The upper limit of transit routers in an LSP is a function of the 8-bit TTL field of the MPLS label, with a maximum value of 255. Both the ingress and egress routers belong to the LSP, leaving 253 other possible hops along the path.

The function of a transit router is quite simple. The router checks all received MPLS packets for an incoming label value, which it then looks up in an MPLS forwarding table. After locating the label, the transit router performs a *label swap operation* by replacing the incoming label with an outgoing label value and decrements the MPLS TTL by 1. The router then forwards the newly labeled data packet to the next hop of the LSP. This entire operation never utilizes the information in the IP data header.

Penultimate Router

One of the transit routers in an LSP—the *penultimate router*—has a special function to perform. This router, which is second to last along the path of the LSP, often performs a *label pop operation* to remove the MPLS information from the data packet. After consulting the MPLS switching table, the router forwards the resulting data, a native IPv4 packet, to the next hop in the LSP after decrementing the TTL value by 1.

Performing this de-encapsulation function on the penultimate router results in scalability. Figure 11.8 shows a network with multiple LSPs established. Three of the LSPs end at Chardonnay. Each of the LSPs has a different penultimate router along the path. If Chardonnay is responsible for de-encapsulating all MPLS packets from the three LSPs, it performs a certain amount of work. This workload increases as the number of LSPs ending on Chardonnay increases. Imagine if 50 LSPs terminate there, or 100, or even 1000. The effort exerted by Chardonnay increases dramatically. If we move the de-encapsulation function to the penultimate router, however, the workload of the label pop operation is spread across a greater number of routers. This *penultimate hop popping (PHP)* system allows an MPLS network to scale to greater proportions.

FIGURE 11.8   Benefits of the penultimate router

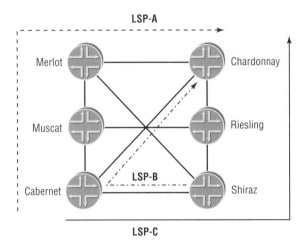

 A Juniper Networks router performs penultimate hop popping (PHP) by default on all dynamic LSPs.

Egress Router

The *egress router* is the end point of the LSP. The egress router receives packets from the penultimate router and performs an IPv4 route lookup operation. The router then forwards the data packet to the next hop of the route. From a directionality perspective, the egress router is downstream to all other routers in the LSP.

Each LSP in the network must have an egress router. As is the case with its ingress partner, only a single egress router may exist per LSP.

Popping the MPLS Label

Our definition of each router's role along the path of an LSP assumes the default JUNOS software behavior of penultimate hop popping (PHP). In this case, the penultimate transit router in the LSP performs the label pop operation. Another option exists for popping the MPLS label from the data packet—ultimate hop popping.

> Ultimate hop popping occurs when the egress router itself performs the label pop operation. This requires the egress router to perform two operations on the data packet: the label pop and an IPv4 lookup to forward the packet. This dual operation places a larger processing burden on the egress router, which prompts the use of PHP.
>
> The technical difference between PHP and ultimate hop popping comes in the action of the egress router. Based on its current configuration, the egress router signals different MPLS labels upstream to the penultimate router. A label value of 3 means the upstream router should perform PHP and forward native IPv4 packets. A label value of 0, on the other hand, tells the upstream router to perform a label-swap operation and to forward the data with an MPLS header attached. (We discuss the definitions of the MPLS label values in the "Labels" section of this chapter.) A Juniper Networks router performs ultimate hop popping when the explicit-null command is applied.

Labels

The forwarding of user data traffic through an MPLS network is accomplished by *label values* assigned by the MPLS routers themselves. This assignment occurs in an upstream direction through a manual or dynamic process. The downstream router, in essence, informs the upstream router what label value to use when sending traffic along the LSP. When the downstream router receives that label value, it swaps the label with the value assigned by *its* downstream router. This exchange of labels between two routers on a single link results in the label value having *local significance* only. This means that a specific value, say 100101, may appear on multiple links in a network simultaneously. This is a similar concept to both ATM and Frame Relay networks and provides for excellent scalability of the network.

The assigned labels are encoded as part of a 32-bit MPLS *shim header* that the ingress router adds to the packet. The router places this header between the IP packet and the appropriate Layer 2 header for the physical link, as shown in Figure 11.9.

FIGURE 11.9   MPLS shim header

Layer 2 Header	MPLS Header	IP Packet

The format of the MPLS header is shown in Figure 11.10 and consists of the following fields:

FIGURE 11.10   MPLS header details

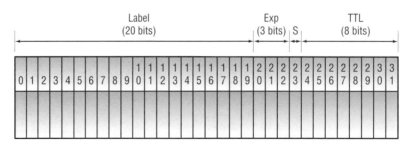

Label (20 bits)   This field contains a locally significant value specifying that a packet belongs to a certain LSP. Possible values range from 0 to 1,048,576.

Experimental Bits (3 bits)   Listed as experimental due to standards work, this field was always intended for use as a Class of Service (CoS) field. The particular type of CoS is still undetermined, hence the experimental title.

Stacking Bit (1 bit)   This field indicates whether an IP packet or another MPLS header follows the current header. A value of 1 represents an IP packet, and a value of 0 means other MPLS headers follow.

Time to Live (8 bits)   The same as the TTL field in an IP header, this prevents looping MPLS packets in the network. Each router decrements this field by 1, and any value of 0 results in a dropped packet. The default action for an LSP is to copy the IP TTL value to the header at ingress and copy the MPLS TTL value back to the IP packet when the label is popped.

The Internet Engineering Task Force (IETF) reserves some label values for standardized use on all MPLS routers. These values are in the range of 0 through 15. Their meanings, as defined by the IETF, are:

0 – IPv4 Explicit NULL   This entry is valid only as a label when an IPv4 packet follows the MPLS header. It indicates that the label must be popped and a route lookup performed for packet forwarding.

1 – Router Alert Label   This entry indicates that the packet should be sent to the Routing Engine for processing; the packet should not be forwarded based on the incoming label value.

2 – IPv6 Explicit NULL   This entry is valid only as a label when an IPv6 packet follows the MPLS header. It indicates that the label must be popped and a route lookup performed for packet forwarding.

3 – Implicit NULL   This label value should never appear in an MPLS header. A router receiving this value from its downstream neighbor should pop the label of all received MPLS packets and forward the remaining data to the downstream router using the information in the local MPLS switching table. This action is performed instead of performing a swap operation on the local router. This label value is used for penultimate hop popping.

4 – 15   These label values are reserved for future use.

Packet Processing

Now that we have the basic terminology under our belt, let's examine how a data packet is actually forwarded through an MPLS network. Figure 11.11 shows a sample network with an LSP and some assigned labels.

FIGURE 11.11 MPLS packet processing

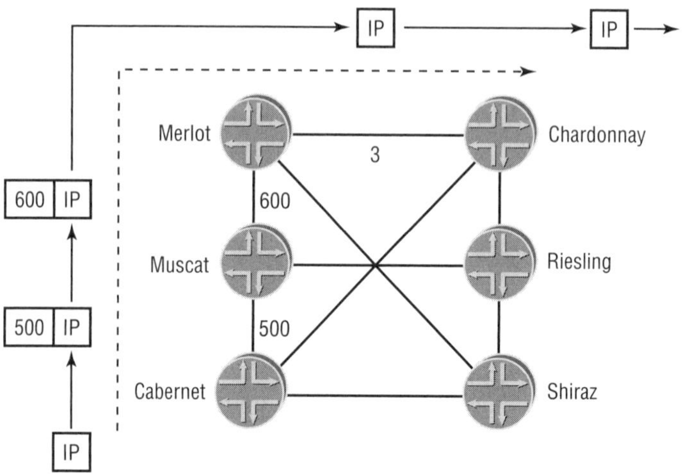

As you can see, an LSP has been established from Cabernet to Chardonnay. All downstream routers have assigned label values to their upstream neighbors; Chardonnay has assigned 3, Merlot 600, and Muscat 500. When an IP packet arrives at the ingress router of Cabernet, the following sequence occurs:

1. Cabernet performs an IPv4 route lookup on the destination IP address. It finds the next hop for the route is the LSP to Chardonnay. An MPLS header is added to the packet with a label value of 500 and forwarded to Muscat.

2. Muscat receives an MPLS packet with a label of 500. It performs an MPLS forwarding table lookup and finds a swap operation. It removes the label of 500 and replaces it with a label of 600. The packet is forwarded to the next hop along the LSP.

3. Merlot receives an MPLS packet with a label of 600. It performs an MPLS forwarding table lookup and finds a pop operation since its downstream peer advertised a value of 3. Merlot removes the MPLS header from the packet and forwards the remaining data (IPv4 packet) to the next hop of the LSP.

4. Chardonnay receives an IPv4 packet. It performs a routing table lookup and forwards the packet to the next hop of the route.

One of the keys to a successful packet transmission is correctly assigned labels. This occurs as part of the establishment of the LSP itself, so let's now discuss those various methods.

Establishing an LSP

An MPLS label switch path is established by one of two methods: static or dynamic. Each method carries with it both advantages and disadvantages, as we see in the following sections.

Static Label Switched Paths

A *static label switched path* requires that each router along the LSP be configured explicitly. This is very similar to static IPv4 routes, where each hop along the path requires a static route.

One benefit to establishing a static LSP is the simple and straightforward manner of its operation. You decide where the LSP should go and what labels it should use, and you assign those resources. Static LSPs also consume fewer router resources than dynamic LSPs do. No signaling protocol is operated, and no state information is required to be maintained. Again, this is similar to static routes, which require fewer resources than routes that use a routing protocol.

Of course, the same reasons for not using static routes in a network also apply to static LSPs. The lack of knowledge about topology changes means that traffic may be black-holed during an outage. Static LSPs are active until you change their parameters in the configuration, and the process of making those changes on multiple routers is prone to error.

Dynamic Label Switched Paths

To achieve visibility into the LSP, use a *dynamic label switched path*. As the name implies, a signaling protocol creates and maintains an LSP with no user intervention. Only the ingress router is configured with the information concerning the LSP; all other routers receive signaling messages during the establishment process.

Your ability to control the setup parameters of the LSP depends primarily on your choice of a signaling protocol. The JUNOS software supports two methods of signaling an LSP, which is our next topic of discussion.

ATM VC versus MPLS LSP

As you read the "The History of Traffic Engineering and MPLS" section earlier in this chapter, you saw the very strong relationship between ATM and MPLS. Partly due to history and partly due to a similar switching paradigm, the concepts are closely aligned. As such, it might be useful to draw some correlations between a virtual circuit (VC) and a label switched path (LSP).

Static LSPs are very similar to ATM permanent virtual circuits (PVCs). Both paths are manually created along each hop and remain *nailed up* until a configuration change alters the path. There is absolutely no flexibility or contingency to the establishment and maintenance of the path. Should a node along the path stop functioning, the entire path fails to function. No fail-over capabilities are in place.

Dynamic LSPs, on the other hand, are very similar to ATM switched virtual circuits (SVCs). Both use a signaling protocol to establish the path, and configuration is needed only at the head-end node. Furthermore, a link or node problem along the path does not bring the path down. The signaling protocol establishes a new path through the network, provided an alternate path exists.

Signaling Protocols

The two signaling protocols supported in the JUNOS software are the Resource Reservation Protocol (RSVP) and the Label Distribution Protocol (LDP). RSVP is a generic signaling protocol that has been adapted for use in MPLS. LDP, on the other hand, was designed explicitly for use with MPLS. The two protocols are fully independent from each other but can be used at the same time in a network.

Resource Reservation Protocol

The IETF designed the *Resource Reservation Protocol (RSVP)* as a method for allowing end hosts to reserve capacity in a network. The theory is that applications required a certain quality of network service standards to operate correctly. RSVP is a method aimed at accomplishing this goal. Widespread use of RSVP for its original purpose never occurred for a number of reasons, one being that ISPs didn't want their customers altering the network configuration. The protocol has been extended to support traffic engineering capabilities and is currently used to establish MPLS LSPs.

Some portions of the original specification are still used, so we cover those first. We then explore more deeply the extensions to the protocol for MPLS use.

RSVP Basics

RSVP uses unidirectional and simplex (one-way) flows through the network to perform its function. The ingress router initiates an RSVP *Path message* and sends it downstream to the egress router. This Path message contains information about the requested resources of the connection. Each router along the path begins to maintain a *soft state* connection for this reservation. You can think of the soft state as a database of current reservations affecting the local router.

When the Path message reaches the egress router, the actual reservation of resources begins. This happens with an *RSVP Resv message*, which is initiated by the egress router and sent upstream to the ingress router. Each router along the path receives the Resv message and sends it upstream, following the route used by the Path message. In addition, more soft state information is added to each local router. Once the ingress router receives the Resv message that matches its original Path message, the unidirectional network path is established.

The established network path remains operational as long as the RSVP soft state stays active. This is accomplished through a refresh mechanism where each local router sends Path and Resv messages to its neighbors for all current states every 30 seconds. This informs those neighbors of active paths and assists them in maintaining their own local soft state. The flow of Path and Resv messages in a network is seen in Figure 11.12.

FIGURE 11.12   RSVP Path and Resv messages

In addition to the `Path` and `Resv` messages, RSVP defines these message types:

PathTear message   The *PathTear message* always travels downstream to the egress router. It removes the established `Path` soft state for all routers receiving the message. A transit node sends this message when an outage occurs. The ingress router may also use it when the path is no longer desired.

ResvTear message   The *ResvTear message* always travels upstream to the ingress router. It removes the established `Resv` soft state for all routers receiving the message. A transit node sends this message when an outage occurs.

PathErr message   The *PathErr message* always travels upstream to the ingress router. It denotes an error along the established path. No soft state is removed by routers receiving this message type.

ResvErr message   The *ResvErr message* always travels downstream to the egress router. It denotes an error along the established path. No soft state is removed by routers receiving this message type.

ResvConf message   The egress router may ask each node along the path for a confirmation that the `Resv` message was received. The *ResvConf message* type provides that confirmation message.

RSVP Extensions

The RSVP extensions to support MPLS LSPs allow label-specific information to be encoded in the `Path` and `Resv` messages. In addition, path maintenance and scalability issues are addressed.

The soft state information described in the previous "RSVP Basics" section remains active on a local router for approximately three minutes. Many ISPs desire a quicker response to network changes and outages than the soft state allows. To combat this issue, extended RSVP uses a *hello mechanism*. Each RSVP router sends a hello message to its neighbors every 9 seconds, by default. When a router stops sending hello messages, its neighbors detect the change in 63 seconds and advertise the appropriate error messages. This extension is backward compatible with the original RSVP specification. Should a neighbor not support the hello mechanism, the soft state timers are used.

When each router sends `Path` and `Resv` messages to refresh the soft state database, it does so for each established path in the database. As the number of paths grows, the local router sends additional messages to its neighbors. For scalability, RSVP now supports *message aggregation*, which allows a router to bundle up to 30 messages into a single packet before sending it to a neighbor. `Path`, `Resv`, hello, and error messages are suitable for this aggregation function.

A primary goal of extending RSVP is to support MPLS LSPs. As such, some of the additions to the protocol specifically account for the establishment and maintenance of traffic-engineered LSPs. The extensions include a number of objects that are encoded within the `Path` and `Resv` messages.

EXPLICIT ROUTE OBJECT

The *explicit route object (ERO)* allows the `Path` message to traverse the network using information that is independent of the IGP shortest path. The ingress router adds the ERO to the `Path` message, and all transit routers must follow the specifications outlined in the object.

A configured ERO may contain only *loose hops*. This specifies that the LSP must transit the specified nodes in the object in the order given. The IGP shortest path is used between the loose hop nodes.

Figure 11.13 shows an LSP using a loose hop ERO. Here, the only specified transit router in the ERO is Merlot, with an attribute of `loose`. The ingress router (Cabernet) and all other transit routers use the IGP routing table to send the `Path` message toward Merlot. Merlot examines the ERO and finds no other specified nodes. It then forwards the `Path` message toward the egress router using its IGP routing table.

FIGURE 11.13   ERO using loose hops

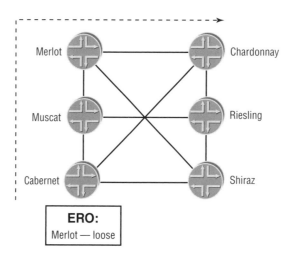

The opposite of a loose hop in an ERO is a *strict hop*. When you use a strict hop, you are informing the network of the exact path you wish the LSP to take. Each router examines the defined ERO and forwards the `Path` message to the next router listed. The next-hop router must be directly attached to the local router for this process to succeed.

Figure 11.14 details an LSP established using a strict hop ERO. Each hop along the LSP path is specified in the ERO. The ingress router determines if Muscat is directly connected to itself. This is the case in our network, so the `Path` message is forwarded to Muscat. Muscat performs the same function. It finds Merlot is directly attached and forwards the `Path` message appropriately. Merlot examines the ERO, determines that Chardonnay is directly attached, and forwards the `Path` message. Chardonnay receives the `Path` message and notices that no more nodes are listed in the ERO and that the egress router address equals a local interface address. It then terminates the `Path` message and generates a `Resv` message back along the path.

FIGURE 11.14   ERO using strict hops

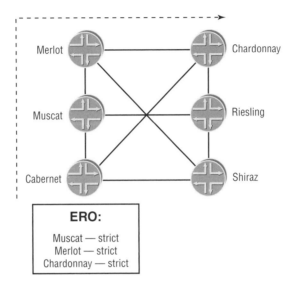

ERO:

Muscat — strict
Merlot — strict
Chardonnay — strict

 WARNING   Failure to have an ERO strict hop directly connected results in an error message. The requested LSP is not established in this condition.

Some situations might call for an ERO that contains both loose and strict hops. This is a perfectly allowable condition that extended RSVP can handle. The requested LSP becomes established when each router has a route to the loose hops and all strict hops are directly connected. Figure 11.15 shows an example of an ERO using both forms of next hops.

FIGURE 11.15   ERO using both loose and strict hops

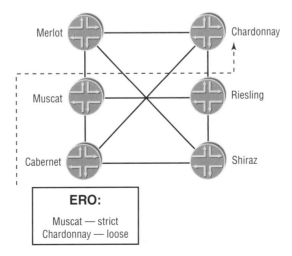

ERO:

Muscat — strict
Chardonnay — loose

In this case, only a single strict hop is configured. Cabernet, the ingress router, finds that Muscat is directly connected and forwards the Path message to the next hop. Muscat examines the ERO and finds that the next hop is loosely defined. It then uses its IGP routing table to forward the Path message. In this example, it arrives at Riesling. Riesling performs a routing lookup to find the loose hop and forwards the Path message to Chardonnay.

LABEL REQUEST OBJECT

The *label request object* is encoded in the Path messages sent to the egress router. This object allows each router to assign a label value to the requested LSP. When the Path message is received, the local router allocates a label and stores it with the Path soft state for that LSP. When the Resv message arrives from the downstream neighbor, the label is advertised upstream in an RSVP label object.

LABEL OBJECT

The *label object* is carried within the Resv messages sent to the ingress router. The object allows each router along the path to advertise its assigned label value to each upstream router.

RECORD ROUTE OBJECT

The *record route object (RRO)* can be encoded in both a Path and a Resv message. The primary purpose of the RRO is loop detection. A router does not forward an RSVP message if the current RRO lists an interface belonging to the local router.

The ingress router generates the Path message and includes the RRO. As the Path message moves downstream, each router along the path adds its outgoing interface address to the RRO. Should a loop be encountered, the Path message is dropped. A PathErr message is generated by that node and sent to the ingress reporting a "routing problem, loop detected" error.

The process works the same in reverse, with the egress router generating a Resv message with an RRO. As the Resv message moves upstream, each router along the path adds its outgoing interface address to the object. If a loop is found, the Resv message is dropped. A ResvErr message is generated by that node and sent to the egress reporting a "routing problem, loop detected" error.

SESSION ATTRIBUTE OBJECT

The *session attribute object* is contained within a Path message. MPLS routers use this object to control the priority, preemption, affinity class, and local-rerouting capabilities of the LSP. In addition, the ingress router may place an ASCII string in the session attribute object. This string assists users in identifying an LSP on each router in the network.

TSPEC OBJECT

The *tspec object* (or traffic specifier object)is also encoded within an RSVP Path message. It contains information such as the requested bandwidth of the LSP. Each MPLS router uses this data to determine whether the LSP should become established. The tspec object also contains the minimum and maximum packet sizes supported along the path of the LSP.

Label Distribution Protocol

The *Label Distribution Protocol (LDP)* is the second method for signaling the establishment of an LSP. Unlike RSVP, LDP is a new protocol designed specifically for use with MPLS.

LDP detects neighbors using a Hello protocol. Once a neighbor is found, an LDP router establishes a TCP session with that peer to exchange label information. Each set of established LDP peers generates a set of labels for inclusion in the LDP database, which is advertised throughout the network. Every LDP router then consults its database to determine the label required to reach every other LDP router in the network.

 Real World Scenario

Policing Traffic in MPLS

When learning about the capabilities of the MPLS signaling protocols, many users focus on the bandwidth request capabilities of RSVP. It is very important to know what the limitations and functions of this request entails.

We've been happily drawing similarities between ATM and MPLS throughout this chapter. This is one case where this comparison breaks down. Bandwidth requests in an ATM network mean that each node along the path actively monitors the traffic flows. Should the amount of traffic exceed the requested amount, the excess traffic is dropped from the network. In short, ATM nodes perform policing functions.

An MPLS bandwidth request, however, does no such thing. No policing functions are performed within the MPLS routers. The purpose of the request is only to determine whether the LSP should be established. There is no inherent guarantee that the requested bandwidth is available in the network.

This is not to say that you can't do policing in an MPLS network. In fact, you can. However, this function must be accomplished outside the MPLS and RSVP protocols. On a Juniper Networks router, policing functions are part of the firewall filter syntax (see Chapter 10, "Firewall Filters").

MPLS Implementation

Now that we've covered the theory of MPLS, let's discuss how the protocol is implemented within the JUNOS software. We first explore how to establish an LSP using a static configuration. Next, we look at how RSVP is used for dynamic signaling. Finally, we discuss how user traffic actually enters and uses the LSP for traffic forwarding.

Configuring a Static LSP

In the "Establishing an LSP" section earlier in this chapter, we stated that each router must be configured to support a static LSP. While this is a good general statement to make, some more detail is needed. In fact, each router requires the ability to support the MPLS protocol as well as interpret MPLS packets received on an interface. When it comes to the LSP itself, the ingress and all transit routers must be correctly configured.

Let's explore the steps required to configure static LSPs within the JUNOS software. We first configure `family mpls` on all the router interfaces. We then enable the MPLS protocol on the router and configure the routers themselves for the static LSP.

Configuring Interfaces

An interface on a Juniper Networks router accepts only IP packets by default. You must configure the router interfaces to recognize other protocol types. In this case, each interface must be aware that MPLS packets are important and should be accepted as well. To do this, you use the `family mpls` command, as in this example:

```
[edit]
user@Cabernet# set interfaces so-0/0/0 unit 0 family mpls
```

The `show interfaces terse` command reveals that Cabernet's interface is now correctly configured:

```
lab@Cabernet> show interfaces terse
Interface       Admin Link Proto Local                 Remote
so-0/0/0        up    up
so-0/0/0.0      up    up    inet  10.100.10.1/24
                            iso
                            mpls
so-0/0/1        up    up
so-0/0/2        up    up
so-0/0/3        up    down
fxp0            up    up
fxp0.0          up    up    inet  10.250.0.121/16
fxp1            up    up
fxp1.0          up    up    tnp   4
gre             up    up
ipip            up    up
lo0             up    up
lo0.0           up    up    inet  192.168.1.1           --> 0/0
                            iso   49.1111.0192.0168.0101.00
lsi             up    up
```

Configuring the Protocol

From the perspective of the Routing Engine, MPLS is just another protocol. As such, it requires some configuration within the [edit protocols] hierarchy. Within this directory, you must assign each transit interface that supports MPLS.

Let's suppose the Muscat router wants all transit interfaces to support MPLS traffic. The configuration looks like this:

```
[edit protocols]
user@Muscat# show
mpls {
    interface all;
    interface fxp0.0 {
        disable;
    }
}
```

Once you commit the configuration, the router creates the mpls.0 routing table and places three entries in it. You can see this by issuing the show route table mpls.0 command:

```
user@Muscat> show route table mpls.0

mpls.0: 2 destinations, 2 routes (2 active, 0 holddown, 0 hidden)
+ = Active Route, - = Last Active, * = Both

0                  *[MPLS/0] 00:11:26, metric 1
                      Receive
1                  *[MPLS/0] 00:11:26, metric 1
                      Receive
2                  *[MPLS/0] 00:11:26, metric 1
                      Receive
```

Referring back to the "Labels" section earlier in this chapter, the three preestablished entries correspond to the IPv4 Explicit NULL (0), the Router Alert label (1), and the IPv6 Explicit NULL (2). Notice that each label has a next-hop value of Receive. This sends all packets matching this value to the Routing Engine for further processing.

This next hop makes sense if you recall the meaning of these special label values. The 0 label means that the receiving router should perform a label pop operation and then perform an IPv4 route lookup. The 1 label requires the receiving router to process the packet by the routing process and not perform a forwarding table lookup. The 2 label means that the receiving router should perform a label pop operation and then perform an IPv6 route lookup.

In reality, when a Juniper Networks router receives a label value of 0, the packet does not go to the Routing Engine. All processing is instead completed in hardware. The incoming I/O Manager ASIC on the Flexible PIC Concentrator (FPC) performs the label pop operation. The resulting IP packet is then turned into J-Cells and stored in packet memory. The Internet Processor ASIC performs a regular IPv4 route lookup on the packet and forwards it to the appropriate next hop.

Configuring the Static LSP

We are now ready to configure the actual LSP. We would like the LSP to operate between Cabernet and Chardonnay, as shown in Figure 11.16. You can see the label values assigned to the links. Cabernet uses label 912 to forward packets to Muscat. Muscat uses label 36 to forward packets to Merlot. Merlot uses label 0 when sending packets to Chardonnay, the egress router.

FIGURE 11.16 Static LSP label assignments

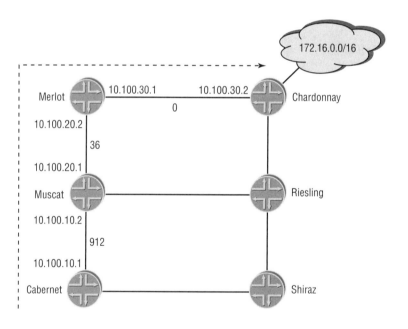

 The IETF reserved label values 0 through 15. The JUNOS software sets aside label values 16 through 1023 for use with static LSPs. A Juniper Networks router can use a dynamic advertisement from a downstream neighbor from within this range. This range simply means that the JUNOS software will never use those values when generating its own dynamic label values.

Next, we configure the ingress router, followed by the two transit routers. The egress router does not need any special configuration at this point. It performs a label pop when it receives the 0 label from the penultimate router.

Configuring the Ingress Router

We want Cabernet to use MPLS to forward traffic to the 172.16.0.0 /16 subnet attached to Chardonnay. The following command accomplishes this goal:

```
[edit protocols mpls]
user@Cabernet# set static-path inet 172.16/16 push 912 next-hop 10.100.10.2
```

The configuration now looks like this:

```
[edit protocols mpls]
user@Cabernet# show
static-path inet {
    172.16.0.0/16 {
        next-hop 10.100.10.2;
        push 912;
    }
}
interface all;
```

The MPLS-specific information for this route now appears in the `inet.0` routing table on Cabernet, as shown here:

```
user@Cabernet> show route table inet.0

inet.0: 11 destinations, 11 routes (11 active, 0 holddown, 0 hidden)
+ = Active Route, - = Last Active, * = Both

10.100.10.0/24     *[Direct/0] 00:42:17
                    > via so-0/0/0.0
10.100.10.1/32     *[Local/0] 00:45:57
                       Local via so-0/0/0.0
10.100.20.0/24     *[IS-IS/15] 00:34:41, metric 20, tag 1
                    > to 10.100.10.2 via so-0/0/0.0
10.100.30.0/24     *[IS-IS/15] 00:33:45, metric 30, tag 1
                    > to 10.100.10.2 via so-0/0/0.0
172.16.0.0/16      *[Static/5] 00:00:33
                    > to 10.100.10.2 via so-0/0/0.0, Push 912
192.168.1.1/32     *[Direct/0] 00:45:57
                    > via lo0.0
```

```
192.168.2.2/32     *[IS-IS/15] 00:41:50, metric 10, tag 1
                    > to 10.100.10.2 via so-0/0/0.0
192.168.3.3/32     *[IS-IS/15] 00:34:22, metric 20, tag 1
                    > to 10.100.10.2 via so-0/0/0.0
192.168.4.4/32     *[IS-IS/15] 00:33:22, metric 30, tag 1
                    > to 10.100.10.2 via so-0/0/0.0
```

All route lookups for 172.16.0.0/16 result in label 912 being added to the packet. The result-ing MPLS information is forwarded to Muscat on the interface so-0/0/0.0.

 A static LSP is assigned to the Static protocol within the routing table, making it no different from a regular static route.

Configuring the Transit Routers

The configuration on each of the transit routers is similar. The incoming interface and label value must be identified. Let's configure the resulting label operation first, followed by the next hop of the LSP.

We configure Muscat first. It should watch for label 912 on its interface to Cabernet—so-0/0/0.0. Muscat should swap label 912 with label 36 and send the packet to Merlot's interface of 10.100.20.2. We use the following commands to accomplish this:

```
[edit protocols mpls]
user@Muscat# set interface so-0/0/0 label-map 912 swap 36
user@Muscat# set interface so-0/0/0 label-map 912 next-hop 10.100.20.2
```

The resulting configuration now appears as:

```
[edit protocols mpls]
user@Muscat# show
interface all;
interface so-0/0/0.0 {
    label-map 912 {
        next-hop 10.100.20.2;
        swap 36;
    }
}
```

The Merlot router is similarly configured as:

```
[edit protocols mpls]
user@Merlot# show
interface all;
interface so-0/0/0.0 {
```

```
    label-map 36 {
        next-hop 10.100.30.2;
        swap 0;
    }
}
```

Once committed, the label operations are visible in the mpls.0 table:

```
user@Merlot> show route table mpls.0

mpls.0: 3 destinations, 3 routes (3 active, 0 holddown, 0 hidden)
+ = Active Route, - = Last Active, * = Both

0                     *[MPLS/0] 00:49:20, metric 1
                         Receive
1                     *[MPLS/0] 00:49:20, metric 1
                         Receive
2                     *[MPLS/0] 00:49:20, metric 1
                         Receive
36                    *[Static/5] 00:00:06
                       > to 10.100.30.2 via so-0/0/2.0, Swap 0
```

The addresses used in the next-hop command represent the address of a directly connected router. This is an important concept since recursive IP route lookups are not performed inside the LSP.

Verifying the Operation

We've already seen that Cabernet has an IP route in inet.0 for the 172.16.0.0 /16 subnet. However, like a static route, this does not prove end-to-end connectivity. Let's see if the ingress router can ping the subnet:

```
user@Cabernet> ping 172.16.1.1
PING 172.16.1.1 (172.16.1.1): 56 data bytes
64 bytes from 172.16.1.1: icmp_seq=0 ttl=252 time=1.059 ms
64 bytes from 172.16.1.1: icmp_seq=1 ttl=252 time=0.976 ms
64 bytes from 172.16.1.1: icmp_seq=2 ttl=252 time=0.941 ms
^C
--- 172.16.1.1 ping statistics ---
3 packets transmitted, 3 packets received, 0% packet loss
round-trip min/avg/max/stddev = 0.941/0.992/1.059/0.049 ms
```

Things look good so far. It is interesting to see the information gathered with the `traceroute` command:

```
user@Cabernet> traceroute 172.16.1.1
traceroute to 172.16.1.1 (172.16.1.1), 30 hops max, 40 byte packets
 1  10.100.10.2 (10.100.10.2)  0.904 ms  0.700 ms  0.657 ms
     MPLS Label=912 CoS=0 TTL=1 S=1
 2  10.100.20.2 (10.100.20.2)  0.753 ms  0.706 ms  0.676 ms
     MPLS Label=36 CoS=0 TTL=1 S=1
 3  10.100.30.2 (10.100.30.2)  0.721 ms  0.675 ms  0.651 ms
 4  172.16.1.1 (172.16.1.1)  0.889 ms  0.750 ms  0.730 ms
```

Note that the MPLS label information is returned as part of the output. These ICMP messages are returned using IP routing lookups and truly prove that our data packets are using the LSP to reach the 172.16.1.1 address.

WARNING Please remember that static LSPs do not have a keepalive mechanism. As such, there is no way to view the LSP to verify its status. The ingress router could start forwarding packets to the LSP even if the other routers are not configured. This will cause packet loss on the transit routers. You must be careful to coordinate your efforts when configuring static LSPs.

Configuring a Dynamic LSP

One advantage of establishing a dynamic LSP is that only the ingress router requires configuration knowledge of the LSP; the other routers in the network do not need any explicit configuration. This is true for the LSP itself; however, all routers in the network do need information about MPLS and the signaling protocols in general. This allows for the setup of the LSP using RSVP `Path` and `Resv` messages.

Let's now look at the steps needed to support RSVP as a dynamic signaling protocol. Like the establishment of static LSPs, each router interface must use `family mpls` and the MPLS protocol needs to be enabled on the router. Each router in the network also enables the RSVP signaling protocol on all required interfaces. From there, the actual LSP is configured on the ingress router. First, we examine a basic configuration and then show you how to use bandwidth requests and assign an explicit route object.

Configuring Interfaces

The interfaces on all MPLS routers in the network should now accept more than just IP packets, which is the default. Each interface should accept and process MPLS packets using the `family mpls` command. The Merlot router accomplishes this goal:

```
[edit]
```

```
user@Merlot# set interfaces so-0/0/0 unit 0 family mpls
user@Merlot# set interfaces so-0/0/2 unit 0 family mpls
```

The show interfaces terse command demonstrates our successful configuration:

```
lab@Merlot> show interfaces terse
Interface         Admin Link Proto Local              Remote
so-0/0/0          up    up
so-0/0/0.0        up    up   inet  10.100.20.2/24
                             iso
                             mpls
so-0/0/1          up    up
so-0/0/2          up    up
so-0/0/2.0        up    up   inet  10.100.30.1/24
                             iso
                             mpls
so-0/0/3          up    down
fxp0              up    up
fxp0.0            up    up   inet  10.250.0.123/16
fxp1              up    up
fxp1.0            up    up   tnp   4
gre               up    up
ipip              up    up
lo0               up    up
lo0.0             up    up   inet  192.168.3.3         --> 0/0
                             iso   49.1111.0192.0168.0303.00
lsi               up    up
```

Configuring the MPLS Protocol

Each transit interface that supports MPLS requires some configuration within the [edit protocols] hierarchy. In this example, we want all transit interfaces on the Chardonnay router to support MPLS traffic:

```
[edit protocols]
user@Chardonnay# show
mpls {
    interface all;
    interface fxp0.0 {
        disable;
    }
}
```

As we saw in the "Configuring a Static LSP" section earlier in this chapter, the router creates the mpls.0 routing table once MPLS is created as a protocol. We can see this table by using the show route table mpls.0 command:

```
user@Chardonnay> show route table mpls.0

mpls.0: 2 destinations, 2 routes (2 active, 0 holddown, 0 hidden)
+ = Active Route, - = Last Active, * = Both

0                  *[MPLS/0] 14:53:33, metric 1
                      Receive
1                  *[MPLS/0] 14:53:33, metric 1
                      Receive
2                  *[MPLS/0] 14:53:33, metric 1
                      Receive
```

Configuring the RSVP Protocol

RSVP is another protocol enabled on the Routing Engine to support dynamic LSPs. Each inter-face receiving and sending RSVP messages requires a configuration in the [edit protocols] hierarchy. A typical router places the same interfaces in both the MPLS and RSVP configuration directories.

Chardonnay now adds its interfaces to the RSVP section of the configuration. The result of the change is:

```
[edit protocols]
user@Chardonnay# show
rsvp {
    interface all;
    interface fxp0.0 {
        disable;
    }
}
mpls {
    interface all;
    interface fxp0.0 {
        disable;
    }
}
```

Many people find the `all` keyword a bit confusing. Which interfaces does it find? How do you know it will be running properly? The JUNOS software does provide some `show` commands to answer those questions. However, from the perspective of MPLS and RSVP, only interfaces configured with `family mpls` are activated for those protocols. In our case, we do want all interfaces, except `fxp0.0`, using the protocols. In your network, you may want to explicitly list interfaces in the protocol configuration. Both solutions are acceptable.

We can check the current status of our interfaces to ensure that each router is supporting both MPLS and RSVP on all interfaces. The Muscat router has been completed, so we'll check it now:

```
user@Muscat> show mpls interface
Interface       State       Administrative groups
so-0/0/0.0      Up          <none>
so-0/0/2.0      Up          <none>


user@Muscat> show rsvp interface
RSVP interface: 2 active
                Active Subscr- Static      Available   Reserved  Highwater
Interface  State resv  iption  BW          BW          BW        mark
so-0/0/0.0 Up        0  100%   155.52Mbps  155.52Mbps  0bps      0bps
so-0/0/2.0 Up        0  100%   155.52Mbps  155.52Mbps  0bps      0bps
```

Both of the transit interfaces are reporting a state of Up. This is the desired state we're looking for. We discuss the bandwidth information in the `show rsvp interface` output in the "Configuring LSP Attributes" section later in this chapter.

Configuring the Dynamic LSP

We're now ready to configure the LSP on the ingress router. We would like the LSP to follow the current IGP shortest path between Cabernet and Chardonnay. The desired network path is shown in Figure 11.17.

Configuring the Ingress Router

The minimum configuration of an *RSVP signaled LSP* requires an ASCII name and the address of the egress router. Suppose you issued the following commands on Cabernet:

```
[edit protocols mpls]
user@Cabernet# set label-switched-path Cab-to-Char to 192.168.4.4
user@Cabernet# set label-switched-path Cab-to-Char no-cspf
```

The configuration on Cabernet now looks like this:

```
[edit protocols mpls]
user@Cabernet# show
label-switched-path Cab-to-Char {
    to 192.168.4.4;
    no-cspf;
}
interface all;
interface fxp0.0 {
    disable;
}
```

FIGURE 11.17 Dynamic LSP network path

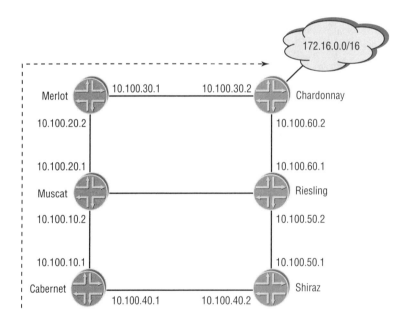

The JUNOS software default for dynamic LSPs is to calculate the path using a Traffic Engineering Database (TED) and the Constrained Shortest Path First (CSPF) algorithm. We have decided that the path should be calculated on a hop-by-hop basis using the IGP routing tables on each router. The no-cspf command disables the default use of the CSPF algorithm. The CSPF algorithm and the Traffic Engineering Database are discussed in the upcoming *JNCIS: Juniper Networks Certified Internet Specialist Study Guide*, also from Sybex (2003).

To verify the establishment of the LSP, we can use the show mpls lsp command on any router. We first check it on the ingress router, Cabernet:

```
user@Cabernet> show mpls lsp
Ingress LSP: 1 sessions
To              From             State Rt ActivePath      P     LSPname
192.168.4.4     192.168.1.1      Up    0                  *     Cab-to-Char
Total 1 displayed, Up 1, Down 0

Egress LSP: 0 sessions
Total 0 displayed, Up 0, Down 0

Transit LSP: 0 sessions
Total 0 displayed, Up 0, Down 0
```

It appears as if the **Cab-to-Char** LSP has an operational status of Up. Notice that the command output also displays LSPs for which the local router is an egress or transit router. A Juniper Networks router can perform all these functions simultaneously, so this output makes sense. By adding the *extensive* option to the command on the ingress router, we see some other useful information:

```
user@Cabernet> show mpls lsp extensive
Ingress LSP: 1 sessions

192.168.4.4
  From: 192.168.1.1, State: Up, ActiveRoute: 0, LSPname: Cab-to-Char
  ActivePath:  (primary)
  LoadBalance: Random
 *Primary                     State: Up
    Received RRO:
          10.100.10.2 10.100.20.2 10.100.30.2
    4 Jul 11 08:44:41  Selected as active path
    3 Jul 11 08:44:41  Record Route:   10.100.10.2 10.100.20.2 10.100.30.2
    2 Jul 11 08:44:41  Up
    1 Jul 11 08:44:41  Originate Call
   Created: Thu Jul 11 08:39:18 2002
Total 1 displayed, Up 1, Down 0

Egress LSP: 0 sessions
Total 0 displayed, Up 0, Down 0

Transit LSP: 0 sessions
Total 0 displayed, Up 0, Down 0
```

The record route object (RRO) from the Resv message is visible in this display. This shows us the exact path the LSP is taking through the network. A quick look at Figure 11.17 reveals that the LSP follows the desired path of Cabernet, Muscat, Merlot, and Chardonnay.

Once a dynamic LSP is established and usable, the router inserts information about that LSP in the routing table structure. Specifically, the router places the egress address of the LSP in the inet.3 routing table. We can verify this with the show route command:

```
user@Cabernet> show route table inet.3

inet.3: 1 destinations, 1 routes (1 active, 0 holddown, 0 hidden)
+ = Active Route, - = Last Active, * = Both

192.168.4.4/32      *[RSVP/7] 01:05:55, metric 30, metric2 0
                     > via so-0/0/0.0, label-switched-path Cab-to-Char
```

The 192.168.4.4 /32 address is the loopback IP address of Chardonnay, so it appears the defaults are working as intended.

Configuring Transit and Egress Routers

No explicit configuration is required on the transit and egress routers to set up a dynamic LSP. After establishing the LSP, you can check its status on these routers by examining the RSVP soft state. Let's check one of the transit routers:

```
user@Muscat> show mpls lsp
Ingress LSP: 0 sessions
Total 0 displayed, Up 0, Down 0

Egress LSP: 0 sessions
Total 0 displayed, Up 0, Down 0

Transit LSP: 1 sessions
To              From            State Rt Style Labelin Labelout LSPname
192.168.4.4     192.168.1.1     Up    1  1 FF  100000  100000   Cab-to-Char
Total 1 displayed, Up 1, Down 0
```

Again, the LSP is operational. This display shows the label values that Muscat received from Merlot (Labelout) and sent to Cabernet (Labelin) for this LSP. This is useful for troubleshooting an LSP's behavior.

NOTE   The label value of 100000 appearing on both the Labelin and Labelout fields might be a bit confusing. The JUNOS software allocates dynamic LSP labels in the 100,000 to 1,048,576 range. As you start your MPLS configuration, you will notice that many label values appear on multiple links for the same LSP. This is what happened here. As the number of LSPs and routers grows in your network, this "pattern" disappears and the label values become more randomized.

Finally, we verify the egress router:

```
user@Chardonnay> show mpls lsp
Ingress LSP: 0 sessions
Total 0 displayed, Up 0, Down 0

Egress LSP: 1 sessions
To              From            State Rt Style Labelin Labelout LSPname
192.168.4.4     192.168.1.1     Up    0  1 FF     3        - Cab-to-Char
Total 1 displayed, Up 1, Down 0

Transit LSP: 0 sessions
Total 0 displayed, Up 0, Down 0
```

Notice that Chardonnay lists a label value of 3 in the Labelin field. Recall from the "Labels" section earlier in this chapter that a value of 3 represents an Implicit NULL. This is the default behavior for the JUNOS software and means that the penultimate router (Merlot) is performing penultimate hop popping (PHP). We can verify this behavior by examining the Merlot output:

```
user@Merlot> show mpls lsp
Ingress LSP: 0 sessions
Total 0 displayed, Up 0, Down 0

Egress LSP: 0 sessions
Total 0 displayed, Up 0, Down 0

Transit LSP: 1 sessions
To              From            State Rt Style Labelin Labelout LSPname
192.168.4.4     192.168.1.1     Up    1  1 FF  100000     3 Cab-to-Char
Total 1 displayed, Up 1, Down 0
```

Merlot has correctly listed a label value of 3 in the Labelout field to support PHP.

Configuring LSP Attributes

At this point, we would like to control the path of the LSP through the network. To accomplish this, we configure an ERO and assign it to the LSP. We also add an RSVP bandwidth request of 15Mbps to the LSP. Since a dynamic LSP is configured only on the ingress router, we make these changes on Cabernet.

An ERO is called a *named path* in the JUNOS software. This is where loose and strict hops are defined. Using Figure 11.17 as a guide, the LSP should now traverse along the Cabernet, Shiraz, Riesling, and Chardonnay routers. We first build the path and define Shiraz as a loose hop:

```
[edit protocols mpls]
user@Cabernet# set path via-Shiraz 192.168.5.5 loose
```

The configuration now looks like this:

```
[edit protocols mpls]
user@Cabernet# show
label-switched-path Cab-to-Char {
    to 192.168.4.4;
    no-cspf;
}
path via-Shiraz {
    192.168.5.5 loose;
}
interface all;
```

The ERO called *via-Shiraz* tells the routers in the network to use the IGP routing tables to forward the Path message from the ingress router to the address of 192.168.5.5 (the loopback address of the Shiraz router). From there, the routers again consult their IGP routing tables to send the Path message from Shiraz to the egress router.

At this point, we use the *primary* option to assign the path to the LSP itself to ensure that the path takes effect. In short, we are telling the ingress router to use this named path as its preferred method for sending Path messages:

```
[edit protocols mpls]
user@Cabernet# set label-switched-path Cab-to-Char primary via-Shiraz
```

This alters the configuration:

```
[edit protocols mpls]
user@Cabernet# show
label-switched-path Cab-to-Char {
    to 192.168.4.4;
    no-cspf;
    primary via-Shiraz;
}
path via-Shiraz {
    192.168.5.5 loose;
}
interface all;
```

The bandwidth request is now added to the LSP configuration:

```
[edit protocols mpls]
user@Cabernet# set label-switched-path Cab-to-Char bandwidth 15m
 [edit protocols mpls]
user@Cabernet# show
```

```
label-switched-path Cab-to-Char {
    to 192.168.4.4;
    bandwidth 15m;
    no-cspf;
    primary via-Shiraz;
}
path via-Shiraz {
    192.168.5.5 loose;
}
interface all;
```

 The JUNOS software uses bits/second as its default value for an LSP's bandwidth. You may alter this default by using the k, m, and g characters to represent kilobits, megabits, and gigabits per second, respectively. In our example, the router translates 15m into 15Mbps of bandwidth.

After committing the configuration, we verify the operational status of the LSP by using the `show mpls lsp` command:

```
user@Cabernet> show mpls lsp
Ingress LSP: 1 sessions
To              From            State Rt ActivePath     P     LSPname
192.168.4.4     192.168.1.1     Up      0 via-Shiraz    *     Cab-to-Char
Total 1 displayed, Up 1, Down 0

Egress LSP: 0 sessions
Total 0 displayed, Up 0, Down 0

Transit LSP: 0 sessions
Total 0 displayed, Up 0, Down 0
```

It appears that our configuration was successful. The LSP is in an Up state and the current ActivePath is via-Shiraz. We can use the *extensive* option to see if the desired network path was taken:

```
user@Cabernet> show mpls lsp extensive
Ingress LSP: 1 sessions

192.168.4.4
  From: 192.168.1.1, State: Up, ActiveRoute: 0, LSPname: Cab-to-Char
  ActivePath: via-Shiraz (primary)
  LoadBalance: Random
```

```
 *Primary   via-Shiraz      State: Up
    Bandwidth: 15Mbps
    Received RRO:
           10.100.40.2 10.100.50.2 10.100.60.2
    4 Jul 11 11:39:44  Selected as active path
    3 Jul 11 11:39:44  Record Route:  10.100.40.2 10.100.50.2 10.100.60.2
    2 Jul 11 11:39:44  Up
    1 Jul 11 11:39:44  Originate Call
   Created: Thu Jul 11 11:37:27 2002
Total 1 displayed, Up 1, Down 0

Egress LSP: 0 sessions
Total 0 displayed, Up 0, Down 0

Transit LSP: 0 sessions
Total 0 displayed, Up 0, Down 0
```

Based on the Resv message RRO, our desired path was selected. This output also displays the bandwidth request of 15Mbps for the LSP. We can verify that the network honored this request by examining a transit router. The show rsvp interface command details the current reservations in the network:

```
user@Shiraz> show rsvp interface
RSVP interface: 2 active
                 Active Subscr- Static      Available   Reserved   Highwater
Interface  State resv   iption  BW          BW          BW         mark
so-0/0/0.0 Up       0   100%    155.52Mbps  155.52Mbps  0bps       0bps
so-0/0/2.0 Up       1   100%    155.52Mbps  140.52Mbps  15Mbps     15Mbps
```

The so-0/0/2.0 interface shows a current Reserved BW of 15Mbps. This is the interface headed to the Riesling router and in the direction of the egress. Remember that LSPs are unidirectional in nature and, therefore, reservations flow in a downstream direction.

Altering the RSVP Protocol

The JUNOS software provides several configuration options you can use to alter the behavior of the RSVP protocol. We quickly talk about what each knob does and look at a configuration example for each.

Hello Interval Timer

The JUNOS software uses the extended RSVP option of sending hello messages to its neighbors. The hello mechanism speeds the detection of router failures in the network. Without it, each router waits for the RSVP soft state to expire before detecting an outage.

For backward compatibility, hello messages are asynchronous in nature. Each router uses the timer advertised from its peer to calculate the hold interval for that neighbor. Should a peer not send hello messages, the local router relies on the soft state for expiring the session. This provides backward compatibility with the original RSVP specification.

The default interval for hello messages is 9 seconds, with a possible range of 1 to 60 seconds. Each router determines the hold interval for each neighbor. When ($2 \times$ `keep-multiplier` + 1) consecutive hello messages are not received, the neighbor is declared dead. By default, the `keep-multiplier` value is 3, which leads to 7 missed hello messages. Using the hello interval of 9 seconds results in a dead interval of 63 seconds for each neighbor.

> RSVP neighbor loss is also detected by a physical layer interface change. When the interface goes down, the RSVP state is removed immediately. The 63-second hold time is used when the RSVP process itself stops operating on the neighboring router.

We can see the hello interval in the output of the `show rsvp neighbor` command. The Chardonnay router is using the default values:

```
user@Chardonnay> show rsvp neighbor
RSVP neighbor: 2 learned
Address          Idle Up/Dn LastChange HelloInt HelloTx/Rx MsgRcvd Status
10.100.30.1         0  1/0    5:04:40         9  5940/5940     238 -
10.100.60.1         0  1/0    2:09:37         9  2529/2529     177 -
```

The interval is changed on Chardonnay's `so-0/0/2.0` interface (10.100.60.1) to 20 seconds:

```
[edit protocols rsvp]
user@Chardonnay# set interface so-0/0/2 hello-interval 20

[edit protocols rsvp]
user@Chardonnay# show
interface all;
interface fxp0.0 {
    disable;
}
interface so-0/0/2.0 {
    hello-interval 20;
}

user@Chardonnay> show rsvp neighbor
RSVP neighbor: 2 learned
Address          Idle Up/Dn LastChange HelloInt HelloTx/Rx MsgRcvd Status
10.100.30.1         5  1/0    5:09:06         9  6027/6027     238 -
10.100.60.1         5  1/0    2:14:03        20  2616/2616     183 -
```

Soft State Refresh Timer

Without the use of the hello mechanism, RSVP routers use the soft state timers to detect network outages. Each router sends Path and Resv messages to its neighbors for each current LSP known to the local router. These messages are sent only between adjacent nodes and do not travel the length of the LSP.

The JUNOS software uses a default value of 30 seconds, with a possible range between 1 and 65,535 seconds. The refresh value is used to calculate the lifetime of the RSVP soft state database. The total lifetime is found using the formula (keep-multiplier + 0.5) × 1.5 × refresh-time. The default values mean that each router waits 157.5 seconds (2.625 minutes), as a worst case, before declaring a network outage.

 The actual time for sending an RSVP refresh message ranges from 15 seconds (0.5 × refresh-time) to 45 seconds (1.5 × refresh-time).

Chardonnay reduces its refresh-time to 15 seconds to speed the expiration of the soft state. This option is configurable at the global RSVP level only.

```
[edit protocols rsvp]
user@Chardonnay# set refresh-time 15

[edit protocols rsvp]
user@Chardonnay# show
refresh-time 15;
interface all;
interface fxp0.0 {
    disable;
}
interface so-0/0/2.0 {
    hello-interval 20;
}
```

We can see the result of this configuration in the output of show rsvp version:

```
user@Chardonnay> show rsvp version
Resource ReSerVation Protocol, version 1. rfc2205
    RSVP protocol       = Enabled
    R(refresh timer)    = 15 seconds
    K(keep multiplier)  = 3
    Preemption          = Normal
```

Multiplier Value

You can use the `keep-multiplier` command to calculate timer values for network outages. Both the hello and soft state timers use the multiplier to determine when to notify neighbors about a failure. The JUNOS software default value for the multiplier is 3, with a possible range between 1 and 255.

To speed detection of outages, Chardonnay alters the `keep-multiplier` for its RSVP process:

```
[edit protocols rsvp]
user@Chardonnay# set keep-multiplier 1

[edit protocols rsvp]
user@Chardonnay# show
refresh-time 15;
keep-multiplier 1;
interface all;
interface fxp0.0 {
    disable;
}
interface so-0/0/2.0 {
    hello-interval 20;
}
```

The `show rsvp version` command shows the effect of this configuration:

```
user@Chardonnay> show rsvp version
Resource ReSerVation Protocol, version 1. rfc2205
   RSVP protocol      = Enabled
   R(refresh timer)   = 15 seconds
   K(keep multiplier) = 1
   Preemption         = Normal
```

Message Aggregation

Each RSVP message sent between neighbors is contained in a separate packet. This includes hello, `Path`, `Resv`, and error messages. Your router can negotiate with its neighbors on an interface-by-interface basis to bundle up to 30 RSVP messages (non-configurable) in a single packet before sending it to that neighbor. This greatly reduces the overhead of running RSVP and provides for greater network scalability.

As you can see here, Chardonnay enables this feature on all of its transit interfaces:

```
[edit protocols rsvp]
user@Chardonnay# set interface so-0/0/2.0 aggregate
```

```
[edit protocols rsvp]
user@Chardonnay# set interface all aggregate

[edit protocols rsvp]
user@Chardonnay# show
refresh-time 15;
keep-multiplier 1;
interface all {
    aggregate;
}
interface fxp0.0 {
    disable;
}
interface so-0/0/2.0 {
    aggregate;
    hello-interval 20;
}
```

Notice that the aggregate command is configured twice on the Chardonnay router. Keep in mind that the JUNOS software uses the most specific reference to a command possible. Since the so-0/0/2.0 interface is listed separately, it doesn't inherit commands applied within the interface all portion of the configuration. This requires us to use the two commands shown to apply the aggregate option to all the transit interfaces.

Authenticating RSVP

You can authenticate RSVP message exchanges between routers. To do so, you use the MD5 authentication mechanism with a key length of 16 characters.

In our example, Chardonnay configures authentication on its so-0/0/2.0 interface with a key of *password*:

```
[edit protocols rsvp]
user@Chardonnay# set interface so-0/0/2 authentication-key password

[edit protocols rsvp]
user@Chardonnay# show
refresh-time 15;
keep-multiplier 1;
interface all {
    aggregate;
}
```

```
interface fxp0.0 {
    disable;
}
interface so-0/0/2.0 {
    authentication-key "$9$2SgZjHkPQ39.PhrvLVb.P5Tz6"; # SECRET-DATA
    aggregate;
    hello-interval 20;
}
```

Bandwidth Reservation Limits

The JUNOS software allocates 100 percent of the physical interface bandwidth for RSVP reservations. You have two methods for altering this default behavior. The first is changing the reservation percentage for the entire physical interface. The second is specifying an actual bandwidth value to be used for a logical interface unit. This second method is very useful for controlling reservations on ATM and Frame Relay circuits.

Chardonnay is currently using the default reservation percentage. We can see this by issuing the show rsvp interface command:

```
user@Chardonnay> show rsvp interface
RSVP interface: 2 active
                 Active Subscr- Static      Available   Reserved    Highwater
Interface   State resv   iption  BW          BW          BW          mark
so-0/0/0.0  Up       0   100%   155.52Mbps  155.52Mbps  0bps        0bps
so-0/0/2.0  Up       0   100%   155.52Mbps  155.52Mbps  0bps        0bps
```

Both methods are used to alter the default reservation availability:

```
[edit protocols rsvp]
user@Chardonnay# set interface so-0/0/0 bandwidth 20m

[edit protocols rsvp]
user@Chardonnay# set interface so-0/0/2 subscription 65

[edit protocols rsvp]
user@Chardonnay# show
refresh-time 15;
keep-multiplier 1;
interface all {
    aggregate;
}
interface fxp0.0 {
    disable;
}
```

```
interface so-0/0/2.0 {
    authentication-key "$9$2SgZjHkPQ39.PhrvLVb.P5Tz6"; # SECRET-DATA
    subscription 65;
    aggregate;
    hello-interval 20;
}
interface so-0/0/0.0 {
    bandwidth 20m;
}
```

We then verify the results:

```
user@Chardonnay> show rsvp interface
RSVP interface: 2 active
                  Active Subscr- Static      Available   Reserved   Highwater
Interface   State resv   iption BW           BW          BW         mark
so-0/0/0.0  Up        0   100%  20Mbps       20Mbps      0bps       0bps
so-0/0/2.0  Up        0    65%  155.52Mbps   101.088Mbps 0bps       0bps
```

The values in the `Subscription` and `Static BW` columns for non-configured options remain unchanged. The result of the configuration is best seen by adding the `Available BW` and `Reserved BW` columns together. As there are no current LSP bandwidth reservations on Chardonnay, we see that the `so-0/0/0.0` interface is using the static value of 20Mbps, and the `so-0/0/2.0` interface calculated 65 percent of the physical bandwidth for a result of 101.088Mbps.

Routing Table Integration

In the "Configuring a Static LSP" section earlier in this chapter, we explicitly assigned the 172.16.0.0/16 subnet to use the LSP across the network. We made no such routing association in the "Configuring a Dynamic LSP" section earlier in this chapter. This was not an oversight on our part. The JUNOS software has a default action for associating IP routes to established dynamic LSPs. In addition, numerous configuration options are available for changing the default behavior. As such, this topic receives its own special treatment at this point.

We first explore how a Juniper Networks router uses LSPs by default. We then describe a few methods for altering the default behavior.

Default Behavior

There is an inherent relationship between LSPs and BGP. The JUNOS software assumes that traffic using BGP routes should also use the LSP for data forwarding. This is useful for engineering transit user traffic across your network.

The BGP route and the established LSP are linked together when the route is installed in the routing table. Recall from Chapter 8, "Border Gateway Protocol," that a BGP route can be used only when the BGP Next Hop attribute is reachable. Under normal circumstances, the BGP process examines the inet.0 routing table to verify this reachability. When an LSP has been established and placed in the inet.3 routing table, the BGP process can examine its contents to determine reachability to the BGP Next Hop. Figure 11.18 shows this process.

FIGURE 11.18 Default routing table integration

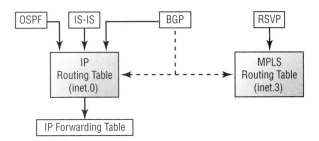

The RSVP information is installed in inet.3. The IGP routes from OSPF and IS-IS are installed in inet.0. As BGP attempts to place a route in inet.0, it examines both inet.0 and inet.3 during its BGP Next Hop resolution. This longest-match lookup process identifies the version of the route with the lowest JUNOS software preference. RSVP installs information with a preference value of 7, OSPF uses a value of 10, and IS-IS uses both 15 and 18. By default, then, the BGP route uses the established LSP as its physical forwarding path across the network. Let's examine this behavior in a sample network, shown in Figure 11.19.

In the case of a preference tie between the routing tables, the JUNOS software prefers the inet.3 table and the LSP.

FIGURE 11.19 Route table integration network

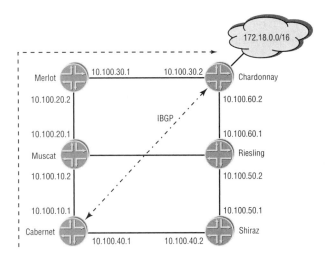

The Cabernet router is peering with Chardonnay using IBGP routing. The 172.18.0.0/16 route is advertised to Cabernet over this connection. The current BGP next-hop value is 192.168.4.4, the loopback address of Chardonnay. We can verify this information by using the show route receive-protocol command on Cabernet:

```
user@Cabernet> show route receive-protocol bgp 192.168.4.4

inet.0: 17 destinations, 17 routes (17 active, 0 holddown, 0 hidden)
+ = Active Route, - = Last Active, * = Both


172.18.0.0/16
192.168.4.4                    0          100 2 I
```

The next hop of 192.168.4.4 is currently assigned to the 172.18.0.0/16 BGP route. No LSP has been established and Cabernet has reachability only to 192.168.4.4 through IS-IS:

```
user@Cabernet> show route 192.168.4.4

inet.0: 17 destinations, 17 routes (17 active, 0 holddown, 0 hidden)
+ = Active Route, - = Last Active, * = Both


192.168.4.4/32     *[IS-IS/15] 07:00:15, metric 30, tag 1
                      to 10.100.10.2 via so-0/0/0.0
                    > to 10.100.40.2 via so-0/0/2.0
```

The BGP route is installed in the inet.0 routing table with a next-hop value of 10.100.40.2 out the so-0/0/2.0 interface:

```
user@Cabernet> show route 172.18/16

inet.0: 17 destinations, 17 routes (17 active, 0 holddown, 0 hidden)
+ = Active Route, - = Last Active, * = Both


172.18.0.0/16      *[BGP/170] 00:04:34, MED 0, localpref 100, from 192.168.4.4
                      AS path: 2 I
                      to 10.100.10.2 via so-0/0/0.0
                    > to 10.100.40.2 via so-0/0/2.0
```

We have configured an LSP on Cabernet that uses Chardonnay as the egress router. The desired path through Muscat and Merlot in Figure 11.19 is enforced with a named path ERO. The egress router address now appears in the inet.3 routing table:

```
[edit protocols mpls]
```

```
user@Cabernet# show
label-switched-path Cab-to-Char {
    to 192.168.4.4;
    no-cspf;
    primary via-Merlot;
}
path via-Merlot {
    192.168.3.3 loose;
}
interface all;
interface fxp0.0 {
    disable;
}

user@Cabernet> show route table inet.3

inet.3: 1 destinations, 1 routes (1 active, 0 holddown, 0 hidden)
+ = Active Route, - = Last Active, * = Both

192.168.4.4/32      *[RSVP/7] 00:00:03, metric 30, metric2 0
                     > via so-0/0/0.0, label-switched-path Cab-to-Char
```

Cabernet now has reachability to 192.168.4.4 through both RSVP and IS-IS:

```
user@Cabernet> show route 192.168.4.4

inet.0: 17 destinations, 17 routes (17 active, 0 holddown, 0 hidden)
+ = Active Route, - = Last Active, * = Both

192.168.4.4/32      *[IS-IS/15] 07:07:55, metric 30, tag 1
                        to 10.100.10.2 via so-0/0/0.0
                     > to 10.100.40.2 via so-0/0/2.0

inet.3: 1 destinations, 1 routes (1 active, 0 holddown, 0 hidden)
+ = Active Route, - = Last Active, * = Both

192.168.4.4/32      *[RSVP/7] 00:01:30, metric 30, metric2 0
                     > via so-0/0/0.0, label-switched-path Cab-to-Char
```

The BGP Next Hop resolution process finds both versions of the next hop and chooses the LSP because of a lower route preference. The 172.18.0.0 /16 is installed in the inet.0 routing table with a next hop pointing to the LSP ***Cab-to-Char***.

```
user@Cabernet> show route 172.18/16

inet.0: 17 destinations, 17 routes (17 active, 0 holddown, 0 hidden)
+ = Active Route, - = Last Active, * = Both

172.18.0.0/16      *[BGP/170] 00:12:22, MED 0, localpref 100, from 192.168.4.4
                      AS path: 2 I
                   > via so-0/0/0.0, label-switched-path Cab-to-Char
```

 Should the LSP become unusable, the BGP Next Hop resolution process installs the route in inet.0 with the IS-IS physical next hop, as before.

Assigning Individual Prefixes to an LSP

In addition to assigning BGP routes to an LSP automatically, you have the option of manually assigning routes. Perhaps the BGP next-hop address does not match the egress address of the LSP. Maybe you prefer to use the LSP to reach some internal non-BGP destination. Both of these scenarios are possible through the use of the install command.

Adding a Route to *inet.3*

The Chardonnay router has added the 172.20.0.0/16 route to its routing table in Figure 11.20. Chardonnay then advertises the two BGP routes to Cabernet.

FIGURE 11.20   Assigning a prefix to an LSP

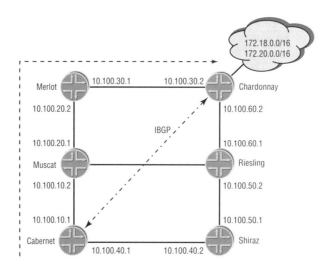

The 172.18.0.0/16 route has a next hop of 192.168.4.4. The 172.20.0.0/16 route has a next hop of 172.16.1.1:

```
user@Cabernet> show route receive-protocol bgp 192.168.4.4 all

inet.0: 18 destinations, 18 routes (17 active, 0 holddown, 1 hidden)
+ = Active Route, - = Last Active, * = Both


172.18.0.0/16
192.168.4.4                0          100 2 I
172.20.0.0/16
172.16.1.1                 0          100 2 I
```

Only the 172.18.0.0/16 route is active in the inet.0 routing table. Since Cabernet does not have reachability to 172.16.1.1, the 172.20.0.0/16 route is currently hidden:

```
user@Cabernet> show route protocol bgp

inet.0: 18 destinations, 18 routes (17 active, 0 holddown, 1 hidden)
+ = Active Route, - = Last Active, * = Both


172.18.0.0/16      *[BGP/170] 00:09:54, MED 0, localpref 100, from 192.168.4.4
                      AS path: 2 I
                    > via so-0/0/0.0, label-switched-path Cab-to-Char


user@Cabernet> show route 172.16.1.1


user@Cabernet> show route hidden

inet.0: 18 destinations, 18 routes (17 active, 0 holddown, 1 hidden)
+ = Active Route, - = Last Active, * = Both


172.20.0.0/16      [BGP/170] 00:12:59, MED 0, localpref 100, from 192.168.4.4
                      AS path: 2 I
                      Unusable
```

The 172.16.1.1 address is assigned to the ***Cab-to-Char*** LSP. The install command places the address within the LSP configuration:

```
[edit protocols mpls]
user@Cabernet# set label-switched-path Cab-to-Char install 172.16.1.1
```

The configuration on Cabernet now looks like this:

```
[edit protocols mpls]
user@Cabernet# show
label-switched-path Cab-to-Char {
    to 192.168.4.4;
    install 172.16.1.1/32;
    no-cspf;
    primary via-Merlot;
}
path via-Merlot {
    192.168.3.3 loose;
}
interface all;
interface fxp0.0 {
    disable;
}
```

The router places the 172.16.1.1 /32 address in the inet.3 routing table as reachable through the **Cab-to-Char** LSP:

```
user@Cabernet> show route table inet.3

inet.3: 2 destinations, 2 routes (2 active, 0 holddown, 0 hidden)
+ = Active Route, - = Last Active, * = Both

172.16.1.1/32      *[RSVP/7] 00:01:54, metric 30, metric2 0
                    > via so-0/0/0.0, label-switched-path Cab-to-Char
192.168.4.4/32     *[RSVP/7] 00:01:54, metric 30, metric2 0
                    > via so-0/0/0.0, label-switched-path Cab-to-Char
```

Cabernet has reachability to the BGP Next Hop of the 172.20.0.0 /16 BGP route and installs the route in the inet.0 table:

```
user@Cabernet> show route 172.20/16

inet.0: 18 destinations, 18 routes (18 active, 0 holddown, 0 hidden)
+ = Active Route, - = Last Active, * = Both

172.20.0.0/16      *[BGP/170] 00:20:56, MED 0, localpref 100, from 192.168.4.4
                     AS path: 2 I
                    > via so-0/0/0.0, label-switched-path Cab-to-Char
```

Adding a Route to *inet.0*

You have decided that traffic destined for the 10.100.60.0/24 route should use the LSP for data forwarding. This link is the Riesling-Chardonnay connection. Currently only an IS-IS route appears in the routing table:

```
user@Cabernet> show route 10.100.60/24

inet.0: 18 destinations, 18 routes (18 active, 0 holddown, 0 hidden)
+ = Active Route, - = Last Active, * = Both

10.100.60.0/24      *[IS-IS/15] 07:51:16, metric 30, tag 1
                     > to 10.100.40.2 via so-0/0/2.0
```

The next hop for the route is 10.100.40.2, Shiraz. In examining Figure 11.20, you find that the *Cab-to-Char* LSP currently follows the Cabernet, Muscat, Merlot, and Chardonnay path through the network. We assign the 10.100.60.0/24 route to the *Cab-to-Char* LSP by using the install command:

```
[edit protocols mpls]
user@Cabernet# set label-switched-path Cab-to-Char install 10.100.60/24 active
```

The configuration now looks like this:

```
[edit protocols mpls]
user@Cabernet# show
label-switched-path Cab-to-Char {
    to 192.168.4.4;
    install 172.16.1.1/32;
    install 10.100.60.0/24 active;
    no-cspf;
    primary via-Merlot;
}
path via-Merlot {
    192.168.3.3 loose;
}
interface all;
interface fxp0.0 {
    disable;
}
```

We use the *active* option to install the specified prefix in the inet.0 routing table instead of the inet.3 routing table. This is a critical step in the process of allowing non-BGP routes to use the LSP. All user data traffic uses the inet.0 table for route lookups. BGP routes in inet.0

have a next hop of the LSP when RSVP installs the egress address in the inet.3 table. Without the *active* keyword, only the inet.3 table is updated and data traffic to the 10.100.60.0 /24 route still uses the IGP shortest path to Shiraz. We've avoided this problem and achieve our desired result.

```
user@Cabernet> show route 10.100.60/24

inet.0: 18 destinations, 19 routes (18 active, 0 holddown, 0 hidden)
+ = Active Route, - = Last Active, * = Both

10.100.60.0/24     *[RSVP/7] 00:05:20, metric 30, metric2 0
                    > via so-0/0/0.0, label-switched-path Cab-to-Char
                    [IS-IS/15] 08:01:02, metric 30, tag 1
                    > to 10.100.40.2 via so-0/0/2.0
```

User data traffic now uses the LSP to Muscat on the so-0/0/0.0 interface.

Summary

In this chapter, we examined the basics of Multiprotocol Label Switching (MPLS). We started with a look at why the protocol was created and how its usefulness has evolved. Our discussion focused on the needs of ISPs to support growing bandwidth demands and the data-forwarding speed needed in that environment. We concluded our look at the history of the protocol by exploring the use of MPLS as a traffic-engineering mechanism.

We then described the terminology and conceptual aspect of MPLS. We defined an MPLS label and a label switched path (LSP), and discussed the functions of ingress, transit, penultimate, and egress routers.

We next examined the methods for establishing an LSP in an MPLS network. We looked at both static and dynamic methods. In addition, we explained how the Resource Reservation Protocol (RSVP) and Label Distribution Protocol (LDP) signaling protocols are used for the dynamic setup of an LSP.

We concluded the chapter by discussing the JUNOS software implementation of MPLS. We saw configuration examples of both static and RSVP signaled LSPs, described methods for altering the RSVP protocol, and discussed ways to place user data traffic into an LSP.

Exam Essentials

Understand the use of MPLS in an ISP network.   MPLS is a method for engineering traffic flows across a network. It uses a switching table lookup to forward traffic based on a label value.

Be able to describe the functions of MPLS routers.   Ingress routers add an MPLS label with a push operation. Transit routers swap label values and forward traffic along the LSP. The penultimate router performs a pop operation by removing the MPLS label and rewriting the TTL field back to the IP packet. The egress router terminates the LSP and forwards traffic based on an IP route lookup.

Identify the methods of LSP establishment.   LSPs are established in one of two ways. Static LSPs are similar to static routes and require configuration of all routers. Dynamic LSPs use a signaling protocol to set up the LSP and require configuration on the ingress router only.

Be able to describe the signaling protocols used in MPLS.   Both RSVP and LDP are valid protocols used to signal an LSP setup. The original RSVP specification was extended to support MPLS requirements. The LDP specification was created specifically for use with MPLS.

List the RSVP objects used for MPLS.   The extended RSVP specification defines the explicit route object, label request object, label object, record route object, session attribute object, and tspec object.

Identify the steps required to configure a RSVP signaled LSP.   The ingress router needs an ASCII name for the LSP and the address of the egress router. You may add other attributes, such as a bandwidth request and an explicit route object, to control the setup parameters of the LSP.

Be able to describe the integration of the JUNOS software routing tables.   RSVP signaled LSPs place the egress router address in the `inet.3` routing table. BGP can use both the `inet.0` and `inet.3` tables to resolve reachability to the BGP Next Hop attribute. The longest-match route with the lowest preference value is used, which is the LSP by default.

Key Terms

Before you take the exam, be certain you are familiar with the following terms:

cell tax	`Path` message
dynamic label switched path	`PathErr` message
egress router	`PathTear` message
explicit route object (ERO)	penultimate hop popping (PHP)
hello mechanism	penultimate router
ingress router	record route object (RRO)
Label Distribution Protocol (LDP)	Resource Reservation Protocol (RSVP)
label object	`ResvConf` message
label pop operation	`ResvErr` message
label push operation	`ResvTear` message
label request object	RSVP `Resv` message
label swap operation	RSVP signaled LSP
label switched path (LSP)	session attribute object
label switching router (LSR)	shim header
label values	soft state
local significance	static label switched path
loose hops	strict hop
message aggregation	traffic engineering
named path	transit routers
overlay network	tspec object

Review Questions

1. What is MPLS used for in today's ISP networks?

    A. ATM compatibility

    B. Traffic engineering

    C. Virtual Private Networks

    D. Class of Service

2. What was the original goal of MPLS?

    A. To increase the router's packet processing speed

    B. To provide traffic engineering

    C. To provide Layer 2 switching within Layer 3 routers

    D. To provide Class of Service to IP traffic

3. What does LSR stand for?

    A. Label Switching Router

    B. Label Swapping Router

    C. Layer 3 Switching Router

    D. Layer 2 Swapping Router

4. What is the functionality of a transit router?

    A. Performs MPLS encapsulation

    B. Forwards traffic based on IP address

    C. Performs a label swap operation

    D. Forwards traffic based on MAC address

5. Where is an MPLS label placed in a packet on a Juniper Networks router?

    A. Before the Layer 2 header

    B. After the Layer 3 header

    C. Between the Layers 2 and 3 headers

    D. Between the Layers 3 and 4 headers

6. What MPLS router performs only a label push operation?

    A. Ingress router

    B. Transit router

    C. Penultimate router

    D. Egress router

7. What MPLS routers perform label swap operations? (Choose two.)

   A. Ingress

   B. Transit

   C. Penultimate

   D. Egress

8. How many bits form an MPLS header?

   A. 16

   B. 20

   C. 22

   D. 32

9. An MPLS header has a stack bit value of 0. What does this mean?

   A. This is the last label.

   B. There is only one more label in the stack.

   C. The TTL has expired and the router needs to pop the label.

   D. There are other labels in the stack.

10. What value is placed in the TTL field by the ingress LSR?

    A. A value of 0.

    B. A value of 255.

    C. The IP TTL value is copied to the MPLS header.

    D. The ingress LSR does nothing.

11. What does a label value of 2 mean?

    A. IPv4 Explicit NULL

    B. Router Alert

    C. IPv6 Explicit NULL

    D. Implicit NULL

12. Which protocols can be used for a dynamic LSP setup? (Choose two.)

    A. IGP

    B. LDP

    C. BGP

    D. RSVP

13. What label values are reserved by the IETF?

    A. Labels 0 to 15

    B. Labels 4 to 15

    C. Labels 0 to 32

    D. Labels 4 to 32

14. What router(s) require LSP configuration for a dynamic establishment?

    A. Ingress

    B. Penultimate

    C. Transit

    D. Egress

15. In which direction is a `Path` message sent?

    A. Upstream to the ingress router

    B. Downstream to the ingress router

    C. Upstream to the egress router

    D. Downstream to the egress router

16. In which direction is a `Resv` message sent?

    A. Upstream to the ingress router

    B. Downstream to the ingress router

    C. Upstream to the egress router

    D. Downstream to the egress router

17. How does RSVP maintain knowledge of the soft state of an LSP?

    A. It uses RSVP authentication.

    B. It uses RSVP hellos.

    C. It refreshes RSVP `Path` and `Resv` messages.

    D. It refreshes `PathErr` and `ResvErr` messages.

18. Into which JUNOS software routing table are RSVP signaled LSPs placed?

    A. `inet.0`

    B. `inet.1`

    C. `inet.2`

    D. `inet.3`

19. What types of hops are allowed in an ERO?

    A. Strict hops only.

    B. Loose hops only.

    C. Both strict and loose hops.

    D. No hops are allowed in an ERO.

20. How is the RSVP reservation information influenced when you configure `subscription` *percentage* on an interface?

    A. It applies to the physical interface.

    B. It applies to the entire router.

    C. It applies to specific LSPs only.

    D. It has no effect.

Answers to Review Questions

1. B. Traffic engineering is the main application of MPLS in today's networks.

2. A. The original IETF goal for MPLS was to increase the router's packet-processing speed.

3. A. LSR stands for Label Switching Router.

4. C. A transit MPLS router performs a label swap operation.

5. C. The JUNOS software uses a shim header that is placed between the Layers 2 and 3 headers.

6. A. The ingress router performs the label push operation in an LSP.

7. B, C. Transit and penultimate routers perform a label swap. The ingress and egress routers never perform this operation.

8. D. MPLS uses a 32-bit header.

9. D. When the S bit position contains a 0, it means that other labels exist in the stack.

10. C. By default, the ingress LSR copies the TTL value from the IP packet to the MPLS packet. The router that pops the MPLS label then copies the MPLS TTL back to the IP packet.

11. C. An MPLS label value of 2 represents an IPv6 Explicit NULL.

12. B, D. Both LDP and RSVP are signaling protocols supported by the JUNOS software.

13. A. The IETF reserved labels 0 to 15.

14. A. Only the ingress router needs specific LSP configuration in a dynamic environment.

15. D. `Path` messages are always sent in a downstream direction to the egress router.

16. A. `Resv` messages are always sent in an upstream direction to the ingress router.

17. C. RSVP refreshes `Path` and `Resv` messages every 30 seconds to maintain the soft state of the LSP in the network.

18. D. The egress address of RSVP LSPs are always placed in the `inet.3` routing table.

19. C. An RSVP ERO may contain both strict and loose hops.

20. A. The `subscription` **_percentage_** command applies to the entire physical interface.

Glossary

1X   First phase of third-generation (3G) mobile wireless technology for CDMA2000 networks.

1XEV   Evolutionary phase for 3G for CDMA2000 networks, divided into two phases: 1XEV-DO (data only) and 1XEV-DV (data and voice).

2-Way   Adjacency state for OSPF that shows bidirectional communication between two neighbors has been established.

3GPP   Third-generation Partnership Project. Created to expedite the development of open, globally accepted technical specifications for the Universal Mobile Telecommunications System (UMTS).

A

accept   JUNOS software syntax command used in a routing policy or a firewall filter. It halts the logical processing of the policy or filter when a set of match conditions is met. The specific route is placed into the routing table or announced to a neighbor. An IP packet is forwarded to the next hop along the network path.

action   Within a routing policy or firewall filter, an action denotes a specific function to perform on a route or IP packet.

active route   Route chosen by a router from all routes in the routing table to reach a specific destination. Active routes are installed into the forwarding table.

add/drop multiplexer (ADM)   SONET functionality that allows lower-level signals to be dropped from a high-speed optical connection.

address match conditions   The use of an IP address as a match criterion in a routing policy or a firewall filter.

Address Resolution Protocol (ARP)   Protocol for mapping IP addresses to MAC addresses.

adjacency   Link-state network neighbor status that represents two neighbors who have exchanged their link-state database information with each other.

Adjacency-RIB-In   Logical software table that contains BGP routes received from a specific neighbor.

Adjacency-RIB-Out   Logical software table that contains BGP routes to be sent to a specific neighbor.

aggregation   Combination of groups of routes that share the same most significant bits into a single entry in the routing table.

Alternate Priority Queuing (APQ) Dequeuing method that has a special queue, similar to SPQ, which is visited each time the scheduler moves from one low priority queue to another low priority queue. The packets in the special queue still have a predictable latency, although the upper limit of the delay is higher than that with SPQ. Since the other configured queues share the remaining service time, queue starvation is usually avoided. See also *Strict Priority Queuing (SPQ)*.

American National Standards Institute (ANSI) The United States' representative to the ISO. See also *International Organization for Standardization (ISO)*.

application-specific integrated circuit (ASIC) Specialized processors that perform specific functions on the router.

area Routing subdomain that maintains detailed routing information about its own internal composition and that maintains routing information that allows it to reach other routing sub-domains. In IS-IS, an area corresponds to a Level 1 subdomain. In IS-IS and OSPF, an area is a set of contiguous networks and hosts within an Autonomous System that have been administratively grouped together.

area border router Router that belongs to more than one area. Used in OSPF. See also *Open Shortest Path First (OSPF)*.

ASBR Summary LSA OSPF link-state advertisement sent by an ABR to advertise the router ID of an ASBR across an area boundary. See also *Autonomous System boundary router*.

AS external-link advertisements OSPF link-state advertisement sent by AS boundary routers to describe external routes that they know. These link-state advertisements are flooded throughout the AS (except for stub areas).

AS path In BGP, the path to a destination. The path consists of the AS numbers of all domains a packet must go through to reach a destination.

Asynchronous Transfer Mode (ATM) A high-speed multiplexing and switching method utilizing fixed-length cells of 53 octets to support multiple types of traffic.

ATM adaptation layer (AAL) A series of protocols enabling various types of traffic, including voice, data, image, and video, to run over an ATM network.

ATM Line Interface (ALI) Interface between ATM and 3G systems. See also *Asynchronous Transfer Mode (ATM)*.

atomic Smallest possible operation. An atomic operation is performed either entirely or not at all. For example, if machine failure prevents a transaction from completing, the system is rolled back to the start of the transaction, with no changes taking place.

attempt OSPF adjacency state seen in a Non-Broadcast Multi-Access (NBMA) network that means the local router is to send a unicast hello packet to a neighbor for which it has not yet received any protocol packets.

authentication center (AUC)   Part of the Home Location Register (HLR) in 3G systems, the AUC performs computations to verify and authenticate the user of mobile phones.

Authentication Header (AH)   A component of the IPSec protocol used to verify that the contents of a packet have not been changed, and to validate the identity of the sender. The actual packet data is not protected. See also *encapsulating security payload (ESP)*.

Automatic Protection Switching (APS)   Technology used by SONET ADMs to protect against circuit faults between the ADM and a router and to protect against failing routers. See also *add/drop multiplexer (ADM)*.

Autonomous System (AS)   A set of routers under a single technical administration. Each AS normally uses a single Interior Gateway Protocol (IGP) and metrics to propagate routing information within the set of routers. Also called *routing domain*.

Autonomous System boundary router   In OSPF, routers that import routing information external to the protocol into the link-state database.

Autonomous System external-link advertisements   OSPF link-state advertisement sent by Autonomous System boundary routers to describe external routes that they know. These link-state advertisements are flooded throughout the Autonomous System (except for stub areas).

Autonomous System path   In BGP, the path to a destination. The path consists of the Autonomous System numbers of all the domains a packet must pass through to reach a destination.

auto-RP   One of three methods of electing and announcing the rendezvous point to group address mapping in a multicast network. A vendor-proprietary specification supported by the JUNOS software.

B

backbone area   In OSPF, an area that consists of all networks in area ID 0.0.0.0, their attached routers, and all area border routers.

backbone router   An OSPF router with all operational interfaces within area 0.0.0.0.

backplane   On an M40 router, component of the Packet Forwarding Engine that distributes power, provides signal connectivity, manages shared memory on FPCs, and passes outgoing data cells to FPCs. See also *flexible PIC concentrator (FPC)*.

backup   Denotes a Routing Engine in a dual Routing Engine chassis that is not currently controlling the router's operations.

backup designated router   An OSPF router on a broadcast segment that monitors the operation of the designated router and takes over its functions in the event of a failure.

bandwidth   The range of transmission frequencies a network can use, expressed as the difference between the highest and lowest frequencies of a transmission channel. In computer networks, greater bandwidth indicates faster data-transfer rate capacity.

base station controller (BSC)   Key network node in 3G systems that supervises the functioning and control of multiple base transceiver stations.

base station subsystem (BSS)   Composed of the base transceiver station (BTS) and base station controller (BSC).

Base Station System GPRS Protocol (BSSGP)   Processes routing and quality-of-service (QoS) information for the BSS.

base transceiver station (BTS)   Mobile telephony equipment housed in cabinets and co-located with antennas. Also known as a *radio base station*.

Bellcore   Bell Communications Research. Research and development organization created after the divestiture of the Bell System. It is supported by the regional Bell holding companies (RBHCs), which own the regional Bell operating companies (RBOCs).

Bellman-Ford algorithm   Algorithm used in distance-vector routing protocols to determine the best path to all routes in the network.

bit error rate test (BERT)   A test that can be run on an electrical point-to-point interface (T1, E1, T3, E3, etc.) to determine whether it is operating properly.

bit field match conditions   The use of fields in the header of an IP packet as match criteria in a firewall filter.

bootstrap router   The single router in a multicast network responsible for distributing candidate rendezvous point information to all PIM-enabled routers.

Border Gateway Protocol (BGP)   Exterior Gateway Protocol used to exchange routing information among routers in different Autonomous Systems.

broadcast   Operation of sending network traffic from one network node to all other network nodes.

Building Integrated Timing Source (BITS)   Dedicated timing source that synchronizes all equipment in a particular building.

bundle   Collection of software that makes up a JUNOS software release.

C

call detail record (CDR)   A record containing data (such as origination, termination, length, and time of day) unique to a specific call.

candidate configuration   A file maintained by the JUNOS software containing all changes to the router's active configuration. It becomes the active configuration when a user issues the `commit` command.

candidate-RP-advertisements   Information sent by routers in a multicast network when they are configured as a local rendezvous point. This information is unicast to the BSR for the multicast domain.

CDMA2000   Radio transmission and backbone technology for the evolution to third-generation (3G) mobile networks.

cell tax   Describes the physical transmission capacity used by header information when sending data packets in an ATM network. Each ATM cell uses a 5-byte header.

CFM   Cubic feet per minute. Measure of air flow in volume per minute.

Challenge Handshake Authentication Protocol (CHAP)   A protocol that authenticates remote users. CHAP is a server-driven, three-step authentication mechanism that depends on a shared secret password that resides on both the server and the client.

channel service unit/data service unit (CSU/DSU)   The channel service unit connects a digital phone line to a multiplexer or other digital signal device. The data service unit connects a DTE to a digital phone line.

chassis daemon (chassisd)   JUNOS software process responsible for managing the interaction of the router's physical components.

circuit cross-connect (CCC)   A JUNOS software feature that allows you to configure transparent connections between two circuits.

Cisco-RP-Announce   Message advertised into a multicast network by any router configured as a local rendezvous point in an auto-RP network. It is advertised in a dense-mode fashion to the 224.0.1.39 multicast group address.

Cisco-RP-Discovery   Message advertised by the mapping agent in an auto-RP network. It contains the rendezvous point to multicast group address assignments for the domain. It is advertised in a dense-mode fashion to the 224.0.1.40 multicast group address.

class of service (CoS)   The method of classifying traffic on a packet-by-packet basis to provide different service levels to different traffic. See also *type of service (ToS)*.

classless interdomain routing (CIDR)   A method of specifying Internet addresses in which you explicitly specify the bits of the address to represent the network address instead of determining this information from the first octet of the address.

client peer   In a BGP route reflection network, a member of a cluster that is not the route reflector. See also *nonclient peer*.

cluster   In BGP, a set of routers that have been grouped together. A cluster consists of at least one system that acts as a route reflector, along with any number of client peers. The client peers mainly receive their route information from the route reflector system. Routers in a cluster do not need to be fully meshed.

Code Division Multiple Access (CDMA)   Technology for digital transmission of radio signals between, for example, a mobile telephone and a base transceiver station (BTS).

command completion   Function of the router's command-line interface that allows a user to enter only the most significant characters in any command. Users access this function through the spacebar or Tab key.

command-line interface (CLI)   The user's interface to the JUNOS software through a console, Telnet, or SSH session.

common language equipment identifier (CLEI)   Inventory code used to identify and track telecommunications equipment.

community   In BGP, a group of destinations that share a common property. Community information can be included as one of the path attributes in BGP update messages.

Competitive Local Exchange Carrier (CLEC)   (Pronounced "see-lek") Company that competes with the already established local telecommunications business by providing its own network and switching.

complete sequence number PDU (CSNP)   Packet that contains a complete list of all the LSP headers in the IS-IS database.

confederation   In BGP, a group of small Autonomous Systems that appears to external Autonomous Systems to be a single Autonomous System.

configuration mode   JUNOS software mode allowing a user to alter the router's current configuration.

Connect   BGP neighbor state where the local router has initiated the TCP session and is waiting for the remote peer to complete the TCP connection.

Connectionless Network Protocol (CLNP)   ISO-developed protocol for OSI connectionless network service. CLNP is the OSI equivalent of IP.

Connector Interface Panel (CIP)   On an M40e or M160 router as well as on a T320 or T640 routing node the panel that contains connectors for the Routing Engines, BITS interfaces, and alarm relay contacts.

constrained path   In traffic engineering, a path determined using the CSPF algorithm. The ERO carried in the RSVP packets contains the constrained path information.

Constrained Shortest Path First (CSPF)   An MPLS algorithm that has been modified to take into account specific restrictions when calculating the shortest path across the network.

context-sensitive help   Function of the router's command-line interface that allows a user to request information on the JUNOS software command hierarchy. It is accessed in both operational as well as configuration modes.

contributing routes   Active IP routes in the routing table that share the same most significant bits and are more specific than an aggregate or generate route.

Control Board (CB)   On a T640 routing node, part of the host subsystem that provides control and monitoring functions for router components.

core   The central backbone of the network.

craft interface   Mechanisms used by a Communication Workers of America craftsperson to operate, administer, and maintain equipment or provision data communications. On a Juniper Networks router, the craft interface allows you to view status and troubleshooting information and perform system control functions.

customer edge device (CE device)   Router or switch in the customer's network that is connected to a service provider's provider edge (PE) router and participates in a Layer 3 or Layer 2 VPN.

customer premises equipment (CPE)   Telephone or other service provider equipment located at a customer site.

Customized Application of Mobile Enhance Logic (CAMEL)   ETSI standard for GSM networks that enhances the provision of Intelligent Network services.

D

daemon   Background process that performs operations on behalf of the system software and hardware. Daemons normally start when the system software is booted, and they run as long as the software is running. In the JUNOS software, daemons are also referred to as processes.

damping   Method of reducing the number of update messages sent between BGP peers, thereby reducing the load on these peers without adversely affecting the route convergence time for stable routes. The protocol accomplishes this by not advertising unstable routes.

data circuit-terminating equipment (DCE)   An RS-232-C device, typically used for a modem or printer, or a network access and packet switching node.

data-link connection identifier (DLCI)   Identifier for a Frame Relay virtual connection (also called a logical interface).

data service unit (DSU)   A device used to connect a DTE to a digital phone line. Converts digital data from a router to voltages and encoding required by the phone line. See also *channel service unit/data service unit (CSU/DSU).*

Data Terminal Equipment (DTE)   The RS-232-C interface that a computer uses to exchange information with a serial device.

Database Description packet   OSPF packet type used in the formation of an adjacency. It sends summary information about the local router's database to the neighboring router.

dcd   The JUNOS software interface process, called the Device Control Daemon.

deactivate   A method of modifying the router's active configuration. Portions of the hierarchy marked as inactive using this command are ignored during the router's commit process as if they were not configured at all.

dead interval   The amount of time an OSPF router maintains a neighbor relationship before declaring that neighbor as no longer operational. The JUNOS software uses a default value of 40 seconds for this timer.

default address   Router address that is used as the source address on unnumbered interfaces.

default route   Route used to forward IP packets when a more specific route is not present in the routing table. Often represented as 0.0.0.0 /0, the default route is sometimes referred to as the route of last resort.

denial of service (DoS)   System security breach in which network services become unavailable to users.

dense mode   A method of forwarding multicast traffic to interested listeners. Dense mode forwarding assumes that the majority of hosts on the network wish to receive the multicast data. Routers flood packets and prune back unwanted traffic every 3 minutes.

dense wavelength-division multiplexing (DWDM)   Technology that enables data from different sources to be carried together on an optical fiber, with each signal carried on its own separate wavelength.

designated router   In OSPF, a router selected by other routers that is responsible for representing the local segment to the remainder of the network, which reduces the amount of network traffic and the size of the routers' topological databases.

destination prefix length   The number of bits used for the network portion of a CIDR IP address.

Differentiated Services Codepoint (DSCP)   The use of the first 6 bits of the IPv4 Type of Service byte. The use of the DSCP for classifying traffic allows an administrator to have 64 unique service levels in the network.

Diffie-Hellman   A public key scheme, invented by Whitfield Diffie and Martin Hellman, used for sharing a secret key without communicating secret information, thus precluding the need for a secure channel. Once correspondents have computed the secret shared key, they can use it to encrypt communications.

Diffserv   Differentiated Service (based on RFC 2474). Diffserv uses the ToS byte to identify different packet flows on a packet-by-packet basis. Diffserv adds a Class Selector Codepoint (CSCP) and a Differentiated Services Codepoint (DSCP).

Dijkstra algorithm   See *shortest path first (SPF)*.

direct routes   See *interface routes*.

disable   A method of modifying the router's active configuration. Portions of the hierarchy marked as disabled (mainly router interfaces) cause the router to use the configuration but stop the pertinent operation of the configuration.

discard   JUNOS software syntax command used in a routing policy or a firewall filter. It halts the logical processing of the policy or filter when a set of match conditions is met. The specific route or IP packet is dropped from the network silently. It may also be a next-hop attribute assigned to a route in the routing table.

distance-vector   Method used in Bellman-Ford routing protocols to determine the best path to all routes in the network. Each router determines the distance (metric) to the destination as well as the vector (next hop) to follow.

Distance Vector Multicast Routing Protocol (DVMRP)   Distributed multicast routing protocol that dynamically generates IP multicast delivery trees using a technique called reverse path multicasting (RPM) to forward multicast traffic to downstream interfaces.

Distributed Buffer Manager ASICs   Juniper Networks ASIC responsible for managing the router's packet storage memory.

Down   OSPF adjacency state that is the starting state for the protocol.

drop profile   Drop probabilities for different levels of buffer fullness that are used by RED to determine if a packet is dropped from a queue or transmitted out an interface.

dual inline memory module (DIMM)   A 168-pin memory module that supports 64-bit data transfer.

Dynamic Host Configuration Protocol (DHCP)   Allocates IP addresses dynamically so that they can be reused when they are no longer needed.

dynamic label-switched path   An MPLS network path established by signaling protocols such as RSVP or LDP.

dynamic random access memory (DRAM)   Storage source on the router that can be accessed quickly by a process.

E

edge router   In MPLS, a router located at the beginning or end of a label-switching tunnel. When at the beginning of a tunnel, an edge router applies labels to new packets entering the tunnel. When at the end of a tunnel, the edge router returns to forwarding the packets using the destination IP address. See also *Multiprotocol Label Switching (MPLS)*.

editor macros (Emacs)   Shortcut keystrokes used within the router's command-line interface. These macros move the cursor and delete characters based on the specific sequence specified.

egress router   In MPLS, the last router in a label-switched path (LSP). See also *ingress router*.

electromagnetic interference (EMI)   Any electromagnetic disturbance that interrupts, obstructs, or otherwise degrades or limits the effective performance of electronics or electrical equipment.

Electronic Industries Association (EIA)   A United States trade group that represents manufacturers of electronics devices and sets standards and specifications.

embedded OS software   Software used by a Juniper Networks router to operate the physical router components.

encapsulating security payload (ESP)   A fundamental component of IPSec-compliant VPNs, ESP specifies an IP packet's encryption, data integrity checks, and sender authentication, which are added as a header to the IP packet. See also *Authentication Header (AH)*.

end system   In IS-IS, the network entity that sends and receives packets.

Equipment Identity Register (EIR)   Mobile network database that contains information about devices using the network.

Established   BGP neighbor state that represents a fully functional BGP peering session.

exact   JUNOS software routing policy match type that represents only the route specified in a route filter.

exception packet   An IP packet not processed by the normal packet flow through the Packet Forwarding Engine. Exception packets include local delivery information, expired TTL packets, or packets with an IP option specified.

Exchange   OSPF adjacency state that means the two neighboring routers are actively sending Database Description packets to each other to exchange their database contents.

Exchange Carriers Standards Association (ECSA)   A standards organization created after the divestiture of the Bell System to represent the interests of interexchange carriers.

explicit path   See *signaled path*.

Explicit Route Object (ERO)   Extension to RSVP that allows an RSVP Path message to traverse an explicit sequence of routers that is independent of conventional shortest-path IP routing.

export   To place routes from the routing table into a routing protocol.

ExStart   OSPF adjacency state where the neighboring routers negotiate who is in charge of the synchronization process.

Exterior Gateway Protocol (EGP)   The original exterior gateway protocol used to exchange routing information among routers in different Autonomous Systems. EGP was replaced by BGP as the size and complexity of the Internet grew.

External BGP (EBGP) BGP configuration in which sessions are established between routers in different ASs.

external metric A cost included in a route when OSPF exports route information from external Autonomous Systems. There are two types of external metrics: Type 1 and Type 2.

F

far-end alarm and control (FEAC) Signal used to send alarm or status information from the far-end terminal back to the near-end terminal and to initiate loopbacks at the far-end terminal from the near-end terminal.

fast reroute Mechanism for automatically rerouting traffic on an LSP if a node or link in an LSP fails, thus reducing the loss of packets traveling over the LSP.

field-replaceable unit (FRU) Router component that customers can replace onsite.

firewall A security gateway positioned between two different networks, usually between a trusted network and the Internet. A firewall ensures that all traffic that crosses it conforms to the organization's security policy. Firewalls track and control communications, deciding whether to pass, reject, discard, encrypt, or log them. Firewalls also can be used to secure sensitive portions of a local network.

first in, first out (FIFO) Queuing and buffering method where the first data packet stored in the queue is the first data packet removed from the queue. All JUNOS software interface queues operate in this mode by default.

flap damping See *damping*.

flapping See *route flapping*.

flexible PIC concentrator (FPC) An interface concentrator on which PICs are mounted. An FPC inserts into a slot in a Juniper Networks router. See also *physical interface card (PIC)*.

floating static route A route that should be used only when all dynamically learned versions of that same route are no longer in the routing table.

flood and prune Method of forwarding multicast data packets in a dense-mode network. This process repeats itself every 3 minutes.

flow control action JUNOS software syntax used in a routing policy or a firewall filter. It alters the default logical processing of the policy or filter when a set of match conditions is met.

forwarding class Internal router designation that represents the queuing service offered to IP packets matching some set of criteria. The forwarding class is assigned to a packet when it enters the router and can be modified by a routing policy or a firewall filter.

Forwarding Engine Board (FEB) In M5 and M10 routers, provides route lookup, filtering, and switching to the destination port.

forwarding information base See *forwarding table*.

forwarding table JUNOS software forwarding information base (FIB). The JUNOS routing protocol process installs active routes from its routing tables into the Routing Engine forwarding table. The kernel copies this forwarding table into the Packet Forwarding Engine, which is responsible for determining which interface transmits the packets.

Frame Relay Layer 2 encoding and addressing mechanism that uses a DLCI to segment logical circuits on a physical transmission media.

from JUNOS software command syntax that contains match criteria in a routing policy or a firewall filter.

Full OSPF adjacency state that represents a fully functional neighbor relationship.

fxp0 JUNOS software permanent interface used for out-of-band network access to the router.

fxp1 JUNOS software permanent interface used for communications between the Routing Engine and the Packet Forwarding Engine.

fxp2 JUNOS software permanent interface used for communications between the Routing Engine and the Packet Forwarding Engine. This interface is not present on all routers.

G

Garbage Collection timer Timer used in a distance-vector network that represents the time remaining before a route is removed from the routing table.

Gateway GPRS Support Node (GGSN) Router that serves as a gateway between mobile networks and packet data networks.

G-CDR GGSN call detail record. Collection of charges in ASN.1 format that is eventually billed to a mobile station user.

General Packet Radio Service (GPRS) Packet-switched service that allows full mobility and wide area coverage as information is sent and received across a mobile network.

generated route A summary route that uses an IP address next hop to forward packets in an IP network. A generated route is functionally similar to an aggregated route.

Global System for Mobile Communications (GSM) A standard for mobile communications networks that delivers high quality and secure mobile voice and data services with full roaming capabilities across the world.

GPRS Tunneling Protocol (GTP)   Protocol that transports IP packets between an SGSN and a GGSN.

GPRS Tunneling Protocol Control (GTP-C)   Protocol that allows an SGSN to establish packet data network access for a mobile station.

GPRS Tunneling Protocol User (GTP-U)   Protocol that carries mobile station user data packets.

group   A collection of related BGP peers.

group address   The IP address used as the destination address in a multicast IP packet. It functionally represents the senders and interested receivers for a particular multicast data stream.

H

hash   A one-way function that takes a message of any length and produces a fixed-length digest. In security, a message digest is used to validate that the contents of a message have not been altered in transit. The Secure Hash Algorithm (SHA-1) and Message Digest 5 (MD5) are commonly used hashes.

Hashed Message Authentication Code (HMAC)   A mechanism for message authentication that uses cryptographic hash functions. HMAC can be used with any iterative cryptographic hash function—for example, MD5 or SHA-1—in combination with a secret shared key. The cryptographic strength of HMAC depends on the properties of the underlying hash function.

hello interval   The amount of time an OSPF router sends a hello packet to each adjacent neighbor. The JUNOS software uses a default value of 10 seconds for this timer.

hello mechanism   Process used by an RSVP router to enhance the detection of network outages in an MPLS network.

High-Level Data Link Control (HDLC)   An International Telecommunication Union (ITU) standard for a bit-oriented data link layer protocol on which most other bit-oriented protocols are based.

High-Speed Circuit-Switched Data (HSCSC)   Circuit-switched wireless data transmission for mobile users, at data rates up to 38.4Kbps.

hold down   A timer used by distance-vector protocols to prevent the propagation of incorrect routing knowledge to other routers in the network.

hold time   Maximum number of seconds allowed to elapse between the time a BGP system receives successive keepalive or update messages from a peer.

Home Location Register (HLR)   Database containing information about a subscriber and the current location of a subscriber's mobile station.

Host Membership Query   IGMP packet sent by a router to determine whether interested receivers exist on a broadcast network for multicast traffic.

Host Membership Report   IGMP packet sent by an interested receiver for a particular multicast group address. Hosts send Report messages when they first join a group or in response to a Query packet from the local router.

host module   On an M160 router, provides routing and system management functions of the router. Consists of the Routing Engine and Miscellaneous Control Subsystem (MCS).

host subsystem   On a T640 routing node, provides routing and system-management functions of the router. Consists of a Routing Engine and an adjacent Control Board (CB).

I

Idle   The initial BGP neighbor state where the local router is refusing all incoming session requests.

import   To install routes from the routing protocols into a routing table.

inet.0   Default JUNOS software routing table for IPv4 unicast routes.

inet.1   Default JUNOS software routing table for storing the multicast cache for active data streams in the network.

inet.2   Default JUNOS software routing table for storing unicast IPv4 routes specifically used to prevent forwarding loops in a multicast network.

inet.3   Default JUNOS software routing table for storing the egress IP address of an MPLS label-switched path.

inet.4   Default JUNOS software routing table for storing information generated by the Multicast Source Discovery Protocol (MSDP).

inet6.0   Default JUNOS software routing table for storing unicast IPv6 routes.

infinity metric   A metric value used in distance-vector protocols to represent an unusable route. For RIP, the infinity metric is 16.

ingress router   In MPLS, the first router in a label-switched path (LSP). See also *egress router*.

init   OSPF adjacency state where the local router has received a hello packet but bidirectional communication is not yet established.

insert   JUNOS software command that allows a user to reorder terms in a routing policy or a firewall filter. It may also be used to change the order of a policy chain.

Institute of Electronic and Electrical Engineers (IEEE)   The international professional society for electrical engineers that sets standards for networking technologies.

Integrated Drive Electronics (IDE)   Type of hard disk on the Routing Engine.

inter-AS routing   Routing of packets among different ASs. See also *External BGP (EBGP)*.

intercluster reflection   In a BGP route reflection network, the redistribution of routing information by a route reflector system to all nonclient peers (BGP peers not in the cluster). See also *route reflection*.

interface cost   Value added to all received routes in a distance-vector network before placing them into the routing table. The JUNOS software uses a cost of 1 for this value.

interface routes   Routes that are in the routing table because an interface has been configured with an IP address. Also called *direct and local routes*.

Interior Gateway Protocol (IGP)   A routing protocol designed to operate within the confines of an administrative domain. Examples include the Routing Information Protocol (RIP), Open Shortest Path First (OSPF), and Intermediate System to Intermediate System (IS-IS).

intermediate system   In IS-IS, the network entity that sends and receives packets and that can also route packets.

Intermediate System-to-Intermediate System (IS-IS)   Link-state, interior gateway routing protocol for IP networks that also uses the shortest path first (SPF) algorithm to determine routes.

Internal BGP (IBGP)   BGP configuration in which sessions are established between routers in the same AS.

Internal Ethernet   Another name for the fxp1 and fxp2 interfaces that provide communications between the Routing Engine and the Packet Forwarding Engine.

International Electrotechnical Commission (IEC)   See *International Organization for Standardization (ISO)*.

International Mobile Station Equipment Identity (IMEI)   A unique code used to identify an individual mobile station to a GSM network.

International Mobile Subscriber Identity (IMSI)   Information that identifies a particular subscriber to a GSM network.

International Organization for Standardization (ISO)   Worldwide federation of standards bodies that promotes international standardization and publishes international agreements as International Standards.

International Telecommunications Union (ITU)   Formerly known as the CCITT, group supported by the United Nations that makes recommendations and coordinates the development of telecommunications standards for the entire world.

Internet Assigned Numbers Authority (IANA)   Regulatory group that maintains all assigned and registered Internet numbers, such as IP and multicast addresses.

Internet Control Message Protocol (ICMP)   Used in router discovery, ICMP allows router advertisements that enable a host to discover addresses of operating routers on the subnet.

Internet Engineering Task Force (IETF)   International community of network designers, operators, vendors, and researchers concerned with the evolution of the Internet architecture and the smooth operation of the Internet.

Internet Group Management Protocol (IGMP)   Multicast protocol used for router-to-host communications. Hosts use IGMP to request multicast data streams from the network. Routers use IGMP to determine whether group members are still present on the local segment.

Internet Key Exchange (IKE)   The key management protocol used in IPSec, IKE combines the ISAKMP and Oakley protocols to create encryption keys and security associations.

Internet Processor ASIC   Juniper Networks ASIC responsible for using the forwarding table to make routing decisions within the Packet Forwarding Engine. The Internet Processor ASIC also implements firewall filters.

Internet Protocol (IP)   The protocol used for sending data from one point to another on the Internet.

Internet Protocol Security (IPSec)   The industry standard for establishing VPNs, IPSec comprises a group of protocols and algorithms that provide authentication and encryption of data across IP-based networks.

Internet Security Association and Key Management Protocol (ISAKMP)   A protocol that allows the receiver of a message to obtain a public key and use digital certificates to authenticate the sender's identity. ISAKMP is designed to be key exchange independent; that is, it supports many different key exchanges. See also *Internet Key Exchange (IKE)* and *Oakley.*

Internet service provider (ISP)   Company that provides access to the Internet and related services.

intra-AS routing   The routing of packets within a single AS. See also *Internal BGP (IBGP).*

I/O Manager ASIC   Juniper Networks ASIC responsible for segmenting data packets into 64-byte J-cells and for queuing result cells prior to transmission.

J

jbase   JUNOS software package containing updates to the kernel.

jbundle   JUNOS software package containing all possible software package files.

J-cell   A 64-byte data unit used within the Packet Forwarding Engine. All IP packets processed by a Juniper Networks router are segmented into J-cells.

jdocs   JUNOS software package containing the documentation set.

jitter   Small random variation introduced into the value of a timer to prevent multiple timer expirations from becoming synchronized.

jkernel   JUNOS software package containing the basic components of the software.

Join message   PIM message sent hop-by-hop upstream towards a multicast source or the RP of the domain. It requests that multicast traffic be sent downstream to the router originating the message.

jpfe   JUNOS software package containing the Embedded OS software for operating the Packet Forwarding Engine.

jroute   JUNOS software package containing the software used by the Routing Engine.

K

keepalive   BGP packet used to maintain a peering session with a neighbor.

kernel   The basic software component of the JUNOS software. It operates the various daemons used to control the router's operations.

kernel forwarding table   See *forwarding table*.

L

label   In MPLS, a 20-bit unsigned integer in the range 0 through 1048575, used to identify a packet traveling along an LSP.

Label Distribution Protocol (LDP)   A signaling protocol used to establish an MPLS label-switched path. LDP uses the IGP shortest-path cost to each egress router in the network and is not capable of utilizing traffic-engineering concepts.

label object   An RSVP message object that contains the label value allocated by the next downstream router.

label pop operation   Function performed by an MPLS router in which the top label in a label stack is removed from the data packet.

label push operation   Function performed by an MPLS router in which a new label is added to the top of the data packet.

label request object   An RSVP message object that requests each router along the path of an LSP to allocate a label for forwarding purposes.

label swap operation   Function performed by an MPLS router in which the top label in a label stack is replaced with a new label before forwarding the data packet to the next-hop router.

label-switched path (LSP)   Sequence of routers that cooperatively perform MPLS operations for a packet stream. The first router in an LSP is called the ingress router, and the last router in the path is called the egress router. An LSP is a point-to-point, simplex connection from the ingress router to the egress router. (The ingress and egress routers cannot be the same router.)

label switching   See *Multiprotocol Label Switching (MPLS)*.

label-switching router (LSR)   A router on which MPLS is enabled and is thus capable of processing label-switched packets.

label values   A 20-bit field in an MPLS header used by routers to forward data traffic along an MPLS label-switched path.

Lightweight Directory Access Protocol (LDAP)   Software protocol used for locating resources on a public or private network.

line loopback   A method used to troubleshoot a problem with a physical transmission media. A transmission device in the network sends the data signal back to the originating router.

link   Communication path between two neighbors. A link is up when communication is possible between the two end points.

link-state acknowledgment   OSPF data packet used to inform a neighbor that a link-state update packet has been successfully received.

link-state advertisement (LSA)   OSPF data structure that is advertised in a link-state update packet. Each LSA uniquely describes a portion of the OSPF network.

link-state database   All routing knowledge in a link-state network is contained in this database. Each router runs the SPF algorithm against this database to locate the best network path to each destination in the network.

link-state PDU (LSP)   Packets that contain information about the state of adjacencies to neighboring systems in an IS-IS network.

link-state request list   A list generated by an OSPF router during the exchange of database information while forming an adjacency. Advertised information by a neighbor that the local router doesn't contain is placed onto this list.

link-state request packet   OSPF data packet that a router uses to request database information from a neighboring router.

link-state update   OSPF data packet that contains one or multiple LSAs. It is used to advertise routing knowledge into the network.

loading   OSPF adjacency state where the local router is sending link-state request packets to its neighbor and is awaiting the appropriate link-state updates from that neighbor.

local preference   Optional BGP path attribute carried in internal BGP update packets that indicates the degree of preference for an external route.

local significance   Concept used in an MPLS network where the label values are unique only between two neighbor routers.

Local-RIB   Logical software table that contains BGP routes used by the local router to forward data packets.

logical operator   Characters used in a firewall filter to represent a Boolean AND or OR operation.

longer   JUNOS software routing policy match type that represents all routes more specific than the given subnet, but not the given subnet itself. It is similar to a mathematical greater-than operation.

loose   In the context of traffic engineering, a path that can use any route or any number of other intermediate (transit) points to reach the next address in the path. (Definition from RFC 791, modified to fit LSPs.)

loose hop   Router in an MPLS named-path that is not required to be directly connected to the local router.

M

management daemon (mgd)   JUNOS software process responsible for managing all user access to the router.

Management Ethernet   Another name for the fxp0 interface that provides out-of-band access to the router.

Management Information Base (MIB)   Definition of an object that can be managed by SNMP.

mapping agent   A router used in an auto-RP multicast network to select the rendezvous point for all multicast group addresses. This information is then advertised to all other routers in the domain.

Martian address   Network address about which all information is ignored.

Martian routes   Network routes about which information is ignored. The JUNOS software doesn't allow Martian routes to reside in the inet.0 routing table.

mask   See *subnet mask*.

master   The router in control of the OSPF database exchange during an adjacency formation.

match   A logical concept used in a routing policy or a firewall filter. It denotes the criteria used to find a route or IP packet before performing some action.

match type   JUNOS software syntax used in a route filter to better describe the routes that should match the policy term.

maximum transmission unit (MTU)   Limit on segment size for a network.

MBone   Internet multicast backbone. An interconnected set of subnetworks and routers that support the delivery of IP multicast traffic. The MBone is a virtual network that is layered on top of sections of the physical Internet.

mean time between failure (MTBF)   Measure of hardware component reliability.

mesh   Network topology in which devices are organized in a manageable, segmented manner with many, often redundant, interconnections between network nodes.

message aggregation   An extension to the RSVP specification that allows neighboring routers to bundle up to 30 RSVP messages into a single protocol packet.

Message Digest 5 (MD5)   A one-way hashing algorithm that produces a 128-bit hash. See also *Secure Hash Algorithm (SHA-1)*.

midplane   Forms the rear of the PIC cage on M5 and M10 routers and the FPC card cage on M20, M40e, M160, and T640 platforms. Provides data transfer, power distribution, and signal connectivity.

Miscellaneous Control Subsystem (MCS)   On the M40e and M160 routers, provides control and monitoring functions for router components and SONET clocking for the router.

mobile network access subsystem (MAS)   GSN application subsystem that contains the access server.

mobile point-to-point control subsystem (MPS)   GSN application subsystem that controls all functionality associated with a particular connection.

mobile station   A mobile device, such as a cellular phone or a mobile personal digital assistant (PDA).

Mobile Station Integrated Services Digital Network Number (MSISDN)   Number that callers use to reach a mobile services subscriber.

Mobile Switching Center (MSC)   Provides origination and termination functions to calls from a mobile station user.

mobile transport subsystem (MTS)   GSN application subsystem that implements all the protocols used by the GSN.

multicast   Operation of sending network traffic from one network node to multiple network nodes.

multicast distribution tree   The data path between the sender (host) and the multicast group members (receiver or listener).

Multiple Exit Discriminator (MED)   Optional BGP path attribute consisting of a metric value that is used to determine the exit point to a destination when all other factors in determining the exit point are equal.

Multiprotocol BGP (MBGP) An extension to BGP that allows you to exchange routing knowledge from multiple NLRI within and between BGP ASs.

Multiprotocol Label Switching (MPLS) Mechanism for engineering network traffic patterns that functions by assigning to network packets short labels that describe how to forward them through the network. Also called *label switching*. See also *traffic engineering*.

N

named-path JUNOS software syntax that specifies a portion or the entire network path that should be used as a constraint in signaling an MPLS label-switched path.

neighbor Adjacent system reachable by traversing a single subnetwork. An immediately adjacent router. A system to which a BGP session is established. Also called a *peer*.

network entity title (NET) Network address defined by the ISO network architecture and used in CLNS-based networks.

network layer reachability information (NLRI) Information that is carried in BGP packets and is used by MBGP.

network-link advertisement An OSPF link-state advertisement flooded throughout a single area by designated routers to describe all routers attached to the DR's local segment.

network LSA OSPF link-state advertisement sent by the DR on a broadcast or NBMA segment. It advertises the subnet associated with the DR's segment.

network service access point (NSAP) Connection to a network that is identified by a network address.

Network Summary LSA OSPF link-state advertisement sent by an ABR to advertise internal OSPF routing knowledge across an area boundary.

Network Time Protocol (NTP) Protocol used to synchronize computer clock times on a network.

Next Hop BGP attribute that specifies the router to send packets to for a particular set of routes.

nonclient peer In a BGP route reflection network, a BGP peer that is not a member of a cluster. See also *client peer*.

notification cell JUNOS software data structure generated by the Distributed Buffer Manager ASIC that represents the header contents of an IP packet. The Internet Processor ASIC uses the notification cell to perform a forwarding table lookup.

Notification message BGP message that informs a neighbor about an error condition and then possibly terminates the BGP peering session.

not-so-stubby area (NSSA)   In OSPF, a type of stub area in which external routes can be flooded.

n-selector   Last byte of an ISO Network Entity Title (NET) address.

Null Register message   A PIM message sent by the first hop router to the RP. It informs the RP that the local source is still actively sending multicast packets into the network should future interested listeners send a Join message to the RP.

numeric range match conditions   The use of numeric values (protocol and port numbers) in the header of an IP packet as match criteria in a firewall filter.

O

Oakley   A key determination protocol based on the Diffie-Hellman algorithm that provides added security, including authentication. Oakley was the key-exchange algorithm mandated for use with the initial version of ISAKMP, although various algorithms can be used. Oakley describes a series of key exchanges called "modes" and details the services provided by each; for example, Perfect Forward Secrecy for keys, identity protection, and authentication. See also *Internet Security Association and Key Management Protocol (ISAKMP)*.

Open message   BGP message that allows two neighbors to negotiate the parameters of the peering session.

OpenConfirm   BGP neighbor state that shows a valid Open message was received from the remote peer.

OpenSent   BGP neighbor state that shows an Open message was sent to the remote peer and the local router is waiting for an Open message to be returned.

Open Shortest Path First (OSPF)   A link-state IGP that makes routing decisions based on the shortest path first (SPF) algorithm (also referred to as the Dijkstra algorithm).

Open System Interconnection (OSI)   Standard reference model for how messages are transmitted between two points on a network.

operational mode   JUNOS software mode allowing a user to view statistics and information concerning the router's current operating status.

Optical Carrier (OC)   In SONET, Optical Carrier levels indicate the transmission rate of digital signals on optical fiber.

Origin   BGP attribute that describes the believability of a particular route. The router that first places the route into BGP should attempt to accurately describe the source of the route.

orlonger   JUNOS software routing policy match type that represents all routes more specific than the given subnet, including the given subnet itself. It is similar to a mathematical greater-than-or-equals-to operation.

OSPF Hello packet   Message sent by each OSPF router to each adjacent neighbor. It is used to establish and maintain the router's neighbor relationships.

overlay network   Network design seen where a logical Layer 3 topology (IP subnets) is operating over a logical Layer 2 topology (ATM PVCs). Layers in the network do not have knowledge of each other, and each requires separate management and operation.

P

package   A collection of files that make up a JUNOS software component.

packet data protocol (PDP)   Network protocol, such as IP, used by packet data networks connected to a GPRS network.

Packet Forwarding Engine   The architectural portion of the router that processes packets by forwarding them between input and output interfaces.

Packet Loss Priority (PLP)   Internal router designation that represents a greater probability of dropping a particular IP packet based on configured class of service settings. The priority is assigned to a packet when it enters the router and can be modified by a firewall filter.

partial sequence number PDU (PSNP)   Packet that contains only a partial list of the LSP headers in the IS-IS link-state database.

path attribute   Information about a BGP route, such as the route origin, AS path, and next-hop router.

PathErr   RSVP message that indicates an error has occurred along an established LSP. The message is advertised upstream toward the ingress router and it doesn't remove any RSVP soft state from the network.

PathTear Message   RSVP message that indicates the established LSP and its associated soft state should be removed by the network. The message is advertised downstream hop-by-hop toward the egress router.

path-vector protocol   A routing protocol definition that describes the direction to the destination and the network path used to reach the destination. This often describes the functionality of BGP.

peer   An immediately adjacent router with which a protocol relationship has been established. Also called a *neighbor*.

penultimate hop popping (PHP)   A mechanism used in an MPLS network that allows the transit router prior to the egress to perform a label pop operation and forward the remaining data (often a native IPv4 packet) to the egress router.

penultimate router   The last transit router prior to the egress router in an MPLS label-switched path.

Perfect Forward Secrecy (PFS)   A condition derived from an encryption system that changes encryption keys often and ensures that no two sets of keys have any relation to each other. The advantage of PFS is that if one set of keys is compromised, only communications using those keys are at risk. An example of a system that uses PFS is *Diffie-Hellman*.

Peripheral Component Interconnect (PCI)   Standard, high-speed bus for connecting computer peripherals. Used on the Routing Engine.

permanent virtual circuit (PVC)   A logical Layer 2 connection between two network devices. The network path is preengineered and configured on each device in the network supporting the PVC.

Personal Computer Memory Card International Association (PCMCIA)   Industry group that promotes standards for credit card–size memory or I/O devices.

Physical Interface Card (PIC)   A network interface–specific card that can be installed on a FPC in the router.

PIC I/O Manager ASIC   Juniper Networks ASIC responsible for receiving and transmitting information on the physical media. It performs media-specific tasks within the Packet Forwarding Engine.

PLP bit   Packet Loss Priority bit. Used to identify packets that have experienced congestion or are from a transmission that exceeded a service provider's customer service license agreement. This bit can be used as part of a router's congestion control mechanism and can be set by the interface or by a filter.

policing   Applying rate limits on bandwidth and burst size for traffic on a particular interface or IPv4 prefix.

Policing Equivalence Classes (PEC)   In traffic policing, a set of packets that is treated the same by the packet classifier.

pop   Removal of the last label, by a router, from a packet as it exits an MPLS domain.

Point-to-Point Protocol (PPP)   Link-layer protocol that provides multiprotocol encapsulation. It is used for link-layer and network-layer configuration.

poison reverse   Method used in distance-vector networks to avoid routing loops. Each router advertises routes back to the neighbor it received them from with an infinity metric assigned.

policy chain   The application of multiple routing policies in a single location. The policies are evaluated in a predefined manner and are always followed by the default policy for the specific application location.

precedence bits   The first three bits in the ToS byte. On a Juniper Networks router, these bits are used to sort or classify individual packets as they arrive at an interface. The classification determines the forwarding class to which the packet is directed upon transmission.

preference   Desirability of a route to become the active route. A route with a lower preference value is more likely to become the active route. The preference is an arbitrary value in the range 0 through 4,294,967,295 that the routing protocol process uses to rank routes received from different protocols, interfaces, or remote systems.

preferred address   On an interface, the default local address used for packets sourced by the local router to destinations on the subnet.

prefix-length-range   JUNOS software routing policy match type representing all routes that share the same most significant bits. The prefix length of the route must also lie between the two supplied lengths in the route filter.

primary address   On an interface, the address used by default as the local address for broadcast and multicast packets sourced locally and sent out the interface.

primary contributing route   The contributing route with the numerically smallest prefix and smallest JUNOS software preference value. This route is the default next hop used for a generated route.

primary interface   Router interface that packets go out when no interface name is specified and when the destination address does not imply a particular outgoing interface.

protocol address   The logical Layer 3 address assigned to an interface within the JUNOS software.

protocol data unit (PDU)   The basic data structure used by the IS-IS routing protocol to form adjacencies and exchange routing information.

protocol families   The grouping of logical properties within an interface configuration. The JUNOS software supports the inet, iso, mpls, and inet6 families.

Protocol Independent Multicast (PIM)   A protocol-independent multicast routing protocol. PIM sparse mode routes to multicast groups that might span wide-area and interdomain internets. PIM dense mode is a flood-and-prune protocol.

protocol preference   A 32-bit value assigned to all routes placed into the routing table. It is used as a tiebreaker when multiple exact routes are placed into the table by different protocols.

provider edge (PE) router   A router in the service provider's network that can have customer edge (CE) devices connected and that participates in a virtual private network (VPN).

provider router   Router in the service provider's network that does not attach to a customer edge (CE) device.

Prune message   PIM message sent upstream to a multicast source or the RP of the domain. It requests that multicast traffic stop being transmitted to the router originating the message.

public land mobile network (PLMN)   A telecommunications network for mobile stations.

push   Addition of a label or stack of labels, by a router, to a packet as it enters an MPLS domain.

Q

quad-wide   A type of PIC that combines the PIC and the FPC within a single FPC slot.

qualified next hop   A next hop for a static route that allows a second next hop for the same static route to have different metric and preference properties than the original.

quality of service (QoS)   Performance, such as transmission rates and error rates, of a communications channel or system.

querier router   PIM router on a broadcast subnet responsible for generating IGMP Query messages for the segment.

R

radio frequency interference (RFI)   Interference from high-frequency electromagnetic waves emanating from electronic devices.

radio network controller (RNC)   Manages the radio part of the network in UMTS.

Random Early Detection (RED)   Gradual drop profile for a given class that is used for congestion avoidance. RED tries to anticipate incipient congestion and reacts by dropping a small percentage of packets from the head of the queue to ensure that a queue never becomes full.

rate limiting   See *policing*.

rate policing   See *policing*.

receive   A next hop for a static route that allows all matching packets to be sent to the Routing Engine for processing.

record route object (RRO)   An RSVP message object that notes the IP address of each router along the path of an LSP.

recursive lookup   A method of consulting the routing table to locate the actual physical next hop for a route when the supplied next hop is not directly connected.

regional Bell operating company (RBOC)   (Pronounced "are-bock") Regional telephone companies formed as a result of the divestiture of the Bell System.

Register message   PIM message unicast by the first hop router to the RP that contains the multicast packets from the source encapsulated within its data field.

Register Stop message   PIM message sent by the RP to the first hop router to halt the sending of encapsulated multicast packets.

reject   A next hop for a configured route that drops all matching packets from the network and returns an ICMP message to the source IP address. Also used as an action in a routing policy or a firewall filter.

Remote Authentication Dial-In User Service (RADIUS)   Authentication method for validating users who attempt to access the router using Telnet.

rename   JUNOS software command that allows a user to change the name of a routing policy, a firewall filter, or any other variable character string defined in the router's configuration.

Request for Comments (RFC)   Internet standard specifications published by the Internet Engineering Task Force.

Rendezvous Point (RP)   For PIM-SM, a router acting as the root of the shared distribution tree.

Request message   RIP message used by a router to ask for all or part of the routing table from a neighbor.

resolve   A next hop for a static route that allows the router to perform a recursive lookup to locate the physical next hop for the route.

Resource Reservation Protocol (RSVP)   Resource reservation setup protocol designed to interact with integrated services on the Internet.

Response message   RIP message used to advertise routing information into a network.

result cell   JUNOS software data structure generated by the Internet Processor ASIC after performing a forwarding table lookup.

ResvConf message   RSVP message that allows the egress router to receive an explicit confirmation message from a neighbor that its Resv message was received.

ResvErr message   RSVP message that indicates an error has occurred along an established LSP. The message is advertised downstream toward the egress router and it doesn't remove any RSVP soft state from the network.

ResvTear message   RSVP message that indicates the established LSP and its associated soft state should be removed by the network. The message is advertised upstream toward the ingress router.

reverse path forwarding   Method used in a multicast routing domain to prevent forwarding loops.

reverse path multicasting (RPM)   Routing algorithm used by DVMRP to forward multicast traffic.

route filter   JUNOS software syntax used in a routing policy to match an individual route or a group of routes.

route flapping   Situation in which BGP systems send an excessive number of update messages to advertise and withdraw reachability of the same NLRI.

route identifier   IP address of the router from which a BGP, IGP, or OSPF packet originated.

route redistribution   A method of placing learned routes from one protocol into another protocol operating on the same router. The JUNOS software accomplishes this with a routing policy.

route reflection   In BGP, configuring a group of routers into a cluster and having one system act as a route reflector, redistributing routes from outside the cluster to all routers in the cluster. Routers in a cluster do not need to be fully meshed.

Router ID   An IP address used by a router to uniquely identify itself to a routing protocol. This address may or may not be equal to a configured interface address.

router-link advertisement   OSPF link-state advertisement flooded throughout a single area by all routers to describe the state and cost of the router's links to the area.

router LSA   OSPF link-state advertisement sent by each router in the network. It describes the local router's connected subnets as well as their metric values.

Router Priority   A numerical value assigned to an OSPF or an IS-IS interface that is used as the first criterion in electing the designated router or designated intermediate system, respectively.

routing domain   See *Autonomous System (AS)*.

Routing Engine   Architectural portion of the router that handles all routing protocol processes, as well as other software processes that control the router's interfaces, some of the chassis components, system management, and user access to the router.

Routing Information Base (RIB)   A logical data structure used by BGP to store routing information.

Routing Information Protocol (RIP)   Distance-vector Interior Gateway Protocol that makes routing decisions based on hop count.

routing instance   A collection of routing tables, interfaces, and routing protocol parameters. The set of interfaces belongs to the routing tables and the routing protocol parameters control the information in the routing tables.

routing protocol daemon (rpd)   JUNOS software routing protocol process (daemon). User-level background process responsible for starting, managing, and stopping the routing protocols on a Juniper Networks router.

routing table   Common database of routes learned from one or more routing protocols. All routes are maintained by the JUNOS routing protocol process.

RSVP Path message   RSVP message sent by the ingress router downstream toward the egress router. It begins the establishment of a soft state database for a particular label-switched path.

RSVP Resv message   RSVP message sent by the egress router upstream toward the ingress router. It completes the establishment of the soft state database for a particular label-switched path.

RSVP signaled LSP   A label-switched path that is dynamically established using RSVP `Path` and `Resv` messages.

S

Secure Hash Algorithm (SHA-1)   A widely used hash function for use with Digital Signal Standard (DSS). SHA-1 is more secure than MD5.

secure shell (SSH)   A protocol that provides a secured method of logging in to a remote network system.

security association (SA)   An IPSec term that describes an agreement between two parties about what rules to use for authentication and encryption algorithms, key exchange mechanisms, and secure communications.

Security Parameter Index (SPI)   A portion of the IPSec Authentication Header that communicates which security protocols, such as authentication and encryption, are used for each packet in a VPN connection.

segmentation and reassembly (SAR)   Method used in ATM to transform IP packets into ATM cells and cells into IP packets.

Serving GPRS Support Node (SGSN)   Device in the mobile network that requests PDP contexts with a GGSN.

Session Announcement Protocol (SAP)   Used with multicast protocols to handle session conference announcements.

session attribute object   RSVP message object that is used to control the priority, preemption, affinity class, and local rerouting of the LSP.

Session Description Protocol (SDP)   Used with multicast protocols to handle session conference announcements.

shared tree   The multicast forwarding tree established from the RP to the last hop router for a particular group address.

shim header   The name used to describe the location of the MPLS header in a data packet. The JUNOS software always places (shims) the header between the existing Layers 2 and 3 headers.

Short Message Service (SMS)   GSM service that enables short text messages to be sent to and from mobile telephones.

shortest path first (SPF)   An algorithm used by IS-IS and OSPF to make routing decisions based on the state of network links. Also called the *Dijkstra algorithm*.

shortest-path tree   The multicast forwarding tree established from the first hop router to the last hop router for a particular group address.

show route advertising-protocol   JUNOS software command that displays the routes sent to a neighbor for a particular protocol.

show route receive-protocol   JUNOS software command that displays the routes received from a neighbor for a particular protocol.

signaled path   In traffic engineering, an explicit path; that is, a path determined using RSVP signaling. The ERO carried in the packets contains the explicit path information.

Signaling System 7 (SS7)   Protocol used in telecommunications for delivering calls and services.

Simple Network Management Protocol (SNMP)   Protocol governing network management and the monitoring of network devices and their functions.

simplex interface   An interface that assumes that packets it receives from itself are the result of a software loopback process. The interface does not consider these packets when determining whether the interface is functional.

soft state   A database structure maintained by an RSVP router to store information about a particular label-switched path.

SONET Clock Generator (SCG)   On a M40e or M160 router as well as on a T320 or T640 routing node, the SCG provides Stratum 3 clock signal for the SONET/SDH interfaces. It also provides external clock inputs.

source-based tree   The multicast forwarding tree established from the source of traffic to all interested receivers for a particular group address. It is often seen in a dense-mode forwarding environment.

source-specific multicasting   As part of the IGMPv3 specification, it allows an end host to request multicast traffic for a group address from a specific source of traffic.

sparse mode   A method of operating a multicast domain where sources of traffic and interested receivers meet at a central rendezvous point. A sparse-mode network assumes that there are very few receivers for each group address.

Split Horizon   Method used in distance-vector networks to avoid routing loops. Each router does not advertise routes back to the neighbor it received them from.

static label-switched path (static LSP)   See *static path*.

static path   In the context of traffic engineering, a static route that requires hop-by-hop manual configuration. No signaling is used to create or maintain the path. Also called a *static LSP*.

static route   A configured route that includes a route and a next hop. It is always present in the routing table and doesn't react to topology changes in the network.

static RP   One of three methods of learning the rendezvous point to group address mapping in a multicast network. Each router in the domain must be configured with the required RP information.

strict   In the context of traffic engineering, a route that must go directly to the next address in the path. (Definition from RFC 791, modified to fit LSPs.)

strict hop   Routers in an MPLS named path that are required to be directly connected to the previous router in the configured path.

Strict Priority Queuing (SPQ) Dequeuing method that provides a special queue that is serviced until it is empty. The traffic sent to this queue tends to maintain a lower latency and more consistent latency numbers than traffic sent to other queues. See also *Alternate Priority Queuing (APQ)*.

stub area In OSPF, an area through which, or into which, AS external advertisements are not flooded.

subnet mask The number of bits of the network address used for the network portion of a Class A, Class B, or Class C IP address.

summary-link advertisement OSPF link-statement advertisement flooded throughout the advertisement's associated areas by area border routers to describe the routes that they know about in other areas.

Switch Interface Board (SIB) On a T320 or T640 routing node, provides the switching function to the destination Packet Forwarding Engine.

Switching and Forwarding Module (SFM) On an M40e or M160 router, a component of the Packet Forwarding Engine that provides route lookup, filtering, and switching to FPCs.

Synchronous Digital Hierarchy (SDH) CCITT variation of SONET standard.

Synchronous Optical Network (SONET) High-speed synchronous network specification developed by Bellcore and designed to run on optical fiber. STS-1 is the basic building block of SONET. Approved as an international standard in 1988. See also *Synchronous Digital Hierarchy (SDH)*.

Synchronous Transport Module (STM) CCITT specification for SONET at 155.52Mbps.

Synchronous Transport Signal (STS) Level 1 Basic building block signal of SONET, operating at 51.84Mbps. Faster SONET rates are defined as STS-*n*, where *n* is a multiple of 51.84Mbps. See also *Synchronous Optical Network (SONET)*.

sysid System identifier. A portion of the ISO Network Entity Title (NET) address. The sysid can be any 6 bytes that are unique throughout a domain.

syslog A method for storing messages to a file for troubleshooting or record-keeping purposes. It can also be used as an action within a firewall filter to store information to the `messages` file.

System Control Board (SCB) On an M40 router, the part of the Packet Forwarding Engine that performs route lookups, monitors system components, and controls FPC resets.

System Switching Board (SSB) On an M20 router, Packet Forwarding Engine component that performs route lookups and component monitoring and monitors FPC operation.

T

TCP port 179   The well-known port number used by BGP to establish a peering session with a neighbor.

tcpdump   A Unix packet monitoring utility used by the JUNOS software to view information about packets sent or received by the Routing Engine.

Terminal Access Controller Access Control System Plus (TACACS+)   Authentication method for validating users who attempt to access the router.

terminating action   An action in a routing policy or firewall filter that halts the logical software processing of the policy or filter.

terms   Used in a routing policy or firewall filter to segment the policy or filter into smaller match and action pairs.

through   JUNOS software routing policy match type representing all routes that fall between the two supplied prefixes in the route filter.

Timeout timer   Used in a distance-vector protocol to ensure the current route is still usable for forwarding traffic. The JUNOS software uses a default value of 120 seconds.

token-bucket algorithm   Used in a rate-policing application to enforce an average bandwidth while allowing bursts of traffic up to a configured maximum value.

totally stubby area   An OSPF area type that prevents Type 3, 4, and 5 LSAs from entering the non-backbone area.

traffic engineering   Process of selecting the paths chosen by data traffic in order to balance the traffic load on the various links, routers, and switches in the network. (Definition from `http://www.ietf.org/internet-drafts/draft-ietf-mpls-framework-04.txt`.) See also *Multiprotocol Label Switching (MPLS)*.

transient interfaces   Interfaces that can be moved from one location in the router to another. All customer-facing interfaces are considered transient in nature.

transit area   In OSPF, an area used to pass traffic from one adjacent area to the backbone or to another area if the backbone is more than two hops away from an area.

transit router   In MPLS, any intermediate router in the LSP between the ingress router and the egress router.

Transmission Control Protocol (TCP)   Works in conjunction with Internet Protocol (IP) to send data over the Internet. Divides a message into packets and tracks the packets from the point of origin.

transport mode   An IPSec mode of operation in which the data payload is encrypted but the original IP header is left untouched. The IP addresses of the source or destination can be modified if the packet is intercepted. Because of its construction, transport mode can be used only when the communication endpoint and cryptographic endpoint are the same. VPN gateways that provide encryption and decryption services for protected hosts cannot use transport mode for protected VPN communications. See also *tunnel mode.*

triggered updates   Used in a distance-vector protocol to reduce the time for the network to converge. When a router has a topology change, it immediately sends the information to its neighbors instead of waiting for a timer to expire.

Triple-DES   A 168-bit encryption algorithm that encrypts data blocks with three different keys in succession, thus achieving a higher level of encryption. Triple-DES is one of the strongest encryption algorithms available for use in VPNs.

Tspec Object   RSVP message object that contains information such as the bandwidth request of the LSP as well as the minimum and maximum packets supported.

tunnel   Private, secure path through an otherwise public network.

tunnel mode   An IPSec mode of operation in which the entire IP packet, including the header, is encrypted and authenticated and a new VPN header is added, protecting the entire original packet. This mode can be used by both VPN clients and VPN gateways, and protects communications that come from or go to non-IPSec systems. See also *transport mode.*

Tunnel PIC   A physical interface card that allows the router to perform the encapsulation and decapsulation of IP datagrams. The Tunnel PIC supports IP-IP, GRE, and PIM register encapsulation and decapsulation. When the Tunnel PIC is installed, the router can be a PIM rendezvous point (RP) or a PIM first-hop router for a source that is directly connected to the router.

type of service (ToS)   The method of handling traffic using information extracted from the fields in the ToS byte to differentiate packet flows.

U

UMTS Terrestrial Radio Access Network (UTRAN)   The WCDMA radio network in UMTS.

unicast   Operation of sending network traffic from one network node to another individual network node.

uninterruptible power supply (UPS)   Device that sits between a power supply and a router (or other piece of equipment) that prevents undesired power-source events, such as outages and surges, from affecting or damaging the device.

unit   JUNOS software syntax that represents the logical properties of an interface.

Universal Mobile Telecommunications System (UMTS)   Third-generation (3G), packet-based transmission of text, digitized voice, video, and multimedia, at data rates up to 2Mbps.

Update message   BGP message that advertises path attributes and routing knowledge to an established neighbor.

Update timer   Used in a distance-vector protocol to advertise routes to a neighbor on a regular basis. The JUNOS software uses a default value of 30 seconds.

upto   JUNOS software routing policy match type representing all routes that share the same most significant bits and whose prefix length is smaller than the supplied subnet in the route filter.

User Datagram Protocol (UDP)   Layer 4 protocol that provides an unreliable, connectionless service between two end IP hosts.

V

vapor corrosion inhibitor (VCI)   Small cylinder packed with the router that prevents corrosion of the chassis and components during shipment.

virtual circuit   Represents a logical connection between two Layer 2 devices in a network.

virtual circuit identifier (VCI)   A 16-bit field in the header of an ATM cell that indicates the particular virtual circuit the cell takes through a virtual path. Also called a *logical interface*.

virtual link   In OSPF, a link created between two routers that are part of the backbone but are not physically contiguous.

virtual local area network (VLAN)   A grouping of end hosts within a single IP subnet. These hosts usually reside on multiple physical segments and are connected through a Layer 2 Ethernet switched network.

virtual path   A combination of multiple virtual circuits between two devices in an ATM network.

virtual path identifier (VPI)   The 8-bit field in the header of an ATM cell that indicates the virtual path the cell takes. See also *virtual circuit identifier (VCI)*.

virtual private network (VPN)   A private data network that makes use of a public TCP/IP network, typically the Internet, while maintaining privacy with a tunneling protocol, encryption, and security procedures.

Virtual Router Redundancy Protocol (VRRP)   On Fast Ethernet and Gigabit Ethernet interfaces, allows you to configure virtual default routers.

W

wavelength-division multiplexing (WDM)   Technique for transmitting a mix of voice, data, and video over various wavelengths (colors) of light.

Wideband Code Division Multiple Access (WCDMA)   Radio interface technology used in most third-generation systems.

weighted round-robin (WRR)   Scheme used to decide the queue from which the next packet should be transmitted.

Index

Note to the Reader: Page numbers in **bold** indicate the principal discussion of a topic or the definition of a term. Page numbers in *italic* indicate illustrations.

Symbols and Numbers

> (angle bracket) in operational mode, 13
> (angle bracket) in set command, 32
- (minus sign) in candidate configurations, 33
+ (plus sign) in candidate configurations, 33
+ (plus sign) in set command, 32
# (pound character) in configuration mode, 23
? (question mark) in help system, 15
* (asterisk) as wildcard, 86
2-Way state in OSPF, **238**, *239*, **534**

A

ABRs. *See* area border routers
accept action, 446, 447–450, **534**
access lists. *See* firewall filters
actions. *See* firewall filters; routing policies
activate (configuration) command, 79
active configurations, **33**
active routes, **150**, **534**
Active state in BGP, **332**
Address Family Identifiers, *207–208*, **207**, **208**
address match conditions, **439–441**, **534**
Address Resolution Protocol. *See* ARP
addresses. *See also* IP addresses
    encoding in PIM protocol, 395–397, *395–396*
    in multicast networks
        Ethernet addresses, 380–383, *381–382*
        IP group addresses, 378–380, *378*
        overview of, 377–378
    static RP addresses in PIM, 410–411
adjacencies
    defined, **284**, **534**
    forming in IS-IS, 284–285, *285*
    forming in OSPF
        adjacency states, 238–239, *239*
        Ethernet links and, 243–244, *243*

        example, 239–240
        overview of, 238
        and troubleshooting, 241
    overview of, 277
Adjacency-RIB-In in BGP, **337**, **534**
Adjacency-RIB-Out in BGP, **338**, **534**
AFI (Authority and Format Indicator), **282**, *283*
aggregated routes. *See also* routing, protocol-independent
    attributes, 118–119
    in BGP, route policies and, 166
    configuration examples, 119–121
    contributing routes, 117
    defined, *116*, **116–117**, **534**
    next-hop options, 118
aggregation, message, in RSVP, 489, **513–514**, **553**
all keyword, 503
AND operator in route filters, 168
angle bracket (>) in operational mode, 13
angle bracket (>) in set command, 32
area border routers (ABRs), **247**, **535**
area match condition (OSPF), **159**
areas, **535**. *See also* IS-IS; OSPF
ARP (Address Resolution Protocol)
    defined, **534**
    multicast and, 380
    viewing ARP tables, 90
AS (Autonomous System)
    AS external LSAs, **250–255**, *251–254*, *256*, **535**
    AS Path attribute, 323, 331–332, **342–343**, **535**
    as-path match condition, 159
    assigning AS numbers, 346, *346*
    defined, **323**, **536**
    GLOP addressing and, 379
ASBR (Autonomous System Boundary Routers), 247, **536**

C

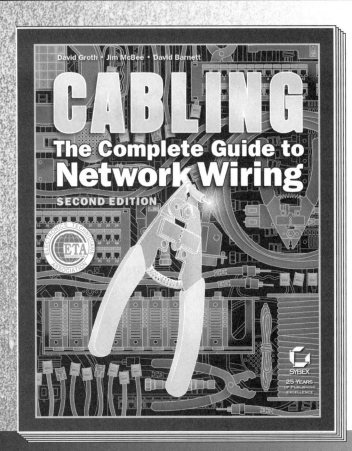

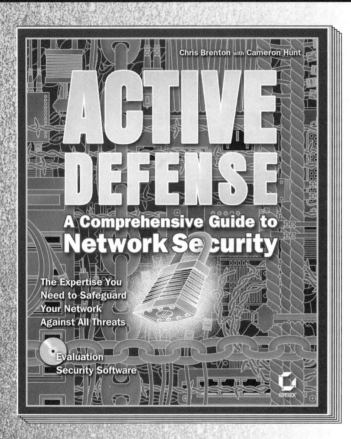

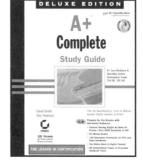

TELL US WHAT YOU THINK!

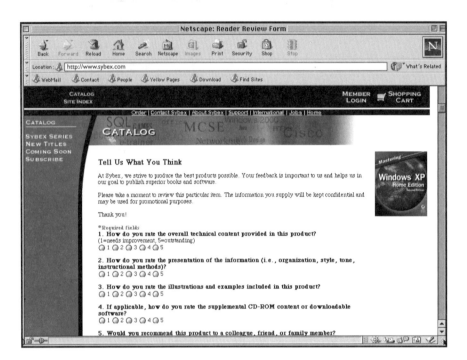

Your feedback is critical to our efforts to provide you with the best books and software on the market. Tell us what you think about the products you've purchased. It's simple:

1. Go to the Sybex website.
2. Find your book by typing the ISBN or title into the Search field.
3. Click on the book title when it appears.
4. Click **Submit a Review.**
5. Fill out the questionnaire and comments.
6. Click **Submit.**

With your feedback, we can continue to publish the highest quality computer books and software products that today's busy IT professionals deserve.

www.sybex.com

SYBEX Inc. • 1151 Marina Village Parkway, Alameda, CA 94501 • 510-523-8233

SYBEX®